International Financial Management

DAVID B. ZENOFF

Associate Professor
Graduate School of Business
Columbia University

JACK ZWICK

Associate Professor
Graduate School of Business
Columbia University

Prentice-Hall, Inc., *Englewood Cliffs, New Jersey*

PRENTICE-HALL INTERNATIONAL, INC., *London*
PRENTICE-HALL OF AUSTRALIA, PTY. LTD., *Sydney*
PRENTICE-HALL OF CANADA, LTD., *Toronto*
PRENTICE-HALL OF INDIA PRIVATE LTD., *New Delhi*
PRENTICE-HALL OF JAPAN, INC., *Tokyo*

13–473017–8
Library of Congress
Catalog Card Number 74–78492

Current printing (last digit)
10 9 8 7 6 5 4 3 2
Printed in the United States of America

PRENTICE-HALL, INC.
PRENTICE-HALL INTERNATIONAL, INC., UNITED KINGDOM AND EIRE
PRENTICE-HALL OF CANADA, LTD., CANADA
J. H. DEBUSSY, LTD., HOLLAND AND FLEMISH-SPEAKING BELGIUM
DUNOD PRESS, FRANCE
MARUZEN COMPANY, LTD., FAR EAST
HERRERO HERMANOS, SUCS., SPAIN AND LATIN AMERICA
R. OLDERBOURG VERLAG, GERMANY
ULRICO HOEPLI EDITORS, ITALY

PRENTICE-HALL INTERNATIONAL SERIES IN MANAGEMENT

Athos and Coffey	Behavior in Organizations: A Multidimensional View
Baumol	Economic Theory and Operations Analysis
Boot	Mathematical Reasoning in Economics and Management Science
Brown	Smoothing, Forecasting and Prediction of Discrete Time Series
Chambers	Accounting, Evaluation and Economic Behavior
Churchman	Prediction and Optimal Decision: Philosophical Issues of a Science of Values
Clarkson	The Theory of Consumer Demand: A Critical Appraisal
Cohen and Cyert	Theory of the Firm: Resource Allocation in a Market Economy
Cyert and March	A Behavioral Theory of the Firm
Fabrycky and Torgersen	Operations Economy: Industrial Applications of Operations Research
Greenlaw, Herron, and Rawdon	Business Simulation in Industrial and University Education
Hadley and Whitin	Analysis of Inventory Systems
Holt, Muth, Modigliani, and Simon	Planning Production, Inventories, and Work Force
Hymans	Probability Theory with Applications to Econometrics and Decision-Making
Ijiri	The Foundations of Accounting Measurement: A Mathematical, Economic, and Behavioral Inquiry
Kaufmann	Methods and Models of Operations Research
Lesourne	Economic Analysis and Industrial Management
Mantel	Cases in Managerial Decisions
Massé	Optimal Investment Decisions: Rules for Action and Criteria for Choice
McGuire	Theories of Business Behavior
Miller and Starr	Executive Decisions and Operations Research (2nd ed.)
Montgomery and Urban	Management Science in Marketing
Morris	Management Science: A Bayesian Introduction
Muth and Thompson	Industrial Scheduling
Nelson (ed.)	Marginal Cost Pricing in Practice
Nicosia	Consumer Decision Processes: Marketing and Advertising Decisions
Peters and Summers	Statistical Analysis for Business Decisions
Pfiffner and Sherwood	Administrative Organization
Simonnard	Linear Programming
Singer	Antitrust Economics: Selected Legal Cases and Economic Models
Vernon	Manager in the International Economy
Wagner	Principles of Operations Research with Applications to Managerial Decisions
Zangwill	Nonlinear Programming: A Unified Approach
Zenoff and Zwick	International Financial Management

TO

OUR

CHILDREN

Preface

The literature of international finance has dealt with the problems of international liquidity and related institutional developments. Scant attention has been paid to the financial problems of business enterprises in their attempts to adapt to international operations. To the extent that increased overseas involvement by the private sector is desirable, this conventional emphasis is regrettable. Firms require new tools for dealing with factors unique to foreign investment decisions. Overlooked opportunities or mistaken judgments are likely to occur if the firm regards the financing of international operations as a mere extension of domestic financial techniques. In view of the increased emphasis on overseas business in recent years, it is both surprising and unfortunate that comprehensive guidelines have not been offered to the practitioner for incorporating uniquely foreign variables into corporate financial procedures.

This book attempts to overcome this deficiency in two ways. First, the international financial behavior of multinational firms is described and critically analyzed. In this connection, the authors have concentrated in both the text and accompanying cases on companies that are noted for their international expertise, in order to identify the most advanced procedures currently being used. Second, the book is conceptual in that it prescribes modifications of conventional procedures and models of financial control to incorporate uniquely foreign variables. The objective of this facet of the book is to provide guidelines that suggest how international financial operations should be conducted and how assets held in different parts of the world ought to be managed. In resolving international problems, financial managers, either explicitly or unwittingly, make important assumptions about their companies with respect to risk posture and external opportunities that have far-reaching implications. An attempt is made here to identify these assumptions precisely, thereby providing firmer ground for resolving questions posed in international financial analysis.

The book is designed primarily for use in a course in international financial management. The course will be offered either in the corporate finance division or in the international business department of a school. Although there are no prerequisites for such a course, the book assumes that the reader has some background in accounting, business finance, and economics. The order of chapters reflects our preference for teaching the course, but the instructor is free to approach them in the order he deems appropriate. Typically, we have assigned both a chapter to read and a case problem for most class sessions. The cases cover substantial institutional material and, focusing on specific problem areas, afford an opportunity for the student to sharpen analytical skills and to make administrative decisions.

We are grateful to the people who assisted us in the development of the book. Lawrence Broadwell is primarily responsible for the import-export chapter. Ricardo Sanchez Aguilar and Judy Hendren have collected and assembled much of the institutional materials in chapters 8 and 9. Jane Colvin, O. J. Heestand, James Jepson, and Samuel Keretsky have each written one or two cases under the supervision of the authors. The Bell Campinas case is published by express permission of the President and Fellows of Harvard College, who hold the copyright. The comments of Kenneth Hurst and our colleague, Michael Adler, have been most helpful to us in revising portions of the book. We are also indebted for the suggestions of our colleague, John C. Burton, and of Jon Stroble, as well as for the assistance of Clara B. Crook. Further, we want to thank those business leaders whose active cooperation made possible the writing of the text and the preparation of case materials drawn from actual situations; unfortunately, in most instances they must remain anonymous. Finally, we wish to acknowledge the moral support and encouragement of our wives, Nancy and Barbara.

While much that is of merit was contributed by the aforementioned, the authors accept sole responsibility for the contents of this volume. Specifically, David B. Zenoff has written chapters 1 through 4, 11, 12, and 14, as well as cases 1, 2, 3, 12, 13, 16, and 19. Jack Zwick has written chapters 5 through 9, and 13, and is responsible for the balance of the cases. In accordance with requests of the cooperating companies, many of the cases have been disguised.

DAVID B. ZENOFF
JACK ZWICK

Contents

Introduction

1

In a world drawn closer by jet air transportation and new forms of instant communication, many large companies are creating global networks of affiliated companies. The required planning and operational decision making for the intricate networks that are evolving necessitate a worldwide perspective. While the advantages of dovetailing manufacturing and sales operations into overseas markets are obvious, the problems of transcending international financial restrictions loom as a large barrier to realizing the potential profitability in establishing such business networks. This book is an effort to identify, evaluate, and overcome these financial problems of modern international commerce.

NEW PROBLEMS FOR THE INTERNATIONALLY ORIENTED COMPANY

In many respects, the international age in commercial relations developed quickly, and most of today's largely international companies evolved from a purely domestic status into a "multinational" one in the short space of seven to fifteen years. It is not surprising, therefore, that many of these firms have not been well prepared managerially for the new directions they have consciously or unconsciously taken. From organizational and control points of view, most of the giant companies had been managing their overseas activities through one or more export departments, whose expertise was limited largely to the transportation, financing, and marketing of a limited line of export goods. If the firm owned one or two foreign subsidiaries, these typically were managed by "old hands" who probably had resided abroad for many years and knew the countries well but who lacked the managerial tools and sophistication that a network of multinational activities requires.

With the exception of a few international petroleum companies, commercial banks, and a small number of manufacturers such as IBM, W. R. Grace, Nestle, Singer, Unilever, and Colgate, little thought appears to have been given to the *concept* of managing a global organization. The fundamental question—how does the management of multicountry businesses differ from the management of domestic organizations—has not been analyzed critically in many instances. As the companies, their management consultants and accountants, and the academic community have begun to study the problems and opportunities of the international enterprise, they have discovered that a paucity of data exists regarding the organization, planning, and management of worldwide activities.

Within the past four or five years, ideas have begun to emerge as a growing group of internationalists within the business, banking, and academic communities has acquired sufficient experience and observations to begin providing new approaches to extant problems. One can now see new patterns of corporate adaptation to the special environmental and commercial requirements of managing a large internationally oriented business. Among these changes, evolution in organizational structures is prominent. Having started with small export departments, the large corporations have usually experimented with some form of international division, with centralized responsibility and control for managing the extensive overseas operations. Subsequently, many firms have experimented with a modification of the international division, often forming one or more geographically dispersed regional headquarters. Companies such as Allied Chemical, Goodyear Tire, Procter & Gamble, Johns-Manville, Chrysler, Celanese, Gillette, Raytheon, IBM, Crucible Steel, and Standard Oil of New Jersey are currently utilizing one or more regional headquarters.[1] Another type of change that has become increasingly evident is the development of a decision-making framework specially suited for use by managers charged with worldwide responsibilities. Accompanying this development has been the increased awareness by international managers of the possible business implications of such variables as

[1] For discussion of organizational adaptations to international business, *see* G. H. Clee and W. M. Sachtjen, "Organizing a World-Wide Business," *Harvard Business Review*, November-December 1964, pp. 55–67; Harold Stieglitz, *Organizational Structures of International Companies*, New York, National Industrial Conference Board, 1965.

inflation, exchange devaluation, cultural differences, and host government domestic policies—often encountered when operations are conducted in different countries. Furthermore, the more experienced and imaginative of the corporate officers have begun to develop a more workable concept for managing a *global* business, with its diverse opportunities and multitude of special environmental complications and problems.

At the present time, functional management specialties are emerging that are serving the needs of the highest organizational levels in multinational companies: international production managers, international marketing managers, international comptrollers, international logistics managers, and international financial managers.

INTERNATIONAL FINANCIAL MANAGEMENT

It is principally to the last of these new functional specialists, the international financial manager, that the contents of this book are addressed. Perhaps the easiest method of conceptualizing the position and role of the international financial manager in many corporate organizations is to use the analogy of a wheel with many spokes. The hub of the wheel represents the parent company headquarters where the most critical decisions and policies are made for the entire organization. Located at the end of each spoke is a subsidiary or branch of the parent company operating in a foreign country. The affiliates are assigned tasks by the international headquarters—perhaps manufacturing a product for the local market, assembling components for reexport, or extracting and processing raw materials—and it is the responsibility of the local management as well as the parent company staff to ensure that each affiliate fulfills the goals for which it has been established.

At headquarters, the financial manager for the entire organization must ensure that adequate financial resources are available to the worldwide network of affiliates, and he must manage the deployment of company-controlled resources so that each of the affiliates and the corporation as a whole are able to achieve their respective objectives. Fulfilling these financial objectives is complicated by virtue of the chief financial manager's geographical detachment from the various foreign affiliates. Language and cultural barriers also contribute to this detachment. Moreover, decisions are made more difficult by differences in countries' tax codes, restrictions and regulations governing capital flows and borrowing arrangements, variations in exchange rates and purchasing-power parities among national currencies, constant exposure to the risk of expropriatory action by foreign governments, and differences in financial customs and attitudes in relation to credit terms, distribution of current income, and disclosure of financial information.

The international financial manager must think in terms of *both* the global organization with its opportunities and worldwide "pool" of financial resources—and the peculiar circumstances, opportunities, and requirements of each individual foreign affiliate. Otherwise results may be suboptimal.

Managing the finances of the total organization necessitates keeping in touch with environmental changes in perhaps sixty-five unique foreign countries, analyzing alternative solutions that are proposed by subordinate managers in the field and by headquarters staff, and maintaining an appropriate balance of priorities between *individual* opportunities and financial requirements abroad and those of the firm *as a whole*.

The financial manager must possess sufficient perspective and analytical skills to fulfill competently these complex and sizable responsibilities. In essence, he must be a *financial* manager and an *international* manager, capable of effecting an overlap between the functional skills that heretofore have been organizationally separated. It is unquestionably true that the domestically oriented business executive must be capable of assimilating a voluminous amount of information in order to make intelligent decisions. Yet, the domestic executive's decisions are perhaps less dependent on detailed analysis of environmental data. The success or failure of a foreign venture is likely to hinge on a valid environmental assessment. Furthermore, the international businessman must search for satisfactory answers to policy questions that have not been considered by academicians or business practitioners in the preinternational business era. How should a minimum acceptable rate of return on investment be established for a *worldwide* company? Should the cost of capital be calculated individually for the parent company and for the respective affiliates that have access to separate financial markets? When an affiliate is prohibited from remitting its earnings to the parent company, should its operating performance be judged on the basis of local earnings or on the stream of remittances that are anticipated when the host country restrictions are lifted?

The complications are extant in all areas of the international financial manager's job. In asset management, the implications of currency devaluation or price inflation or creeping expropriation require thorough and close evaluation. Controlling foreign operations to ensure compliance with headquarters' directives is often made more difficult by the fact that traditional budgeting procedures are upset by environmental changes and the employment of foreign nationals as subsidiary managers.

The Purpose of This Book

This volume is addressed to the problems cited above and, more broadly, to the entire realm of international financial management. In part, it purports to describe many of the current financial practices of international management. It also recommends comprehensive approaches to fulfilling the responsibilities of financial management in a multinational setting. There are very few articles yet developed on this topic,[2] and no book-length treatment of either contemporary managerial practices or normative theory exists. International finance has thus far been a subject of economics, in which a macro orientation has been applied to such problems and prospects as the foreign exchange market, the International Monetary Fund, the adequacy of the supply of international liquidity, the dollar-exchange system, and reform of the present payments mechanism. The purpose of this volume is, therefore, to fill the void for the observer of international business management and for the manager of a firm where an internationalist's approach is warranted.

The discussion of international financial management will concentrate, in the main, on those aspects of the financial manager's functions that are somehow altered or complicated by business transactions that transcend national borders. The justification for taking this somewhat specialized "international" point of view can be understood in terms of the uniqueness of transnational commercial activity, the current state of corporate financial management, and the existing theory of finance. As discussed earlier, direct foreign investment and the responsibilities of managing a worldwide network of manufacturing and marketing operations have taken on major importance for a growing number of United States, Canadian, and European firms in the past fifteen years. Astute planning and control of these far-flung investments require systematic procedures to minimize suboptimal decision making in such areas as project assessment, design of financial structures, evaluation of performance, and international fund movement. At a suitable level of abstraction, the existing theory of domestic financial management provides suggestions for making optimal decisions in all areas of finance, both domestic and international. Yet, the theory has limited utility. It does not aid the businessman in solving specific problems such as whether a "swap" is better than an "exposed" loan or whether funds should be remitted by a foreign affiliate in dividend or royalty form or in assessing the likelihood of expropriatory action in a particular environment. The authors propose to extend existing theory in order that the added international variables can be explicitly included in the manager's decision parameters.

This volume assumes a managerial point of view throughout, stressing the two basic ingredients of *multinational* tasks:

[2] For a representative sampling of recent articles, *see* Dan T. Smith, "Financial Variables in International Business," *Harvard Business Review,* January-February 1966, pp. 93–104; John Veroen, "How ITT Manages Its Foreign Exchange," *Management Services,* January-February 1965, pp. 27–33; Gerhard Mueller, "The International Accounting Problem," *The Accounting Review,* January 1963, pp. 142–147; James Shulman, "When the Price Is Wrong—By Design," *Columbia Journal of World Business,* May-June 1967, pp. 69–76; David Zenoff, "Remitting Funds from Foreign Affiliates," *Financial Executive,* March 1968, pp. 46–63; Jack Zwick, "Models for Multicountry Investments," *Business Horizons,* Winter 1967, pp. 69–74.

1. Using a *global* approach to analysis and decision making
2. Employing tools of analysis that are suited to the development of appropriate financial policies and action-oriented decisions.

The treatment of some aspects of financial management, such as capital budgeting and asset management, builds upon the existing body of domestic financial theory. In other areas, as in the management of international fund movements and the assessment of foreign environmental risks, it has been necessary to break new ground.

The Setting for International Financial Management

The importance of international trade and commercial transactions for the members of today's world community is readily documented. As Table 1–1 suggests, more than $200 billion worth of goods and services are currently being traded among the hundred-plus nations, and this total is growing by about 5 per cent a year. It is estimated that the book value of direct foreign investment—the privately owned foreign business assets—is increasing by about 10 per cent a year and presently totals approximately $130 billion. Although international commerce has been important since the beginning of the European countries' colonialization movements hundreds of years ago, the post-World War II era has brought the age of international business to the forefront of international relations, economic development, and managerial science. The record of private direct foreign investment in the post-1946 period is probably most clearly reflected by the activities of United States companies, which currently account for about one-half of the world's total. While the international activities of certain Japanese, European, and Canadian firms are evident to the observer of international business (and, indeed, to their competitors!), the size and extent of their overseas holdings, as well as the number of non-United States companies that are now international in their orientation, are considerably smaller than United States holdings overseas. It has been estimated, for example, that the book value of England's private foreign direct investments at the end of 1966 was $12.5 billion, that of Canada $3.5 billion, West Germany $2.8 billion, Switzerland $2.6 billion, and France $1.8 billion—whereas the total for the United States was $54.6 billion.[3]

It is evident in Table 1–2 that United States companies began to acquire foreign business assets long before the end of World War II (by 1928, more than 1,300 United States firms owned foreign affiliates[4]), yet it was not until after 1946 that the absolute size and the rate of

[3] Among the reasons that can be hypothesized for the United States dominance in private foreign direct investment is the fact that during the first ten to fifteen years after World War II, European and Japanese companies were principally occupied with the reconstruction of their own economies, whereas United States firms were able to begin expanding abroad by the early 1950's.

[4] Frank Southard, *American Industry in Europe,* New York, Houghton Mifflin Co., 1931.

TABLE 1–1

World Exports of Goods and Services by Geographical Areas, 1959–1967
(millions of U.S. $)

AREA	*1959*	*1960*	*1961*	*1962*	*1963*	*1964*	*1965*	*1966*	*1967*
World total *	101,500	113,400	118,600	124,700	136,000	152,600	165,400	181,400	190,300
Industrial Countries (U.S., U.K., Japan, Canada, Industrial Europe)	69,020	78,790	83,220	87,490	95,330	107,940	118,430	130,780	137,680
Other developed	7,150	7,700	8,280	8,600	9,530	10,710	11,100	12,270	13,200
Less developed	25,300	26,900	27,100	28,600	31,200	34,000	35,800	38,400	39,400
Latin America	9,050	9,370	9,650	10,210	10,840	11,520	12,050	12,790	11,100
Middle East	4,400	4,860	4,880	5,350	5,830	6,620	7,140	7,770	8,400
Asia	7,320	7,740	7,570	7,730	8,550	8,870	9,320	9,800	10,000
Africa	4,350	4,720	4,750	5,120	5,700	6,650	7,040	7,700	7,700

* Excluding the Soviet area and Cuba.
Source: *IMF International Financial Statistics.*

increase in the book value of foreign direct investment began to increase significantly.

The data in Table 1–2 show that Canada and Europe were the areas receiving the most attention by the internationally oriented United States investors. Except for Latin America—principally Venezuela, Brazil, and Mexico—the less-developed countries have not received large flows of private capital from the United States. Although the extractive sectors—petroleum, mining, and smelting—have always been prominent in direct foreign investment activities, the manufacturing industries have been most important in terms of the book value of assets abroad.

Hidden by these aggregate figures are several interesting characteristics of United States investment abroad. More than two-thirds of the recent growth in foreign business assets has been financed by locally obtained funds. Typically, parent companies have provided equity capital and technical know-how to start a foreign affiliate, but thereafter they have used funds from local operations and foreign-denominated debt to sustain the subsidiaries.[5] Another characteristic of the investment activity has been the popularity of the European Common Market countries. Since 1960, these countries have received more attention from United States investors than any other single area. Among the manufacturing industries that have become international-minded, chemical, motor vehicle, food processing, electric equipment, and pharmaceutical companies have been the most active.

Although there are thousands of companies with one or more subsidiaries in foreign countries, the bulk of the value of foreign-owned assets is accounted for by about 250 firms—almost all of which are among the largest in their industries. The return on foreign investments, which reached the 15–19 per cent range in the early 1950's, recently has averaged about 11–12 per cent.

For a large number of the companies that are today heavily committed to overseas operations, their real start came after 1946. Often, companies' experience and approaches followed this sequence: Europe, Japan, Canada, and a few other overseas markets of size attracted their attention, but through the mid-1950's the overriding objectives and resource commitment were concentrated on the formidable pent-up demand in the United States. Hence, foreign opportunities were relegated to a second-class status and were exploited in what might be termed the "noncommittal" ways, i.e., exportation, foreign licensing agreements, and small portfolio investments. The principal intent was to minimize the involvement of company executives—a scarce company resource—and the amount of corporate assets placed at risk.

[5] For the current data, see the U.S. Department of Commerce *Survey of Current Business;* also, Judd Polk, Irene Meister, and Lawrence Veit, *U.S. Production Abroad and the Balance of Payments,* New York, National Industrial Conference Board, 1966; David B. Zenoff, "Remittance Policies of U.S. Subsidiaries in Europe," *The Banker,* May 1967, pp. 418–424.

TABLE 1–2

Book Value of United States Direct Foreign Investment by Geographical Areas and by Industry, 1897–1967

(in billions of $)

AREA	*1897*	*1908*	*1914*	*1924*	*1929*	*1936*	*1946*	*1950*	*1955*	*1960*	*1965*	*1966*	*1967*
Total:	.6	1.6	2.65	5.4	7.5	6.7	7.2	11.8	19.4	32.8	49.3	54.7	59.3
Canada					2.0	1.9		3.6	6.8	11.2	15.2	16.9	18.0
Latin America					3.5	2.8	3.1	4.6	6.0	8.4	9.4	9.9	10.2
Europe					1.4	1.3	1.0	1.7	3.0	6.7	14.0	16.2	17.9
Middle East and Africa					.1	.1	.2	1.0	1.5	2.0	3.4	3.7	4.0
Asia					.4	.3	na	.3	.6	1.2	2.0	2.2	4.3
Oceania					.1	.1	na	.3	.6	1.0	1.8	2.0	2.5
Other areas					.1	.1	.4	.3	.9	2.3	1.5	3.8	2.4
INDUSTRY													
Manufacturing					1.8	1.7	2.4	3.8	6.6	11.2	19.4	22.0	24.1
Petroleum					1.1	1.1	1.4	3.4	5.9	10.9	15.3	16.3	17.4
Mining and smelting					1.2	1.0	.8	1.1	2.2	3.0	3.8	4.1	4.8
Public utilities					1.6	1.6	1.3	1.4	1.6	2.5	2.1	2.3	2.4
Trade					.4	.4	na	.8	1.3	2.4	4.2	4.7	5.0
All others					3.4	2.9	2.6	1.3	1.8	2.8	4.6	5.2	5.6

Sources: *Survey of Current Business;* Cleona Lewis, *America's Stake in International Investment,* Washington, D.C., The Brookings Institution, 1938; U.S. Department of Commerce, *U.S. Business Investment in Foreign Countries,* 1960.

With the passage of time, the income from exporting and licensing activities grew, as did the chief executives' appreciation of foreign opportunities. At the same time, the middle managers' knowledge of how to tap overseas opportunities expanded. By the late 1950's, enlarged profit-making opportunities abroad coupled with falling rates of return (in some industries) at home set the stage for the enduring rush to invest in production and sales facilities in foreign countries. As a consequence, several sizable corporations' sales and profitability today are heavily dependent on operations which transcend national borders.

The internationally oriented firms, which have become more popularly known as multinational,[6] are domiciled in England, Switzerland, Germany, Japan, United States, Canada, and France. Typically, they derive no less than one-fourth of their total earnings from foreign investments (in some as much as 85 per cent comes from abroad) in addition to perhaps another 10 per cent from export activities. Many have manufacturing and/or assembly operations in at least fifteen different countries and sales offices in as many locations. If we use the definition suggested in footnote 6, such non-financial firms as the following can be classified as multinational: General Motors, Standard Oil of New Jersey, Ford Motor, General Electric, du Pont, Royal Dutch Shell, Unilever, British Petroleum, Nestle, ICI, Farbenfabriken Bayer, Dow Chemical, Brown Boveri, Philips Gloeilampen-fabrieken, Colgate, Mitsubishi, Foremost Dairies, Coca Cola, Chas. Pfizer, Singer, Corn Products, Alcan Aluminum, Massey-Ferguson, Hoffmann-LaRoche, Olivetti, General Foods, ITT, Westinghouse, IBM, Richardson-Merrell, Socony Mobil, Volkswagen, International Harvester, and Saint-Gobain. This list is by no means exhaustive.

Not only have manufacturing and extractive companies expanded abroad, but commercial banks, management consultants, advertising agencies, and accounting firms have extended their sphere of operations as well. Most service businesses limited the scope of their operations to a few foreign countries prior to the mid-1950's, but the tremendous volume of foreign activity by their traditionally domestic clients, beginning in the 1960's, induced—or perhaps "forced"—the banks, accountants, advertising agencies, and so on, to go international themselves.[7] In reviewing the

[6] Defining a multinational corporation can lead to considerable disagreement among academicians and businessmen. Probably in the purest sense, a firm cannot be considered to be multinational until its *ownership* as well as the geographical distribution of its operations and management outlook are worldwide. Because no more than a handful of companies could be so characterized, the term "multinational" has recently become identifiable with the large, increasingly internationally oriented companies whose ownership and top echelons of management are decidedly *uni*-national (usually American), but whose foreign affiliates number at least fifteen and whose foreign earnings account for twenty-plus per cent of the total company profits. It is this latter definition which will be used in this book.

[7] For an account of the international experience and objectives of the service firms, *see* Marvin Bower, "Personal Service Firms Venture Abroad," *Columbia Journal of World Business,* March-April 1968, pp. 49–58.

financial statements of large corporations, it is common to discover that a foreign affiliate of the parent company's auditors has performed the audit of the corporation's subsidiaries in Manila, Mexico City, or Brussels. Similarly, it is becoming increasingly common to read about large United States and European banks joining ranks in order to better serve their multinational clients, and to compete against other giants which have already taken this step. A now significant number of United States, Canadian, and European banks have opened foreign branches, subsidiaries, and advisory centers and have created special staffs of internationalists that can provide counsel to their nonfinancial clients and suggest new methods of raising or investing corporate funds in foreign areas. In addition, the multinational banking institutions such as First National City Bank of New York, Chase Manhattan Bank, Bank of America, and Morgan Guaranty Trust Company have expanded export financing capabilities throughout the world and have established foreign investment subsidiaries that make equity investments in foreign businesses.

Accompanying the international expansion of nonfinancial and financial institutions that started in the mid-1950's has been the growth and maturity of the so-called international money and capital markets in Europe. While London had traditionally served as the world's—and certainly Europe's—financial center, the uniqueness of its position and capabilities began to disappear after World War II when the stability and convertibility of the English pound sterling came under recurrent doubt. At the same time the role and respect of the United States dollar were universally elevated and the sophistication and financing capacity of New York as a financial center continued to grow. For about fifteen years after the war's end, the dollar—along with sterling—fulfilled the roles of the world's reserve currencies, and the United States, the role of the world banker. But even during the ascendency of the United States position, certain forces were operative which eventually led to the prominence of European capitals such as Zurich, Paris, and Amsterdam as international financial centers. The development of national, if not international, capital and money markets in Europe has been a postwar objective of both European and United States leaders. It was believed that greater European financial self-sufficiency was a requisite to the continued growth of the private sector and the overall viability of the European Economic Community, and that it would also relieve the strain on New York's ability to meet private and governmental financing requirements.

An impetus to rapid European capital market development was provided in the early 1960's when recurrent balance-of-payments deficits forced the United States to impose a series of voluntary and mandatory restraints on the use of the New York financial markets to satisfy foreign fund requirements. With the closing of the United States market as a source of long-term funds for most foreign borrowers—both public and private—and later the imposition of restrictions on borrowings by affiliates of United States companies, pressures have been placed on European centers to supply international financing. The response of the European markets to the challenge has exceeded virtually all observers' most optimistic expectations. Markets in Europe have been able to fulfill a large segment of the demand for medium and long-term funds, and such terms as "Eurodollar" and "Eurobond" have become an important part of the international financial manager's vocabulary.

A REVIEW OF HYPOTHESIZED EXPLANATIONS FOR INVESTMENT ACTIVITY

A number of explanations for the popularity of international business in the post-World War II period have been proffered.[8] Many companies have been lured by the prospect of opening new and profitable markets abroad. As the market characteristics in foreign countries became more similar to those in the United States, companies have been induced to enter into some kind of commercial exchange with them. As can be confirmed by an examination of international trade statistics,[9] the bulk of international trade traditionally and currently is among nations with similar levels of income and consumer traits. Thus, in direct investment activities, the United States companies have been inclined to establish most of their foreign affiliates in Canada and Europe where local market demand is similar to demand conditions at home. Table 1–2 suggests that with the exception of a few less-developed countries (Brazil, Australia, Argentina, Chile, India, and Mexico), about four-fifths of the total United States foreign direct investment has been in the so-called developed nations. Until recently most of the funds committed to the less developed areas had been in search of raw materials—mostly by petroleum and mining companies.

Associated in various ways with the desire to sell more goods abroad have been the economic and political forces in the host countries. Companies that during prior years were able to reach foreign markets solely by exportation have been required to establish or acquire local manufacturing facilities. In some countries, increased tariff restrictions and more restrictive quotas on imports have been responsible for the shift in em-

[8] There have been several studies on the motivation for direct investment abroad. *See,* for example, Raghbir S. Basi, *Determinants of United States Private Direct Investments in Foreign Countries,* Bureau of Economic and Business Research, Kent State University, Ohio, 1963; Yair Aharoni, *The Foreign Investment Decision Process,* Boston, Division of Research, Harvard Business School, 1966; Stephen Hymer, *The International Operations of National Firms: A Study of Direct Foreign Investment,* Cambridge, M.I.T. Press, 1960; Raymond Mikesell, *U.S. Private and Government Investment Abroad,* Eugene, Ore., University of Oregon Books, 1962.

[9] The monthly IMF *International Financial Statistics* and the United Nations *World Trade Yearbook* are valuable sources of trade data on most countries. For a recent theoretical interpretation of the patterns of world trade, *see* Staffan Burenstam Linder, *An Essay on Trade and Transformation,* John Wiley & Sons, Inc., New York, 1961.

phasis from exporting to investing. Nationalistic sentiment and preference for locally made goods have had a similar effect.

It is interesting that *defensive* motivations have been cited as rationale for much foreign investment. Many companies have suggested that their overseas investments reflect attempts to forestall or combat local competition (owned by indigenous principals in some cases, and foreign competitors, in others). Increasing transportation costs or foreign import duties—which increase the landed price of exported products—have threatened to reduce the price competitiveness of many companies' exports. This sentiment was reflected in the remarks of the president of the American Cyanamid Company, a sizable United States multinational firm, when he explained the purpose and direction of his company's sizable foreign investment activity in the mid-1950's and 1960's.

> At the moment Cyanamid is exporting synthetic resins to 40 countries, but believes that if it is to maintain its five to ten per cent overseas plastics growth rate, more emphasis must be placed on local production in view of increasing import restrictions.[10] . . . Competition from producers abroad and the pressures arising from dollar exchange allocations have prompted Cyanamid to install facilities in . . . Argentina, Brazil, and Mexico for the production and refinement of antibiotics, sulfa drugs, and other pharmaceuticals.[11]

Other factors and variables have been influential in the foreign investment decisions of American companies. Foremost among these are:

1. The desire of a high-level executive to see his company become international in scope and in outlook. Thomas Watson of the IBM Company and George Eastman of the Eastman Kodak Company are notable examples.
2. The expectation that local production and marketing of one or more products will assist in the exportation of other products to that market as the result of increased consumer awareness of the company's brand name or reputation and because of the company's increased marketing capability resulting from more on-the-spot activity and management experience.
3. The objective of spreading the parent company's fixed costs over a wider marketing area. As the number and size of foreign operations increase, the parent company believes that it may be able to allocate a significant amount of the expenses incurred in research and development, as well as general management, to the various affiliates, thus increasing the contribution to the headquarters' overhead.

Important Environmental Circumstances

From a macro point of view, there have been a number of important environmental changes and trends in the past thirty-five years that have contributed to the general interest of business in foreign trade and in-

[10] *Journal of Commerce*, April 6, 1964, p. 5.

[11] Remarks of K. C. Towe to Security Analysts of San Francisco, November 29, 1956.

vestment and that have fostered the growth of both. In the extractive industries, the growth in world demand for raw materials such as petroleum, sulphur, copper, tin, and bauxite have encouraged companies to intensify their explorations for new deposits throughout the world. Both supply and demand considerations have been important for manufacturing companies. On the one hand, the increasing availability of skilled laborers in Europe, Latin America, and Asia, whose wages have been considerably lower than in the United States, has enabled companies to manufacture or assemble components or finished products for the United States or foreign markets at a lower unit cost than could otherwise be experienced. On the demand side, a number of recent phenomena have served to increase the outside demand for goods and services previously restricted to the home market: In Europe and Japan, the postwar reconstruction has been extensive, successful, and rapid; from the outset these countries have provided the world with a large demand for capital and consumer goods, and since 1950 they have been able to produce a wide variety of price competitive, high-quality products for export. Throughout the 1950's and 1960's, the Japanese and a number of European economies experienced the highest real growth rates in the world; they provided expanding and sizable markets for other countries, and they were highly productive sources of goods and services for trading partners. Recently, as had been the case in the 1920–1940 period, these countries have engaged in a rapidly increasing amount of direct foreign investment in the United States, Latin America, Asia, and the Middle East.[12] The growth in number and size of regional economic trading groups, beginning in the late 1950's with the European Common Market, has provided an observable stimulus to the growth of many member countries' economies, interregional and international trade, and international investment. Whereas the most dramatic results have taken place in the European Economic Community, nations of the European Free Trade Association, the Central American Common Market, and to a lesser degree the Latin American Free Trade Association have also seen evidence of such gains in GNP, investment, and trade.

Another environmental force which has led to increased international trade and capital flow has been the steadily improving access that the goods and services of countries have had to the markets of other countries. Beginning in the mid-1930's, and continuing in scope and intensity after the end of World War II, most of the major trading countries in the world have gradually reduced the levels of import duties and have (more slowly) abolished some nontariff barriers. At the present time, under the rules and objectives of the General Agreement on Tariffs and Trade (GATT), periodic international bargaining sessions are held wherein countries agree on a reciprocal basis to reduce even further their

[12] At the end of 1967, the total book value of European- and Japanese-owned direct investment in the United States was $7.1 billion.

restrictions on imported goods. Although the spirit of protectionism and isolationism is by no means dead—witness the considerable pressure within the United States in 1967, 1968 and 1969 for undoing the tariff concessions granted in the Kennedy Round—the record makes it clear that the amount of protection afforded domestic producers in virtually all of the economically advanced countries has steadily diminished during the past thirty years. The result has been an increase in the volume of world trade with a concomitant growth in the international flow of capital.

A fourth contributing force to the growth of international commerce has been the increasing demand among the less-developed nations for the goods and services produced by the developed ones. The higher aspiration levels have stemmed from a variety of circumstances and forces: political independence, improved communication and transportation, higher levels of real per capita income, and increasing amounts of international travel and intercultural exposure. The outcome has usually been a growing demand for capital goods and industrial supplies to fuel the economic development programs of these nations, as well as an increasing demand for consumer goods that reflects the slowly improving standards of living. These requirements have been filled in two ways: through local manufacture owned and managed (in whole or in part) by foreign investors, and by exportation from the more economically advanced countries.

A fifth stimulant to the growth of international business activity has been the recent development of international and national institutions which facilitate these types of commercial transactions. The International Monetary Fund, through its resources and rules, has helped develop financial stability in the international payments system as well as means by which many nations could weather payments difficulties without having to resort to severe and comprehensive current and capital account restrictions. The World Bank group and a number of regional public and private development banks have had positive impact on the economic growth of individual nations, the viability of individual projects, and the feasibility of international investment projects. As mentioned earlier, the GATT has helped provide the ground rules and a forum for periodic discussion to reduce trade barriers. National credit institutions that provide financing to indigenous exporters, governmental insurance agencies that provide insurance against investors' risks in foreign operations, and countries' intelligence services which offer businessmen useful data and advice on exporting activities or foreign investments have all contributed to the recent growth in expanding business horizons.

THE STRUCTURE OF THE BOOK

The volume's design bears some resemblance to existing books in domestic financial management. The discussion in chapters 2, 3, and 4 focuses on the various types of environmental risks which are often encountered in international commercial transactions—exchange control, inflation, devaluation, and expropriation. In chapter 2, the dimensions of environmental risks are defined together with their business implications. Chapter 3 provides a methodology for projecting the likelihood of the occurrence of environmental adversity. In chapter 4, the types of defensive and adaptive corporate policies which might be used to protect against environmental contingencies are discussed.

In chapter 5, attention is focused on evaluating prospective foreign investments where the existence of the international variables necessitates modification of traditional methods of domestic project analysis. The chapter explores such topics as how to estimate foreign investment costs and how to assess corresponding earnings streams given such complicating factors as restrictions on remittances of earnings, exchange rate changes, and threat of property loss. Chapter 6 considers the issues relevant to the selection of an appropriate capital structure for a foreign subsidiary. The capital structure question is complicated since the multinational investor must account for the influence of differences in national customs and laws as they relate to the debt-equity balance, access to local capital and money markets, environmental risks, and requirements for parent company guarantees.

In chapter 7 the focus is on working capital management in foreign affiliates. The principal topic is how to manage the tradeoff between the requirement of the enterprise for liquid assets and the necessity of protecting the affiliate's assets from purchasing power erosion. The next three chapters are largely descriptive. Chapter 8 concentrates on banking institutions as sources of finance and investment outlets for short-term funds possessed by multinational corporations. The chapter includes a discussion of the growing capabilities of multinational banks to assist the business executive in solving a variety of financial problems. Chapter 9 considers nonbank sources of capital and instruments of finance which are employed by the internationally oriented firm. International money and capital markets are discussed and analyzed. The intent is to familiarize the reader with the existing nonbank financial institutions and the manner in which they function. Chapter 10 provides a description of the approaches and instruments used in export financing.

Chapters 11, 12, and 13 are managerial in orientation. Chapter 11 deals with the management of fund remittances from foreign subsidiaries. It reviews existing corporate practices, and then enumerates a comprehensive approach to deciding upon the appropriate amount and form of transnational funds flows between individual subsidiaries and the company pool of funds. Chapter 12 focuses on management control. As suggested earlier, the design of a suitable system of control for a multinational company is complicated by the forces at work in the international business environment. The chapter discusses how these environmental factors can be harnessed in order that performance can be appraised and controlled. Chapter 13 is concerned with the problem of reporting foreign results to higher echelons of multinational management. Price level changes and currency devaluations can distort financial statements prepared according to conventional procedures. The question then becomes, what method will provide a clear and realistic picture of overseas results, and what systems of reporting will provide both operating level personnel and headquarters management with the information they require for effective control? The final chapter, 14, projects the authors' views of how the international business environment is likely to evolve during the next five to ten years and considers the implications of these trends and changes for the international executive.

To supplement the text, the book also includes several case studies drawn from actual business situations. The cases afford the reader an opportunity to see more clearly the characteristics of international financial problems. The cases cover a wide variety of topics, industries, and geographical locations in order to provide the reader with a somewhat representative sampling of business situations. They can be used to develop skills in solving international financial problems.

BIBLIOGRAPHY

Aharoni, Yair. *The Foreign Investment Decision Process.* (Boston: Harvard Business School, Division of Research, 1966).

Benoit, Emile. "Interdependence on a Small Planet," *Columbia Journal of World Business,* Spring 1966.

Farmer, Richard. *International Business: An Operational Theory.* (Homewood, Ill.: Richard D. Irwin, Inc., 1966).

Fayerweather, John. *Facts and Fallacies of International Business.* (New York: Holt, Rinehart and Winston, Inc., 1962).

Hymer, Stephen. *The International Operations of National Firms, A Study of Direct Foreign Investment.* (Unpublished Ph.D. dissertation, M.I.T., 1960).

Kolde, Endel J. *International Business Enterprise.* (Englewood Cliffs, N.J.: Prentice-Hall, Inc., 1968).

Martyn, Howe. *International Business.* (New York: The Free Press, 1964).

Mikesell, Raymond F. *U.S. Private and Government Investment Abroad.* (Eugene: University of Oregon Books, 1962).

Moyer, Reed. "Foreign Investment Grows, Changes, Prospers," *Columbia Journal of World Business,* March-April 1968.

Penrose, E. T. "Foreign Investments and the Growth of the Firm," *The Economic Journal,* June 1956.

Robinson, Richard D. *International Business Policy.* (New York: Holt, Rinehart and Winston, Inc., 1964).

———. *International Management.* (New York: Holt, Rinehart and Winston, Inc., 1967).

Robock, Stefan, and Kenneth Simmonds. "What's New in International Business?" *Business Horizons,* Winter 1966.

Servan-Schreiber, J. J. *The American Challenge.* (New York: Atheneum Publishers, 1968).

Case I
INTERVIEW WITH WILLIAM RITTMAN

The following is a transcript of a May 1967 interview with William C. Rittman, vice-president of Richardson-Merrell, Inc. At the time of the interview, Mr. Rittman had central management responsibility for the company's international manufacturing and financial departments, and he was a member of the Finance and Audit Committees. Prior to joining the company in 1962, Mr. Rittman had been executive assistant to the president of the international division of another large pharmaceutical company. He is a graduate of Harvard College and Harvard Law School.

The company, whose 1967 sales exceeded $300 million, produces and sells ethical drug products and the Vicks line of cold remedies throughout the United States and in approximately fifty other countries.

Q. What typically has motivated the company to invest abroad?

A. Well, in selling abroad you usually start out by appointing an exclusive distributor in a foreign country. When the sales subsequently reach a certain minimum level, you normally put in your own sales organization, which in turn leads to further boosts in sales. Eventually you run into problems of supply; transportation costs or import duties preclude further import activity, which leads to the setting up of a plant. It is a typical evolutionary process in this industry.

Q. Would you calculate a rate of return if you became sufficiently interested in a foreign market?

A. We always calculate a rate of return as a routine procedure. Whether we allow it to influence us is something else again. We have a standard formula for measuring return on investment. And we have a rule of thumb that the money be returned in five years. And this doesn't mean returned to the U.S., it means income earned by the subsidiary. But I don't think, for example, that if the rate of return in a good foreign market, as measured by our formula, were to be less than 20 per cent or longer than a five-year payback, that it would deter us because this is not a large capital-consuming industry. You can go into a country with a relatively small amount of money, and perhaps with a PL480 loan[1] and overdraft facilities, you can launch yourselves on a very thin equity and earn your way . . .

Q. When you calculate a payback figure, what is the base figure you use? Equity funds? Or any capital the parent company makes available to the subsidiary?

[1] A PL480 loan is made in local currency by the United States government to American firms operating in certain less-developed countries.

A. The base figure is any funds that we make available to a new subsidiary. Initially, these funds would be the equity. We might establish the foreign operation on a thin equity, then supply it with ingredients required for production, taking into consideration its inability to pay on a current basis. In the beginning years, we might allow the subsidiary to run six, nine, or twelve months credit. Technically, the credit should be part of the investment, but we have not included such credit in the payback formula, which I think is a shortcoming in our approach.

Q. When you mentioned "thin capitalization," do you mean a small amount of equity, or a small amount of equity relative to the amount of credit?

A. A small amount of equity relative to the amount of credit.

Q. Do you compare alternative overseas investment possibilities as part of your capital budgeting approach?

A. I know of no case where we have made comparisons. It would be neglecting—if the two projects were worthwhile—an obvious market to select only the better one. And money is seldom a problem.

Q. Are you saying, then, that there has never been a *need* to compare opportunities?

A. I guess that's really the answer. We might compare the projected operating results with our experience in other markets. At the present time, we are working hard to perfect a concept of return on investment, and there is a big discussion going on now as to whether it is a control mechanism itself or whether it is a means of measuring the effect of our controls. A part of the discussion is how to make a comparison between operations in two countries—do we measure it on *net* worth or on total assets? You get into all kinds of arguments over what should be the base. I don't know where we will end up, but I think it is something we must try to do. It would probably alert us to defects of local operation if we found that the return on investment in one country was higher than in another. That fact alone would cause us to look more carefully into the lower rated country and perhaps find some way to improve it.

Q. Is the present base or rate-of-return formula any different from that used for domestic investment?

A. There is an enterprise-wide study being made. And it is being implemented first in the domestic divisions. At the present time we are trying to get the general managers of each domestic division to agree on an appropriate base for calculating rate of return for their divisions. We are running into differences of opinion. For example: suppose you bought an existing product that had no foreign sales but had fairly substantial U.S. sales. Suppose you paid X million dollars for good will. Now, when the international division develops a large volume of sales abroad, the question is: In its investment base should the domestic division be charged with the *entire* amount of good will, or, should it be the entire amount less some amount which the international division has taken advantage of? One argument is that because there were no foreign sales when you bought the product, there was no foreign good will . . .

Q. When you are making an evaluation of a project located in a less-developed country, how are the risks of devaluation, expropriation, or inflation worked into your evaluation of whether or not to make the investment and how to best manage the operation if you do invest?

A. Well, let's take Pakistan, for example, where there may be a devaluation within the next three to five years because the rupee is worth considerably less than its stated foreign exchange value. Here, you would be investing at a time when you believed a devaluation was coming. What are the things you could do? You might set the initial price of your products higher than normal because following a devaluation there is always an increase in manufacturing costs. And following devaluation there are always frozen prices—at least drug industry prices are frozen. In essence you would establish initial prices uneconomically high and take on the burden of competing with inflated prices. But when the devaluation came and when costs inevitably rose afterwards, you would be in a better position to continue operating profitably. In addition you could immediately buy concrete, steel, and any construction material required for your new plant that would be likely to move up in price as a result of the devaluation. You could order them now, even though normally you would want to order as construction progressed and perhaps take advantage of price fluctuations as they occurred.

Q. Even if you think devaluation might be a year and one-half away?

A. There would be a gamble on this and in this case I would say "yes" because I think the Pakistan currency is far out of line and, of course, one never gets any indication of when devaluation will come. But, I could tell you a fascinating story about a different foreign country where a little six-year-old boy advised me about a week ahead that there was a devaluation coming. His father was the head of a Swiss bank in that country. . . . Now, another action you could take: Assume you would be going into a joint venture and, while the investment would be made with dollars, it would be converted into rupees before being invested in the new company. In other words, the company would be a rupee-capitalized company, and let's say your share of the equity was 75 per cent and your obligation was to put up 476,000 rupees. Were you to invest your capital at today's exchange rate of 4.76:1, you would be obliged to provide $100,000. If you could wait and somehow delay your part of the investment, and the rupee devalued, you could buy 476,000 rupees with something less than $100,000. You might arrange this by subscribing to the full 476,000 rupees but request the Pakistan affiliate to call up the money in 10 per cent dribbles as needed to construct the plant. If there were a devaluation before all of your investment had been supplied, a part of your contribution would go in at a more favorable rate of exchange. Now, you might run into problems here, because this would be against the interest of your local partner. So whether you could succeed with this is doubtful but it might be considered.

Q. As you think about any recent foreign investment decisions in less-developed countries, do you try to evaluate how risky the proposition is relative to investments that were made before, or others that were being contemplated?

A. I have read much about comparison and evaluation of risk in foreign investment, and it simply does not fit my experience in this industry. The answer seems to be that it is very difficult to measure risk in any meaningful way. We invest abroad whenever there is a market for our products which can only be supplied locally. And there are markets from which we might conceivably shy away, where the risk is all too obvious.

Q. In looking at investment possibilities in less-developed countries, how important are incentives or concession that the host governments have been offering to foreign private investors in either inducing you to make the investment or in affecting the form in which you make the investment?

A. They have had virtually no effect on our decisions, although they have been an interesting aspect of the evaluation of foreign opportunities. They cause our accounting department a great deal of trouble in computing the savings, but they do not induce us to invest if we don't want to invest.

Q. Is this because the savings haven't been large enough?

A. They haven't really been large enough. Take, for instance, India. It offers a tax exemption on income equal to 6 per cent of the capital base. If you had a million-dollar investment, only $60,000 would be exempt, which means you would save only about $30,000 after taxes. The savings lasts for five years, and if you discount the value, it's hardly worth more than a $10,000 present value. This in itself is not much of an incentive, but a market of 400 million people is!

Q. Have there been occasions when government representatives from less developed countries have approached the company to try to induce you to consider investing there?

A. No.

Q. To what extent do countries' barriers to foreign investment, and regulations of the way that business must be managed, affect your evaluation of the desirability of investing in a particular country?

A. I think that many foreign governments operate under a misapprehension of what a host government can do for business. Probably the biggest barrier is the insistence that the foreign investor should not have a majority interest in the local company. I can understand the emotions involved, but from the foreigner's standpoint he thinks, for example, of his Japanese company as a part of his "family," and not as a separate, isolated operation. The Japanese, of course, only see what is in front of them and don't think of it as part of anything. My experience has been that when a foreign investor sits here in New York and decides what foreign operations he is going to concentrate on, he invariably gives more attention to the 100-per-cent-owned operations than to the 50-per-cent-owned ones. I said earlier that we have never had to select countries to invest in because of a shortage of money. But we do have a shortage of *people*, and this is why we are selective and why we decide on priorities. This industry is very dynamic, and we have to institute changes quickly, and therefore we need to be in control of our subsidiaries. Furthermore, the interests of the local people are usually different. They often want to pull out every nickel from the company that they can, whereas we are building for the long pull. This is understandable because those of us here who are making decisions are not using our own money, whereas for the other fellow it may be everything he and his family own.

Q. In addition to the requirement for local partners as a barrier to investment, what about restrictions on remittances?

A. I don't think this would be a barrier if the market was attractive enough, because I consider all these things as transitory. I would assume that there is a valid reason to restrict remittances. For example, many companies have invested substantial amounts of money in Japan *without* having any right to remit at all. They hope that the remittance restriction will pass in due time, and there is evidence that it will.

Q. In less-developed countries with a low rate of capital formation and relatively underdeveloped capital and money markets, what forms and sources of financing do you use for your foreign affiliates?

A. PL480 funds have been a very substantial source of financing. In most underdeveloped countries, you will find a World-Bank-sponsored activity that lends money for an infrastructure-type activity, but it will not finance consumer goods. One also often finds a government-sponsored industrial development bank that will lend medium term money to local businesses, but the bank generally wants to participate in the activity—they may want to put someone on the board of directors or offer planning help which you don't really need. So, PL480 money is a very attractive source of medium-term funds—eight to ten years. It provides for a grace period at the beginning, during which a plant can be built. There is no maintenance-of-dollar-value required, so the borrower is protected from devaluation and has a firm rate of interest with no escalation-of-rate clause.

Q. Are there any serious problems in getting a PL480 loan?

A. There is a long form to fill out, and there is a lot of coordinating to be done, which makes it a three-to-six-month process.

Q. Are there any restrictions on the use of PL480 funds?

A. In essence the government wants these funds to be used for fixed assets. However, if there is a fixed asset investment involved, the borrower is allowed to "plus up" the amount borrowed to cover working capital requirements. But, they will seldom lend for working capital alone. Also, PL480 funds may not be used to finance imports. One can purchase only locally made products. Then there are restrictions as to the amount that can be loaned based on the equity of the subsidiary company, and this varies from country to country. Normally, it's one dollar of 480 money for one dollar of equity. Where they have plenty of money, and they do in some countries such as India and Pakistan, they will lend up to 140 per cent of equity.

Q. In addition to PL480 funds, do you borrow short-term funds from local banks?

A. Short-term money is loaned on a demand or overdraft basis by the banks, but the banks seldom make a demand, particularly if you are dealing with an American bank abroad with which you may have dealings around the world. It would be very unusual for one of the New York banks to indicate that you must immediately return the entire draw that had been made on your overdraft account.

Q. Do you deal only with American banks abroad?

A. No; our banking arrangements always include a national bank because we usually use banks for collection purposes. The American banks traditionally locate in the capitals or in the major cities, and they seldom have a banking network throughout the foreign country. Therefore, we require a national bank with a number of branches because when goods are sold, the payment is often made to the local branch of the bank.

Q. But do you also establish relations with the American bank branches?

A. We very frequently do this for our overdraft facilities. We may have a joint overdraft with an American bank and a local bank, and we have an understanding with them that no matter which one we go to, they may share in supplying the funds. In exchange for that flexibility, we may have to commit ourselves to giving each of the banks an equal amount of our foreign exchange business. I am not sure why,but this is a very attractive type of activity for banks; they like to handle foreign exchange transactions.

Q. What do you mean?

A. Well, if one of our foreign affiliates is importing, banks like to handle the currency aspects of the transactions. There is apparently a volume of credit or money the banks pile up that they can use while that transaction is taking place. In other words, when one is importing and turns over local currency, there is a period when that currency is idle in the bank and it is just free money to them.

Q. Do you have to secure your borrowings in any way in less-developed countries?

A. We have been asked to give parent company guarantees, particularly by the American banks.

Q. Do you also utilize inventory as collateral for loans?

A. We may be required to hypothecate our inventory in support of an overdraft which gives the bank a type of rolling claim on the inventory. This means they can come in and take it over at any time. If things get really tough and the sub's balance sheet is weak—this hasn't happened to us, but I have heard of it—the bank will come in and place a big sign up on the warehouse, and the sub can't get back in the warehouse until it gets its balance sheet back in order. I might say that a local overdraft is generally limited to 75 per cent of the fair market value of the inventory—fair market value or book value, whichever is lower. So, one couldn't be borrowing against a lot of obsolete inventory. And the banks do come in and examine the inventory from time to time. They are very well secured. Inventory is the most liquid item on one's books. You might argue that the banks should also allow accounts receivable as security but they say that they can't be responsible for the parties with whom you trade.

Q. In an inflationary environment, how high an interest rate might you pay?

A. In Brazil during the hard period it was necessary to have relations with a number of banks, each of which would ration out a part of the money at 12 per cent, the maximum legal rate of interest. It was possible to obtain these funds from banks, but only on the understanding that you would also borrow on a promissory note basis. The promissory notes would range from a 20 to 40 per cent rate of interest, and they would be short term—thirty days, forty days, or sixty days. The banks would agree to renew the notes, but they added handling charges. In addition at renewal you had to agree to leave a specified amount of the loan on deposit. So, it's one thing to say what the stated rate is, but if you add in all these other costs, the effective rate is far above the rate as stated on the note. Then, there is another type of financing which is called "discounting accounts receivable." You sell X something and invoice him. He accepts and signs a document which is really a bill of acceptance that you have given him credit for, say, ninety days. You can take the bill of acceptance to the bank and sell it to the bank. But that is expensive. In Brazil, it has run 40 to 60 per cent. And, you cannot get rid of your liability on the bill. If the customer doesn't pay, you have to pay.

There is yet another source of funds in Latin America: the "financieras," which are not really a part of the banking structure. They are financial institutions that sell their own bonds. In Brazil they might have been selling them at 30 per cent interest, and relending the money at say 40 per cent.

Summing up, in Brazil a company naturally starts out with 12 per cent money at the bank, but it gets so little of it that it is a joke. Then there are the promissory notes, the discounting of accounts receivable, and finally the borrower is pushed to the "financieras." Hence, a firm may have outstanding debt with effective interest ranging from 12 to 60 per cent, with an average between 40 to 45 per cent. You must add to this the time of top level people, nursing the project, keeping track of obligations, and running to the bank because occasionally some of the notes aren't renewed.

Q. Have you ever borrowed from any international agencies or regional development banks?

A. No. They normally do not lend to producers of consumer goods.

Q. I have heard it said on a number of occasions that as we look to the future of U.S. investment abroad, there will be more use made of joint ventures. How would you assess the likelihood of this occurring in the future?

A. I don't know who said that; businessmen wouldn't say it, perhaps government people and professors would, but I have never been able to understand why. It seems to me that with freedom of capital movement, a requirement that U.S. business establish joint ventures abroad is retrogressive. There are only one or two governments in the world which are making such a demand, and I just don't know why a joint venture holds all that attraction.

Q. Would you consider going into partnership when you make a foreign investment?

A. I am opposed to it because I think that it inevitably develops conflicts of interests which inhibit the growth of the company. Let me give you a few examples of the kind of conflict a company might run into. Let us say that you have a joint venture in Chile which processes and packages pharmaceutical products. It does not manufacture any of the basic ingredients because of the small size of the market. You manufacture the ingredients in the U.S. for your domestic requirements, and you sell part of the output to the Chilean subsidiary. What price do you charge Chile? No matter what you charge, there will be a conflict. Now, let's consider Europe and assume you had a number of joint ventures within the EEC. How are you to divide up that six-country market among partners? I just don't know what the answer to that is, but I can give you a lot of cases where the joint venture cripples the viability of the local operation. . . . And, in many cases—especially the less-developed countries—the joint venture often results in one rich foreign national getting wealthier.

Q. Because it wouldn't be widely held?

A. Seldom would it be widely held. In most less-developed countries you could list on a single sheet of paper the families that would be potential partners in a joint venture.

Q. What restrictions or regulations have less-developed countries placed on the capital structures of the subsidiaries which are established?

A. In both India and Pakistan the amount of the foreign investment in any new project is limited to the value of the machinery and equipment that must be *imported*. For example, if you decide to organize a company with an equity base equal to the local currency equivalent of $500,000, and if $200,000 were required to import machinery and equipment, the host governments would allow you to own only 40 per cent of the company. In other words, they permit the foreign investor to acquire that portion of the equity which represents what the country would otherwise have to supply out of its own foreign reserves to put the company into operation.

Q. How about the working capital requirements?

A. You can't take in working capital. The Indian government, for example, will not approve a higher foreign investment than is required to import equipment. Normally, you would think they would want foreign exchange, but they look at the investment as a one-shot deal of obtaining foreign exchange once against a permanent obligation to pay out dividends to foreigners.

Q. Is there anything an investor can do to get around his restriction in the design of the affiliate's capital structure?

A. Not really, although some have tried. For example, it might be possible to establish the capital of the company at an amount of which the foreign machine and equipment requirements would be the percentage of the company that you wanted. In other words, let's assume $200,000 is the cost of imported equipment. If the foreign investor desired 66 2/3 per cent of the equity, he would then try to establish the capital of the company at $300,000. But he would be locked in on other fronts because once having established the capital base, there are local rules of thumb for lending money which relate to a firm's capital base. PL480 money may be available only on a one-to-one basis; overdraft money, which I mentioned before was limited to 75 per cent of the fair market value of the inventory, is also limited in some countries to a percentage of the capital base. Hence, although it might be possible to obtain the desired percentage of the equity by scaling down the capital of the company, this may cripple the entire financial structure of the company . . .

Q. Do investors ever overstate the initial capacity requirements for a plant and therefore bring in more plant and equipment than is needed?

A. In under-developed countries, particularly India and Pakistan, the governments determine how much installed capacity they desire for every type of activity. This is somewhat unrealistic, but they set out to do it. In our industry, for example, they would establish a maximum amount of installed capacity to manufacture pharmaceutical tablets. As each prospective investor applies to produce tablets, he will state the capacity he desires, and he will be licensed to produce a portion of the target. The government approves only what they have left to license out. Eventually, they will have it all licensed. A licensed firm is not supposed to install more than the amount for which it is licensed. This can get very tricky because invariably you cannot find machinery with rated capacity for exactly what you have been licensed to do. A decision then has to be made whether or not to come in with lower rated machinery or higher rated. If a firm comes in with higher rated, it may be accused of misleading the government. Moreover, a machine's rated capacity is achieved only under ideal conditions, with no breakdowns or labor stoppages. (In India they have holidays depending upon whether the moon was out the night before. You may turn up at the plant the next day and find nobody there because the moon had been out.) So, ordinary prudence necessitates bringing in more capacity.

Q. What tools do you use, or what methods to assess the likelihood of an exchange devaluation in a country in which you have a subsidiary?

A. I don't know of any valid tools. This is certainly anything but an exact science. You can find thousands of opinions. In countries where devaluation is a potential, we keep in contact with banks which have economists who have ways of analyzing the economic environment. We ourselves try to measure the degree of inflation, and we get many opinions as to how far out of line the exchange rate has become. . . . I think if you look at the Mexican case, the last two devaluations occurred when the Mexican currency in terms of dollars was 40 per cent out of line.

Q. When *what* is out of line?

A. Let's say as a starting point a meal in the U.S. costs $1, and you can get the same meal in Mexico for the peso equivalent of $1. If five years later that same meal in Mexico costs $1.25 in pesos, but remains $1 in the U.S., you might say that Mexican money in terms of dollars had devalued by 25 per cent. Of course, the dollar devalues too but since it is the base mark, we hold it constant. . . . I have been told that Mexico runs its economy by deliberately debasing the buying power of the peso in terms of dollars by 4 per cent a year. They will allow this to accumulate until it reaches 40 per cent, and then they will devalue the peso.

Q. What index would you use? Are any published?

A. Well, of course, there is always a free market for every currency both within the country and outside, and you can get an idea from that of what the outside world thinks a local currency is worth. The free money market is a very good barometer of local inflation. It doesn't follow that a country will devalue by the amount of the inflation because the very act of devaluation is inflationary. If a country is dependent on imports—as many of the less-developed countries are—and if it devalues its currency, it will have to pay more in terms of local currency for its imports. This will result in an increase in the price of everything. So, even though the rupee is out of line as it is in Pakistan, one finds many very responsible people saying that the country cannot afford to devalue.

Q. When you expect a devaluation to occur—and of course, you can't be certain when—let's say within a year, do your subsidiaries take any special measures to try to minimize your loss in dollar value?

A. The only way to protect yourself on devaluation is to have locally borrowed funds which exceed the subsidiary's devaluable assets . . . the so-called financial assets which consist of cash and items that are going to be changed into cash such as accounts receivable and inventory. . . . When there is a devaluation, you write down the financial assets in terms of dollars. So you take a loss on those. Fixed assets you don't devalue in terms of dollars because you assume that the dollar value of bricks and mortar is maintained no matter what happens to the local currency. On the liability side you also devalue liabilities, which means a gain because the dollar cost of your local obligation is reduced by the devaluation. Hence, it is only the extent to which the loss on devaluable assets exceeds the gain on devaluable liabilities that you get hurt. When you are exposed to a situation where you think there is a devaluation problem, you go as heavily in debt as you can. And, you don't pay your accounts payable any faster than you collect your accounts receivable.

On the U.S. parent company's financial statements . . . if you leave earnings in the higher risk countries, you may not want to include them in the final net income figues reported to shareholders. Instead you may put the foreign profits into a reserve for foreign operations and then if you get hit with a devaluation, you are able to charge the loss on devaluation to this reserve, and therefore you might say one is able to even out the impact of a devaluation. All of this, of course, must have the blessings of your public accountants and must be fully reported to your shareholders.

The Nature of Environmental Adversities in International Business and Their Implications for the Firm

2

The conduct of business across national boundaries has built in extra dimensions of risk[1] which are rarely encountered in domestic business transactions. The financial manager of an international company must therefore have an appreciation of what the added risk elements are, under what circumstances they may occur, what their implications are for the firm, and how they can best be handled. In part, the prescription calls for better understanding the risk elements so that a clearer picture can emerge of the range and nature of possible results—that is, a more precise probability distribution of the likelihood of various possible outcomes. The remaining facet of the manager's assignment involves preparing for the risk elements or reducing their impact upon the company.

This chapter will discuss the nature and business implications of three types of international environmental phenomena which frequently add dimensions of risk to business operations abroad:

1. The possibility of losing company-owned assets and/or freedom to operate in a foreign country as a result of foreign governmental policy
2. The possibility of host country or lending country balance-of-payments

[1] A distinction is drawn in the literature between "risk" and "uncertainty." *See*, for instance, Frank H. Knight, *Risk, Uncertainty, and Profit*, Boston, Houghton Mifflin Co., 1921. For our purposes, this distinction is ignored.

problems which may result in restrictions on the movement of funds between national jurisdictions and result in a loss in the dollar value of the assets and profitability of a foreign affiliate

3. The possibility of price inflation in foreign localities that may seriously impede the firm's ability to conduct successful operations

The next chapter, chapter 3, will focus on what the businessman can do to assess the likelihood of occurrence of these environmental adversities in the near term. The discussion in chapter 4 will then include a recommended range of actions which can be initiated to minimize or avoid adverse consequences to the firm as the result of unfavorable environmental conditions.

The Possibility of Losing Company-Owned Assets and/or Freedom to Operate in a Foreign Country

When a firm invests or engages in a commercial venture in its own or a foreign country, it does so subject to the state's power of *eminent domain.* In recent years, such international commercial activity has been carried out between the industrialized nations of the free world without fear of an improper condemnation by the respective host nations. In these countries it is axiomatic that seizure of alien property must serve a public purpose, must not be discriminatory, and must be compensated for at the full value of the property in convertible currencies, without undue delay.

Adherence to the first two principles prevents the seizure from being illegal, whereas the third principle precludes the act from being confiscatory. These concepts of protecting the acquired rights of foreign investors is a traditional principle of international law and has been incorporated into the national legislation of the capital exporting countries. The investor's position *vis à vis* the lesser developed nations is not often so secure.

Many of the newly emerging nations argue that the foregoing rules are not entirely applicable to their status, for theirs is a unique position wherein the rights and security of foreign investors were acquired at a time when today's leaders were not able to control their national destiny. In turn, this group of countries has adopted the position that expropriations must be for a public purpose and must not be discriminatory. However, in the case of a general expropriation designed for social and economic reform, the traditional concept of "adequate, effective, and prompt payment" has often been rejected.

Furthermore, many countries, particularly those of Latin America, invoke the "Calvo doctrine," by which a foreigner agrees to seek redress only in the local courts and not to seek diplomatic assistance from his own country. These countries refuse to allow foreigners greater rights than those of nationals. Essentially, a foreign investor receives treatment as a national, even if this falls below the so-called international minimum standard.[2]

The less-developed countries of the world clarified their legal position on expropriation in the December 14, 1962, Resolution of the United Nations General Assembly on "Permanent Sovereignty over National Resources." Section 4 of that resolution stated:

> Nationalization, expropriation or requisitioning shall be based on grounds or reasons of public utility, security or the national interest which are recognized as overriding purely individual or private interests, both domestic and foreign. In such cases the owner shall be paid appropriate compensation, in accordance with the rules in force in the State taking such measures in the exercise of its sovereignty and in accordance with international law. In any case, where the question of compensation gives rise to a controversy, the national jurisdiction of the State taking such measures shall be exhausted. However, upon agreement by sovereign States and other parties concerned, settlement of the dispute should be made through arbitration or international adjudication.

It is important to note that "appropriate" compensation does not necessarily mean "adequate, effective, and prompt."

The seizure of foreign property, whether or not within the power of *eminent domain* of sovereign states, has served many purposes. In its most extreme form it has constituted a fundamental part of the political ideology of a new ruling party. The belief in the "socialization of the means of production" made such seizures inevitable following the Russian Revolution of 1917 and, more recently, following the Cuban acceptance of communist doctrine. Expropriation has included compensation to achieve widespread economic and political reform. In 1938 the Mexican government took the oil properties of American citizens as a step in a selective program of land reform; after prolonged negotiations with the United States, Mexico paid compensation. Sometimes expropriation has occurred as a retaliatory measure designed to express distaste for a deteriorating relationship between nation-states. The nationalization of the Suez Canal which followed the withdrawal of American and British aid from the Aswan Dam project may have been such a response. Normally, however, the major reason for expropriatory action is host

[2] Normally, expropriated property is considered to be lost for the foreseeable future or forever. However, the recent case of Indonesia suggests that important exceptions can occur. "Jakarta: Three years ago, Indonesia's tough Communist labor unions struck the Unilever soap and margarine factories here demanding that the government seize control and oust the 'neo-colonialist' British supervisors. The government did just that. Three months ago, Indonesia's post-Sukarno regime announced plans to return the facilities to foreign management after a six month transition period. The workers demonstrated again: Bring back the foreigners immediately. Once more, the government consented." *Wall Street Journal*, April 18, 1967, p. 32.

country discontent with the benefits accruing from foreign-owned industries.[3]

The governments have often become impatient with what they consider limited payback or outright exploitation of their natural resources (whether they be bananas, oil, or iron ore) by foreigners, and there are many examples in the past thirty-five years of governmental seizures or forced changes affecting the terms of the foreigners' presence.[4] One observer has adroitly described the welcome of foreign investors in terms of a time horizon, calling it "an asset with a fixed maturity."[5] In essence, Gabriel's thesis is that an international investor is foolish to believe that his operations in any given country will *continue* to be greeted by the host government with the degree of enthusiasm received initially. Changes occur over time. The host country may develop alternative sources of technology and capital. The growth strategy of the nation may shift from one which courts foreign investment at almost any price to one of hard-headed business calculations wherein the foreign investor is welcome but only if he brings in *and maintains* a highly valued resource which is otherwise unavailable locally. The foreigner's days are thereby marked if his presence does not continue to be appreciated by the local administration. This host country sentiment is readily observable in the following editorial entitled "Decapitalization" that appeared in the Mexican press in 1967.

> The strong entrance of foreign capital into Mexico's food processing industry seems to indicate a weakening of stated government policy that foreign investment should be complementary to national investment rather than in direct competition with national investment or displacing that investment altogether with a given segment of the economy.
>
> The recent purchase of Clemente Jacques by United Fruit is an excellent example of foreign investment that represents decapitalization as the result of purchasing an established firm with a fair percentage of the local market.
>
> Earnings that have accrued to Mexican owners and/or stockholders will now be channeled directly out of the nation. The foreign investor exports an average of 70 per cent of his earnings yearly.

[3] The reader should be aware of the dangers in simplifying the reasons for various of the expropriation cases in recent history. Normally expropriation has resulted from a *number* of contributory causes. To obtain a more detailed account of several cases, *see* U.S. Congress, Committee on Foreign Affairs, *Expropriation of American-Owned Property by Foreign Governments in the Twentieth Century,* Washington, D.C., U.S. Government Printing Office, 1963.

[4] *See,* for example, Charles Kepner and Jay Soothill, *The Banana Empire: A Case Study of Economic Imperialism,* New York, Vanguard Press, Inc., 1935; Roger W. Benedict, "Tiger in the Tank of Peruvian Fields," *Wall Street Journal,* March 20, 1968, p. 14.

[5] Peter Gabriel, "The Investment in the LDC: Asset with a Fixed Maturity," *Columbia Journal of World Business,* Summer 1966, pp. 109–120.

> Although a higher percentage of reinvestment would be appreciated, it is only natural to expect the foreign investor to take out the lion's share of his profits; after all, these profits were his investment incentive. But displacement of national capital followed by drainage of profits to owners outside Mexico is one thing, whereas returns to the foreign investor whose capital has been used to create a needed industry that did not exist before is something else.
>
> Present legislation tends to be ambiguous and leaves much of the final decision to the individual official in charge of a given case. There is a need for clear legislation outlining government policy on foreign investment, possibly creating a joint commission of public officials and private initiative to channel foreign investments into projects that represent true capitalization rather than displacement and decapitalization.
>
> As Mexico increases its potential via better distribution of local earnings and bigger export markets through LAFTA, there will be a natural tendency for the foreign investor to deemphasize putting money into new, necessary, but problematical industries, and rather to concentrate on purchasing established firms already solidly rooted in a growing local market which can look forward to the bigger market of LAFTA.
>
> As the Mexican government pushes exports and as goods produced in Mexico become more competitive internationally, more foreign firms will be tempted to buy into Mexican companies with the idea of setting up a closed circuit from Alaska to Tierra del Fuego.
>
> In recent months the government has—and justly so—warned local manufacturers that they must compete in price and quality. The government has also hinted that margins of tariff protection may be modified to eliminate those manufacturers who are taking advantage of Mexico's protectionist policies.
>
> Very few people would disagree with SIC's desire to promote greater competition, higher quality goods, and lower prices to the consumer. But if the secretary is going to utilize protectionism as a lever for obtaining better, cheaper, made-in-Mexico goods, he should also give local producers some sort of assurance [that] their competitors will not be U.S. or European firms which can meet SIC's demands for lower prices by merely taking a loss and writing it off taxes at home.

Added to these possible reasons for nationalization of foreign property is a list of complaints which local businessmen or their governments have and have had about business investment by other than local principals. The following sample of arguments will serve to illustrate how—rightly or wrongly—the stage can be set in a given country for pushing out foreign companies: [6]

1. Foreign companies can compete unfairly because they have access to virtually unlimited supplies of capital resources.

[6] If the reader is not well acquainted with the type of objections American businesses have encountered in Europe, Canada, and Japan, and in many of the less-developed nations, he may wish to consult any of the following: Walter Guzzardi, Jr., "Why the Climate is Changing for U.S. Investment," *Fortune*, September 15, 1967; Raymond Vernon, "Multinational Enterprise and National Sovereignty," *Harvard Business Review*, March-April, 1967, pp. 156–163; Alan Johnstone, *United States Investment in France: An Investigation of the French Charges*, Cambridge, M.I.T. Press, 1965.

2. The remittance of dividends, royalty payments, and fees to the parent company constitutes a damaging and endless drain on the host country's balance of international payments.

3. The foreign investors have, in some industries and some countries, allegedly gained control, thereby exposing the capital-importing country to the dangers of monopolistic practices, and strategies dictated by Washington, D.C.

As an example of some of these sentiments: "Latin Americans will lose control of their economies to huge international corporations unless measures are taken to prevent it, Gustave Magarines, secretary-general of the Latin American Free Trade Association, warned Friday. He said international corporations have invested more than four billion dollars in this area and that their annual sales are in excess of eight billion dollars—about four-fifths of Latin America's total exports. Countries must work on the principle that although certain limits should be imposed on foreign capital, it is very much needed for development since the region does not have enough, he said. But, he added that unless guidelines are fixed, Latin America will be running the risk of engaging in a ruinous competition of concessions to get foreign capital. Perhaps the best formula, Magarines added, is the joint association of foreign and regional capital." [7]

4. The foreign investor is often unmindful of existing business practices and therefore makes business life uncomfortable or even impossible for the indigenous entrepreneur or industrial worker. These complaints are frequently voiced *vis à vis* cut-throat competition for market share, or the practice of laying off workers when sales decline, or the policy of attracting a significant share of the best quality managers and workers by paying higher than average salaries.

5. From the macro point of view, it is widely feared by host country officials that the so-called multinational company may make business decisions in its own interest which will ignore the possibly adverse effects of such decisions on the individual host country. The XYZ Company, for example, may decide to increase production of tires in Nigeria because of low factor costs there and concurrently decrease production in Canada where labor rates are high. For the firm, selecting between alternative opportunities on a worldwide scale is sound business practice; for Canada, however, many hundreds of workers may be out of jobs because the decision maker presumably is a disinterested foreigner.

As might be expected, host countries, which for any one or combination of reasons become disenchanted with the presence of a foreign-owned corporation, may take measures short of outright expropriation to improve the situation. The following is a well-publicized example:

[7] "Corporate Giants Pose Threat to Economy," *The News* (Mexico City), January 20, 1968.

Lima, Peru, November 30, 1967: Peru Wednesday froze all funds of the U.S.-owned International Petroleum Company (IPC) on deposit in banks of this country. The Finance Ministry ordered the freeze after IPC failed to make a 125,000-dollar payment on an alleged 144-million-dollar back-tax debt to the government. The payment was due November 28. IPC has contended that the 144 million—which it denies it owes, would represent its gross profits over the past fifteen years in the operation of Peru's oil fields. The government was authorized by Congress last September to nationalize IPC's holdings and to negotiate future exploration rights with the American concern, a subsidiary of Esso Standard Oil, New Jersey. In a message to Congress . . . Prime Minister Rebagliati said IPC's holdings are "property of the state" which intended to exercise "its full rights" in order to preserve "national dignity and interests." [8]

Sometimes the host country's remedy is intended solely as a type of one-shot adjustment of the terms by which the foreigner is permitted to remain. Mexico, for example, to encourage greater local exploration and development of sulphur by the Mexican affiliate of the giant United States-owned Pan American Sulphur Company, realigned the export quotas it granted to the industry and, in essence, made any increase in the size of the quotas dependent on the company's discovery of new deposits.[9] On the other hand, over a period of time a host government may impose a series of conditions on foreign investors which may be viewed by the government administration or the businessman as a step-by-step approach to force or induce the foreigner to withdraw or to alter significantly his mode of operations. This action is frequently termed "creeping expropriation."

The state has at its disposal a wide number of measures to accomplish its purpose.[10] It may, for example, limit or temporarily check a locally incorporated affiliate from remitting profits to its parent company abroad; it may limit the company in its importation of supplies, finished goods, or components. The state may severely restrict the number of foreign managerial or technical personnel that may enter the country, or it may discriminate against foreign-owned operations in the administration of income, sales, and excess profits taxes. The approach that has been utilized in India, Mexico, and Japan, for instance, is to apply pressure on many international firms having local subsidiaries to sell a part of their equity in affiliates to indigenous investors.

A brief description of a shift in the Mexican government's approach

[8] "Peruvians Freeze Funds of U.S.-Owned Oil Firm," United Press International, November 30, 1967.

[9] R. F. Mikesell, "Healing the Breach over Foreign Resource Exploitation," *Columbia Journal of World Business*, March-April 1967, pp. 25–32.

[10] For a more complete discussion of creeping expropriation, *see* A. A. Fatouros *Government Guarantees to Foreign Investors*, New York, Columbia University Press, 1962; National Industrial Conference Board, *Obstacles and Incentives to Private Foreign Investments, 1962–1964*, Studies in Business Policy, No. 115, New York, 1965; "What Mexicanization Means," *Business Week*, November 26, 1966.

to foreign investors in the early 1960's provides an excellent illustration of what creeping expropriation may mean.

> First of all, the government began to buy a number of private enterprises in which foreigners had a heavy interest. These included the two remaining foreign-owned electric power companies . . . two chains of movie theaters . . . in which a former United States citizen had a heavy interest; and the United States-held controlling interest in a major Mexican steel company. . . . The policy of selectively buying out foreign interests was supplemented by a policy of pressing foreign investors . . . to surrender majority control to Mexican private or public holders. Pressure was applied in various ways. In mining, where a few United States companies still dominated the field . . . a new principle of discriminatory taxation was adopted, favoring mining companies with majority Mexican ownership. In the award of government contracts, the pressure was exerted simply by refusing to buy the products or services of foreign-controlled Mexican enterprises, irrespective of price. . . . Attempts to force the rate of import replacement became much more vigorous. . . . The withholding of import licenses was, of course, one obvious case. This technique was used most spectacularly in the case of the automobile assembly industry, which was still organized on a basis of importing about 80 per cent of the value of the assembled vehicle. . . . The Mexican government introduced the concept of an annual import budget. Another means of hurrying the import-replacement process was a more stringent application of Mexico's tax-exemption law.[11]

Despite these examples, all such government policies are not motivated by the desire to push out foreign investors. No doubt this has been the case in a number of countries and will be a proper interpretation of certain confrontations in the future. However, it is probably much more accurate to think of such policy measures as being a part of a country's overall development strategy or response to a buildup of internal or external pressures that necessitate utilization of policy tools designed to induce certain modes of business behavior. As an example, the policy of Mexicanization pursued by the government of Mexico for many years was given the following interpretation by the Mexican Minister of Industry and Trade in 1967:

> The "Mexicanization" of industry is a concept applied to the capital structure of firms that are established in Mexico. The basis of this concept is that the total or at least majority of that capital should be in the hands of Mexican citizens. . . . Because they constitute basic fields in the national economy, the law reserves exclusively to the federal government the petroleum industry, basic petrochemicals, electric power, railroads, and telegraphic communications. In those activities that are not reserved exclusively for the state, there are some fields where the government allows the establishment of firms in which foreign investors may participate on the condition that at least 51 per cent of the capital stock is held by Mexican citizens. These fields pertain to activities

[11] Raymond Vernon, *The Dilemma of Mexico's Development*, Cambridge, Harvard University Press, 1965, pp. 120–22.

> closely connected with the basic ones or which are of particular importance to the nation. . . . Except in the cases already mentioned, foreign capital is free to invest in any productive enterprise without any limitations other than those that apply also to Mexican investors. However, new firms who wish to apply for tax exemptions or reductions must have a majority of Mexican capital in order to qualify under the Law of New and Necessary Industries. Also, when a proposed new industrial enterprise expects to import equipment or raw materials requiring import permits, the projects must have prior approval . . . and it will be insisted that there be a majority of Mexican capital when the firm in question is going to operate in fields where there are already firms having majority Mexican capital holdings.
>
> In the remaining cases, a Mexican majority is not required if and when (1) the activity of the firm . . . will aid substitution of imported goods or because it proposes to export goods; (2) the proposed site for the new firm is highly beneficial; (3) substantial benefits would accrue to the economic and social interests of the country.[12]

A decline in raw material export receipts by a less-developed country may bring on import restrictions as well as fiscal policy tools designed to bring about industrial diversification and growth. The implementation of an import substitution policy by a country to speed up development of certain key industries may put pressure on certain investors (including foreigners) to produce better quality products with lower unit costs, expand the product line, and/or increase the skill level of its employees. In these cases, the emphasis is *not* on the ownership of the firm, but on the economy's requirements for meeting a stated objective. For the international businessman, it makes a difference whether or not the objective of the host government is to get rid of him or rather to make him a more welcomed citizen. In either case, however, it is important that the manager understand

1. What the implications are likely to be for his operation
2. The likelihood of the host government's implementing certain policy measures or continuing existing ones
3. What can be done to adapt to the changing situation and to minimize the adverse consequences for the firm

The Possibilities of a Loss in the Dollar Value of Foreign Assets and Earnings, and Restrictions on the International Movement of Funds: Devaluation and Exchange Controls as Policy Measures of Foreign Governments

A. THE PROBLEM DEFINED

During most of 1965, 1966, and 1967 there was considerable conjecture in England and throughout the world that the British currency, the pound

[12] Octaviano Campos Salas in an interview in *Latin America*, 1967, pp. 112–13.

sterling, would be devalued. In April 1968 Uruguay devalued its peso from 200 to the dollar to 250:1, which was the country's fifth devaluation in thirteen months. In August 1968 the government of Chile devalued the escudo for the fifteenth time in eight months. Also in mid-1968 the Philippines placed the following restrictions on importers:

> The Central Bank of the Philippines imposed a cash margin deposit requirement, to be effective until the end of 1968, for the opening of import letters of credit in the following proportions: 50 per cent for essential producer and consumer goods, 75 per cent for semiessential producer goods, 100 per cent for nonessential producer goods and semiessential consumer goods, and 175 per cent for nonessential consumer goods and unclassified items. Imports under documents against payment, documents against acceptances, and open account arrangements were also subject to the deposit requirement. These advance deposits were to be held for 120 days upon filing the letter of credit and were to be released at the time of the issuance of the release certificates for the imported goods.

These examples and many others that can be cited illustrate conditions that have faced and (in other countries) still face the financial managers of multinational companies. Policy decisions must be made regarding how to deal with the types of situations described, and day to day decisions must be reached on the likelihood of an affiliate's experiencing devaluation or exchange controls and the steps which should be taken to avoid loss or difficulties for the firm. This section of the chapter discusses the nature of these policy measures.

Currency devaluation and exchange control risks are discussed under one heading because in many ways they are similar: both may be considered to be discretionary policy measures taken by the host country; and both frequently result from external economic forces and pressures which induce national policy-makers to consider the utility of one or both measures as tools of last resort. Normally both devaluation and controls are directly related to the state of the country's balance of international payments.

From prior knowledge the reader will recall that there may be numerous reasons for a country to experience a deficit (or surplus) in its balance of payments.[13] Among the commonly cited causes are:

1. *Inflation* within the domestic economy that tends to make export products uncompetitive in world markets, imports increasingly attractive, and that discourages the inflow of private capital and often leads to capital flight by anxious citizens [14]

[13] For the reader who desires to make a more complete review of balance of payments concepts and relationships, *see* Delbert A. Snider, *Introduction to International Economics,* 4th ed., Homewood, Ill., Richard D. Irwin, Inc., 1967; "The Bookkeeping of the Balance of Payments," *Morgan Guaranty Survey,* May 1962, pp. 2–11.

[14] For a concise description of the possible impact of inflation on a nation's external accounts, *see* Graeme S. Dorrance, "Rapid Inflation and International Payments," *Fund and Bank Review,* June 1965, pp. 65–70.

2. *Business cycles* in either the local economy or in the outside world that can significantly alter a nation's demand for imported goods or foreign countries' demand for the exports of a given country

3. *Structural problems* within the economy that may preclude successful competition in the world markets—as is often alleged to be the cause of England's recent balance-of-payments difficulties—or, as is characteristic of most less-developed countries, an excessively heavy reliance on the export earnings of one or two products such as coffee or cocoa, with accompanying instability in the inflow of foreign exchange

4. The process of *economic development*—a combination of structural problems, susceptibility to the business cycles of the advanced countries, and sometimes inflationary pressures, characteristically involving a lengthy period of heavy reliance on imported goods and a concurrent buildup in annual debt service obligations to the outside world. Internal disorders, such as the 1968 French student and worker riots and strikes, may sufficiently disrupt a nation's international trade patterns and induce an outflow of short-term capital of such magnitude as to cause a serious deficit in the balance of payments.

No nation can indefinitely endure balance-of-payments deficits, for at some point in time its capacity for financing them—either through the exportation of gold, foreign exchange reserves, or the inflow of so-called accommodating capital—will be exhausted. In anticipation of that date, countries which are experiencing such problems will take steps to put an end to the deficits. In general, there are four major categories of adjustments which can be made:

1. Changes in the relative levels of national income
2. Changes in the exchange rates of the home currency *vis à vis* the rest of the world
3. Changes in the relative level of domestic prices
4. Imposition of controls on the current and/or capital accounts.

In Table 2–1 a detailed presentation is made of the *specific* policy measures which fall within the foregoing general categories. In this chapter, the focus is limited to changes in the exchange rate of the host country currency and the use of quantitative controls, the two discretionary measures which are peculiarly international in character from the point of view of the businessman with foreign interests.

Exchange rate devaluations that may be effected by individual countries are, in general, intended to lower international cost-price levels, thereby reducing the price of exported goods to the rest of the world while concurrently increasing the cost to domestic consumers of imported goods and services. The ensuing change in a devaluing country's autonomous international expenditures and receipts will be dependent upon the elasticity of the demand and supply of foreign exchange and, over a period of time, on the country's ability to maintain relatively stable internal prices.

TABLE 2–1

Policies and Measures Prescribed for Correcting Balance of Payments Deficits

DOMESTIC MONETARY POLICY

1. Stop increasing domestic bank assets
2. Reduce domestic bank assets
3. Retard domestic bank assets
4. Raise short-term interest rates
5. Raise long-term interest rates
6. Allow prices to decline

PRICE AND INCOME POLICY

7. Keep price level stable
8. Allow wage rates to decline
9. Keep wage rates stable

COMMERCIAL POLICY

10. Raise tariffs and other import barriers
11. Introduce or raise export subsidies
12. Tie foreign loans to exports

FISCAL POLICY

13. Increase personal income taxes
14. Reduce business taxes (to attract foreign and domestic exportable capital)
15. Reduce government spending at home

FOREIGN SPENDING, LENDING, AND INVESTING

16. Reduce government spending abroad
17. Reduce government grants abroad
18. Reduce government lending abroad
19. Discourage private long-term capital exports
20. Control private long-term capital exports
21. Encourage private long-term capital imports
22. Discourage private short-term capital exports
23. Encourage private short-term capital imports
24. Control private short-term capital exports

EXCHANGE RATE POLICY

25. Ration foreign exchange or prohibit certain payments
26. Devalue the currency against foreign exchange (and gold)

Source: Fritz Machlup, *Real Adjustment, Compensatory Corrections, and Foreign Financing of Imbalances in International Payments,* Reprints in International Finance, No. 2, International Finance Section, Princeton University, Princeton, N.J., September 1965.

During the past few years there have been numerous examples of exchange rate devaluations and widespread anticipations of their occurrence. (In fact, during the period 1948–1967, *ninety-six* countries underwent one or more devaluations of their exchange rates!) In the case of

England cited at the beginning of this discussion, the country ran a continuous balance-of-payments deficit for many years and, in the eyes of the world, it had dangerously low gold and foreign exchange reserves with which to maintain the par value of the pound sterling. This is exemplified by the following excerpt from the Associated Press story on November 17, 1967:

> UK SEEKING INTERNATIONAL AID TO SHORE UP POUND
>
> LONDON. (AP). Britain pressed on Thursday night with secret moves to rally massive new international support for its wobbly pound with some signs suggesting government leaders are split on the rescue operation.
>
> The rate for sterling slumped to 2.783 dollars—only five points above the floor—after Chancellor of the Exchequer James Callaghan refused in Parliament to confirm or deny that loans worth 1 billion dollars or more are imminent.
>
> One authoritative source said Prime Minister Harold Wilson's labor cabinet is divided over terms under which some friendly countries are offering support.
>
> Some members were said to want to stave off the threat of pound devaluation at almost any cost.
>
> Others were reported equally ready to use the sanction or threat of devaluation as a means of getting the best terms possible.
>
> Almost all British leaders agreed that a forced, untimely devaluation of sterling monetary arrangements exposed most other currencies, including the dollar, to the risk of unwanted cutbacks too.
>
> It was a day of high drama in the city of London's foreign exchange market and in and around Parliament.
>
> On the foreign exchange market the pound took a sensational switchback ride as rumors circulated about the Wilson government's bid for new sources of credit.
>
> At one point the pound soared 16 points, to 2.7848 dollars.

During the 1960's the inability of the British economy to significantly and permanently improve its external accounts despite a variety of public policy measures designed to bring about structural change, to lower domestic prices, and to impede the outflow of capital on both current and capital accounts, led to the recurrent expectations of a devaluation of the pound.

The devaluation of the Finnish markka in October 1967 appeared to stem from similar circumstances. The governor of the Bank of Finland explained that in the preceding years, rising costs, income, and prices had "exceeded the limits that could have been permitted in view of the maintenance of Finland's international competitive position." This situation resulted in a vigorous growth of demand for imported goods, while exports expanded more slowly than imports. The result was a large balance-of-payments deficit that the country was no longer able to finance. In the mid-1960's Finland tried to improve the situation by pursuing contractive domestic economic policy—using monetary and fiscal policy to curb internal demand, as well as special policies to control imports and to stimulate exports. These efforts were somewhat effective in countering the balance-of-payments trend, but the nation's internal costs were too high. Investment declined, unemployment grew, and overall economic activity slowed considerably. By 1967 it became clear to the government policy-makers that unless an exchange devaluation was instituted—in addition to other selective policies designed to improve the external accounts—"it would have been some time before an expansionary economic policy could have been introduced." Hence, on October 12, 1967, the markka was devalued by 23.8 per cent.[15]

A much different situation has existed in Brazil. For almost a decade that country has experienced continuing rapid internal price inflation. Given its basic position as a less developed economy with heavy reliance on the outside world for goods and services and with excessive dependence on coffee exports to earn its foreign exchange, Brazil's incessant price inflation has aggravated the country's balance-of-payments problems. As can be noted in Table 2–2, which compares Brazil's price level changes with its official rate of exchange, the government has been forced to devalue the cruzeiro many times.

TABLE 2–2

The Cost-of-Living Index and the Official Rate of Exchange for Brazil, 1958–1967.

YEAR	*COST OF LIVING*	*CRUZEIROS PER U.S. DOLLAR* *
1958	100	138.5
1959	137	203.8
1960	185	205.1
1961	256	318.5
1962	390	475.0
1963	684	620.0
1964	1270	1850.0
1965	2050	2220.0
1966	3380	2220.0
1967	4190	2715.0

* Note: the figures given are end-of-year for the free market cruzeiro.
Source: IMF *International Financial Statistics.*

Exchange controls, which may take a variety of forms, are discretionary policy measures that can be employed to counter the free market forces affecting a country's balance of international payments. Normally, one or more control devices are employed to ration a limited supply of foreign exchange among those in the economy who demand it. As such, the system will involve discriminatory treatment of some parties within the foreign exchange market; in some cases exchange controls may favor exporters over the country's importers, whereas in others it may discrimi-

[15] *International Financial News Survey,* November 10, 1967.

nate against the goods of a foreign country whose currency is in short supply in the deficit nation.

At the present time and throughout the twentieth century, there have been many nations which have, for some combination of reasons, employed exchange controls. Less-developed countries such as Brazil, Argentina, Chile, Colombia, Indonesia, Thailand, Pakistan, the Philippines, Vietnam, and India have utilized controls for many years, and a number of the so-called advanced countries including France, Japan, and Italy have recently resorted to a number of restrictions on current and/or capital accounts.[16] The most widely utilized approach for controlling a country's limited reserves of foreign exchange is a system of multiple exchange rates. As the name implies, the host government establishes two or more rates of exchange between its currency and say, the United States dollar, and specifies the rates at which certain transactions will take place. In effect, multiple exchange rates permit selective devaluation of the local currency, for an artificially low rate of exchange applied to an international transaction will result in either a subsidy or an extra cost to the enterprise, depending on the nature of its transactions.

Let us review, for example, the case of Colombia in early 1967. The country utilized three separate rates of exchange:

	Pesos:Dollar
1. Coffee export rate	9.94:1
2. Other export and import rate	13.50:1
3. Free market rate	16.30:1

The government permitted the importation of certain "approved" goods at the preferred rate of 13.50:1. Other imports were paid for at the free rate of 16.30:1. Coffee exporters, on the other hand, in effect taxed by the government, were permitted to realize only 9.94 pesos for each dollar of export earnings.[17] Presumably the rationale for the multiple exchange rate system was three-fold:

1. To discourage certain types of imports, and thus conserve foreign exchange reserves

[16] There are a number of sources which discuss exchange controls: Leland B. Yeager, *International Monetary Relations,* New York, Harper & Row, Publishers, 1966, ch. 7; Jorge Marshall, "Exchange Controls and Economic Development," in H. S. Ellis, *Economic Development for Latin America,* New York, St. Martin's Press, 1961; Margaret G. de Vries, "Multiple Exchange Rates: Expectations and Experiences," *IMF Staff Papers,* July 1965, pp. 282–313; Eugene A. Schlesinger, *Multiple Exchange Rates and Economic Development,* Princeton Studies on International Finance, No. 2, May 1952. For a comprehensive coverage of the existing foreign exchange restrictions, *see* the *IMF Annual Report on Exchange Restrictions,* Washington, D.C.

[17] Cited in George Parker, *The Analysis of Private Capital Expenditures in Developing Economies,* Stanford University Business School, unpublished Ph.D. dissertation, 1967, p. 109.

2. To obtain revenues for the government from the production and exportation of coffee
3. To discourage excess coffee production.

One of the advantages of employing multiple exchange rates versus other types of quantitative controls is that it affords the government flexibility and selectivity in the implementation of fiscal policy.

The businessman can expect to encounter numerous other forms of controls in addition to multiple exchange rates. In some cases the host government may completely *prohibit* certain types of international transactions either through formalized regulations or through the subtleties of administering less restrictive policies. In Japan, for example, a number of United States companies have complained that their so-called yen companies [18] were not permitted to remit any dividends to the parent companies for many years. In other countries remittances of dividends are restricted to a percentage of the subsidiary's current earnings or capital base. For example, in a northern European country, foreign and domestically owned companies are required by law to allocate 10 per cent of their annual net profits to a reserve fund until the reserve reaches 25 per cent of share capital. In a recent year, dividends to both domestic and foreign recipients were limited to 6 per cent of capital, or the average dividend for the prior three years, until the reserve equaled 10 per cent of capital. Frequently the complaint is registered against many less developed countries that the ground rules for defining an acceptable capital base are changed from one fiscal period to another or are never made clear to the foreign investor so that he can understand what remittances will be permitted in the future.

Controls used to prohibit or lessen the importation of nonessential goods may take a number of additional forms. Many Latin American countries, for example, have required importers to deposit in local currency a certain proportion of the cost of desired imports before they enter the country. Although the deposit is subsequently released after the goods have been imported, the disadvantageous implications for working capital management are clear. As an illustration of how restrictive this type of exchange control can be, in 1962 Chile required advance deposits with rates being 10, 100, 200, and 1,000 per cent of the CIF value of the imports, depending on their essentiality. The deposits, which were to be made at the time the imports were registered with the Central Bank, were retained for 90 days. [19]

A variation of the above is a foreign exchange auctioning system conducted by the host government with the objective of limiting imports. As

[18] "Yen" companies could be established in Japan prior to July 1963 without their being required to obtain explicit permission by the Japanese government.

[19] Samir Makdisi, "Restrictions on the Movement of Funds Within Latin America," *IMF Staff Papers,* March 1963, pp. 186–217.

described in the following excerpt from the study, *International Enterprise in a Developing Economy,*[20] Brazil utilized a so-called agio system to discourage nonessential imports as well as to earn the government a profit from its foreign exchange transactions:

> The agio system, adopted in 1953, was actually a system for auctioning exchange commitment certificates (PVC's) . . . which entitled the holder to apply for exchange cover. The dollar or other foreign credits thus purchased were then acquired at the official parity rate . . . 18.92 cruzeiros to the dollar. The foreign exchange was actually acquired through the holder's private bank in Brazil from the Bank of Brazil. The total cruzeiro cost of dollars on the agio markets therefore included (1) the holder's bid price for the PVC, (2) 18.92 cruzeiros per dollar, and (3) stamp and brokerage fees totaling 0.975 per cent. . . . The price in cruzeiros, which a firm was obliged to bid in order to buy on the agio markets, depended on the effective demand on that particular day and on the allotment of foreign exchange made available daily by the . . . federal government.
>
> One other feature combined with the above factors to determine bid prices. For the purpose of exchange purchase, two categories of goods prevailed in 1958. All commodities considered by the Brazilian government as essential . . . fell into the "general" category and were listed as such. All other commodities . . . fell into the "special" category. . . . Dollars purchased in the special category cost about twice those purchased in the general category.

As another example, in October 1967 Peru instituted an exchange certificate system whereby exporters were required to deliver to the Central Bank 100 per cent of the FOB foreign exchange value of their shipments. They received, in turn, certificates of exchange that could be sold to importers for use in payment for registered imports and certain specified remittances. The exchange rate for these certificates was pegged at 38.70 whereas the sol was otherwise not supported by the government and declined to 43.20 by the following March.

From the foregoing survey and discussion of devaluation and the forms which exchange controls can take—and there are almost an infinite variety which can be devised by host governments—it should be clear to the reader how a host government's concern for its balance-of-payments deficit and low foreign exchange reserves may move the government to utilize one or more forms of adjustment in an attempt to remedy the situation. Additionally there are other pressures that may give rise to a system of exchange controls.

In a basic sense we may classify most of the other reasons under the general heading of "furthering economic development objectives." A country which desires to foster the growth of its industry may, for instance, provide protection to local companies against imported goods,

[20] Claude McMillan, Jr., Richard F. Gonzales, Lee G. Erickson, *International Enterprise in a Developing Economy,* East Lansing, Michigan State University, 1964, pp. 185–86.

thereby creating a monopolistic position for the local entrepreneur,[21] and encourage or induce reinvestment of current earnings. Similarly, if the objective is the creation or expansion of the domestic export industry, a system of exchange controls may, in addition to the benefits named above, provide a subsidized rate of exchange to exporters, thereby increasing local currency earnings. Controls may also provide revenues to the government that it may not otherwise be able to raise. As Margaret de Vries has pointed out:

> In countries where taxes on commodity exports or duties on commodity imports cannot be applied for political reasons, or where income taxes either do not exist or are inadequate, multiple exchange rates are often believed to be a convenient means of taxation. Payment of a tax when exchange is sold to exchange control authorities, or of surcharges when exchange is purchased, is more readily enforceable than payment of other types of taxes.[22]

Outright nationalism may be an important factor. Countries that desire to limit foreign-owned enterprises either in general or in specified industries may impose a system of discriminatory controls that discourage would-be investors and drive out existing ones. The latter event would be a case of creeping expropriation.

B. POSSIBLE BUSINESS IMPLICATIONS OF EXCHANGE CONTROLS AND CURRENCY DEVALUATION

The preceding discussion identified many of the reasons for a host country's decision to devalue its currency or institute a system of foreign exchange controls. These government policy decisions are as likely today as they were immediately after World War II when the world economy and the internal conditions of individual nations were suffering from shock, war disaster, and economic disequilibrium. Despite the dramatic economic and social recovery of the past 25 years by many countries and the admirable work done by postwar international institutions and through multilateral cooperation, the conditions still exist (or may develop) in almost every country of the free world that pressure a government administration into taking relatively drastic remedial or corrective balance-of-payments actions. A considerable proportion of the nations are still struggling to make themselves economically viable and are today —as they were thirty years ago—heavily dependent on a few primary goods for their national income and foreign exchange receipts. Inter-

[21] For an account of how the Philippine's leading entrepreneur viewed the importance of exchange controls in his own personal rise, *see* "An Interview With Ramon Del Rosario," in David B. Zenoff, *Private Enterprise in the Developing Countries,* Englewood Cliffs, N.J., Prentice-Hall, Inc., 1969.

[22] Margaret G. de Vries, *op. cit.*

national price instability, periodic declining commodity terms of trade, heavy external indebtedness, and internal inflation still characterize many countries and continue to necessitate, under a system of pegged exchange rates, currency controls and devaluation.

A reading of the daily press will vividly remind the student of international business that balance-of-payments deficits continue to plague mighty industrial nations, too; speculation against deficit countries is still an important and uncontrollable phenomenon; hoarding of gold is just as popular an activity as it ever was, and methods of adjusting balance-of-payments disequilibria still appear to subordinate domestic objectives to external ones.

In considering the possible implications for a business located in a country that has just undergone an exchange rate devaluation, it is important to identify first the possible general economic effects as they may pertain to the firm and then to focus on some of the balance sheet and profit-and-loss-statement considerations.

One of the intended results of a devaluation is to increase the local currency cost of imported goods and services. The effects on a local enterprise will depend on the extent to which it relies on imported goods and services, the extent to which its competitors do, and the amount of competition provided by imported finished goods. How much domestic prices rise in response to a devaluation is another critical variable. Other things equal, domestic price performance after exchange rate devaluation can be expected to be a function both of the government's efforts to restrain price increases and the extent to which the economy is dependent on imported goods and services. For the firm, a rise in domestic price levels—if it occurs—may nullify some of the gains which resulted from the devaluation, or, in the case of a company which was relatively well insulated from rising costs, the higher general price level may result in larger per unit contribution if the firm raises its prices.

Devaluation may also lead to general uncertainty about the future rate of exchange, and the country may experience widespread capital flight with a consequent decrease in domestic consumption and money supply. Some parties who anticipate another devaluation may be induced to invest heavily in durable goods whose local prices are expected to increase when the next devaluation occurs. For the economy as a whole, and for a given firm, the possible after-effects of these actions will range from a slowdown in business investment and sales to selective increases in sales and profits, depending on the nature of the general response to the devaluation, the borrowing requirements of the firm, and the nature of its product line.

Looked at from still another viewpoint, a successful devaluation may be expected to lead to greater export volume for the local economy and more demand for locally produced goods versus imports. This increased activity would produce more income for the economy as a whole and for the firm whose sales and profitability are a function of the growth in national income.

One may expect that devaluation will increase the local currency cost of foreign indebtedness by the amount of the devaluation. Hence, a company which contracted for the importation of $1,000 worth of foreign-made components when the exchange rate was $1 = 1LC will have to pay LC2,000 if its country's currency is devalued to $1 = 2LC in the period between placing the order and receiving the goods. Similarly, an intracompany loan made in dollars will cost the foreign subsidiary twice as much in local currency if there is such a devaluation between the time the indebtedness is incurred and repaid.

To the parent company, devaluation of a foreign currency will reduce the dollar value of the foreign affiliate's local earnings unless the effect of the devaluation is to raise local currency profits by as much or more than the percentage amount of the devaluation. Similarly, the dollar value of the affiliate's monetary assets is reduced by the amount of the change in the exchange rate.

The imposition of exchange controls in a foreign host country can have two general types of effects upon a multinational firm:

1. It can increase the cost of doing business
2. It can restrict the freedom to conduct certain types of transactions.

The use of import surcharges, advance deposits, an auction system, or multiple exchange rates that discriminate against imports can be expected to increase the costs of imported supplies and components to the subsidiary and/or tie up a part of the affiliate's liquid assets. The requirement to purchase foreign exchange at a free market rate that is higher than the official rate in order to make profit remittances will in effect be an extra cost of doing business for the affiliate and will require executive time to negotiate transaction approval from the local governmental authorities.

In terms of restricting a firm's freedom of operations, exchange controls can affect many types of transactions. The importation of certain required supplies or parts may be prohibited altogether or restricted in volume in a given fiscal period, thereby causing the firm to curtail production and/or to incur the opportunity cost of stocking out. Controls over capital transfers may preclude remittances of dividends, royalties, or fees to the parent company, or repayment of principal on intracompany loans. Also from a financial manager's viewpoint, exchange controls may tie up company-controlled funds within a particular country in which there is no attractive project in which to earn a satisfactory rate of return. Concurrently the worldwide company may encounter working capital problems because of inability to transfer funds from an affiliate; or the global company may be forced to forego an attractive external investment opportunity because of a capital shortage resulting from blocked funds in a particular country.

In summary, although it may not be said that the imposition of exchange controls by a host country or its decision to devalue its currency *must* lead to adverse circumstances for local business enterprise, there are distinct possibilities that the use of either or both of these measures may have costly consequences for individual firms and for the economy as a whole, as well as increasing uncertainty in the local business environment. The adept internationally oriented businessman must appreciate the possible consequences of these measures, and he must be able to forecast their occurrence and take appropriate measures to protect his firm against possible loss.

The Possibility of Price Inflation in the Foreign Host Country with the Chance of Serious Impediment to the Affiliate's Ability to Conduct Profitable Operations

Experience has demonstrated that business operations in an inflationary environment are normally subject to more uncertainty and greater operational problems than are usual in a noninflationary economy. The international financial manager is likely to encounter inflation—in various degrees—in many countries around the globe, and an important part of his overall responsibility is to ensure that his firm is well prepared to operate in these troublesome situations. This section of the chapter is devoted to an examination of the nature and forces of inflation.

A. INFLATION DESCRIBED AND ANALYZED

In the ensuing discussion we shall use the term "inflation" to describe a 5 per cent or greater rise in the general price level of a country in which the markets for goods and factors of production are permitted to function freely without abnormal interference by the government in the establishment of selling prices.[23] As suggested in Table 2–3, in recent years there have been numerous countries which have experienced inflation.

An examination of recent history reveals that inflation is neither a modern-day phenomenon nor one restricted to the lesser developed countries. In the post-World War I period, Germany suffered from price in-

[23] Questions of semantics can easily be raised in deciding precisely what constitutes inflation. An interesting attempt to resolve this difficulty is found in R. J. Ball, *Inflation and the Theory of Money,* Chicago, Aldine Publishing Co., 1964, Ch. I.

TABLE 2–3

Average Annual Increase in Consumer Price Index for Selected Countries, 1955–1965

COUNTRY	*AVERAGE ANNUAL INCREASE (in %)*
Israel	5.3
India	5.4
Finland	5.6
Taiwan	6.4
Spain	6.9
Turkey	8.1
Peru	8.1
Colombia	10.0
Korea	11.3
Bolivia	21.1
Chile	22.5
Argentina	23.5
Brazil	29.7

Source: United Nations, *Monthly Bulletin of Statistics*; First National City Bank of New York.

creases as high as 20 per cent per *month.* In the late 1930's China's prices were doubling each year. In the period from 1938 to 1945, Switzerland experienced a rise in its wholesale price index of 107 per cent and of 52 per cent in its cost-of-living index. From the late 1940's to the early 1960's France was forced repeatedly to devalue the franc, largely because of persistent internal price inflation. In 1968–1969 France again faced internal price increases of close to 15 per cent. And from late 1967 to 1969 United States domestic economic policy was preoccupied with choosing policy tools to curb the buildup of inflationary pressures:

> The more talk that goes on in the United States about future galloping inflation and future galloping growth, the sharper becomes the current inflation. It is now running at an annual rate of nearly 4 per cent and nobody . . . sees any let-up before next spring at the earliest, even with a tax increase, tight money or what have you. . . . Next year given the tax increase, it should be 4 per cent plus; without restraint it could go to 5½ per cent with considerable overheating.[24]

To be able to deal effectively with the effects of inflation, as well as to evaluate the likelihood of inflation commencing, continuing, or terminating in a particular economy, the businessman must have a fundamental understanding of what the forces and causes are that often lead to inflation. In the following pages it will be possible to present only a brief account of the many causes of general price level increases. Even experts disagree regarding the precise causes of inflation in a given situation. Without delving into the apologetics of the various schools of thought,

[24] "Over-Inflated Economy?" *The Economist,* October 21, 1967.

the ensuing discussion provides a guide to the businessman regarding the many causes that *may* be relevant in given situations.

The experiences of many less-developed countries that at some time have encountered relatively severe price inflation suggest that price increases usually result from a combination of economic forces that are largely outside the control of the respective governments, although in some instances inflation is used as a *tool* of government policy to promote economic development. In the former category, the following conditions and forces are contributory:

1. Rapidly increasing populations coupled with increasing disposable incomes and higher aspiration levels have resulted in increasing demand pressures for goods where there are relatively limited and inadequate domestic productive facilities.

2. Balance-of-payments problems and generally low levels of foreign exchange reserves have frequently necessitated restrictions on the quantity and type of consumer goods that could be imported to satisfy the demand not met by local production.

3. The general unresponsiveness of the supply of food to the demand of rapidly growing urban centers resulting from low agricultural productivity, short-run supply inelasticities in the rural sector, and inadequate channels of distribution and transportation facilities have led to price increases.

4. Ambitious government spending for economic development programs and social overhead capital, which frequently require deficit financing because the method and administration of local taxation are unable to provide sufficient revenues for the public sector, have contributed to inflation.

5. The conditioned responses of individuals and corporations used to combat inflation cause it to feed upon itself. When people become convinced that saving is not worthwhile, the aggregate problem of financing capital formation is aggravated. Available funds are invested in durable goods and inventories. Manufacturers and retailers make every effort to raise their prices before costs increase, and wage earners bargain hard to have their remuneration pegged closely to the cost-of-living index. In effect, inflation may occur independent of economic realities where behavior and expectations are based on past experience rather than current facts.

6. With certain goods having thin markets, which result from a low level of industrial activity, moderate shifts in demand can lead to relatively large fluctuations in the prices for these products.

7. Tightly controlled production and distribution of a number of goods among a small group of principals can cause noneconomic variations in price levels stemming from monopolistic pricing practices.

8. Balance-of-payments problems which lead to exchange controls or devaluation can cause higher local currency prices for imported goods and frequently contribute to a rise in the general cost of living.[25]

As noted above, inflation has also been utilized as a government tool in a number of less developed countries. Although there are many economists and politicians who see great dangers and costs to a society which experiences price inflation, there is a school of thought, one including several prominent political economists as well as influential government leaders, that believes a controlled inflation can produce several important benefits for a developing country. Anticipation of these benefits—a sampling of which is provided below—has led many, principally Latin American administrations, to utilize large-scale deficit financed spending programs to trigger a general price rise. While the record of successes and failures of such attempts is difficult to interpret and is no doubt mixed, numerous countries have learned through experience that a mild inflation is difficult to produce. Many attempts have led to runaway price increases bearing no resemblance to the controlled variety originally intended.

For those who nonetheless favor utilizing inflation as a method to further established social and economic goals, the expected benefits include:

1. An inducement to entrepreneurs to raise and invest funds because of the illusion of greater profitability through selling prices that will rise more quickly than the costs of doing business.

2. Increased capital formation and GNP that will result from the widespread propensity to invest available funds in inventories and durable goods.

3. Larger government revenues that will stem from increased corporate and personal taxable income.

4. The probability of a redistribution of wealth in favor of the wealthier and entrepreneurial classes with a concomitant greater likelihood that the new funds will be saved and productively invested.

Outside of the group of less-developed countries, inflation may result from a number of situations and conditions. In time of war,[26] national mobilization, or internal political uncertainties, governments must control available resources, adding significantly to the existing demand for factors of production and goods. Uncertainties shorten the time horizons of corporations and individuals, inducing them to invest in consumer durables and inventories as stores of wealth instead of holding liquid

[25] For a discussion of the possible effects of devaluation on the country's internal prices, *see* Egon Sohmen, "The Effect of Devaluation on the Price Level," *Quarterly Journal of Economics,* May 1958, pp. 273–283.

[26] In wartime, even the neutral countries are likely to experience inflationary pressures, which are transmitted internationally. In World War II, almost no country escaped general price level increases. Leland Yeager, *op. cit.,* p. 335.

asset balances. Furthermore, the redirection of national resources to a mobilization objective will restrict the supply of consumer goods at a time when there is likely to be relatively full resource utilization. Normally these forces lead to inflated prices for available goods.

Industrialized countries experiencing relatively full employment of labor and capital are susceptible to inflation from an autonomous increase in demand which may originate within the economy or the outside world. An example of this was the heavy defense spending by the United States government for the Vietnam war in a period of relatively full employment. An enlarged demand for the country's export products or a spurt in inventory and capital goods spending may lead to the widely noted situation of "too much money chasing too few goods." Similarly, government deficit financing and lax monetary policy in a full employment economy can result in heightened expectations of economic growth and inflating prices —with concomitant increases in corporate stockpiling of inventories and individual purchases of durable goods. With short-run supply inelasticity *vis à vis* both price and income, the enlarged demand and increasing velocity of money will lead to a generally higher level of domestic prices. Where unionization is strong, increases in wage levels are usually pegged to upward changes in the cost-of-living index and to inflated corporate profits. Hence, if unchecked by government measures, a spiraling effect of some sort and some duration may be expected to follow.

In addition, a country with a surplus balance of international payments can in some situations import inflation. A surplus of exports over imports results in less real goods and services available for purchase within the domestic economy. The foreign trade multiplier can be expected to operate in an expansionary direction. And, as the host government purchases surplus foreign exchange from local citizens in order to keep the exchange rate stable, its actions enlarge the domestic money supply; under a fractional-reserve banking system, governmental purchase of foreign exchange expands the volume of bank reserves, which in turn allows for a multiple expansion of the money supply.

Based upon the unpredictability of:

1. Government policies
2. The future extent and severity of the inflation
3. The impact that inflation will have on the local economy
4. The problems and situations that will confront the firm,

business planning will become more difficult and less reliable than under noninflationary circumstances. The business manager will be forced to make many more decisions under conditions of greater uncertainty than otherwise is the case.

B. POSSIBLE BUSINESS IMPLICATIONS OF PRICE INFLATION IN A FOREIGN HOST COUNTRY

The impact inflation may have on an affiliate of a multinational firm depends on inflation's effect on the overall business environment. We have already discussed the possible balance-of-payments impact; the countries' exports will become less price-competitive in world markets, whereas domestic products and services will become increasingly less attractive than the lower-priced imports. Capital inflows on private account may well slow down because of entrepreneurs' hesitations about investing in an uncertain, inflation-ridden economy. Meanwhile, there may be extensive speculative capital flight into more stable foreign convertible currencies. All of these forces may trigger the use of exchange controls or currency devaluation with their mixed effects upon the country as a whole and on the business community.

If inflation causes general unrest among the lower and fixed income groups and among influential business leaders, political instability may ensue. A parade of different administrations may come to power to take up the task of bringing prices back to more normal levels with stability. People in general, as well as business firms, will characteristically become defensive and inflation-minded, pursuing a number of operational policies designed to minimize the impact of inflation. Investment in durables, fixed assets, and inventories can be expected as well as disinvestment in cash and near cash assets. Within the limits of local credit control, widespread and continuous efforts to operate as largely as possible on borrowed capital will predominate. Price increases and methods to effect rapid turnover of funds will be utilized. In general, the private sector is typically preoccupied with methods to effect a rapid turnover of funds.

In this setting, the financial manager may expect to be confronted with any or all of the following conditions and situations:

1. A general unavailability of credit and/or substantially higher credit costs. Long- and medium-term borrowing may be impossible, and required short-term capital will be found only after extensive shopping on very short terms at high rates of interest with requirements for compensating balances and the inclusion of "roll-over" charges. Accounts receivable will build up and collection periods will lengthen, while creditors will offer inducements and put on the pressure for prompt payment of outstanding balances.

2. The value of financial assets in terms of purchasing power will diminish as inflation continues; but concurrently the real cost of local borrowing to the firm will decrease as prices increase.

3. Price controls may be imposed on some or all industries and, depending upon their design, the affiliate may experience a profit squeeze if prices are restricted more than costs.

4. Conversely, firms may experience illusory profits because depreciation and amortization schedules are based upon outdated historical costs and inventories. The result may well be an unduly burdensome income tax liability.

5. Increasing remuneration demands from the local labor force may lead to (1) higher wage bills for the firm, or (2) if the employees' demands cannot be adequately met, a continuing turnover in personnel with the usual accompanying difficulties and costs to the enterprise of an unstable labor force.

6. Another personnel problem concerns the compensation policy for expatriates employed by the subsidiary. As local prices increase, real income will fall below the equivalent income that could have been earned elsewhere in the company system. Adjustments may therefore be required. But the questions arise: (1) On what basis should the adjustments be made? (2) Who should pay them, the affiliate or the parent company?

7. If a devaluation of the currency takes place, the cost of imported inputs to the local affiliate will increase. Also, if the affiliate must compete against imported goods in the local market, its sales volume may suffer if unit prices are not held down.

8. With general price increases in the local economy, the subsidiary that depends upon domestically produced components or supplies will find that its cost of goods sold as well as other expenses are increasing, although the precise timing of the increases may be quite unpredictable.

Summary

Environmental adversities frequently encountered in international business are normally less important for managers of purely domestic operations. It is necessary that the financial manager of an internationally oriented company be familiar with such phenomena as currency devaluation, exchange controls, severe price inflation, and expropriatory action by host governments. He must be able to forecast their occurrence, anticipate their impact on the firm, and take suitable actions to minimize their unfavorable consequences.

Chapter 2 has focused on the nature of these environmental adversities and on their possible implications for foreign affiliates of multinational companies. Emphasis has been given to the interrelationships between the causes of devaluation, price inflation, exchange controls, and expropriatory actions, and to the fact that these events should usually be viewed as policy tools available to host governments, although any of them may result from forces and pressures which are beyond control of the local public policymakers.

The impact that any of these phenomena have upon a firm will depend on the circumstances surrounding the firm and producing the event. Normally they will add uncertainty to the businessman's horizon, and often the consequences can be loss of business profits and loss in asset values. It behooves the international executive to strive to understand the reasons for the occurrence of exchange controls, devaluation, inflation, and expropriation so that he can properly assess their importance to his organization and decide what actions to take. The next chapter tackles the problem of formulating an approach to forecasting foreign environmental conditions, and chapter 4 presents methods of minimizing possible adverse consequences for the firm if one or more of these contingencies are expected.

BIBLIOGRAPHY

Ashton, David J. "U.S. Investments in Canada: Will the Shoe Drop?" *Worldwide P and I Planning*, September-October 1968.

Baer, Werner, and Isaac Kerstenetzky. *Inflation and Growth in Latin America.* (Homewood, Ill.: Richard D. Irwin, Inc., 1964).

Bernstein, Marvin. *Foreign Investment in Latin America: Cases and Attitudes.* (New York: Alfred A. Knopf, Inc., 1966).

Christie, G. C. "What Constitutes a Taking of Property under International Law," *British Yearbook of International Law,* 1962.

Fayerweather, John. "19th Century Ideology and 20th Century Reality," *Columbia Journal of World Business,* Winter 1966.

Gabriel, Peter. "The Investment in the LDC: Asset with a Fixed Maturity," *Columbia Journal of World Business,* Summer 1966.

Gordon, Lincoln, and E. L. Grommers. *U.S. Manufacturing in Brazil.* (Boston: Harvard Business School, Division of Research, 1962).

Gudin, Eugenio. "Multiple Exchange Rates: The Brazilian Experience," *Economica Internationale,* August 1956.

Haberler, Gottfried. *Inflation—Its Causes and Cures.* (Washington, D.C.: American Enterprise Association, 1961).

Hansen, Bent. *Inflation Problems in Small Countries.* (Cairo: National Bank of Egypt, 1960).

International Monetary Fund. *Annual Report of Exchange Restrictions.* (Washington, D.C.).

Johnstone, Allan W. *United States Investment in France: An Investigation of the French Charges.* (Cambridge: M.I.T. Press, 1965).

Kart, K. L. "Latin-American Land Reform: The Uses of Confiscation," *Michigan Law Review,* Vol. 63, 1964.

Makdisi, Samir. "Restrictions on the Movement of Funds within Latin America," in Lee C. Nehrt, ed., *International Finance for Multinational Business.* (Scranton, Pa.: International Textbook Company, 1967).

Mikesell, Raymond. *Inflation in Latin America.* (Washington, D.C.: U.S. Congress, Subcommittee on American Republics Affairs, 1967).

Miller, John. "Devaluation of Foreign Currencies," *The Controller*, August 1956.

Morse, Chandler. "Potentials and Hazards of Direct Investment in Raw Materials," in Marion Clawson, ed., *Natural Resources and International Development*. (Baltimore: Johns Hopkins Press, 1965).

Servan-Schreiber, J. J. *The American Challenge*. (New York: Atheneum, 1968).

U.S. Library of Congress. *Expropriation of American-Owned Property by Foreign Governments in the Twentieth Century*. (Washington, D.C.: U.S. Government Printing Office, 1963).

de Vries, Margaret. "The Magnitudes of Exchange Devaluation," *Finance and Development*, no. 2, 1968.

Case 2
DEBENHAM INDUSTRIES

In September 1968, Jack Berliner, international treasurer for Debenham Industries, a United States capital goods manufacturer, was reviewing a request for a $75,000, one-year intercompany loan by the company's Brachilean subsidiary. Mr. Berliner considered the evaluation of the request to be somewhat complicated by the recurring price inflation in Brachile and the periodic exchange rate devaluations of the country's currency. In recent years, whenever the Brachilean affiliate—or any of the others located in an inflationary environment—requested outside funds, the parent company had authorized the use of locally denominated debt in the belief that the company's interests would be better served this way than by providing the capital through an intercompany loan.

The September 1968 request for funds from Brachile also included a memo from the affiliate's comptroller which contained cost data intended to assist the headquarters management in their selection between the alternative methods of financing foreign operations—an intercompany loan versus borrowing from local sources—when the affiliates were subjected to severe price inflation and repeated exchange devaluations. Mr. Berliner was intrigued with the possibilities of being able to make more use of available data in solving financial management problems, and he, therefore, decided to experiment with the Brachilean cost data to ascertain their usefulness and to assist him in evaluating the subsidiary's loan request.

The New Methodology

The new approach suggested by Brachile was intended to facilitate a comparison of:

1. The potential exchange loss to the parent company if it loaned funds to an affiliate and devaluation of the Brachilean currency occurred
2. The cost to the company of borrowing from Brachilean sources at relatively high interest rates because of the prevailing inflation in that country.

According to the Brachilean affiliate's comptroller, Tables 1 and 2 (pages 58 and 59) indicate the cost to the company expressed in dollars, of a local currency (LC) loan of 100 to the Brachilean affiliate by each of the two methods of financing under consideration (intercompany loan and local borrowing) and under various assumed exchange rates and interest rates.

The comptroller intended Table 1 to show the dollar cost of an *intercompany loan* equivalent to LC100. The table arrays possible dollar costs of such a loan, depending on the prevailing LC/$ exchange rates at the beginning and end of the year. The body of the table reflects the after-tax dollar cost possibilities of such a loan to the company as a whole when repaid in one year at various assumed rates of exchange.

As an example of the use of Table 1, an LC100 loan made when the exchange rate was 3.6:1 and repaid one year later at a 4:1 exchange rate would have a net cost to the company of $3.19. In Table 1, this cost figure can be located at the intersection of line 3.6 and column 4.0.

The Brachilean comptroller explained that Table 2 shows the cost, expressed in dollars, of LC100 borrowed locally for one year at various assumed interest rates ranging from 12 to 30 per cent. The left-hand column in the table contains various assumed rates of exchange at the time the loan is made. The other columns indicate the after-tax dollar cost to the company of a one-year loan at various interest rates. Table 3 provides the basis for the construction of Tables 2 and 3.

As an example, a one-year LC 100 loan made when the rate of exchange was 3.6:1, at 18 per cent interest, would cost the company $3.35 (located at the intersection of line 3.6 and column 18 per cent).

Solving the Immediate Problem

To properly evaluate the current loan request from Brachile, Mr. Berliner obtained the company economist's projections of the likelihood that the Brachilean exchange rate would be at various levels *vis a vis* the dollar on September 30, 1969. They are shown in the following chart. (Prevailing rate, September 1, 1968, LC3.2 = $1.)

Possible ending exchange rates (9/1/69) (LC/$)	*Probability of occurrence*
3.2	.05
3.4	.00
3.6	.30
3.8	.30
4.0	.20
4.2	.10
4.4	.04
4.6	.01

Questions

1. Evaluate the overall utility of the Brachilean manager's approach to deciding on affiliate financing.
2. What information and considerations in addition to the foregoing cost calculations should enter into his decision?
3. Assuming a 22 per cent interest rate in Brachile in September 1968, what should be Mr. Berliner's decision?

Table 1

Dollar Cost of an Intercompany Loan, which is Equivalent to LC100 at 8 Per Cent Rate of Interest, Shown at Various Beginning and Ending Rates of Exchange

BEGINNING EXCHANGE RATES	*ENDING EXCHANGE RATES (LC:$)*														
	3.2	3.3	3.4	3.5	3.6	3.7	3.8	3.9	4.0	4.1	4.2	4.3	4.4	4.5	4.6
3.2	$1.50	2.13	2.73	3.29	3.82	4.32	4.80	5.25	5.68	6.09	6.48	6.85	7.21	7.54	7.87
3.3		1.45	2.05	2.61	3.14	3.64	4.12	4.57	5.00	5.41	5.80	6.17	6.52	6.86	7.19
3.4			1.41	1.97	2.50	3.01	3.48	3.93	4.37	4.78	5.16	5.53	5.89	6.23	6.55
3.5				1.37	1.90	2.40	2.88	3.33	3.76	4.17	4.56	4.93	5.28	5.62	5.95
3.6					1.33	1.83	2.31	2.76	3.19	3.60	3.99	4.36	4.71	5.05	5.37
3.7						1.29	1.77	2.22	2.65	3.06	3.45	3.82	4.18	4.51	4.84
3.8							1.26	1.71	2.14	2.55	2.94	3.31	3.66	4.00	4.33
3.9								1.23	1.66	2.07	2.46	2.83	3.18	3.52	3.84
4.0									1.20	1.61	2.00	2.37	2.72	3.06	3.38
4.1										1.17	1.56	1.93	2.28	2.62	2.94
4.2											1.14	1.51	1.86	2.20	2.53
4.3												1.11	1.47	1.81	2.13
4.4													1.09	1.43	1.75
4.5														1.06	1.39
4.6															1.04

Table 2

Cost Expressed in Dollars of Borrowing LC100 Locally at Various Rates of Interest

ASSUMED EXCHANGE RATES	*INTEREST RATES* 12%	14%	16%	18%	20%	22%	24%	26%	28%	30%
3.2	$2.51	2.93	3.35	3.77	4.19	4.61	5.02	5.44	5.86	6.28
3.3	2.44	2.84	3.25	3.65	4.06	4.47	4.87	5.28	5.68	6.09
3.4	2.36	2.76	3.15	3.55	3.94	4.33	4.73	5.12	5.52	5.92
3.5	2.30	2.68	3.06	3.44	3.83	4.21	4.59	4.98	5.36	5.74
3.6	2.23	2.60	2.98	3.35	3.72	4.09	4.47	4.84	5.21	5.58
3.7	2.17	2.53	2.89	3.25	3.61	3.97	4.34	4.70	5.06	5.42
3.8	2.11	2.46	2.81	3.16	3.51	3.85	4.23	4.58	4.94	5.29
3.9	2.06	2.40	2.75	3.09	3.44	3.78	4.12	4.47	4.81	5.15
4.0	2.01	2.35	2.68	3.02	3.35	3.69	4.02	4.36	4.69	5.03
4.1	1.96	2.29	2.61	2.94	3.27	3.59	3.93	4.25	4.58	4.90
4.2	1.91	2.23	2.55	2.87	3.19	3.50	3.83	4.15	4.46	4.78
4.3	1.87	2.18	2.49	2.80	3.12	3.42	3.74	4.05	4.36	4.67
4.4	1.82	2.13	2.43	2.74	3.04	3.35	3.65	3.95	4.26	4.56
4.5	1.78	2.08	2.39	2.68	2.97	3.27	3.57	3.87	4.17	4.46
4.6	1.74	2.04	2.32	2.62	2.91	3.20	3.49	3.79	4.07	4.37

Table 3

The Method and Assumptions Used by the Brachilean Comptroller to Calculate the Costs of Dollar and Local Currency Loans

INTERCOMPANY DOLLAR LOAN

Assumptions Used

A. Intercompany dollar loans made @ 8 per cent per annum rate of interest
B. Beginning exchange rate: LC3.60:1
   Ending exchange rate: LC4:1
C. Local income tax rate: 33 per cent
   U.S. Income tax rate: 50 per cent
D. U.S. $ imputed interest cost: 3.4375 per cent

	Subsidiary's books	*U.S. books*	*Consolidated books*
1. Interest expense: 8% of $27.777 (equals LC100 @ 3.6:1)	($2.222)	$2.222	
2. Loss on exchange:			
$27.777 @ 3.6:1 = LC100			
$27.777 @ 4.0:1 = LC111.108			
Loss LC11.108			
Loss @4.0:1	($2.777)		($2.777)
3. Total income (expenses)	($4.999)	$2.222	($2.777)
4. Income tax rates	33%	50%	
Amount of tax	($1.650)	$1.111	($ .539)
5. Profit (loss) after taxes	($3.349)	$1.111	($2.238)
6. Imputed interest @ 3.4375% on $27.777			($0.954)
7. After-tax cost of loan			$(3.192)

LOCAL CURRENCY LOAN

Assumptions Used

A. Prevailing rate of exchange: LC3.60:$1

B. Local interest rate: 18% p.a.

1. Amount of loan		LC 100	
2. Annual interest expense		LC 18	
3. Local tax rate	33%		
4. Amount of local taxes		LC 6	
5. After-tax expense		LC 12	= $3.35

Case 3
AMERICAN VEHICLES CORPORATION

American Vehicles Corporation, S.A., was a marketing and assembly operation in Abroland, a Latin American less-developed country about equal in size to the state of Utah with a population of approximately twelve million. The firm was one of thirty wholly-owned foreign subsidiaries of a United States vehicle manufacturer, the American Vehicle Corporation (AVC). Worldwide sales were about $650 million in 1968, of which 45 per cent was accounted for by overseas operations.

AVC made all of the major policy decisions for its overseas affiliates,[1] leaving to the subsidiary managers responsibility for day-to-day operating problems, maintenance of workable relationships with the host country governments, and the supplying of information and advice to the parent company on the status of local operations and suggested modifications in existing company policies.

Since its establishment in 1954, AVC, S.A., had sold more than 60,000 jeep-type vehicles in Abroland. Annual sales had increased from only 500 vehicles in the first year to somewhat more than 15,000 in 1968. The ability of AVC, S.A., to sell so many of its "Speedys" in this relatively small and backward country was generally attributed to three factors:

1. The Speedy had been priced at the local currency equivalent of only $1,300, which was many hundreds of dollars cheaper than any of the other automobile manufacturers' models and within the reach of the country's upper class and growing middle-income group.
2. The Speedy had two features which made it especially suitable for Abroland. It had excellent weight-hauling characteristics for its size and was popular among farmers for transporting produce to urban markets, light manufacturers for pick-ups and deliveries of supplies, and drivers who used the Speedy as a taxicab which could carry up to six passengers at a time.

[1] An important example of worldwide policy was the requirement that 45 per cent of each subsidiary's earnings after foreign taxes were to be remitted to the parent company as dividends.

The vehicle also had been designed to have the high road clearance required to navigate the country's unimproved roads that would otherwise have become impassable to motor vehicles during the three-month rainy season.

3. AVC, S.A., had never had any significant competition in the local market. The small size of the market precluded any automobile manufacturer from producing locally. Vehicles exported[2] to Abroland were typically far too expensive for the local populace because of the high costs of transportation, the 125 per cent *ad valorem* tariff on all imports of assembled automobiles, and the relatively high FOB price of American or European automobiles.

Furthermore, other vehicle producers were unable to follow AVC and ship manufactured assemblies to Abroland for local assembly and completion; competitors' retail prices would still have exceeded the local currency equivalent of $1,900, and few cars other than those made by AVC were built with the required high road clearance.

AVC, S.A., imported so-called knocked-down assemblies from the parent company for $1,000 and assembled them at the rate of approximately 300 per week. Three hundred semiskilled and skilled nationals were employed in the assembly process. Most of the company's work force had received on-the-job training with AVC, S.A., in addition to special evening classes in auto mechanics which the firm provided for its new employees. The company also employed twenty secretaries, ten foremen and four department managers. Only two Americans, the subsidiary general manager and financial manager, were on the AVC, S.A., staff.

At the current level of operations, the company paid out the local currency equivalent of about $700,000 per year in wages to its work force, $250,000 annually to lease its block-long building, incurred overhead and administrative expenses of $350,000 a year, $400,000 for paints, lubrications and supplies purchased locally, and almost $300,000 in business taxes and licenses. In addition, AVC, S.A., paid corporate income taxes which were based on a two-step rate schedule: 30 per cent for the first $5 million in earnings and 50 per cent thereafter.

AVC was one of a small number of foreign-owned companies in Abroland. The dearth of foreign private investment reflected the fact that more than one-half of the country's population resided in the traditional, rural sector which was largely outside of the money economy and the existing transportation and communications networks. Despite the absence of foreign capital inflows, the economy had managed to finance imports of goods and services by exporting between $105-130 million a year of agricultural and mineral products, an activity supplemented by its receipts of bilateral aid from a small number of North American and Western European countries (see Exhibit 1).

Beginning in 1966, however, the country's exports to its traditional markets began to decline and by early 1969 foreign exchange reserves had fallen to their

[2] In recent years approximately 1,000 United States and European-made cars had been imported annually. These were expensive models purchased by high government leaders and wealthy businessmen.

lowest level since 1940, $82 million. The decline in foreign demand for Abroland's mineral production reflected a shift by some of its industrial consumers to a newly produced synthetic material which was being widely promoted by a large European chemical company. Abroland also exported an agricultural commodity used in the production of certain types of plastics; in late 1968 demand for the commodity began to slacken as a result of a slowdown in industrial activity in the United States.

In early 1969 Elliot Robinson, manager of AVC, S.A., decided to discuss the country's balance-of-payments problems with his long-time acquaintance M. D. Sade, the finance minister of Abroland. Robinson had heard an increasing number of rumors about the possibilities of exchange controls or currency devaluation and he wanted to investigate their validity. Sade and Robinson had known each other since 1959 when they met at a management development seminar sponsored by an American business school. From that time on, the two men had made an effort to get together periodically and discuss the problems and prospects of the local business community. For each man, these meetings provided an opportunity to informally exchange information and to test out their respective ideas for changes in public policy.

At their meeting in March 1969, Robinson explained his suspicions and was handed a draft of some new legislation Sade said he planned to introduce (see Exhibit 2). After Robinson had had time to cursorily read through the draft, he inquired about the likelihood of its being introduced to the national legislature in its present form and in the near future. He was told:

> We have to take *some* action to alleviate the strain on our balance of payments position, and the Prime Minister has tentatively concluded that we might as well begin with the curtailment of private capital outflows. I personally have mixed feelings about a policy of this type because I know it can scare off foreign investors that we so desperately need. On the other hand, we do have a serious problem to solve *today*, and it's my responsibility to find a workable and timely solution.

On his way back to his office, Elliot Robinson considered what he should do. He was reasonably certain that if he could develop some convincing arguments for modifying certain features of the proposed legislation, the finance minister would be receptive to making a few alterations. Robinson also believed that the legislature would quickly pass any bill which M. D. Sade proposed if it would help to alleviate the balance-of-payments pressures.

Questions

1. If the legislation were passed in its present form, what effects, if any, would it have on AVC, S.A.?
2. What arguments, reasoning, and strategy would you recommend that Robinson utilize in attempting to influence M. D. Sade?
3. If the legislation is passed in its present form, what should Robinson do in the short run to overcome the company's problems?
4. As an extension of the foregoing question, taking a five-to-ten-year view, what recommendations should Robinson make to AVC headquarters?

EXHIBIT 1

Selected Abroland Balance-of-Payments Accounts by Year, 1958-1968 (in millions of dollars)

Year	*Exports*	*Imports*	*Receipts from bilateral aid*	*Total official foreign exchange reserves*
1958	128	134	32	104
1959	123	141	31	106
1960	127	142	26	105
1961	121	140	28	105
1962	124	144	29	102
1963	129	138	34	112
1964	122	143	35	114
1965	124	145	37	116
1966	116	143	34	108
1967	110	146	35	94
1968	109	146	37	82

EXHIBIT 2

Draft of Legislation to Limit Remittances by Affiliates of Foreign Companies in Abroland

I. Affiliates of foreign companies will be allowed each year to remit funds to foreign stockholders according to the schedule shown below.

Remittance rating	Allowable remittance as per cent of profits after local income taxes
80-100	80
60- 79	50
40- 59	20
20- 39	10
0- 19	5

The total remittance rating will be the sum of the ratings of the two subratings that measure the contribution of individual firms to the local economy—their balance of payments effect and their national income effect.

II. Balance of payments effect (E_{bp}) will be rated on the following scale:

E_{bp}	Rating
200 or more	50
150-199	40
125-149	30
110-124	20
100-109	10
below 100	0

The balance of payments effect is to be measured as the ratio of foreign exchange earned and saved by the firm to foreign exchange used by the firm. Symbolically,

$$E_{bp} = \frac{FX \text{ (earned and saved)}}{FX \text{ (used)}} \times 100$$

where

> *Foreign exchange earned* will be considered to be the amount received by the firm from the sale of exports.
>
> *Foreign exchange saved* will be measured in terms of the foreign exchange value of products deemed to be essential import substitutes. A product will be given an "essential" rating only if it is clear that in its absence, the further economic development of the country would be severely hindered or precluded.
>
> *Foreign exchange utilized* will be that expended on imported capital equipment, materials and supplies, and salaries of foreign technical and managerial personnel.

III. Contribution to national income (C_{NY}) will be rated on the following scale:

C_{NY}	Rating
250 or more	50
200-249	45
150-199	40
125-149	30
100-124	20
90- 99	10
below 90	0

The contribution to national income is to be measured as the ratio of domestic value added by the local firm (VA) to foreign exchange utilized by the firm in its production process (FX used). Symbolically,

$$C_{NY} = \frac{VA}{FX \text{ (used)}} \times 100$$

where

> *Domestic value added* will be the sum of wages, salaries, rent, interest on loans, and taxes paid locally.

Forecasting International Environmental Adversities

3

With the background on international environmental adversities and their implications for the firm provided in the previous chapter, the focus shifts in this chapter to the manager's task of forecasting environmental changes in a foreign country in which his company has business interests. Our primary objective is to assist the international manager in (1) identifying important forces and trends in the host country that in the future may impinge on local operation, and (2) assessing the likelihood of their occurrence.

The discussion commences with consideration of how to forecast price level inflation in a foreign economy. The second section suggests an approach to projecting currency devaluation and the imposition of exchange controls by a host country. The third section focuses on expropriatory actions by foreign governments and methods of assessing their likelihood.

FORECASTING INFLATION

From the discussion in chapter 2, it is obvious that a great premium is to be placed on the ability to forecast the commencement, duration, severity, and termination of inflation in a given country. While known methods of forecasting are still inexact, it is possible to make a useful analysis of the forthcoming fiscal period(s), and such analysis, combined with outside advice from banks and consultants, can help the manager to decide upon a suitable course of action for the affiliate. In forecasting inflation the approach recommended is to analyze the elements that govern *changes* in the host country's general price level. The key forces and factors for each country must be identified, examined, and finally, evaluated in terms of their relative importance in conditioning the environment. In this section a number of the key elements will be noted with suggestions for identifying changes that occur. No attempt is made to assess their respective importance in causing changes in a country's price levels, for conditions differ from country to country.

1. A program of continuous deficit spending by the host government should be carefully noted. Normally the methods of financing programs, overhead, and individual projects are announced publicly by the appropriate public authorities, as are the government's fiscal budget and new debt obligations.

2. An increase in the money supply, consisting of demand deposits plus money in circulation, can be monitored by reviewing IMF data and reports released by the central bank or the host country treasury department.

3. A substantial increase in business spending over previous periods can be anticipated from the reports of government agencies or private service organizations (banks, consultants, newspapers) which conduct periodic studies of business capital spending and inventory plans for the forthcoming fiscal periods. Also, if the local bank rate for private borrowings increases more rapidly than the central bank discount rate, it may signal a surge in business demand for bank funds.

4. A change in private expectations about the general price level is important to recognize. Through bank studies of firms' plans, analysis of consumer demand in the marketplace, and the demand for funds, the manager should attempt to ascertain if (a) producers are withholding their stocks from the market in anticipation of high prices, (b) companies in general are investing heavily in inventory in anticipation of cost increases, (c) companies and individuals are borrowing now or lining up overdraft facilities in anticipation of tight and more expensive credit conditions in the near future.

5. Restrictions on imported goods and government policies intended to stimulate the local economy and export industries may lead to general price increases. Normally they are announced publicly in the newspapers, are known to the businessman whose position is directly affected, and can be forecasted by recognizing deteriorations in the balance of trade, balance of payments, and level of foreign exchange reserves.

6. The government's attitude toward inflation as a tool of development or economic growth, as a necessary evil to be tolerated, or as a phe-

nomenon to be combatted can be ascertained (a) by how it has dealt with price rises in the past, (b) from newspaper interviews with top-level politicians and advisors or their public statements, and (c) from articles written by those in charge of monetary and fiscal policies on the general impact of inflation in similarly situated economies.

The reader is reminded that there are very distinctive schools of thought about why inflation occurs, how it should be treated, and what is its value in the development process. In a given country the policy-makers may favor provoking or maintaining some amount of domestic inflation.[1]

7. Pressure for higher wages on a widespread basis can be recognized and anticipated by (a) knowledge of forthcoming labor contract renegotiations in key industries or companies that are widely regarded as setting the pace for other firms, (b) an increase in the price of food and other basic goods, which is usually transmitted into demands for higher pay or is the basis for automatic increases in wages, (c) the overall strength of labor's position in important industries.

8. The possibility that host governmental agencies will be able to take effective action to preclude or curb price level increases must be analyzed from both a political and a technical standpoint. The position and strength of the administration's critics *vis à vis* inflation and anti-inflationary policies can be well monitored by following local politics in newspapers and in the political arena. The technical ability can be assessed by analyzing the strength that the central banking agency has over domestic financial institutions, the administrative effectiveness of the government in collecting income and turnover taxes from businesses and individuals, and the relative importance of the government budget to the total volume of domestic consumption and savings.

In this regard a useful method of assessing the likelihood of general price level increases is to examine key changes in the balance sheets of the host country's central banking institution. The statements, which are issued monthly or quarterly, will normally include the following major accounts:

Assets	*Liabilities and capital*
Net foreign reserves (gold, foreign exchange)	Currency
Domestic assets	Domestic liabilities
Loans to banks	Bank deposits
Loans to the public	Public deposits
Loans to the government and its agencies	Government deposits
	Capital and reserves

[1] For a summary of the most prominent views, *see* Werner Baer and Isaac Kerstenetzky, *Inflation and Growth in Latin America,* Homewood, Ill., Richard D. Irwin, Inc., 1964.

If, for example, the manager notes that the central bank has increased its holdings of government obligations—perhaps reflecting an increase in public sector spending, he must then determine what other changes have occurred in the accounts of the bank to compensate for the buildup of domestic assets. One possibility, of course, is a corresponding increase in currency in circulation, bank deposits, or government deposits, which might suggest a buildup of inflationary pressures.

9. The likelihood of wartime inflationary pressure being generated locally or transmitted to the host country, can be assessed through local and foreign news media, following the host country's domestic politics and foreign relations, and by analyzing how closely the local economy is tied to the events of the outside world, such as supplying critical raw materials to major cold or hot war belligerents.

10. The local employment conditions should be followed. The extent to which the local economy is employing available labor, finance capital, and productive capacity, and the availability of unemployed factors of production can be gleaned from periodic reports by the government and from the firm's own experiences in obtaining additional inputs for its operations.

As suggested earlier it is impossible to develop a checklist for use in forecasting changes in the general price level. There is no universally applicable list, for conditions vary between countries and the requirement and ability to analyze particular indicators will differ appreciably from one area to the next.

FORECASTING DEVALUATION AND EXCHANGE CONTROLS

As explained in chapter 2 currency devaluation and exchange controls are discussed together because in many important ways they are similar: both may be considered to be discretionary policy measures of the host country; both frequently result from external economic forces and pressures which impel their use as tools of last resort; and, normally, devaluation and exchange controls are directly related to the state of the nation's balance of international payments.

Forecasting controls and devaluation in a foreign country is very difficult. In effect, the businessman is attempting to second-guess the implementation of discretionary governmental policies, which, in turn, are dependent on all of the following factors:

1. The decision-making characteristics of those with authority
2. The outlook and type of advice provided to the government by advisors
3. The conditions, pressures, and forces which are considered by the decision-makers and their advisors, and the perceptions of these people regarding current trends and appropriate policy responses

4. Economic considerations within the country and in the outside world which impinge upon the local economy
5. Political forces, pressures, and trends within the country and outside which may temper policy decisions
6. The required secrecy about official deliberations on devaluation.

The international businessman and his advisors may perceive conditions differently from government policy-makers. Entrepreneurs may place more emphasis on certain of the variables than do their counterparts in government. They may be unaware of what the civil servant is thinking about in terms of current conditions and suitable measures. As complicated and involved as these forecasting problems may be, the businessman must nonetheless attempt to project future conditions since the success and safety of overseas operations are normally largely dependent on the ability of management to adapt to environmental differences and changes over time. Corporate experience and the logic of careful management analysis suggest that in most cases it is possible to develop a useful forecast of environmental changes. The business manager can normally identify most of the relevant decision variables confronting the government policy-makers and subsequently prepare a careful and thorough analysis of the implications for future policy.

The recommended approach to exchange rate and exchange control forecasting consists of three steps:

1. The relevant environmental variables are initially identified
2. The businessman next reaches tentative conclusions regarding the steps he would take *if* he were the government policy-maker
3. The decisions reached in step two are, in a final step, tempered by the businessman to reflect how the politician is likely to react to the same information.

Earlier it was explained that a country considers imposing exchange controls or devaluing its currency in the face of inflation, balance-of-payments problems, and difficulties associated with economic development. A business manager must examine the list of possible reasons and determine if any of them are likely to be relevant in the particular situation under consideration. Those reasons that are relevant should be thoroughly examined. For purposes of explanation and illustration, the following discussion assumes that *all* of the possible reasons for devaluation or exchange controls are relevant. Each will be discussed, with emphasis given to the quantitative and qualitative indicators to which the manager might refer in making predictions.

Inflationary conditions or inflationary trends may bring on devaluation or exchange controls for one of two reasons:

1. Inflationary pressures may aggravate the country's balance of payments
2. The inflation may disrupt the economic development program by diverting domestic demand from locally produced goods and by diverting outside demand away from locally produced export products.

The principal signals of a buildup of inflationary pressures have already been enumerated. Therefore, the following abbreviated discussion is meant to highlight the relationships between inflation and exchange controls or devaluation and the method for forecasting them.

The reader will recall that four quantitative indicators suggest the extent of inflationary pressures:

1. The domestic cost-of-living index
2. The growth in domestic money supply (currency in circulation plus demand deposits in the domestic banking system)
3. The extent and trend in deficit financing of government programs and overhead
4. Trends in domestic wage levels.

In Tables 3–1 and 3–2, the cost of living and money supply statistics are arranged together with exchange rate figures for Mexico and Uruguay. The data permit a visual correlation between exchange rate stability and these two indices of inflation. While undoubtedly there are other factors that will influence the movement of a currency's exchange rate, the Mexican and Uruguayan illustration of a stable and unstable situation, respectively, suggests that at least during the period 1960–1967, there was a strong relationship between internal price levels and exchange stability.

TABLE 3–1

Exchange Rates, Money Supply, and Cost of Living in Mexico, 1960–1967

	1960	*1961*	*1962*	*1963*	*1964*	*1965*	*1966*	*1967*
Official rate of exchange (pesos per U.S. $)	12.50	12.50	12.50	12.50	12.50	12.50	12.50	12.50
Changes in money supply (1958 = 100)	126	135	153	177	208	220	247	269
Changes in cost of living (1958 = 100)	108	105	108	108	111	116	121	122

Source: IMF *International Financial Statistics.*

TABLE 3–2

Exchange Rates, Money Supply, and Cost of Living in Uruguay, 1960–1967

	1960	*1961*	*1962*	*1963*	*1964*	*1965*	*1966*	*1967*
Official rate of exchange (pesos per U.S. $)	11.03	10.98	10.98	16.40	18.70	59.90	76.20	200.00
Changes in money supply (1958 = 100)	192	234	227	292	415	841	1193	2434
Changes in cost of living (1958 = 100)	202	223	248	357	483	908	1360	na

Source: IMF *International Financial Statistics.*

The data show that exchange rate stability in Mexico was accompanied by relatively little change in the internal cost of living and in money supply, whereas in Uruguay the exchange stability lasted for only three years during which the internal price levels and money supply were relatively stable. Thereafter, as inflationary pressures grew at a more rapid pace, the currency exchange rate was debased on several occasions and to an increasing extent.

Balance-of-payments conditions and trends are the most frequently mentioned contributing factors in connection with exchange devaluation or controls. In this aspect of environmental forecasting, the two key factors to be analyzed by the manager are:

1. The size and duration of a deficit in the balance of payments
2. The ability of the country to finance the deficit over a period of time.

The investigation should inquire into the cause of the present deficit, whether or not the conditions responsible for the deficit are likely to persist, and if they are, the magnitude of the anticipated deficit. The appropriate follow-up questions should be: How has the deficit been financed thus far? Is the country likely to be able to rely continuously on these means of financing the disequilibrium? What are the alternative and complimentary sources of finance?

The October 1967 devaluation of the Finnish markka is an interesting case in point. An earlier discussion brought out that Finland had experienced recurring serious balance-of-payments difficulties starting in 1964 because of rising costs, income, and prices. For a number of years the government attempted to correct the external disequilibrium by restrictive monetary and fiscal policies. However, by mid-1967 not only were these internal measures considered too costly to the economy, but the country's leaders believed that the means were running out to finance further deficits. Most of Finland's drawing facilities at the IMF were exhausted, and as can be noted in Table 3–3, the total amount of official reserves—which could be used to maintain the par value of the markka—had diminished significantly since the end of 1964. If one discounts the value of the $31 million IMF gold tranche position, because drawings had by 1967 exceeded this amount, the volume of Finnish gold and foreign exchange reserves in August 1967, one month prior to the devaluation, were less than one-half of what they had been only two and one-half years earlier when the problems first became severe.

Additional numerical indicators can also be used to analyze a country's external position. The historical trends and changes in the current and capital accounts of the country's balance of payments can be examined with special emphasis on import and export totals, inflows of private and governmental capital for investment and aid purposes, outflows of short-term capital which might be associated with known rumors of devaluation or controls—so-called capital flight—and outflows of capital

TABLE 3–3

Official International Liquidity of the Bank of Finland, 1960–1967 (millions of U.S. $)

	1960	1961	1962	1963	1964	1965				1966				1967		
						I	II	III	IV	I	II	III	IV	I	II	August
Bank of Finland Assets	279.7	286.4	249.3	292.7	383.9	358.3	299.9	284.3	289.2	247.8	213.7	198.5	188.7	161.4	188.5	182.8
Gold	41.1	46.9	60.9	60.6	85.4	85.4	84.6	84.6	83.6	57.6	55.4	55.4	45.0	47.7	46.8	46.7
IMF gold Tranche position	14.3	14.3	14.3	14.3	14.3	14.3	14.3	14.3	14.3	31.3	31.3	31.3	31.3	–	–	–
Foreign exchange	224.3	225.2	174.1	217.8	284.2	258.6	201.0	185.4	191.3	158.9	127.0	111.8	112.4	113.7	141.7	136.1

Source: IMF *International Financial Statistics.*

TABLE 3–4

Rate of Exchange for Uruguay Currency, 1960–1967 (pesos : dollar)

	1960	1961	1962	1963	1964				1965				1966				1967			
					I	II	III	IV	I	II	III	IV	I	II	III	IV	I	II	III	IV
Free rate	11.03	10.98	10.98	17.35	19.50	19.50	21.25	24.32	33.90	59.00	70.00	69.20	65.10	63.70	68.50	76.50	86.20	88.80	124.00	199.00
Official rate	11.03	10.98	10.98	16.40	16.40	16.40	16.40	18.70	24.00	24.00	24.00	59.90	59.90	63.80	68.30	76.20	85.90	88.30	99.00	200.00

Source: IMF *International Financial Statistics.*

to service both private and governmental indebtedness. The historical trend and the present level of official reserve assets (foreign exchange and gold) and known governmental borrowing power at the IMF and under ad hoc credit facilities already arranged with one or more foreign countries should be noted. The manager should analyze the spot and forward rates of the country's currency on the foreign exchange market —if trading is extant—and on the black market if one exists to ascertain:

1. The relative willingness of private parties to hold the local currency versus a foreign currency.
2. The willingness of private parties to contract for future receipts of the local currency.

A comparison of the official and free rates of exchange for the currency of Uruguay during the period 1960 to 1967 illustrates the signals which a businessman may note of local distrust in the existing exchange rate. The reader will recall that Uruguay has had difficulty in maintaining the par value of its peso. Often a two-rate system has been used wherein the official rate was established by the government, and the free rate reflected the supply and demand in the market place for pesos versus foreign exchange. In Table 3–4 note the spread between the Uruguayan official and free rates which developed in advance of a devaluation of the official rate.

Periodic attention to changes in the spread between the official and the free rates of exchange can provide important clues to impending devaluation or the imposition of more restrictive exchange controls.

A host country's difficulties in servicing its external indebtedness may result in the imposition of exchange controls as the country attempts to increase its capacity to service such obligations.[2] It is characteristic of the less-developed countries that they are unable to generate sufficient capital from internal sources to meet their urgent requirements for sustenance and growth. To be able to import raw materials, technology, supplies, marketing and organizational know-how, capital equipment, foreign expert personnel, and working capital, these countries must supplement the locally generated capital with borrowings from abroad. In the past fifteen years, the amount of these capital inflows from both private and public sources has grown to billions of dollars annually, and although the amount is not nearly sufficient to meet the rapidly expanding current account deficits of the less developed world, the amount is gigantic when one considers the repayment and service obligation that is concomitantly acquired by the capital-importing nations. Table 3–5 provides an indication of both the size and the growth of external public indebtedness of

[2] This section of the chapter is reproduced by permission of Intercontinental Publications. The discussion originally appeared in the article by David B. Zenoff, "Environmental Forecasting Is a Tricky Business," *Worldwide Projects and Installations Planning*, September-October 1968.

TABLE 3–5

External Public Debt Outstanding of Forty-eight Developing Countries, 1962–1966, by Area (billions of U.S. $)

AREA	*DEBT OUTSTANDING*				
	1962	*1963*	*1964*	*1965*	*June 1966*
Latin America	8.57	9.46	10.00	11.32	11.46
South Asia	4.75	5.95	7.57	8.44	9.41
East Asia	0.93	1.29	1.40	1.74	1.95
Africa	1.93	1.91	2.34	2.75	2.92
Southern Europe and Middle East	3.83	4.27	4.81	6.07	6.02
Total	20.01	22.88	26.12	30.32	31.76

Source: International Bank for Reconstruction and Development.

TABLE 3–6

External Public Debt Service of Forty-eight Developing Countries, 1962–1966, by Area (billions of U.S. $)

AREA	*SERVICE PAYMENT*				
	1962	*1963*	*1964*	*1965*	*1966* *
Latin America	1.49	1.40	1.68	1.78	1.85
South Asia	0.23	0.28	0.40	0.34	0.44
East Asia	0.07	0.07	0.08	0.13	0.19
Africa	0.11	0.14	0.14	0.16	0.19
Southern Europe and Middle East	0.40	0.44	0.54	0.55	0.63
Total	2.30	2.33	2.84	2.96	3.30

Source: I.B.R.D.
* Estimated.

a large group of developing countries in a recent period, and Table 3–6 shows the growth in external debt service requirements associated with the public debt.

If one adds to these totals the flow of *private* financial resources, about $4 billion in 1967, and the concomitant service requirements, it becomes apparent how sizable and serious the matter of servicing external indebtedness has become. A United States AID projection of foreign indebtedness and service requirements for all of the developing countries suggests that by 1970 the annual interest and amortization obligations will be $5.2 billion, and by 1975, $6.8 billion.[3]

The amount of foreign indebtedness and the severity of the service ob-

[3] As quoted in Pieter Lieftinck, *External Debt and Debt-Bearing Capacity of Developing Countries*, Essays in International Finance, no. 51, Princeton, N.J., Princeton University, March 1966.

ligation will, of course, vary from country to country. But it is a relatively safe assumption that for almost all of the less-developed nations, the management of external debt will continue to be a pressing problem, for it may well amount to as much as one-sixth of the country's gross national product. Where foreign debt service is a problem, the implications for the economy and for the international investor may be critical. The economy will be continually pressured to develop contingency sources of foreign exchange as well as an increased volume of internal savings. The government may have to resort to increased local taxation, methods to discourage consumption, higher barriers to imported capital and consumer goods, and exchange controls to limit the amount of private capital outflow.

The financial manager must forecast the likelihood of the debt service problem's reaching the point of necessitating restrictive government policies so that plans can be made to accommodate the policies' impact on local operations and to minimize any deleterious effects. The discussion and examples that follow are intended to provide a guide to analyzing the future severity of a host country's debt service problem.

The financial manager must focus his attention on the short-run relationship between a country's external debt service *capacity* and its service *obligation*. The long-run outlook is also important, but there are so many variables impinging on the situation that it is not realistic for the manager to expect to develop an accurate ten- to fifteen-year forecast. In the near term, the debt service question involves assessing an economy's liquidity relative to its payment schedule. Liquidity, in this sense, is composed of:

1. The availability of local savings that can be utilized to meet the public and private sectors' respective service obligations
2. The ability of the economy to transfer the local currency savings into a payments medium which is acceptable to foreign creditors.

Internally generated savings are largely a result of government budgetary policies—the government's ability to force the public to save via taxation and mandatorily reduced consumption, and the decisions made by corporations and individuals to forego current consumption or investment in favor of saving. This, in turn, is largely determined by such factors as the business climate, the availability and characteristics of savings institutions, and the cultural disposition toward savings.

The so-called external liquidity of a country is usually measured by the sum of its officially held monetary gold, foreign exchange reserves, and its ability to borrow from abroad. Because the less developed countries' problems with debt service mainly result from deficient external liquidity, the present discussion will focus on the external liquidity situation. The primary determinants of a country's external liquidity at a given point in time are threefold:

1. The foreign exchange receipts from the export of goods and services
2. The amount of foreign exchange used to import goods and services from the outside world
3. The inflows and outflows of long- and short-term capital on private and government accounts.

Forecasting activity *vis à vis* a country's ability to service its foreign-held debts must, in large part, be focused on anticipated changes and trends in these major external accounts.

In the broadest sense the analysis which is recommended consists of matching up the projected service obligations for the period in question with the volume of national liquidity which is anticipated. If the country's service capacity appears to be clearly in excess of the projected debt burden, the host government will probably be able to meet its external obligations without resorting to extraordinary measures. If, on the other hand, the nation's debt service capacity appears to be insufficient to meet its external responsibilities, the businessman should begin to anticipate public policy changes.

Estimating debt service obligations for a given period is not an extremely difficult task. The central bank, department of commerce, or foreign exchange authority of the country publishes schedules of all known public and private external indebtedness. The government's estimate can be used as a starting point. It normally should not be considered to be all-inclusive because a private company's remittance decisions can vary from one period to the next, and even in those countries that have relatively stable patterns of foreign trade and capital flows, it is possible that one or more contingencies such as crop failure, military actions, or external business cycles will disrupt at least one of the major balance-of-payments accounts. Therefore, the financial manager is advised to establish ranges for a host country's projected debt service capacity.

In debt service forecasting the manager might begin by consulting central or commercial bank data for the most current level and composition of the nation's external liquidity. In the case of the anonymous country Moritzland,[4] which will be used as an example in this discussion, the data as of January 1, 1967, were: gold $194.6 million; foreign exchange, $366.5 million; International Monetary Fund quota, $270 million (of which $67 million was the gold tranche position). In addition the country had an exchange stabilization agreement with the United States, giving it drawing rights of up to $75 million, and a $90 million credit from the United States Export-Import Bank. The former agreement was due to expire in one year, and the latter in two. These totals are not

[4] The reason for the use of a mythical country, Moritzland, rather than an actual nation as an illustration is that the reader will not bring into the ensuing discussion and analysis preconceived notions of the country's debt service and balance of payments position. The authors believe such notions might be disconcerting.

by themselves particularly revealing *vis à vis* the nation's ability to meet debt service, but they are a starting point for further analysis.

The next step is to forecast the foreign exchange receipts for Moritzland that will result from its exportation of goods and services. In this context it will be useful to look at a trend line of the value of exports over a period of time, their historical and current composition, and the major buyers of Moritzland's goods and services. The purpose is to obtain leads to other environmental and institutional conditions that should also be examined and to attempt to assess the vulnerability of the export sector to significant changes—either more or less favorable to the economy.

In Table 3–7 one is able to follow the progress of the nation's exports from 1958 through 1966 (which we assume is the date at which the manager began his forecasting actively).

TABLE 3–7

Total Value of Moritzland Exports of Goods and Services, 1958–1966, (millions of U.S. $)

YEAR	*1958*	*1959*	*1960*	*1961*	*1962*	*1963*	*1964*	*1965*	*1966*
Total Exports	708	721	740	804	900	936	1,022	1,114	1,186

The major conclusions that can be drawn from this data are:

1. Exports have increased in every year
2. The rate of annual increase has varied from 2 to 11 per cent
3. There is no clear pattern in the rate of increase in the most recent years, although since 1960, the annual increase was most frequently above 5 per cent, with the average about 7½ per cent.

In Table 3–8 the composition of exports is given.

From this data a number of important observations may be made relative to the analysis of debt service capacity. First, it is significant that primary products from the agricultural and mineral sectors account for about 80 per cent of the nation's exports. Second, the percentage of primary versus manufactured products in the export total had not shifted in the past five years. Third, a few of the primary goods account for a very important percentage of total export revenues; cotton (19 per cent), coffee (7 per cent), tomatoes (5 per cent), sugar (5 per cent), livestock and meat (6 per cent), corn (4 per cent), sulfur (3 per cent), zinc (4 per cent), and petroleum (3 per cent) are the most important. Fourth, a few of the most important export products (cotton, coffee, tomatoes, livestock, and corn) have demonstrated relatively large year to year variability in the value of their export earnings. Fifth, a few of the more important export sectors have shown a relatively large increase in their absolute and relative size among the exported goods; namely, tomatoes, corn, and chemicals.

TABLE 3–8

Exports by Major Commodity Groups, 1958–1966 (millions of U.S. $)

COMMODITY	*1958*	*1959*	*1960*	*1961*	*1962*	*1963*	*1964*	*1965*	*1966*
Cotton	190	199	158	160	218	196	170	215	221
Coffee	79	63	72	72	70	49	95	73	83
Tomatoes	23	24	26	14	20	25	34	35	60
Sugar	17	15	53	69	43	60	77	59	57
Corn							16	77	47
Livestock and meat	12	10	10	16	21	27	43	55	67
Petroleum	29	29	20	33	38	37	39	40	39
Sulfur	23	24	28	29	30	34	38	34	35
Fish	32	39	34	44	46	52	54	45	51
Lead	35	34	34	37	26	27	23	28	28
Zinc	20	25	30	27	28	30	43	43	42
Manufacturing chemicals	na	na	na	na	26	31	26	36	41
Other manufactured goods	na	na	na	na	80	100	97	97	124
Others	248	259	275	306	204	268	267	280	294
Totals	708	721	740	804	900	936	1022	1114	1186

In terms of predicting Moritzland's future export revenues, as well as the stability of individual products, a number of follow-up questions and areas of inquiry would be indicated to gain a more complete basis for forecasting foreign exchange receipts. Are there government plans or current efforts to further diversify the structure of the economy? With such a high percentage of exports representing primary products as is typical of most less-developed nations, the export capability as well as the national income of the country are vulnerable to price instability and possibly falling prices in the world marketplace. In this regard it is also important to try to assess the reasons for the variability in export earnings of such goods as cotton, coffee, tomatoes, and livestock and the likelihood of such variability occurring in the future. Are any of these or other primary products a part of an international commodity scheme in which price ceiling and floors have been determined, export quotas established, or foreign markets assured? Are the exports of Moritzland given duty-free or preferential treatment in gaining access to certain important foreign markets? To what extent will this treatment affect prices and volumes of goods sold? If the country is the leading exporter of one or more commodities, how does this competitive position affect its ability to control world prices and increase (or at least stabilize) export volumes? Is there an extraordinary world demand developing for any of the country's products such as might be the case with lead or copper for wartime use? Has there been—or is there likely to be—a significant change in the tariff rates or quota amounts which affect the entry of Moritzland goods into its major foreign markets? Examples of such changes range from beneficial reductions in barriers following a GATT international tariff negotiating session like the Kennedy Round to the partial or complete closing of markets to imports.

Additional examination of the export sector would include a determination of the reasons for the recent rapid growth in export receipts of tomatoes, corn, and chemicals. Are the increases due to higher world prices—and if so, can these prices be expected to be maintained in the future? Is the primary reason a recent increase in production of these products or an increased inducement to produce them for export as well as domestic markets? Or, is the rapid rise in international trade the result of the opening of new markets abroad? Because tomatoes, corn, and chemicals now form an important segment of Moritzland's foreign trade, an effort must be made to understand why these items have become so important so that the businessman will have a more secure basis for predicting what their volume will be in the future.

A final type of follow-up investigation regarding exports pertains to the production of primary goods. Is the weather expected to be favorable to agricultural production? Is there any danger of pestilence destroying crops such as hoof-and-mouth disease, so costly to a number of cattle-producing nations in late 1967 and early 1968? Are there any significant mineral explorations or commercial developments within that industry that might be expected to add to its capacity to export? Fortified with this type of information, the manager will have the basis for projecting export revenues for the period he is studying.

An examination of the current account of the balance of international payments also shows that Moritzland has been able to earn sizable foreign exchange receipts from its tourist industry. Hence a part of the financial manager's forecasting activity must include analysis of this industry and any other type of commercial transaction that may result in a significant credit to the nation's current account. (In a country like Israel, for example, not only tourism would be important, but also unilateral remittances from abroad.) The tourism data for Moritzland over the past eleven years are provided in Table 3–9. They indicate that the numbers of tourists and the revenue from their visits have been steadily and rap-

TABLE 3–9

The Number of Foreign Tourists Visiting Moritzland, and Associated Foreign Exchange Earnings, 1956–1966 (in thousands of tourists and millions of U.S. $)

	YEAR										
	1956	*1957*	*1958*	*1959*	*1960*	*1961*	*1962*	*1963*	*1964*	*1965*	*1966*
Number of Tourists	588	614	640	682	692	719	835	940	1,074	1,199	1,528
Receipts	na	na	na	na	153	155	179	210	240	278	320

idly increasing over the years, and that tourism now accounts for about thirteen per cent of the inflows on current account.

Analysis of this source of foreign exchange should be designed to ascertain whether or not the historical increase in tourism receipts is likely to continue. Data from the national department of tourism are normally available and can provide a reliable basis for such projections. One important factor is to determine if the host country is scheduled to be the host to a world's fair or a large athletic event that will draw an extraordinarily large number of foreign visitors, and what efforts the nation is making to attract such events and more foreign tourists.

On the other side of the current account ledger, the financial analyst must also forecast the foreign exchange that will be utilized in the forthcoming period to purchase goods and services from abroad. The analytical procedures are similar to those for the exportation of goods and services. The basic task is to determine if there will be a significant change in the level of imports compared to the most recent period. The recommended approach is to examine trade statistics and determine whether there are any noticeable trends in the pattern of imports as a whole and in their composition. The analyst should then examine the current trends within the economy and national commercial policy to ascertain whether or not there are any fundamentally new or different forces that would increase or impede the nation's purchases from abroad. For Moritzland Table 3–10 provides some of the required data.

TABLE 3–10

Moritzland Imports by Major Commodity Groups, 1962–1966 (millions of U.S. $)

COMMODITY	*YEAR*				
	1962	*1963*	*1964*	*1965*	*1966*
Consumer goods	$ 229	283	300	299	288
Food and beverages	36	71	40	32	33
Automobiles, parts	98	114	147	152	143
Other consumer goods	96	99	113	115	112
Producer goods	914	957	1,193	1,261	1,321
Raw and semifinished materials	378	416	487	551	588
Capital goods	536	541	706	710	733
Total imports	$1,143	1,240	1,493	1,560	1,609

One observation that can be made is that while the total value of imports has grown every year, the *rate* of increase has varied considerably from as low as 3 per cent to as high as 20 per cent. Secondly, only about one-fifth of total imports has consisted of consumer goods, whereas about one-third are raw materials to feed the nation's industries. Approximately one-half of the imports are capital goods. The table shows that while imports of raw and semifinished materials increased more rapidly than total imports, the relative importance of consumer goods has dwindled gradually from slightly more than one-fifth of all imports to slightly less than one-fifth. Finally, with the exception of 1964, the size of the year-to-year increase in capital goods imported has remained relatively unchanged. Examined in composite, the data reflect an industrializing country that has probably put severe restraints on consumer goods imports in order to permit needed purchases of producers' goods. The growth in imports reflects primarily a growth in demand for materials and supplies of the type needed to fuel the country's existing industrial base that the typical less-developed nation is not able to produce itself.

The next step in the analysis is to supplement the foregoing data with information on the changes that have occurred—or that are anticipated—in trade restrictions and within the respective sectors that account for a significant volume of total imports. If, for example, it was learned that a new basic industry was being established, the manager might expect this to be a one-shot rise in capital good imports and a subsequent sustained increase in raw and semifinished materials. If the new industry produces consumer goods such as automobiles, then presumably within a few years there would be a significant decrease in the volume of vehicle imports. In a broad scope analysis, the businessman should also obtain forecasts of the national income for the period in question to correlate changes in the level of imports with those in overall economic activity—if such a relationship has been identified for the host country.

The third major determinant of a country's external debt service capacity is its net international flow of capital. For purposes of the present analysis, the net capital figure is determined by adding all of the inflows and outflows of capital—private and public, short- and long-term—excluding those payments to foreigners which represent repayment of private debt obligations or are dividends to foreign owners of local businesses. As was true for the current account analysis, the objectives are to identify the extant patterns of capital flows, develop an understanding of the flows, and then determine if any significant changes are likely to take place in the time period for which the forecast is being made. Data of the type required are available in the monthly International Monetary Fund *International Financial Statistics* and from the host country's central and leading commercial banking institutions.

The required capital account figures can be found in the Moritzland balance of international payments. Care must be taken to add only the capital figures that represent actual *flows* of funds and not to include such categories as reinvested earnings that are not current flows. When recent international flows have been identified, one can try to determine what has taken place and why. For example, if in a given period there was what appeared to be an abnormally large volume of short-term capital outflow, the businessman might investigate the reason and learn that there had been a wave of devaluation fears during the fiscal period and that the balance-of-payments data reflected "hot money" in search of a more secure haven. By putting together this information and using it with an overall evaluation of the country's balance-of-payments stability and reserve level, the financial analyst can evaluate whether or not such hot money flows are likely to occur with frequency and in the near term.

The pattern of long-term capital inflows representing direct investment by foreign entrepreneurs should similarly be examined. What historical pattern—if any—is observable, and what has been the basis for the inflow that has occurred? Is the Moritzland government still as receptive to foreign investment, or is there new legislation pending that may scare off new direct investment from abroad? What types and amounts of foreign aid does Moritzland receive, and what are the future aid commitments of the capital rich countries? When the sources of foreign assistance are identified, a review of the donors' aid programs and authorized disbursements during the fiscal period under review will provide some of the information which the businessman seeks. The objective is always one of identifying existing patterns and sources of potential inflows and outflows and combining this data with supplementary information from other sources to form the framework for estimating what the net capital account figure will be in the short run.

When the estimating activity for the capital and current accounts is completed, it is possible to put together the findings and projections and to estimate the probable debt service capacity of Moritzland. As indicated earlier, the suggested procedure is to use as a starting point the existing levels of the nation's international liquidity and then to add to or subtract from it the various projections of major balance-of-payments accounts. Assume, for example, that in the period for which the projection is being made, revenues from exports are estimated to be $1,250 million; tourist receipts, $400 million; and imports, $1,700 million. When added to the country's existing official reserve assets (gold, foreign exchange, and IMF gold tranche position), $628 million, the most probable Moritzland debt service capacity will be $578 million. Because this total is only an approximation subject to all of the inaccuracies of forecasting balance-of-payments accounts, the businessman should make additional estimates of debt service capacity that he also believes are possible. In this way he can work out a range of projections believed to encompass the actual figure in the future period.

Against these projections the financial analyst can compare the level of forecasted debt service. To the government schedule of official service obligations can be added the analyst's own estimate of what will be the outflow of dividends and debt service on private account. The latter figure may be developed in the following manner: information can be compiled on the volume of past remittances; the book value of foreign investors' affiliates in Moritzland and the annual profits after taxes are recorded; important recent institutional changes which may have a bearing on remittance decisions are noted. (These may include the balance of payments program in the United States, tight credit conditions in Moritzland or the country of the parent company, the extent of exchange risks in one of the countries, and/or a new foreign investment law in Moritzland that affects investors' confidence or permitted remittances.)

This information provides the basis for identifying patterns in recent remittances and for projecting future changes in current business practices. It may be noted, for example, that in the aggregate dividend payments normally total between 45 and 55 per cent of the affiliates' net income and 15 per cent of their book value. Or, if no such relationship can be established between remittances and earnings or book value, it may be possible to identify a pattern in the year-to-year change in aggregate remittances—say, a 4-to-6 per cent annual increase over the past five years.

After he has projected the most likely range of private remittances, the manager should add to these totals the schedule of official debt service for the period to obtain an estimate of the nation's total service obligations. These should be compared to the range of projections made earlier of gross debt service capacity. If the projected service obligations are less than the forecasted debt service capacity, the businessman can assume that the host country will not need to use exchange controls or devalue the local currency on the basis of its external indebtedness. If, however, the outcome of the comparison between capacity and obligations indicates that the nation's capacity will be insufficient, the manager must then attempt to identify what steps the government might take to ward off a liquidity crisis.

A government caught in such a squeeze could attempt to increase its reserves or borrowing power through a variety of means such as:

1. Negotiating for standby credits from outside sources
2. Imposing restrictions on importations
3. Restricting the export of foreign exchange on capital account
4. Encouraging greater foreign exchange earnings via increase exportation of the nation's goods and services.

An evaluation of what approach(es) the host country would be likely to take should include consideration of a number of factors. The internal politics in Moritzland may weigh heavily in the chief executive's decision. If an election is forthcoming, he may be politically fearful of imposing severe restraints on the populace or of antagonizing important business leaders. Or the deciding factor may be the government policy-maker's view of the *technical* attractiveness of utilizing one or more of the measures. Does the politican have confidence in the public sector's ability to influence favorably the volume of exports and tourist receipts in the short run? Would a more meaningful approach be the negotiation of

IMF credits or special borrowing rights from one or more nations on an ad hoc basis?

Answers to questions of this type will depend upon the administration's analysis of the feasibility of each possible approach. Although the businessman is unlikely to have access to the same amount and quality of information as does the government decision-maker, the businessman can reach his own tentative conclusions about the technical attractiveness of some of the host country's policy choices utilizing the data he developed earlier in forecasting debt service capacity. The manager can also make an evaluation of the announced official attitude toward preservation or establishment of credit-worthiness in the world financial community. What has been its history of debt service? What is the attitude concerning credit-worthiness and prudent fiscal management among foreign nations and investors? If, as is the case of many less developed countries, top priority is given to image building among the community of nations, the manager might be able to define more narrowly what the government's choice of policy alternatives will be.

To summarize the foregoing discussion: evaluation of the likelihood of a foreign affiliate's being restricted or injured by the use of exchange controls or devaluation in the host country depends on analysis of the nation's future debt service capacity and obligations in the period under review. As suggested, an orderly analysis can normally be made from data available to the businessman. The objective will be to ascertain whether debt service capacity is likely to be sufficient, and if not, what steps the government is most likely to take to meet the impending crisis.

The manager must also appreciate that economic development programs often dictate the use of exchange controls and/or devaluation to help achieve the established objectives. It is difficult to recommend quantitative indicators that may help the manager ascertain how well the development program is going and whether devaluation or controls will be required to give added impetus. Probably the best method for obtaining useful clues is to become familiar with the official development plan and to identify which sectors are to be emphasized in the current and forthcoming fiscal periods. A next step involves deciding if exchange controls or devaluation would be appropriate as primary or emergency policy tools to stimulate sectoral development. Finally, utilizing all available intelligence sources such as official governmental progress reports, unofficial opinions of bureaucrats, and the observations of banks, consultants, and international agencies (where their opinions are known), the businessman can evaluate how well the stated objectives are being achieved via the use of current public policy measures.

External forces and pressures emanating from foreign institutions or the host country's relationships with outside institutions may play an important role in determining whether or not a country's currency will be devalued or controls used. The "rules of the game" of the International

Monetary Fund, for an important example, act to restrict a country's freedom to devalue its currency, both in amount and in frequency of change, and to impose certain type of controls. While in fact there have been a number of nations which have either overlooked the rules, never formally agreed to them, or else have obtained the Fund's approval to devalue or impose controls, the business manager who is trying to forecast future government actions can, at least for the more economically developed nations, take comfort in the prospect that devaluation or exchange controls will be measures of last resort for curbing balance-of-payments problems. This was the situation for the three-year period prior to the devaluation of the British currency in 1967, and for France during the international currency crisis in late 1968.

For developed countries such as England and France, the matter of forecasting will therefore include an examination of what *other* policy measures have been tried—and are yet to be used—before a final decision will have to be made on devaluation or controls.

Another source of external pressure to avoid these policy measures *or* to implement them can come from governments and institutions granting foreign aid. One can normally assume that both bilateral and multinational sources of economic assistance will utilize their leverage to induce recipient countries to establish certain types of development objectives and/or to utilize certain types of policy measures.

There can be no safe bets that the external institutions will always caution less-developed nations to avoid devaluation or controls. In fact in 1965–1967 it was widely rumored that India's devaluation of the rupee resulted from intense pressure from the United States to take such action, even though the Indian government was not so inclined. In particular instances it may be possible for the manager to second-guess or obtain factual information on what measures are being recommended to the recipient nations. Occasionally luck plays an important role. William Rittman, vice-president of Richardson-Merrell, Inc., in an interview (see p. 18) told of his having learned in advance of the planned devaluation of a country's currency from a six-year-old playmate of his child, who was the son of the president of a Swiss bank.

The threat of loss of foreign confidence in a nation's currency may be sufficient reason for some nations to avoid devaluation or controls. England and the United States are examples. Their currencies have long been considered to be reserve currencies by the rest of the world, and in order to fulfill this designation and to have the privileges and the benefits which accrue to the world's bankers, each of these countries has had to use all available methods to stabilize its exchange rates and to convince the world in general that devaluation would never occur.

At the opposite end of the spectrum, many of the less-developed countries trying to attract foreign investment as a part of their sales program to the outside world will declare that their currency is stable and that foreigners will not be subject to debilitating restrictions on the remittance of funds or on their ability to import required supplies, equipment, and goods. The manager of an existing affiliate is probably well aware of the host country's claims and offers of an attractive local investment climate. As a part of his forward planning, the international manager should follow the government's efforts and public relations programs to ascertain if the government still considers exchange freedom and stability to be important objectives, and if there is any change in the host's emphasis of these environmental safeguards to foreigners.

As was mentioned earlier, it is up to the manager in each particular case to decide how much importance to attach to changes in any of the environmental conditions that are noted by analysis of the economic indicators. In evaluating whether or not the government policy-maker would come to the same conclusion as he, the businessman can often make effective use of the rhetorical question: what would the country and the decision-maker have to gain or lose by devaluing the local currency or by imposing restrictions on international fund transfers? In the attempt to answer his own question, the analyst often identifies additional decision variables that he had previously overlooked and also disciplines himself to a rigorous and realistic cost-benefit analysis—viewed from two points of view:

1. The country's welfare
2. The policy-maker's welfare.

The matter of anticipating how large a forthcoming devaluation will be is an extension of the foregoing analysis. By utilizing the same information and answering (or attempting to answer) the following questions, the manager should be able to establish a most likely range for the amount by which the par value will be changed.

1. What is the government's attitude toward repeated devaluations? If devaluation is viewed as a matter of course, as appears to be true (in a simplistic sense) in many inflation-plagued Latin American countries today, the manager might expect that continued inflation would bring about periodic devaluations whose size will bear a similar relationship to the size of the recent price increase as did previous devaluations to the amount of then current rises in the general price level. Uruguay and Chile are examples. Uruguay devalued the peso five times in the thirteen-month period of March 1967 to April 1968, from 99:1 to 250:1. Chile devalued the escudo more than twenty times in 1968.

On the other hand, if the manager believes that the host government is *reluctant* to devalue its currency now or in the future—most likely because it does not wish to disturb investors' confidence—the size of a forthcoming devaluation that the government finds to be inevitable because of maladies basic to the economy may be relatively large, designed to overcompensate for current conditions with the expectation that one big devaluation now will preclude having to make a series of changes over the ensuing year or two.

2. What is the attitude and policy of the present administration towards inflation? If it is permissive or encourages inflation, then most probably the host country will experience repeated balance-of-payments difficulties, and as discussed above, the manager may expect a series of par value changes which may be pegged in some way to the amount of short- or medium-term price rises. If, on the other hand, the government is bound to a noninflationary policy, the prospect of devaluing the local currency by a large amount—say, more than 20 per cent—will be viewed unfavorably because an economy that is tied to imported goods and services runs a risk of domestic price inflation when it devalues its exchange rate. *Ceteris paribus*, the larger the devaluation, the greater the problems with inflationary pressures.

3. What are the fundamental reasons for expecting an exchange devaluation? The rationale for devaluation in the manager's mind should provide a clue to the size of the rate change, if it develops. For example, if inflation has been damaging the country's balance-of-international-payments position, the amount of the devaluation may be designed to overcome the nation's international disadvantage caused by price increases. This, of course, does not mean that a 37 per cent rise in prices within the past sixteen months will necessarily lead to a 37 per cent change in the par value. It does, however, give the manager some basis for arriving at a range of expectations. If, to continue with the example, the nation's balance of trade was in equilibrium or favorable before the price increases began, and the trade deficit is seen to be the basic problem for the overall balance of payments, other things being equal, the manager would be justified in looking forward to an exchange rate change of at least thirty-plus per cent.

If the devaluation is expected because of structural problems within the economy that have led to unsatisfactory export performance and relatively too great a dependence on imports, an analysis of the domestic price elasticity of demand for imports and the price elasticity of demand of the major consumers of its exports might provide the basis for zeroing in on a reliable estimate of the size of the devaluation.

> One of the main reasons exchange policy management has proved so difficult [for Argentina] in practice is that . . . its main exports are also basic domestic wage goods: principally meat, grains, fresh fruit, textile fibers, and leather. Imports, on the other hand, are chiefly raw materials, intermediate products, and capital goods, few of which are directly competitive with domestic output (because of exceedingly high tariffs on competitive imports) and most of which are essential

for maintaining or expanding the level of economic activity. Exchange rate adjustments therefore have an immediate impact on the general cost of living, thus generating pressure from the country's strongly organized labor unions for wage increases, which quickly tend to be passed on, together with the rise in other costs in the form of higher prices by strongly cartelized producers. Under these circumstances it is exceedingly difficult for devaluation to bring about a significant change in relative prices, lasting long enough to help induce the desired shift in demand and in the allocation of resources between domestic and internationally traded goods necessary to solve the balance-of-payments problem.[5]

Occasionally countries are so dependent on other nations for either imports or export markets that a currency devaluation by one or more of the other countries will often necessitate the same action by the dependent country to bring its international trade back to the status quo. In this kind of situation, knowledge of the other countries' actions would probably provide a useful guide to estimating the amount by which the local currency will be changed.

In the case of England's devaluation of the pound sterling in late 1967, twenty-two countries closely tied economically to Great Britain also devalued their currencies. Seventeen countries altered their exchange rates by the exact amount of the British devaluation, 14.3 per cent, two nations devalued by about one-half of the amount, and three countries devalued by about one-fifth.

FORECASTING EXPROPRIATORY ACTIONS BY THE HOST GOVERNMENT

The threat of having a company's foreign properties expropriated is so critical and permanent a risk that any steps that can be taken to forecast the likelihood of such host country action will be of significant assistance in protecting the firm's assets and improving the business environment for the affiliate. The objective of the forecasting activity is to gain information so that the decision- and policy-maker will be better able to identify the possible outcomes of particular actions and to estimate the probability of their occurrence.

Whereas in some areas of business analysis the manager can reduce to quantifiable form environmental data and market forces, the matter of anticipating treatment by a foreign host government is a somewhat illusive and nebulous one, and therefore must be handled in a largely qualitative manner. Based upon a study of the current trends in host country-foreign investor relations, as well as the recent history of expro-

[5] Richard D. Mallon, "Exchange Policy: Argentina," Report No. 33, *Economic Development Series*, Cambridge, The Center for International Affairs, Harvard University, 1966.

priation and creeping expropriation,[6] the authors suggest a four-step approach to projecting possible host government policies. First, the manager should study the present administration's attitudes and policies toward private property, private enterprise, foreign investment, and investment by United States-owned companies (or whichever is the nationality of the parent company). Second, an evaluation should be made of the country's political stability. Is the present administration likely to continue, and if not, by what means and with what people will the present government be replaced? Third, analysis of major economic trends is warranted to ascertain the likelihood of contingencies arising (or continuing) that might alter the government's present view of foreign investors. Finally, an in-depth investigation is required by the manager to determine the relative strength and future security of his own affiliate in the economic and political climate characterized in the three foregoing exercises.

To pursue the suggested approach, the manager can draw upon a wide variety of sources of information. Local branches of international banks as well as the headquarters intelligence units of these institutions have generally been found to be of immense value to the businessman in keeping abreast of foreign conditions. United States government agencies (or those of the country in which the parent company is incorporated) can be expected to compile current economic and political information on the countries in which they have representation, much of which is available to the businessman through such channels as the periodic publications or commissioned studies by the Department of Commerce, Agency for International Development, or Department of Agriculture, and possibly through informative conversations with staff members of such organizations. The United States Chamber of Commerce of the respective country, a semiprofessional association of managers representing various United States-owned affiliates, often presents an excellent forum for exchanging information and testing ideas. International and local service firms such as accountants, management consultants, and advertising agencies can also be expected to supply their clients with useful information on local conditions. Finally, local businessmen and government administrators are sometimes in a position and are willing to supply information.

Analyzing the Host Government's Attitudes

The first step in evaluating future investor-host country relations is to study the administration's attitudes and policies toward private property,

[6] In addition to the sources of information on host country-foreign investor relations cited in ch. 2, nn. 3–6, the reader may also wish to see Victor Urquidi, "Some Implications of Foreign Investment for Latin America," in Claudio Veliz, *Obstacles to Change in Latin America*, London, Oxford University Press, 1966; William Whyte, "Heroes, Homework and Industrial Growth," *Columbia Journal of World Business*, Spring 1966, pp. 51–58; E. Penrose, "Foreign Investment and the Growth of the Firm," *Economic Journal*, June 1956.

private enterprise, foreign investment, and foreign investment by United States companies. The key here is to identify favorable or unfavorable *trends* which will affect the climate in which the subsidiary will operate (or from which it will be excluded). What, for example, would the international investor conclude from the following "Arusha Declaration" made in 1967 by Mwalimu Julius K. Nyerere, president of Tanzania?

> The policy of Tanu is to build a socialist state. The principles of socialism are laid down in the Tanu constitution, and they are as follows . . . That in order to ensure economic justice the State must have effective control over the principal means of production; and . . . To see that wherever possible the Government itself directly participates in the economic development of this country . . . to see that the Government exercises effective control over the principal means of production and pursues policies which facilitate the way to collective ownership of the resources of this country . . . How about the enterprises of foreign investors? It is true we need these enterprises. We have even passed an act of Parliament protecting foreign investments in this country. . . . We expect to get money through this method. But we cannot get enough. And even if we were able to convince foreign investors and foreign firms to undertake all the projects and programs of economic development that we need, is that what we actually want to happen? . . . How can we build the Socialism we are talking about under such circumstances? [7]

Obviously it is not an accomplishment to use hindsight and refer to recent examples of expropriations where the expropriations in such countries as Cuba, Indonesia, Peru, Egypt, Chile, Argentina, Ceylon, and Iran were preceded by buildups of antiforeigner feelings, the socialization of industry, and sometimes land reform programs. Nevertheless, in each of these cases there *was* evidence of a change in the government's attitude toward privately owned property and/or foreign investment *prior* to the overt act of confiscating property. These indicators, which may forecast future change, must be monitored by the businessman and included in his overall intelligence system.

Judging from past experience, an alert observer of a foreign business scene would be well advised to be mindful of past election promises of the incumbent administration and to study carefully the platforms of rising political figures. Is so-called reactive nationalism [8] a popular political football which an aspiring politician must use as a base of support? If it is, and campaign promises are made, how likely are they to be carried out, and in what form? How much pressure will be placed on the new leader to carry out campaign slogans?

[7] Excerpts from "The Arusha Declaration," released by the United Republic of Tanzania News Service, Mission to the United Nations, New York, *See also:* David B. Zenoff, "Interview with G. L. Mehta," *Private Enterprise in the Developing Countries,* Englewood Cliffs, Prentice-Hall, Inc., 1969.

[8] For a brief description of the form "reactive nationalism" has taken in the Philippines and the problems it may cause foreign entrepreneurs, *see* David B. Zenoff, " 'Filipino First'—A Dangerous Policy?" *Far Eastern Economic Review,* May 31, 1962.

Consider the following example in late 1967:

> Stockholm—The state must direct the flow of capital investment in industry. That was the outcome of the first extraordinary congress of the Swedish Social Democratic Party since 1907. Though nationalization is out, increased control of investment is in. And it is the policy on which the Socialists are hoping to base a new election victory in 1968. The congress was called to decide how the party, in office without a break since 1932, could stop the decline in electoral support which many observers believe will bring the opposition parties to power next year. . . . In their efforts to win back the political initiative, the Social Democrats are pulling out all the stops, backing up the plans to control capital investment by cashing in on widespread Swedish hostility to U.S. policies in Vietnam and lashing into Swedish big business.[9]

An important question concerns the extent to which the host country depends on the foreign investor's country for economic aid or trade, military advice, or political support. For example, Peru's exports of sugar account for about 6 per cent of total exports; fully 80 per cent of the sugar exports go to the United States. If such dependence exists, the manager can ask how likely is it that the present or a future administration will flaunt the United States government by confiscating the property of an American-owned company or by drastically altering the terms upon which the foreign investor is welcomed? Since 1962, with the passing of the Hickenlooper Amendment to the Foreign Assistance Act of 1961, the United States government has signified its intent to withhold or suspend foreign aid to any country that expropriates the property of United States citizens or corporations that are at least 50 per cent American-owned unless that country takes adequate steps within six months to provide appropriate compensation. The amendment also covers certain forms of creeping expropriation which include actions short of actual takeover of United States assets but which have the same effect as expropriation.[10]

Enforcement of the law would be controversial, and the businessman cannot be certain how vigorously the executive branch will, in any given case, carry out the intent of Congress which some have labeled "gunboat diplomacy." Nevertheless, the political and economic ties between the country in which an investment has been made and the country of the parent company constitute an important substantive area where continuing analysis is required. And while it may be tempting to assume almost blindly that the stronger the dependency of the host country upon foreign government aid or private capital inflows, the greater will be the security of foreign investment within that country, there are too many examples which suggest that complacency can be dangerous. For example, in 1968

[9] H. J. Barnes, "Swedish Socialists Seek State Investment Control," Copley News Service, November 1967.

[10] Richard B. Lillich, "The Protection of Foreign Investment and the Foreign Assistance Act of 1962," *Rutgers Law Review,* No. 17, 1963, pp. 405–427.

Peru was depending on the United States as an important market for its exports, and for more than $30 million in foreign aid; yet Peru was threatening to confiscate many millions of dollars in assets of an American-owned petroleum company.

The multinational investor should also examine the current pattern of governmental attitudes toward foreign investment and ascertain what pressures are exerted on the chief governmental policy-makers. Are there powerful leftist groups operating at the highest levels of government who are campaigning to minimize the importance of foreign-owned operations (e.g., Peru in 1968)? What is the attitude of the leader's technical advisors toward private enterprise and the importation of private capital? In Mexico, for example, it has been reported that many government "tecnicos" are of the opinion that

> (1) industrialization is best accomplished through the use of domestic capital rather than foreign capital, (2) capital formation in an unregulated private economy proceeds by trial and error . . . therefore, extensive error is certain and the related costs are borne by society through bankruptcy, high monopoly costs and prices, or chronic idle capacity. By contrast . . . public investment proceeds from reason and study. (3) Mexico's remaining needs for foreign technology and capital are sufficiently limited that it can afford to bargain hard regarding the terms on which these needs should be provided. The ideal channel by which foreign technology should be brought into the country . . . is not through direct investment but through licensing agreements.[11]

A related area for investigation is the government's economic development plan and the extent to which formalized strategies rely upon private enterprise and foreign investment. While there is no guarantee that the approach cannot be changed in mid-stream or that differing degrees of emphasis upon sectoral development may be given in the future, there is much to be said for making a careful analysis of the announced plans. International institutions such as the World Bank, United Nations, the International Monetary Fund, and bilateral aid-granting agencies representing capital exporting countries usually are willing to advance funds only after careful study of the recipient's development plan. Within the realm of reason, the lender expects the recipient country to follow the strategies laid out in the master plan and to achieve the stated objectives. Similarly, for the more developed countries of Western Europe and Japan, economic planning has inherently the intention of guiding sectoral and geographical development as well as providing a framework for the implementation of fiscal and monetary policies. Although one must readily admit that economic planning is at this point a very inexact art, the businessman can still expect that in the absence of a major contingency (such as a war, drought, or world business recession) most host governments

[11] Raymond Vernon, ed., *Public Policy and Private Enterprise in Mexico*, Cambridge, Harvard University Press, 1964, pp. 144–149.

will try to follow the development strategies which they have formally approved, with the intention of achieving or surpassing announced goals and thereby pleasing constituents and foreign observers.

Evaluating Political Stability in the Host Country

Studies of foreign investment behavior[12] have suggested that large multinational companies consider political stability within a foreign country to be one of the principal preconditions for direct investment. The reason is obvious. If an affiliate is to have an opportunity to earn a satisfactory rate of return on the funds invested, there must be a reasonable certainty that apart from purely commercial considerations, the foreign operation will have both a long life span and a suitable investment climate. Because these two conditions are in essence controlled by the host country's governmental machinery, it is vital that the foreigner have confidence that the administration which approves the investment will *continue* in existence, or that its successor will have a similar outlook.

For the manager of an existing operation, the need is no less great for an atmosphere of political stability. While the manager cannot be expected in most cases to influence the local political climate, he can make a continuing analysis of it with a view toward assessing the likelihood of future alterations in what he perceives to be the present governmental attitude toward his operation. In effect his analysis of local political stability (which must include consideration of who is the most probable successor to the current incumbent) results in a subjective judgment regarding the probability of continuation of the status quo.

Estimating the Likelihood of the Occurence of Contingencies

Before the manager settles upon his best general estimate of the short- and perhaps medium-term outlook for host country-foreign investor relations, he must allow for contingencies. In essence he must make a survey of the general economic position of the host country, as well as its military security, in order to ascertain the likelihood of a disrupting economic downturn or military encounter. Of particular relevance to the local investment climate are:

1. A troublesome deterioration in the nation's balance of payments
2. A significant downturn in national income
3. An increase in defense spending or an outright armed encounter with another nation.

Any of these phenomena could be expected to have indirect or direct repercussions for the foreign investor.

[12] For studies of foreign investment practices and experiences of many large corporations, *see* Yair Aharoni, *The Foreign Investment Decision Process,* Boston, Harvard Business School, Division of Research, 1966; R. S. Basi, *Determinants of United States Investment Abroad,* Kent State Bureau of Business Research, 1963.

Balance-of-payments problems could lead to such adverse policy measures as:

1. Restrictions on the importation of supplies, equipment, or finished goods
2. Controlled remittances of dividends, royalties, or fees
3. Increased pressures for larger and more rapid implementation of local manufacture
4. Antagonistic feelings toward foreign investment in general, placing on it—with or without justification—the onus for the country's external difficulties.

Consider the recent case of Argentina:

> The stop and go performance of the Argentine economy during the last fifteen years has been closely related to balance-of-payments difficulties. Each period of expansion has been cut short by an external payments crisis. . . . Every conceivable policy has been applied at one time or another to tackle the balance-of-payments problem, from strict quantitative regulations to prior import deposits and exchange surcharges, from multiple exchanges to freely fluctuating rates. The frequent changes in policy have reflected not only the rapid turnover of government officials with different policy prescriptions but also the successive failure of the measures previously adopted, sometimes because they were ill-conceived, frequently because they were not executed together with a consistent set of other policies, occasionally because of external factors beyond the control of policy.[13]

A downturn in national income may have similar results. The national development plan may be partially or wholly abandoned, and new emphasis placed on sectors or regions or methods of development that do not favor the foreign investor. Taxes may be increased. The government may insist that the local labor content of the investor's product be increased. Military troubles may lead to even more severe restrictions on the foreigner, with possible complete loss of property. Increased military spending may lead to balance-of-payments or national income difficulties and the kinds of business restrictions discussed above. Much more seriously, the nation's relations with the home country of the investor may deteriorate, and political leaders, as a matter of foreign policy, may nationalize all foreign investors' property. Or, as a matter of national mobilization in the time of military conflict, the host country may nationalize or dictate production plans to foreign (and domestically) owned industries.

Assessing the Relative Strengths and Security of the Affiliate Itself

Utilizing the framework suggested by the article, "The Investment in the LDC: Asset with a Fixed Maturity," [14] the foreign investor must ap-

[13] Richard D. Mallon, *op. cit.*

[14] Peter Gabriel, "The Investment in the LDC: Asset with a Fixed Maturity," *Columbia Journal of World Business*, Summer 1966, pp. 109–120.

praise not only the environment in which he is operating, but his *own* bargaining power *vis à vis* the host government.

The appraisal, which must be a continuing one, consists of asking two basic questions:

1. Is the foreign affiliate considered to be a good citizen and therefore tolerable?
2. Does the host government continue to *need* its presence?

An example of the good citizen approach is suggested by Eastman Kodak's action when in 1967 the company announced the following policies in conjunction with its investment of $20 million in a new manufacturing company in Mexico:

1. The equity of the affiliate will be made available to Mexican investors when the affiliate becomes profitable and can pay dividends.
2. The location of the plant will be Guadalajara, not Mexico City, in line with the Mexican government's official policy on decentralization of industry away from the nation's capital city.
3. The affiliate will attempt to use the greatest possible amount of locally supplied raw materials.
4. The Mexican company will offer extensive training to the Mexican employees and no more than ten non-Mexican supervisors will be used even in the initial stages of production.[15]

A number of observers have suggested, however, that being a good citizen is a necessary but *not sufficient* basis for the continued acceptability of a foreign-owned venture.[16] The key to the maintenance of security in a country is a "yes" answer to the second query above: does the host government continue to *need* its presence?

A subsidiary's ability to retain an essential status in the eyes of a host government can normally be expected to depend on:

1. The degree to which its product or service is valued by the host
2. The competitive edge held over other foreign or local producers of a similar good
3. The cost to the economy of local production of the product as opposed to importation or abstention.

An experienced businessman can normally expect to make a relatively exacting appraisal of his basic strength in these three regards because he will utilize the same types of market intelligence that he requires for planning the sales and promotion of his company's output. Such benchmarks as local market share, extent and type of local competition, rapidity of technological and style changes, the price competitiveness of im-

[15] *Business Latin America,* Business International Corporation, Aug. 3, 1967.

[16] *See,* for example, Raymond Mikesell, "Healing the Breach over Foreign Resource Exploitation," *Columbia Journal of World Business,* March-April 1967, pp. 25–32.

ported products, and the number of local entrepreneurs who possess the know-how (perhaps as a result of having worked for the foreigner) to join a directly competing enterprise should provide the foreign investor with an adequate feel for the relative solidarity of his position.

Owing to the fact that outright or creeping expropriatory actions by a host government can be of extreme importance to the foreign affiliate, *continuous* evaluation and forecasting cannot be overemphasized. At first blush, the rather formalized framework for making such an evaluation which is recommended above may appear to be a full-time and awesome task for the subsidiary or international division management. This is not the authors' intention. Instead, the foregoing discussion is meant to be a guideline for the financial manager's team and to provide the rationale and a feel for the design of such an unending inquiry. Once the approach has been designed and the responsibilities for implementation assigned, there is no doubt that the exercise of double-checking the security of the firm will become fully and readily incorporated into the day-to-day tasks of managing a successful enterprise abroad.

Summary

The most important conclusion which should emerge from this chapter is that *it is possible* for the international businessman to improve his decisions by collecting and analyzing environmental data with an eye to forecasting changes that may take place in the future. Often it is very difficult to compile a sufficient volume of timely and accurate statistics that relate to a particular host country; at other times, even armed with a sizable mass of information, the manager will find that he experiences great difficulty in piecing it together and using it to form a prediction about the future. Nevertheless, intelligent decision making requires information so that the manager may select wisely among alternative solutions. An important difference between purely domestic operations and international operations is the sensitivity of business outcome to a multitude of environmental factors. The international manager is required to pay close attention to changes in foreign conditions and to the possibility of encountering critically important environmental forces.

BIBLIOGRAPHY

Baer, Werner, and Isaac Kerstenetzky. *Inflation and Growth in Latin America.* (Homewood, Ill.: Richard D. Irwin, Inc., 1964).

Doody, Francis S. *Introduction to the Use of Economic Indicators.* (New York: Random House, Inc., 1965).

Gabriel, Peter P. "The Investment in the LDC: Asset with a Fixed Maturity," *Columbia Journal of World Business,* Summer 1966.

Haberler, Gottfried. *Inflation—Its Causes and Cures.* (Washington, D.C.: American Enterprise Association, 1961).

Hodgson, Ralphael W., and Hugo E. Uyterhoeven. "Analyzing Foreign Opportunities," *Harvard Business Review,* March-April 1962.

International Financial Statistics. (Washington, D.C.: International Monetary Fund). Monthly.

Lee, Maurice W. *Macroeconomics: Fluctuations, Growth, and Stability.* (Homewood, Ill.: Richard D. Irwin, Inc., 1967).

Lieftinck, Peter. *External Debt and Debt-Bearing Capacity of Developing Countries.* (Princeton: International Finance Section, March 1966).

Robinson, Richard D. *International Business Policy.* (New York: Holt, Rinehart and Winston, Inc., 1964).

Techniques of Economic Forecasting. (Paris: Organization for Economic Cooperation and Development, 1965).

Case 4
LAMONT INDUSTRIES, INC.

Office of the President
Memorandum to: Country managers of Lamont's worldwide subsidiaries
From: President
Subject: Balance-of-payments analysis

In order to facilitate the handling of the various foreign currencies in which Lamont deals, we are attempting to improve our forecasting of exchange rates and regulations. Possible future exchange fluctuations and the easing or worsening of exchange controls are of great importance to our financial policies in each country where we have subsidiary operations.

As one means of forecasting, we are planning to experiment with balance-of-payments projections. Although the balance-of-payments figures published by the International Monetary Fund are useful as historical information, they do not provide enough indications of future trends. Our research department will, therefore, make three-month, six-month, and one-year projections of the balance of payments for the countries in which we operate. We hope that these projections will help us in determining the possible development of the country's exchange position.

In order to assist our research department in this kind of work, we request that you provide us with a balance-of-payments analysis for country *X*.

The balance-of-payments analysis should include:

1. The trends of the country's balance of payments during the past five years
2. An explanation of these trends based on the analysis of the more important items in the balance of payments
3. The projection of the balance of payments for the current year (using any actual data already available)
4. Explanatory comments on your forecast.

In order to be most useful to our research department in its future forecasting, your analysis should set forth the main structural features of country X's economy as they affect the balance of payments. It should also indicate the relationship between the balance of payments and internal economic developments, as well as world economic factors. The trade pattern and trade relations of country X, the importance and the competitive position of its exports on world markets, and the nature and essentiality of its imports may be crucial in forecasting its balance-of-payments prospects. The report should discuss the major factors influencing country X's exchange rate and its exchange controls.

Case 5
THE CLIFFORD COMPANY

In early 1963 the Clifford Company, a Swiss-based company with extensive overseas investments, began to develop a generalized formula approach to gaining a measurement of the degree of risk existing in any foreign currency at a point in time. The technique was devised as a consequence of continuing concern among executives of the company with foreign currency devaluation and the accompanying dollar value erosion of certain company assets. A formula approach was chosen for ease of application and consistency. Basically, the system as described below involves five economic indicators, each having a weighting factor that is granted in various numerical degrees according to the favorable or unfavorable trends within each indicator. Accompanying the five factor descriptions below are the values given for significant trend categories. A perfect score signifying overall excellent currency health would be 100; however, of twenty-two situations analyzed, in no case did a total exceed 85.

The specific weights were arbitrarily assigned although not completely without basis, for this study involved detailed observation of a number of indicators and their interrelationships. It was felt by the analysts who developed the approach that the assigned weights reflect properly the relative importance of the factors.

The factors chosen for presentation, the thinking that led to their choice, and the weights assigned each (Exhibit 1) are as follows:

1. Reserves

Monetary gold plus foreign exchange plus IMF gold tranche position. These are a reflection of the solvency, in effect, of a country in regard to its ability to meet international obligations. These can, of course, be represented by debt repayment obligations, profits, and royalty remittances, and so on. A foreign investor's direct concern is whether or not he will be able to retrieve the proceeds derived from proposed dollar investments quite apart from the investment proposal's internal attractiveness.

The IMF gold tranche position is included (gold tranche being the maximum amount which can be borrowed without having to make unusual arrangements) because it acts as a reserve which can be drawn upon with virtual certainty. However, there are circumstances in which the IMF may refuse to lend. For this reason, a category, given five points, is included to reflect a deteriorating situation where no outside assistance is available.

Reserves are assigned a total of 40 out of 100 because of their clearly critical effect upon the external value of a given currency. In no observed situation did a nation avoid devaluation, or the institution of other measures tantamount to devaluation, when a severe drop in reserves was experienced. The intermediate values (0-35) were determined arbitrarily, although the various categories are found significant by observation of various situations.

2. Money Supply

Currency in circulation plus demand deposits. Normally, there is a close correlation between the internal supply of money and cost of living. In the ideal classical sense a nation should experience an increase in production to match increases in demand at home. With increases in production there is usually a reduction in unemployment and, as a result, a higher level of real income. Theoretically, it can happen without inflation. However, actual experience suggests that wages and other forms of payment tend to move upward at a more rapid rate than output. This leads to a supply of money, usable for making payments, that grows faster than the supply of goods. Generally a situation results that leaves too much money available to buy too few goods. Hence, prices are bid up and inflation results.

In countries where capital and consumer goods must be imported, the value of the goods is inflated in internal currency terms while it remains stable in dollar or other hard currency terms. Eventually the dollar becomes increasingly expensive, causing further import price increases and, in addition, making it increasingly more difficult for the exporter to find markets and thus to earn foreign exchange. If this kind of situation continues, an adjustment must eventually be made, probably via the introduction of trading obstructions or devaluation.

The situation is particularly likely in countries where it is considered politically advantageous for governments to embark on vast deficit spending programs financed by the printing press, as in Brazil.

Money supply is assigned a total of 20 out of 100 points. The often direct correlation between this factor and cost of living is accounted for by weighting them equally. They are mentioned separately, however, because there are a number of situations where the correlation is not evident. Excessively unfavorable trends in either category may or may not undermine the other, although the existence of either, at rates deemed excessive, can lead to external pressures on a currency.

The breakdown within this category results from a review of nine countries, primarily Latin American, with emphasis on rate of increase in money supply over five years, rate of increase in cost of living over five years, and frequency and extent of devaluations over five years.

3. Cost of Living

The significance of the internal purchasing power of a given currency is self-evident. An erosion of value at home cannot help but be eventually reflected externally, provided there is not a similar relative decline in the internal value of important trading currencies.

As stated above, there may or may not be a direct correlation between cost of living and money supply. Because of the inconsistency of the interrelationship between the two, each is assigned 20 out of 100 points.

Some general conclusions as to the rate of deterioration in the internal value of a given currency were derived from the annual First National City Bank Monthly Economic Letter review of currency value erosion. The relative weights were obtained from an analysis of this review as to frequency of and extent of devaluations in the forty-three countries reported.

4. Trade Balance

Dollar volume of international trading activities. The relationship between these items is critical, for most countries, to the reserve position. Exports form, generally, the most important source of foreign exchange earnings, and imports the most important source of drainage. While it may not be possible to state categorically that a continuing deficit is intolerable, it is probably safe to say that in the long run such a situation is most unhealthy. A trend toward a deficit position in international trading accounts is, in a vast majority of cases, an indication of troubled times ahead. Spain is an exception, at least temporarily, for a 1959 devaluation led to a phenomenal tourist boom which has more than compensated for a growing trade deficit. However, dependence on so fickle a source of earnings as tourist traffic does not replace indefinitely a sound, competitive trade-based economy.

A value of 10 points was given this category because of the usual importance of trade to the foreign exchange balance. Countries were classified as either good, indifferent or bad depending upon their trade balance.

5. Official versus Free Market Rates of Exchange (Exchange Spread)

The "official" rate in this comparison is that rate at which most government-authorized transactions take place. It should not be equated with the IMF established rate which is meaningless in some countries like Uruguay, where the official rate is set in the free market. In countries using a fluctuating free market rate for all transactions, trends in this rate over the month are used.

The purpose of the comparison is to observe the value placed upon a given currency by outsiders whose interests are neither politically nor emotionally tied to overvaluing their currencies while outside traders tend to exaggerate their weaknesses by undervaluing the currencies. Nevertheless, a sudden or persistent widening of this spread would serve as an indication of increasing apprehension over the near future, thus providing a signal which may be of use in timing new investments.

A total value of 10 was assigned the exchange spread with intermediate values for variations up to 10 per cent discount and over 10 per cent discount. The 10 per cent bench mark is an arbitrary one that, by observation, seems to indicate a significant shift in outsider value appraisals.

Experience with the formula (Exhibit 2) proved it to be consistent and, within limits indicated below, a valid indicator of currency health in twenty-one of twenty-two situations. Only in Canada, prior to a devaluation in 1961, did the formula fail to provide an accurate indication of a situation at a given point in time. Exhibit 3 is an analysis of the events preceding the Canadian devaluation and some discussions as to why the formula, as is, failed.

In the other twenty-one situations displayed, the following significance can be attached to various formula results:

75–100	Strong
65–75	Bears watching, perhaps closer analysis
45–60	Definite risk, some adjustment necessary
0–45	High risk, devaluation or equivalent expected

While significant consistency is apparent in the formula resulting, it must be mentioned that only quantitatively measurable factors are used. Political philosophies and feasibilities can vary tremendously from country to country and can cause authorities to refrain in acting in ways which might be economically prudent. Only a fairly intimate knowledge of the local political climate can provide a complete assessment of the degree of risk existing in any national currency.

The rather comprehensive nature of the formula approach, in contrast with a series of independently formed charts of the individual factors used, appears to eliminate a significant portion of the inherent differences between advanced and developing nations. Very often economically advanced nations will react differently to similar situations, primarily because of their basically healthier positions and the sophistication of their monetary authority. There are also, normally many more avenues open to the developed countries should a need arise for a drastic step to be taken in an effort to relieve pressure on their currencies. Confidence alone, built over a period of stability, contributes greatly to relative ease in finding solutions, as does the more extensive information system which often enables authority to make defensive moves before crises develop.

However, by reducing all the factors to a single numerical indicator that reflects currency strength, the qualitative matter of relative economic monetary development and sophistication becomes less critically important. A low value, i.e. below 60, resulted in devaluations whether in France, Spain, Syria, or Brazil. On the other hand, the Canadian experience may suggest that the advanced nations must be watched far more carefully for signs of intrinsic weaknesses because in these countries good economic sense may outweigh political and/or emotional attitudes and permit a devaluation before deep crises result.

EXHIBIT 1

Currency Risk

FACTORS:	*RELATIVE WEIGHTS:*
1. Reserves	40
2. Cost of living	20
3. Money supply	20
4. Exchange	10
5. Balance of trade	10

Reserves:
(3 years or since last devaluation)

a. Rising trend	40
b. Consistent stability	35
c. Sporadic or improving	30
d. Slow decline	20
e. Rapid decline (IMF-US)	10
f. Rapid decline (no help)	5
g. Negative (chaos)	0

Cost of Living: Five-year Trend
(compound per cent per annum)

a. Stable (0 -1.5%)	20
b. Rising (1.5%-3.5%)	15
c. Rising (3.5%- 6%)	10
d. Rising (6% - 15%)	5
e. Rising (over 15%)	0

Money supply: Five-year trend
(compound per cent per annum increase)

a. Stability	20
b. Rising (2% - 4%)	15
c. Rising (6% -10%)	10
d. Rising (over 10%)	5
e. Chaos (i.e. Brazil)	0

Balance of trade: Three-year trend

a. Export surplus	10
b. Stability (with exchange cushion)	10
c. Deficit (stable, slight)	5
d. Deficit (expanding rapidly)	0

*Exchange (*spread between official and free market): Six-month trend*

a. Less than 10%	10
b. More than 10%	5
c. No correlation	0

*Where a fluctuating free market governs all transactions, the trend over six months is used.

EXHIBIT 2

Formula Application: 20 Countries, 22 Situations

		1. Australia 1957-1962	2. U.K. 1957-1962	3. New Zealand 1957-1962	4. Switzerland 1957-1962	5.* Canada 1955-1960	6.* Germany 1955-1960	7.* Netherlands 1955-1960	8. U.S.A. 1957-1962	9. Portugal 1957-1962	10. Philippines 1957-1962	11. Denmark 1957-1962
Reserves	40	33	30	30	40	35	40	35	20	35	20	25
Money supply	20	26	20	15	10	15	5	10	20	10	10	10
Cost of living	20	13	15	15	15	15	15	15	15	15	15	10
Trade balance	10	3	5	10	5	5	10	5	10	5	5	5
Exchange spread	10	10	10	10	10	10	10	10	10	10	10	10
	100	85	80	80	80	80	80	75	75	75	60	60

		12.* Syria 1957-1962	13.* Argentina 1957-1962	14.* Uruguay 1954-1958	15.* Spain 1954-1958	16.* Brazil 1957-1962	17.* Mexico 1948-1954	18. Mexico 1957-1962	19. Japan 1957-1962	20. Peru 1957-1962	21.* France 1953-1958	22. France 1958-1962
Reserves	40	15	30	20	10	0	30	30	35	40	10	40
Money supply	20	10	5	5	5	0	5	10	5	5	10	10
Cost of living	20	20	0	0	5	0	5	10	10	5	10	10
Trade balance	10	5	5	5	5	5	0	10	10	10	5	10
Exchange spread	10	5	5	10	5	0	10	10	10	10	5	10
	100	25	45	60	30	5	50	70	70	70	40	80

*Notes:
5. 17% devaluation in 2nd quarter, 1961
6. 5% revaluation in 1st quarter, 1961
7. 5% revaluation in 1st quarter, 1961
12. 11% devaluation in 3rd quarter, 1962
13. 63% devaluation in 2nd quarter, 1962; thereafter free market also official
14. 49% devaluation in 2nd quarter, 1959
15. 43% devaluation in 2nd quarter, 1959
16. 31% devaluation in 2nd quarter, 1963; 32% devaluation in 3rd quarter, 1962; 13% devaluation in 2nd quarter, 1962; 7% devaluation in 4th quarter, 1961; etc.
17. 45% devaluation in 2nd quarter, 1954
21. 20% devaluation in 2nd quarter, 1958; 17% devaluation in 4th quarter, 1958; Total devaluation—40%

EXHIBIT 3

Canada: Comments on the 1961 Devaluation

As indicated in Exhibit 2, the Canadian dollar appeared a very strong currency, yet it was devalued by some 17 per cent over a period of time. A close review of the classic indicators did not reveal any serious trouble. Yet the Canadian dollar was widely regarded as being intrinsically weak. The problems were among those usually thought of as being cause for devaluation, i.e. persistent trade deficits and continuing substantial deficit spending by the government. Also, the internal economic outlook was not good, with unemployment at 7 per cent, down from a 1960 high of 11 per cent, both figures seasonally adjusted.

Internally Canada suffered cumulative fiscal deficits in the full five years through 1961/1962 of approximately $2.8 billion dollars, a huge amount for a nation whose annual federal budget is about $6 billion dollars. This would be comparable to a United States cumulative deficit, over the same period, of some $26 billion dollars. That this was not reflected in any excessively increased money supply was probably because of the efficiency of the payment system (resulting in a smaller need in absolute increases in money) and rising income taxes.

Reserves were, statistically, stable for some eight years prior to the devaluation because of investments and heavy short-term borrowing abroad. Not evident from the generally published statistics was a cumulative trade deficit over the period of 1948 to 1960 of $1.25 billion dollars and an "invisible" deficit of $7.1 billion. Thus the cumulative external current account deficit, 1948-1960, was a staggering $8.35 billion.

A key problem for Canada was the increasing difficulty its exporters found in holding overseas markets. With the Canadian dollar at a premium over the United States dollar and with world surpluses in oil, copper, and uranium, important Canadian exports, plus a suffering gold-mining industry and paper and pulp sales threatened by Soviet dumping, the outlook for Canada was not bright. Thus the devaluation route, taken before a crisis could develop, was a useful and wise solution. Also, with reserves at the United States $2-billion mark, Canada was not in a position to embark on a protracted support program for the Canadian dollar. dollar.

It is probable that, given an absence of any action to reverse generally unfavorable trends, the Canadian formula result has begun to deteriorate. Canada was, and remains, in a position unique among advanced nations. There is no parity or IMF establishing floor to which the bank of Canada is committed. Thus, the Canadian dollar was allowed to slip gradually until a rate of exchange deemed appropriate was reached. Had Canada been committed to intervention, reserves would have shown a marked reduction and caused a significantly lower formula.

Responding to Environmental Adversities

4

The two preceding chapters focused on the types of environmental adversities which international investors can expect to encounter, their possible implication for the firm, and a methodology for assessing the likelihood of encountering these situations. The discussion emphasized that the international businessman should be able to understand the forces at work when inflation, devaluation, exchange controls, or expropriation occur so that he can make a thorough attempt to forecast the future business climate, to establish appropriate objectives, and to take precautionary measures when warranted. The present chapter will continue where the last terminated by discussing methods and measures that an international corporation can use to adjust and adapt to high risk situations.

Reducing the Prospects of Expropriatory Action by the Host Country

This section discusses the *action*-oriented and policy-making ingredients in an affiliate's program to minimize the possibility of being forced out of business in a particular country. In this regard it is important to keep in mind the current objectives and major economic and social trends in foreign countries in general. Allowing for differences in emphasis from one country to the next, and between the industrial and the less developed nations, the following three goals summarize the attitudes and policies which international investors can expect to find abroad:

1. A desire to increase the nation's per capita income through increased productivity rates and greater employment of local factors of production.

2. A desire to strengthen the nation's international position, with less dependence on the goods and services provided by the outside world, and larger and more stable earnings from the country's exports.

3. A desire to gain and maintain more control over the national economic destiny through less reliance on foreign-owned financial capital, technical know-how, management, organizational, and marketing capabilities.

If one accepts this simplistic summary of national aspirations, the implications for the international investor who wishes to remain secure and unharassed in a foreign environment are relatively clear. The host country must perceive that it is benefiting from the presence of a foreign-owned enterprise to such an extent that no other arrangement would be more favorable for attaining the national objectives.

The task for the corporate public relations staff is self-evident. The host country—which means the government, the populace at large, local suppliers, consumers, and the employees of the affiliate—must not fail to recognize and duly appreciate all of the benefits which have accompanied the foreigner's presence. For the corporate policy-maker and international manager, the path to be followed is also well marked. Commensurate with the nature of the company's overall operations, the affiliate's operating strategies and day to day policies must be designed to insure that the host country will perceive that it *is* in fact aided by the foreign-owned enterprise.

It is impossible to prescribe a set of failsafe guidelines that will befit the myriad of peculiar circumstances of individual companies in different national jurisdictions. Nevertheless, evidence from the reports of internationally oriented companies, disinterested observers, and foreign countries' investment legislation, suggests the kind of operational strategies and policies which warrant serious consideration by most foreign affiliates.[1]

[1] For an elaboration of the rationale of using many of these approaches and a review of companies' experiences with them, *see* Thomas Aitken, Jr., *A Foreign Policy for American Business*, New York, Harper & Row, 1962; John Fayerweather, *The Executive Overseas*, Syracuse, Syracuse University Press, 1959; William R. Fritsch, *Progress and Profits, The Sears Roebuck Story in Peru*, Washington, D.C., Action Committee for International Development, 1962; *The Atlantic Community and Eco-*

1. Foreign-owned affiliates should, as a general rule, hire an increasing number of local persons for positions initially held by Americans or other representatives of the parent company management. In essence, this recommendation refers to *technical* and *managerial* positions, implying a responsibility to *develop* the requisite skill levels among the local nationals.

2. Foreign parent companies should geographically *disperse* research and development operations, so as to provide this type of employment as well as to increase the professional competence of foreign nationals.

3. Foreign firms may be well advised to sell a part of the ownership of their foreign affiliates to private or public representatives of the host countries.

4. Foreign-owned affiliates should attempt to develop and to utilize *local* sources of supply for their raw material and component requirements and to encourage the development of local entrepreneurship.

5. Wherever possible the foreign-owned affiliate should endeavor to export its products or services so as to increase the export earnings of the host economy.

These recommendations, which are only illustrative of many possibilities, are what might be called good citizenship policies. They clearly are in the interest of the host country and, as such, can be expected to be evaluated as "pluses" for the affiliate in any governmental cost-benefit evaluation of its contribution. Yet, as a number of companies have learned, being a good citizen is not *in itself* a sufficient basis for warding off expropriatory actions by the host country. Hence, attention must be turned to a second aspect of risk reduction and adaptation: namely, means of buying protection against unfavorable governmental actions. Protection, as the term is hereafter used, can refer to two types of action:

1. Operational policies and organizational approaches to overseas investments that make expropriatory actions extraordinarily difficult or risky for the foreign country
2. Contractual guarantees that serve to minimize the likelihood of unfavorable host country policies *vis à vis* the foreign investor, or that provide for compensation to the investor should his properties suffer from certain types of host country actions.

These forms of protection will be discussed in turn.

---

nomic Growth, Report of the Conference, December 12–15, 1965, The Atlantic Council of the United States, Washington, D.C., 1966, pp. 25–34; Richard D. Robinson, *International Management,* Holt, Rinehart & Winston, Inc., New York, 1967; R. F. Mikesell, "Healing the Breach over Foreign Resource Exploitation," *Columbia Journal of World Business,* March-April 1967, pp. 25–32; Lynn Townsend, "Aesop's Golden Goose Couldn't Compare," *Columbia Journal of World Business,* Summer 1966, pp. 103–108.

Since many foreign nations have alternative sources from which to receive investment capital and know-how, as well as an increasing sophistication in exacting attractive commercial terms from international investors, the multinational firm finds itself increasingly obliged to find methods of making its affiliates *indispensable* to the countries in which they are located.

Twentieth century investment experience and the history of host country-foreign investor relations suggest that two strategic approaches can be recommended to today's investors:[2]

1. Maintain technological superiority over local enterprises and, if possible, over other competing foreign firms. Implied is the requirement to introduce technological improvements on a *continuing* basis into the host countries.

2. If appropriate, organize international operations in such a way that individual foreign affiliates are integrated into a worldwide production, logistical, and marketing system. Without this integration (such as exists in the petroleum industry), the respective foreign subsidiaries are likely to be unable to operate or compete successfully.

The second principal form of protection frequently available to the international investor is investment guaranty insurance. Although the potential investor may receive assurances from the host country that he can freely withdraw profits, repatriate invested capital, operate his business without interference, and receive full compensation in the event of expropriation, changes in the political and economic climate of the recipient country or the partiality of its judiciary may ultimately deprive the investor of his property and/or freedom to operate as previously. Recognizing the dangers inherent in international operations while at the same time attempting to encourage the flow of private capital to less developed areas, the governments of some countries, notably the United States, Australia, Germany, Japan, Norway, Austria, France, and Denmark, have established insurance coverage schemes which protect certain designated activities from certain prescribed adversities. Such insurance schemes are also being contemplated by other countries such as Belgium, the Netherlands, and Switzerland. Eventually some form of multilateral investment insurance may also be available to the international investor.

[2] The extractive industries have the lengthiest experience in foreign investment activity, and they have the most difficult adaptations to make abroad. For some interesting reading on a few specific examples, *see* J. R. Powell, *The Mexican Petroleum Industry*, Berkeley, University of California Press, 1956; the National Planning Association case studies on United States business performance abroad, including: Wayne C. Taylor, *The Creole Petroleum Corporation in Venezuela;* Cambridge, M.I.T. Press, *Stanvac in Indonesia*; Stacy May, *The United Fruit Company in Latin America*; and, S. Kannappan, *Aluminum Limited in India.*

In the United States, the Agency for International Development (AID) can provide a corporation beneficially owned by a majority of Americans or a wholly-owned foreign subsidiary investment guarantees for new investments or for the expansion of existing facilities in those countries that have entered into special bilateral agreements with the United States. (Presently, the United States has entered into seventy such agreements.)

The American investor currently may apply for two major types of insurance,[3] specific risk guaranties and extended risk guaranties. In essence, the specific risk coverage includes inconvertibility, expropriation, and war, revolution, or insurrection. Application may be made for any or all of these coverages, with the maximum available protection being 200 per cent of the value of the investment, or 100 per cent of the value of a loan to an affiliate and applicable interest. In the case of licensing type agreements, coverage is equivalent to the total amount of royalties and fees that could be expected over the life of the agreement. The annual cost of such insurance is about 1 per cent of the amount of coverage.

The extended risk guaranties are available for portfolio type investments, longer-term loans made by the parent companies to their foreign subsidiaries, and equity investments. Coverage is broader than the specific risk program, including both business and nonbusiness risks, with compensation limited to 75 per cent of the scheduled maturities of a loan and interest due, and 50 per cent of the original amount of an equity investment. While the extended risk guaranties do not cover losses arising from fraud or misconduct of the investor, they *do* include currency devaluation and forms of creeping expropriation for which specific risk coverage is not available.

A number of problems can arise in conjunction with making application for investment guaranties and with securing compensation from them. Under the programs of most lending countries, the international investor may encounter either of the following broad problem areas:[4]

[3] A third major category of AID insurance is the foreign housing guaranty; because it is not directly relevant to this discussion, it has not been described in the text. More information on the AID programs and the problems that have been associated with their administration can be found in: AID, *Specific Risk Guaranty Handbook*, Washington, D.C., 1966; AID, *Extended Risk Guaranties of Loans for Private Projects*, Washington, D.C., 1964; Fred L. Kirgis, "Extended Risks and Latin American Housing Guaranties: Foreign Assistance through Business Risk Protection for Private Enterprise," *Virginia Law Review*, March 1967, pp. 285–292, 295–297, 326; Lawrence A. Collins and Aaron Etra, "Policy, Politics, International Law and the United States Investment Guaranty Program," *The Columbia Journal of Transnational Law*, vol. 4, no. 2, 1966, pp. 240–296.

[4] For an elaboration of these problems *see* Collins and Etra, *op. cit.*; A. A. Fatouros, *Government Guarantees to Foreign Investors*, New York, Columbia University Press, 1962; Marina Von Neumann Whitman, *Government Risk Sharing in Foreign Investment*, Princeton, Princeton University Press, 1965.

1. The processing of guaranty applications as well as those that seek compensation for alleged injury may become embroiled and entangled in government bureaucracy, required procedures, and intergovernmental negotiations, thereby encumbering the foreign investor with costly delays.
2. As with the administration of justice under domestic and international law, the interpretation of national guaranty programs by judicial tribunals may be unknown to the investor when he contracts for protection.

In addition to the investment guaranty legislation of the lending countries, a number of recipient countries have also enacted laws which contain guaranties for foreign investors. In essence these laws identify certain acceptable industries and areas in which foreign investment is welcomed, and they provide for a number of operational limitations as well as investment inducements for the foreigners. One of the inducements is the assurance that in the event of expropriation the investor will be given prompt and adequate compensation.

Among the most comprehensive guaranties in this respect are those contained in Article 32 of the Korean Foreign Investment Encouragement Law of 1960, as amended:

> 1. The assets of registered enterprises under this Law shall not be subject to any compulsory expropriation or any form of compulsory transfer of ownership, except appropriation by the Government for a public purpose.
> 2. In the event of the expropriation of the assets under the preceding paragraph by the Government, just compensation shall be paid for in accordance with law. Such compensation shall be in an effectively realizable form and shall represent the full equivalent of the property taken.
> 3. The investor shall have the right to remit abroad without delay any sums of money received as payment for action taken under this Article free of taxes or fiscal charges.

Such indications of welcome and promise of workable government-investor relations are, of course, of some psychological value to investors. Nevertheless, the legal and material worth of host government promises of this nature are relatively limited. This limitation stems from two characteristics of international investment activity:

1. The continuous threat of expropriation that the investor must face over long periods of time results not so much from arbitrary actions the host government is free to take or not to take, but rather from the general *instability* affecting institutions, policies, and practices that is inherent in the very conditions of less developed nations [5]

[5] Trade and Development Board, Committee on Invisibles and Financing Related to Trade, *Stimulation of the Flow of Private Capital: Promotion of Private Foreign Investment in Developing Countries,* United Nations Conference on Trade and Development, New York, April 4, 1967, p. 30.

2. Even if an investor obtains guaranties from a foreign nation, his newfound security may fall victim to the peculiar logic of international law wherein a state's promise made in contractual form with a foreign citizen can be broken *without* its committing any generally recognized legal wrong [6]

These considerations lead to the final section of the discussion on expropriatory risks. If the international investor is the victim of such actions on the part of a foreign government, what are his legal rights and what remedies might he seek?

The Rights of the Expropriated International Investor and Possible Approaches for Seeking Redress

The precise methodology for seeking legal redress in the event of expropriation at the hands of a foreign state is, of course, best known and handled by professional legal counsel. Nevertheless, the financial manager of an internationally oriented company must be aware of the possible consequences for his firm if one or more of its foreign affiliates suffers a loss of property or the ability to operate. This type of knowledge will be factored into the manager's techniques for assessing the risks confronting foreign affiliates and for determining the most suitable methods for avoiding injury. The following discussion focuses on the legal rights of the international investor, the problems he may experience in seeking remedies for loss he has encountered, and a few of the international institutions that are likely to become increasingly important to investors faced with the problem of recovering damages from a foreign state.[7]

When is governmental action that the investor finds injurious in fact a violation of public international law? Public international law is composed of so-called conventional international law and customary international law. The first type arises when two or more nations enter into a treaty prescribing rules to govern certain types of activities. Because there are relatively few such treaties related to the problem of avoiding injury to an international investment, particular attention will be paid to the second type of public international law, customary international law. It values rules which through practice, recognition, and application

[6] See A. A. Fatouros, *op. cit.*

[7] This section draws on discussions held with Tom Farer of the Columbia University Law faculty. An elaboration of the principles covered in the text can be found in the following sources, the first of which also includes a thorough examination of the legal aspects of nationalization: Konstantin Katzarov, *The Theory of Nationalisation,* The Hague, Martinus Nijhoff, 1965; Francis J. Nicholson, "The Protection of Foreign Property under Customary International Law," *Boston College Industrial and Commercial Law Review,* Spring 1965.

over the years are regarded as controlling the activities of nations. They are not necessarily recognized by a particular treaty, but an international court will nevertheless adhere to those principles as governing a dispute.

Under the traditional view of the United States and several capital-exporting nations, expropriation is valid if the host state provides the investor full, prompt, and effective compensation. This, in effect, means that if an investment is worth $300,000, the investor must be given $300,000 in a convertible currency at the time the property is confiscated.

Since the end of World War II, a forceful critique of this traditional view of expropriatory action has emerged. It has been forwarded by the less-developed countries. Presently, a number of scholars in the advanced nations also support a somewhat different concept, arguing against a general rule requiring full, prompt, and effective compensation. If the expropriation is designed to achieve general social and economic purposes—perhaps to revise economic and social relationships within the society, as in Cuba—the government is not required to provide full compensation. (The Communist countries would argue that no compensation must be paid. The LDC's could generally state that partial compensation would be appropriate.) In part, the LDC advocates of this view have argued that since they did not create contemporary economic and social relations, which instead are the product of external forces, they should not be held responsible for their actions. The governments of the LDC's should not be precluded from pursuing what they perceive to be in their countries' interests. Expropriation of foreign-owned properties should be appreciated as one of numerous state actions deemed to alter the existing relationships.

The existence of conflicting views under customary international law means that if an international investor is able to find an international tribunal to which it can take a claim of expropriation without full compensation, it is *questionable* whether or not the tribunal will find that full compensation *must* be given *if* the property was expropriated as part of a general program of national resource reallocation. *Discriminatory* expropriation, however, is a different matter. The developed countries and most of the legal scholars in the less developed ones agree that if only French properties are expropriated, but not German or United States properties, the act is inconsistent with customary international law and gives rise to the requirement for compensation. Discriminatory expropriation is invalid.

How can one determine what constitutes fair and adequate compensation when international law provides for it? The host government may take the position that the fair value is represented by the amount of the initial investment or that amount less depreciation of assets. The investor may attach a greater value to the lost properties, considering the affiliate to be a going concern with established marketing channels and promotional know-how and an anticipated stream of future earnings. Moreover, what constitutes prompt payment—one month, one year, or even a longer period after the properties were nationalized? These and other problems of administration and interpretation of public international law complicate expropriatory proceedings for the multinational investor.[8]

Even if a company's foreign properties are expropriated in a discriminatory manner, a major hazard to the vindication of a claim is the requirement under international law that the firm first exhaust all *local* remedies before seeking diplomatic assistance from the government of the parent company. (Even in the case of the recent Cuban expropriations, the United States State Department required aggrieved citizens to demonstrate that they had exhausted whatever remedies the Cuban government made available, no matter how inadequate.) The procedure, therefore, is for the investor to go into the courts of the foreign state and claim that the seizure of his property was illegal, and that legal compensation is required. Until the host country has had the opportunity to hear the claim, to react to it, and to provide compensation, the investor's own government is not permitted to enter into formal diplomatic negotiations, nor can the investor have access to an international tribunal or an arbitration tribunal. One obvious result of this requirement is to provide the nationalizing state with a delaying tactic. While the state is not explicitly refusing to honor the claim, it is able to create lengthy delays in litigation which can become costly to the claimant.

Once an injured investor has exhausted all possibilities in the courts of the foreign state, he may decide to pursue a remedy through the act of "espousal." When a claim is espoused, the government of the investor (in the case of the United States, the State Department is the appropriate agency) agrees [9] to assume the role of a direct negotiator with the foreign government on behalf of the aggrieved citizen. Complete control of the ensuing international negotiations, including the terms and amount of payment, is assumed by the State Department. Hence, to a large extent, the success or failure of this procedure appears to be contingent upon the existing state and trend of relations between the interested countries.

Until very recently a corporate investor's case was ended if his government decided not to espouse his claim. There was no international tribunal to which the corporation could turn, because such forums were thought to be available only for disputes between *nations*, not between a nation and a citizen of another state. During the past few years a gradual recognition that an investor may have some rights *vis à vis* a

[8] *See* William C. Brewer, "Protection of United States Investments Abroad: The Investment Guaranty Program," *George Washington Law Review*, December 1963.

[9] When a claim has been submitted, the State Department of the United States has the authority to accept or refuse to provide such assistance. If it refuses, its decision is final, because the claimant cannot secure any judicial review of the case. It has been alleged that *political* considerations frequently exert a strong influence over the decision of whether or not to utilize the nation's political leverage as the backing for a citizen's claim against a foreign country.

foreign state, probably due to the universal desire to increase the flow of private investment capital to the less developed countries, has been manifested in two ways. First, in the Hague a permanent court of arbitration whose secretariat maintains a list of arbiters has, since 1962, been willing to hear disputes between investors and states. International investors (as well as countries) can be served by the center and may ask to have an arbitral tribunal created from the list.

Second, in 1966 the International Bank for Reconstruction and Development established the International Center for the Settlement of Investment Disputes. In the words of the board of governors, it was designed to "establish . . . facilities and procedures which would be available on a voluntary basis for the settlement of investment disputes between contracting States and nationals of other contracting States through conciliation and arbitration."[10] The Center, with a present membership in excess of fifty contracting countries, is too new to be evaluated. If it is to be useful, its special value would be to the international investor who, at the time an investment is made, can negotiate with a host country for an agreement that all disputes between them will be submitted to the Center for binding judgments. The forum will apply whatever law the parties have previously determined to be controlling. Free from the ideological debate of the United Nations and the delicate political problems that are often involved in diplomatic procedures, and enjoying the good reputation of the World Bank, the Center conceivably can fill the needs of the international investor for an impartial and fair international forum.[11]

Methods of Protecting the Firm against Anticipated and Unanticipated Devaluations and Exchange Restrictions

Upon completion of a short- and longer-range forecast of the possibilities of significant changes in the foreign business environment, the man-

[10] Resolution No. 214 of the Board of Governors of the International Bank for Reconstruction and Development.

[11] A description of the operational procedures of the Center can be found in the following sources: S. Boskey and P. Stella, "Settling Investment Disputes," *The Fund and Bank Review: Finance and Development*, September 1965, pp. 167–174; A. Broches, "Development of International Law by the I.B.R.D.," *American Society for International Law Procedures*, vol. 59, 1965; Michael Moore, "International Arbitration between States and Foreign Investors—the World Bank Convention," *Stanford Law Review*, vol. 18, 1966, pp. 1359–1380. A general discussion on arbitration between investors and countries is found in G. C. Doub, J. N. Hazard, *et al.*, "Arbitration between Governments and Private Firms," *American Society for International Law*, vol. 69, 1961; *ICSID Regulations and Rules*, Washington, D.C., International Centre for Settlement of Investment Disputes, 1968.

ager must decide upon the most appropriate method of defending against adversities while concurrently working to achieve the profit-making objectives established for the respective affiliates. Three categories of defenses may be devised to deal with the prospect of controls on foreign transactions or devaluation:

1. *General defensive measures* appropriate wherever such contingencies are considered possible, even if not likely, within the forthcoming eight to twelve months
2. *Special defensive measures* if devaluation or controls are forecasted for the ensuing six- to eight-month period
3. *Contingency measures* after a devaluation has occurred or controls have been imposed.

In the latter case, the objective is to protect the local affiliate from further operational difficulties and losses and to ensure a better adaptation to the new business environment. Each of these types of measures will be discussed below as they relate to devaluation and to exchange controls.

GENERAL DEFENSIVE MEASURES *VIS À VIS* EXCHANGE CONTROLS

When exchange controls are expected within the forthcoming year, an affiliate of a multinational company may be directed to take a number of measures designed to protect it from losses and difficulties which might otherwise be incurred. The basic objectives of such measures are twofold:

1. To provide the affiliate with an operational and financial stance with which it can weather and remain successfully operative under a system of controls
2. To minimize the amount of loss and costs that may be experienced by the firm *as a whole* if controls are imposed.

It is generally desirable to prearrange suitable sources of domestic and foreign exchange financing that will be required during a period of controls. The headquarters and the subsidiary are advised to solidify their positions with local and international banks, to make provisions for lines of credit, and to discuss a number of contingency measures that can be implemented in cooperation with the financial institutions. In part the protective step involves a shopping around for credit—a practice familiar to all businessmen. Also, the action may entail:

1. The immediate placement of funds on deposit to obtain a secure position with one or more banking institutions
2. The establishment of overdraft facilities in advance of the time they are actually required—if permitted by the local government

3. Application for locally denominated "Cooley" funds, which are available to some United States firms through the Agency for International Development, usually for five to ten years at a locally competitive rate of interest.[12]

Also with an eye to lining up sources of funds, affiliates that will require foreign exchange to import goods or to make remittances to their parent companies may consider beginning some type of export activity in order to earn convertible currencies for future use. Some countries with exchange controls will permit local exporters to retain a portion of their receipts for subsequent international transactions. Other nations using exchange controls make a local firm's access to foreign exchange contingent upon the firm's earning a certain amount of foreign exchange.

Another means of ensuring that required international transactions may be conducted if controls are imposed is by formally negotiating such permission with the host government in advance. This procedure is most common with new investments, but many companies—especially those held in highest regard by the local administration—have negotiated remittance agreements even for existing affiliates.

The general defensive measures designed to minimize loss and costs to the firm include:

a. The immediate establishment of bases for future remittances to the parent company. If it is anticipated that dividends, royalties, management fees, and repayment of an intercompany loan will be paid by the affiliate to the parent company during the forthcoming one to two years, the groundwork for such remittances should be laid well in advance of governmental restrictions. There are a variety of methods that can be used to establish that international remittances are necessary business transactions and that they represent a reasonable amount. One approach is to formalize in contractual form all *quid pro quo* arrangements between the affiliate and the parent. As a follow-up, the agreement can be presented to the local taxation authorities to gain their approval of the payment as a tax deductible expense. If controls are subsequently implemented, the affiliate can make the claim to the foreign exchange agency that the government has already recognized the remittance as a legitimate and reasonable transaction. A different method with essentially the same purpose is to develop a systematic basis for assessing charges on local affiliates so the rationale for having to make certain payments to the parent firm can be readily demonstrated to questioning government officials. This is often done to substantiate the

[12] Many companies have used "Cooley" loans abroad, and they represent an important source of funds which should not be overlooked by the international manager. A reasonably current description of the leading procedures and restrictions can be found in *Financing Foreign Operations,* New York, Business International Corporation, updated at about six-to-eight-month intervals.

amounts billed by the international headquarters staff for its time devoted to the management and problems of individual subsidiaries. Another approach to legitimatizing foreign remittances is to establish a readily observable relationship between the amount to be paid and a sales or profit-type figure for the affiliate. For example, royalties might always be 3 per cent of gross sales, dividends 18 per cent of after-tax profits, repayment of intercompany loans $20,000 per fiscal period or 50 per cent of dividends, whichever is larger. The possibilities for establishing bases for future remittances are many. The important point is to act immediately in establishing the precedent, so that if exchange controls are imposed, the affiliate will have documentation and a history of such practices to support its requests for continued remittances.

b. Where commensurate with the local requirements for working capital and funds for near-term capital expansion, efforts should be made to minimize the amount of funds held in a country that may impose exchange restrictions. The decision on allocating locally generated funds between the affiliate and the company's worldwide pool of funds is discussed later in chapters 5 and 11. At this juncture it is necessary to add only that management alert to the timing of international fund flows can help to minimize the total amount of company-controlled funds held within the jurisdiction of a country suspected of considering the imposition of exchange restrictions. In this regard, an officer of the internationally oriented Morgan Guaranty Trust Company emphasized:

> Many thousands of dollars can be saved by a company that can accurately project and forecast its cash receivables and payables. . . . The major problem . . . is to anticipate the receipt of these funds, to convert them at the best possible rates, and then to speed up their availability to [the rest of the company]. . . . The problem is not unique, since most subsidiaries abroad do not have foreign-exchange and money-market experts on their staffs. . . . Consequently when funds are received by a company's subsidiary, they are credited to the subsidiary's account in its local foreign bank; at some later date the local manager instructs the foreign bank to charge the account and remit the funds to the bank account of the U.S. parent company. It has happened that a parent company will first become aware that a subsidiary's funds are available to it when it receives the mailed credit advice from its U.S. bank. In turn, the U.S. bank may have received its advice from its correspondent abroad, not by cable but by air mail or even sea mail, many days after the initial deposit. . . . This is a costly (and it can be a dangerous) way to handle one's business.[13]

As a corollary it can be said that wherever commensurate with appropriate marketing practices, attempts should be made to speed up the

[13] Lee N. Shaw, "Coping with Foreign Exchange Problems in International Operations," in William Falcon, ed., *Financing International Operations,* New York, American Management Association, 1965, pp. 58–59.

collection of the affiliate's accounts receivables in order to minimize at a given point in time the liquid assets that must be held.

c. A final suggestion for minimizing exposure to the effects of exchange restrictions involves the handling of intercompany sales. If goods are to be sold to an affiliate located in a country of which the firm is wary, the supplier should seek one of the following protective terms in his contract with the customer:

1. The customer must provide a confirmed irrevocable letter of credit in the currency of the supplier before the supplier is obliged to commence manufacture
2. The customer will pay for all imported material with a convertible currency before the supplier is required to begin manufacture.

GENERAL DEFENSIVE MEASURES *VIS À VIS* DEVALUATION

In a relatively low risk situation regarding a currency devaluation, the approaches recommended to management are almost identical to those discussed in connection with exchange controls.

The basic objective is to minimize the exposure of the affiliate to loss in the event of a devaluation while not jeopardizing the continued successful operation of the enterprise. The suggested method is to minimize the subsidiary's holdings of cash and other locally denominated near cash assets whose dollar value would diminish by the amount of a devaluation; and to avoid or minimize its foreign indebtedness, whose effective local-currency cost to the affiliate will increase by the same percentage as the devaluation. Also the dependence of the affiliate on local sources of debt capital whose dollar cost will diminish after a devaluation should be increased. An additional measure which might be considered at this stage is to negotiate "exchange repurchase" agreements with the host government. The agreements are, in effect, insurance policies against exchange loss wherein the government provides a guarantee to the foreign investor that he will be able to purchase a convertible currency at a fixed rate of exchange for an agreed upon future period.[14]

SPECIAL DEFENSIVE MEASURES *VIS À VIS* EXCHANGE CONTROLS

If the investor's forecast shows the possibility of exchange restrictions within the forthcoming six to eight months, the necessity for taking precautionary measures is more urgent. In addition to the approaches

[14] See A. A. Fatouros, *op. cit.*, chs. 5, 12. In Colombia, the Central Bank charges investors 1 per cent per annum or less for this guaranty; *see* George Parker, *The Analysis of Private Capital Expenditures in Developing Economies*, Stanford University Graduate School of Business, unpublished Ph.D. dissertation, 1967, pp. 106–107.

enumerated earlier, the manager should consider substituting additional local financing for intercompany loans and advances, raising local prices, and altering the transfer price on goods sold by the parent or another jurisdictionally separated affiliate to the subsidiary. As will be discussed in the chapter on managing international remittances, the manager's flexibility in altering transfer prices is not altogether unrestricted; however, analysis should be made of the costs and benefits to the firm *as a whole* of raising the transfer prices to the affiliate—*if* the local government will permit—in order to provide an avenue to remove funds from the suspect country. The costs to be considered will result from:

1. The increased local borrowing that is likely to be characterized by a relatively high rate of interest
2. The loss in sales revenues that may ensue if the higher cost to the affiliate is passed on to the local consumers.

If the affiliate has indebtedness to the parent company, it should also consider—subject to host country permission—speeding up the repayment of principal (and any interest due) prior to the imposition of restrictions. The wisdom of taking this action will depend on the utility of having the money available to the affiliate during the period of expected remittance blockage versus the benefits of its being available to the worldwide corporate pool of funds. Such factors as competitive uses for the funds and the availability of externally supplied capital and its cost will have to be considered in this connection.

SPECIAL DEFENSIVE MEASURES *VIS À VIS* DEVALUATION

When an adverse change in the exchange rate is foreseen, a local affiliate may take a number of steps to protect the dollar value of its operations to the parent company and to decrease the cost of the devaluation to the subsidiary. In order to protect the dollar value of the local earnings, the manager may—if possible—negotiate to obtain exchange repurchase agreements described earlier, purchase forward dollars or a desired stable convertible currency on the foreign exchange market if forthcoming remittances or payments are planned, speed up the timing and perhaps the size of the affiliate's dividend to the parent company—conceivably by using locally borrowed funds to finance the transaction—and attempt to convert the subsidiary's current assets into a hard currency to be so held until after the devaluation has occurred.

All of these transactions, which constitute "hedges," involve a cost to the company—that is, a known cost is incurred to protect against a risk of unknown size. The manager must decide whether or not to hedge by comparing the expected cost to the firm if a devaluation occurs and no hedge is taken with the cost of the premium required on exchange repurchase agreements; or the cost of the premium if forward dollars are purchased; or the cost of borrowed funds if they are required to finance an early and/or unusually large dividend.

A different set of special defensive measures is designed to minimize the impact and thereby the cost of a devaluation on the affiliate by preparing it for a devaluation. Each of these measures has in common the timing of transactions so they will occur *prior* to the date when the devaluation is expected. The measures to be considered are:

1. Building up the affiliate's inventory of imported supplies, equipment, and/or components whose local currency costs would increase with a devaluation, as well as increasing the supply of locally produced goods whose prices are expected to increase soon after a devaluation, perhaps because they contain a high import content [15]

2. Speeding up the timing of the repayment of foreign indebtedness because the local currency cost of postdevaluation indebtedness will have increased by the same percentage as the devaluation

3. Relying more heavily on locally denominated debt, including that arranged through a dollar credit swap where the parent company makes an interest-free dollar loan to a host country banking institution; and the bank, in turn, lends an equivalent amount of local currency to the company's subsidiary, for a stated period of time, often at a relatively low interest rate. At maturity the transactions are reversed at a predetermined rate of currency exchange. The subsidiary has thereby had the use of locally denominated debt funds—and hedged its devaluation risks—and the parent company, at no exchange risk to itself, has facilitated the foreign loan.

In all of these approaches the firm pays for protection. The costs of protection must be identified by the manager and then compared with the expected cost of devaluation to determine which, if any, of these measures is appropriate in a given situation. The buildup of inventory and supplies ties up working capital with a calculable opportunity cost to the firm. Hurried repayment of foreign indebtedness has similar opportunity costs to the subsidiary and may necessitate supplementary borrowing with associated debt service expenses. The dollar credit swap similarly has two types of costs—interest charges paid by the local subsidiary (and on some occasions a commission charged by the bank) and an opportunity cost to the parent company whose funds are held by the local bank during the period of the loan. It would be wise for the financial manager to investigate other methods of supplying risk-

[15] It should be recognized that if local prices are subsequently raised, the stockpiling policy will presumably lead to increased taxable income—and a larger local income tax liability.

free funds to the affiliate. It might borrow from local nonbank institutions or directly from the parent company, which conceivably could protect its funds against exchange rate change by simultaneously acquiring forward dollars on the foreign exchange market to be delivered when the loan to the affiliate matures. The costs associated with this type of transaction—termed a foreign currency swap—are two-fold:

1. The return foregone on tied-up parent company funds
2. The premium that might have to be paid to acquire forward dollars, at the time the swap is arranged.

CONTINGENCY MEASURES *VIS À VIS* EXCHANGE CONTROLS

If exchange restrictions are imposed, the local subsidiary of a multinational firm will basically be confronted with two new interrelated problems: how to protect and maintain its profitability and how to move funds out of the host country to the parent company.

The matter of protecting and maintaining subsidiary profits involves utilizing internally generated funds that normally are remitted to the parent company but are tied up due to capital restrictions. The manager must determine how most effectively to utilize the blocked funds. Several solutions can be suggested, their suitability being dependent on the specifics of the case, the objectives of the affiliate, the severity and duration of the controls, the nature of the business, and the conditions and opportunities within the host country. Two possible uses of surplus funds consist of investing in capital equipment or inventory, as a hedge against expected price increases, or investment in promotional activities to increase the future salability of the affiliate's product line. Both actions are in fact investments in the subsidiary, designed to increase its forthcoming profitability when exchange controls are lifted. If all such internal investment opportunities are exhausted, the manager might then consider three other types of local portfolio investments:

1. Purchasing commercial or government paper, which in many countries will yield as high as 10 per cent
2. Investing in local real estate, which usually appreciates in value as domestic prices increase
3. Lending funds to other local companies that are willing to pay an attractive rate of interest and can offer the security required.

Another aspect of the problem of protecting local profitability during a period of exchange controls relates to the shortage of imported goods and the attendant rise in prices which controls may produce. The matter of operating in an inflationary environment will be discussed in detail in the next section. At this juncture the reader should recognize the environmental problems that may result from controls, as well as the possibility of having to raise the prices of the affiliate's product line to keep ahead of increasing costs.

The second fundamental problem caused by the imposition of exchange controls concerns the difficulty of moving funds from the host country to the company wide pool of funds. The solutions that will be suggested may in part subvert the intent of the host nation in establishing restrictions and represent departures from both the spirit and letter of local regulations. In the first category are these methods:

1. Raising the transfer price on goods sold to the affiliate by the parent company or by another of the company's foreign subsidiaries.

2. Subject to international prices and local government permission, exporting goods from the affiliate at a low transfer price to another of the company's overseas operations, which will enable the importing subsidiary to earn an abnormally large profit that can subsequently be remitted to the company pool of funds.

3. Making local currency funds available to another company's foreign-owned subsidiary in the host country in exchange for an equivalent dollar transfer by the other company's international headquarters to the lender's parent organization.

Among the methods that will more nearly remain within both the letter and spirit of the host country's restrictive regulations are the following:

1. Where the remittance of dividends is in some manner limited by the size of the capital base or the amount of current earnings, changing tax accounting procedures, e.g., revaluing fixed assets in order to increase depreciation charges thereby reducing taxes—may facilitate larger remittances.

2. Some countries permit and even encourage foreign-owned affiliates to purchase so-called dollar bonds issued by the host country. The bond subscriptions are in local currency, and at maturity are repayable with interest in dollars. (In Chile, for example, companies that subscribed to the government's issues received a 5 per cent yield, but had to wait five years until their local currency funds could be converted into dollars.)

3. Where dividend remittances are severely or altogether restricted, the affiliate can attempt to remit increasing amounts of funds in other forms. If intercompany indebtedness can be clearly established, the exchange authorities have often permitted regularly scheduled amortization of the principal plus a reasonable amount of interest payment on the outstanding balance. Similarly, clearly documented contractual licensing agreements for the transfer of technical know-how or industrial property rights to the subsidiary often will be respected by the control author-

ities. Owing to the typical deference given to these arrangements, their importance can be considerable in arranging for international fund remittances.

CONTINGENCY MEASURES *VIS À VIS* DEVALUATION

Once an exchange devaluation has taken place, and no further short-run changes are anticipated in the country's currency, the local enterprise should attempt to adapt its marketing, production, and financing techniques to the new environment. In the aftermath of devaluation, import prices will of course be higher, exports more competitive in world markets, and it is very likely that some degree of general domestic price inflation will ensue. In anticipation of these conditions the local affiliate will probably benefit from increasing its prices in the domestic market—if there are no controls—to keep ahead of increases in local costs and to overcome the increased local currency costs of imported inputs. A second defensive measure involves shifting production processes and a part of the product line away from goods that require a high import content. Consideration should also be given to starting or increasing export activity if there is a relatively high degree of price elasticity of demand for the affiliate's product line.

Methods of Adjusting to Inflation and Combating Its Adverse Effects

An affiliate operating under inflationary conditions must contend with two interrelated problems that result from rapid increases in the general price level:

1. Protecting the profit-making capability of the firm
2. Preserving the real value of its existing assets.

The specific methods of accomplishing these objectives will vary from country to country depending on government regulations, the type and strength of competition, and the nature of the subsidiary's operations. It is therefore useful to indicate only general guidelines that can be expected to be applicable in any inflationary environment.

Protecting the profit-making capability of the firm takes on special significance in an inflationary situation because of the persistent and relatively rapid increase in the costs of doing business. To overcome this key problem two basic approaches can be used. The first relates to an appropriate *pricing policy,* and the second to *controlling costs.* The objective of an inflationary pricing formula is to keep unit sales revenues increasing at least as rapidly as unit costs, while concurrently not jeopardizing the company's ability to make sales. (This, in turn, is largely dependent on the rate of growth of customers' monetary incomes. If, for example, wages lag behind price, demand can be expected to decline.) It is recommended that a unit price be charged that will be high enough to allow for the replacement of the item in inventory as well as yield a satisfactory contribution to overhead on the day the funds from the sale are actually received. As illustrated by the example below, if this approach is not followed, a firm will probably find that over the course of two or more inventory cycles, it will be losing money even though it makes a profit on the sale of a unit in the first time period.

For purposes of illustration assume that in the first time period the direct cost of producing an electric motor is LC100 and that because of inflationary conditions the cost of production is expected to increase to LC200 in the subsequent period. If the affiliate initially prices the motor at LC150, it will cover the *initial* costs and make a contribution to overhead, but it will *not* earn sufficient revenues to cover the expenses incurred in producing the second motor. If, as is usually the case under inflationary conditions, the inflow of cash receipts from the sale of the first item is delayed until, say, the third time period—because customers will find it to their advantage to withhold payment for as long as possible—the purchasing power to the producer of the LC150 price will have deteriorated so that it may cover only *one-third* of the direct costs associated with manufacturing motors in the third time period. Hence, over three time periods the company will be able to stay ahead of rising prices and have an opportunity to cover both indirect and direct costs *only* if it prices each period's goods on the basis of what replacement cost plus desired contributions to overhead will be when cash is received.

Another troublesome decision to be made concerns *when* and *to what* extent unit prices should be raised as prescribed above. A doctrinaire approach cannot be recommended for the ability of an enterprise to raise prices and the advisability of doing so depend on existing government regulations, the extent and type of competition, the income and price elasticity of local demand, and the amount of inflation. Specific pricing decisions will therefore have to be made according to local conditions. A useful guide for many companies is to try to make numerous small increases on a continuing but unannounced basis, which are designed to arouse as little customer attention and annoyance as possible, while concurrently keeping the consumer guessing as to when the next increase will come and keeping ahead of relevant cost increases.[16]

The second strategy in trying to protect the subsidiary's profit-making capability is to control costs. In addition to the methods appropriate in a noninflationary environment there are two which may take on spe-

[16] An instructive and interesting example is the Corn Products Company's pricing policies in Brazil. *See* "When Cruzeiros Spiral—Think Dollars," *Business Week*, March 13, 1965, pp. 107–110.

cial importance where the price level is increasing rapidly. One method involves investing heavily in supplies and inventories whose future costs and resale values to the firm are expected to increase over time. In deciding on this step the subsidiary's anticipated saving from stockpiling must be compared with the associated opportunity costs of tied-up funds. It should be appreciated, however, that in an inflationary environment many companies find themselves short of working capital and are unable to locate sufficient credit facilities in the local community; hence, stockpiling inventory and supplies may not be feasible or may represent a cost-reducing method with only limited opportunity.

The second method for curbing expenses has limited application, but may be useful in a few countries which permit it, i.e., revaluing the affiliate's fixed assets to represent more realistically their replacement value. The objective of such a move would be to increase the amount of current depreciation expenses that, in turn, will reduce the firm's local tax liability.

The need for protecting the company's existing monetary assets represents the second fundamental problem that results from ongoing inflation. The situation arises because a unit of local currency that is either owned or whose receipt is known will depreciate in purchasing power over time. Hence, the purchasing power of a subsidiary's cash, near cash assets, and accounts receivable can be expected to diminish for as long as local prices are increasing.[17] The general policy implication for a company so situated is to try to keep current assets at the lowest possible level. The corollary to this guideline is to utilize a relatively large amount of locally denominated debt funds to finance monetary assets. The impact of inflation on a company's liabilities is exactly the reverse of its effect on monetary assets. The real cost of local currency indebtedness can be expected to diminish as domestic prices rise.

One must be prudent in exercising these anti-inflationary approaches, for there are obvious costs and risks associated with inadequate current assets and excessive local borrowings. A company whose cash and near cash balances are too low may be unable to meet current obligations. If accounts receivable are trimmed significantly by restricting credit to customers, the result may be severe losses in sales volume with concurrent reductions in profitability. Even in an inflationary environment too much indebtedness may be incurred, and a company may be unable to meet its current obligations. Or, to cite a similar risk which results from a somewhat different situation, indebtedness incurred during a period of rapid price inflation may be manageable only so long as the firm's revenues are rising quickly and sizably. If inflationary pressures subside or

[17] An interesting exception appears to be the so-called inflation-proof savings accounts which have sprung up in Finland, China, Israel, and France. The rate of interest that is paid on these deposits is tied to the cost-of-living index, so that the real value of longer-term savings is protected against inflation. *See* Sirkka Hamalainen, "Inflation-Proof Savings Accounts in Finland," *Banker's Magazine,* Autumn 1965, pp. 56–60.

if price increases are curbed altogether and companies and individuals are no longer desirous or able to continue their high level of consumption, companies with a large volume of current debt may find themselves unable to generate adequate cash inflows through the collection of accounts receivable to meet maturing debt obligations.

One action to limit the size of a subsidiary's investment in current assets consists of offering sizable discounts to customers for prompt payment of debts where the discount is worth more to the customer than the cost of borrowing funds to make the payments. Discounting accounts receivable with a financial institution to provide prompt receipts from sales that have been made is another possibility. Stretching affiliate payables may be feasible. Finally the subsidiary might simply reduce the volume of local activity.

Summary

For purposes of exposition, the discussion in this chapter and preceding ones has tended to treat expropriatory action, inflation, devaluation, and exchange controls as though they were relatively separate phenomena that the international investor might expect to encounter one at a time in given countries. In fact, two or three of these environmental conditions are likely to occur simultaneously because they often result from the same or similar economic, political, and social conditions within a country or in the outside world, and because host governments sometimes find it appropriate to use one (e.g., devaluation) as a discretionary measure to complement another (e.g., exchange controls).

The task of forecasting environmental conditions and deciding upon the most appropriate types of protective and adaptive action is complicated precisely because devaluation, inflation, exchange controls, and expropriatory actions are interrelated and can occur concurrently. If, for example, it is believed that the local currency may be devalued within the forthcoming six months, a suitable course of action might be to speed up the timing and increase the size of the affiliate's dividend remittance. However, at the same time, the host country may be experiencing

1. Severe price inflation that has caused a shortage of local credit
2. Exchange controls that limit the amount and type of remittance payments
3. Antiforeign investor feelings, which suggest that large remittances may further antagonize the host country residents and government.

Should a large dividend be paid? The decision will depend in part on how the investor views the future. Will the exchange restrictions persist, or will they be lifted? Will inflation continue at the present rate, or will it subside? Are the antiforeigner feelings just a passing phase in current politicos' speech making, or are they likely to lead to damaging legislation and regulations? Only after these questions that pertain to the environment have been answered will the manager be able to consider alternative remedies.

Despite the problems of conducting business across national borders, the payoff to multinational companies—in terms of added profitability and sources of manpower or raw materials—are usually large enough to warrant a continuation of foreign investment and operations. Therefore, financial managers must learn to adapt to the unique international variables and contingencies so that their companies' international objectives can be realized.

The discussion in this chapter emphasized that methods of adaptation and risk minimization require, first, an understanding of the type and nature of the adversities that may be encountered, and second, an appreciation of the forces and pressures that lead to environmental difficulties for the firm. With this information the manager can attempt to predict future environmental conditions so that appropriate operational policies can be considered, and final decisions made that account for all of the relevant critical variables.

It is important that the reader appreciate that in international financial management as in purely domestic business, environmental forecasting and designing appropriate responses are *inexact* sciences. Nevertheless, the statement made by the treasurer of a large multinational firm—"we don't try to forecast, we just try to be prepared"—represents a relatively unresourceful and unimaginative approach to management responsibilities. Despite all of the difficulties inherent in trying to predict business conditions in a foreign country, the payoffs can be substantial for the firm that takes a logical, careful, and thoughtful approach to controlling the environmental adversities which surround virtually all business decisions.

The courses of action that are most appropriate will vary from situation to situation, depending upon local conditions, opportunities, government policies, competition, and objectives. Hence, the utility of the guides for action that have been enumerated throughout the chapter should be viewed in *general* terms. They may help point the way to specific business responses to specific environmental threats.

BIBLIOGRAPHY

Amerasinghe, C. F. *State Responsibility for Injuries to Aliens.* (New York: Oxford-Clarendon Press, 1967).

American Bar Association Committee on International Law. "The Compensation Requirement in the Taking of Alien Property," *The Record of the Bar Association of the City of New York,* vol. 22, 1967.

"Avoiding Expropriation Loss," *Harvard Law Review*, vol. 79, 1966.

Balekjian, W. H. *Legal Aspects of Foreign Investment in the European Economic Community.* (Dobbs Ferry, N.Y.: Oceana Publications, Inc., 1967).

Falcon, William D. *Financing International Operations.* (New York: American Management Association, 1965).

Fatouros, A. A. *Government Guarantees to Foreign Investors.* (New York: Columbia University Press, 1962).

Haight, G. W. "O.E.C.D. Resolution on the Protection of Foreign Property," *International Lawyer*, vol. 2, 1968.

Hobbing, Enno. "The Good Corporate Guest Helps Build the Home," *Columbia Journal of World Business*, September-October 1967.

Landau, Henry. "Protection of Private Foreign Investments in Less Developed Countries—Its Reality and Effectiveness," *William and Mary Law Review*, vol. 9, 1968.

Lillich, Richard B. *The Protection of Foreign Investment.* (Syracuse, N.Y.: Syracuse University Press, 1965).

Lowenfeld, Andreas F. "Diplomatic Intervention in Investment Disputes," *Proceedings of the American Society of International Law*, vol. 96, 1967.

Mummery, David R. "The Content of the Duty to Exhaust Local Judicial Remedies," *American Journal of International Law*, vol. 58, 1964.

Robinson, Richard D. *International Management.* (New York: Holt, Rinehart, and Winston, Inc., 1967).

Schwebel, Stephen H., and J. G. Wetter. "Arbitration and the Exhaustion of Local Remedies," *American Journal of International Law*, vol. 60, 1966.

Servan-Schreiber, J. J. *The American Challenge.* (New York: Atheneum, 1968).

Verroen, John. "How ITT Manages Its Foreign Exchange," *Management Services*, January-February 1965.

Von Neumann Whitman, Marina. *Government Risk-Sharing in Foreign Investment.* (Princeton: Princeton University Press, 1965).

Case 6
GENERAL LIGHTING COMPANY

General Lighting (GL) is one of the world's leading companies. It manufactures a broad line of electrically oriented consumer and industrial goods ranging from small transistor radios to complete cyclotron installations. Although GL headquarters is in New York, a substantial part of its manufacturing activity is carried out in other countries. Its product line, in whole or in part, is sold and serviced in virtually every country in the world.

In 1968 GL's sales were slightly more than $500 million, up 12 per cent from the previous year. Seventy-six per cent of 1968 sales were in the United States and Canada, whereas Latin America and the rest of the world accounted for 13 per cent and 11 per cent respectively. The 1968 earnings were $40 million, representing a 14 per cent increase over 1967.

The GL product line includes three categories of products: consumer goods, components, and scientific and industrial equipment. In 1966 consumer goods accounted for 60 per cent of GL sales, components for 23 per cent, and scientific and industrial equipment for the remaining 17 per cent. The consumer goods category included products for lighting ranging from simple incandescent and fluorescent bulbs to highly advanced lighting sources for special applications, a wide range of domestic electrical appliances, radio, television, and record-playing equipment, and phonograph records. The components category consisted of such products as electron tubes, resistors, transistors, and small electric motors. These components, which were generally manufactured in large volumes, were used internally in the manufacture of GL's electrical and electronic products and sold to other concerns. GL scientific and industrial products included such items as industrial television systems, computers, radio and television transmitters, scientific instruments, electric welding apparatus and electrodes, and a wide range of pharmaceutical and chemical products.

GL can be described as a federal organization. Eleven main divisions and a great number of country organizations form a federation of GL companies. The main divisions, with headquarters in New York, are responsible for the development, manufacture, and marketing of the product lines assigned to them. The country organizations, which have their own boards of management, are responsible for the sale of GL products in their national markets and development and manufacturing activities carried out within their countries. These country organizations are part of the International Division.

Each division is self-supporting and contains its own staff group. Division executives are held responsible for planning the course of their divisions and for operating them successfully. Although plans and problems are discussed regularly with headquarters personnel, central management's greatest influence arises through performance appraisal. Performance is evaluated by a number of financial methods as well as by less formal factors.

All divisions including the International Division are responsible for generating investment projects and are expected to abide by a 10 per cent DCF cutoff rate.[1] Projects below this rate are actively discouraged and usually rejected, even though they require less than $150,000 and could consequently be approved by division management without central management review.

This case is concerned with the steps taken by headquarters management of the International Division in developing an investment proposal for the Indian subsidiary. The Indian company (GLI) had expanded more or less continuously since 1949 and by 1963 surpassed the equivalent of $15 million in sales. The

[1] Discounted cash flow.

affiliate was wholly-owned by GL, although management, with the exception of the local treasurer, consisted entirely of Indians.

Late in 1962 GLI was issued a license by the Indian Minister of Commerce and Industry to construct a plant with capacity to produce 200 turbine engines each year. Preliminary analysis suggested that the investment would be sufficiently profitable, although the outcome was heavily dependent on concessions made under India's third five-year plan. Important elements of this plan were income tax concessions to attract new investment, protection of local industry through import restrictions together with high tariffs, the establishment of production goals in the major industries with encouragement and assistance to reach these objectives and screening of new or expanded production facilities to protect local industry from disruptive competition.

In March 1963 new data were received that changed substantially the monetary calculations for the proposed project. The Indian government imposed a 20 per cent excise tax on certain materials important to the production of turbines. Additionally, the 25 per cent development rebate originally offered GLI was reduced to 20 per cent and the import duty on several machines and equipment essential to the project was increased from 5 to 10 per cent. At the same time the tax on anticipated royalties paid by GLI to the parent company was reduced from 62 per cent to 50 per cent. Although these new developments reduced the expected profitability of the proposed project, calculations revealed that the discounted cash flow still exceeded 10 per cent and planning for the project therefore continued.

In this regard, management of the International Division decided to postpone asking the Indian Ministry of Commerce and Industry for required approvals of the financial plan and technical assistance agreement between GLI and the parent company until the possibility of commercial bank financing had been explored. A staff assistant in New York was advised to prepare an application for an Export-Import Bank loan, and management in India was advised to await further instructions from headquarters. Inquiries at commercial banking sources revealed that private financing would require ICA guarantees that, in turn, could be obtained only after detailed applications were filed with the International Cooperation Administration.

While the Export-Import Bank and ICA applications were being prepared during March and April of 1963, the Ministry of Commerce and Industry indicated that the license for the turbine plant would be rescinded unless the plant capacity was enlarged from 200 to 300 units. A check with other companies operating in India revealed that their pending licenses had also been revised. The change in government policy reflected the Indian planners' desire that new projects support their own foreign exchange requirements. Companies that implemented projects in accordance with the revised licenses would be forced to export since capacities would exceed current levels of demand in India. Foreign exchange obtained from the exports could then be used to pay for imported machinery and raw materials and to service nonrupee-denominated debt.

During the late spring and early summer of 1963 the turbine project was reanalyzed at headquarters to ascertain the implications of the new government policy. New analyses were based on two sets of assumptions: first it was assumed that the proposed turbine plant would be run at 300-unit capacity and that all products in excess of present Indian sales estimates would be sold in export markets at prevailing world prices. When foreign exchange earnings from this policy became inadequate to meet import and nonrupee debt servicing requirements, products other than turbines manufactured by the Indian affiliate would be exported to cover these foreign exchange requirements. Under a second set of assumptions it was presumed that the plant would operate at the 300-unit capacity as in the first case and that all excess production in India would be sold in world markets to generate foreign exchange. The second case differed from the first, however, in that the parent company would increase its dollar investment in the Indian affiliate to the extent export sales of turbines alone proved inadequate to meet foreign exchange requirements. Under both sets of assumptions, the project appeared substantially less attractive on a present value basis, although expected returns still exceeded the 10 per cent cutoff rate.

An important complication arose during the summer of 1963 with respect to the commercial bank financing that had been previously arranged. To enlarge the plant in accordance with the government's request that the project support its own foreign exchange requirement by export sales meant extending the loan repayment schedule. The commercial bankers were advised of this problem and asked by headquarters management to consider the possibility of extending their payback terms. Unfortunately the banks refused to assent to this request, and management consequently concluded that all debt financing must be obtained from the Export-Import Bank.

During July and August of 1963 detailed equipment lists were compiled of all items to be imported for the turbine project and forwarded to India for review by the Indian affiliate. Simultaneously, more information was gathered to be submitted to the Indian government for the additional required approvals and the Export-Import Bank loan application. Headquarters staff also began to analyze in detail the differences in profitability depending on whether all foreign exchange requirements would be met with exports or if only turbine production in excess of Indian demand would be exported and the parent company would make additional investments to meet remaining foreign exchange requirements. An elaborate series of calculations emerged indicating different discounted cash flows depending upon: a) the magnitude of parent equity investment in the project, and b) on the extent to which the profits foregone through loss of turbine export sales by other GL affiliates due to Indian turbine exports were included as a charge against the project. The results of these analyses together with an outline of the debt-equity ratio for the entire Indian affiliate were transmitted to the treasurer's office at the corporate level for analysis.

Management in the International Division in collaboration with the corporate treasurer's office concluded that the project was most likely to be economically attractive if the equity investment was maximized. Using equity it would be possible to avoid the necessity of exporting products manufactured in India at a loss in order to generate foreign exchange to service and repay dollar loans. As a consequence substantial time and effort were spent exploring possible ways to reduce the project's foreign exchange requirements. More specifically, a number of American and European-based companies were approached during the following six months to explore the possibility of equity partnership in the Indian affiliate or, alternatively, the establishment of separate businesses in India to provide turbine components, thereby reducing the magnitude of GL's investment in production facilities.

While the search for a partner or component supplier was underway, a French consulting team visited India and completed a study of India's planned investment in heavy industry. Management of the Indian affiliate advised headquarters executives that the French consultants were in the process of preparing a report back in Paris and were likely to recommend that the turbine plant be located in Trombay rather than in the Bombay area as GL had envisioned. More important, company spokesmen in India believed that the Frenchmen would recommend that the plant be in the public rather than in the private sector. The president of the International Division immediately flew to Paris in an attempt to reason with the French planners before their report was completed and he subsequently departed for India to discuss the situation with the Ministry which had jurisdiction over the matter. The president returned to New York confident that the French planners would not recommend that GL's license be revoked even though the turbine project would presumably be contrary to the overall plan they intended to propose.

In August 1964 GLI received notification that the government of India had approved the financing plan for the turbine project *as originally submitted.* GLI management immediately informed the government authorities that the license for the original 200-unit facility had been revoked during April of the previous year and that a 300-unit plant had been proposed and authorized in accordance with the request that new projects support their own foreign exchange requirements by export sales. Indian government officials agreed to expedite their reconsideration of the finance plan and in October 1964 the plan was approved.

As soon as the government advised GLI of this approval, a meeting of International Division executives was convened in New York to consider the exact nature of the project. It was agreed that the unsuccessful search for an equity partner should be abandoned as further delays in project implementation might result in revocation of the government license. At the same time it was recognized that a number of significant specific aspects of the project had not yet been made definite. For example:

a. No license had been obtained from the government of India to permit importation of the equipment necessary for the project
b. No copper supply had been arranged even to the stage of a draft contract
c. Steel allocations for both structural shapes and reinforcing bar would have to be obtained from the Indian government
d. Cement allocations would have to be obtained from the Indian government
e. Specific assurance would have to be obtained from the Indian government that sufficient supplies of electricity and water would be available to the project.

The International Division executives recognized that it was unlikely that all of these matters could be settled in advance of a formal presentation of the project to the corporate board. Rather it would be necessary to submit to the board a proposal contingent on satisfactory conclusion of whatever matters still remained pending at the time of presentation.

An ad hoc staff committee was formed in New York to assemble data for a formal presentation to the board. Members of this committee reviewed plant cost data prepared by an engineering firm fourteen months earlier. (This study of plant design and cost specifications had cost $192,000.) Agreement was reached regarding the appropriate price assumptions for both sales in India and export turbine sales. Decisions were made regarding the best estimates of raw materials costs and set-up costs in order to quantify the present situation.

While this data was being assembled, headquarters management submitted the revised financial application to the Export-Import Bank for approval. The Export-Import Bank asked for additional biographical data on various individuals connected with the Indian affiliate, and management of GLI was directed to assemble the required information.

Early in 1965 management of GLI cabled New York advising headquarters management of major upward revisions in Indian taxes. Subsequently, the impact of the changed taxes on the proposed project were studied both in India and New York. Management of the Indian company made a direct but informal protest of the proposed tax increase, pointing out its substantial effect on the attractiveness of the project under consideration. It was felt that the protest might enable GLI to obtain relief from the severe export requirements imposed by the approvals already received from the Indian government.

A full-dress reanalysis of the project was completed by March 1965 on the basis of all available information regarding the details of the proposed loan agreement, the cost and revenue assumptions agreed upon earlier, and the best available interpretation of the new Indian tax law. It was recognized that the Indian tax law would not be passed for several weeks, but the authorities in India had advised management that any changes made by the Indian parliament with respect to the taxes would probably be minor.

In April 1965 headquarters management received the Export-Import loan agreement, although the task remained of negotiating with Export-Import Bank and AID on minor points. An attempt was made to induce the lenders to adjust the loan repayment schedule to reflect the delays in starting the project and the reduced cash inflows occasioned by higher Indian tax rates than had originally been assumed.

Problems with the loan agreement were ironed out, and discussions regarding possible relief from the forced export requirement were concluded by July 1965. It was then possible to assemble all the data and to present the project to the corporate board for its approval. To conform with established procedures, a parallel analysis was developed by an International Division staff assistant for an alternative course of action to implementing the turbine project. The alternative assumed that the Indian affiliate would do nothing instead of constructing the turbine plant. The predicted outcome associated with this alternative was clearly undesirable. In effect it was suggested that the fate of GLI depended heavily on the implementation of the turbine project; if this proposal were rejected, the Indian government could not be expected to review favorably subsequent requests for entry into newly established industries.

In August 1965 a fifty-page description and analysis of the proposal was delivered to the corporate board for their approval or disapproval at the monthly meeting scheduled for the following week together with other proposals that had been submitted by the various divisions. The proposal was approved and construction of the plant began during the fourth quarter of 1965. Barring delays in the construction schedule, it was anticipated that GLI would be able to achieve six months of turbine production in 1968 with actual start-up early in the second quarter of that year.

Case 7
LAMCO—Part A

In 1953 a group of retired American businessmen began negotiations with Liberian authorities for a concession relating to iron ore prospecting in southeastern Liberia. The concession was granted to a Liberian company, now called the Liberian American-Swedish Minerals Company (LAMCO), in which the Liberian government held half the capital stock in the form of gratis shares—1,000,000 "A" shares. The concession gave LAMCO the right over a period of five years to prospect for iron ore and other minerals anywhere in Liberia and to stake claims up to an aggregate area of 500 square miles. LAMCO was entitled to exploit such deposits for a period of seventy years dating from the signing of the concession. In return, LAMCO was exempted from all forms of taxes and duties in Liberia. The other half of the LAMCO shares—1,000,000 "B" shares—was issued to the International African American Corporation (IAAC), a corporation organized by the American promoter group. The two classes of stockholders shared equally in the LAMCO profits to be distributed annually in the form of dividends. The "B" shareholders elected six of the eleven directors on the Board of LAMCO and had the responsibility for the administration and financing of the venture.

Grangesberg and the Swedish Syndicate

IAAC immediately sought to ally itself with a partner who could supply both capital and special mining expertise. In the fall of 1954, after several abortive attempts, IAAC approached Grangesberg. This step was taken at the suggestion of the Liberian government, which was attracted by Sweden's reputation as a technically well-developed country without great political power aspirations.

Grangesberg was one of the largest business enterprises in Sweden and had over sixty years experience in the mining, selling, and shipping of iron ore. Its 50 per cent affiliate, Malmexport AB, was the largest iron ore merchant in Europe. In addition to the mining and marketing of iron ore, Grangesberg's activities consisted, among other things, of mineral prospecting in various parts of the world, shipowning, railway and port operation, production of iron and steel, steel construction, related engineering, and hydroelectric power production.

In 1955 an agreement was reached between IAAC and the Swedish LAMCO Syndicate, a Swedish consortium which Grangesberg had formed for the purpose of the agreement. The Syndicate consisted of six Swedish firms: Grangesberg, Atlas Copco AB, AB Nordstroms Linbanor, Skanska Cement AB, AM Ifoverken, and Svenska Entreprenad AB Sentab. Each company was engaged in an activity which related to the LAMCO project—prospecting, planning construction work, supply or equipment, marketing and shipping ore, and so on.

The Syndicate acquired one half of the IAAC interest in LAMCO—500,000 "B" shares—and agreed to organize the future exploration work in Liberia. All the costs of the work were to be divided between the Syndicate and IAAC.

Near the end of 1955,after extensive drilling,it was determined that the ore in southeastern Liberia was no more than a relatively thin surface layer and not worth exploiting. However, a second investigation in the high and relatively inaccessible Nimba Mountains revealed the presence of a very large deposit of high-grade iron ore, and it was agreed to exploit this area despite substantially larger capital requirements.

The constantly growing financial burdens involved during the exploratory and initial planning stages of the project led to changes in the ownership arrangement between IAAC and the Syndicate. IAAC and the Syndicate agreed that the Syndicate's holding of LAMCO "B" shares would be increased from 50 per cent to 60 per cent. The Syndicate also agreed that it would, throughout the survey period, advance all costs, including those of IAAC, and assume the responsibility for the arrangement of the financing of the project.

The Stockholms Enskilda Bank, a Swedish bank experienced in international financial transactions, acted as financial advisor to the Syndicate with respect to LAMCO's financing program and was subsequently contracted to act as exclusive financial advisor to LAMCO.

The Swedish Syndicate formed together with IAAC a tax-exempt holding company in Canada known as the Liberian Iron Ore, Ltd. (LIO) to which the parties transferred all their shares of LAMCO. In return, the Syndicate and IAAC took over 60 per cent and 40 per cent respectively of the shares in LIO. LIO was formed to make loans to LAMCO and to hold its stock. The Stockholms Enskilda Bank also acted as financial advisor to LIO. The project assumed form under the strong influence and expertise of the Swedish Syndicate and Grangesberg, in particular. Grangesberg and LAMCO formed an agreement under which Grangesberg was to act as exclusive sales agent for LAMCO's share of the ore mined by the joint venture. The enterprise was formally brought under unified direction in 1959 when the Grangesberg Company, on behalf of the participants in the venture, undertook to answer for the management of the whole project both with regard to construction of the railroad, harbor, mine, roads, etc., and with regard to the future extraction.

The estimated total investment cost required for the enterprise increased as the planning and surveying stage progressed. The facilities to be installed or constructed to achieve production from Nimba at an annual rate of at least 6 million tons included mining, crushing, and handling facilities at the Nimba mine site; a 165-mile standard gauge, single track railroad between the Nimba mine area and Lower Buchanan, a town on the Atlantic Ocean about 63 miles southeast of Monrovia; a harbor of 42-foot depth to accommodate ships of up to 45,000-ton cargo capacity at Buchanan; extensive harbor facilities including an ore storage area, a loading dock, and equipment for handling and loading ore; and auxiliary facilities such as power generation and transmission facilities and repair shops, and housing, schools, churches, hospitals, commissaries, communication facilities, water supply and sewage treatment plants, airports and service roads to accommodate the technical, supervisory, and working forces. The total cost to LAMCO was estimated at $190,961,200. (See Exhibit 1 for map.)

Two immediate and related problems confronted the LAMCO enterprise: financing the project and marketing the iron ore. Notwithstanding the involvement of the Stockholms Enskilda Bank, it became apparent that a considerable proportion of the financing would have to be raised by long-term borrowing in the American market. To cover the operating and capital cost of the project alone, it was estimated that at a world price of approximately $8 per ton of ore, at least 5 million tons of ore would have to be marketed annually. And the securing of long-term contracts for the marketing of the ore was anticipated as a necessary condition for the financing of the project.

LAMCO therefore deemed it desirable to arrange a joint venture with an American firm requiring ore, and negotiations were started with Bethlehem Steel Corporation. Bethlehem Steel, the second largest iron and steel enterprise in the world, depended heavily on iron ore imports. In the late 1950's its reserves were almost depleted. Bethlehem was also one of Grangesberg's oldest and at times biggest ore customers, a firm with which cordial trading relations had been long established.

The Joint Venture

The negotiations with Bethlehem led to a joint venture agreement in which the parties defined their rights, powers, and obligations as to the financing, operation, and management of the mining and other activities to be conducted under the concession. LAMCO took a 75 per cent interest and Bethlehem a 25 per cent interest in the venture. The capital cost of the project and the cost of operation for producing the regular shares each party would receive from the project was to be paid by the parties in the 75-25 per cent proportions. (See Exhibit 2.)

In addition to the obligations of the parties to pay their respective shares of the cost of production, the agreement provided that Bethlehem, if LAMCO so requested, was obligated to buy a quantity of ore received from the project not exceeding 1.5 million tons per year at the price of $7 per ton FOB Liberian port or such lower price as corresponded to LAMCO's cost of the ore for the year. If, in any year, production exceeded 4 million tons, the maximum amount which Bethlehem was obligated to buy from LAMCO was to be reduced by 250,000 tons for each 1 million tons of annual production above 4 million. After the third year of operation, Bethlehem also had an option to buy up to a maximum of 750,000 tons per year at a price corresponding to LAMCO's cost plus $1 per ton. If the production exceeded 4 million tons, the maximum amount of ore which Bethlehem had the right to purchase under this provision was to be reduced by 125,000 tons for each 1 million tons of annual production in excess of 4 million.

In accordance with the terms of the agreement in 1961, Bethlehem paid $4.5 million to LAMCO as an entrance fee in the joint venture. In addition Bethlehem reimbursed LAMCO in 1961 for expenditures made by LAMCO on account of Bethlehem's interest in the project to December 1960 amounting to $6,929,787.

In addition to agreeing to purchase ore, Bethlehem agreed to act as the joint venture purchasing agent in the United States, procuring equipment which was required for the project. Bethlehem's participation in the joint venture helped LAMCO establish contacts with other United States firms. The LAMCO-Bethlehem joint venture entered into contracts with Raymond International of New York for the construction of the railroad, the harbor, and various access roads at a cost of approximately $40 million.

Other Contracts

Other long-term contracts differed in their construction from that with Bethlehem. No other ore-buying firm took direct part as investor in the LAMCO project. In 1960 Grangesberg, on behalf of LAMCO, entered into a long-term contract with thirteen major producers of pig iron in West Germany. The Ruhr contract provided that from 1963 through 1965, each buyer agreed to purchase a specified tonnage of Nimba iron ore at a specified price per ton; from 1966 through 1979, the buyers agreed to purchase a total of 2,500,000 tons of ore. From 1966 until 1979, 2,000,000 tons of the ore were to be sold at a formula price based upon operating expenses of the project, replacement costs, interest, and amortization expenditures and a fixed return of equity capital. An aggregate of 500,000 tons of ore were to be sold at a price corresponding to current market conditions to be agreed upon yearly between LAMCO and each buyer. LAMCO had the right, until January 1, 1968, to change the price negotiated annually to the formula price for the years beginning January 1, 1969. In the event that LAMCO did not exercise this right, the buyers were free to cancel their respective shares of the market-priced ore from January 1, 1969.

Each buyer had the right to terminate the provisions of the contract applicable to him in the event that the Concession Agreement were changed or in the event that the Liberian government levied direct charges on the buyers or their shippers in such a manner that the terms and conditions for deliveries became considerably less favorable to the buyers. LAMCO and each of the buyers were relieved from their respective obligations to deliver or receive ore for the duration of any case of force majeure, including strikes and lock-outs.

All payments for ore were to be made in United States dollars. If dollar payment became impossible because of government restrictions, LAMCO and each buyer would attempt to agree on payment in German or other currency reasonably appropriate for both parties. If no agreement could be reached, and if none of the proposals made by either party as to a currency were held to be reasonably appropriate by the arbitral tribunal referred to below, the contract would be suspended for the duration of the governmental restrictions up to a period of two years and could thereafter be terminated by LAMCO.

Controversies in connection with the Ruhr contract were to be decided by an arbitral tribunal in accordance with the rules of the International Chamber of Commerce.

In 1961 a five-year contract was also signed with French buyers for 500,000 tons per year. Other short-term contracts allocated approximately a million tons per year to Italian and Belgium buyers.

Conditions in Liberia

Liberia provides many incentives to foreign investment: there are virtually no restrictions on foreign exchange or trade (with the exception of transport and land ownership) or on the kind of enterprise in which foreign business may engage. There are no controls on the import or export of capital or foreign exchange regulations; royalties, earnings, or dividends may be transferred abroad without restriction or limit. Imports and exports are also relatively free from controls. There are no import quotas, although special licenses are required to import certain products such as firearms, ammunition, and pharmaceuticals. Imports that are regarded as especially necessary for development purposes are entirely exempt from import duties: construction materials, feeds, fertilizers, some industrial equipment, and all mining equipment.

Combined with rich and abundant supplies of natural resources, Liberia is a natural area of interest for foreign investors. Its domestic, social, and economic environments, however, are not similarly conducive to direct foreign investment.

Liberian laborers, who come primarily from remote tribal areas of the country, are largely illiterate and unfamiliar with simple mechanical principles. Modern, large-scale projects require them to handle comlicated machinery, work in a high-speed, continuous industrial process and sometimes to live in large communities whose requirements are very much different from their previous environment. Communication of simple factual information from management to laborer is extraordinarily complicated, as there is such a high incidence of illiteracy, and there are twenty-five different tribal languages among workers.

In Liberia political form differs radically from actual substance. Liberia has a constitution and governmental forms—executive, legislative, and judicial—modeled after the United States institutions but without the slightest resemblance in actual operation. Some 5 per cent of the Liberian population—the Americo-Liberians —control the country and govern the tribes, about 95 per cent of the population, on a colonial pattern of indirect rule. Tribal Liberians in the hinterland were subject to a sociolegal system different from that of the coastal Americo-Liberians. In 1964 the system of county administration was reformed, and the status of the districts in the interior was raised to that of the coastal countries. A number of younger educated tribal leaders occupied positions formerly held as sinecures by Americo-Liberians. The tribal peoples also gained representation in the House of

Representatives, though in numbers far smaller than their 9 to 1 numerical preponderance might have warranted.

Economic and political rewards are distributed to a similarly narrow social strata. Approximately one half of Liberia's national income accrued directly to foreign households and business firms. Another quarter accrued directly or indirectly to the small and privileged group of Liberians, probably no more than 3 per cent of the total. The great mass of Liberian households and business firms —approximately 97 per cent—received the remaining quarter of national income. Although increasing numbers of tribal peoples have received education and have begun to work for wages, many Americo-Liberians consider them ill-prepared and undeserving of a greater share in the fruits of economic progress, let alone a stronger voice in their own government. Despite President Tubman's program of "national unification," the coastal community of the Americo-Liberians and the tribal communities in the hinterland remained essentially distinct entities.

In the late 1950's and early 1960's Liberia appeared to be politically stable and secure. The initiative of President Tubman was decisive. He had formulated the Open Door Policy to foreign investors and had strongly supported Liberia's orientation toward Western political and economic systems. Yet if Tubman were to leave office, the movement to the left by nearby African countries could be expected to have some impact on future developments.

The government of Liberia was anxious to continue the economic boom which had been stimulated by loans and foreign investors; however, it was less inclined to accept economic development by proxy. Foreign investors had dominated the economic scene. The large rubber plantations—representing a total investment of approximately $60 million—were owned by foreigners. The Liberian government was part owner of all iron ore ventures, but foreigners had supplied all but $10 million of the $250 million invested in iron ore projects as of 1960. Virtually all commercial and banking activity were financed and managed by foreigners. Liberia's public buildings, roads, ports, and airports were largely or wholly financed by foreigners.

The concession revenues and customs duties relating to foreign investment accounted for the bulk of government inflows. These inflows in turn enabled the government to build roads, schools, and power facilities. Yet the foreign investments did not have an appreciable effect on other sectors of the economy. The modern commercial sector of Liberia consisted primarily of American rubber plantations, American and European mining companies, American, Israeli, and Italian construction firms and Lebanese wholesalers and retailers. Virtually all highly skilled and professional positions in the money sector of the Liberian economy were held by foreigners. The Liberian government was the only significant employer of skilled and professional Liberians. The Americo-Liberians were restricted to positions in government, law, commercial transports, and real estate. The tribal Liberians (about two-thirds of the population) received the bulk of their livelihood from subsistence level farming. Commercial activity and cash crops were minor sources of income in tribal life.

Thus Liberia's development had been given direction and impetus by foreign personnel as well as by foreign financing. By 1960 Liberia was anxious to develop its own skilled labor force. The government stressed the indirect benefits that concession activity could bring to the Liberian economy—i.e., employment of tribal Liberians, payment of taxes, and training and technical assistance activities.

The Concession Agreement

In view of the aspirations of the contracting parties, on April 28, 1960, a new concession agreement was announced simultaneously with the joint venture agreement between LAMCO and Bethlehem.

Major points in the concession agreement were:

> LAMCO and Bethlehem agree to furnish such capital, equipment and materials as are necessary in their opinion for the economic, practical, and profitable development of the concession granted by the Concession Agreement and to use their best efforts to provide skilled personnel for engineering, operating, and management functions. to train Liberian citizens for such functions, to give preference to skilled Liberian citizens, and to use Liberian citizens, if sufficient numbers are available, for unskilled labor. LAMCO and Bethlehem further agree, within ten years of the date of the Concession Agreement to investigate in good faith and consult fully with the Liberian Government, and if in the opinion of LAMCO and Bethlehem it is economical and profitable to do so, to create mineral processing and manufacturing facilities in Liberia.
>
> LAMCO and Bethlehem will pay to the Liberian Government an annual rental of 6¢ per acre ($38.40 per square mile) for land included within the Concession Areas.
>
> The Concession Agreement requires the annual distribution to LAMCO's stockholders of LAMCO's net profits, computed by deducting from annual gross business income (1) the cost of production of ore sold by LAMCO (including exploration costs and intangible development costs); (2) depreciation computed (at LAMCO's option) on the straight-line method, the declining-balance method, the sum-of-the-years-digits method or the unit-of-production method; (3) to the extent not included in the foregoing, annual charges for reserve funds for capital expenditures, working capital and maintenance, annual interest charges and sinking fund payments or other repayments of the principal amount of loans, capital losses, and contributions in Liberia; and (4) any items, in addition to the foregoing, constituting ordinary and necessary business expenses.
>
> LAMCO has authorized the payment to the Liberian Government of the sum of $250,000 per year, payable monthly commencing April 1, 1959, as an advance against future dividends. LAMCO has agreed to pay to the Liberian Government in each of the first two years of production a royalty in an amount which, together with any dividends paid by LAMCO to the Government out of income in such year, will equal 50¢ per ton of ore or other minerals produced and shipped by LAMCO in such year. Dividends payable by LAMCO to the Government are not limited to 50¢ per ton in respect of any year.
>
> The Concession Agreement provides, in effect, that dividends received by the Liberian Government will be in lieu of any other royalties, of any export or import duties, and of any income or other taxes of any kind which may be levied by the Government against LAMCO, against Raymond in respect of the contract with Raymond for railroad and harbor construction, or against any managers of LAMCO or the Joint Venture. A separate agreement between the Liberian Government and Bethlehem provides for an income tax of 50 per cent of the net income as defined in such agreement, from Bethlehem's 25 per cent interest under the Concession Agreement. All dividends and distributions on LAMCO's Class B Stock, and payments of interest, principal, and premium by LAMCO or Bethlehem, may be converted at any time from Liberian currency, if a Liberian currency other than the U.S. dollar had been established, at the then prevailing free market rateof exchange and paid in United States dollars or any other currency, that LAMCO and Bethlehem, and any agent or manager, may freely receive and dispose of funds in any currency irrespective of any currency or exchange control regulations imposed by the Liberian Government, that no income

tax shall be assessed on shareholders or creditors of LAMCO (except to the extent such persons are taxable as Liberian citizens and residents) on income received as such, and that such persons shall be entitled to transfer their funds out of Liberia free of income and other taxes or duties of any kind.

The Concession Agreement will expire by its terms on November 18, 2023, but may be extended or renegotiated by agreement among the Liberian Government, LAMCO,

EXHIBIT 1

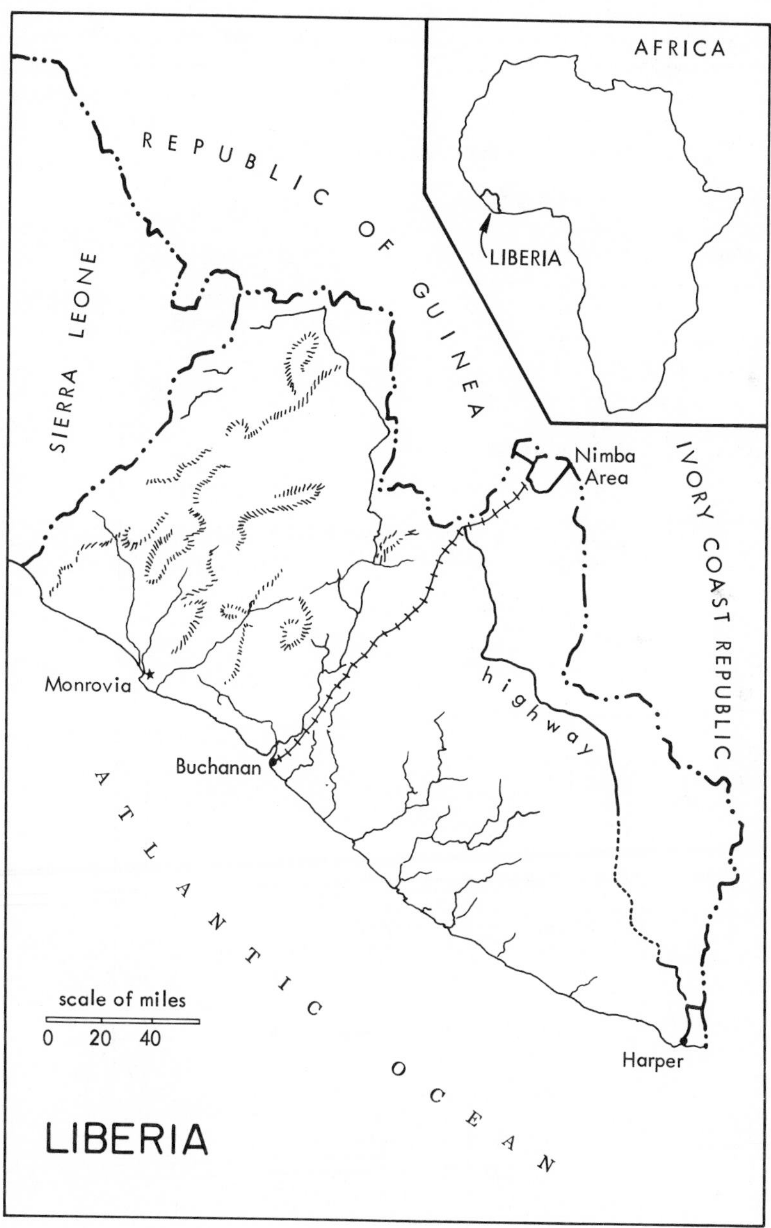

and Bethlehem at any time. The Concession Agreement provides that any dispute between the Liberian Government and LAMCO and Bethlehem or either of them which cannot be settled by mutual agreement will be submitted to arbitration, each side selecting one arbitrator, and such arbitrators or, failing agreement, the President of the International Chamber of Commerce, selecting the third arbitrator.

Upon termination of the Concession Agreement all mineral rights contained in the concession and all roads, railroads, air strips, harbors, and docks constructed by the Joint Venture, LAMCO, or Bethlehem under the Concession Agreement shall become the property of the Liberian Government and all other assets shall remain the property of LAMCO and Bethlehem or either of them and may be exported from Liberia or sold without payment of any duty or other taxes, subject to the Liberian Government's rights of first refusal to purchase any of such assets located in Liberia at the reasonable value thereof.

EXHIBIT 2

Participants in the LAMCO Joint Venture

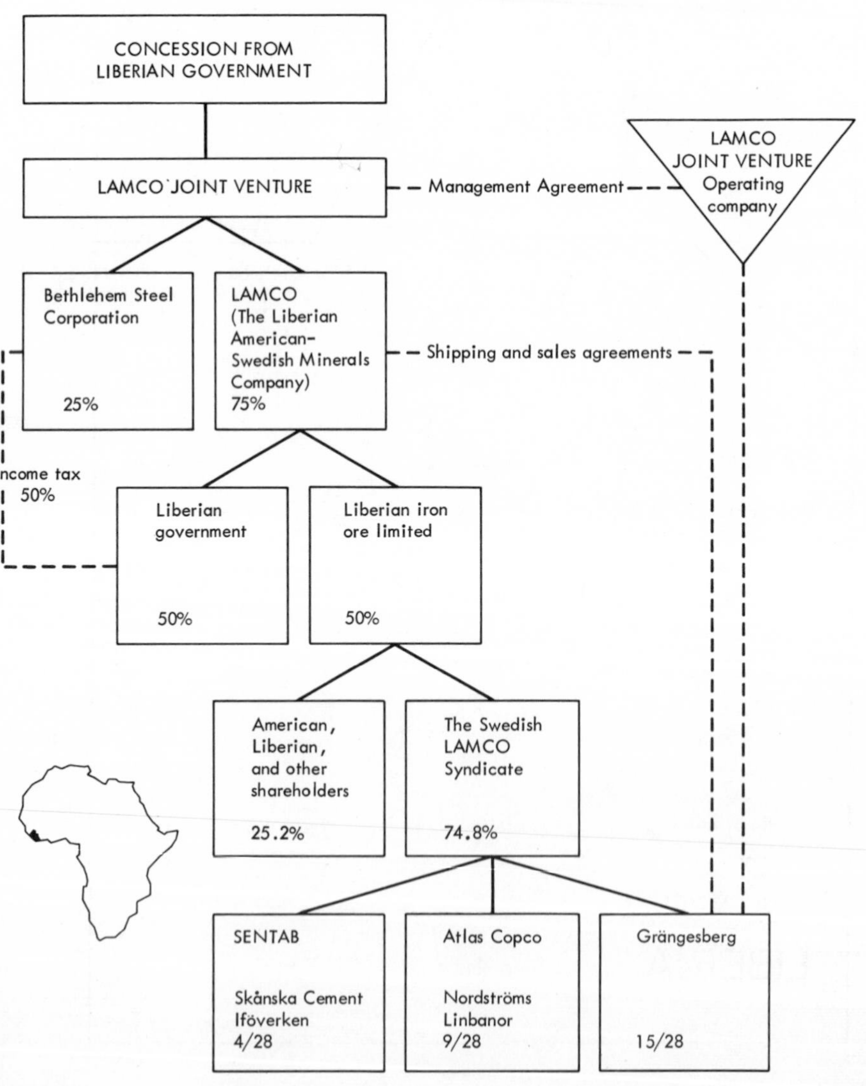

Evaluating Direct Investment Opportunities

5

"In view of the capital scarcity and high interest rates in Mexico what must a project earn to assure adequate returns? Is a 30 per cent rate of return sufficient to compensate for the 'high political risks' which affect our commitments in India? What incremental profits are required to protect our investment from the alarmingly high rate of inflation in Brazil? Should our firm give a higher priority to expansion plans in Brazil or Nigeria?" These are the types of questions which confront the manager responsible for the investment policy of an international corporation.

Although some of the difficulties these questions pose are not unique to the international field, the broader range of risk factors encountered abroad complicates the decision process. Additionally, as we shall see in this chapter, several aspects of the investment decision must be modified once national boundaries are crossed. Besides the additional factors that have to be taken into account, the very terms in which the investment problem is described and appraised must be altered. Developed and refined in relation to national companies, capital budgeting theory must be expanded and modified in order to be compatible with the facts which face international investors. Chapter 5 develops a capital budgeting framework appropriate for the analysis of international opportunities.

To analyze any investment opportunity systematically in some precise meaning of the term, a prospective investor needs the following information:

1. An awareness of the alternatives
2. A precise notion regarding the extent to which he has freedom of choice among the alternatives
3. Insight into the probable consequences of these choices.

Succeeding pages of this chapter suggest how formal decision aids might be used to help obtain this information. First an approach to defining investment alternatives in foreign environments is outlined. Next a method for estimating the alternatives' financial consequences is described. A third section of the chapter incorporates uncertainty into the analysis in order that the best alternative can be identified.

A company's first investment in a particular country is the most difficult to analyze using formal decision aids. The riskier the country, the more difficult quantitative analysis becomes. Therefore, a purely hypothetical instance is considered in which an investor contemplates a first venture in a comparatively risky country.[1] If this type of foreign opportunity can be analyzed using formal aids, so can others.

For purposes of illustration, assume that an American manufacturer of transistors is considering an investment opportunity in Argentina. The time of the decision is 1969. Attention is concentrated on the final decision either to go ahead with the factory in Argentina or not to go ahead, although earlier decisions obviously influence this ultimate "go-no-go" decision. The schematic that appears on page 145 suggests the range of possible preliminary screening[2]: The criteria used in these preliminary screenings are beyond the scope of our inquiry.

Also, in order to simplify matters it is assumed that the decision maker is an individual rather than a committee or a group of individuals.[3]

THE PRESUMED ENVIRONMENT

Before postulating investment alternatives, the prospective investor needs to make some assumptions regarding future market and financial conditions in Argentina. As a point of departure, the decision-maker develops a demand forecast for transistors manufactured in Argentina. This forecast consists of "best guess" estimates for each year over some arbitrary time period, say ten years. The forecast emerges from a study

[1] Although the illustration is fictitious, it draws heavily upon the types of considerations which concern actual companies.

[2] The preliminary screening process is described in Jack Zwick, "Is Top Management Really on Top?" *Columbia Journal of World Business*, Winter 1966, pp. 87–96.

[3] These limiting assumptions are important, but they do not affect the concepts discussed here.

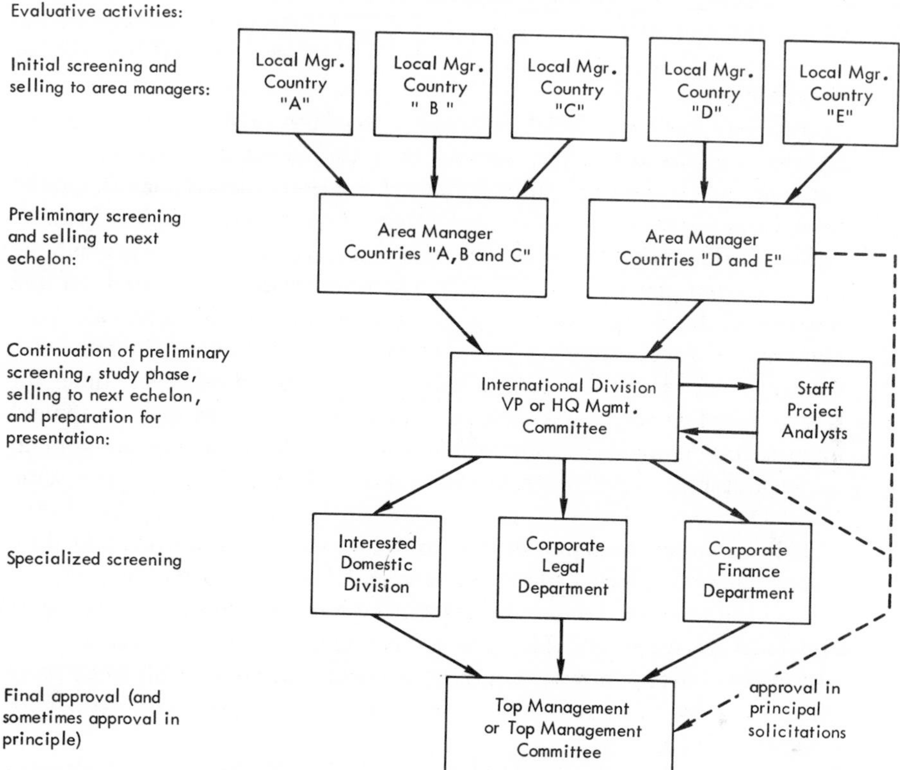

* The early screening activities are circumvented to greater or lesser degrees when project ideas originate at headquarters.

of factors such as the following: past and present consumption of transistors in the principal segments of the Argentine market; import and export patterns; tariff regulations—duties on transistor imports; existing sources of transistor supply; evidence of growth in demand—growth in population, growth of industries that use transistors, etc.; the potential for transistor sales in nearby countries and the feasibility of serving these markets through exports (in this connection the potential effect of common market arrangements on transistor demand would be analyzed); the history and rationale of price changes; and present and potential techniques of promoting and distributing transistors.

Next he develops schedules of relevant, anticipated exchange rates.[4] The investments made in Argentina and anticipated remittances to

[4] An approach to appraising future exchange rates has been proffered in chapter 3.

headquarters or to other countries involve transactions in the foreign exchange markets. Imported raw materials, transistors manufactured in Argentina for export, technical fees, royalties, and dividends all move through the exchange markets. It is necessary to develop a forecast of the applicable exchange rate for each type of transaction, as the translated monetary values are of ultimate interest in appraising project desirability.

Although both an official rate and a free rate exist in Argentina, the prospective investor might assume that the original investment commitment, subsequent investments, and the various transactions stemming from these investments will occur at the then prevailing official rates.

Many transactions involving foreign exchange allocations are subject to duties and special taxes. For instance, equipment imported for the purpose of local manufacture is subject to special exchange rate concessions. After considering such factors the prospective investor develops a series of foreign exchange rate projections over time for raw material imports, export sales, dividend remittances and equipment importation. A single rate is insufficient because different rates are applied to the different types of transactions (even if they occur at the same time).

It is important to separate the various types of transactions and their respective anticipated conversion rates for another reason. In some instances the rates are subject to negotiation between prospective investors and local governments. The prospective investor needs to know what aspects of conversion relief are most important in view of his investment plans in order to know what to ask for during negotiations with government officials.

So far the discussion of Argentine financial conditions has dealt with the various rates of exchange, duties, and taxes likely to be applied to transactions. It is necessary to consider another aspect of Argentine financial conditions before turning to the investment alternatives themselves, i.e., the size and the timing of the foreign exchange allocations that are likely to be made available for the transactions. This is perhaps the most difficult and worrisome projection of all for the prospective investor who is concerned with eventually transferring cash flows from Argentina to headquarters or to other countries.

To the extent that the prospective investor is willing to base his projection of available foreign exchange on present conditions, he examines existing statutes pertaining to such factors as remittances of earnings, technical fees, royalties, and advances. He analyzes the country's remittance record in the past, which in the case of Argentina is not very reassuring. (Currencies were blocked for several years during the Peron regime.) Companies often discuss remittance attitudes with local government officials to improve their assesments. A most important item of information is whether or not convertibility insurance is available and, if so, whether at a reasonable cost.

To ascertain the *ability* of the country to provide the desired foreign exchange, in contrast to its willingness, the prospective investor might base his projection on such indices as the country's reserve position, money supply, cost of living, and trade balance. Inflationary estimates might also be based on these or similar indices. These assessments are difficult. Yet the prospective investor must make judgments regarding the timing and availability of required foreign exchange in order to analyze the alternatives from the home nation point of view. (The reasons for advocating this point of view are explained shortly.)

IDENTIFICATION OF ALTERNATIVES

The decision maker is rarely cognizant of a variety of alternative opportunities from which to choose either in the domestic or foreign setting. Alternatives do not arise simultaneously but sequentially, and the authors' observations have suggested that alternatives are reviewed sequentially because of internal and external time pressures. The decision-maker at any one time is severely constrained in terms of the number of investment opportunities available for comparison. Cyert and March have reached similar conclusions.[5]

Consider the cost of the hypothetical transistor manufacturer. Probably the only possibilities which he perceives are the opportunities to manufacture transistors in Argentina, or not to manufacture them in Argentina, or to postpone his decision. If he decides to go ahead with manufacture, he must also decide what size manufacturing facility to construct and additionally how to finance the venture. Although this illustration simplifies matters, it reveals the extent of choice normally perceived by the decision maker. The analysis here accepts this predicament as an organizational fact of life.[6]

Despite the fact that the decision maker's search is probably limited, he is able to list a great many choices. Without much analysis, however, he discovers that many of the possible choices are unattractive. For example, one approach to manufacturing transistors may require too high a component of skilled labor for Argentina. This, and other possible choices, are quickly eliminated.

[5] Richard M. Cyert and James G. March, *A Behavioral Theory of the Firm*, Englewood Cliffs, N.J., Prentice-Hall, Inc., 1963.

[6] No formal decision aids are proposed to increase the intensity and degree of search, although the literature contains suggestions along these lines. For example, *see* A. Charnes and W. W. Cooper, "The Theory of Search: Optimum Distribution of Search Effort," *Management Science*, V, 1958, pp. 44–50; and H. A. Simon, "A Behavioral Model of Rational Choice," *Quarterly Journal of Economics*, LXIX, 1955, pp. 99–118.

Among the remaining choices one alternative might be to construct a factory of a certain design to produce X number of transistors daily. Initial plants of other sizes might also be considered. The choices of not manufacturing or postponing the decision may imply continuing to export transistors to Argentina from the United States for some period of time.

So far the foreign opportunity analysis has been identical to domestic analysis except that added environmental information has been required for foreign analysis and some of the data have been more difficult to obtain. At this juncture, however, it is important to carry the process of postulating investment choices further for foreign opportunities than is customarily necessary for domestic opportunities. The reason is that in the foreign environment the initial investment choice rarely portrays the nature of foreign commitments which the decision maker is contemplating. The transistor example illustrates the point. The domestic investor frequently has substantial latitude with regard to the reinvestment of net inflows generated by the "initial commitment" choice. To the extent that such freedom of choice is anticipated at the time of the initial investment decision, it is appropriate to evaluate the financial worth of the initial commitment without immediate reference to the form which reinvestment of the net flows is likely to take.

THE REINVESTMENT ASSUMPTION

Argentina is an attractive investment climate for the transistor manufacturer largely as a result of the tariff protection afforded local manufacturers. The prospective investor knows that the Argentine government is likely to maintain the protective tariff to conserve scarce foreign exchange only so long as local transistor production is sufficient to satisfy local demand. Additionally he realizes that the factories he is considering for Argentina are too small in size to compete in world markets. He will operate at a loss at prevailing world prices without tariff protection. Thus, the monetary consequence of each of the initial investment choices is largely dependent upon whether or not he decides to expand his Argentine factory in the future. Moreover, he knows that reinvestment in Argentina is unavoidable since Argentine exchange regulations disallow the repatriation of cash flows in excess of annual earnings. Of necessity some cash flows must be reinvested in Argentina. Finally the investor may very well decide to set up the new venture on a narrow financial base to minimize his exposure, which will necessitate the reinvestment of initial profits to strengthen the venture.

Consequently it is highly desirable that the prospective investor look beyond his first proposed commitment and include all subsequent reinvestments provoked by the initial investment. The reinvestments required to protect or strengthen the initial commitment over the ten-year arbitrary time period are analyzed explicitly prior to making the first commitment.

Frequently executives have intimated that failure to look beyond the initial investment decision overseas has been a mistake. The measures of financial worth that have been employed have made the implicit, simplifying assumption that initial commitments are the only necessary commitments. This dubious assumption has led to distortions in return measures to the extent that irretrievable flows could not be continuously reinvested at adequate rates. In point of fact original investments have frequently been followed by a snowballing of subsequent investments, many of which have been involuntary; and the return measures have failed to depict either the size or the time pattern of the required additional financial, managerial, and technological commitments provoked by the initial investments. In the authors' opinion, many of the subsequent commitments could have been foreseen and should have been considered explicitly at the time of the initial evaluations.

Including all required reinvestments in his analysis, the prospective investor places an appropriate emphasis on future financial flexibility. As the Argentine project throws off cash, he may wish to reinvest the cash in other countries, pay dividends to stockholders in the home country, repay debt obligations, or reinvest in Argentina. The profits of the initial Argentine commitment are of maximum value to the investor only if he is afforded the flexibility to choose among these alternatives.

First commitments plus required reinvestments are defined as realistic investment alternatives (or investment alternatives) in contrast to initial investment choices. The investment alternatives that the decision maker identifies imply varying degrees of ability and willingness to supply transistors to satisfy Argentine demands over time. In effect, they are alternative market strategies.

One strategy, for example, might be to supply 75 per cent of the Argentine market and to maintain this market position. Another strategy might be to build a specific size plant thereby capturing 35 per cent of the market, but thereafter not expanding and, as a result, gradually losing market position both in relative and absolute terms.

The important judgment in postulating and screening alternatives is to determine whether the proposed courses of action are likely to be feasible in view of anticipated environmental constraints. For instance it is unrealistic to presume that a small plant can be constructed in Argentina and that afterwards all cash flows can be remitted to headquarters thereby avoiding reinvestment. As noted previously, the Argentine government restricts remittances to the amount of annual earnings. All such unrealistic alternatives are disregarded in subsequent analysis. After realistic investment alternatives are postulated, their monetary consequences can be estimated.

Two important limitations of the approach outlined above should be mentioned before turning to the computation of financial desirability. First, to simplify matters it has been assumed that Argentine transistor demand and financial conditions—conversion rates and foreign exchange allocations—are independent of whatever investment alternatives the decision maker adopts. The size and timing of the proposed investment commitments themselves may affect those environmental factors in a developing country.

Second, the decision maker has assumed that he will follow *one* of several proposed courses of action over time even though he knows that in all probability this course will be altered from time to time after operations begin. Because of these limitations, the postulated alternatives are only approximations of conceivable action.

FINANCIAL CONSEQUENCES OF THE INVESTMENT ALTERNATIVES

Earlier paragraphs have alluded to possible distortion in the return measure caused by focusing on initial investment choices rather than on realistic investment alternatives. As noted, the degree of distortion depends on the income-generating potential and ultimate remittability of the required reinvestment expenditures. Another potential source of distortion is occasioned by measuring returns in terms of peso cash flows that the project generates rather than in terms of inflows available to the investor.

Inflows available to the investor, hereafter called "available inflows," are defined as project inflows that the investor is free to convert into hard currencies and transfer elsewhere. In effect available inflows are the monies that can be remitted after providing for required reinvestments.

Regardless of whether the parent investor wishes to maximize stockholders' wealth, profitability, power, or something else, he undoubtedly expects to recover his investment outlays and related profits from Argentina through the exchange markets. Information concerning the likelihood of obtaining foreign exchange and estimates of the peso exchange rate for various types of transactions have been developed during the course of the investor's environmental assessment. Whereas return yardsticks based on peso cash flows in Argentina ignore this information, the advocated "net available inflows" measure includes these insights and thus best reflects the prospective investor's ultimate return expectations.

It is advisable to measure returns in terms of net available inflows for another reason as well. If evaluation focuses on peso returns in Argentina, there is a possibility that intercountry effects will be neglected. An opportunity with an adequate profit potential in Argentina might be implemented instead of a more profitable or less risky prospect in another country. Or the effect of the Argentine project on operations in other countries may be ignored. (Intercountry effects complicate the international evaluation process and are examined in detail in the appendix to this chapter.) To define an optional investment policy it is essential that the entire budgetary procedure be conceived in relation to the interests of the parent investor rather than in the interests of individual affiliates. The net available inflow measure assures parent investor orientation.

The inflow component of the prescribed return measure, "available inflows," consist of estimated cash flows available for transfer after adjusting for time and projected currency conditions. The outflow element, "required outflows," comprises all convertible currency outlays (or equivalents) required to launch and sustain proposed alternative after making the necessary time and currency adjustments. Additionally, certain imputed items to be discussed later are included in the net available inflows measure.

The net present value (NPV) criterion is advocated for appraising the financial desirability of the proposed investment alternative.[7] The difference between the present value of available inflows and the present value of required outflows is the "present value of net available inflows," or simply, the present value. It is this element which ultimately interests us. Clearly the rate chosen to discount required outflows and available inflows is critical in determining the results. If the discount rate is very large, decisions will be biased against projects characterized by long economic lives. The problems in determining the appropriate discount rate will be discussed in chapter 6. For now this rate will be defined as the minimum acceptable rate of return at which the interest of the investor will not be damaged. This is the rate that equals the company-wide marginal cost of capital.

The decision rule for net present value is that any alternative with a positive present value is acceptably profitable. In the case of mutually exclusive alternatives the project with the highest present value is best.

PROJECT CASH FLOWS

Recognizing that projects are effectively strategies involving several investments, the prospective investor begins his financial analysis of each alternative by considering the determinants of project cash flows. In effect he simplifies matters initially by concentrating on the project, temporarily disregarding inflow aspects of associated plans for financing alternatives. The hypothetical investor first prepares a pro forma statement of project receipts and disbursements for each of the years in the evaluative period. Such a statement for the transistor manufacturer

[7] Although we believe this is the best criterion for measuring returns, especially for international ventures, the various steps outlined in the chapter can be used in conjunction with other return criteria as well.

appears in Table 5–1. The types of information upon which the projections in the table are based appear below:

transistor sales in Argentina
transistor export sales from Argentine facilities
transistor imports into Argentina
tariffs
cost of raw materials
cost of transporting raw materials
cost of transporting transistors from factories to consumers
depreciation
set-up costs
time factories are on stream
factory capacities
cost of factory production as a function of factory capacity
collection experience
cash requirement for operations
general selling and administrative expenses
Argentine duties and income taxes

As one might expect, the principal receipt element in Table 5–1 consists of collections of accounts receivable. These collection estimates are dependent upon sales and price projections and anticipated collection experiences. The investor's attitudes about the presumed environment materially affect the collection projections. For example, anticipated inflationary pressures in Argentina might be expected to lengthen the collection period or further devaluations might be expected to increase domestic demand for transistors.

The profit-from-export-sales element in Table 5–1 may consist of gains obtained at the expense of the investor's facilities in other countries, which in the absence of the Argentine project might have made these sales. This imputed loss element is included in the analysis at a later stage, and for the time being profits from Argentine export sales are accepted at face value. Note that although the investor can ignore the exchange mechanism during most of his analysis of project receipts and disbursements, he must explicitly consider exchange rate conditions in connection with the anticipated transistor exports.

The cost of various fixed assets is included among project disbursements. After the large outlays required during the first twenty-four months to build and equip the proposed plant, disbursements are reduced to $300,000 per annum, which represents estimated repair and maintenance outlays. Since the prescribed return criterion looks beyond the initial commitment and includes required reinvestments, the anticipated plant expansion during 1971 is also included in the projection of fixed asset disbursements.

A problem arises in connection with "costing" used equipment which

TABLE 5–1

Analysis of Project Cash Flows for Transistor Project *

	1969	*1970*	*1971*	*1972*	*1973*	*1974*	*1975*	*1976*	*1977*	*1978*	*1979*
PROJECT RECEIPTS											
Collections of AR			2,500	11,000	13,000	12,500	12,000	11,000	11,000	11,000	11,000
Profits from export sales			10	400	1,020	1,160	1,230	1,790	1,790	1,790	1,790
Imputed terminal value											1,000
Total Receipts			2,510	11,400	14,020	13,660	13,230	12,790	12,790	12,790	12,790
PROJECT DISBURSEMENTS											
New fixed assets	2,800	9,000	300	300	300	300	300	300	300	300	300
Plant expansion			4,500								
Transfer of used fixed assets †	400										
Set-up costs			200	100							
Raw material outlays			850	3,480	1,890	1,770	1,690	1,530	1,570	1,570	1,570
Labor			240	1,060	1,720	1,720	1,680	1,740	1,740	1,740	1,740
S & A			260	1,400	1,400	1,400	1,400	1,400	1,400	1,400	1,400
Supervisory fee			70	280	280	270	260	250	250	250	250
Local taxes			−1,200	3,185	3,095	2,985	2,915	3,275	3,315	3,355	3,390
Total disbursements	3,200	9,000	5,080	9,805	8,685	8,445	8,245	8,495	8,575	8,615	8,650
PROJECT NET RECEIPTS	−3,200	−9,000	−2,570	1,595	5,335	5,215	4,985	4,295	4,215	4,175	10,220

* Peso cash flows have been converted to dollar equivalents ($000).
† Valued at fair market value.

the investor intends to transfer to the Argentine facility. The used equipment has value of $100,000 on the investor's books. Yet under certain circumstances the Argentine government will allow the investor to capitalize this equipment at the peso equivalent of $1 million—an amount equal to the cost of new equipment. The used equipment has gradually become technologically obsolete in the home country, and the investor is eager to transplant the machines to an environment with a less advanced technology. The question that arises concerns the appropriate amount to charge the Argentine project for the used equipment. A check with equipment manufacturers in the home country reveals that the used equipment has a $400,000 trade-in value; and since the investor intends to replace the used equipment with new equipment at home, he charges the Argentine project $400,000. Thus for evaluative purposes the proposed venture is charged with the opportunity cost of the used equipment.

Estimates are obtained for the other cost factors including local taxes, and these estimates are incorporated in the cash flow projections. The effects of tariffs and deposit requirements applicable to imported raw materials are reflected in the estimates together with liberal depreciation allowances that reduce Argentine tax payments. Notice, for example, that in 1971 after two loss years the investor receives a tax rebate instead of an assessment.

ESTIMATES OF AVAILABLE INFLOWS

Thus far the analysis has ignored the exchange mechanism except to consider the cost of imported raw materials and the sales value of anticipated transistor exports. Since the preferred return criterion—present value of net available inflows—focuses on all flows as they move through the exchange, the analysis is now expanded.

The prospective investor has already forecast peso exchange rates and available foreign exchange allocations over time. These projections and the estimates of net receipts in Table 5–1 are the basis for the net available inflow forecast in which the investor is ultimately interested. One additional ingredient is necessary to derive forecasts of available inflows: information regarding financial plans.

During review of the various regulations pertaining to foreign investment in Argentina, the investor discovers that a particular financial plan for a given alternative affects these elements of the opportunity:

1. The cost of the assets required to implement the alternative
2. The operating costs in Argentina under the alternative
3. The magnitude of the dividend remittance privilege.

For example under existing Argentine law the hypothetical investor can avoid a 30 per cent exchange premium imposed on equipment imports by paying for required equipment with dollars (or other hard currencies).[8] Thus the dollar cost of required assets is a function of how the assets are financed.

The decision maker has been assured by Argentine officials that the Argentine Tariff Commission will approve an application for a 10 per cent reduction in the duties imposed on imported raw materials if the investor finances the required equipment with dollars. Also, if equipment is financed with dollar equity commitments, the Argentine affiliate will have a larger equity base and consequently, will pay lower Argentine excess profit taxes that are levied on peso earnings in excess of 30 per cent of paid-in capital and surplus. In such ways, the selected financial plan affects operating costs and ultimate dollar inflows.

Aside from the fact that ability to pay dollar dividends partially depends on debt servicing requirements (and in this way the financial plan influences remittances), the remittance privilege in Argentina is tied to the size of the paid-in capital base. If the dollar equity commitment is small, the remittance allowance will also be small. Furthermore, parent dollar loans to the Argentine affiliate can only be repaid out of foreign exchange earned by the Argentine affiliate. The Argentine affiliate must make export sales to obtain the foreign exchange with which to repay the parent loans, and a significant proportion of these sales may occur at distressed prices.

The prospective investor presumes that these or similar restrictions are likely to persist in the future and that he must broaden his definition of the alternatives. In effect the original investment alternative is the basis for several mutually exclusive alternatives depending on the number of viable financial plans the prospective investor identifies. For example, the investor in consultation with his financial advisors might identify three possible financing schemes: 60 per cent parent equity and 40 per cent local debt; 50 per cent parent equity and 20 per cent local debt, the 30 per cent balance consisting of dollar-denominated advances and borrowings; and a 50–50 joint venture with a local partner who together with the parent investor supplies 60 per cent of the financing with the remaining 40 per cent consisting of local debt.

After viable, alternative financial plans are identified for the transistor project, the investor develops separate receipt and disbursement projections for each alternative financed in a particular way. A series of required outflow and available inflow schedules is obtained by combining the receipts and disbursement projections in Table 5–1 with data pertaining to each financing plan. Required outflow and available inflow estimates for the transistor illustration financed *in a particular way* are arrayed in Table 5–2. Different estimates would be obtained for each financing plan.

[8] This type of inducement, as well as others noted below, is fairly typical in developing countries where foreign exchange is scarce.

TABLE 5–2

Analysis of Available Inflows for Transistor Project Financed in a Particular Way
(in thousands of U.S. $)

	1969	1970	1971	1972	1973	1974	1975	1976	1977	1978	1979
Available inflows											
Project throw-off *	−3,200	−9,000	−2,500	1,875	5,615	5,485	5,245	4,545	4,465	4,425	4,390
Terminal value †											6,080
Bank loans	3,400	9,000	1,800								
TOTAL AVAILABLE INFLOWS	200	–	−700	1,875	5,615	5,485	5,245	4,545	4,465	4,425	10,470
Required outflows											
Loan repayment				1,200	1,200	1,200	1,200	1,200	1,200	1,200	1,200
U.S. income taxes †	−200	−200	350	950	2,340	2,240	2,000	1,670	1,670	1,670	1,800
U.S. taxes–supervisory			36	146	146	140	135	130	130	130	
Dividend withholding taxes	−55	−55	101	286	684	650	612	480	475	475	
After-tax export sales loss †				200	200	200	200	200	200	200	
Know-how contribution †	191										
TOTAL REQUIRED OUTLAYS	−64	−255	487	2,782	4,570	4,430	4,147	3,680	3,675	3,675	3,000
NET AVAILABLE INFLOWS	264	−255	−1,187	−907	1,045	1,055	1,098	865	790	750	7,470
Discount factor (10% rate)	1.00	.91	.83	.75	.68	.62	.56	.51	.47	.42	.39
Net present value	264	−232	−985	−680	711	654	615	441	371	315	2,913
CUMULATIVE VALUE	264	32	−953	−1,633	−922	−268	347	788	1,159	1,474	4,387

* Unblocked cash flows available for payment of royalties, fees, dividends, or reinvestment.
† Imputed value.

"Project throw-off" summarizes project net receipts which the investor is free to use as he chooses—i.e., inflows available for payment of royalties, fees, dividends, or reinvestments. Project throw-off is equivalent to net project receipts plus supervisory fees (taken from Table 5–1) so long as the combined amounts do not exceed the maximum allowable remittances.[9] In other words, the figures derived earlier are regarded as available to the extent that the earlier figures are expected to be unblocked.

Like most investors our hypothetical transistor manufacturer has developed projections for a limited planning period, ten years, instead of attempting to forecast project results indefinitely into the future. Consequently, it is necessary for him to assign some value to the proposed investment at the end of this arbitrary planning horizon. It would be inappropriate to disregard the expectation that project assets will have value at the end of 1979 either as a going concern or through asset liquidation. Therefore he imputes a value to project assets at the end of 1979 and includes this terminal value as an available inflow item.

Several imputed items are also included among required outflows. As noted previously, the investor's plants outside Argentina are likely to lose business to the Argentine project and the after-tax export sales loss in Table 5–2 reflects this consideration. Amenability to United States taxes depends on both the profitability of the Argentine venture and on the magnitude of Argentine tax assessments. Note in Table 5–2 that United States tax liability is reduced in 1969 and 1970 by virtue of the losses that the new venture sustains. The United States tax code allows the investor to defer tax payments on income which originates in Argentina until dividends are remitted by the Argentine affiliate. Consequently the United States taxes included among required outflows exceed the investor's estimates of actual United States tax payments to the extent that profits are reinvested in Argentina. (The United States tax figures thus include outlays required to make project cash flows transferable.)

The $191,000 of know-how contribution is an additional imputed value. In a sense the investor's skill in manufacturing and distributing transistors is a sunk cost. The know-how was acquired earlier in connection with domestic transistor production and since no additional expenditures are necessary to transfer this know-how to Argentina, one might argue that the past know-how costs are irrelevant to the appraisal of the Argentine opportunity.[10] Yet there are potential costs associated with transferring know-how to other environments. As skills in the transistor business are acquired by foreign nationals, the investor ex-

[9] Supervisory fees are included in project throw-off since they accrue to the parent investor in a country whose government authorizes such remittances.

[10] Obviously there are some supervisory costs associated with transferring technological skills. These costs are charged to the project as supervisory fees.

poses himself to the possibility of competition in the foreign market as well as in other countries. The Argentine plant might be expropriated. Native Argentineans might learn the transistor business and later establish an independent, competitive business to serve Argentina as well as export markets. These and other such possible adversities suggest the desirability of assigning an imputed cost to the know-how transfer as our hypothetical investor has done. Obviously the assignment of dollar values to the imputed items discussed above is based on the subjective judgments of the investor. The investor brings to bear his best estimates regarding opportunity costs, potential future costs, and likely future values. The fact that these judgments of necessity are tentative does not obviate the need for the assessments, as the corresponding project elements are crucial to the analysis.

The remaining required outflows consist of United States taxes on anticipated supervisory fees and scheduled loan repayments. The loan repayments pertain to the specific financing plan included in Table 5–2. Note that anticipated interest expenses associated with this financing plan are not included in the flow projections since, in this instance, it is assumed that the discount rate used for time adjustment incorporates capital costs into the analysis; reducing project receipts by subtracting interest charges would amount to double counting. Under certain circumstances, however, elements of financial costs should be included in the flow projections. For reasons outlined in the next chapter, the investor might select a financing plan locally for the transistor project which is more costly than an identical debt-equity mix arranged outside the country of investment; in effect, he decides on a plan that is more expensive than the firm-wide cost of capital. If the investor does not employ the least costly financial instruments available to the company as a whole, the financial premiums he agrees to pay should be included in Table 5–2 as outflows, since the discount rate only adjusts for minimal capital costs.

All the required outflows are converted from pesos to hard currency equivalents using the estimated exchange rates at the time the flows are expected to occur. In a concluding step the required outflows estimated for each year are subtracted from the projections of available inflows yielding an estimate of net available inflows for each of the ten years. Using the predetermined company-wide cost of capital as the discount rate (in our illustration the 10 per cent rate), present value of net available inflows is computed. Since the cumulative present value at the end of the planning horizon is positive, the illustrated opportunity is acceptably profitable. (Although the cumulative present value is positive for most of the ten years in the illustrated case, the cumulative present value must only be positive by the final period of the planning horizon for the project to be acceptably profitable.)

Unfortunately our hypothetical investor is not yet in a position to decide whether the project as defined in Table 5–2 should be implemented. Alternatives must be considered. Moreover, the implications of business, financial, and environmental risk elements have been totally ignored.

RISK

Thus far the analysis of alternative investment opportunities has been based on a single set of presumed environmental, financial, and business conditions which were postulated in advance. More specifically, each factor affecting project outcome has been summarized in single net inflow predictions for each time period. In effect, by suppressing all information concerning the riskiness of the alternative, the analysis has assumed that the dollar net inflows are certain to occur.

In reality the prospective investor is highly uncertain regarding the presumed environmental conditions. A change in some environmental factors might have a decided effect on the financial consequences of a particular alternative. For this reason it is recommended that the more promising investment alternatives be reexamined to obtain insights into their inherent risks. The reexamined alternatives might very well consist of different versions of the transistor project or the single transistor scheme financed in different ways.

Some firms attempt to adjust project estimates for risk either by arbitrarily reducing inflow projections or by using a higher discount rate than would be used for a less risky proposal. Both of these methods raise serious problems. Arbitrarily reducing inflows, a so-called conservative adjustment, merely makes a particular opportunity appear less attractive. The fact that the investor is uncertain regarding the project's outcome implies that results ultimately may be less favorable *or more favorable* than originally assumed. Therefore, understating the present value of risky opportunities is a means of avoiding risk, not of evaluating it. It might be that individually risky opportunities would prove not only to be extremely profitable, but also would contribute to reducing the overall risk facing the investor.[11] The principal objection to raising the discount rate to account for risk is that it assumes that risks before and after implementing the project are identical. This assumption is valid only in the special case when the expected returns for the new project have a zero covariance with existing returns.

[11] The overall risk confronting the investor depends on the covariance between the cash flows of existing investments and the new investments which are implemented rather than on the variances associated with the cash flows from individual investments. The effects of diversification on risk have been examined by Harry M. Markowitz in *Portfolio Selection: Efficient Diversification of Investments,* New York, John Wiley & Sons, Inc., 1959 and more recently by William Sharpe in "Capital Asset Prices: A Theory of Market Equilibrium under Conditions of Uncertainty," *Journal of Finance,* September 1964, pp. 425–42.

Additionally, experience has suggested that these risk adjustment techniques can become excessive. Discounting the future returns of a risky investment by 15 per cent instead of 10 per cent naturally reduces the proposal's cumulative present value. But why not use 20 per cent or 30 per cent or some other arbitrarily selected discount rate? When the risk adjustment involves reducing the project projections, an additional problem arises. An investment proposal is likely to be initiated by someone familiar with the project or country where the opportunity is to be implemented. To get the project approved, this individual must typically enlist support at several management echelons.[12] Note the stages of evaluation depicted in the schematic on page 145.[13] At each echelon of management the individual making the evaluation may adjust the projections downward in the interest of conservatism. By the time the proposal reaches the ultimate approving authority, the successive reductions may have withered out most of the venture's anticipated profitability.

The risk adjustment approach we advocate requires the investor to estimate several possible outcomes for a proposed alternative instead of developing a single, best guess set of projections.[14] In addition to the series of estimates contained in Table 5–1 and Table 5–2, the investor predicts what will happen to project receipts, project disbursements, required outflows, and available inflows if environmental conditions differ from those originally assumed.

For example, the investor might develop predictions of project cash flows and net available inflows using as a basis the following assumptions:

1. Transistor sales prove to be 15 per cent lower than originally assumed
2. Transistor prices are 15 per cent lower than the initial projections after 1970 due to the removal of tariff protection
3. The peso-dollar conversion rate is 20 per cent lower than initially assumed.

The present value implications of such changes in environmental conditions are analyzed in the context of schedules identical to those devised originally for the best guess case. Still other sets of environmental assumptions are postulated in order that the financial implications of these conditions can also be assessed.

In a subsequent step the investor assigns probabilities to the likely occurrence of the various environmental conditions that he has postulated and analyzed earlier. The investor assumes that these are the only possibilities. In other words he assumes that there is a 100 per cent probability that one of the sets of assumed environmental conditions will

[12] *See* Jack Zwick, *op. cit.*

[13] *Ibid.*

[14] The recommended approach is described in detail in Robert Schlaifer, *Probability and Statistics for Business Decisions.* New York, McGraw Hill, 1959.

prove accurate and that the estimated present value calculation based on that set of environmental assumptions will in fact result.

Then the investor arrays the various possible outcomes and associated probability estimates as in Table 5–3. The expected value of each possible outcome is the present value of the possibility multiplied by the subjective probability that that possibility will occur. The expected value of the probability distribution is the weighted average of the possible outcomes where the weights are the probabilities. It is the central value of the distribution. For example, note in Table 5–3, which arrays the possible present values for Case 1 together with associated probabilities, that the expected net present value is $1,888. What this means is that, assuming the frequency distribution is valid as a probability distribution, the investor can expect an average net present value of $1,888 for an investment characterized by these returns and risk conditions. Some investments will be better, others worse.

TABLE 5–3

Analysis of Conditional Outcomes ($000)
Case 1

CONDITIONAL OUTCOMES (*cumulative present values*)	×	SUBJECTIVE PROBABILITIES	=	WEIGHTED PRESENT VALUES
$ 345		5%		$ 17
840		20%		168
1,765		35%		618
2,290		15%		344
3,100		25%		775
		100%		$1,888 Expected present value

Now, let us compare Case 1 with a different alternative (Case 2) portrayed in Table 5–4. Our hypothetical investor might very well have predicted the outcomes and associated probabilities in Case 2 for the transistor opportunity if he assumed that the project would be financed in a more conservative manner. Clearly this is a less risky alternative, as its net present value is expected to fall within a much narrower range than for the first example (Case 1).

Risk is described by the dispersion of possible outcomes. The wider the dispersion, the riskier the investment. The standard deviation is a generally accepted measure of dispersion.[15] It is the square root of the

[15] Such an assumption may, however, be unreasonable as Markowitz conjectured (*loc. cit*). J. Fred Arditti, "Risk and the Required Return on Equity," *Journal of Finance,* March 1967, established investor response to skewness (the 3rd moment); and there is speculation that investors may prefer lower kurtosis (tighter distributions) to higher kurtosis (the 4th moment). In our discussion these factors are ignored.

TABLE 5–4

Analysis of Conditional Outcomes ($000)
Case 2

CONDITIONAL OUTCOMES (*cumulative present values*)	×	*SUBJECTIVE PROBABILITIES*	=	*WEIGHTED PRESENT VALUES*
$ 462		10%		$ 46
712		25%		178
1,086		25%		272
1,628		20%		326
2,265		20%		453
		100%		$1,275 Expected present value

sum of the squared differences between each possible present value and the expected present value, and it is weighted by the subjective probability associated with the possible present value. The standard deviation calculations for Cases 1 and 2 are shown in Table 5–5. Notice that the risk as measured by the standard deviation is greater for the first alternative than for the second. The standard deviation for Case 1 is 92.7 in comparison with 82.8 for Case 2.

REACHING A CONCLUSION

The investor has now generated sufficient data to make a decision. He has developed a measure of financial desirability (expected present value of available inflows) and a measure of risk (standard deviation) for each alternative. Remember that the alternatives consist not only of different conceivable projects but of each project financed in different ways. The only question remaining concerns the relative importance that the investor attaches to maximizing profitability versus minimizing risk. Different investors facing the same opportunities may have quite different attitudes toward risk due to subjective attitudes and objective circumstances. An investor with total resources of $10,000 is likely to regard a loss of $10,000 as more serious than a gain of $10,000 would be beneficial. In this situation the investor with limited resources might avoid any opportunity with the possible loss of $10,000 no matter how small the probability of loss. On the other hand, an investor with $1 million might be amenable to a project with an equal probable loss or gain of $10,000. In short, the impact of a loss may not be measurable in money, but in the ability of the firm to absorb the loss.

How then can our hypothetical investor decide whether the transistor project, financed in a particular way, is worthwhile? The cumulative

TABLE 5–5

Standard Deviation Calculations for Cases 1 and 2

Case 1

CONDITIONAL OUTCOMES	− EXPECTED PRESENT VALUE	= DIFFERENCE	$(DIFFERENCE)^2$	× PROBABILITY	= PROBABILITY × $(DIFFERENCE)^2$
$ 345	1,888	2,233	4,986,289	5%	249,314
840	1,888	1,048	1,098,304	20%	219,961
1,765	1,888	123	15,129	35%	5,295
2,290	1,888	402	161,604	15%	24,241
3,100	1,888	1,212	1,468,944	25%	367,236
				Variance =	866,047

$\sqrt{866} = \$92.7$ = standard deviation

Case 2

CONDITIONAL OUTCOMES	− EXPECTED PRESENT VALUE	= DIFFERENCE	$(DIFFERENCE)^2$	× PROBABILITY	= PROBABILITY × $(DIFFERENCE)^2$
$ 462	1,275	813	1,036,575	10%	103,658
712	1,275	563	717,825	25%	179,456
1,086	1,275	188	239,700	25%	59,925
1,628	1,275	353	450,075	20%	90,015
2,265	1,275	990	1,262,250	20%	252,450
				Variance =	685,504

$\sqrt{686} = \$82.8$ = standard deviation

present value indicates that the project is sufficiently profitable, but are the risks too high? Furthermore, if the risks are tolerable, how can the investor decide between Cases 1 and 2 which represent two financial plans for implementing the transistor project? The tables suggest that Case 1 has a higher expected present value but Case 2 is less risky.

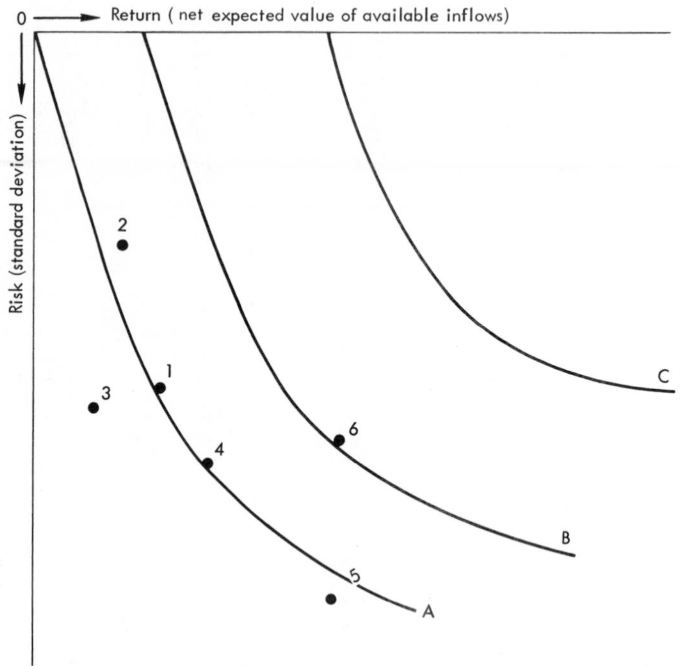

What is needed is a utility curve for the investor which reflects his attitude toward risk and profits.[16] In the diagram a risk preference function is drawn for our hypothetical investor. The dots in the diagram represent investment alternatives plotted according to risk (standard deviation) and return (net present value). Only alternatives with positive net present values are plotted in the diagram. (Unless expected returns exceed the discount rate, the opportunity is automatically rejected.) The three lines, A, B, and C, shown in the diagram represent

[16] For a discussion of the application of utility theory to capital budgeting, *see* C. J. Grayson, "The Use of Statistical Techniques," in *Financial Research and Management Decisions,* ed. Alexander A. Robichek; R. M. Adelson, "Criteria for Capital Investment: An Approach Through Decision Theory," *Operational Research Quarterly,* March 1965, pp. 19–50; C. J. Grayson, *Decisions Under Uncertainty: Drilling Decisions by Oil and Gas Operators,* Boston, Division of Research, Harvard Business School, 1960; Robert O. Schlaifer, *Probability and Statistics for Business Decisions,* New York, McGraw-Hill Book Company, 1959; and Harold Bierman, Jr., Charles P. Bonini, Lawrence E. Fouraker, and Robert K. Jaedicke, *Quantitative Analysis for Business Decisions,* rev. ed., Homewood, Ill., Richard D. Irwin, Inc., 1965, ch. 21.

the investor's attitude toward risk and profits. Each line is an indifference curve reflecting the added returns required to compensate the investor for increments of risk. The investor is just as willing to accept opportunity 4 as 1 shown in the diagram since both fall on the same indifference curve.

Line A represents the investor's least acceptable return for risk trade-offs. Therefore, all opportunities to the left of line A, e.g., alternative 3, are rejected. Although the expected profits for opportunity 3 exceed capital costs, returns are insufficient to compensate for the degree of risk. All opportunities represented by dots to the right of line A are acceptable and should be implemented unless some of the alternatives are mutually exclusive.

If the investor must choose between mutually exclusive alternatives, opportunities on line B are preferable to those on line A. So too in comparing B and C, points on C are preferred to points on B. If, for example, the investor must decide between alternatives 1 and 2 (these dots might represent Cases 1 and 2 from the transistor illustration—the hypothetical project financed in two different ways) the investor prefers 2 to 1; although expected returns are greater for 1, opportunity 2's substantially lower risk makes it preferable. Similarly, alternative 6 is clearly preferable to project 4 since it has the same risk but higher expected returns. Alternative 5 has the highest expected returns on the diagram but is unacceptable due to its high risk.

Summary

The assessment of an international opportunity consists of several steps. Project receipts and disbursements are analyzed after first identifying realistic investment alternatives. Then required outflow and available inflow measures can be devised that adequately reflect the parent investor's concern for financial flexibility. Within this context the present value of net available inflows must be positive for an alternative to be acceptably profitable. In subsequent steps, or in conjunction with the earlier stages of analysis, different inflow predictions and probability assessments are made to facilitate risk appraisal. After expected returns and risks are paired for each alternative, these important project characteristics can be analyzed in terms of the particular investor's willingness to assume risk.

The budgeting format described in this chapter has assumed that the prospective international investor is able (and can afford) to make several sets of forecasts and environmental judgments. If the prescribed techniques prove impracticable, less demanding techniques can be used in conjunction with the basic theoretical framework. Any financial manager can adapt the prescribed analytical approach to the situation in his company by developing specific budgeting procedures appropriate to his organization setting. Regardless of the specific budgeting techniques used, adherence to the dictates of the conceptual framework set forth in this chapter should assist the international investor in identifying the most attractive opportunities called to his attention.

BIBLIOGRAPHY

Adelson, R. M. "Criteria for Capital Investment: An Approach Through Decision Theory," *Operational Research Quarterly,* March 1965.

Aharoni, Yair. *The Foreign Investment Decision Process.* (Boston: Harvard Business School, Division of Research, 1966).

Angell, J. W. "Uncertainty, Likelihoods, and Investment Decisions," *Quarterly Journal of Economics,* February 1960.

Arditti, J. Fred. "Risk and the Required Return on Equity," *Journal of Finance,* March 1967.

Aubrey, Henry G. "Investment Decisions in Underdeveloped Countries," *Capital Formation and Economic Growth.* (New York: National Bureau of Economic Research, 1955).

Bierman, Harold, Jr., and Seymour Smidt. *The Capital Budgeting Decision.* (New York: The Macmillan Co., 1966).

———, Charles P. Bonini, Lawrence E. Fouraker, and Robert K. Jaedicke. *Quantitative Analysis for Business Decisions.* (Homewood, Ill.: Richard D. Irwin, Inc., 1965), ch. 21.

Bugnion, J. R. "Capital Budgeting and International Corporations," *The Quarterly Journal of AIESEC International,* November 1965.

Charnes, A., and W. W. Cooper. "The Theory of Search: Optimum Distribution of Search Effort," *Management Science,* October 1958.

Cord, J. "A Method for Allocating Funds to Investment Projects When Returns Are Subject to Uncertainty," *Management Science,* October 1964.

Cyert, Richard M., and James G. March. *A Behavioral Theory of the Firm.* (Englewood Cliffs, N.J.: Prentice-Hall, Inc., 1963).

Dean, J. *Managerial Economics.* (Englewood Cliffs, N.J.: Prentice-Hall, Inc., 1951).

Edwards, W. "Utility, Subjective Probability, Their Interaction and Variance Preferences," *Journal of Conflict Resolution,* May 1962.

Farrar, Donald E. *The Investment Decision Under Uncertainty.* (Englewood Cliffs, N.J.: Prentice-Hall, Inc., 1962).

Friedland, S. *The Economics of Corporate Finance.* (Englewood Cliffs, N.J.: Prentice-Hall, Inc., 1966).

Gaddis, P. "Analyzing Overseas Investments," *Harvard Business Review,* May-June 1966.

Good, I. J. "How Rational Should a Manager Be," *Management Science,* July 1962.

Grayson, C. J. *Decisions Under Uncertainty: Drilling Decisions by Oil and Gas Operators.* (Boston: Harvard Business School, Division of Research, 1960).

———. "The Use of Statistical Techniques," in *Financial Research and Management Decisions,* Alexander A. Robichek, ed.

Haner, F. T. "Determining the Feasibility of Foreign Ventures," *Business Horizons.*

———, and H. Uyterhoeven. "Analyzing Foreign Opportunities," *Harvard Business Review,* November-December 1960.

Lee, James A. "Cultural Analysis in Overseas Operations," *Harvard Business Review,* March-April 1966.

McDonald, J. G. "Minimizing the Risks of Moving Abroad," *Business Horizons,* Spring 1961.

Markowitz, Harry M. *Portfolio Selection: Efficient Diversification of Investments.* (New York: John Wiley and Sons, Inc., 1959).

Schlaifer, Robert O. *Probability and Statistics for Business Decisions.* (New York: McGraw-Hill Book Company, 1959).

Simon, H. A. "A Behavioral Mode of Rational Choice," *Quarterly Journal of Economics,* February 1955.

Zwick, Jack. *Aspects of the Foreign Capital Rationing Procedures of Certain American Manufacturing Corporations.* Unpublished Doctoral Dissertation, Harvard Business School, 1964.

———. "Is Top Management Really on Top?" *Columbia Journal of World Business,* Winter 1966.

APPENDIX

Evaluating Multicountry Investments *

Most companies make overseas investment decisions primarily on a country-by-country basis. Each country is considered as a separate production and marketing entity, and, with few exceptions, investments are justified largely in terms of the potential size and profitability of operations within the country. Any exports from a given country in which new operations are to be based are considered more or less as a necessary evil until the local market can support full capacity activity. New operations, therefore, are proposed when conditions in a single-country market seem justified without evaluation of possible alternative schemes for supplying that market.[1] If the expected profitability of the direct investment exceeds the investor's minimum return standards and is greater than the rewards associated with continuing to export to the country, the investor generally decides to make the direct investment.

*The appendix is based on Jack Zwick, "Models for Multicountry Investments," *Business Horizons,* Winter 1967.

[1] In several observed instances the financial consequences of constructing new facilities in a country have been compared with the profitability of continuing to export to that country.

The country-by-country approach to analyzing foreign investment opportunities has an important weakness. Regarding a specific country as a separate market leads to the selection of a scheme that maximizes returns in that country regardless of the implications of the decision on company prospects in surrounding countries. Consequently, a suboptimal investment decision may be reached; although returns are maximized for operations in a given country, aggregate returns for the larger multicountry market are lower than might otherwise be the case. The conventional approach—which fragments multicountry markets—is not well suited to analysis of investment opportunities in countries subject to various degrees of economic integration. The more complex the situation, the more difficult it is intuitively to select the optimal investment scheme. Consider, for example, the problem which formation of the Latin American Free Trade Association (LAFTA) poses for a large American company we will call Universal.[2]

Universal at present (1967) manufactures an industrial product in Brazil. In 1966 the company produced and distributed 7 million units in Brazil relying on a single plant, the capacity of which was 7.2 million units. In 1966 Universal management authorized expansion of the plant to 10 million units, and further expansions are now being considered. The company's export sales from the United States to LAFTA countries in 1966 amounted to 6.5 million units.

Company analysts estimate that the market for Universal's product in the LAFTA countries will grow from 80 million units in 1966 to 185 million units by 1970 and to 600 million units by 1980. Universal's current share of the markets in LAFTA countries is 17 per cent.

In a recent meeting sales managers forecast that Universal would be able to sell 35 million units per annum in the LAFTA area by 1970 and 75 million units by 1980 *if* supplied from plants within the LAFTA countries. The amount that could be sold if the product were supplied only from the United States and from the single Brazilian plant would be considerably less than these figures.

It seems clear to Universal management that additional plants to supply these growing markets should be constructed before the markets are preempted by competitive plants located within the LAFTA countries. Yet how many plants should be constructed, where should they be located, and how large should each plant be? These questions are further complicated by uncertainties regarding when free trade for Universal's product among the LAFTA members will commence. This appendix outlines an approach to the types of investment questions posed for a company like Universal by the formation of multicountry markets.

The Recommended Approach

The attempt to devise an optimal production and marketing scheme for a multicountry market consists of several steps. First alternative schemes are postulated. The alternative schemes are precise production and marketing plans that imply varying degrees of ability and willingness to satisfy multicountry demands over time. The best production and distribution plan for each alternative is isolated and summarized in cash flow work sheets, and time-adjusted measures of financial return are then computed for each scheme. In a concluding step (or in conjunction with the earlier steps) the return measures for each proposal are adjusted for uncertainty, and the best scheme is identified.

A sample scheme for the Universal Company in the LAFTA countries might

[2] LAFTA was formed in 1960 and is now negotiating tariff concessions among the members—Argentina, Bolivia, Brazil, Chile, Colombia, Ecuador, Mexico, Paraguay, and Uruguay. The removal of trade barriers is scheduled to be completed by 1972.

include present operations plus construction of a 16-million-unit plant in Mexico to be completed by 1969, a 4-million-unit plant in Argentina by 1970, and an 8-million-unit expansion of the Brazilian plant by 1972. An alternative plan might include continuation of present activities plus construction of a 14-million-unit facility in Mexico to be completed by 1970. Another possibility for Universal might be to do nothing—that is, to serve the Brazilian market with the existing plant and to continue exporting from the United States.

For each plan the investor identifies, different allocation possibilities exist. Output can be varied among the plants or distributed in different ways among the countries. The decision problem is to identify the allocation plan that satisfies demand requirements in each country over time within the capacity of each plant while maximizing net cash inflows for the particular scheme. This type of allocation problem can be solved using a linear programming technique called the transportation method.[3] Basically this technique involves solving a finite number of transportation problems for all plants, each with a different combination of possible output allocations. It is an enumeration method in which the annual cash flow implications for alternative allocation plans are measured. The following variables are included in the prescribed analysis:

1. Sales in each country each year
2. Tariffs in each country each year
3. Transportation costs—port to plants, port to port, and port to customers
4. Costs of raw materials each year
5. Capacity of plants
6. Plant costs as a function of plant capacities
7. Time periods during which plants come on stream
8. Sales price in any country each year
9. Tax rates in each country each year—income and dividend withholding
10. Cash, accounts receivables, and inventory requirements in each country each year
11. Depreciation for plants
12. Sales and administrative costs in each country
13. Economic lives of plants and terminal values for assets
14. U.S. corporate tax rates each year
15. Time period when free trade becomes effective in each country for the product in question
16. Fixed investment requirements and start-up costs for plants.

To illustrate the technique, assume that the Universal Company is analyzing the first plant mentioned—that is, the scheme that requires the construction of new plans in Mexico and Argentina and expansion of the Brazilian plant. Also assume that these plants are designed to serve five LAFTA countries—Argentina, Brazil, Chile, Colombia, and Mexico. Given the sales estimates for each of the five countries and the capacities of the three plants, *one* possible allocation plan is shown in Table 1. The plan requires that Argentine demand be satisfied by supplying 1,000 units from the Argentine plant and 2,000 units from the pro-

[3] For a discussion of this approach *see,* for example, David W. Miller and Martin K. Starr, *Executive Decisions and Operations Research,* 2nd ed., Englewood Cliffs, N.J., Prentice-Hall, 1960, pp. 260–277.

posed expansion of the Brazilian plant; Chilean demand is satisfied by production of 5,000 and 2,000 units in Mexico and Argentina, respectively. Like all allocation plans, this one is characterized by unique cash flow projections since both inflows and outflows are affected by production and distribution arrangements. The net cash inflows for this allocation plan are predicted, using as basic ingredients the variables listed in the previous paragraph. Hypothetical inflow estimates for the allocation plan in Table 1 are shown in Table 2. The total net cash inflow, $5,440, is compared with the inflow estimates of other allocation plans after adjusting the respective inflow estimates for the time value of money, and the plan with the highest net cash inflow is identified as the best production and marketing arrangement for this particular scheme.

In identical fashion it is possible to select the best allocation plans for the other schemes such as constructing a single 14-million-unit plant in Mexico or doing nothing. In a final step the alternatives are compared, and the scheme with the highest net cash inflow is selected as the best strategy for serving the multicountry market.

It should be noted that the prescribed allocation solution focuses on all inflow and outflow estimates for a given scheme rather than only on individual plant costs and revenues. Consequently, the indicated solution may require that some plants operate in ways that maximize net cash inflows for the scheme as a whole, but that do not maximize the returns of individual plants.

TABLE 1

Countries Served by Allocation Plan 1

COUNTRY	PLANT IN MEXICO	PLANT IN ARGENTINA	EXPANSION OF PLANT IN BRAZIL	SALES ESTIMATES FOR EACH COUNTRY
Argentina		1,000	2,000	3,000
Brazil	3,000		6,000	9,000
Chile	3,000	2,000		5,000
Colombia	3,000	1,000		4,000
Mexico	7,000			7,000
Total Plant Capacities	16,000	4,000	8,000	28,000

TABLE 2

Net Cash Inflows to Each Country from Allocation Plan 1

COUNTRY	PLANT IN MEXICO	PLANT IN ARGENTINA	EXPANSION OF PLANT IN BRAZIL	NET CASH INFLOWS
Argentina		$205	$ 400	$ 605
Brazil	$605		1,325	1,930
Chile	700	400		1,100
Colombia	585	210		795
Mexico	1,010			1,010
All Countries				$5,440

Case 8
COMPAGNIE GENERALE COMESTIBLE

In May 1969 John Carron, the treasurer of Compagnie Générale Comestible (CGC) was considering a proposal to can and process fish in Gelibolu, Turkey. A report describing the prospective investment had been received in February 1969 from Giles Donahue, managing director of the company's middle-eastern division, headquartered in Istanbul. In addition to Donahue's report, Mr. Carron had obtained a critique of the report from Omar St. Jean, a headquarters staff assistant, and a rebuttal of St. Jean's criticisms by Donahue. It remained for Mr. Carron to evaluate the testimony and to make a recommendation to the board of management.

Compagnie Générale Comestible was a Belgium company which manufactured cereals, canned foods, frozen foods, and confectionary products. In 1968 CGC's total assets were in excess of 50 billion francs and the common stock plus retained earnings of the company amounted to more than 40 billion francs. Sales during 1969 were expected to reach 55 billion francs with attendant profits after taxes of almost 4 billion francs. Headquartered in Antwerp, the company had established manufacturing and distribution facilities throughout the Common Market, Great Britain, South Africa, and Turkey. The managing director in each country was responsible for both manufacturing and sales of all CGC products within the country. Major decisions, such as approvals of plans and budgets, required the agreement of the country managing director and the headquarters board of management.

To assure continuous growth of company sales and income the managing directors outside of Belgium had been encouraged to identify attractive investment possibilities and, after completing a cursory analysis of the prospects, to forward related data and preliminary conclusions to corporate headquarters. It was Mr. Carron's responsibility to evaluate the various projects which flowed into headquarters and to present attractive proposals to the board of management for ultimate disposition.

The Turkish Affiliate's Proposal

In February Mr. Carron had received the following memorandum from Mr. Donahue in Istanbul:

Dear John:

For some time I have been studying the possibility of our entering the fish business in Turkey. The more I look into the subject the more convinced I become that we have a unique opportunity for profits from both domestic and export sales which can be realized within a reasonably short period of time and return our original investment many times over. As you may know, Turkey's fishing grounds rank second only to Norway's in European productive capacity. Yet Turkey is far behind the European producers because of antiquated fishing vessels, a shortage of seagoing trawlers, and insufficient facilities to can the fish or to convert fish into by-products.

It's been estimated that over 500,000 tons of fish pass between the Black Sea straits twice a year moving from the Black Sea to the Sea of Marmara and back. Moreover, large tonnages of a wide variety of fish are found in the Turkish waters of the Black Sea, the Aegean Sea, and the Mediterranean. Both salt water and fresh water fish are equally prevalent and include the principal varieties—e.g., mullet, anchovy, turbo, swordfish, blue fish, bass, sardines, tuna, sturgeon, shad, trout, perch, and pike. Of particular significance is the availability in Turkish waters of shrimp, prawns, lobsters, oysters, and sturgeon.

The shortage of refrigeration facilities here has severely limited the local demand for fish. Even more important has been the canning problem. Of the sixty-five canneries in Turkey only a dozen can fish, the majority preferring to concentrate on fruits and vegetables. Canning costs have been high in the past because Turkey has had to import its tin plate requirements. Yet the new steel mill constructed at Eregli recently is beginning to supply tin plate whose availability should enhance significantly the country's ability both to can and to provide end products at a price that will encourage much greater consumption than at the present time.

You might find this hard to believe, but authorities here estimate that the average Turk consumes less than one can per year of all types of canned foods at the present time. I am certain that if we use modern canning techniques and promote fish products aggressively, it will be possible to provide products at a cost low enough to induce substantially higher rates of domestic consumption than at the present time. We should have a big jump on the competition since their equipment for the most part is outmoded and requires a great deal of hand operations to supplement the machinery. The local producer's high cost of production resulting from inefficient techniques will continue to be an important barrier for them. Moreover, fish canning and processing is a minor operation for existing producers (about 15 per cent of their total output).

Now, let me turn to the exciting part of the marketing picture. At the present time a large proportion of the Turkish fish catch is exported, even though virtually nothing has been done promotionally to induce the purchase of canned or fresh/frozen fish abroad. Right now, most of Turkey's fish exports are going to surrounding countries. An enormous and virtually untapped market consists of the European countries which CGC is ideally equipped to serve. After your recent visit, I don't need to tell you how good the native fish dishes are! Turkey's present "associate membership agreement" with the Common Market will certainly provide a competitive advantage over other exporting countries. The well-known excellent flavor of Turkish species together with the low and competitive price position can be expected to strengthen our position.

Rather than drone on in this memorandum let me show you what we think sales figures look like. I can provide a justification for the numbers later. It suffices to suggest here that both the demand and sales figures for the proposed project are conservative. (See Table 1.)

Table 1
Projected demand and sales for next five years
(in thousands of metric tons)

		DEMAND		*SALES*	
Year		*Domestic*	*Foreign*	*Domestic*	*Foreign*
1971	Fresh and frozen fish	122	40	3.0	2.0
	Canned fish	0.8	10	0.5	4.5
1972	Fresh and frozen fish	130	50	1.0	2.5
	Canned fish	1	15	0.5	5.0
1973	Fresh and frozen fish	138	60	1.5	2.5
	Canned fish	1	20	0.5	5.5
1974	Fresh and frozen fish	146	68	1.0	2.5
	Canned fish	1.8	25	1.0	6.0
1975	Fresh and frozen fish	160	100	1.0	2.5
	Canned fish	2.0	30	1.0	6.0

To exploit the existing and growing demand (especially in foreign markets), I suggest that we procure fish from local suppliers and confine our activities to a) the production of tin cans, b) fish canning, and c) fish processing. Since the cans produced in Turkey have been very primitive, they would never meet European standards. Tin plate required for canned production is now available locally, and the government has prohibited the importation of cans. Consequently, all companies active in canning food must now produce their own cans since there is no can producer per se. The plant should be located in Gelibolu which is the main fish supplier of the country. Water, electricity, and native labor are readily available in Gelibolu.

I think we should build a plant with a 10-thousand-ton capacity and plan for initial production of 8 thousand tons, increasing output to 10 thousand tons by 1973. The cost of such a plant will run approximately 14 billion Turkish lire (TL) and certainly would not exceed 17 billion TL. The government can be expected to react favorably to the project since we will be using local labor and raw materials and generating a lot of foreign exchange by virtue of our export emphasis. In the major landing centers the fish are sold wholesale at auctions which are supervised and managed by the local municipalities. Although we could buy the fish ourselves, I suggest that we use the so-called middlemen to act as agents on a commission basis. In this way we can reduce our permanent overhead while utilizing fully the middlemen's experience and established long-time personal relations with the local fishermen. With respect to personnel, we should employ only a small permanent group of workers and supplement them during the peak seasons with an additional labor force. We will need approximately twenty skilled and eighty unskilled employees on a permanent basis which will cost approximately 2 billion TL per annum including the various required social and fringe benefits.

The projected output, costs, revenues, taxes, and profits for the first three years of operations should look something like this: (see Tables 2 and 3).

Table 2
Projected output
(in thousands of tons)

	1971	1972	1973
Fresh and frozen fish (marketing)	3.0	3.5	4.0
Canned fish	5.0	5.5	6.0
Totals	8.0	9.0	10.0

Table 3
Projected revenues
(000 TL)

	1971	1972	1973
Net sales*	25,000	29,000	33,000
Cost of fish	10,000	12,000	13,000
Packing material	1,093	1,305	1,182
Labor	1,972	2,100	2,220
Plant overhead (10%)	457	457	457
Cost of production	13,422	15,862	16,859
Gross margin	11,578	13,138	16,141
Less: Administrative cost	1,560	1,560	1,560
Less: Contingency†	5,600	5,600	5,600
Profits before taxes	4,458	6,018	8,981
Less: Corporate tax (36%)	1,605	2,166	3,233
Profits after taxes	2,853	3,852	5,748
Net return on investment: (000 TL)	2,853 / 14,000 = 20%	3,852 / 14,000 = 28%	5,748 / 14,000 = 41%

* Estimated sales revenue is based on average minimum price of fish in the Common Market countries during the last five years (=330 kurus).

† Contingencies for various local taxes + transportation costs + power, water, etc. + adjustments in administrative salaries and bonuses; the cost of temporary labor forces is also included in contingency.

As you can see, returns should be extremely high with return on investment in the range of 20 per cent, 28 per cent and 41 per cent in 1971, 1972, and 1973 respectively. Therefore I hope you will give this proposal your immediate attention.

If the board of management can approve the project by the end of 1969, it should be possible to start construction early in 1970 and have planned activities on stream by the beginning of 1971.

I am quite enthusiastic about this one and hope that we can get a reading in the not too distant future.

Best regards,

Giles Donahue (signature)

Mr. Carron turned the memo over to his assistant Omar St. Jean, who made a number of adjustments in the figures supplied by Donahue.

In his report, Mr. St. Jean first determined the total investment required. He accepted the Turkish figures for the cost of the land, building, and equipment. He added, however, a 25 per cent allowance for installation costs, inflation during the period of construction, and also as a general reserve for underestimation. Thus the estimated cost of the project was increased from 14 billion TL to 17.5 TL.

Next Mr. St. Jean added an allowance of 6.125 billion TL for working capital, bringing the total investment up to 23.625 billion TL. He did not know why Mr. Donahue had omitted cash, receivables, and inventory requirements from his memo but inquiries in Antwerp confirmed his suspicion that one could count on approximately 35 per cent of assets being tied up in these categories.

Another entirely new cost factor which Mr. St. Jean added was an allowance for training expenses. In his discussions with headquarters production people, Mr. St. Jean learned that it would probably be necessary to maintain three engineers on location in Gelibolu for six months to train the production crews in the tin can section, in the fish canning plant, and in the fish processing section. This would cost approximately 150,000 TL for salaries and relocation expenses. Mr. St. Jean made no further adjustments to the cost figures, and the total investment required stood at 23.775 billion TL. It was assumed that CGC would provide the necessary funds for the investment since no difficulties were anticipated in recovering dividends from Turkey.

Mr. St. Jean next turned his attention to the economic life of the fixed assets which Mr. Donahue neglected in his cost calculations. Inquiries with equipment manufacturers revealed that the average life of the building and the various types of equipment was about fifteen years, and consequently an annual depreciation charge of 1.167 billion was tacked on to the annual cost estimates (17.5 divided by 15).

Mr. St. Jean also noticed that the Turkish figures assumed that the relationship between cost of production and sales was the same for 1971, 1972 and 1973. This seemed to him to be overly optimistic for several reasons. Presumably it would be necessary for the Turkish affiliate to incur above average promotional costs and aggressive pricing policies to break into both the domestic and export markets. Also one could anticipate higher than average production costs during the initial phase of operation. Moreover, it seemed logical to Mr. St. Jean that production costs would automatically be higher during the first couple of years before capacity production was reached. Recognizing that such judgments of necessity were arbitrary, Mr. St. Jean decided to assume that gross margins during 1971 and 1972 would be 9.262 billion TL and 11.824 billion TL respectively, or 20 per cent and 10 per cent below Mr. Donahue's predictions.

The staff assistant next recomputed the profits for the proposed venture using the same format as Mr. Donahue. His figures appear in Table 4.

Mr. St. Jean then calculated rates of return for the project on a time-adjusted basis. Specifically, he computed the present value of anticipated net inflows for the project at a discount rate of 20 per cent. Mr. St. Jean decided that a 20 per cent rate after taxes should be the cut-off rate. This figure was a company goal,

Table 4
Projected revenues
(000 TL)

	1971	*1972*	*1973*
Gross margin	$9,262	$11,824	$16,141
Less: Depreciation*	1,167	1,167	1,167
Less: Administrative cost	1,560	1,560	1,560
Less: Contingency	5,600	5,600	5,600
Profits before taxes	935	3,497	7,814
Less: Corporate taxes (47%)†	439	1,644	3,673
Profits after taxes	$ 496	$ 1,853	$ 4,141
Net return on investment‡:	496 / 23,625[3‡] = 2%	1,853 / 23,625 = 8%	4,141 / 23,625 = 18%

* Mr. St. Jean added depreciation to Mr. Donahue's cost calculations.
† Mr. St. Jean added anticipated Belgium taxes to the 36 per cent Turkish taxes which Mr. Donahue had predicted.
‡ Mr. St. Jean substituted 23,625 for the 14,000 in Mr. Donahue's calculations to reflect the additional investment elements.

and he had seen a number of investment proposals in recent weeks which would yield at least this amount. The results of his calculations are shown as Exhibit 1.

On the basis of his calculations Mr. St. Jean decided that the Turkish project was not to be recommended since it failed to achieve a satisfactory rate of return on capital, i.e., its net present value was negative.

Before reaching a decision on the proposal Mr. Carron decided to send Mr. St. Jean's report to the Turkish affiliate for comments. Excerpts from Mr. Donahue's reply are presented below:

Clearly, Mr. St. Jean's study uses some management techniques which we consider novel, to say the least. Naturally I am not in a position to challenge these present value methods or their relevance to our situation. On the other hand, I do feel qualified to comment on some of Mr. St. Jean's assumptions. Skillful as Mr. St. Jean has been in bringing the various projections back to their present values, he has also shown a serious ignorance of some essential aspects as they pertain to our Turkish operations.

First, it is totally unnecessary to add 6.125 billion TL of working capital to the capital investment on which you require a 20 per cent return. Like other businesses here, we operate with much smaller proportions of working capital than is customary in Europe. Besides, it is a common business practice to rely on local commercial banks for working capital needs—which will cost us no more than 5 per cent after adjusting for taxes. Such leverage is entirely normal as well as highly desirable for us in Turkey as well as for you in Antwerp. Finally, the investment in working capital will certainly not take place until 1971 and 1972 instead of in 1970 as Mr. St. Jean's analysis assumes.

Second, although we agree that depreciation should be included in the analysis as Mr. St. Jean suggests, isn't depreciation an expense? Apparently Mr. St. Jean's present value procedure treats depreciation as a benefit. If his procedure is valid,

EXHIBIT 1

Present Value Analysis of Turkish Project
(000 TL)

Year	*Investment*	+	*Profit after Turkish and Belgian Taxes**	+	*Depreciation*	=	*Cash flow*	X	*20% PV factor*	=	*PV of cash flow*
1970	(23775)		0		0		(23,775)		1.000		(23,775)
1971	0		496		1,167		1,663		.833		1,352
1972	0		1,853		1,167		3,020		.694		2,096
1973	0		4,141		1,167		5,308		.579		3,073
1974	0		4,547		1,167		5,714		.482		2,754
1975	0		4,774		1,167		5,941		.402		2,388
1976	0		5,013		1,167		6,180		.335		2,070
1977	0		5,264		1,167		6,431		.279		1,794
1978	0		5,527		1,167		6,694		.233		1,560
1979	0		5,803		1,167		6,970		.194		1,352
1980	0		6,093		1,167		7,260		.162		1,176
1981	0		6,398		1,167		7,565		.135		1,021
1982	0		6,768		1,167		7,935		.112		389
1983	0		7,106		1,167		8,273		.093		769
1984	0		7,461		1,167		8,628		.078		730
1985	0		7,834		1,167		9,001		.065		585
15 yrs.											
											Net present value = (166)

* Mr. St. Jean assumed that profits would increase at a 5 per cent annual rate after 1973.

why then use the straight-line method? We have quite a bit of flexibility in setting our depreciation schedule here in Turkey, and it will be entirely legal to amortize the building costs in fifteen years and all the equipment in five years. Additionally we can obtain permission to deduct a double depreciation charge during the first year.

Third, we may be able to reduce the required investment significantly by buying the equipment on credit and constructing the building in a section of Gelibolu that comes under the program of the State Planning Organization. Under this program we can obtain long-term loans at very favorable interest rates. Although such loans would probably require a CGC guarantee, they would add to our leverage and thereby substantially improve the return on investment.

Fourth, turning to the profit margin which Mr. St. Jean deflated in the interest of conservatism, I believe our margins in the original memo were quite conservative. I did not include in the original figures the effects of export incentives which the Turkish Council of Ministers has recently established. Without question this project would be eligible for significant tax refunds that are being offered to promote exports. This tax relief would increase our after tax margins by roughly 5 per cent.

While on the subject of taxes I question the validity of applying Belgium taxes to this project. Belgium taxes are not assessed unless we remit profits to CGC and, as you well know, the board of management has invariably suggested that we use our profits for expansion or new projects.

One final question: What happens to the proposed investment after fifteen years? Presumably, according to Mr. St. Jean's present value analysis, everything ends after fifteen years. Why not twenty years instead of fifteen? Even if there's adequate justification for selecting fifteen years for analysis, I am convinced that the fish operations will be of value to CGC after the fifteen years have elapsed.

Considering all of Mr. Donahue's remarks, Mr. Carron concluded that the Turkish proposal raised some significant policy dilemmas which could be expected to reoccur as other proposals were submitted to headquarters for appraisal. He decided, therefore, to give the Turkish proposal more than his usual attention in order to develop some general guidelines for dealing with these issues in the future. At the same time he hoped to obtain answers to Mr. Donahue's questions and to pass judgment on the Turkish proposal as quickly as possible in order to minimize hard feelings and misspent energies.

Case 9
WILLIAMSON COMPANY, S. A.

In August of 1965 the president of the Williamson Company's international division was reviewing a Brazilian investment proposal prepared by a staff analyst. Although there were certain problems inherent in the proposal, the president was seriously considering the venture because of Brazilian exchange restrictions. The Williamson Company was engaged in other Brazilian activities which were generating substantial cruzeiro flows. Because these cruzeiros could not be converted to dollars and repatriated, and because the cruzeiro was depreciating rapidly, it was particularly important that the Williamson Company find suitable, additional investment outlets within Brazil.

The Compos lumber project involved acquiring a 50 per cent interest in Compos Industrial, S. A., an operating softwood saw mill located on the upper Amazon, in addition to a 50 per cent interest in Cia Agricola y Industria Rangoona, a large hardwood stand located north of Rio de Janiero on which would be established both a saw mill and veneering activity.

There was a growing export potential for Brazilian lumber as a result of its quality and favorable price. The generation of substantial profits could be anticipated both locally in cruzeiros and externally in dollars from these related acquisitions.

This proposal envisaged utilizing available, presently nonremittable, cruzeiro funds. The recovery of the cruzeiros invested in Compos lumber and Cia Agricola y Industria Rangoona was estimated to be possible within one year from generated profits. The staff analyst's report follows.

Background

USAWA, a well-known, substantially American-owned holding company domiciled in Rio (see Exhibit 1 which contains a profile of Williamson's potential partner) has offered Williamson an opportunity to join with them in these two lumber ventures. They have conducted extensive studies of all aspects involved and have satisfied themselves as well as Williamson's Brazilian personnel that this project is not only economically feasible, but offers the promise of significant profits. USAWA's present activities qualify them for such appraisals but nonetheless, it should be noted that appropriate Williamson personnel, both in Brazil and at United States headquarters, have reviewed and generally concur in the contents of these studies.

Additionally, USAWA owns Utopia Wood Product, Ltd., located at Twin Rivers, Canada, which has guaranteed to purchase 1 million board feet per month of the exported Brazilian lumber at an established favorable price.

Description

Compos Lumber Company, S.A., is a share company with a capital of 9 million cruzeiros represented by 9,000 shares. It is engaged in sawmill operations, principally in virola (softwood) timber logs purchased from suppliers. The mill is located 125 miles up the Amazon from Belem.

The assets and their appraisal consist of the following: 1 large masonry building containing 4 circular saws, one engine, one band saw, planers, lathe, milling machines, chopping machines, etc.; a landing dock 140 feet long that allows for a 15-foot draft; two steam launches for pulling barges; one 160-ton pontoon; one barge of 450-ton capacity; one barge of 90-ton capacity; a warehouse containing spare parts and materials; a company store with provisions for employees; a radio transmitter; a tractor; one large building for residence of managerial staff; one large brick warehouse; and an office in Belem containing filing cabinets, a radio transmitter, desks, typewriters, a safe, calculating machines, and so on. These items have been appraised on a replacement value basis at 98 million cruzeiros (U.S. $160,000).

Compos is presently cutting and marketing approximately $10,000 worth of virola per month, exported principally to Europe. The owners are willing to accept the cruzeiro equivalent of U.S. $100,000 cash. It has been ascertained that it would be advisable to add an additional fan saw and to cover with corrugated roofing a certain portion of the landing dock. These improvements would be at an estimated cost of $15,000, to which we estimate a working capital need of $10,000, making the total investment in Compos $125,000.

With the recent change in the official cruzeiro exchange rate it is expected that the export price per 1,000 board feet for virola is approximately U.S. $51, broken down as follows:

Cost of lumber	$ 2.50
Cost of transportation to mill	5.00
Labor cost	5.00
Overhead	6.00
Treatment cost	2.00
Loading expenses	4.00
Export expenses	11.50
Profit	15.00

Adding to the FAS price per 1,000 board feet of $51 the sum of $39 for ocean freight and landing costs to Canada and assuming a retail price of $140 per 1,000 board feet ($15 below present rates), it is evident that a $50 overage per 1,000 board feet is possible on exports from Compos to Canada. By invoicing through some third location such as Panama, it is expected that USAWA and Williamson could jointly accumulate substantial dollar funds.

Additionally, it is assumed that approximately a third of the lumber production from Compos will be unsuitable for export but readily marketable within Brazil. Our calculations do not take into account the profit which would be made on selling this lumber within Brazil.

Please refer to Exhibit 2 outlining the recovery of our joint investments in Compos per the contemplated production schedule. It will be noted that full recovery of our acquisition and improvement cost appears possible out of the projected cruzeiro earnings on exports alone.

As Exhibit 3 suggests, more than $400,000 in dollar overages are contemplated to be accumulated externally within the first year, and these will accrue to the extent of at least $500,000 per year thereafter.

Cia Agricola y Industria Rangoona

This company is wholly owned by USAWA and is valued at $1 million. It consists of 8,467 hectares of which only 5,000 hectares or 12,700 acres are considered as timber stands worthy of exploitation. Appraisals indicate that 165,000 board feet per hectare of commercially valuable hardwood are obtainable for approximately 825 million board feet. By types of species of interest for export, it is calculated that the holdings contain 573,000 cubic meters or 22,910,000 board feet. On a stand basis this represents a value of United States $1,265,000 without giving consideration to either lumber marketable internally or the value of the land itself.

Both the land and timber presumably are investments unlikely to suffer erosion of value as a result of continued inflation. The company is registered for agricultural purposes that provide beneficial local tax advantages. Once the land has been cleared the area is most suitable for cattle raising and systematic planting of marketable commodities such as corn, cocoa, and wheat. The company is chartered for export activities and has a permit for cutting lumber. The property does contain a small saw mill although this is inactive at the moment. It is proposed that this installation be improved and that a veneering operation be incorporated. The cost of these improvements would approximate $350,000 in equipment. Of this amount, $200,000 is available in Brazil, payable in cruzeiros, and the balance obtainable from Germany on five-year terms for the cruzeiro equivalent of $150,000. Additionally, working capital to the extent of a cruzeiro equivalent of $50,000 would be needed to finance the purchase of logs and meet initial payroll and administrative expenses.

For as long a period of time as is physically and economically feasible to do so, logs will be purchased from outside suppliers in order to maintain the Rangoona timber reserve. Without reforestation, the Rangoona property contains over a ten-year supply of the specific lumber and veneers that would be required by Williamson's São Paulo affiliate at a production level of 150,000 cabinets per year. It is expected that the cost of the Rangoona installation would be recovered from export profits alone in approximately seven months after commencing operations per the indicated production schedule.

Financial Appraisal

Compos (sawmill – as improved including working capital)		$ 125,000
Rangoona $1,500,000 (timber, land and present mill)		
350,000 (improvements and veneer equipment)		
50,000 (working capital)		1,900,000
	Total assets	$2,025,000
50% of Assets		$1,012,500
Cost to Williamson for 50%		812,500
Differences or assets cost-free to Williamson		$ 200,000

Projected Annual Return on Investment Before Taxes

	$ Profits locally in Cruzeiros	*$ Profits externally*	*Total*
Compos	$180,000	$ 600,000	$ 780,000
Rangoona	180,000	750,000	930,000
	$360,000	$1,350,000	$1,710,000
	50% of Profits – $855,000		
Annual estimated return on investment before taxes: 113%			

Proposed Plan for Acquisition Payment

Step 1: Williamson's São Paulo affiliate lends on two equal interest-free notes the cruzeiro equivalent of $125,000 to USAWA in return for which an option on 50 per cent of Compos is received. Step 2: Williamson's Brazilian affiliate contracts in cruzeiros the $200,000 locally available equipment necessary to develop Rangoona and assigns this equipment to Rangoona. Step 3: Williamson's Brazilian affiliate contracts in cruzeiros over a five-year payment term at the official exchange rate for the $150,000 of equipment from Germany needed to develop Rangoona and assigns the equipment to Rangoona. Step 4: Williamson's Brazilian affiliate pays the cruzeiro equivalent of $50,000 to Rangoona for working capital after installation of equipment. Step 5: USAWA repays Williamson's Brazilian affiliate one note for $62,500 or the cruzeiro equivalent from USAWA's half share in initial earnings either locally or from foreign-generated overages from exports from Compos. Upon receipt of this payment, Williamson-Brazil will cancel the second note as well. Step 6: Williamson's Brazilian affiliate pays the $350,000 balance due USAWA for the 50 per cent Rangoona interest out of Williamson-Brazil's half share in initial earnings either locally or from foreign-generated overages from exports from Rangoona.

Williamson's Brazilian affiliate will then have incurred a net cruzeiro outlay of:

$262,500	
200,000	
150,000	(over five years)
50,000	
$462,500	

For this $462,500, Williamson-Brazil will receive a 50 per cent interest in assets valued at $2,025,000 on which, after approximately one year's time to allow for installation development and full payments from earnings, they should expect to earn $855,000 before taxes, or a return on assets employed of 185 per cent.

Comments

Williamson presumably is encountering difficulties in receiving dollar obligations and profit remittances from Brazil. The company is accumulating cruzeiro funds that, unless converted, invested, or otherwise employed, are depreciating in their relationship to the dollar because of devaluation and inflation in Brazil.

This proposal offers a means for

1. Converting these cruzeiros into an inflation-proof investment
2. Generating additional cruzeiro funds that can be utilized to assist in financing ordinary Williamson activities in Brazil and in reducing the affiliate's abnormally high interest expenses on local borrowings
3. Accumulating substantial dollar earnings in locations offering favorable or nonexistent tax rates. Such earnings might then be reinvested or reemployed to advantage in other markets to help Williamson's overall development and expansion programs.

USAWA, like Williamson, possesses a reservoir of personnel familiar with lumbering operations. We visualize the establishment of a joint management office at Solom, which would exercise operational control over these two facilities and be responsible to both USAWA in Rio and Williamson's Brazilian affiliate in São Paolo for their success.

Recommendation

Analysts in the international division are of the opinion that this is an excellent opportunity, particularly insofar as it can be accomplished in cruzeiros entirely within the present and projected existing resources of Williamson-Brazil and represents no new dollar investment. We are satisfied both with its economic feasibility and possibilities for growth and profit.

To implement this proposal, we suggest that we enter immediately into a formal letter of intentions with USAWA and that we authorize Williamson-Brazil to implement execution of the two notes to USAWA.

EXHIBIT 1

Profile of the Potential Partner: USAWA

USAWA is a holding company located in Rio which maintains offices in New York, Tokyo, London, Geneva, Bangkok, and Rangoon. The company is engaged in and owns the following operations: a company mining and exporting diamonds; a company engaged in wheat importations; a company manufacturing furniture sold both internally and exported from Brazil; a company mining and exporting quartz; a company of fishing boats and a freezer plant for lobster exports; a company engaged in harvesting and export of nuts; a company in cigar manufacture and distribution including exports; a pharmaceutical company; a lumber operation in Canada; a lumber operation in Colombia; a land development company in Venezuela; an import-export company in Venezuela; and a liquor manufacturing complex in Brazil making scotch, gin, and bourbon under licenses from leading American distillers. The owners of USAWA are Frederick Fellini and George C. Scott.

USAWA has been active in Brazil for over thirty years and both Fellini and Scott are respected members of the American community. USAWA's worth has been estimated as between $20 and $40 million dollars.

EXHIBIT 2

Recovery of Investment in Brazil
($15 per 1000 board feet)

	PRODUCTION SCHEDULE			
	Production 1000/b. ft.	*Cumulative production*	*Profits $ in Brazil*	*Cumulative profits*
July 1965	200	200	$ 3,000	
August	200	400	3,000	$ 6,000
September	400	800	6,000	12,000
October	500	1,300	7,500	19,500
November	600	1,900	9,000	28,500
December	700	2,600	10,500	39,000
January 1966	800	3,400	12,000	51,000
February	900	4,300	13,500	64,500
March	1,000	5,300	15,000	79,500
April	1,000	6,300	15,000	94,500
May	1,000	7,300	15,000	109,500
June	1,000	8,300	15,000	124,500

EXHIBIT 3

Recovery of Compos Investment in Dollars

	Production 1000/b. ft.	*Foreign overage*	*Cumulative*
July 1965	200	$10,000	
August	200	10,000	$ 20,000
September	400	20,000	40,000
October	500	25,000	65,000
November	600	30,000	95,000
December	700	35,000	130,000
January 1966	800	40,000	170,000
February	900	45,000	215,000
March	1,000	50,000	265,000
April	1,000	50,000	315,000
May	1,000	50,000	365,000
June	1,000	50,000	415,000

EXHIBIT 4

Rangoona Production and Profit Projections

		Month	*1000's board ft. per month*	*$ – Local profit in Cruzeiros*	*$ – External profit*	*Total profit*	*Cumulative*
Hardwoods				@$10	@$25		
Cost	$ 60	1st	100	1,000	2,500	3,500	
Export	70	2nd	200	2,000	5,000	7,000	10,500
Retail	125	3rd	300	3,000	7,500	10,500	21,000
Freight	30	4th	400	4,000	10,000	14,000	35,000
Overage	25	5th	500	5,000	12,500	17,500	52,500
			thereafter $17,500 per month				
Prime Veneers				@$10	@$80		
Cost	$ 90	1st	100	1,000	8,000	9,000	
Export	100	2nd	200	2,000	16,000	18,000	27,000
Freight	25	3rd	300	3,000	24,000	27,000	54,000
Retail	205	4th	400	4,000	32,000	36,000	90,000
Overage	80	5th	500	5,000	40,000	45,000	135,000
			thereafter $45,000 per month				
Printable Veneers				@$5	@$10		
Cost	$ 35	1st	200	1,000	2,000	3,000	
Export	40	2nd	400	2,000	4,000	6,000	9,000
Freight	20	3rd	600	3,000	6,000	9,000	18,000
Retail	70	4th	800	4,000	8,000	12,000	30,000
Overage	10	5th	1000	5,000	10,000	15,000	45,000
			thereafter $15,000 per month				

Annual profit before taxes from exports: $77,500 X 12 = $930,000

Affiliate Financial Structures: Criteria for Selection and Cost Implications

6

The previous chapter offered a format for evaluating direct investment opportunities; using this format the investor could consider the various opportunities called to his attention and thus identify the best investment candidates. An important task remains in planning for international investment. Whereas chapter 5 treated the alternative financing plans as givens, the investor must in point of fact identify the best financial schemes for proposed ventures (or affiliates). He must examine both cost and risk implications for various financing alternatives. Choosing optimal financial plans for affiliates and the company as a whole, the investor minimizes financial costs and avoids foreign exchange and other risks that he considers intolerable. Moreover, analysis of financial implications has an important bearing on the ultimate acceptability of the projects whose cash inflows and outflows have been examined in accordance with the dictates of chapter 5.

This chapter discusses the considerations that are most important in determining capital structure and suggests ways to evaluate financing alternatives. Although the approach is identical, the considerations differ somewhat when the investor looks for temporary (or short term) financing rather than for financing that affiliates require more or less continuously. Therefore chapter 7 explores financing of seasonal or temporary needs separately after the considerations that relate to permanent financing have been analyzed.

THE COMPANY-WIDE COST OF CAPITAL

As the previous chapter implied, the company-wide marginal cost of capital estimate should ultimately be used as a discount factor in appraising venture profitability. One can argue that the investor should use a discount factor higher than the cost of capital to allow for uncertainties in calculating net present value. Yet as Stonehill and Nathanson point out,[1] adjusting for international uncertainties by modifying the discount rate has serious defects. Robichek and Myers have reached a similar conclusion.[2]

The company-wide marginal cost of capital calculation already reflects investor attitude toward uncertainty, as this calculation is based on investors' assessment of probable future earnings and takes into account investors' aversion to risk. Therefore, so long as an individual foreign affiliate (or the project that an affiliate intends to implement) is not expected to change the frequency distribution of company-wide returns, the company-wide cost of capital calculation should be used for discounting purposes. Uncertainty is explicitly dealt with in the return-risk-utility analysis of project net inflows as outlined on pages 159–165 of chapter 5. To use a discount rate higher than the analytically determined cost of capital would be both conceptually erroneous and redundant. On the other hand, when the investment activities of a foreign affiliate (or the proposed new venture of an on-going affiliate) are expected to change the frequency distribution of returns, an adjustment in the company-wide cost of capital calculation is required. So that the following analysis can be presented as simply as possible, we will assume for the time being that a new foreign investment proposal does not change the general risk characteristics of the firm as perceived by investors and that consequently the company-wide cost of capital calculation can be used for discounting purposes. Later in the discussion this assumption will be removed.

For some years financial theorists and practitioners have debated the issue of what constitutes an appropriate debt-equity ratio for the firm.[3] No one denies that the best debt-equity mix minimizes overall capital

[1] Arthur Stonehill and Leonard Nathanson, "Capital Budgeting and the Multinational Corporation," *California Management Review*, Summer 1968, pp. 39–55.

[2] Alexander A. Robichek and Stewart C. Myers, *Optimal Financing Decisions*, Englewood Cliffs, N.J., Prentice-Hall, Inc., 1965, pp. 79–93.

[3] *See*, for example, Franco Modigliani and Merton H. Miller, "The Cost of Capital, Corporate Finance and Theory of Investment," *American Economic Review*, June 1958; David Durand, "The Cost of Debt and Equity Funds for Business," National Bureau of Economic Research, reprinted in Ezra Solomon, ed., *The Management of Corporate Capital*, New York, The Free Press, 1959, pp. 91–116; Modigliani and Miller, "The Cost of Capital, Corporate Finance and the Theory of Investment: Reply," *American Economic Review*, September 1959.

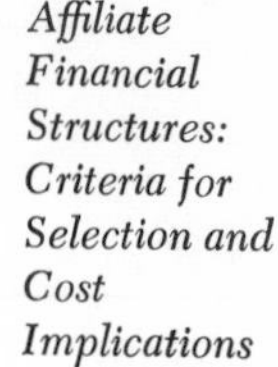

costs but the impact of leverage on capital costs is disputed and empirical evidence on the subject is inconclusive.

There is widespread agreement among financial theorists that initial increments of debt lower capital costs notwithstanding the lack of empirical confirmation.[4] Debt is characterized by obligations to pay interest and repay principal regardless of business conditions. Although debt servicing requirements increase a firm's chances of insolvency, the risks which initial increments of debt impose are considered to be less important than the advantages derived from debt's low explicit cost. As debt proportions are increased, however, the advantage of leverage diminishes. Stockholders become increasingly concerned about the risks that increments of debt servicing requirements impose. Stock prices decline, increasing the explicit cost of common equity, and this increase offsets the cost saving attributable to debt. Eventually increases in the proportion of debt have an adverse effect on capital costs. Shareholder concern regarding increased burden requirements mounts, and common stock prices begin to deteriorate significantly, contributing in this fashion to higher overall capital costs. These costs of capital conclusions can be summarized graphically.

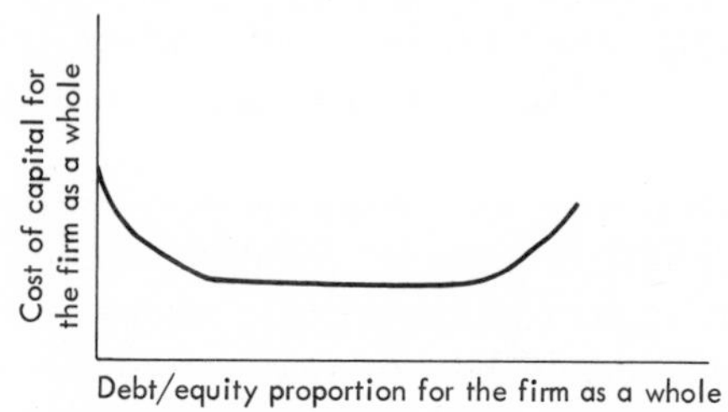

The implication that follows is that the firm should try to assess parent shareholders' and lenders' attitudes regarding appropriate debt limits and confine overall borrowings to the debt-equity range which minimizes overall capital costs. If the financial structure is kept within this range and if projects that are accepted and implemented yield more than the company-wide cost of capital, the firm is able to increase the market price of its common stock. This appreciation in share values occurs because the firm has accepted projects that are expected to produce

[4] *See* John Lintner, "Dividends, Earnings, Leverage, Stock Prices and the Supply of Capital to Corporations," *Review of Economics and Statistics*, August 1962; Alexander Barges, *The Effect of Capital Structure on the Cost of Capital*, Englewood Cliffs, N.J., Prentice-Hall, Inc., 1963; Ronald F. Wippern, "Financial Structure and the Value of the Firm," *Journal of Finance*, December 1966; Fred D. Arditti, "Risk in the Required Rate on Equity," *Journal of Finance*, March 1967; William Beranek, *The Effect on Leverage on the Market Value of Common Stocks;* and Myron J. Gordon, *The Investment, Financing and Valuation of the Corporation*, Homewood, Ill., Richard D. Irwin, Inc., 1962.

returns greater than those required by parent investors at the margin.

The company-wide cost of capital is as relevant to the international investor as to his domestic counterpart. He must decide what is the appropriate debt-equity range for the firm as a whole. This judgment is complicated, however, by virtue of accounting practices which may hide international borrowings and related burdens, thus insulating the international firm from adverse shareholder and lender reactions. If the international firm consolidates parent and affiliate financial statements, the debts of affiliates are shown explicitly in the firm's balance sheet and have a visible influence upon the firm's financial condition. On the other hand, if nonconsolidated practices are followed, the existence of such debts may be concealed from both shareholders and lenders of the parent company and may have only a negligible influence upon the financial situation of the latter. Therefore the international firm issuing nonconsolidated reports must appraise the extent to which parent shareholders and lenders are likely to become aware of incremental affiliate debt in order to judge the impact of such debt on capital costs.

If high proportions of debt are used to finance foreign affiliates, a suboptimal debt-equity mix for the corporation as a whole may result. Leverage abroad may contribute to a decline in share prices at home, thus raising the company-wide cost of capital. Additionally, investor preference for capital raised in the country where the financing is to be used may subject the firm to higher capital costs than would otherwise be the case.

It is our contention that any premiums paid by the firm to finance foreign affiliates (or affiliate projects) should be charged directly against the foreign proposals under consideration. In other words, foreign affiliates (or affiliate projects) should be expected to bear all incremental costs resulting from financing plans that are suboptimal from the point of view of the company as a whole. Hence, to the extent that foreign affiliates' financing plans contain more expensive debt or equity instruments than are available to the firm elsewhere or contribute to debt-equity ranges which raise the company-wide cost of capital, all incremental financial costs are included among project outflows for purposes of the capital budgeting decision.

Thus the company-wide cost of capital as we define it does not necessarily represent the configuration of actual financing costs incurred by the firm. Rather it is a normative cost measure which reflects what overall financing costs would be *if* the firm obtained its debt and equity capital in the least expensive markets in ideal proportions.[5] It

[5] The financial literature is replete with discussions concerning how to measure the firm's cost of capital. *See*, for instance, James C. Van Horne, *Financial Management and Policy*, Englewood Cliffs, N.J., Prentice-Hall, Inc., 1968, pp. 109–43, for an excellent discussion of approaches and problems associated with attempting to approximate the firm's cost of capital.

is the company-wide cost of capital calculation that is used as the discount rate for capital budgeting decisions unless the proposed project under consideration is expected to change the business risk complexion of the firm as a whole. In the event that a particular foreign project is expected to alter the general risk characteristics of the firm, the company-wide cost of capital as previously defined also changes, and the discount rate in turn must be altered. For the time being we will assume that the acceptance of a particular project will not change overall business risk characteristics of the firm and that the company-wide cost of capital is the appropriate rate to be used for discounting purposes.

Business risk aside, the international firm may for reasons outlined below select financing plans for particular foreign affiliates (or for the projects these affiliates launch) that are more expensive than the company-wide cost of capital. These cost premiums, frequently unavoidable in international operations, are included among project outflows in the assessment of venture profitability. To include these cost premiums the international firm must first identify possible financial schemes for its foreign affiliates, measure the costs of these financing schemes and, finally, isolate the differences (if any) between these costs and the rate implied by the company-wide cost of capital calculation. The following sections of this chapter deal with the selection of financing schemes for specific foreign affiliates and with the measurement of related financial costs.

Frequently factors outside management's control make it advisable for affiliates to be financed in such a manner that they can service debt requirements themselves without reliance on parent cash flows. Risk of expropriation and resource blockage, tax considerations, and other limitations on intercompany loans may force the firm to think in terms of separate financial structures for affiliates in different countries. Under these circumstances the size of equity commitments in individual affiliates cannot be based on an assessment of debt capacity for the entire firm and parent shareholder reaction. Rather, debt policy must be based on consideration of cash flow characteristics in each local environment. Estimated cash flows must be sufficient in each environment to provide for amortization of the debt if the local affiliates are to be self-sufficient. In these instances debt capacity must be defined with reference to each entity instead of in relation to the firm as a whole.

The actual debt-equity decisions for the international firm are based on a number of interrelated considerations. Debt limitations may be imposed by government authorities or lenders. Capital restrictions, transfer costs, or headquarters control procedures may necessitate the evaluation of financial needs on an affiliate by affiliate basis. In other words, the financial markets are segmented, precluding the selection of an optimal mix for the firm as a whole. Subject to these constraints, the investor must first assess the firm's (or each affiliate's) debt capacity and then select the debt-equity mix for the firm as a whole (or for each affiliate) which minimizes capital costs. Despite such efforts the resulting financial costs may exceed the company-wide cost of capital and consequently necessitate adjustments in the flow projections used to evaluate affiliate (or project) profitability.

HOW MUCH EQUITY?

Many companies try to finance affiliates abroad with a minimum of equity capital. Even companies that are conservatively financed at home often seek high degrees of leverage for their affiliates abroad (large debt proportions). Indeed, for some companies the attainment of high degrees of affiliate leverage is a precondition for investment. The rationale for this commonly observed attitude differs from company to company. Some firms whose supply of equity capital is limited find that leveraging their affiliates abroad is the best way to stretch their equity investment. Some of the smaller firms among the more than 100 companies included in the National Industrial Conference Board Study have indicated that capital requirements at home limit expansion activity abroad. Financial limitations have been cited as a major constraint on foreign investment and the *raison d'être* for several firms' reliance on licensing.[6] Other firms have a sufficient supply of equity but are constrained by capital restrictions such as the Foreign Direct Investment Regulations in the United States, and as a consequence are compelled to borrow abroad to finance affiliate operations. Still other firms, having indicated that adequate equity capital is available or could be obtained for foreign investments that are considered worthwhile, prefer to minimize equity commitments in order to reduce financial risks.

Researchers in the NICB study have concluded that companies relatively new to the direct investment field, in contrast to more experienced multinational firms, prefer loans to equity and that undercapitalization of foreign ventures is a common practice among these companies.[7] Apparently the newcomers believe that cash inflows from foreign affiliates can be obtained more readily in the form of interest and debt repayment than in the form of dividends. In other words, from the point of view of the parent investor loans constitute retrievable commitments whereas equity investments in affiliates are more permanent. Another explanation for companies' preference for debt relates to the contention that parent equity commitments are regarded as free resources by affiliate managers and that repayment obligations associated with loans prove to be useful in motivating and controlling local personnel.

Whether the firm likes or dislikes borrowing, its ability to leverage affiliates' operations is usually restricted. In some cases debt-equity

[6] *U.S. Production Abroad and the Balance of Payments*, NICB, 1966, p. 54.
[7] *Ibid.*, p. 85.

limits have been set explicitly by government authorities. Venezuela has frequently been mentioned by investors as a country that strenuously objects to high debt proportions when it appears that the large debt increments are being used to support dividend payments to the parent companies. In most countries experiencing balance-of-payments problems, officials object to thinly capitalized affiliates. In some instances the debt limits are set by banks, which refuse to provide further financing to undercapitalized affiliates. Further debt limitations relate to certain countries' restrictions on dividend remittances based on formulas relating to affiliates' equity accounts. Several companies in the NICB study have reported one or more instances of having been subjected to pressure by local governments to transfer funds from subsidiaries' surplus accounts into their capital accounts. The segregation of capital in this fashion becomes important since in many countries dividend remissions are restricted to the amounts reflected in the earned surplus accounts; the less equity available for segregation the smaller the dividend allowance. Still other debt constraints relate to the shortage of acceptable equity alternatives. Sometimes loans are unavailable or only available on terms which jeopardize the success of affiliate operations. Public debt flotations, even in highly developed countries, are frequently too difficult to place or too expensive to constitute a feasible method of raising capital for an affiliate. Thus the extent to which equity commitments can be minimized is usually limited. As a result, the international investor may be unable to obtain the proportion of debt financing that the company-wide cost of capital conclusion dictates.

WHOSE EQUITY?

In addition to the decision regarding appropriate debt-equity proportions, the investor must consider whether equity capital should be contributed exclusively by the parent investor or by the parent in conjunction with outsiders. For a number of reasons the international firm frequently solicits outside equity participation. In some instances the reasons for joint ownership are similar to those that result in mergers among domestic firms. A firm with limited capital of its own may solicit equity capital from other sources especially if debt financing alternatives are limited or foreclosed. When a firm exhausts possible debt alternatives as a means of reducing its stake in a venture, it can further reduce its resources at risk by enlisting the financial support of a partner. In some instances nonfinancial considerations make joint ownership advisable. Foreign partners may be able to supply valuable assistance in obtaining local financing or provide business assistance. Local partners may contribute production and distribution facilities, management talent, or access to important customers.

Yet in a large number of cases, environmental complexities provoke ownership patterns that the investor would avoid in the domestic setting. A local partner is required to obtain desired tax status or tariff protection. Joint ownership helps to reduce the risk of expropriation or to assure favorable treatment by officials. In India, Japan, Mexico, and Spain exclusive or even majority ownership by foreign interests has become impracticable. Other countries are following suit.

Sometimes the local ownership requirement is fulfilled by enlisting the host government or government-affiliated institutions such as development banks as participants. This mixed venture route is frequently used in the case of large or politically strategic projects. Examples of mixed venturing include the Eregli Steel Mill in Turkey, which is owned jointly by three American firms, the Turkish government, and Turkish citizens. Other examples include the Chilean copper mines in which Kennecott participates and the Liberian-American-Swedish Minerals Company (LAMCO), an iron-mining corporation owned jointly by the government of Liberia, a Swedish company, an American company, and private shareholders in several countries.

Multinational ownership of either the mixed venture or exclusively private sector variety is becoming more common with the development of international financial consortia. To satisfy local ownership requirements and to create a large area of common interest with the host society, several firms including Chrysler, Celanese, Liggett and Myers, Cannon Mills, Union Carbide, Dupont, Phillips Petroleum, Reynolds Aluminum, Richardson-Merrell, and the Eregli group have sold stock in affiliated companies to local nationals. Some firms such as General Motors, Lever Brothers, Volkswagen, and IBM have listed parent stock on the local stock exchange to increase local participation. Still other firms including General Electric have sold convertible bonds offshore which are expected eventually to increase foreign holdings of parent stock. In a few instances parent stock has been used to pay for acquisitions abroad, and this stock has subsequently been listed locally.

By way of contrast to these situations in which widespread outside ownership has been sought, the vast majority of joint ventures involve the parent investor and a single or few other participants. Offering shares privately to a few suppliers, distributors, customers, or financiers has enabled investors to improve relations with these interest groups. Frequently shares have been offered to local management. This has been particularly important when local management has insisted on participation as a condition of employment.

In some cases joint ventures have been arranged with a few local partners expected to offer little or no assistance to the proposed businesses. The joint ownership arrangements have been regarded as a necessary evil to enter the particular national markets, and the arrangements can be traced to firms' inability to obtain widespread local ownership. In some of these instances where local laws permit, it has been possible to issue nonvoting stock to local owners giving them a full share in profits while leaving control with the investors holding the voting stock. Other devices such as the separate, wholly-owned distributing company which is the exclusive purchaser at a previously established price of the venture's output have been used to retain control.

It is beyond the scope of this section to examine in depth the rationale and relative virtues of various joint ownership arrangements. Our principal point, not to be obscured by the abbreviated discussion of joint ownership, is that the firm must frequently identify distinct equity packages for its affiliates and that these packages often involve outsiders. Different conditions throughout the world, many of which are beyond the control of the investor, influence patterns of ownership. Situations in various countries must be analyzed on an *ad hoc* basis to ascertain appropriate ownership schemes.

Where exclusive ownership is either impracticable or undesirable, the investor tries to devise ownership schemes that create the largest possible area of common interest between him and his joint venture associates. To the extent that this attempt is successful and the various ownership groups have similar expectations, equity costs are unaffected by outside participation. Joint ownership has merely resulted in a smaller equity holding by the parent investor than would otherwise have been the case. On the other hand, to the extent that expectations are dissimilar among the participants, equity costs differ, and these differences cannot be ignored. Larger (or smaller) return expectations of outside shareholders should be included explicitly in flow projections used to appraise project desirability.

WHICH EQUITY INSTRUMENTS?

After deciding what constitutes the best mix of parent and outside equity financing, the investor must next weigh the comparative advantages of parent loans and advances versus common stock as methods of self-financing. There are different ways in which the parent company can provide for the financing of an affiliate, and the methods selected can have important fiscal consequences.

Ordinarily the parent investor acquires common equity in an affiliate by contributing cash or other assets such as machinery, inventory items, patents, trademarks, and know-how. Likewise the parent investor's common equity is increased when an existing affiliate ploughs back earnings. By making equity contributions the parent investor acquires the right to repatriate dividends (or a proportion of the dividend declaration in the case of a joint venture) from its affiliates.

The parent investor may also make loans or advances to affiliates. There are several parent lending devices. The affiliate may receive formal loans directly from the parent or from another affiliate. The multinational investor may make loans indirectly through a subholding company in some fiscal haven such as Liechtenstein, the Bahamas, Liberia, Panama, or Switzerland. Tax savings can sometimes be realized by forwarding equity capital to a subholding company that in turn advances needed capital to affiliates in the form of loans or advances. Loans or advances may be made indirectly to affiliates from banks that in turn receive deposits from other affiliates or the parent.

Two prevalent parent lending devices relate to affiliates' inventory needs. In one case the parent sells merchandise to the affiliate but does not receive payment until later, even though the affiliate may very well sell the merchandise in the interim. Under this open account method of inventory financing, the inventories on the affiliates' books are offset by corresponding current liabilities that fluctuate according to the magnitude of affiliate needs. These open account loans may or may not bear interest. An alternative to open account inventory financing consists of parent loans to affiliates that are authorized when requested to facilitate inventory purchases. These loans generally appear on affiliates' books as long- or intermediate-term credits. Parent inventory financing of the latter type has appeared most conspicuously on the books of affiliates that in turn must extend substantial credits to their customers. Both inventory lending devices have permitted parent companies some flexibility in the management of affiliates' overall capital structures. For example, remissions by an affiliate to the parent could take the form of dividends where tax considerations and earned surplus position warrant or, alternatively, represent a reduction in affiliate indebtness to the parent.

The loans or advances as common equity substitutes have afforded certain advantages. Usually parent loans have been subordinated to other affiliate indebtedness, and consequently the financial risks of the affiliates have not increased by virtue of the loans. The fiscal advantage of the loans has related to the ability to remit from affiliates via interest and loan repayment rather than via dividend declarations. Consequently, parents have obtained inflows from affiliates without subjecting the affiliates to taxes on dividends. Moreover, interest on the parent loans has reduced affiliate earnings, thereby reducing the parent investor's amenability to taxes levied on such earnings. Thus it has been possible to increase the available inflows and to minimize parent taxes by financing affiliates through loans rather than equity.

Yet since the enactment of the 1962 Revenue Act in the United States, American-based companies must prove conclusively—by meeting a series of tests—that loans extended to affiliates are indeed bona fide loans and not simply contributions to equity if the interest on the loans is to be exempt from United States taxes on income. Hence, companies have been forced to refrain from extending credits on informal terms to affiliates without fixed repayment schedules and, in some cases, without interest. Similarly, tax authorities in other countries have begun to force the collection of interest from borrowing affiliates and have begun to insist that affiliates provide schedules for the amortization of the debt in order that the loans be regarded as debt rather than equity capital.

Other considerations make intercompany loans less attractive than they might first appear. If the affiliate's income tax rate is based on profits in relation to common equity or if dividend remittances are restricted to some proportion of equity funds, the problems and added costs caused by parent lending may outweigh related benefits. The parent may wish to avoid subordinating affiliate advances and loans and, as a consequence, parent lending may adversely affect the affiliate's credit position.

From the parent investor's point of view, equity capital supplied to affiliates has the same cost regardless of whether it takes the form of loans, advances, or common stock. Parent resources are obtained from a common pool of risk capital supplied by the investor's stockholders. The firm's cost of equity capital is based on the expectations of these stockholders, and this cost is not directly influenced by the particular instrument selected by management to transfer resources to various affiliates.

The advantages and disadvantages of alternative instruments for supplying equity capital to affiliates can be traced to associated inflow and outflow implications. Although the cost of the parent equity commitment is the same regardless of the common stock/parent loan mix selected for an affiliate, affiliate net inflows can be minimized by choosing the mix which has the most favorable fiscal consequences. This selection is made within the context of the cash flow worksheets described in chapter 5. The effects of various common stock-parent loan alternatives on affiliate profits, taxes, and remittance privileges are included in the calculations of available inflows. The combination which yields the highest expected net available inflows is identified as the best self-financing scheme.

LOCAL VERSUS IMPORTED DEBT?

A venerable rule of thumb is that international companies should rely on local debt financing to the greatest possible extent. Especially in countries characterized by unstable economic conditions and recent histories or future prospects of inflation and devaluation, investors have typically tried to minimize the dollar portion of their commitments and to maximize the local currency portion. Although in some instances affiliates might have been able to obtain financing relatively cheaply in capital markets outside the host country, affiliate management (or headquarters management) usually has ignored this option. Similarly, the parent investor has refused to borrow dollars or other convertible currencies for investment in affiliates plagued by inflation. In the most extreme instances borrowing quotas in local currencies have been established for the affiliates and investment requests have been denied unless they could be internally financed using local resources.

The explanation for this posture relates in large part to financial managers' desire to avoid foreign exchange losses. When devaluations occur the servicing requirements on debts denominated in outside currencies increase. In effect, the outside debts grow as larger magnitudes of local currencies are required to pay interest and to retire principal. For example, a British pound could have been used to repay $2.80 worth of debt on November 17, 1967. After the devaluation on November 18, the same pound could retire only $2.40 worth of externally denominated debt.

Another explanation for the observed reluctance to finance affiliate activity with imported borrowings relates to parent investors' desire to motivate and control affiliate operations from a distance. Many companies participating in the NICB study have argued that ready availability of equity capital from the parent is not conducive to maximum performance on the part of affiliate managers; the burden of meeting loan obligations is considered a useful incentive.[8] Parent management can indirectly impose greater control over affiliate investment policy by insisting that affiliates obtain their own local financing. Such a policy to some extent shifts the responsibility for evaluating affiliate financial requests from parent management to sources of financing in the local environment. Additionally, it is frequently contended that managers of nonfinancial firms should concentrate on operating characteristics of the business rather than on financial risk taking. Hence, foreign exchange risks should be avoided.

The conventional accounting treatment of foreign exchange losses also helps to explain management's preference for local borrowing. Realized or unrealized foreign exchange losses are typically reported as extraordinary items in financial statements if they are of material size. It is understandable that treasurers prefer to avoid the incurrence of such losses since directors and stockholders are likely to be unusually responsive to write-offs of this type that can be clearly identified in the financial statements and about which observers have sometimes voiced strong opinions. A foreign exchange loss is likely to make a more pronounced impression on observers than losses occasioned by more customary adversities such as technological obsolescence. The following comment of a treasurer in a speech made recently to a group of security analysts reflects this attitude: "The extraordinary exchange losses which had plagued us for a number of years and which in 1959 exceeded $18 million have disappeared." A few years earlier the company had begun to borrow local currencies in significant amounts to minimize exposure. The fact that the company has paid substantial interest burden premiums to borrow in soft

[8] *Ibid.*

currencies countries and that these premiums, in effect, have been substituted for the former foreign exchange losses was not mentioned by the treasurer.

The vast majority of companies in the NICB study expressed the opinion that the advantages of local debt outweigh the higher cost of these instruments. Company spokesmen argue that the local debt's higher cost is typically recovered through higher prices and that although profit margins could theoretically be increased by raising less costly extended financing, the higher costs of local borrowing are justified by virtue of the protection against devaluation and possible laxity of local management that local borrowings afford.[9]

Thus for a variety of reasons an international investor may adopt a local borrowing rule. In making this decision, however, the investor should be fully aware of its consequences. The investor must recognize that it is frequently impossible to obtain adequate local financing. In countries where the exchange risk is significant, normal sources of capital are usually loathe to negotiate long-term or even medium-term credit. Public issues of bonds are virtually impossible to place since locally denominated credits offer investors no protection against depreciation and devaluation. Consequently, adherence to a local debt only policy may stunt the growth of affiliates forced to depend on local sources of financing for planned expansions.

Moreover, the commitment to a policy of local borrowing to avoid foreign exchange risks is usually quite costly. Even short-term bank loans denominated in local currencies carry interest rates that seem unusually high by United States standards, although the true cost of local borrowing may be greatly reduced by anticipated deterioration in the local currency. The cost of insurance against foreign exchange losses can be measured as the interest rate differential between locally denominated debt and otherwise identical hard currency instruments. In recent years these interest rate differentials have been substantial. For example, during 1967 when high quality borrowers could obtain United States dollar loans in the 5½–6 per cent range, similar obligations denominated in cruzeiros or Argentine pesos might cost as much as 40 per cent. Hence, a policy that saddles affiliates with large blocks of locally denominated debt may very well deprive both the affiliates and the parent company of substantial profits.

In some instances it has been possible to avoid foreign exchange risks while supplying affiliates with imported debt financing. Various hedging instruments have been devised that enable investors under certain circumstances to make available hard currency financing and at the same time to insure against the losses caused by devaluation. Usually these hedging

[9] *Ibid.*, p. 102.

devices have been available on a short-term basis only (90 or 180 days) and for this reason the instruments have been unsuitable for permanent financing. Additionally, hedging is costly—as the next chapter on temporary financing indicates.

Although preferences for local debt and hedging devices are understandable, the investor should carefully appraise the related consequences. Potential costs should be analyzed both in terms of higher financial charges and investment opportunities foregone. To the extent that unhedged risks are tolerable, the cost of insuring against foreign exchange losses can be compared with anticipated benefits. To make such a comparison the investor must revert to his earlier predictions of interest rates, inflationary indices, and impending devaluations. The reader can refer to page 145, a schematic for risk assessment and avoidance, as well as to the text in chapter 3 which contains suggestions for developing these environmental projections.

A systematic comparison of the relative costs of local versus imported borrowings begins with an analysis of interest rate differentials and anticipated variations in relative price levels.[10] Momentarily ignoring the effect of changes in exchange rates, the real cost of local borrowing can be represented by subtracting the rate of anticipated inflationary gain or loss from the rate of interest charged by local lenders. That is:

Borrowing Cost = interest rate − rate of inflation or deflation

$$\text{EBC} = I_x - \left[\frac{p^1{}_x - p^0{}_x}{p^0{}_x}\right]$$

where EBC = Explicit borrowing cost (the real cost of debt except for the possible impact of debt increments on common equity costs)

I_x = the effective rate of interest in country x (the stated rate of interest adjusted for invisibles such as compensating balance requirements)

$p^1{}_x$ = estimated end-of-period price level in country x and

$p^0{}_x$ = initial price level in country x

For example, assume that the firm can borrow locally in country x at 30 per cent per annum. Management expects prices in country x to rise 20 per cent. Hence, the cost of explicit borrowing is 10 per cent (30 per cent minus 20 per cent).[11]

[10] The approach suggested here is similar in most respects to the analysis of borrowing costs recommended by Richard Robinson, *International Management*, New York, Holt, Rinehart & Winston, Inc., 1967, pp. 110–13.

[11] Note that if the expected rate of inflation exceeds the effective rate of interest, borrowing costs are negative.

As a next step, the explicit cost of imported debt from country y can be calculated. It consists of the effective rate of interest in country x.

If the investor is considering debt obtainable in country y as an alternative to local financing in country x, the relation between interest charges and price levels in country x are compared with the rate of interest in country y. For example, the investor might conclude that the cost of borrowing in country y is only 7 per cent, since loans can be obtained from banks at an effective 7 per cent rate.

Placing local and imported borrowing alternatives side by side, the alternatives can then be compared:

EBC in country x

$$\frac{I_x P^0_x - [P^1_x - P^0_x]\,.100}{P^0_x} \qquad\qquad \frac{I_y}{P^0_y}$$

where the symbols are defined as previously. In our example the explicit borrowing cost in country x is 10 per cent. In country y money can effectively be borrowed for 7 per cent. The relative rates would suggest that imported debt from country y is preferable due to the anticipated cost savings.

Yet our analysis thus far has ignored one crucial consideration—that is, the possibility of changes in the currency exchange rate between countries x and y. Borrowing from country y during the year is 3 per cent cheaper only if the exchange rate remains the same during the year. If on the other hand, there is a devaluation in country x, borrowing in country y is indicated only if the loss caused by the devaluation is less than the effective cost differential. In general terms the investor should borrow in country y if

Explicit cost saving is greater than *estimated exchange loss*

$$\overbrace{EBC_x - EBC_y} > \overbrace{\frac{R^1_x - R^0_x}{R^0_x}}$$

where R^1_x = estimated exchange rate for currencies of countries x and y at end of period

R^0_x = initial exchange rate for currencies of countries x and y and

EBC_y and EBC_x = defined as previously

In the context of our example a devaluation in country x of more than 3 per cent would obviate the cost advantage of borrowing in country y. Obviously if country y's currency is devalued in relation to country x's, the advantage of financing in country y is further enhanced.

Thus, the investor must relate his previous calculation of the differential in local versus imported borrowing costs to predictions of exchange rate conditions. If the rate of exchange deterioration is expected to exceed the differential in explicit borrowing costs, local borrowing is indicated. Otherwise the indicated cost savings favor imported borrowing. Obviously the investor can also substitute probability distribution estimates for the single point estimates of relative price levels and exchange rates in the calculations.

Comparing the various elements that contribute to the ultimate costs of local versus imported borrowing, the investor is able to select the alternative which he expects to be least costly. Adhering to the dictates of the prescribed format, the investor uses imported debt whenever explicit cost savings are expected to exceed foreign exchange losses. To the extent that these predictions prove accurate the firm incurs lower financing costs than would otherwise be the case. Additionally, willingness to finance affiliates with imported debt may enable the investor to undertake projects that could not be financed following a local borrowing only rule. Thus in addition to reducing borrowing costs, a policy that permits the assumption of foreign exchange risks may very well contribute to more expansive involvement abroad.

Regardless of whether the investor is willing to assume foreign exchange risks or not, he must estimate explicit borrowing costs for capital budgeting purposes. The real cost of debt can be computed as follows: the explicit cost of borrowing is equivalent to the effective interest rate minus the expected rate of increase in the local price level if the debt instrument is denominated in the local currency. If imported debt is used the explicit cost consists of the effective interest rate adjusted for both price level increases and expected deterioration in the exchange relationship between the imported currency and the local currency. Anticipated foreign exchange losses must be considered in calculating the cost of imported debt since repayment of this debt involves movement through the exchange market at the rates that prevail when payments are made.

Clearly the financial risk posture of the investor ultimately affects borrowing costs. The investor's willingness (or unwillingness) to assume foreign exchange risks influences the financial package that he selects for foreign affiliates. If the investor is willing to assume foreign exchange risks he can choose between local and imported debt on the basis of comparative cost and risk calculations. The investor who is unwilling to assume foreign exchange risks is restricted merely in terms of the number of borrowing alternatives. Using either cost or risk avoidance criteria to identify appropriate sources of borrowing, the investor computes the explicit cost of the selected borrowings. In the case of imported borrowings, changes in the anticipated exchange rates are explicitly included in the cost calculations together with effective interest rates and price level judgments. Naturally borrowing costs are lower for the investor willing to assume foreign exchange risks unless local borrowing in a particular instance proves to be cheaper than credits obtained from sources outside the country. If hedging devices are employed to insure against foreign exchange risks, cost premiums paid may also be implied.

ADJUSTMENTS IN CASH FLOW ESTIMATES TO ACCOUNT FOR COST PREMIUMS

The investor is now ready to incorporate financial cost implications in the capital budgeting decision. Of necessity this step has been postponed until a series of interrelated decisions could be made regarding capital structure for a particular foreign affiliate. First it has been necessary for the investor to appraise the desirability of outside participation in affiliate ownership, a decision that in all likelihood was based on both financial and nonfinancial considerations. If joint ownership was deemed advisable, it has also been necessary for the investor to decide on the appropriate proportion of outside equity capital. Control implications, legal considerations, anticipated fiscal consequences, and assessments of capital availability have influenced this judgment. The total amount of equity capital prescribed for the affiliate reflects the investor's judgments regarding company-wide (or affiliate) debt capacity, government and lender limitations on borrowing, cash flow characteristics of the affiliate's contemplated activities, and the likely impact of leverage on company-wide capital costs. The investor's choice of self-financing instruments—common stock, advances, and parent loans—has been resolved after consideration of transfer cost implications. Similarly, decisions regarding local versus imported debt reflect the investor's risk posture, earlier identification of borrowing alternatives and appraisal of comparative borrowing costs. Thus by making a series of decisions regarding capital structure ingredients, the investor has been able to identify the appropriate financing plan for the particular foreign affiliate (or affiliate project). As we saw earlier, willingness or unwillingness to assume foreign exchange risks has influenced the selection of a financial package for a particular foreign affiliate. Naturally, unless local borrowing and credit swaps have proven to be cheaper than unhedged positions, financial costs are lower for the investor following cost minimization rather than risk avoidance criteria.

The explicit costs of debt and equity instruments proposed for the particular foreign affiliate (or affiliate project) can now be compared with corresponding explicit costs for debt and equity obtained in the least costly markets to which the international investor has access. All cost premiums associated with the proposed financing plan are treated as incremental outflows in the cast flow projections used to assess affiliate (or project) profitability.

RISKY INVESTMENTS: THEIR EFFECT ON COMPANY-WIDE COST OF CAPITAL CALCULATIONS

Chapter 5 suggested approaches for dealing with the uncertainty inherent in proposed direct investment opportunities without adjusting the discount rate (the company-wide cost of capital). It is important at this juncture to consider the effect of changes in the general risk characteristics of the international firm on the company-wide cost of capital. If the international firm accepts and implements a project which increases the business risk characteristics of the firm as a whole, the cost of parent equity capital is likely to increase; as investors become aware of the increased risk, share prices will decline. At the same time, the cost of debt capital (both locally and externally) may also increase since lenders are likely to demand higher interest rates to compensate for the increased risk in the company. When the general risk characteristics of the firm change as the result of a new project, it is no longer appropriate to evaluate all investment opportunities using a single, company-wide cost of capital. Consideration must be given to the effect of the acceptance of a proposed investment opportunity on the company-wide cost of capital.

A logical approach to the required adjustment has been suggested by G. David Quirin in *The Capital Expenditure Decision.*[12] Quirin argues that a change in the risk characteristics of the firm as a whole causes a change in the company-wide cost of capital used as the discount rate. The risk characteristics of the firm as a whole are measured as follows:

1. First, the investor computes the standard deviation of the probability distribution of net inflows for all company investments, including the proposed project under consideration
2. Then the calculated standard deviation is divided by the mean of this probability distribution
3. The resulting measure, the coefficient of variation, suggests the degree of risk inherent in the firm's investment activities and is used to adjust the company-wide cost of capital calculation
4. The adjusted company-wide cost of capital calculation is then used as the discount factor to measure the net present value of all existing investments plus the new proposed investment.

Unless the proposed investment opportunity maintains or increases the net present value of the firm's portfolio of investments, it is rejected.

Summary

In chapter 6 we have argued that ordinarily a single, company-wide cost of capital measure should be used as the discount factor in apprais-

[12] *See* G. David Quirin, *The Capital Expenditure Decision,* Homewood, Ill., Richard D. Irwin, Inc., 1967, pp. 223–49.

ing foreign affiliate (or project) profitability. The exception to the rule involves proposed projects that are expected to change the general risk characteristics of the international firm and that consequently increase company-wide capital costs. If proposed projects fall into the latter category, the company-wide cost of capital measure should be adjusted accordingly for purposes of project evaluation.

The company-wide cost of capital is an imputed measure. It reflects what the international firm's financial costs would be if the least costly combination of financial instruments to which the firm has access were selected. For a variety of reasons the international investor is likely to select a combination of financial instruments for its numerous foreign affiliates that have costs in excess of the ideal company-wide cost of capital measure. Restrictions in various capital and money markets, government regulations regarding ownership and financial arrangements, and investor attitude regarding the assumption of risk may contribute to a more costly financial structure for the firm as a whole. Subject to the various constraints which confront the international firm, appropriate financial plans for individual affiliates and for the firm as a whole should be identified. The costs that characterize these financial plans should then be measured. Finally all cost premiums associated with the plans should be included in the outflow projections developed to appraise affiliate (or project) profitability.

BIBLIOGRAPHY

Arditti, Fred C. "Risk and the Required Return on Equity," *Journal of Finance*, March 1967.

Barges, Alexander. *The Effect of Capital Structure on the Cost of Capital.* (Englewood Cliffs, N.J.: Prentice-Hall, Inc., 1963).

Beranek, William. *The Effect on Leverage on the Market Value of Common Stock*, Madison, Wis.: University of Wisconsin, Bureau of Business Research and Service, 1964.

Bodenhorn, Diran. "On the Problem of Capital Budgeting," *Journal of Finance*, December 1958.

Durand, David. "Costs of Debt and Equity Funds for Business: Trends and Problems of Measurement," reprinted in *The Management of Corporate Capital*, Ezra Solomon, ed. (New York: The Free Press, 1959), pp. 91–116.

Financing Foreign Operations, Business International Corporation.

Financing International Operations. (New York: American Management Association, 1966).

Fisher, Edward P. "Financing Foreign Operations," *Financial Executive*, October 1964.

Friedland, J. Seymour. *The Economics of Corporate Capital*, Part II. (Englewood Cliffs, N.J.: Prentice-Hall, Inc., 1966).

Gordon, Myron J. *The Investment, Financing and Valuation of the Corporation.* (Homewood, Ill.: Richard D. Irwin, Inc., 1962).

Lintner, John. "The Cost of Capital and Optimal Financing of Corporate Growth," *Journal of Finance,* May 1963, reprinted in *Foundations for Financial Management,* James Van Horne, ed. (Homewood, Ill.: Richard D. Irwin, Inc., 1966), pp. 460–478.

———. "Dividends, Earnings Leverage, Stock Prices and the Supply of Capital to Corporations," *Review of Economics and Statistics,* August 1962.

Miller, Merton H., and Franco Modigliani. "Cost of Capital, to Electric Utility Industry," *American Economic Review,* June 1966.

———. "The Cost of Capital, Corporation Finance and the Theory of Investment," *American Economic Review,* June 1958, reprinted in *Foundations for Financial Management,* James Van Horne, ed. (Homewood, Ill.: Richard D. Irwin, Inc., 1966), pp. 367–405.

———. "The Cost of Capital, Corporation Finance and the Theory of Investment: Reply," *American Economic Review,* September 1958. "Taxes and the Cost of Capital: A Correction," *Ibid.,* June 1963. "Reply," *Ibid.,* June 1965.

Mock, Edward J. "Financing Overseas Subsidiaries and Evaluating Their Earning," *Business Topics,* Summer 1964.

Polk, Judd, Lawrence Meister, and Laurence Veit. *U.S. Production Abroad and the Balance of Payments.* (New York: National Industrial Conference Board Study, 1966).

Quirin, G. David. *The Capital Expenditure Decision.* (Homewood, Ill.: Richard D. Irwin, Inc., 1967), chs. 5, 6.

Robichek, Alexander A., and Stewart C. Myers. *Optimal Financing Decisions.* (Englewood Cliffs, N.J.: Prentice-Hall, Inc., 1965), pp. 79–93.

Robinson, Richard D. *International Management.* (New York: Holt, Rinehart and Winston, Inc., 1967).

Schwarts, Eli. "Theory of the Capital Structure of the Firm," *Journal of Finance,* March 1959, reprinted in *Foundations for Financial Management,* James Van Horne, ed. (Homewood, Ill.: Richard D. Irwin, Inc., 1966), pp. 413–433.

Smith, Dan T. "Financial Variables in International Business," *Harvard Business Review,* January-February 1966.

Van Horne, James C. *Financial Management and Policy.* (Englewood Cliffs, N.J.: Prentice-Hall, Inc., 1968).

Wippern, Ronald F. "Financial Structure and the Value of the Firm," *Journal of Finance,* December 1966.

Case 10
ZWEISS ASSOCIATES

In the summer of 1967 the board of directors of Zweiss Associates was studying the latest developments in the negotiations being conducted with the Provisional Government of Sebaca. The negotiations concerned the ownership and financial arrangements for a fully integrated steel mill to be located in Sebaca. The project had been originally conceived by three major United States companies, Zweiss Company, Carsons Company, and MacKenzie International, that formed a joint venture, Zweiss Associates, for the development of the project.

The Steel Mill

The integrated steel mill including coke ovens, blast furnaces, oxygen process, steelmaking, and rolling mills was envisioned to produce initially 400,000 metric tons of ingots per year from local raw materials, and with rolling and finishing facilities, to process 300,000 ingot tons into 210,000 tons of flat rolled products for the Sebacan domestic market. It was also intended that the mill sell 75,000 metric tons of ingots per year to a steel plant owned by the Sebacan government. The mill was to be designed to accommodate an ultimate expansion to one million tons of products per year as Sebaca's requirements for flat rolled steel products increased. Statistical projections and physical surveys indicated that Sebaca's iron and steel requirements would increase quickly and would reach an annual level of at least 1½ million tons by 1976.

Zweiss Associates had earlier contracted with the Sebacan government to engineer and supervise all phases of the construction of the plant. Zweiss Company was the prime contractor for the engineering and construction of the plant and additionally was engaged to manage the plant for a fee once commercial operations began. Carsons Company and MacKenzie International were subcontractors providing machinery and equipment for the project not supplied by Zweiss. Sebacan labor and Sebacan subcontractors were to be employed under the supervision of Zweiss Company. Except for the items which could be purchased on favorable credit terms from European countries, all machinery and equipment were to be purchased in the United States.

From a preliminary comparison of costs, it was envisaged that Zweiss would probably supply the blast furnace, the oxygen furnace shop, and the material handling system at a cost of approximately $70 million; Carsons Company, the mechanical equipment for the combination mill, hot strip mill, cold mill, temper mill, and the cleaning and finishing lines at a cost of $15 million; and MacKenzie International, the power plant, generators, and all the necessary mill motors and controls for $35 million.

It had been decided that the plant would be situated in Dvola, Sebaca, because of the proximity of iron ore and coking coal deposits. Privately conducted ore surveys indicated that a total of 7,650,000 tons of proven high quality ore reserves were available, an amount sufficient to operate the mill at initial capacity for approximately twenty years.[1] It was planned that ore would be supplied from privately owned mines that would be developed either by the owners themselves or as a joint effort with the project. Coal was to be supplied from government owned coal mines. Limestone was to be produced for the mill by private contractors who would deliver the limestone to the plant by truck or rail. Power was to be supplied from a government power plant.

Although the initial plant would be relatively small and thus somewhat costly in terms of investment per unit of production, it was agreed that the products of the mill would be sold at a price sufficient to give the company a satisfactory return after taxes and expenses from the outset. Both the Sebacan government and Zweiss Associates recognized that this would require pricing the plant's products above the costs of imported materials duirng the early stages of production but believed that the program for rapid expansion of volume would result in lower unit costs and would make competitive pricing possible. The Sebacan government had tentatively agreed to allow Zweiss Associates to establish a pricing policy that would guarantee an income of not less than 30 per cent of the book value of the plant's capital shares, with the limitation that one-half of net earnings be retained for expansion. A pro forma profit and loss statement appears as Exhibit 1.

Total initial capital required for the project was estimated at $200,000,000. Because of the magnitude of the capital requirements, Zweiss Associates sought major amounts of funds from government sources. The United States government in 1965 had tentatively agreed to help finance the project through the Agency for International Development (AID). Because of AID's special interest in this project and previous large-scale loans for industrial development in Sebaca, Zweiss Associates anticipated that a large share of the financing could be obtained from the government agency.

Negotiations between the Sebacan government and Zweiss Associates had begun in 1965.

Investment Climate in Sebaca

In the early 1950's Sebaca could still be classified as a developing nation. GNP growth was 4 per cent; 80 per cent of the population of 34 million was engaged in agriculture. Per capita income was $425. Yet more than one half of national income accrued to less than 10 per cent of the population, and 60 per cent of the population was illiterate.

Sebaca's principal exports consisted of agricultural products subject to wide price fluctuations and elasticity of demand. Industrial development had progressed only marginally under state control. The state-owned industries in which 65 per cent of nonagricultural workers were employed constituted 40 per cent of Sebaca's industrial capacity. For the most part, however, the industries were inefficient and inadequate for Sebaca's future development. Private investment

[1] Probable ore reserves totalled 17,750,000 metric tons.

was limited to small-scale enterprises, as the domestic supply of capital could not be mobilized easily due to uncertainty and inflationary conditions; private investors preferred investment opportunities abroad. Foreign direct investment was also insignificant.

In 1956 the Sebacan government inaugurated its first Five-Year Plan to induce more rapid industrialization. By establishing import-substituting industries, the government hoped to ease the pressure on its foreign exchange position and to relieve the economic chaos in the larger cities by providing employment for agricultural workers who had emigrated to the crowded cities.

Also in 1956 the government and the World Bank established an Industrial Development Bank to accelerate the growth of private industry and the development of a Sebacan capital market.

The forced transition from agrarian to industrial economy was especially difficult. The external credits available to the country as well as its own supply of foreign exchange were insufficient to carry out the degree of industrial expansion at the rate which the government had planned. In an effort to maintain its program the government resorted to deficit financing and obtained additional external credits. By 1964 foreign debt had attained unmanageable proportions especially in view of the severe inflation. The cost of living had doubled from 1959, and the value of the currency on the free market, that had developed in response to the inflated economy had declined greatly.

In 1964 the government consulted the IMF and following its advice implemented a stabilization program in the same year. Yet deficiencies in the government monetary and fiscal policies persisted. Unemployment and inflation continued, and by 1965 the additional foreign exchange credits granted by the IMF to Sebaca were exhausted.

A poor harvest in the fall of 1965 added to Sebaca's economic problems. Economic discontent found expression in political opposition to the Modugno regime and culminated in a popularly supported coup d' état and the establishment of a provisional government in May 1966.

To halt inflation and to conserve foreign exchange necessary to meet their commitments, the provisional government rigorously implemented IMF recommendations, including an attempt to balance the budget, elimination of extraordinary expenditures, and the restriction of nonessential imports. The provisional government actively sought direct private foreign investment as a means to continue the industrialization program and to achieve the now moderated goals of the original Five-Year Plan.

Project Benefits

Because of the long- and short-term contributions that it would make to the economy, the provisional government was especially interested in the steel mill. Foreign exchange savings could be made directly by the domestic production of steel and indirectly by the domestic production of secondary industrial goods. New employment opportunities would be created not only in the mill but also in the many secondary industries that could be expected to develop in the consumer durable industries, transportation industries, and agricultural equipment industries.

The state-owned iron and steel industry established in 1949 for the production of rails, sections, and structurals for the railway and construction industries had never been able to produce enough iron and steel to satisfy the country's increasing needs. During the previous twenty years steel imports, including mill and finished iron and steel products, had increased from 65 per cent to 75 per cent of consumption. For the past five years an average of $12 million per year of foreign exchange had been spent for the importation of the types of mill products that were to be produced at the new plant.

A reliable and eventually low cost supply of raw materials would invigorate and expand the production of consumer durables by encouraging Sebaca's established manufacturers to expand production facilities. New producers would be encouraged to start production. Other types of secondary industries could be established throughout the country, making employment available to villages in which agricultural overemployment was endemic.

The established freight and passenger transportation network provided by the railroad could be expected to improve and develop as more flat products for new rolling stock and rail replacements were made available.

Farm implements and machines are constructed from flat mill products, and the establishment of an industry that produced modern equipment could be expected to improve the supply and quality of farm equipment, which would stimulate the adaptation of more modern farming techniques.

Most important, the steel mill, developed in part by foreign private capital, would stimulate new foreign private capital investments that in turn would help to mobilize domestic capital resources.

The direct and indirect benefits from the project would also redound to the credit of United States private and government investors. This was especially significant, as the United States government was anxious to maintain favorable relations with the Sebacan government. From the United States government's point of view, the project not only would aid the economic viability of a strategically valuable country, but also would strengthen a vital link in an important chain of defense.

The Position of the Provisional Government

The provisional government agreed to honor legislation passed in 1966 by the Sebacan National Assembly that stipulated that the imports for the project would be exempted from various kinds of excise taxes and customs duties and that raw materials purchased by the project directly or indirectly from government-controlled enterprises would be priced in a fair manner.

The provisional government also assured Zweiss Associates that the project would be protected by the Sebacan Foreign Investment Encouragement Law of 1960 which granted *inter alia*, equity holders of companies the right of unrestricted repatriation of profits and capital.

The provisional government also made known its intention to continue the plans started in the Modugno regime for the establishment of a Mining Development Bank to help finance independent ore miners and thereby ensure a constant supply of raw material for the plant.

Zweiss Associates were also assured by the provisional government that the latter intended to make the investments for the development of the country's infrastructure which the Modugno regime had promised—in particular, provision of adequate rail, highway, and ocean transport, including ore boats, docks, and port facilities to meet the transportation requirements of the project. The provisional government also restated the assurance made by the previous regime that it would use its own funds to build the units needed to house the plant's operating personnel, and that independent Sebacan developers would provide facilities for housing construction workers. Zweiss Associates had estimated that these infrastructure projects that the government promised would cost approximately $90 million.

The provisional government, however, would not agree to the ownership and financial package which the Modugno regime had accepted. This previous arrangement specified that the project would be owned primarily by Sebacans and United States shareholders and that the debt/equity ratio would be approximately 3:1. (See Exhibit 2.) Details of the earlier financial proposal were as follows:

> The Modugno government proposed to subscribe initially to $28.9 million, or 57.6 per cent of the equity although it would elect only four of the nine directors of the company. Within five years after the commencement of operations, the government was to make half of its shares available to Sebacan private investors. As the government sold off its shares, the number of directors that it could elect would be correspondingly reduced from four to two.
>
> The arrangement proposed by the Modugno government also stipulated that $9.3 million of equity would be initially offered to the Sebacan private sector, entitling the private shareholders to elect two of the nine directors. To encourage the Sebacan private investors to buy shares, the Modugno regime proposed that all privately held Sebacan capital shares should receive a 6 per cent dividend from the date of paid-in subscription. The incentive funds were to be advanced by the government as described below. The Modugno regime further indicated a willingness to pick up the unsubscribed shares offered to the Sebacan private sector, although these shares would carry no voting power.
>
> Zweiss Associates were asked to subscribe for $10.2 million or 20.3 per cent of the equity. Other private United States suppliers were expected to subscribe for $1.7 million or 3.4 per cent of the equity; Zweiss Associates were asked to absorb any of the shares offered but not subscribed by the other United States suppliers. The United States private investors would elect three members to the board of directors.
>
> The approximately $158 million debt was to be funded by (1) $110 million from AID for twenty years at 5 3/4 per cent; (2) $17 million from various European Suppliers; (3) $17 million in loans from the Sebacan Government for twenty years at 5 3/4 per cent; (4) $9 million worth of interest capitalized during construction; (5) $740,000 noninterest-bearing loans by the Sebacan government with the interest equivalent used to pay the 6 per cent divided on paid-in capital stock of Sebacans; and (6) $4,260,000 of debentures to be subscribed by private United States investors.

The provisional government could neither understand nor accept the acquiescence of the Modugno regime. Historically the industrial sector of the Sebacan economy had been controlled by the government. It was inconceivable to the provisional government that as vital an industry as steel should be controlled privately by foreigners and by Sebacans who had no knowledge of management decision making.

Nor was the provisional government sympathetic to the position that AID had indicated a preference for private control of the project, expecially since it and other United States loan agencies had previously helped to finance government-owned industries. Regardless of the ownership of the mill, the substantial sums involved in the sale of United States goods and services would aid the United States balance-of-payments position. And the whole project would certainly warm the cockles of the hearts of United States government officials who were interested in influencing the alignment of Sebaca in the Cold War.

The provisional government was equally dissatisfied with the financial structure of the project. It was unsure whether the people of Sebaca would subscribe to $9.3 million worth of capital shares. Although the government believed that there was sufficient wealth in the private sector to absorb the shares, it felt that potential investors would be reluctant to take the shares until the viability of the venture had been assured notwithstanding the 6 per cent dividend. It would be more realistic and successful, the provisional government argued, to offer equity to the private Sebacan sector only after the project had proven successful.

The provisional government was also reluctant to pick up any unsubscribed shares, increasing its already large investment without increasing its control over the project. Its equity participation ($28.9 million) plus investment in infrastructure (approximately $90 million) plus $35 million in other loans and advances did not, according to the provisional government, add up to a subordinate role in the control of the venture.

The provisional government was also displeased with the financial package for other reasons. Zweiss Associates, it felt, were not carrying an equitable proportion of the financial costs in light of their position as major suppliers of goods and services to the project. Specifically, their participation in the equity financing represented only a fraction of the total amount of machinery, equipment, and engineering services that they were to provide in the construction of the plant. While Zweiss Associates were to spend a maximum of $11.9 million for equity, they were to receive over $120 million for their equipment, machinery, and services.

The New Proposal of the Provisional Government

In the light of these arguments the provisional government recommended an ownership and financial package that included several changes:

1. Initial provisional government control of the venture. The provisional government would initially subscribe to a controlling amount of capital shares of the venture and as soon as the private market was ready the government would sell its shares to the Sebacan public
2. An approximate increase of $10 million in equity participation by Zweiss Associates and
3. Zweiss Associates could establish a pricing policy that would guarantee an income of not less than 30 per cent of the book value of the plant's capital shares except that one-half of net earnings must be retained for expansion in Sebaca and the pricing protection would terminate as soon as the long-term debt was liquidated.

Zweiss' Position

Zweiss Associates were not unsympathetic to the posture of the provisional government. However, the whole project assumed a different character in the light of the new financial and ownership proposal of the provisional government. United States Congressional pressure was already beginning to develop in response to AID's planned participation in the project. Despite assurances from the IMF and the United States State Department that the provisional government was exceedingly competent and that it was applying in good faith all the measures necessary to stabilize the economy, several influential United States Congressional leaders expressed general concern over AID's involvement in publicly controlled projects abroad, and in particular, in the Sebacan steel mill venture.

Although this project was large and therefore likely to be subject to Congressional review, Zweiss Associates were of the opinion that an AID loan could be obtained within the framework of the provisional government's counter proposal. One positive factor concerned the expressed willingness of the Sebacan provisional government to distribute shares to private investors as soon as there was a prospect of market acceptance. A second positive factor concerned the strategic location of Sebaca and the definite possibility of Sebaca's receiving financial aid from the Soviet Union in the event that United States participation fell through.

Yet despite the probable participation of AID, Zweiss Associates were not sure that what was best for AID was necessarily best for its interests. Concern centered on several factors. In the first place the new government was a revolutionary regime and had yet to establish itself in an underdeveloped country. Domestic economic requirements and international economic commitments required that the government allocate its scarce resources quite carefully. Given Sebaca's limited financial resources, Zweiss Associates recognized that the expenses of this project would compete with other needs of the economy and that an unfavorable resolution of priorities could result in the slowdown or indefinite postponement of necessary infrastructure development. Zweiss Associates were quite conscious of the extent to which completion of the steel complex was dependent on the fulfillment of government promises.

Although the investors had management responsibility in the project, control of the venture by the government raised potential problems. Once the project had commenced operations, for example, any of a number of developments could lead the government to withdraw support of the guaranteed 30 per cent return on equity. One such possible development could conceivably revolve around the maintenance of artificial prices that, in the economic environment of Sebaca, could result in inflation, increases in raw material and transportation prices, and consequent curtailment of demand.

These factors assumed greater importance in light of the provisional government's counter proposal that requested the United States investors to increase substantially their equity participation in the project. The larger their participation, Zweiss Associates realized, the more dependent they were on the viability of the project in order to recover their investment.

Zweiss Associates realized that the after-tax contribution to profits of the

$120 million worth of goods and services sold to the project would amount to almost $20 million concentrated in the second and third year of plant operation. Yet many things could happen within these two or three years.

Naturally Zweiss Associates were reluctant to withdraw from the project completely. Much time, money, and effort had been devoted to negotiations, explorations, and feasibility studies.

EXHIBIT 1

Sebacan Steel Plant
Projected Profit and Loss Statements
Based on Financial Plan
Accepted by Modugno Regime (dollar figures in thousands)

	YEAR		
	1	*2*	*3*
Sales value of products	$71,051	$76,979	$80,951
Estimated expenses*			
Cost of sales	27,602	29,724	28,906
Selling, general, administrative expense	3,078	2,585	2,533
Depreciation	10,867	10,867	10,867
Operating period interest	10,377	9,756	9,137
Amortization – deferred interest	521	521	521
Allowance – doubtful accounts	260	40	
Total expenses	$52,705	$53,493	$51,964
Net income – before bonuses and taxes	18,346	23,486	28,987
Bonuses and incentives (5%)	569	728	899
Taxable income	$17,777	$22,758	$28,088
Provision for income tax (36%)	6,399	8,202	10,112
Net income	$11,378	$14,556	$17,976

* Interest calculations based on financial plan proposed by Zweiss Associates and accepted by Modugno Regime.

EXHIBIT 2

Sebacan Steel Plant
Capital Structure Accepted by Modugno Regime
(dollar figures in thousands)

	Amount	Per cent of total capital	Per cent of equity
Debt			
AID —twenty years— 5 3/4%	$110,204*	52.9	
European suppliers' credits —eight years	17,000	8.2	
	$127,204	61.1	
Subordinated Sebacan loan twenty years — 4 3/4%	16,871	8.1	
Interest capitalized during construction	8,925†	4.3	
Noninterest-bearing advance by Minister of Finance for payment of 6% dividend on paid-in capital stock	742	0.4	
	$153,743	73.9	
Debentures			
Class A — four years — 7% with warrants convertible into capital stock	1,700	0.8	
Class B — seven year — 7% — guaranteed by sponsors	2,550	1.2	
Total debt	$157,993	75.9	
Capital Stock			
Sebacan public sector	$ 28,900	13.9	57.6
Sebacan private sector	9,350	4.5	18.7
Total Sebacan	$ 38,250	18.4	76.3
Zweiss Associates	10,200	4.9	20.3
Other U.S. suppliers‡	1,700	0.8	3.4
Total capital stock	$ 50,150	24.1	100.0
Total initial capital	$208,144	100.0	

* It is assumed that principal and interest on $26,500,000 of these loans would be paid in United States dollars and that principal and interest on the balance, $83,704,000 would be paid in Sebacan currency.

† Interest during construction would not be payable currently (except for debentures) but would be capitalized and amortized with borrowings.

‡ Zweiss Associates would agree to subscribe for any of these shares not taken by other United States suppliers.

Case 11
LAMCO—Part B

On November 15, 1963, President William Tubman of Liberia led a distinguished international group including H.R.H. Prince Bertil of Sweden, officials of the Liberian government, industrialists, financiers, and contractors in ceremonies dedicating the LAMCO joint venture iron ore project. These ceremonies climaxed a decade of effort devoted to the exploration, financing, and construction of mine, railroad, port, and community facilities in Liberia—one of the greatest industrial undertakings in the history of Africa. This major project was undertaken by a joint venture between LAMCO and Bethlehem Steel Corporation in which LAMCO had a 75 per cent interest and Bethlehem a 25 per cent interest. Liberian Iron Ore, Ltd. (LIO), owned 50 per cent of the outstanding shares of LAMCO while the Liberian government owned the other 50 per cent of the outstanding LAMCO shares. (Relationships among the participating parties were described in detail in Part A of the LAMCO case, and diagrammed on page 142.)

Commercial operations began in July 1963, and iron ore production of the joint venture amounted to approximately 2,400,000 tons in 1963. During 1964, its first full fiscal year of commercial operations, LAMCO produced 6,875,000 tons of ore, and in 1965 output reached 8,316,000 tons of ore. During 1965 ore was delivered to customers in Germany, United States, Belgium, Italy, France, the United Kingdom, Japan, Sweden, and the Netherlands under term contracts extending through 1967 or later. These contracts had been arranged by the Grangesberg Company of Sweden, manager of the LAMCO joint venture, and the exclusive sales agent for LAMCO's share of the ore mined by the joint venture. Exhibit 1 breaks down the iron ore sales by country. Comparative financial statements for 1964 and 1965 and notes to the financial statements are shown as Exhibits 2 and 3.

It was recognized during the construction period—1961-1963—that LAMCO must step up ore production from the contemplated 6,000,000 ton capacity in order to meet anticipated sales commitments. The decision was taken in 1962 to increase the budgeted capacity of the project from 6,000,000 to 7,500,000 tons. An additional expansion was approved in 1965 to enlarge future productive capacity to 10,000,000 tons. Because the original design and planning of the project contemplated a capacity of 10,000,000 tons per year when this output level became economically feasible, the cost of the additional physical facilities was comparatively small when contrasted with $191 million required to launch the 6,000,000-ton original project. The expansion consisted principally of additional mining equipment, ore shovels, and trucks; more rolling stock and expanded signal control systems for the railroad; and some expansion of the industrial buildings and community facilities. Notwithstanding the advanced planning for the expansion of capacity, the mining enterprise represented a basic investment of more than $275 million by the end of 1965, and the financial sponsorship of a variety of institutions and individuals was required to support this very substantial investment.

Financing

A series of financings were required to complete the development stages of the project during the 1961-1963 period. LAMCO, on June 14, 1961, entered into credit agreements with the Swedish Syndicate and LIO; the Export-Import Bank in Washington; Kreditanstalt für Wiederaufbau of Frankfurt; and the First National City Bank of New York. Based on the estimated $191 million cost to the joint venture of a 6-million-ton facility, LAMCO's 75 per cent contribution amounted to approximately $143,222,100. Additional expenses, for which LAMCO was alone responsible, including financing charges, commitment fees, interest during construction, and certain other expenses, raised LAMCO's total financial requirement to approximately $152,152,000.

Approximately $88 million (58 per cent) of the total required capital was borrowed in the form of long-term credits, whereas the balance, $63 million (42 per cent) was advanced by the participants in the project from their own resources in various forms. LAMCO received:

1. $1 million from the sale of Class B stock to LIO
2. $10,250,000 in advances from the Swedish Syndicate and IAAC
3. $4,500,000 from Bethlehem as an entrance fee in accordance with the terms of the Joint Venture Agreement (see Part A, the LAMCO case)
4. $38,000,000 in loans from the Swedish Syndicate, evidenced by $38 million principal amount of subordinated debentures
5. $30 million from the Export-Import (Exim) Bank evidenced by 5 3/4 per cent Series A Notes
6. DM208,450,000 (U.S. $52,112,000) from Kreditanstalt für Wiederaufbau, Frankfurt, evidenced by First Lien Collateral Trust Bonds Series B. (Kreditanstalt applied for and obtained a guaranty from the government of West Germany that insured Kreditstalt against default by LAMCO in the service of its loan if default were caused by government action or other events of a political nature within Liberia. The Exim Bank and Kreditanstalt agreements each provided that LAMCO could not obtain loans from either, unless a pro rata amount of the total loan provided by the other was obtained concurrently)
7. $5,700,000 from the First National City Bank evidenced by 6 per cent Series C Notes. (FNCB entered into a guaranty contract with the International Cooperation Administration (ICA) of the United States in which ICA protected FNCB against loss on its loans to LAMCO due to expropriation. LAMCO could not obtain the loan from FNCB until it had received the full $30 million and DM208,450,000 provided for in the Exim Bank and Kreditanstalt Agreement)
8. $10,590,000 was budgeted from cash generated from sales of LAMCO's

share of the ore to be produced during the period between commencement of commercial operations and the completion of the 6-million-ton capacity

(To the extent that internally generated sources proved inadequate because of delays in commencement of commercial operations or because sales were insufficient, the cash would be obtained from short-term borrowing sources.)

The loans were secured primarily by collateral in the form of LAMCO property and were not guaranteed or underwritten by LIO shareholders or by the Liberian government. The lenders, therefore, assumed a substantial share of the commercial and political risks involved. The wide distribution of risk and capital was made possible by American and German government investment guarantees and other institutions specifically organized to grant long-term financial credits to enterprises in developing countries.

Also during the construction period,at the instigation of both the Liberian government and the Export-Import Bank, LAMCO management became aware of the importance of spreading ownership interests in the project as widely as possible throughout Liberia. Accordingly, 298,696 shares of common stock were offered in 1961 to Liberian citizens at a price of $12.30 per share (which represented more than a 20 per cent discount from the then current market price). Payment for the shares was made in installments, $4.80 per share being paid in cash at the time of the subscription, and the balance paid at the rate of $2.40 per share in cash in three years plus $.30 per share for expenses. The Liberian government through the Liberian Development Corporation, guaranteed the obligations of those who subscribed and agreed to purchase any unsubscribed shares. The offering resulted in subscriptions of 100,585 shares by approximately 1,900 Liberians. Since this offering was only partially successful, management felt that Liberian citizens, particularly those in rural areas, should be given another opportunity to subscribe to shares. Consequently LAMCO had a second offering of 198,111 shares during 1963, again underwritten by the Liberian Development Corporation. When this offer expired at the end of 1963, 6,567 shares had been purchased, bringing the total or private Liberian shares to 107,202.

In connection with the $27,500,000 required to expand the production facilities to 7,500,000 tons, the existing creditors—Kreditanstalt, the Export-Import Bank, and First National City Bank agreed to increase their loans to LAMCO by 15 per cent or in the aggregate by $13,172,000. The extended credit from these sources gave rise to the Series D Notes, the Series E Bonds, and the Series F Notes respectively. At the same time the creditors insisted that the equity investors also increase their commitments, in effect requiring LAMCO to provide approximately $8,500,000 of additional funds. The Swedish LAMCO Syndicate provided $7,741,000 through the purchase of senior debentures and the remaining inflows were obtained principally from cash generated by the sale of iron ore during the last half of 1963.

In 1965 LAMCO sought an additional $51,400,000 of external financing to further enlarge and diversify its productive capacity. The major contribution to the financing was obtained from the Exim Bank, which authorized a loan of

$23,130,000, again for the purchase in the United States of machinery, equipment, and services which LAMCO required. As a 25 per cent participant in the LAMCO joint venture, Bethlehem Steel also contributed $12,850,000. LAMCO's 1965 retained earnings contributed another $4,420,000. The remaining $11,000,000 was financed by LIO from the proceeds of the capital stock offering made in March 1966 and from LIO's retained earnings. LIO loaned LAMCO this $11 million, receiving in return an equal principal amount of 6 1/4 per cent junior subordinated debentures due in 1985 ($2 million of the junior subordinated debentures were outstanding by the end of 1965). LIO shareholders were offered the right to subscribe to 659,171 additional shares of capital stock at $14.50 per share, 74.8 per cent of which were subscribed by the Swedish LAMCO Syndicate on a preemptive basis. The remaining 165,999 shares (25.2 per cent of 659,171 shares) were issued publicly in March of 1966 by an underwriting group headed by the First Boston Corporation, White, Weld, and Company, Inc., and the Stockholms Enskilda Bank.

Community Development

A high priority objective of the joint venturers has been to provide modern dwellings and community services for all personnel at the Nimba and Buchanan sites. By 1965 more than 800 dwellings of different types had been completed, and an equal number was planned for the late 1960's to replace all existing construction-camp housing. A scientifically and architecturally modern hospital had been completed by Nimba. International schools were opened in Nimba and Buchanan offering instruction in English and special mother-tongue training for non-English-speaking students. During November of 1966, President William Tubman visited Yekepa and dedicated a church, a school, and "The Open Door," the community's theatre and assembly hall, named for the President's policy that has attracted foreign private investment to help Liberia develop its resources. Other community development construction projects included a sewage treatment plant, site preparations for water and sewage lines, a community assembly hall, and the paving of main roads in the residential areas.

The company attempted to "Liberianize" its labor force, and by the end of 1965 approximately 85 per cent of the 3,754 employees were Liberian citizens. A training program was established in 1964 to prepare Liberian employees for positions of responsibility within the organization. The program provided vocational and on-the-job training, apprenticeships, and scholarships. Correspondence courses were also offered to compensate for lack of formal education and to expand opportunities for job advancement.

Future Prospects

Notwithstanding the intensive training program for Liberians, LAMCO has found it necessary to recruit foreigners to work in critical areas of its operations. At the beginning of 1966 more than 600 aliens representing twenty different nationalities were employed by the company. Liberian government officials continually sought reductions in the non-Liberian workforce despite the concession

The new Lutheran church at Yekepa—Christ the King Church

Erland Waldenstrom, chief executive of the Grängesberg Company and manager of the Joint Venture, and President and Mrs. William V.S. Tubman of Liberia at the dedication of Christ the King Church.

agreement which guaranteed LAMCO the right to employ foreigners wherever necessary. President Tubman's son was retained as a public relations consultant.

More significant, economic discontent was reflected in a rash of strikes which occurred in 1963 against the Firestone Rubber plantation operation in Liberia. In February 1965 a wildcat strike by ore truck drivers developed into a general strike at LAMCO's Nimba facilities. With the assistance of the Liberian government, the National Mineworkers Union of Liberia was formed to represent the workers, and mining operations were continued during the negotiations. In June 1965 a two-year collective bargaining agreement with the union was concluded, granting an average pay increase of approximately 12 per cent retroactive to May 1, 1965. Although the LAMCO strike was settled without interruption in ore deliveries, strikes against other companies created serious problems. Emergency powers were granted to President Tubman by the legislature which authorized him to forbid strikes that threatened state security, to prohibit Liberian labor unions from receiving financial aid from abroad without permission, and to suspend *habeas corpus* when dealing with illegal strikes. Conceivably the severity of this legislation, combined with troop intervention, could provoke more serious labor reaction and opposition to the government and foreign concessions.

Labor's pressure in advancing its claims was evidence not only of economic discontent, but also of a broader social revolution that was beginning to challenge the old power relationships. The Liberian economy was overextended. To finance its development projects, the government had borrowed from a variety of sources, expecting to repay the loans with anticipated revenues from the operations of the concessions in its expanding economy. The increased debt, however, coincided with a drop in the world price for rubber and iron ore and diminution of foreign investment as the installations of the various foreign projects neared completion.

Recently (1966) Liberia has been forced to request special assistance from the International Monetary Fund in arranging to extend the repayment period of outstanding obligations. With one quarter of its revenues earmarked for debt servicing, Liberia has reduced investment in its public sector, laying off workers recruited to build railroads, roads, and mining facilities. There is unemployment at several iron ore mines and in Monrovia itself. School and hospital construction has been curtailed. Economic hardship and disillusionment have resulted. Conceivably, revolution could replace the evolutionary form of development which has characterized Liberia in the past unless these problems are resolved.

EXHIBIT 1

LAMCO Distribution of Ore by Country

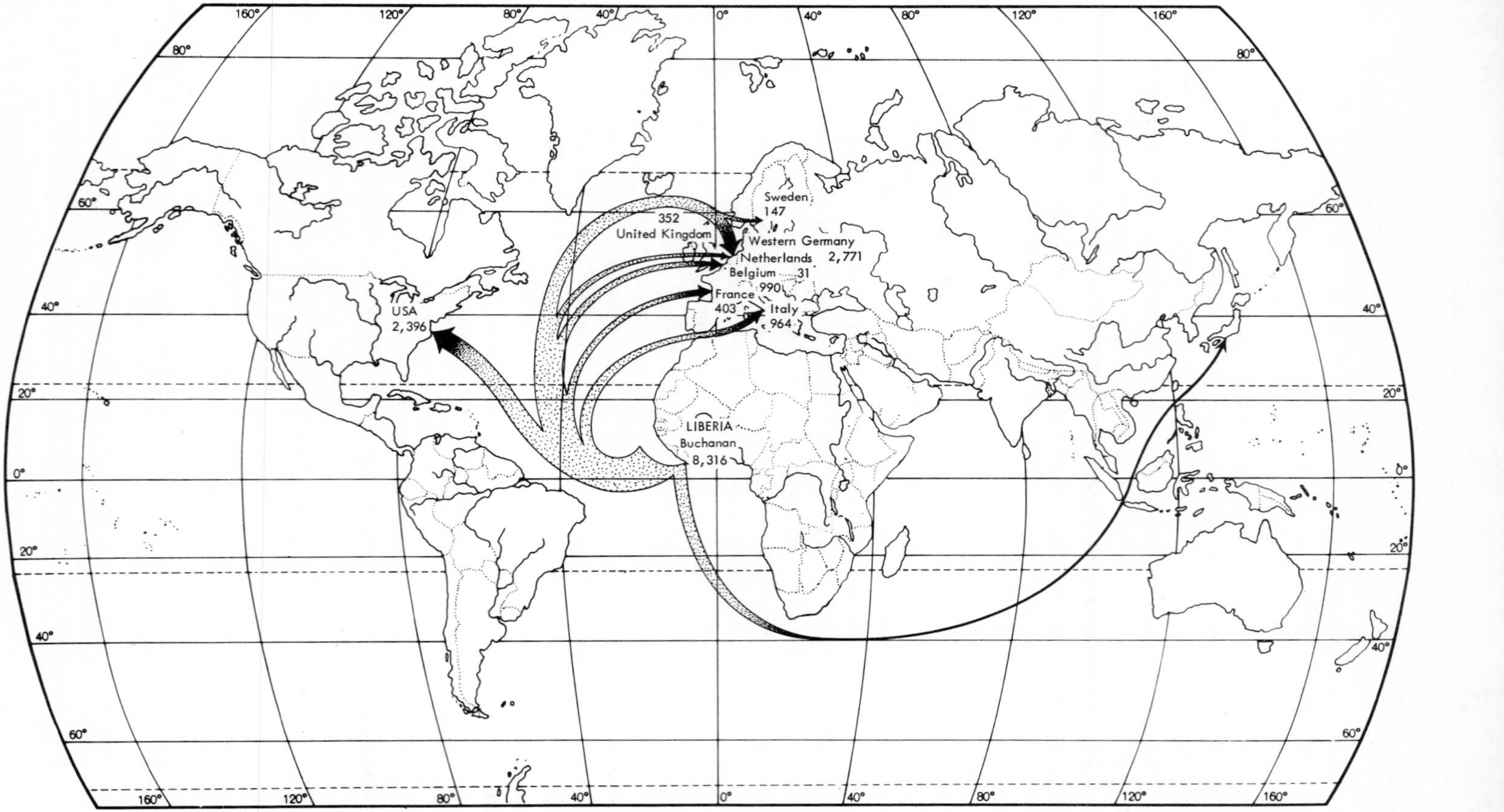

EXHIBIT 2

The Liberian American-Swedish Minerals Company
Balance Sheet (including LAMCO's undivided 75 per cent share of the Assets and Liabilities of the LAMCO Joint Venture)

Assets	DECEMBER 31 *1965*	*1964*
Current assets		
Cash	$ 4,256,558	$ 1,715,875
Accounts receivable		
Trade	2,913,763	3,802,265
Other	528,240	453,657
Inventories (Note 2)		
Ore	2,295,242	1,593,207
Materials and supplies	4,021,116	4,383,724
Prepaid expenses	122,393	31,270
Total current assets	14,137,317	11,979,998
Property and equipment, at cost (Note 3)		
Railway	46,177,491	46,159,746
Harbor	24,115,049	21,679,659
Roads and airstrips	5,986,970	5,784,956
Buildings	20,378,519	19,233,489
Rolling stock	8,815,205	8,229,945
Special purpose structures, machinery, and equipment	34,665,600	34,123,964
Motor vehicles	1,993,513	1,634,597
Boats	844,387	844,347
Heavy duty equipment	3,924,333	3,870,711
	146,901,067	141,561,414
Less – Depreciation	13,640,299	7,955,950
	133,260,768	133,605,464
Construction in progress	3,479,737	4,367,533
	136,740,505	137,972,997
Unamortized exploration and development costs, interest during construction and mining concession (Note 4)	26,798,270	27,408,034
Advance payments to contractors and others	186,013	183,711
Sundry investments	18,750	
Advance payments on account of future dividends		583,333
	$177,880,855	$178,128,073

EXHIBIT 2 (cont.)

Liabilities and capital

Current liabilities		
Short-term tank loans		$ 12,500,000
Accounts payable	$ 2,321,453	2,189,198
Accrued liabilities	892,352	236,962
Accrued interest	1,889,235	4,967,389
Current maturities of long-term debt	3,962,500	4,912,250
Profit credited to stockholders	1,809,705	500,000
Total current liabilities	10,875,245	25,305,799
Long-term debt (Note 5)	142,484,631	133,236,884
Capital		
Capital obligation, noninterest-bearing, payable only in the event of liquidation	12,855,662	12,855,662
Capital stock – authorized and issued (Note 6)		
Class A – 1,000,000 shares $1 par value	1,000,000	1,000,000
Class B – 1,000,000 shares $1 par value	1,000,000	1,000,000
Capital in excess of par value (no change since 1960)	4,500,000	4,500,000
	19,355,662	19,335,662
Reserves, per accompanying statement		
In accordance with Section 5.17 of First Supplemental Bond Indenture	483,767	146,880
For capital expenditures and working capital	4,681,550	82,848
	5,165,317	229,728
	24,520,979	19,585,390
Contractual commitments and contingent liabilities (Note 7)	$177,880,855	$178,128,073

Note: A substantial portion of the above assets have been pledged under an indenture to secure long-term debt (Notes 5 and 8).

Auditor's report

To the Board of Directors of The Liberian American-Swedish Mineral Company: In our opinion the accompanying balance sheet and the related statements of profit and loss and appropriation and disposition of net profit present fairly the financial position of The Liberian American-Swedish Minerals Company at December 31, 1965, and the results of its operations for the year, including its 75 per cent undivided share in the assets and liabilities and cost of production of the LAMCO Joint Venture, in conformity with generally accepted accounting principles applied on a basis consistent with that of the preceding year. Our examination of these statements was made in accordance with generally accepted auditing standards and accordingly included such tests of the accounting records and such other auditing procedures as we considered necessary in the circumstances.

New York, February 24, 1966 — Price Waterhouse & Co.

Statement of profit and loss (including LAMCO's undivided 75% share of the costs of production of the Joint Venture) (Note 1)	*FOR THE YEAR ENDED DECEMBER 31* 1965	1964
Sales	$42,594,831	$33,642,369
Cost of sales		
Production costs	11,319,357	9,758,846
Depreciation (Note 3)	6,168,767	5,975,376
Amortization of intangibles (Note 4)	914,473	759,163
Insurance	268,200	250,591
	18,670,797	16,743,976
Inventory of ore at beginning of period	1,593,207	
Inventory of ore at end of period	(2,295,242)	(1,593,207)
	17,968,762	15,150,769
Gross profit	24,626,069	18,491,600
Selling, general, and administrative expenses		
Selling and other commissions (Note 7)	1,707,239	691,468
General and administrative expenses	660,888	412,233
Insurance	280,505	293,915
Loss on retirement and sale of fixed assets	116,354	254,472
	2,764,986	1,652,088
Income from operations	21,861,083	16,839,512
Royalty to Liberian Government (Note 1)		2,453,328
Interest expense (net)	9,517,425	9,472,517
	9,517,425	11,925,845
Net profit	$12,343,658	$ 4,913,667
Statement of appropriation and disposition of net profit (in accordance with the Concession Agreement) (Note 1)		
Net profit as shown by the statement of profit and loss	$12,343,658	$ 4,913,667
Deficit at beginning of period		(3,683,939)
		1,229,728
Appropriations by board of directors in accordance with the Concession Agreement:		
To reserve in accordance with First Supplemental Bond Indenture Section 5.17:		
Calculated at April 30, 1965		146,880
Calculated at February 15, 1966	336,887	
To reserve for capital expenditures and working capital	4,598,702	82,848
	4,935,589	229,728
Profit as defined by the Concession Agreement for the year credited to stockholders	$ 7,408,069	$ 1,000,000

EXHIBIT 3

Notes to the Financial Statements
December 31, 1965

Note 1 — General:

LAMCO is incorporated under the laws of the Republic of Liberia and its accounts are maintained in U.S. dollars, currency of Liberia.

LAMCO participates with Bethlehem Steel Corporation (Bethlehem) in a joint venture to develop and mine iron ore deposits in the Nimba Mountains in Liberia under a concession granted by the Government of the Republic of Liberia (Government). LAMCO has a 75% interest and Bethlehem a 25% interest in the joint venture. The financial statements of LAMCO reflect LAMCO's 75% undivided share amounting in total to $168,735,112 (net) in such assets and liabilities at December 31, 1965.

The concession expires November 18, 2023 and provides that annually the net profits of LAMCO, as defined in the Concession Agreement, are to be distributed to the owners of the Class A and B shares. The Concession Agreement definition of annual net profits permits the creation of certain reserves; further, from January 1, 1965, under the terms of the indenture covering the Series A, B, C, D, E and F bonds and notes described in Note 5, as long as such bonds and notes are outstanding the company may not distribute as dividends certain amounts depending on the amount of A and D notes outstanding and other factors. The maximum that may not be distributed under this provision is $466,260 per year. The amount shown in the attached financial statements as "Profit as defined by the Concession Agreement credited to shareholders" is after making the necessary provisions for this requirement and other appropriations to reserves in accordance with the Concession Agreement.

The terms of an agreement consented to by Liberian Iron Ore Ltd. (LIO) dated as of January 1, 1965 between LAMCO and the Government provide for quarterly advance payments to the Government as holder of the Class A shares of up to 50 cents per ton of ore produced and shipped from Liberia out of the profits of LAMCO as defined in the agreement. To the extent that profits are available after the payments to the Government, the holder of the Class B shares will receive equal payments. Any remaining profits will be distributed to the shareholders by the declaration of dividends with the first $1,083,333 payable to the Government being used to repay the "advance payments on account of future dividends" carried on the balance sheet of LAMCO. For the year ended December 31, 1964, $500,000 was credited to this account, and for the year ended December 31, 1965, $583,333.

The Concession Agreement also provides that no taxes, export duties or import duties on materials and supplies relating to the developing and mining operations of the concession are to be assessed against LAMCO by the Government and that dividends to Class B shareholders, other than citizens or residents of Liberia, are to be free of Liberian taxes; and payments of dividends, and of interest and principal to creditors, will be allowed to be made to parties outside Liberia without restrictions.

Note 2 — Inventories:

Ore inventories are stated at average cost which is not in excess of market. Inventories of materials and supplies are stated at average cost.

Note 3 — Property and Equipment:

Except for certain minor items, buildings, roads and airstrips, railway and harbor are situated in concession areas.

Note 4 — Exploration and Development Costs:

These items are being amortized on a unit of production basis over proven and probable reserves. Additions amounted to $304,709 in 1965.

Note 5 – Long-Term Debt:

Bonds and notes:	
Series A Notes 5¾%, due 1965-1980, authorized $30,000,000	$ 29,100,000
Series B Bonds 6¾%, due 1965-1980, authorized DM 208,450,000 (at DM 4 = $1) $52,112,500	50,600,000
Series C Notes 6%, due 1965-1967, authorized $5,700,000	4,200,000
Series D Notes 5¾%, due 1968-1980, authorized $4,500,000	4,500,000
Series E Bonds 6¾%, due 1968-1980, authorized DM 31,268,000 (at DM 4 = $1) $7,817,000	7,817,000
Series F Notes 6%, due 1968, authorized $855,000	855,000
	97,072,000
Less – Current maturities	3,962,500
	93,109,500
Senior Debentures 6¼%, due 1968-1980, authorized $7,741,000	7,741,000
Subordinated Debentures 6¼%, due 1985, authorized $38,000,000	38,000,000
	138,850,500
Other long-term debt:	
Deferred interest payable on Subordinated Debentures, accrued during construction at 4.167%, due 1967-1968 (current maturity, $961,253, is shown under accrued interest)	1,634,131
Advance received from LIO on account of Junior Subordinated Debentures	2,000,000
	3,634,131
Total long-term debt	$142,484,631

Maturities of long-term debt for the years 1966-1970 amount to $4,923,753, $5,643,127, $7,252,504, $8,169,000 and $8,731,500, respectively.

Among the terms governing the issue of the Series A notes, the Series B bonds, the Series C notes, the Series D notes, the Series E bonds and the Series F notes (referred to below collectively as the "bonds") contained in the indenture relating thereto are:

(a) The bonds are secured by a first lien on the Class B stock of LAMCO owned by LIO and on LAMCO's 75% interest in the Nimba project.

(b) The holders of the Series B and E bonds have the right, exercisable to December 31, 1966, to request LAMCO to exchange these bonds which are payable in German marks for bonds payable in U.S. dollars.

(c) No dividends may be declared or paid nor may any distribution be made on any capital stock unless the Guarantee of the Swedish LAMCO Syndicate is in effect in the amount of $15,000,000 or the principal amount of the bonds outstanding whichever is lower or the Guarantee shall have terminated in accordance with its terms.

(d) The bonds are repayable semiannually on June 1 and December 1 during the years set forth above and the Series B and E bonds and Series C and F notes benefit from the operation of a sinking fund calling for the redemption of such bonds and notes in amounts varying from approximately $3,000,000 in 1965 to a maximum of approximately $6,000,000 in 1974 and $5,800,000 in 1975; thereafter in amounts from approximately $2,500,000 in 1976 to $3,000,000 in 1980.

Among the terms governing the issue of the senior debentures are:

(a) The senior debentures constitute "senior indebtedness" to the 6¼% subordinated debentures due 1985, but are subordinated as to payment of principal and interest, to the extent and in the manner set forth in the debentures, to the prior payment in full of the bonds.
(b) The senior debentures are to be redeemed by operation of a sinking fund which provides for the retirement of $298,000 semiannually in each of the years 1968 through 1979 and of the remaining debt in 1980.
(c) The holder of senior debentures who was a holder of senior debentures initially issued has the right to request LAMCO to exchange these debentures which are payable in U.S. dollars for debentures payable in Swedish kronor or in German marks of the Federal Republic of Germany.

The Swedish LAMCO Syndicate (Syndicate) and individual members of the Syndicate hold all the outstanding senior debentures.

Among the terms of the indenture covering the subordinated debentures are:

(a) Commencing in 1965 interest became payable quarterly at 6¼% per annum. The interest payments are subject to "interest net income" as defined in the indenture being available therefor.
(b) The subordinated debentures are subordinated as to payment of principal and interest to the prior payment in full of "senior indebtedness" (bonds and senior debentures) and as to payment of interest to the advance dividend payments described in Note 1.
(c) The subordinated debentures are redeemable on not less than 30 days' notice at LAMCO's option at any time after all the bonds have been retired or by operation of a sinking fund which provides for the retirement of $2,000,000 principal amount of debentures in each of the years 1976 through 1984.

The Swedish LAMCO Syndicate holds $37,664,000 of the outstanding subordinated debentures.

The Export-Import Bank of Washington has authorized the establishment of a credit in favor of LAMCO in an amount of $23,130,000. These obligations of LAMCO will be designated Series G notes and will be issued under and be secured by the lien of the indenture covering the Series A, B, C, D, E and F notes and bonds. Such obligations will be payable in twenty-five semiannual instalments commencing not later than December 1, 1968 and will bear interest at the rate of 5½% per annum. LAMCO will be obligated to make annual prepayments of the Series G notes under a formula based on annual net profits, in amounts not to exceed $1,900,000 in 1970, $2,100,000 in 1971, $2,500,000 in 1972, $3,400,000 in each of the years 1973 and 1974, $4,000,000 in each of the years 1975 through 1978, $3,700,800 in 1979 and $1,850,400 in 1980, but in certain circumstances such prepayments may be deferred until specified conditions are satisfied.

Under an agreement dated as of January 1, 1966, between LIO and LAMCO, LIO will purchase from LAMCO $11,000,000 principal amount of its 6¼% Junior Subordinated Debentures due December 1, 1985. Among the terms governing the issue of the Junior Subordinated Debentures are:

(a) The payment of principal and interest on the Junior Subordinated Debentures is subordinated in right of payment to the prior payment in full of "senior indebtedness" (being, at present, the bonds, the senior debentures and the subordinated debentures).
(b) Interest at 6¼% per annum will be payable quarterly to the extent of "available interest net income" as defined in the agreement.
(c) The Junior Subordinated Debentures are redeemable on not less than 30 days' notice at LAMCO's option at any time after all the bonds have been retired or by operation of a sinking fund providing for the retirement of $550,000 principal amount of debentures in each of the years 1976 through 1984.

Note 6 — Capital:

The Class A shares are held by the Government of the Republic of Liberia and the

Class B shares are held by LIO. The Class A shares elect five and the Class B shares elect six of LAMCO's eleven directors.

The certificate of incorporation of LAMCO requires that at least 60% of its capital stock must at all times be owned by the Government of the Republic of Liberia, or citizens or corporations of Liberia, the United States of America, or Canada.

Note 7 – Contractual Commitments and Contingent Liabilities:

LAMCO has contracts for the sale of ore which in 1966 and 1967 will cover approximately 5.5 million tons. Most of these contracts will expire in 1968. One contract covering a minimum of 2.5 million tons, annually, extends to 1979 with an option of renewal by the buyer to 1999 and another contract for 900,000 tons expires in 1974.

Other contractual commitments are:

	Service	*Contracting Party*	*Fee*
(i)	Management of the Nimba project for indefinite period, cancellable on two years' notice after 1978	Trafik AB Grängesberg-Oxelösund	7.5 cents per ton of ore delivered plus expenses
(ii)	Sales agent; agreement expiring December 31, 1978	Trafik AB Grängesberg-Oxelösund	2% of net invoice price, f.o.b. Liberian port, on sales of first 5,000,000 tons; 1% of sales in excess of 5,000,000 tons
(iii)	Securing long-term ore contract for LAMCO by making substantial investment in Esperance-Longdoz; expiring 1974	Triton Limited—controlled by international consortium in which Trafik AB Grängesberg-Oxelösund has 5/8 interest	Commission on ore contract for minimum of 765,000 tons and maximum 990,000 tons annually of $1.25 per ton for 1965-1968; 50 cents per ton 1969-1970 and 25 cents per ton 1971-1974
(iv)	Financial advisor for indefinite term, cancellable on 90 days' notice	Stockholms Enskilda Bank	On reasonable and customary basis. Last instalment of $150,000 per annum on agreed fee to end of construction period was paid June 30, 1964. Fees for services thereafter to June 30, 1966 have been agreed at $150,000 per annum
(v)	Guarantee fee re Swedish Syndicate Guarantee of LAMCO indebtedness	LIO	A quarterly fee of ¼ of 1% of $15,000,000 or principal amount of bonds outstanding whichever is lower

The Joint Venture will expand its existing facilities in Liberia to achieve a total annual production capacity of at least 10,000,000 tons of ore. The expansion program involves the erection of a washing plant with an annual capacity of at least 10,000,000 tons, a pelletizing plant with an annual capacity of at least 2,000,000 tons and other industrial and residential buildings and facilities, the installation of additional ore handling and stockpile facilities, and the purchase of additional mining, railway and other equipment. Construction of the new facilities commenced at the end of 1965, and is expected to be completed by the end of 1967.

The estimated total cost to the Joint Venture of the expansion program is $51,400,000, and LAMCO's 75% contribution to these costs, under the terms of the Joint Venture Agreement, as amended, would be approximately $38,550,000. The Joint Venture has entered into construction and procurement contracts amounting to $25,000,000 in connection with the expansion.

Note 8 – Pledge of Assets:

Under the terms of the bond indenture and with the consent of Bethlehem, LAMCO has pledged all its right, title and interest in the Concession Agreement, Joint Venture Agreement, Management Agreement, and the sales contract with German ore buyers and has entered into a chattel mortgage, as supplemented, covering its interest in tangible personal property in Liberia used in connection with the Nimba project.

Working Capital Management

7

The objective of working capital management is to protect the purchasing power of assets and to maximize return on investment. The management of cash, accounts receivable, inventories, and near cash assets such as negotiable securities is complex in any business. It is substantially more complex for the multinational firm. The present chapter describes and analyzes the complicating international factors and suggests approaches and procedures for resolving them.

THE COMPLICATING VARIABLES

Inflation is a primary complicating factor in international working capital management. Many government officials are unable to control inflation in their respective countries or favor mild inflation as a policy tool. Consequently the purchasing power of companies' financial assets (cash, near cash, and receivables) erodes. Faced with this problem intelligent management strives to protect its financial assets, usually by minimizing investment to the extent that successful operations will allow. Yet conservation of financial assets proves difficult. The investment in receivables increases even if it remains in the same proportion to sales. Buyers clamor for additional credit, and the firm must reply to these demands. If the firm refuses, it may lose valued customers. If it accedes to the demands, the purchasing power of the additional receivables declines each day that buyers manage to delay payment.

Minimizing vulnerable balances through prompt remission of earnings in inflation-ridden countries may prove equally difficult. Even if local authorities have not and are unlikely to impose barriers to the transfer of assets abroad, a number of difficulties may arise. For example, local partners in any joint venture may well protest the attempts of foreign owners to reduce liquid asset balances. One can hardly expect local partners to be enthusiastic as liquidity cushions are drawn down. The possibility of a clash between joint venture partners may be very great when lucrative investment opportunities elsewhere induce multinational partners to minimize their working capital commitments, whereas local owners believe that the local ventures offer the best returns on investment available to them.

Ownership arrangements may pose problems in other circumstances as well. In an effort to protect the exchange rate, local authorities sometimes classify remittances greater than an arbitrary percentage of equity as capital repatriation. The effect on a foreign corporation will vary with the intent of the governmental regulation. In some cases the multinational partner who insists on remittances will inadvertently enhance the control position of local partners. In other cases the excess remittances will be taxed at a higher rate, or all earnings may be taxed more heavily as a penalty for minimizing capital contributions to the local economy.

Taxes and tariffs are a source of great concern where inflation increases the threat of devaluation. Intelligent planning becomes increasingly difficult when the next step in government efforts to maintain the exchange rate is unknown. Import duties are a likely government target in the struggle to balance trade. A rising tariff barrier hurts both local operations and affiliates of closely knit international networks. Uncertainty regarding tariff and exchange rate levels can be even more demoralizing to conscientious management than actual changes as management attempts to protect financial assets.

Similarly, higher taxes on all businesses may be expected as part of the effort to curb inflation. Foreign-owned firms are likely to be subjected to special pressures to restrain cash remissions. As stated above, extra taxes on dividends frequently occur when the local economy is overheated. Depending on the form of the tax and the state of economic development in the taxing country, the tax might not be deductible from tax liabilities in the United States for the American-based company. In the words of one authority on taxation, "changes in the tax-paid credit arising out of the 1962 Revenue Act have created one of the most critical problem areas. . . . When a dividend is received from a subsidiary in an industrialized country, the parent company pays a higher tax. . . . When the dividends are paid by a less developed country corporation, the parent corporation is allowed a deduction and a foreign tax credit."[1]

Finally a host of legal controls and regulations may be imposed to limit the firm's effective control over working capital. Import controls can be especially damaging to a subsidiary that depends on raw material imports. The imposition of multiple exchange rates may be used to penalize remissions and imports without actually blocking them; thus managers are compelled to accumulate unproductive cash balances or to use less desirable local sources of supply. Price controls, on the other hand, may spur the affiliates to accumulate as much raw material as it can afford before devaluation forces up the price of imports; this essentially defensive move proves desirable notwithstanding increased inventory carrying costs.

As the government attempts to curb inflation, some official tightening of credit may also be expected. Consequently, the affiliate's efforts to balance liquid assets with local currency debts become more tenuous. Government conscription of the money supply, rising bank reserve requirements, and increasing central bank rediscount rates all serve to boost effective interest rates and make local borrowing more difficult. Often local managers are forced to deal with several banks in order to minimize borrowing costs. Under these circumstances reliance on a single lender is especially unwise. As the extent of the affiliate's indebtedness becomes known, few banks are willing to assume the full risk of default alone; banks that are willing to comply with lenders' requests exact charges that fully compensate for both inflationary pressures and lending risk. Working with a syndicate of lenders, however, requires extra time and effort to maintain contacts, keep books, and meet all payments promptly.

All too often managers of overseas affiliates have learned too late that local currency profits are real only after conversion into dollars. Inflation, devaluation, penalty taxes on excessive remittances, blocked accounts, multiple exchange rates, and hostility of foreign governments have been known to turn local currency profits into losses upon translation or remission. In his detailed analysis of swap transactions, Claude Macmillian states the problem of working capital management in foreign environments quite succinctly. A quotation from his article follows:

> The difficulty is in short-run discrepancies (between fluctuations in asset purchasing power and in the total exchange rate), a source of constant concern to the manager of an American subsidiary in a soft currency area. Repayment of loans, imported materials and components, internal budgetary planning and financial reporting to the parent firm all are complicated by the fact that fluctuations in exchange

[1] Walter H. Diamond, "Doing Business Abroad—And Living with the Tax Impact," *Management Controls,* vol. 14, no. 9, September 1967, p. 216.

rates and fluctuations in the purchasing power of soft currency are not in phase in the short run.

In 1958 many U.S. firms had one of their best years in Brazil. But as a consequence of violent short run fluctuation, the dollar profits into which their cruzeiro earnings were converted made it one of their worst years.[2]

WORKING CAPITAL AND THE SELECTION OF CASH CENTERS AND PROFIT HAVENS

In several important respects working capital decisions presume the predetermination of cash flow centers and tax payments. In the most obvious demonstration of this relationship, management will not choose to hold cash in a country noted for violent political upheavals and rampant inflation. Rather, it will siphon off local cash balances as rapidly as possible to a more stable environment. Net working capital (liquid assets minus liquid liabilities) is minimized in less stable areas of the international network.

Many factors affect the location of cash centers and, hence, the management of working capital. Perhaps most important is the local government's ability and its attitude toward foreign-based firms. Laws requiring partial ownership of alien corporations by nationals of the host country or by the government itself, hostility of the courts toward foreign business claims, and disclosure requirements may all militate against the operation of an affiliate as a cash center. Tax laws in the country of operation and in the parent country also play an important role in the decision. Aggregate tax levels, penalty rates on excessive dividend remittances, provisions affecting the taxable base of income, and the timing of the tax (upon earnings or upon remission of earnings) are crucial considerations.

Management must also consider a variety of economic factors in selecting cash centers. The stability of local currency values is paramount among these. It is necessary to recall, however, that the exact timing of a change in the exchange rate is rarely predictable. Governments take great pains to avoid speculation against their currencies. Even *The Economist* did not expect the November 1967 devaluation of the British pound. It is frequently essential, therefore, to engage in hedging operations to assure that remittance schedules, foreign debt payments, and trade obligations can be discharged. Hence the existence of an active forward market as well as suitable money market instruments for the deployment of temporary excessive resources is important. The availability of investment guarantees may be crucial and is affected by both economic and political factors, as is the local government's ability to control inflation and economic growth.

[2] Claude Macmillian, "Swap as a Hedge in Foreign Exchange," *California Management Review*, 1965, p. 59.

Finally, factors peculiar to the structure and style of operation of individual firms may dictate management policy on working capital. The unpredictable need for funds at various points in a network of international affiliates may require that certain locations maintain large liquid balances. Sometimes headquarters must forego investment opportunities in areas with surplus funds in order to retain the flexibility needed to meet exigencies elsewhere. For some affiliates the level of working capital varies inversely with the degree of stockholder pressure for repatriation of dividends. On the other hand, in many joint ventures high levels of liquid assets will accumulate due to the aforementioned efforts of local partners to maximize the foreign investor's financial commitment to the enterprise. Headquarters must consider each of the variables discussed above in deciding on a working capital posture for each affiliate and for the network as a whole.

Attesting to the importance of cash planning and controls in the international organization, a spokesman for Mobil Oil Company reports that great savings for Mobil have resulted from coordinated borrowing and pooling of affiliates' cash resources.[3] Mobil's short-term borrowing guidelines place responsibilities for local assessments on the affiliate managers. External lending possibilities meanwhile are analyzed by regional service units, division treasurers, or headquarters staff. Wherever possible Mobil balances off the cash shortages and surpluses of each affiliate to obtain the requisite levels of working capital. Residual cash resources are channeled to identified cash centers.

LINES OF AUTHORITY

If foreign subsidiaries are not run as cash centers, local managers have limited opportunities to retain and invest surplus cash resources as they see fit. It is nonetheless important for headquarters management to make clear to local managers certain basic tenets of working capital management. Until recently Pan American Airways suffered significant asset deterioration because its sales managers throughout the system were not conscious of the exchange rate vulnerability created by the "Fly now, pay later" plan. For similar reasons Pan American occasionally lost money on bookings for other airlines by accepting soft currency deposits and paying the other carriers immediately from their own hard currency reserves.

It should be stressed to the local managers that profits in the local environment are distinctly different from cash in the parent investor's pockets. The local managers must be encouraged to adopt an international outlook and concentrate efforts on minimizing asset deterioration due to inflation. Headquarters management should foster this

[3] Edward P. Fisher, "Financing Foreign Operations," *The Financial Executive*, October 1964, pp. 14–15.

outlook by developing a system of controls to measure the effectiveness of a manager's handling of international transfers. Suggestions for the evolution of such a system are proffered in chapter 12. Finally local managers must be provided with access to expertise on available methods of financing. Making local executives responsible for asset deterioration and exchange losses seems to be a key to the resolution of many working capital problems, a point discussed in depth in chapter 12.

Both affiliate and parent should keep abreast of exchange rate movements. Each lends a particular perspective on local and worldwide trends and contributes to the other's understanding. Crucial decisions on the timing of transfers and the balancing of current accounts can also be made with the help of outside analysts such as economists and trusted bankers.

REDUCING VULNERABILITY TO INFLATION AND DEVALUATION

When it becomes evident that inflation will continue and devaluation is imminent, managers should consider the following adaptations. First, cash balances should be minimized. Remissions should be accelerated, especially if authorities appear likely to institute exchange controls. If debt is outstanding to the parent company or an external institutional leader, repayment should be hastened. If controls are already in force, local managers should be given the authority to reinvest any excess funds, thereby trading for assets that are not so vulnerable as cash. At the same time, care must be taken to avoid angering local authorities by transferring funds at a sensitive time. Remittances by way of the black market (although perhaps practicable under certain circumstances) are especially dangerous in this regard. Working capital managers must remember that alien firms are always vulnerable to economic reprisals and that even accepted practices by indigenous or local businessmen may be unwise for foreign-owned affiliates.

As suggested earlier, receivables should usually be reduced to the extent local operating circumstances permit under inflationary conditions. There may be worthwhile opportunities, however, for management to profit by reversing this rule. Sometimes local buyers will ignore higher prices and respond to credit offerings enthusiastically. In addition, extra service charges and cost of living clauses can be written into credit agreements in some instances, making receivables less vulnerable than cash to the effects of inflation and devaluation. The only receivables that management can ignore entirely when exchange rates are threatened are export credit sales invoiced in external currencies. These may be considered invulnerable, unless in some way related to the local currency, and a possible source of windfall local currency profits.

As in the case of receivables management, the rule that certain companies follow under inflationary conditions is to minimize investments in inventories. Yet inventories can also be managed more profitably in some cases by ignoring the general rule. Certain types of materials are not so susceptible to economic deterioration as others. Subsidiaries that are dependent on imports may wish to buy surplus materials before anticipated devaluations increase costs. Predicted exchange controls or tariff increases may also provide incentive to import. In reaching a decision on inventory levels, managers must balance off the above factors against careful calculations of inventory carrying costs—i.e., costs of storage, financing, insurance, physical deterioration, and the possibility of angering the host government. For a well-based decision, management must use past experience and all the intelligence it can gather to predict price and exchange rate levels. Naturally inventory replacement costs rather than historic costs must be borne in mind when management adjusts prices after a devaluation.

The final current asset category of particular concern to working capital managers consists of prepaid expenses. Deposits on materials, insurance premiums, and other business expenses generally should be kept as small as possible. One exception to this rule may be deposits on imported goods. At times foreign suppliers' insistence on prepayment provides a convenient excuse to move money out of the country while a favorable exchange rate persists. In other circumstances prepayments may represent the only investment open to a company that wishes to avoid holding cash. Usually, however, the multinational firm can obtain better returns on its cash balances than suppliers will offer in discounts for prepayment.

TEMPORARY FINANCING OF WORKING CAPITAL NEEDS

An important facet of working capital management consists of the analysis of individual foreign affiliates' needs for temporary financing. A distinction is drawn here between temporary or discontinuous needs and permanent financial needs. (The previous chapter dealt with the selection of financial resources which affiliates require more or less continuously.) It has been suggested in the financial literature that assets amortized over long periods should be financed with permanent resources.[4] For example, a building with an estimated economic life of twenty years should be financed with long-term debt instruments and/or equity. Conversely, current assets such as inventories and receivables should be financed using short-term instruments such as demand notes and overdraft facilities that are less permanent.

This presumption regarding the propriety of short-term and long-term

[4] *See,* for instance, Bion B. Howard and Miller Upton, *Introduction to Business Finance,* New York, McGraw-Hill Book Co., 1953, pp. 310–14.

financing is subject to serious question in the domestic setting. The working capital cycle of a particular firm may be long by conventional standards. The General Telephone Company generates receivables with twenty-five-year repayment terms in connection with its sale of telephone systems. The time span between the acquisition of raw materials and the sale of finished product, and thus the creation of receivables, is several years in various lines of business such as large-scale construction and the production of alcoholic beverages. Under these circumstances the financing of current assets or working capital with short-term instruments may or may not be provident.

Moreover, a large percentage of business investment in inventories and receivables is more or less permanent. Although individual items in inventory and accounts receivable may be converted into cash in relatively short periods of time, other inventory items and newly created receivables replace these items, and consequently the need for working capital financing is continuous. Our point here is that the choice between short- and long-term financing on the basis of asset classification is by no means clear even in the domestic setting. The maturity characteristics of assets defy general classification and even after maturity characteristics for a particular firm have been identified, the choice between short-term and long-term financing resources does not automatically follow. In point of fact the General Telephone Company has financed its twenty-five-year receivables through the placement of commercial paper with maturities in the range of 180–270 days.

Once multinational considerations are allowed to enter the discussion the venerated rule regarding short-term versus long-term financing becomes even more tenuous. Long-term sources of financing are typically scarce or unavailable in most of the developing countries and in many countries classified as developed. Consequently, firms may not have the luxury of choice between financing instruments of different maturity characteristics. Where choice between financial instruments is limited, reliance on short-term financing often becomes mandatory. Under these circumstances identification of short-term financing instruments in affiliates' capital structures reveals little regarding management's preferences regarding maturity characteristics of financial instruments.

Equally important, opinions differ among firms with regard to the propriety of using short-term financing for permanent needs. To follow General Telephone's practice of financing long-term receivables with short-term commercial paper would be unacceptable to many corporate treasurers. Because attitudes regarding the selection of debt instruments differ among companies where choice exists and because choice does not exist in many instances, we define temporary financing in a special way here. For our purposes temporary financing is whatever a particular firm regards as temporary. Hence, the short-term financing of General Telephone's twenty-five-year receivables is permanent since the firm plans to rely on short-term resources for this purpose on a continuous basis. Long-term debt can be temporary if a firm plans to refund or retire it in the near future. Now let us turn to the logistics of temporary financing, which is an integral part of working capital management.

WHY TEMPORARY FINANCING?

Temporary financial needs arise for a variety of reasons. A firm constructs a new plant in country *X* and requires "bridge" financing until the new operation begins to generate revenues. Conditions in the local money and capital markets are unattractive. Temporary financing is desired until permanent financing on more attractive terms become feasible. For example, many firms borrowed short-term Eurodollars during 1967 and 1968, hoping to refund these obligations with longer term Eurocurrency issues at later dates under more favorable issuing conditions. The investor searching for a local partner may rely on temporary debt financing until an appropriate partner with sufficient capital to retire the loan can be identified.

In other instances, as in solely domestic business, operating requirements of the business itself suggest reliance on temporary financing. In many businesses inventories and receivable needs are partially seasonal. Retailers frequently require abnormally large inventories prior to a peak selling period such as the Christmas season. Immediately after Christmas abnormally large receivables portfolios are attributable to selling activities during this peak period. Frequently it is desirable to meet such seasonal needs with temporary financing, often called self-liquidating financing. These financial needs are self-liquidating in the sense that they diminish automatically as receivables are collected.

Other temporary financing needs relate to the unique inventory and receivable requirements that arise in developing countries. Many governments insist upon prior deposits in connection with raw material imports. Frequently larger stocks are necessary to support operations because of transportation problems, unpredictable suppliers, and import requirements. Similarly, as suggested earlier, infant or otherwise inefficient money markets together with inflationary pressures can contribute to abnormally large receivables portfolios. Extension of credit becomes a primary sales weapon, and customers delay payments to turn inflation and money scarcity to advantage. Although the contention can be seriously questioned, many firms regard these incremental investments in inventories and receivables as temporary and argue that these needs should be financed with temporary resources.

Still another rationale for reliance on temporary financing relates to the international investor's expectation that the local currency will be devalued or blocked. Suspicion of an impending currency crisis may provoke the multinational investor to defer a decision regarding long-term financial structure for an affiliate or to reverse previous financial arrangements regarded as permanent. The investor worried about local currency conditions relies temporarily on locally denominated instruments regardless of their explicit cost. The presumption is that high costs are temporarily justified in view of the protection afforded against devaluation or exchange restrictions.

In other instances temporary financing has served as window dressing to comply with governmental restrictions and requirements. For example, some American-based companies have sought Eurocurrency loans in order to comply with the letter of the President's guidelines program that is intended to curtail capital outflows from the United States. Borrowing foreign exchange at intermittent intervals, sometimes for extremely short periods of time, firms have been able to report to the United States Government reduced magnitudes of capital outflows.

SOURCES OF TEMPORARY FINANCING

One of the best ways to provide for temporary needs is to stretch existing resources. It is possible to maintain sales levels with smaller investments in inventories as a consequence of more stringent inventory control procedures. Similarly, conscientious credit evaluation and credit collection procedures can sometimes facilitate reduction of the accounts receivables portfolio without contributing to corresponding reductions in sales revenues. Perhaps cash balances can be reduced with greater reliance on commercial banks' overdraft facilities. Other asset categories may also be reduced. In each instance where reduction in assets is contemplated it is important to analyze the revenues and related returns associated with the asset categories and to predict the likely consequences of reducing asset investments. To the extent that assets can be reduced, the liberated cash balances can be used to finance temporary needs.

Another avenue open to the international firm in search of additional temporary resources relates to its payments practices. It is sometimes possible to delay paying various social security contributions, taxes, and import customs duties. Likewise, supplier credits can in some instances be extended without jeopardizing relations or incurring costly penalties in terms of foregone discounts. The firm is likely to have more influence regarding suppliers' credit terms than with respect to the terms of institutional lenders. Obviously the cost of any discounts foregone must be carefully considered in evaluating the propriety of delaying supplier payments. By increasing payables and accruals denominated in local currencies when costs and external relations allow, international investors may be able to stretch temporary financial resources at nominal costs.

The possibility of accepting prepayments from customers may be viewed in the same light as stretching current liabilities and accruals. By and large, prepayments are costless liabilties and should be taken whenever offered. Yet as many companies have painfully discovered, the affiliate must have a ready use for cash received in prepayment. An affiliate is in a better position with receivables partially protected by price level adjustment clauses than with cash holding that it is unable to reinvest.

LOCALLY DENOMINATED RESOURCES

Having minimized local asset commitments and having stretched payables and accruals to the extent that is practicable, the multinational investor might next explore the possibility of obtaining locally denominated debt for its affiliates' temporary needs. To the extent that locally denominated credits can be obtained on reasonable terms, affiliate needs can be accommodated without incurring the risk of exchange rate fluctuation. The most logical source for short-term local financing is the commercial bank. Usually an affiliate that needs additional cash will approach its local commercial banks first. Indeed, many farsighted local managers arrange large overdraft facilities with banks well in advance of actual needs when they sense that protective measures and overheated economies are likely to reduce liquidity substantially. Most commercial banks provide overdraft facilities, and these are generally the cheapest local credits available. Commissions on compensating balances notwithstanding, rates charged by the commercial banks are comparatively low due to the relatively large-scale operations and the lending rate ceilings imposed by government authorities. Because of the attractiveness of local bank financing it is not surprising that multinational investors frequently borrow from numerous banks at the same time in spite of related administrative complexities and occasional adverse effects on bank relations.

When overdraft facilities are exhausted, it is sometimes possible to obtain local currency loans by factoring receivables and customers' drafts or by pledging inventories. Almost without exception banks and other financial institutions buy receivables and customers' notes with recourse, thus saddling the borrowing firm with the risk of customer default or delinquency. In general the willingness of banks to discount receivables depends on their ability to rediscount the notes at the central bank. Banks' interest in receivables financing typically wanes when the rediscount window is closed, and under these circumstances it sometimes is necessary to approach nonbank lending institutions that factor receivables at substantially higher rates. Recently International Factors, a consortium of financial institutions organized by the First National Bank of Boston, has begun to provide extensive receivables evaluation and financing facilities, in some instances extending credits against receivables without recourse. Inventory financing is somewhat more cumbersome than receivables financing by virtue of the usual requirement that pledged items be secured in bonded warehouses. In some instances it is possible to meet lenders' standards by segregating inventory on the premises and placing them under the supervision of a bonded custodian. The warehouse receipts obtained when inventories are placed in a public warehouse can sometimes be used as securities for additional bank loans.

The opportunities to obtain secured financing using assets other than receivables and inventories are expanding in numerous countries. Mortgage banks and other term lending institutions are occasionally willing to extend credit against existing fixed assets where title is clear. Several financial institutions have entered the leasing field during the past two years, although for the most part development has been confined to the United States and European countries. Where leasing companies have been established it has occasionally been possible to sell existing assets and to lease them back, thus obtaining needed local currency resources.

A growing practice of multinational firms in need of local financial resources consists of the issuance of commercial paper or promissory notes. For the most part the notes of multinational firms have been placed privately with local financial institutions although a few major companies have established separate finance subsidiaries whose purpose is to place such paper directly with the ultimate investors. Moreover, the finance subsidiaries of firms with well-known names and international reputations have in some instances been able to place substantial volumes of notes without the added attraction of parent guarantees. As one might expect, the ability to sell commercial paper and promissory notes is largely dependent on the reputation of the firm in question, its financial position, and conditions in the local money markets at a given point in time.

Other sources of local financing are also important. Throughout the world there is a wide variety of nonbank lending institutions such as financieras, mortgage banks, finance companies, and private groups that sometimes are willing to extend credit when traditional sources are uncooperative. One important source is the local affiliate of nonfinancial companies that temporarily have excess cash resources. The existence of excess cash is common in countries with currency restrictions; certain affiliates have been unable to remit (or remission has been unattractive due to high transfer costs), and these affiliates are interested in investing their surplus resources. Frequently local affiliates with different patterns of seasonal financial requirements have been able to lend to each other on mutually advantageous terms. Other local sources are more difficult to exploit. Bond markets are virtually nonexistent in countries plagued by persistent inflation. Development banks and United States-owned Cooley amendment funds are intended for long-term investments that will spur local economic growth.

THE COST OF LOCAL BORROWING

A comparative cost analysis of local borrowing alternatives is straightforward. As suggested in chapter 6, local borrowing costs for a given alternative consist of the effective rate of interest adjusted for the rate of inflation in the country supplying the borrowing currency.

It is important to remember that loans obtained from local institutions afford protection against exchange rate fluctuation as the cost calculation assumes only if interest and principal repayments are denominated in the local currency. It is not uncommon for lenders to require that borrowers repay in full or in part in another currency, in which case the borrower assumes the exchange rate risk. Similarly, the borrower is left with the exchange risk where lenders demand "maintenance of value clauses" which insist that repayment in the local currency be equivalent in external purchasing power to the amount originally lent.[5]

IMPORTED RESOURCES

Unavailable or costly local financing options pose two interrelated problems. First, should financing be imported in view of the intended use? Second, if funds are to be imported, where should they be obtained? As intimated earlier, surplus liquidity frequently exists elsewhere in the company; the parent or other affiliate may have excess cash or near cash assets that can be readily transferred. Recall Mobil Oil's testament that substantial cost savings have resulted from coordinated deployment of network cash resources.

Often, however, the ability to transfer firm resources across national boundaries is restricted. Transfers in excess of specified amounts are prohibited by the local authorities or discouraged by such measures as the Presidential Guidelines Program in the United States. Where allowed, the movement of funds from one affiliate to another may involve significant transfer costs—that is, additional tax liability in a variety of forms, foreign exchange losses, and interruption of financial control procedures. Consequently it becomes necessary to assess probable transfer costs in advance and to compare these costs with the alternative charges imposed by lenders outside the company network.

To a significant extent the magnitude of transfer costs depends on the

[5] If the maintenance of value clause is stated in terms of local purchasing power, the borrower assumes the cost of price level deterioration but is not held responsible for changes in external exchange rates.

multinational firm's legal and financial structure as well as on the structures elected for individual affiliates. Typically these structures have emerged over long periods of time in response to sequential opportunities to expand abroad. Control and tax considerations have tended to dominate decisions regarding selection of organizational structures. The ease with which funds can be transferred from one affiliate to another has often been overlooked or given lower priority in the decision process. It is not surprising, therefore, to hear international bankers indicate that a large proportion of their loans are made to companies which in the aggregate do not need cash. Transfer costs are prohibitively expensive, and the companies elect to borrow for individual affiliates rather than to move network cash balances from other areas with surpluses.

If transfers are permissible, the multinational firm must compare costs to ascertain whether resources should be supplied by the parent, another link in the international network, or by an institutional lender outside the ultimate borrower's country. The following elements are relevant to such an analysis:

1. The "opportunity cost" if the parent or other affiliates are supplying the resources—that is, the rate of return which could be obtained if the resources were used alternatively
2. Transfer costs
3. The effective borrowing cost (EBC) where institutional lenders are supplying the required resources—that is, the stated rate of interest adjusted for invisibles such as compensating balance requirements
4. Inflationary gains (or losses)
5. Foreign exchange gains (or losses).

To calculate costs for temporary imported financing, one simply follows the procedures outlined in chapter 6. Recall that:

$$\text{EBC} = I_y + X_y$$

where EBC = the effective borrowing cost

I_y = the effective rate of interest in the country supplying the financing

X_y = the rate of devaluation of country x's currency in relation to the currency of the country supplying the financing

Note that an element of the cost calculation relates to expected fluctuations in currency exchange rates. Whenever imported monies are converted into soft currencies, the exchange risk must be considered. Indeed, exchange rate considerations may outweigh all other elements in the cost calculation. Depending on the investor's willingness to assume exchange risks in connection with temporary financing, resources may be provided on a hedged or unhedged basis.

HEDGING DEVICES

In essence, hedging is a type of insurance. Entering into a *forward contract* for the delivery of a specified currency on a named date—the purchase of hard currency equivalents for future delivery—the multinational investor can eliminate or minimize the risks arising from unfavorable exchange rate fluctuations. In countries where forward exchange markets flourish, contracts can be drawn enabling the multinational investor to make loans, indirectly or directly, to affiliates in local currency units without incurring foreign exchange risks.

Usually forward exchange contracts are not readily available for periods longer than eighteen months. When made available for longer periods of time the contracts become quite expensive. Rarely will an exchange contractor agree to provide currency at a distant future date without a substantial discount in his favor from the present exchange rate. Additionally, forward contracts involving soft currencies are usually difficult or impossible to arrange. Hence the investor unable to arrange a forward contract becomes interested in swap transactions.

In the case of a *foreign currency swap* the multinational investor buys the required amount of local currency in the foreign exchange market and simultaneously enters into a forward contract to sell this amount of local currency at a future, specified date. Thus the parent investor is assured of recovering the foreign exchange at a predetermined exchange rate. Ideally the date of sale under this forward contract corresponds to the date when the affiliate is prepared to repay the parent or network loan. The ability to tailor delivery dates to affiliate borrowing needs depends on swap conditions in the country in question. A mature and active forward market may permit a wide variety of alternative settlement dates. Yet in some countries the only possibility may consist of executing a forward contract of a specific size for 90 or 180 days. Moreover, the central banks in certain countries disallow swaps or restrict the duration of swap contracts usually to six months.

The *credit swap* is kindred to foreign currency swaps in that simultaneous loans are made in two currencies. It is particularly useful, however, in countries characterized by dollar shortages and tight credit conditions. A credit swap consists of the following elements: A bank in the host country makes a loan to an affiliate in need and assumes the foreign exchange risk in connection with the loan. The bank in return is granted a free hard currency loan outside the country and is allowed to charge interest on the offsetting loan to the affiliate. The period of the offsetting credits, the interest rate on the affiliate's borrowings, and the exchange rates for the transaction are settled in advance. Typically it is necessary to loan a larger amount to the foreign bank than the latter lends to the local affiliate by virtue of differential exchange rates applied to the two phases of the transaction. The advantages to the multinational firm are twofold: first, funds are obtained for the affiliate in need without assuming foreign exchange risk; and second, the process is quite simple—the multinational firm merely arranges for hard currency funds to be credited to the local bank account of the foreign bank. Thus no difficult and time-consuming transfers of funds are undertaken.

The volume of credit swaps has fluctuated widely with changes in government attitude toward this lending device. The volume of currency swaps and variations on the basic swap agreement, on the other hand, are unknown. Most swap agreements are concluded in secret. Hence there is little published data to guide the novice negotiator in bargaining with foreign banks or individuals.

As noted previously, the swap transaction presumably insulates the investor against the risk of exchange rate fluctuations. The reader should bear in mind, however, that a hedging device only affords protection against adverse exchange rate developments so long as contractual obligations are honored. Historically there have been instances in which swap agreements and forward contracts have not been honored, and obviously in these instances the promise of protection has proven empty. Yet in the vast majority of cases in which devaluations and currency restrictions have subsequently occurred, the earlier agreements have been kept, for, among other reasons, the reputations of the financial institutions and their ability to conduct business subsequently depend on strict adherence to contractual terms.

It is possible to enter swap transactions in numerous countries as Table 7–1 suggests.

CALCULATING THE COST OF A SWAP

There are two cost elements associated with the currency swap transaction: the opportunity cost attributable to the parent resources that are tied up and the discount price for the foreign exchange sold to close out the transaction. Note in Table 7–1 that in some instances a foreign currency commands a premium in the forward market, in which case the cost of the swap represents the opportunity cost assigned to parent funds minus the premium obtained on the forward contract. For example, a 15 per cent opportunity cost plus a 2 per cent discount sustained in the forward market indicates an overall cost for the currency swap of 17 per cent per annum.

The cost computation for a credit swap is slightly more complicated. Recall that in the credit swap transaction the multinational firm opens a deposit in favor of the foreign bank with which the swap is contracted

TABLE 7–1

Forward Discount and Premiums for Six-Month Currency Swaps in Major Active Markets July 1967 (in % per annum)

	DISCOUNT	PREMIUM
EUROPE		
Austria	.125	
Belgium	.400	
France		.375
Germany		1.000
Denmark	.500	
Italy		.250
Netherlands	.120	
Norway	.500	
Sweden	.250	
Switzerland		.870
U.K.	.700	
LATIN AMERICA		
Mexico	2.500	
Peru	12.000	
Uruguay (restricted)		
Venezuela	2.000	
FAR EAST		
Australia	.250	
Japan	.250	
Philippines	5.500	
Canada	.125	

and that the foreign bank in turn makes available local currency to the affiliate in need. At the conclusion of the swap transaction, the foreign bank repays the external currency to the multinational investor, and the latter repays the local currency loan, thus closing out the transaction. A typical credit swap transaction might appear as follows: affiliate in country *B* requires the local currency equivalent of $500,000 at the current exchange rate of LC3:$1—in other words, LC1.5 million. The exchange rate applied by the local bank in consummating the swap, however, is only LC2:$1. Consequently, to obtain LC1.5 million for the affiliate in country *B*, the multinational investor must open a $750,000 credit in favor of the foreign bank. The foreign bank charges the multinational investor 10 per cent per annum on the LC1.5 million made available and pays no interest whatever on the $750,000 that the investor has credited to the foreign bank's United States account.

Under these hypothetical conditions the cost of the credit swap will appear as follows if we assign a 15 per cent opportunity cost to the parent resources that are tied up: the opportunity cost at 15 per cent on $750,000 is $112,500; and the 10 per cent interest charge on the LC1.5 million

(LC150,000) is \$50,000 at the prevailing rate of LC3:\$1. Thus the total cost is \$162,500 on a loan equivalent of \$500,000 or 32.5 per cent.

Clearly the credit swap is an expensive proposition. The credit swap transaction would only be attractive if the multinational investor insisted on a hedged position and less costly covered positions were unavailable.

COMPARISON OF HEDGED AND UNHEDGED ALTERNATIVES

Unfortunately the preceding analysis of lending costs is inadequate if the multinational investor is willing to assume foreign exchange risks. The foregoing hypothetical illustrations suggest that an external loan costs the parent 15 per cent per annum (the opportunity cost), whereas the credit swap which affords protection against exchange fluctuation costs roughly 32 per cent. Yet the reflective investor cannot choose between these lending alternatives solely on the basis of comparative costs. The hedged and unhedged alternatives are not comparable by virtue of the protection the credit swap affords and the exposure which the direct loan alternative implies.

To compare the hedged and unhedged alternatives the investor must explicitly consider possible fluctuations in exchange rates. The direct loan is 17 per cent cheaper (32 per cent − 15 per cent) only if the exchange rate remains the same—that is, the direct loan does not contribute to a foreign exchange loss. If the exchange rate remains constant, the investor who elects the credit swap makes a mistake in the sense that he pays for insurance which is unnecessary.

To incorporate the investor's assessment of future exchange rate developments into the analysis, we might simply add to the explicit cost of the unhedged direct loan the implied cost occasioned by expected exchange rate deterioration. In this fashion both the hedged and unhedged alternatives could be placed on a comparable evaluative basis. For example, the investor might conclude that exchange rate deterioration is likely to result in a 10 per cent foreign exchange loss if the direct loan is made, and hence the effective cost of the direct loan is 25 per cent. In an important respect, however, such an analysis of the direct loan would be unsatisfactory. In effect the investor has hypothesized that a single possible exchange rate will prevail on a specific future date, and the 25 per cent effective cost assumes that this rate and no other will prevail. In reality the investor is likely to be highly uncertain regarding the precise degree of deterioration in exchange rates, and for this reason the cost calculation is artificial.

Since the investor may be unable to predict future exchange rate developments with confidence, we recommend an alternative approach to analysis which emphasizes the importance of the exchange rate development to the selection of hedged or unhedged lending alternatives. In effect the prescribed approach enables the investor to identify the future exchange rate that equates the cost of the hedged and unhedged alternatives—that is, the exchange rate that increases the cost of the unhedged lending possibility to the level of the hedged lending alternative. The decision-maker can then compare the identified, equilibrating foreign exchange rate with his own subjective estimate of likely exchange rate developments. If he concludes that it is highly unlikely that exchange rates will deteriorate to the equilibrium exchange rate level, he chooses the unhedged alternative, since it probably will be less costly. He selects the hedged alternative whenever his subjective assessment suggests that there is a significant chance for exchange rates to deterioriate beyond the equilibrating rate. The prescribed analysis is conducted for the best hedged and unhedged alternative which the multinational investor has previously identified; straightforward analysis of cost elements has permitted him to identify the least costly hedged and unhedged arrangements.

To illustrate the approach, let us again assume that the affiliate needs LC1.5 million and that the credit swap, as actually discussed above, has proven to be the least costly lending alternative which affords protection against foreign exchange losses. Further assume that the best unhedged alternative is the direct loan from the parent and that the after-tax cost of the parent advance, ignoring momentarily any possible foreign exchange loss, is 15 per cent per annum. The costs of the two alternatives can be placed side by side in an equation in which the unknown, x, represents the exchange rate that equilibrates the costs of the two alternatives:

$$\overbrace{x75{,}000 + (x500{,}000 - 1{,}500{,}000)}^{\text{Parent advance cost}} = \overbrace{x112{,}500 + 150{,}000}^{\text{Credit swap cost}}$$

$$x = 3.57$$

where

$x75{,}000$ = the LC cost equivalent of the parent advance (\$500,000 × 15 per cent opportunity cost)

$x500{,}000 - 1{,}500{,}000$ = the potential foreign exchange loss re the parent advance (note that if the prevailing rate of LC3 = \$1 is maintained, there is no foreign exchange loss (1,500,000 – 1,500,000 = 0)

$x112{,}500$ = the LC cost equivalent re the \$750,000 deposited in favor of the local bank participating in the swap (\$750,000 × 15 per cent opportunity cost)

150,000 = the interest paid in local currency re the 1,500,000 credit extented by the local bank at 10 per cent per annum

In other words, if the foreign exchange rate is LC3.57:\$1 when the affiliate repays the loan to the parent, the parent advance or the credit swap is equally attractive. The multinational investor would be indifferent between the two financing alternatives. If the investor believes that it is highly unlikely that the foreign exchange rate will deteriorate to LC3.57:$1 from the prevailing rate of LC3:$1, he selects the parent advance since it is likely to prove less costly. If on the other hand, the investor anticipates a substantial devaluation during the period of the loan resulting in a foreign exchange rate of greater than LC3.57:$1, he opts for the credit swap. In the latter case the investor's subjective evaluation of the currency situation results in the selection of the insured alternative.

TEMPORARY INVESTMENT OF CASH AND NEAR CASH ASSETS

Until comparatively recently corporate treasurers usually restricted portfolio investments to the safest and most liquid money market instruments available. In the United States, for example, temporary investment of redundant assets was limited largely to treasury bills. The commercial banks and other financial institutions were the first to explore seriously the opportunities for more aggressive portfolio management in the liquid asset area. During the past ten years the normative theories of Markowitz and others have lent support to the portfolio manager in the search of higher returns.[6] Markowitz's diversification thesis has indicated that certain relatively risky investments are not only warranted because of higher expected returns but also because these risky opportunities contribute to a total investment portfolio characterized by lower overall risks than would otherwise be the case. Recently many treasurers of nonfinancial companies have begun to manage their liquid asset portfolios more aggressively.

Rather than discuss the recent literature pertaining to portfolio management, our objective here is to suggest the range of opportunities available to the portfolio manager of a multinational company. The portfolio diversification theories are as relevant to the multinational manager's activities as to the domestic manager's. Clearly the range of money market instruments from among which the investor may choose is broader than is the case for the manager who restricts himself to a single national market. There is a wide variety of government obligations with different rates of interest and maturity patterns. The obligations of private financial institutions are too numerous to describe specifically. The typical investor might select among such investment instruments in numerous countries as the following: deposits in commercial banks, finance houses, and other financial institutions; government obligations such as treasury

[6] For a discussion of the portfolio selection problem *see,* for example, Harry M. Markowitz, *Portfolio Selection: Efficient Diversification of Investments;* William F. Sharpe, "A Simplified Model for Portfolio Analysis," *Management Science,* January 1963, pp. 277–93; Geoffrey P. E. Clarkson, *Portfolio Selection: A Simulation of Trust Investment,* Englewood Cliffs, N.J., Prentice-Hall, Inc., 1962; and Buckner A. Wallingford, "A Survey and Comparison of Portfolio Selection Models," *Journal of Financial and Quantitative Analysis,* vol. 2, June 1967, pp. 85–106.

bills; acceptances; certificates of deposit; the purchase of prime notes or commercial paper. The criteria for choice among these various instruments includes: relative rates of return; maturity dates; the existence of a secondary market to permit liquidation before maturity; currency of denomination; market depth and breadth; investment quality of instruments; and transfer cost implications.

Frequently the multinational investor concludes that higher yields can be obtained by investing in a country other than where liquid resources are held. If the funds are transferred on an unhedged basis, the investor incurs a foreign exchange risk. Alternatively it is possible for the portfolio manager to cover this position in the forward market or via a currency swap transaction. Assume for example that redundant assets exist in the Netherlands but that it is possible to invest the funds in the French money market, thus obtaining a higher yield on instruments of similar investment quality. If the funds are shifted to the French money market to take advantage of interest rate differentials by buying French francs on the exchange market, the investor exposes himself to a possible foreign exchange loss. If, however, the investor hedges this risk by selling an equivalent amount of French francs in the forward market for delivery on the date when the French investment matures, the exchange risk is fully hedged. Usually the exchange rate obtained in the forward market is lower than the one paid in the spot market. In our illustration a more favorable rate would be applied in the spot market when the multinational investor bought French francs than would be applied in the forward transaction where francs are sold for future delivery. Yet if the interest rate differential between francs and guilders is greater than the hedging cost, the investor can obtain a higher return by carrying out the transaction in full even though he assumes no additional currency risk. Although these portfolio practices have offered profitable opportunities for both investors in search of higher returns and for the financial institutions whose foreign exchange departments have provided cover, government restrictions on capital outflows have narrowed the practice recently. For example, most American companies have discontinued this practice because of the Presidential Guidelines Program that restricts capital outflows.

Summary

Throughout the previous discussion of international complexities and opportunities in working capital management it has been apparent that three crucial elements underlie effective control of financial assets and liabilities. First, the multinational investor must carefully estimate the exchange rate movements in various countries in light of the information received from numerous sources and base ultimate decisions regarding the transfer of financial assets both on these estimates and the relative needs of the entire network of affiliates. Second, the investor must establish clear lines of accountability for asset deterioration and exchange losses. Third, an equitable and straightforward system of controls must be developed to help measure the performance of working capital managers. Our discussions in multinational companies have suggested that where these conditions exist, the management of working capital in international business loses much of its mystery. It is possible to assess working capital investment practices for each affiliate comparatively dispassionately. A logical basis exists for decisions regarding ultimate borrowing sources and acceptable terms for temporary borrowings. And finally the portfolio management of network liquid assets can be based both on individual affiliates' liquidity needs and on global money market conditions to the extent that exchange restrictions and controls permit.

BIBLIOGRAPHY

Archer, Stephen H. "A Model for the Determination of Firm Cash Balances," *Journal of Financial and Quantitative Analysis,* March 1966.

Bean, Virginia L., and Reynolds Griffith. "Risk and Return in Working Capital Management," *Mississippi Valley Journal of Business and Economics,* Fall 1966.

Clarkson, Geoffrey P. E. *Portfolio Selection: A Simulation of Trust Investment.* (Englewood Cliffs, N.J.: Prentice-Hall, Inc., 1962).

Colin, Park, and John W. Gladson. *Working Capital.* (New York: The Macmillan Company, 1963).

Diamond, Walter H. "Doing Business Abroad—And Living with the Tax Impact," *Management Controls,* Bulletin of Peat Marwick Mitchell and Company, New York.

Eiteman, Wilford J., and James N. Holtz. "Working Capital Management," in *Essays on Business Finance,* 4th ed., Karl A. Boedecker, ed. (Ann Arbor, Mich.: Masterco Press, 1963).

Fisher, Edward P. "Financing Foreign Operations," *The Financial Executive,* October 1964.

Gole, V. L. "The Management of Working Capital," *Australian Accountant,* June 1959.

Griswold, J. A. *Cash Flow Through a Business.* (Hanover, N.H.: Amos Tuck School of Business Administration, Dartmouth College, 1955).

Macmillian, Claude. "Swap as a Hedge in Foreign Exchange," *California Management Review,* 1965.

Sharpe, William F. "A Simplified Model for Portfolio Analysis," *Management Science,* January 1963.

Walker, Ernest W. "Towards a Theory of Working Capital," *Engineering Economist,* January-February 1964.

Walter, James E. "Determination of Technical Solvency," *Journal of Business,* January 1959.

Case 12
ALBO ENTERPRISES

Albo Enterprises, S.A., was a wholly-owned Swiss subsidiary of a United States multinational capital goods manufacturer. The Swiss firm performed three principal functions in Albo's worldwide activities:

1. It was the headquarters for the firm's European operations
2. It was a holding company, the legal parent company for Albo's three wholly-owned affiliates in Germany, England, and Italy
3. It served as the central distribution point for components imported from the United States plants for ultimate use in the manufacture and assembly performed by the three European subsidiaries.

On July 18, 1968, the vice-president for finance of Albo, S.A., David Deutsch, assembled the most recent financial statements submitted by the European affiliates, which included their balance sheets, profit and loss statements, and projected funds flow. Deutsch noted that each affiliate had idle cash balances that, according to their plans, would not immediately be employed. After having been assured by the Albo headquarters in New York that these balances would not have to be remitted to the United States in accord with the general provision of the Foreign Direct Investment Regulations, Mr. Deutsch decided that the subsidiaries should invest their excess cash balances in a manner that would earn a return for the enterprise.

The English subsidiary had balances of £1 million that were available for 30 days. Albo-Italy held L1 billion available for 90 days, and the German affiliate's DM10 million would not be required in the operations for 180 days.

Exhibit 1 contains a brief description of various European debt instruments as well as a description of time deposits in the Eurodollar market. Exhibit 2 indicates the current yields. Exhibit 3 graphs recent movements of short-term interest rates. The spot and forward rates for the respective currencies for 30, 90, and 180 days are provided in Exhibit 4. Exhibit 5 contains the company economist's one-year forecast of the probability of exchange devaluation or revaluation for the lire, pound sterling, and Deutsche mark, respectively. Exhibit 6 includes relevant data on income and withholding taxes.

Questions

1. What factors should Mr. Deutsch consider in deciding how to best use the affiliates' idle cash balances?
2. What are the alternative methods of employing the funds?
3. What criteria should Mr. Deutsch use as guidelines for his analysis?
4. What, if any, plan of action should Mr. Deutsch adopt?

EXHIBIT 1

General Description of Various European Countries' Available Debt Instruments*

I. Switzerland

There is in Switzerland no market in bankers acceptances, in commercial and sales finance paper, nor in treasury bills available to the corporate treasurer for investing surplus funds.

Demand deposits

Depending upon the client relationship, the "big five" banks and some cantonal, local, and nonincorporated private banks accept interest-bearing demand deposits. There are no minimum or maximum deposit requirements.

Time deposits

These same banks also accept time deposits, the most frequently employed medium for the investment of surplus funds in Switzerland. Maturities may be for three, six, nine, twelve, eighteen, and twenty-four months and even longer in some instances. However, deposits for longer than ninety days are rarely accepted as they are subject to a .06 per cent stamp tax on the face amount up to six months and .12 per cent over six months, and a 3.00 per cent coupon tax on the interest. There are no maximum limits, but 100,000 francs ($23,000) is generally regarded as a minimum amount. Rates of interest vary with maturity and amount.

The banks further offer callable deposit facilities providing for withdrawal at the option of the bank or the depositor. These deposits do not have a fixed maturity. A ninety-day callable deposit provides for withdrawal ninety days after notice is given either by the lender or borrower. Rates also vary according to maturity and amount. A ninety-day callable deposit currently bears interest at 3.75 per cent per annum.

Residents and nonresidents alike may maintain foreign currency time deposits in Swiss banks at current market rates. For all time deposits 27 per cent withholding taxes are deducted from the interest earned.

Government and municipal bonds

Government and municipal bonds are available on the stock exchanges, but in small amounts. Bonds maturing in 1968-1969 now afford a yield between 3.00 per cent and 3.25 per cent per annum depending on the credit standing of the issuer.

* Rates are approximate due to the fluctuating nature of the market.

II. Italy

There is in Italy no market in bankers acceptances, commercial paper, nor in short-term bonds issued by banks available to the corporate treasurer for investing surplus funds.

Demand deposits

Banks pay interest on deposits under the interbank agreement that fixes maximum rates. They currently pay interest at 0.50 per cent annually on demand deposits and at 2 per cent annually on such deposits with average annual balances of more than £ ½ million ($8,000).

Time deposits

On time deposits most banks currently pay interest as follows:

Three to six months	2.25 per cent
Six to twelve months	3.63
Twelve to eighteen months	3.75

On balances of more than £ 100 million ($160,000), the rates may be 0.50 per cent per annum higher.

Government securities

Most Treasury bills are sold through the Bank of Italy to banks, which keep them in their own investment portfolios; but amounts may be available to other investors through these banks. Certain outstanding government obligations with stipulated maturities of seven to nine years may also be purchased at prices now affording annual yields of about 5 per cent tax free.

III. England

The London money market is highly organized and more comprehensive than any financial market in continental Europe. However, the treasurer of a company does not have as wide a choice of media for the investment of surplus funds as his American counterpart.

Demand deposits

British banks do not pay interest on demand deposits. Some interest-bearing time deposits, however, may be withdrawn at very short notice.

Time deposits

London clearing banks accept time deposits in sterling at seven days' withdrawal notice with interest at 2 per cent below the Bank Rate regardless of the length of the time or the amount of deposit. There are no rigid rules on minimum deposits; it depends on the client's relationship with the bank.

Unlike clearing banks, merchant banks and the London branches of British overseas and American and other foreign banks accept sterling time deposits for specified periods at rates varying with the term. Arrangements may be made for withdrawal of such deposits on one day's notice. The minimum amounts accepted for time deposits vary between £ 50,000 and £ 100,000 ($120,000-$240,000). Present rates for time deposits are as follows:

One day's notice	8 per cent
Two days' notice	8 3/8 per cent
Seven days' notice	8 1/2 per cent
One month's fixed	8 1/8 per cent
Three months' fixed	8 per cent

Deposits with local authorities

Local authorities (counterparts of municipalities in United States usage) make a practice of borrowing funds in the short-term market and issuing to lenders their deposit receipts that are in registered form and non-negotiable. Such receipts are generally considered prime in the London market. Some companies make use of this means of investing their surplus funds, although such investments cannot be considered liquid as depositors may not withdraw or purchase any quantity of bills of specific maturity in less than forty-five days. The yield on Treasury bills of forty-five-day to ninety-one-day maturities is presently 7½ per cent and the rate on shorter maturities from 1/16 per cent to 1/8 per cent less.

Government bonds

Government bonds, maturing up to five years, presently yield close to 7.50 per cent to redemption. Yields in the medium-term (five to ten years) range now also run slightly below 7.50 per cent. The choice of maturities is not as broad as in the United States.

Bankers acceptances

The use of bankers acceptances or bank bills for the investment of corporate surplus funds is not widespread. The rate for ninety-day bills is usually the Treasury bill rate plus .25 per cent. Therefore, they are not as attractive as Treasury bills, unlike the case in the United States, nor are bankers acceptances always available in the maturities desired.

Trade bills

Although a market for such bills exists in the United Kingdom, they are not sold to the investing public, but are discounted with the discount houses who generally hold them in their own portfolios to maturity.

Tax reserve certificates

Tax reserve certificates are offered by the Bank of England for purchase by corporations in anticipation of tax payments in multiple of £5 par value with interest at the rate of 4 3/8 per cent* tax free. Interest is allowed for each com-

* 3 per cent if redeemed for cash rather than in payment of tax.

plete calendar month, but is not allowed on any certificate outstanding for more than twenty-four complete months. Principal and interest can be tendered in payment of taxes even after twenty-four months from the date of issue.

Advances to United States parent or associated company

At one time the Bank of England permitted United Kingdom subsidiaries of foreign companies to make loans to their parent or associated companies provided the loan or advance could be charged against earned surpluses available for payment of dividends, but presently the Bank of England will not normally give permission for such loans.

IV. Germany

In the absence of a market for bankers acceptances and commercial paper, the treasurer of a company established in Germany has a relatively limited choice of media for investment of surplus corporate funds.

Demand deposits

German commercial banks currently pay interest rates of .50 per cent to .75 per cent on Deutsche mark demand deposits depending on the type of account. Interest may, however, now be paid only on deposits maintained by German residents.

Time deposits

The main investment medium for the corporate treasurer is Deutsche mark time deposits. The interest rates currently paid on such balances of German residents regardless of the size of the deposit are shown below:

Call	1½ per cent
30 days	3 per cent
90 days	3½ per cent
180 days	4½ per cent
360 days	4½ per cent

Interest may not be paid on time deposits maintained by nonresidents, a restriction put into effect recently by the German Federal Bank. As it is aimed at nonresident-owned balances, it does not apply to German subsidiaries of foreign companies.

Treasury obligations

Treasury bills and noninterest-bearing Treasury bonds with maturities up to two years are available only to domestic banks, but corporate investors may buy from the banks outstanding two-four year Treasury notes having six to twelve months' maturity. The yield is about 4½ per cent, but the market supply is limited. New issues of two-four year Treasury notes are sold from time to time and are also available to corporate investors; recent issues were sold to return about 5 per cent. The minimum amount available is DM100,000 ($25,000), and the customary trading unit is DM1 million ($250,000).

Twenty-year bonds of the federal and state governments and such public bodies as the railroads and the postal system currently yield 6 per cent. Blocks of outstanding bonds maturing in about five years occasionally become available in the market at prices yielding about 5.50 per cent.

V. Short-Term Eurodollar Investments

A deposit in a foreign bank or in an overseas branch of an American bank represents the principal means of investment in Eurodollars. These depositaries normally will accept deposits for varying maturities, including "call," two days' notice, seven days' notice, and any whole number of months up to five years. The bulk of the deposits are for periods of one year or less. It is frequently possible to negotiate options for withdrawals prior to final maturity that require a prepayment penalty if the option is exercised.

The yields for new deposits vary from day to day. The rates paid for Eurodollar deposits on July 18, 1968, by foreign branches of United States banks were: 6 per cent for 30 days, 6 3/8 per cent for 90 days and 6 5/8 per cent for 180 days.

EXHIBIT 2

Current Yields on Ninety-Day Investments on July 18, 1968

	90 Days
Treasury bills:	
Germany	4.50
Italy	3.05
Switzerland	3.00
United Kingdom	7.50
Three-month bank deposits:	
Germany	3.50
Italy	2.25
Switzerland	3.75
United Kingdom	8.00

EXHIBIT 3

Short-Term Interest Rates

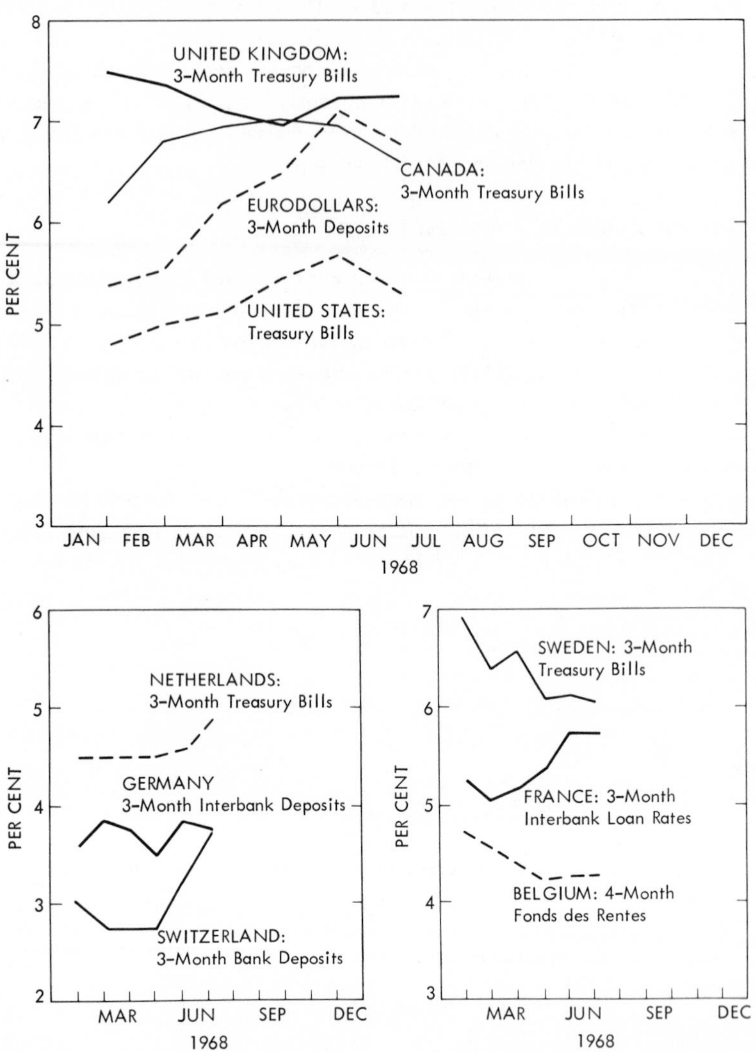
UNITED KINGDOM:
3-Month Treasury Bills
CANADA:
3-Month Treasury Bills
EURODOLLARS:
3-Month Deposits
UNITED STATES:
Treasury Bills
PER CENT
8
7
6
5
4
3
JAN FEB MAR APR MAY JUN JUL AUG SEP OCT NOV DEC
1968
NETHERLANDS:
3-Month Treasury Bills
GERMANY
3-Month Interbank Deposits
SWITZERLAND:
3-Month Bank Deposits
PER CENT
6
5
4
3
2
MAR JUN SEP DEC
1968
SWEDEN: 3-Month
Treasury Bills
FRANCE: 3-Month
Interbank Loan Rates
BELGIUM: 4-Month
Fonds des Rentes
PER CENT
7
6
5
4
3
MAR JUN SEP DEC
1968

EXHIBIT 4

Foreign Exchange Rates

	SPOT RATES PER UNIT	SWAP DIFFERENCE—PER CENT PER ANNUM*		
		1 month	3 months	6 months
England	$2.3912	2.46% disc.	2.61% disc.	3.3% disc.
Germany	.2495	3.07% prem.	2.95% prem.	2.26% prem.
Italy	.001606	.28% prem.	.87% prem.	.47% prem.
Switzerland	.2324	1.22% prem.	1.89% prem.	2.03% prem.

* Swap difference—defined as the percentage difference between selling or buying a foreign currency today (called spot) and either repurchasing or selling that currency at a future date, normally 30, 60, 90, or 180 days from the date of the original sale or purchase. For example, if spot sterling is selling at $2.3912 and at $2.3765 three months forward, the discount would be approximately 2.46 per cent per annum, as determined by the following formula:

$$\frac{\text{(spot) } 2.3912 - 2.3765 \text{ (forward)}}{2.3912 \text{ (spot)}} \times 4 \text{ (factor for converting to per annum basis)} = 2.46\%$$

EXHIBIT 5

Economist's Forecast of Exchange Rate Changes

	PROBABILITY OF CHANGE IN EXCHANGE RATES OF VARIOUS AMOUNTS (FROM 2/18/68 TO 1/18/69)						
Currency of:	*+10%*	*+5%*	*0*	*−5%*	*−10%*	*−15%*	*−20%*
Germany	.1	.2	.7				
Italy			1.0				
Switzerland	.05	.1	.85				
United Kingdom			.5	.1	.2	.2	

EXHIBIT 6

Relevant Tax Information

The following rates of tax were in effect on July 18, 1968, for interest income earned within the respective countries.

Country in which interest income earned:	*Income tax levied on resident companies*	*Withholding tax levied on nonresident companies*
United Kingdom	40%	41%
Switzerland	7.2%	30%
Germany	15% , 51%*	15%
Italy	32%	32%

*The 15 per cent rate applied to distributed income, the 51 per cent rate to undistributed income.

Case 13
CHAMPION MANUFACTURING COMPANY

The Champion Manufacturing Company (CHAMCO) of Chicago, Illinois, was one of the largest United States producers of electrical lighting fixtures for home and industrial uses. The company sold a broad line of fixtures ranging from $17 to $340. In 1966 the company's sales were close to $300 million; 10 per cent was accounted for by overseas affiliates. Since the mid 1930's CHAMCO had been engaged in export and foreign licensing activities. By the early 1960's it owned a minority interest in more than fifty foreign companies to which it had granted licenses to manufacture CHAMCO lighting fixtures for local markets.

In June 1965 the president of the company, acting on the advice of an international business consulting firm, established an international division within CHAMCO and brought in R. M. Morrison, a retired Navy admiral, to manage the new division. Throughout the company's thirty years of business involvements with foreign markets, CHAMCO's highest echelons of management had always considered sales and earnings abroad to be a marginal activity. The foreign operations were managed on a decentralized basis with each of four functional vice-presidents assuming worldwide responsibility for the interests of their respective divisions. Whenever problems arose or when major decisions had to be made for the foreign commitment, the vice-presidents and the president discussed the matter as a group and decisions were reached by informal consensus.

By late 1964 the CHAMCO president had begun to doubt the wisdom of continuing this method of managing the company's international business. He had been informed by the company's accountants that their earnings from abroad were considerably less than those received by other large firms. By coincidence a few months later CHAMCO received the "E" award from the United States Department of Commerce for its export performance; this occurrence served to heighten the president's interest in strengthening the company's position in foreign markets. In 1965 a consulting team was invited to look over CHAMCO's approach to international licensing, exporting, and investment, and to recommend new or different techniques for managing and becoming engaged in foreign commerical activities. The consultants advised CHAMCO to form an international division which would have complete control of CHAMCO's activities abroad.

When R. M. Morrison joined the company as Vice President for International Operations, he was told by the corporate president that he would have free rein to manage and overhaul international operations. Morrison hired as his administrative assistant Clair Crook, who had five years experience abroad as a commercial attache with the United States Department of State and whose education included an MBA degree in finance and international business. Morrison assigned Crook the task of making a three-month study of the company's entire international operations. This study would be used as the basis for Morrrison's subsequent appraisal of existing methods of operation and corporate policies. Crook was instructed to draw up a report on each of the company's commitments abroad that would include:

1. The original justification for CHAMCO's involvement
2. The management policies and procedures utilized in controlling each foreign operation
3. Problem areas that warranted prompt attention and required solutions
4. Recommendations for action.

For his initial assignment Crook investigated the CHAMCO licensing agreement and minority equity position in Champion do Brasil, S.A., in São Paulo, Brazil. His sources of information were company records, the original investment proposals, and conversations with staff members in the offices of the treasurer and comptroller. The information Crook gathered is presented below.

By 1957 the Brazilian market was effectively closed for foreign manufactured lighting fixtures as the result of import and foreign exchange controls and the effective competition of a domestic fixtures industry. A number of United States fixtures manufacturers that considered Brazil a potentially important market had established manufacturing operations there in the late 1950's in anticipation of severe import restrictions. Hence, in 1957 CHAMCO entered into a licensing agreement with a recently formed company (which was later renamed Champion do Brasil, S.A.) giving the latter the right to manufacture a limited line of CHAMCO fixtures. The Brazilian company was owned by Fernando Maquinas, a Brazilian, and Enrique Landau, an Argentine. Maquinas had been the local distributor for an American farm equipment manufacturer in the 1950's, after which time and for several years, he had been the CHAMCO distributor in Brazil. He was independently wealthy, the cousin of a high government official, and he devoted a considerable portion of his time to managing his coffee plantation and raising prize cattle on a model farm. Maquinas was described by CHAMCO's treasurer as "an excellent salesman, but an extremely proud man who was resentful of criticism, suggestions, or even questions about the rationale for his mode of operations." Landau was considered a top quality engineer. He had held licenses from CHAMCO since 1954 to manufacture lighting fixtures in Argentina, Chile, and Peru.

In mid-1958, the Latin American principals offered CHAMCO an opportunity to become a one-third partner in the Brazilian firm. The offer was accepted, and the rationale for the acceptance recorded in the minutes of the meeting held by the CHAMCO executive committee is as follows:

> 1. An investment of this type would be in line with the existing practice of obtaining 5 to 35 per cent of the equity of many of our licensees. These investments assist the company in developing closer relations with its licensees and in sharing to a greater extent the profits from foreign sales.
> 2. The Brazilian licensees have reported to us that the present shortages of working capital would limit their ability to aggressively promote CHAMCO fixtures in the near term, unless we were to supplement their cash position.
> 3. Under Brazilian law equity investments made by foreign companies in their Brazilian licensees would enable the latter to obtain licenses to import components and machine tools that in our case are required by Maquinas and Landau.
> 4. We consider Brazil an important market. It has a large population and has a growing middle class, an increasing amount of housing construction, and a demonstrated consumer acceptance of CHAMCO lighting fixtures.
> 5. Our investment in the Brazilian company would be a natural. Maquinas is a strong salesman, Landau has the manufacturing expertise, and CHAMCO can provide the required capital and product design.
> 6. To preclude any criticism of "Yankee Imperialism," CHAMCO should not obtain more than a minority position in the equity of any foreign business.

The agreement by which CHAMCO became a one-third partner included the following considerations: the capitalization of the existing Brazilian company was increased from Cr100 million to Cr240 million (240,000 shares of Cr1,000 par value common stock). CHAMCO's investment was $500,000. The other two partners each obtained 80,000 shares by contributing Cr10 million in cash, being credited Cr50 million for their investment in the business in 1956 and receiving Cr20 million credit for contributing a 220,000-square-meter parcel of land. The land had been purchased for Cr59 million (approximately $425,000) at the existing rate of exchange in 1956 as a site for the plant and for possible resale if its value increased. CHAMCO approved a request by its new partners to revalue the book value of the land to reflect its appreciated cruzeiro value. The three partners agreed to share equally in the profits of the company, and their intention was to distribute enough of each year's earnings to provide at least a 10 per cent rate of return based on the par value of the equity. CHAMCO was to continue to receive a royalty payment for making its fixtures available. The royalty payment was to be 3 per cent of the cruzeiro sales of the company, converted to dollars at the existing rate of exchange on the day payment was due, June 30 and December 31 of each year. If for any reason payment had to be delayed, CHAMCO would receive 6 per cent interest on the outstanding balance. The Brazilian partner, Maquinas, received commissions equal to 10 per cent of the company's sales as his compensation for being the general manager and marketing manager of the subsidiary. Landau, the third partner, would provide the production expertise in return for a $2,000 monthly salary. The subsidiary would be largely an assembly operation utilizing components shipped from suppliers in the United States that would be assembled, painted, and packaged for local consumption.

About two years after the partnership was formed, the subsidiary experienced a series of financial difficulties. Outside suppliers, which were relied on heavily, were frequently late in shipping goods to the subsidiary, which necessitated its carrying large "safety" inventories. The suppliers demanded sixty-day terms, but the retail dealers to whom the lighting fixtures were sold frequently ran their credit up to 180 days. The Brazilian economy had been experiencing rapid increases in the price of most goods (see Exhibit 1), and for CHAMCO do Brasil, increasingly more funds were required to carry the same physical volume of inventory. Caught in a credit squeeze, the Brazilian affiliate was forced to increase its indebtedness, often at a cost of 1.75 per cent *per month.* Exhibits 2 and 3 summarize the subsidiary's financial statements for the period 1960-1964. In an effort to relieve the pressure on the operation, a meeting was called in 1961 of the principals at which the Latin Americans suggested that each of the three should agree to forego the royalties, commissions, and unpaid loans which were owed to them by the business. CHAMCO, which had not received payment of royalties due to it during the first two and one-half years, waived its share of royalties for the period 1958-1960, while the others did the same for unpaid commissions and advances. Because the values of the principals' waivers were not identical, it was agreed that an amount of funds equal to the difference in waivers would be taken out of the company's future profits and used to repay CHAMCO and Maquinas before any further dividends were declared. Hence, as of June 1961, the subsidiary's records showed the following liabilities to have been written off the books:

	CHAMCO	Maquinas	Landau
Royalties due	Cr13,327,821		
Notes payable			Cr7,711,899
Commissions		Cr9,751,018	
Less amount to be taken out of future earnings	Cr5,615,921	Cr2,039,119	
Net amount waived	Cr7,711,899	Cr7,711,899	Cr7,711,899

At the same meeting it was decided to increase the amount of local processing of the imported lighting fixtures in order to be less dependent on imports. To accomplish this objective, additional funds were required to purchase raw materials and more complex machine tools needed for local processing. An agreement was reached to increase the capitalization of the company to Cr500 million. CHAMCO and Landau stated that they would invest Cr130 million each, but the Brazilian partner claimed that he was short of funds and asked for additional time to increase his share of the equity. He was granted an option to bring his investment up to one-third of the total equity by August 1963. In the interim the ownership of the company was revised to reflect the new contributions:

CHAMCO	42%
Landau	42%
Maquinas	16%
	100%

CHAMCO made its investment in three installments of approximately $200,000. By mutual consent Landau matched each of the CHAMCO payments with the equivalent in dollars, approximately thirty days later. By the time the $1 million had been exchanged for cruzeiros, it had produced Cr36,330,000 more than the Cr260 million required under the new agreement. Landau's investment had produced more cruzeiros than the CHAMCO contribution because of the thirty-day time difference in payments and a declining rate of exchange for the cruzeiro (see Exhibit 4). The two principals agreed to divide evenly the excess of cruzeiros, and Cr18,165,000 was credited to their accounts for future increases in capital. The fund was considered a dollar loan to the business by each of the principals, and it carried an 8 per cent annual rate of interest. They tentatively agreed to leave the funds in the business, but about six months later Landau drew out his share. CHAMCO's account was never touched.

In an effort to raise additional capital for the subsidiary, two-thirds of the large parcel of land belonging to the company was put on the market. One small section was sold at Cr3,000 per square meter, on terms of 10 per cent down, 40 per cent in thirty days, and the balance in twenty four months at 12 per cent interest. No other sales were made, presumably because there were too few investors with enough liquidity to purchase that large a tract.

As shown in Exhibit 3, the subsidiary's sales and earnings in cruzeiros increased steadily and dramatically during the period 1962-1964. In order to finance the growing volume of business, it became necessary for the Brazilian partner, Maquinas, not only to devote a major portion of this time to arranging for short-term borrowings, but in addition to endorse personally the notes of the firm. By 1964 the cost of such indebtedness reached 3½ per cent a month, which reflected the rapid rate of general price increases throughout the country. On several occasions Maquinas and Landau had written to CHAMCO and requested assistance in arranging for the required financing. They suggested that CHAMCO loan funds to the subsidiary or enter into a swap arrangement with a Brazilian bank. On both accounts the CHAMCO management refused, replying that it had never received royalty or dividend payments from the subsidiary and that the company followed the policy of not providing financial assistance to foreign affiliates in which it owned less than 50 per cent—other than to extend liberal terms on goods which the parent company actually sold to its affiliates.

The lack of remittances to CHAMCO reflected the subsidiary's tight working capital position as well as the government's restrictions on royalty payments to foreign licensors. In 1964 Brazil instituted a requirement that all licensing arrangements in which a foreigner owned the patent must be registered with the Brazilian government in order for royalties to be paid. Champion do Brasil had applied for such approval in 1964 but no word had ever been heard from the government. One CHAMCO manager told of his own experience in trying to secure approval for the affiliate to remit funds. During his annual visit to Brazil, he had been ushered into a large room to meet the appropriate government administrator; there he found "the entire wall covered with stacks of unprocessed applications, all the way up to the ceiling."

The unpaid royalties (and the 6 per cent interest accrued on the balance) had been recorded on the subsidiary's books as an amount equal to 3 per cent of the affiliate's annual net sales. The Brazilian partner privately acknowledged that the amount owed CHAMCO was larger than that recorded because the posted cruzeiro figure did not accurately reflect the *dollar* obligation to CHAMCO—but he doubted that he could borrow further if the local bankers became aware of the actual amount of the indebtedness.

A problem which faced the subsidiary was how to price its goods to remain competitive and keep ahead of the rapidly rising costs. To curb inflationary pressures the government had asked companies to limit their price increases to 6 per cent per year. Firms that adhered to this voluntary restraint received a reduction in their corporate income tax rates from the standard 28 per cent to 20 per cent as well as:

1. An increase in their weekly foreign exchange quota for imports
2. Increased credit facilities with the Banco do Brasil
3. Authorization to use all of the exchange generated by exports to pay for import requirements.

Since 1962 Maquinas had dogmatically maintained the 6 per cent pricing policy because his cousin held a high government office, and he felt morally obliged to cooperate with the government's program. For a while CHAMCO was agreeable to this approach because it expected to benefit from the tax incentive program. However in 1965 a member of the CHAMCO treasurer's staff raised the question of whether or not it would be advisable to try to persuade Maquinas to forego his patriotism in favor of higher prices. However, it was recognized that if the Brazilian would agree, a new pricing policy would have to be designed—one that would provide guidelines regarding both the *amount* and the *timing* of price increases.

When Clair Crook was in the process of organizing the notes he had taken on Champion do Brasil, S.A., he began to evaluate what should be included in his report to Mr. Morrison. Several of the subsidiary's transactions had appeared to be of doubtful value to CHAMCO, as were many of the agreements and commitments made by the parent company. Furthermore Crook was undecided as to how well the Brazilian affiliate had actually fared over the past few years. Its financial statements were not consolidated with those of the parent corporation for purposes of public reporting, and therefore no attempt had ever been made to translate the cruzeiro accounts of the affiliate into dollars.

The more he thought about his report, the more confident he became that he should answer the basic question, "In what manner and how effectively had CHAMCO been able to manage and protect its investment in Brazil?" And the answer to that would require an analysis of how well CHAMCO had been able to measure the consequences of the inflationary environment and to deal with them.

EXHIBIT 1

Price Indices in Brazil, 1960-1965 (1960 = 100)

Year	*Wholesale prices (including coffee)*	*Wholesale prices (excluding coffee)*	*Cost of living*
1960	100	100	100
1961	140	138	138
1962	211	213	211
1963	371	370	370
1964	686	687	686
1965	1,032	1,072	1,100

EXHIBIT 2

Balance Sheet, Champion do Brasil, S.A., 1960-1964
(in thousands of cruzeiros)

	1960	*1961*	*1962*	*1963*	*1964*
Current assets					
Cash	12,484	12,871	122,995	88,596	195,526
Net receivables	201,346	357,897	683,669	528,228	749,248
Advanced payments to suppliers	10,387	22,641	12,962	10,049	
Exchange deposits for imports*	4,092	13,784	64,023	14,679	28,341
Inventories†					
Raw materials and parts	94,675	209,885	400,198	509,709	720,250
Finished stock	13,343	43,710	37,248	48,932	202,582
Fixed assets					
Land	30,620	30,620	31,220	110,483	295,021
Net plant and equipment‡	10,234	38,316	45,539	57,997	147,534
Other assets					
Advance payments to Maquinas		33,240	77,324	48,507	48,274
Prepaid rent§			43,086	33,150	30,290
Total assets	377,181	762,946	1,518,264	1,450,330	2,416,066
Current liabilities					
Accounts payable	63,539	95,374	260,068	280,481	507,895
Trade notes payable	29,729	71,689	33,448	26,838	37,353
Bank loans payable	16,063	22,274	17,399	21,333	98,329
Notes payable – financing			414,994	189,700	576,846
Accrued liabilities					
Taxes	2,100	6,116	24,821	22,633	73,657
Salaries and wages	859	1,293	3,863	6,387	12,947
Royalties	20,455	23,517	88,161	88,161	88,161
Commissions	4,436	21,119	152,853	195,055	289,029
Capital stock and reserves					
Capital stock and surplus	240,000	503,417	504,492	601,577	713,684
Reserve for future capital increase (CHAMCO)		18,165	18,165	18,165	18,165
Total liabilities and capital	377,181	762,964	1,518,264	1,450,330	2,416,066

Notes to Champion do Brasil Balance Sheet:

* There are financial surcharges of 10 per cent on dollars purchased for imports and 30 per cent for dollars purchased for financial transactions. The company records as exchange premiums the deposits made to obtain exchange contracts for future importation.

† Inventories of raw materials, purchased components, and finished products are valued at cost on a first-in-first-out basis; finished products include cost of raw materials and purchased components only.

‡ Depreciation calculated on the straight-line method at the maximum annual rates permitted for income tax purposes.

§ At the end of 1962 the corporation advanced Cr43,086,000 to a local firm to enable it to purchase the building presently rented by the company. This amount will be amortized in rent payments up to 1969.

EXHIBIT 3

Selected Profit and Loss Accounts for Champion do Brasil, S.A., 1960-1964
(in thousands of cruzeiros and as a per cent of sales*)

	1960	*%*	*1961*	*%*	*1962*	*%*	*1963*	*%*	*1964*	*%*
Net sales	526,732	100.0	659,529	100.0	1,750,177	100.0	2,331,913	100.0	4,082,626	100.0
Cost of goods sold	400,000	76.0	481,384	73.0	1,217,198	69.0	1,545,191	66.0	2,600,293	64.0
Gross profit	126,732	24.0	178,145	27.0	532,979	31.0	786,722	34.0	1,482,333	36.0
Commissions on sales	41,360	8.0	76,075	12.0	200,494	12.0	247,733	11.0	252,768	6.0
Total gross profit	85,372	16.0	102,070	15.0	332,485	19.0	538,989	23.0	1,230,565	30.0
General expenses	66,998	12.5	68,338	10.0	96,235	5.5	207,619	9.0	152,708	4.0
Operating profit	18,374	3.5	33,732	5.0	236,250	13.5	331,370	14.0	1,077,857	26.0
Deductions:										
Interest on accounts payable and notes payable	15,944	3.0	23,244	4.0	44,076	2.5	66,583	2.4	205,265	5.0
Other bank charges	17,339	3.4	31,780	5.0	80,086	4.6	134,348	6.0	364,071	9.0
Depreciation	1,783	0.2	4,860	0.7	15,004	.8	18,132	0.8	19,224	0.4
Other income	20,109	4.0	27,227	4.1						
Net profit	3,417	0.6	1,075	0.1	97,085	5.5	112,107	4.8	489,297	12.0

* Note: Numbers are rounded

EXHIBIT 4

The Free Market Cruzeiro: Dollar Exchange Rate, by Quarter 1958-1965

Year, end of quarter		*Cruzeiros per U.S. dollar rate*
1958	I	106.7
	II	132.8
	III	156.3
	IV	138.5
1959	I	141.6
	II	148.5
	III	167.5
	IV	203.8
1960	I	191.9
	II	187.2
	III	190.8
	IV	205.1
1961	I	276.5
	II	261.5
	III	298.0
	IV	318.5
1962	I	318.0
	II	359.5
	III	475.0
	IV	475.0
1963	I	475.1
	II	620.0
	III	620.0
	IV	620.0
1964	I	1,368.5
	II	1,200.1
	III	1,621.5
	IV	1,850.0
1965	I	1,850.0
	II	1,850.0
	III	1,850.0
	IV	2,220.0

Source: IMF *International Financial Statistics.*

Case 14
BELL CAMPINAS, S.A.*

At its August 1962 meeting the board of directors of Bell Manufacturing Company, a consumer hard goods producer, voted to increase the company's investment in its Brazilian subsidiary, Bell Campinas. Bell had been active in foreign markets for many years. In fact some Bell products were better accepted abroad than domestically in product lines in which the company was a latecomer. In 1961 72 per cent of total sales were in foreign markets.

Bell Campinas was organized in 1959 to assemble and distribute refrigerators in Brazil. Although sales in Brazil had increased substantially each year (see Exhibit 1), the market had grown only in conjunction with the availability of consumer credit. Bell had experienced a similar association of the growth of consumer credit and advancing consumer hard goods sales in other countries, including the United States. Liberal credit terms were extraordinarily important to inflation-conscious Brazilian consumers, who insisted on incurring indebtedness to turn the galloping price rise to advantage. Management had decided in July to extend installment purchase terms from twelve to twenty four months to assure sales. To finance the refrigerator sales forecast for the first six months of Bell's fiscal year on the extended credit terms, Bell Campinas would need 1,875 million cruzeiros (Cr) or $5,137,000 at the pegged "free" rate then existing of 365 cruzeiros to the United States dollar[1] (Exhibit 1). Other funds needs would be met from Campinas' internal sources.

The parent company was only willing to commit equity capital to Bell Campinas to the extent of 80 per cent of plant and equipment book value, 20 per cent of cash and receivable contracts, and ninety days of inventory requirements. These equity participation limits, set in the summer of 1961 for all Bell subsidiaries operating in inflationary economies with weak currencies, reflected top management's desire to limit Bell's exposure to exchange losses. These limits applied to investments made subsequent to the decision. (The cost of excessive exposure is reflected in Bell Campinas' profitability in fiscal 1960 and 1961 when equity was the only significant source of the subsidiary's funds—Exhibits 1 and 2.) In compliance with this standard it would be necessary to obtain Cr $1,500,000,000, from outside sources in this instance. At the conclusion of the

* This case, Bell Campinas, S.A., EA-F 270R, was prepared as the basis for class discussion rather than to illustrate either effective or ineffective administration.

[1] Throughout the postwar period Brazil had had one of the world's most complex multiple exchange systems. Former President Quadros moved to establish a single free exchange rate. Aside from special arrangements concerning coffee and cacao exports, this had been achieved. Yet the pegged free rate had not kept pace with basic economic forces tending to accelerate the rate of cruzeiro deterioration. This had given rise to an active parallel market. The so-called free rate was pegged by the Bank of Brazil, the only institution permitted to deal in foreign exchange at this time. If Bell were to provide dollars (or other foreign exchange) for its subsidiary, these funds could move legally only through the Bank of Brazil at the pegged rate. In the parallel market during August the exchange rate was approximately Cr555 per United States dollar. Transactions in this market were not sanctioned by the Brazilian Government.

August meeting the board had asked the vice-president of finance, Mr. Senturia, to prepare a financing plan.

Mr. Senturia realized that his recommendation must take into account Brazil's inflation, the weakening exchange rate, and the impact of taxation. The financing plan must enable Campinas to survive government and monetary regulations. At the same time it must accommodate Bell Campinas' return visits to the Brazilian money markets. In sum, his recommendation must reflect the company's intention to remain in Brazilian markets for many years.

Brazil had enjoyed a recent period of considerable growth, a development made all the more remarkable in view of the imbalance prevailing in the economy. Inflationary conditions had caused the cost of living to increase fifteen-fold since 1948. The inflation encouraged imports and discouraged exports by making domestic prices higher than international prices. Consequent painful balance-of-payments corrections had entailed severe import restrictions. Despite this turbulence in the economy, the country's industrial output had increased 100 per cent in real terms between 1946 and 1962.

In 1960 and 1961 the pace of inflation had accelerated. The following governmental expenditures, among others, contributed to a large deficit in each of these years: substantial financial resources had been required to support the increasing coffee inventory; the construction of the new capital, Brasilia, had cost the government 73 billion cruzeiros; ex-President Kubitschek had undertaken large-scale industrial projects. Finally, government administration had been inefficient. These deficits were financed substantially by monetization of the public debt, i.e., by the creation of bank deposits and the issuance of paper money (see Exhibit 3), and it was this which fueled the inflation. By the same token this period was one of considerable expansion of the banking system's claims on the government. The prospects for further inflation in 1962 were aggravated by a 40 per cent wage increase approved for federal employees.

In 1961 the already high level of annual government deficits was stepped up in the budgets for 1962 and 1963. In addition, Premier Neves publicly noted in 1962 that the proposed budgets failed to take into account the cost of projected 40 per cent wage increases as well as the rapidly increasing deficits of the railway system. The rate of the free cruzeiro had weakened from 40 to the dollar in 1953 to an average of 74 in 1955, 90 in 1957, 205 in 1960, and to 315 in 1961.

Chronic inflation had colored the evolution of Brazilian financial institutions and had imposed limitations on the availability of funds for industrial concerns. Although the stock of money had increased markedly in recent years (Exhibit 3), the growth of commercial bank deposits was inhibited because of the imposition of an interest rate ceiling on commercial bank loans that handcuffed the banks in competition for deposits. Unaffected by rate restrictions, private finance companies were better able to obtain cruzeiro deposits. Other financial institutions such as savings banks, insurance companies, and pension funds had preferred investments in real estate to commercial loans, as the former provided an effective hedge against inflation. As a result only an infant capital market existed for would-be industrial borrowers to utilize as a means of effecting the financing required for large-scale and rapid transfers of real resources to growth industries.

Also, government spending to finance enlarged coffee inventories, massive real estate projects, and the burgeoning administrative apparatus of government tended to deprive industry of the economy's real resources.

In July of 1962 the Brazilian Superintendency of Money and Credit (SUMOC) issued a directive which in effect gave the Bank of Brazil a monopoly on legal foreign exchange transactions. This measure, coupled with existing import and export remittance regulations, provided the government with substantial control of foreign exchange in its attempt to preserve hard currency reserves. Bell could readily provide Campinas with foreign capital in the form of currency or banking transfers because the Bank of Brazil needed hard currencies. Mr. Senturia was not at all certain, however, that future remittances from the subsidiary to the parent company could move through this market. The Bank of Brazil was unwilling to cover foreign exchange transactions at the present time – i.e., the Bank would exchange cruzeiros for dollars but would not in return exchange dollars for cruzeiros.

The latest SUMOC directive was merely one of many restrictive measures likely to be introduced during this troubled time. The exchange market was knotted by currency regulations that imposed an artificial rate of exchange and inhibited currency movements. Bell's foreign exchange during August would of necessity move through the official market at Cr$365 per United States dollar without cover or through the parallel market illegally at approximately Cr555 per United States dollar without cover. Since the Brazilian government officials reviewed corporate financial statements frequently and in detail, it was both difficult and risky to circumvent the required procedure of requesting authorization for dollar investment from the Bank of Brazil.

A number of alternative paths to accomplish the projected currenty transfer had emerged from discussions with Bell's bankers and a number of similarly situated corporate treasurers. The alternatives proved numerous enough that it became necessary to group them for analytical convenience into those entailing exchange rate risk and those not doing so. Two possibilities, a direct loan from the parent company to Bell Campinas and the establishment of a financing subsidiary, fell into the former category. Several possibilities, enumerated below, involved little or no exposure to deteriorating exchange rates.

The first of the alternatives bearing currency risk would have the parent company make available to the Brazilian subsidiary a bank draft for the amount required in United States dollars. This amount would then be sold for free cruzeiros to the Bank of Brazil. The Brazilian company would need to repay these funds in subsequent months by repurchasing United States dollars in the free market when cover later became available at the then prevailing exchange rate. On one prior occasion Bell Manufacturing had made a loan of $100,000 to its Brazilian subsidiary in November 1960 to be repaid in July of 1961. This amount was sold in the free exchange market at the rate of 205 cruzeiros to the dollar, and this gave the Brazilian subsidiary 20 million cruzeiros. In order to repay in July 1961, the subsidiary had to pay 30 million cruzeiros to buy the $100,000 at the then existing exchange rate of 300 cruzeiros to the dollar.

It was the Bell policy to charge 10 per cent per annum payable in dollars on all loans made to its subsidiaries. Interest on Bell Campinas borrowing, however, was deductible in computing profits subject to the Brazilian corporate profits tax, which for Campinas would be approximately 30 per cent.

A second alternative involving minimal exchange risk was the swap transaction. A swap loan was an arrangement between the Bank of Brazil and the United States parent of the Brazilian subsidiary. The United States parent would lend a given amount in dollars to the Bank of Brazil, depositing the dollars in its New York account. The Bank of Brazil in return would make a loan in Brazil of an equivalent number of cruzeiros to Bell Campinas. The exchange rate that the Bank of Brazil would apply would be less favorable to Bell than the prevailing free exchange rate. (On a previous occasion, when the rate was Cr$265 per United States dollar and commercial banks were permitted to engage in swap transactions, a Brazilian bank, Banco do Campinas, applied a rate of Cr$210 per dollar; thus Bell had to deposit $100,000 in order to provide Bell Campinas with Cr$21 million, while at the free rate it would have had to exchange only $79,245.)

The Bank of Brazil rates for swap transactions varied between Cr$180 and Cr$200 per dollar during August. Longer contracts and larger amounts commanded more favorable rates. If the transaction could be arranged, Mr. Senturia was confident that Bell could obtain a six-month swap loan sufficient to cover Bell Campinas' additional receivables need of Cr$1.5 million (excluding the parent's equity contribution) at a rate of Cr$180 per United States dollar. There would be no interest charged on either the dollar or cruzeiro balance. Since the swap loan would tie up Bell dollar funds, however, a 10 per cent interest charge per year payable in dollars would be required of Bell Campinas on the dollars deposited in New York. This interest payment would not be tax deductible in Brazil because this dollar deposit was not loaned to Bell Campinas. The interest payment would, perforce, be exposed to the vagaries of the free exchange rate of cruzeiros for dollars.

The possible methods of meeting Bell Campinas' funds needs without exposure to the risk of currency deterioration all relied upon financing within the financial structure of Brazil, thereby avoiding the need to trade currencies and undergo currency risk.

As one alternative without currency risk the Brazilian subsidiary might have been able to borrow its cruzeiro requirement from local banks. Under the influence of a ceiling rate imposed by SUMOC, the interest rate currently charged by Brazilian commercial banks was 14 per cent after additional charges were included. The advantage of this method was that the subsidiary could repay the loan in cruzeiros, benefitting from any inflation and avoiding the risk of exchange losses.

The major drawback with this method, however, was that local banks did not have an abundant supply of cruzeiros.[1] In general they were only willing to make loans for relatively small amounts up to Cr$5 million and for periods not to exceed 120 days. The local bank in some instances expected the parent company

[1] Cruzeiros in large measure were deposited in private finance companies that were not subject to the SUMOC directive and therefore were able to exact a 30-40 per cent lending rate per annum.

to maintain compensating balances and allow it to handle the borrower's commercial transactions. If this expedient were adopted, Mr. Senturia felt that the local subsidiary should not enter into loan agreements with more than twenty local banks because of these unwanted complications.

It was also possible either to discount Bell Campinas' receivables with recourse at Brazilian commercial banks or to borrow cruzeiros from local private finance companies. In both cases Bell Campinas could readily obtain the required cruzeiros. Mr. Senturia's assistant had computed the cost of discounting the receivables to be 30 per cent after including income lost in internally financed receivables. Eighteen per cent of the 30 per cent cost would be deductible in computing profits subject to Brazilian corporate taxes. It would cost approximately 36 per cent per annum to borrow cruzeiros from private finance companies, all of which would be deductible.

The final alternative consisted of establishing a finance company in Brazil to facilitate Bell Campinas' borrowing outside the existing financial institutions. Under this arrangement Bell Campinas would issue bills of exchange cosigned by the finance company and denominated in cruzeiros.[2] These bills could be sold to investors on the Brazilian stock market, where such bills were actively traded. With an investment of $1 million in the proposed finance company, which would guarantee the bills of exchange, it was felt that Bell Campinas would be able to issue bills in excess of its immediate working capital requirements.

Bell Campinas would be charged 10 per cent per annum for the finance company's investment, which would tie up Bell funds. In addition, Bell Campinas would incur the cost of discounting the bills of exchange. (In August 1962, six-month bills of exchange denominated in cruzeiros were being discounted at 18 per cent per annum in Rio.) The vice-president believed these cost components would be tax deductible since all funds would be advanced to Brazilian corporations.

With the background information collected and alternative financing methods identified, Mr. Senturia had now to make his recommendation. He recognized that in large measure the appropriate financing method would depend on future economic and political development in Brazil. More particularly, since the alternatives available varied in the amount of funds exposed to currency exchange rate risk, anticipations about the pace of inflation and the resultant deterioration of exchange rates must play a major role in the policy choice. With the number of possibilities posing a bewildering problem, Mr. Senturia decided to first choose the best of the alternatives not involving exchange risk and then compare it with each of the two possibilities entailing risk. A possible means of choosing the best in this last comparison would necessitate an estimate of losses or gains anticipated during the six months on the alternative with currency risk.

[2] A bill of exchange is a common form of commercial draft drawn between parties to foreign trade. The draft signifies the indebtedness of one of the parties to the other. Bills of exchange are marketed in most financial centers throughout the world. They usually are sold at a discount.

EXHIBIT 1

Bell Campinas, S.A.
Selected Financial Data
(in millions of cruzeiros)

	Fiscal (August 31) 1960	1961	1962	Forecast for first 6 months of fiscal 1963
Time sales	1,253	2,043	4,218	2,816
Total sales	1,794	2,524	5,943	3,118
Year-end time sales receivables*	787	1,541	2,704	4,579
Net earnings subject to exchange fluctuation	517	884	2,185	1,206
Return on net worth subject to exchange adjustment	24%	30%	71%	
Return on investment after adjustment for foreign exchange loss	2%	7%	42%	

*Ending balance.

EXHIBIT 2

Bell Campinas, S.A.
August 31
(in millions of cruzeiros)

	1960	1961	1962
Assets			
Cash	168	198	203
Time sales receivable	787	1,541	2,704
Accounts receivable	414	517	648
Foreign receivables		4	3
Deposits for exchange	8	17	21
Compulsory deposits		36	49
Advances, merchandise—long-term			27
Inventory	79	96	118
Finished			
In-process	268	312	411
Fixed assets	943	1,821	2,059
Total	2,667	4,542	6,243
Liabilities			
Notes payable—bank overdrafts			3
Bills discounted			3
Accounts payable (short-term)	483	812	1,749
Accounts payable (long-term)			1,245
Reserve for federal taxes	30	81	165
Other liabilities		103	61
Legal reserves	102	147	141
Other reserves	268	373	409
Common stock	1,531	1,531	1,531
Earned surplus	253	895	936
Total	2,667	4,542	6,243

EXHIBIT 3

The Rate of Inflation in Brazil

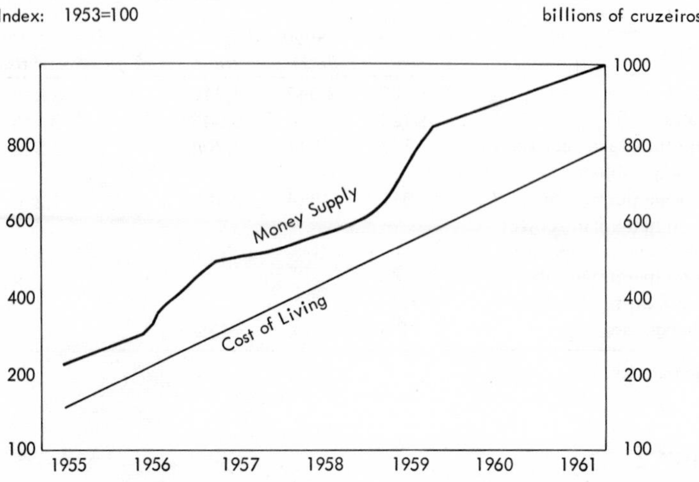

Source: International Monetary Fund

Sources and Instruments of International Finance: Part I

8

This chapter and the next two are concerned with the types of financing available to the international enterprise. These chapters describe the principal sources, instruments, and methods of financing foreign commercial transactions. The division of materials in chapters 8 and 9 is by source, with chapter 8 concentrating on commercial bank financing and chapter 9 on noncommercial bank sources and instruments. The concluding institutional chapter, 10, deals with the important subject of export financing.

Commercial banks are the single most important source of financing for the international enterprise. The range of services provided by banks is multifaceted and differs from country to country. In part the differences reflect various stages of development and sophistication in the national money and capital markets. Historical factors also help to explain the variations in commercial banking structures and government policies.

This chapter portrays the types of financing facilities that commercial banks characteristically provide the international concern. Initially, local currency accommodations are examined with a sequential discussion of short-term, medium-term and long-term instruments denominated in particular national currencies. The analysis next focuses on the short-term, medium-term and long-term instruments denominated in foreign currencies. In this connection, the entire Eurocurrency phenomenon—its evolution, current characteristics, and prospects—are examined. In a final section of the chapter the diverse activities of commercial banks' affiliated institutions are arrayed.

To illustrate characteristic terms and variations among countries, the instruments employed in the EEC countries are described. The rationale for this choice relates to the importance of European countries and the common market to the international investor. (It would have been impracticable to detail commercial bank lending activities in all countries.) A concluding section of the chapter summarizes the typical banking practices in Latin America, Asia, and Africa, in order to provide perspective. In reality there are more similarities than differences among the financial instruments used in various countries. The principal distinctions relate to credit availability and rates rather than to procedure in most instances. Obviously the rates and terms discussed in the chapter are subject to change, and the reader is cautioned to regard them as merely illustrative. In an actual borrowing situation the prospective borrower must consult the lending sources for current quotations and terms.

SHORT-TERM NATIONAL CURRENCY FINANCING

Short-term credit is the mainstay of commercial bank lending. Although exceptions are numerous, credits that mature within one year or less are used principally to finance inventory and receivables—i.e., working capital needs. They are frequently self-liquidating in the sense that sufficient cash flows are generated to repay the credits as inventories are converted into receivables and receivables are collected over the business cycle. Short-term loans are logical media for commercial banks whose deposits are subject to immediate withdrawal or withdrawal on short notice. Bankers naturally examine the prospective borrower's liquidity position in assessing the prospect of short-term credit repayment. This is usually the key facet of the banker's analysis. The principal short-term instruments used by banks in accommodating international firms' borrowing requests consist of the following: overdrafts, discounted bills, short-term loans, rediscountable short-term loans and undertakings.

Overdrafts

Overdrafts are the most commonly used financial tool in Europe. An overdraft is a line of credit which allows the customer to write checks in excess of the amount previously deposited up to some limit predetermined in the overdraft agreement. This limit is fixed subsequent to the bank's analysis of the international firm's request, needs, and prospective cash flows. By its very nature, an overdraft is a one-day demand loan although, due to practice and convention, overdrafts are frequently rolled over for considerable periods of time. The borrower promises to repay the amount overdrawn plus interest on the borrowed proceeds. There are also turnover commissions and service charges although many banks, including most foreign branches of U.S. banks, will waive these charges for their better customers. The characteristics of overdraft facilities in several European countries are outlined below.

Overdraft financing is the most expensive form of short-term financing in *Belgium.* Interest charges are related to the central bank's rate for advances on long-term government bonds. Yet it is common for the exact terms to be negotiated and ultimately to be dependent on the international concern's credit standing. As a guide, the overdraft rate is generally in the range of 1 per cent in excess of the prevailing Banque Nationale rate. Banks also may charge a commission of ¼ to 1 per cent per year on the total line of credit in consideration for making the line available. Assuming complete utilization of the overdraft facility, the total annual cost might be as high as 9 per cent in late 1968. For prime borrowers, however, the cost would be appreciably lower.

By way of contrast with Belgium, overdraft facilities in the *U.K.* are the cheapest and most commonly employed short-term financing arrangement. The British overdraft may be unsecured or secured by a guarantee or by hypothecated assets. The overdraft rate is tied to the Bank of England's rediscount rate (the bank rate). Rates range from ½ to 2 per cent above the bank rate, usually with an agreed upon minimum and occasionally with a predetermined maximum.

Overdrafts are a more expensive medium than trade bills or promissory notes in *France*. Banks usually extend direct, unsecured short-term credit by allowing international concerns to overdraw their accounts up to an agreed upon maximum. The borrower pays interest only on the amount of financing actually utilized. Overdrafts are not typically supported by a formal commitment from the bank and are subject to an additional commission of 1 per cent for a written commitment. The overdraft rate for prime borrowers consists of a basic rate calculated daily in relation to the overdraft balance and a monthly commission of .5 per cent applied to the highest debit balance outstanding during the month. The total cost approximated 7 per cent in late 1968.

In *Germany* the overdraft is the most common type of loan granted to industry, constituting roughly 60 per cent of the total loans and advances outstanding. Overdraft drawings occur against prearranged lines of credit that are usually valid for six months and secured only by the customer's signature. The rate in Germany is usually 3 per cent above the discount rate (or 7 per cent in late 1968). The actual cost in a particular situation, as in other countries, depends on the borrower's credit standing. Fees in addition to the basic rate include a ⅛ per cent turnover commission on the used line, a 1.5 per cent additional commission in the event the borrower overdraws his line without bank consent, plus a commitment commission of up to 3 per cent levied in connection with any unused portion of the overdraft facility.

In *Italy* the overdraft rate is fixed by the bank cartel at approximately 3.5 per cent above the discount rate. In late 1968 the rate for prime borrowers was in the 7 per cent range unless collateral was offered to support the overdraft facility. In the latter instances rates as low as 6 per cent were obtained in addition to a ⅛ per cent commission per quarter levied in connection with the highest amount borrowed during the quarter. Overdraft accommodations are renegotiated with commercial banks at least once a year.

In the *Netherlands* overdrafts are one of the least expensive short-term borrowing methods and dominate the short-term market. Usually borrowers repay drawings under overdraft arrangments in fixed amounts each month so that total drawings are repaid by the end of agreed upon periods. Invariably fixed in relation to the De Nederlandische Bank discount rate, the overdraft rate may include additional turnover charges that average .5 per cent. In late 1968 the total charge averaged 7 to 7.5 per cent. Usually a minimum overdraft rate is set, below which charges cannot drop in the event of a reduction in the discount rate.

In *Switzerland* the extreme popularity of overdrafts is attributable to the fact that the instrument is not subject to stamp taxes as are short-term notes. Although renewals are possible, this type of credit is seldom granted for periods in excess of one year. In late 1968 the overdraft rate payable quarterly was 5.25 per cent on daily outstanding balances. In addition a quarterly commission of ¼ per cent is levied in connection with unsecured overdrafts and is computed on the highest quarterly debit balance. Secured overdrafts are subject to a ⅛ per cent quarterly reduction in commissions.

Discounted Bills

The trade bill is a security device characterized by clearly understood legal safeguards that is used to finance transactions in goods taking some time to complete. Discounting is a technique of borrowing under which a firm draws a bill on its commercial bank. The discount is the margin between the ready money paid and the face value of the trade bill. It is calculated as an annual rate in relation to the maturity value of the note. Frequently promissory notes, as distinct from trade bills, are used in short-term financing. The principal distinction between promissory notes and trade bills is that the former is in the form of a promise to pay whereas the latter is in the form of an order to pay.

Trade bills and promissory notes vary widely with respect to amount, the time to maturity, and the credit standing of the maker. All of these factors help to explain the variations in rates quoted for these instruments by commercial banks. The characteristics of trade bill discounting in several European countries are depicted below.

In *Belgium* discounting trade bills is less expensive than overdraft financing. There are two techniques for discounting bills. The purchaser may take the bill and ask his bank to pay the bill to the seller or, alternatively, the seller may discount the bill drawn upon the purchaser with his own bank. The discounting cost is identical, but in the first instance the purchaser bears the cost, whereas in the second the seller bears the cost. The financing cost for bills with 120 days maturity is the central bank's discount rate plus .5 to 1 per cent, depending on the borrower's standing. The cost was approximately 4.75 per cent in late 1968. Other charges include a stamp tax of ½ per mill and occasionally a 1 per mill flat commission charge. Bills with longer than 120 days to mature command a higher basic discount rate to which must be added the commissions and charges.

In the *U.K.* most bills range in maturity from sixty to ninety days, although bills occasionally carry maturity dates of up to 180 days. Borrowers with a high credit standing are able to offer bills with their own signature alone. By way of contrast less credit-worthy companies must have their bills accepted by two merchant banks acting as acceptance houses and levying a .5 to 2 per cent commission charge. This charge is in addition to the basic discount of approximately .25 per cent below the bank rate.

In *France* the discounting of trade bills is the most important form of short-term financing. Maturities usually fall within a thirty- to ninety-day range. Bills can be rediscounted with the central bank, which helps to explain commercial banks' willingness to deal in bills. In late 1968 the prime rate on discountable bills was 5.1 per cent. Recently a new short-term credit facility called Mobilization of Commercial Credit has emerged. Under this arrangement credit for the borrower's entire turnover is guaranteed. To use this facility the borrower adds up all his invoices with a maximum eight- to ten-day spread in payment deadlines and notifies the bank of the amount of bills due on given dates. The bank immediately opens a credit line to cover the required amounts. The company merely signs a promissory note that is discountable on the spot and need not show the borrowers' invoices to the bank. The cost of this facility is comparable to normal discounting. For an additional fee banks can provide collection services as well.

In *Germany* the discount rate is fixed according to the amount involved and ranges between 1 and 3 per cent above the central bank rediscount rate for rediscountable bills and between 3 and 4 per cent for bills not rediscountable. To be eligible for rediscounting, bills must have a maturity of no longer than ninety days and bear three good names—the drawer, the drawee, and the discounting commercial bank.

In *Italy* commercial banks accept three types of paper—bills of exchange, financial notes, and commercial drafts—during the course of normal discounting business. Bills of exchange and financial notes carry the same discounting rates. Bills of exchange with maturities of up to 120 days are officially discounted at 1.5 per cent above the discount rate. Bills maturing in the 120 to 180-day range should, according to cartel rules, be discounted at 1.75 per cent above the official discount rate. Longer term bills are discounted only if the title to the goods is reserved; these bills are discounted at 2.25 per cent above the official discount rate. Commercial drafts are subject to higher discount rates. For commercial drafts maturing in thirty days the charge is 1.75 per cent above the discount rate. Those maturing within thirty to ninety days are charged the basic discount rate plus 2.25 per cent. In practice, however, the effective discount rates appear to range between 1 per cent and 1.25 per cent higher than the above-mentioned theoretical rates prescribed by Italy's bank cartel.

The discounting of bills is comparatively rare in the *Netherlands*. There is practically no market for bills that are not eligible for rediscounting at the central bank. The eligibility requirements are that bills should mature within 105 days, bear three good names, be denominated in guilders, and payable in the Netherlands at a location where there is an office of the central bank. The discount rate is based on the bank's yield for overdrafts. The rate of discount for commercial bills is about .25 to .15 per cent lower than the interest rate for overdrafts. Late in 1968 the discount rate was in the 6.5 to 7 per cent range in comparison to 7.5 per cent for overdrafts.

Bills are discounted in *Switzerland* usually at a rate .5 per cent in excess of the Swiss central bank rate. Additional charges include a ⅛ to ¼ per cent commission plus a ½ per mill stamp duty for each 180 days of maturity or fraction thereof. The above-mentioned rate and charges would apply to a high-quality client, and fractional increases in charges would be levied against the less credit-worthy. Although bill financing is not particularly prevalent in Switzerland, most activity is concentrated in the maturities of ninety days or less. Occasionally bills of 180 days are negotiated or shorter-term bills renewed to cover extended periods.

Short-Term Loans

A significant proportion of short-term bank financing is conducted on a nonsecured basis—that is, in the absence of collateral. The percentages of such lending vary from country to country and reflect differences in individual bank policy and central bank regulations. Secured loans are extended when the potential borrower is of questionable credit risk or when the amount to be financed exceeds what the bank considers to be prudent on an unsecured basis. In the case of secured loans the costs are influenced by the quality of the collateral and other covenants such as subordination or guarantees. Various types of short-term loans are extended—straight short-term loans, rediscountable short-term loans, special rediscountable short-term loans, and undertakings or deferred tax financing.

The *U.K.* commercial banking system is beginning to relax its opposition to short-term loans, and lending exempt from repayment on demand is becoming more prevalent. British commercial banks provide short-term loans at a cost tied to the Bank of England rate rather than at fixed rates. Generally, however, it is easier to obtain short-term loans from merchant banks or foreign banks in London than from British commercial banks.

Short-term loans on a secured basis are available in *Germany*. Banks usually impose lending limits equivalent to 75 per cent of the market value of fixed interest-bearing securities or 50 per cent of the market value of common stock. Interest rates are similar to overdraft charges. In the *Netherlands* and *Switzerland* commercial banks do not generally make short-term loans for a fixed amount and for a stipulated period against promissory notes; this is merely a matter of practice and does not represent any legal prohibition.

In *Italy* commercial banks make short-term loans in the 90- to 180-day maturity range on a secured basis. The collateral usually consists of merchandise or securities. In this connection the ownership to goods is often surrendered as guarantee for credits on open account, and secured overdraft rates normally apply. The short-term loans can be rolled over several times but with each renewal the interest rate and other provisions are subject to revision. When securities are used as collateral, the theoretical interest rate is fixed by the bank cartel as follows:

1. If the securities are government bonds, the interest rate is .75 per cent above the official discount rate, and the amount loaned may range between 80 and 90 per cent of the market value of the securities
2. If the securities are listed on the stock market and are actively traded, the interest rate becomes the discount rate plus 3 per cent, and the loan is limited to 60 to 70 per cent of the collateral's market value
3. If the securities are not listed, the loan rate is 3.25 per cent above the discount rate, and the advance against such securities may be restricted to 50 per cent of their value.

In reality effective lending rates range between .25 and 2 per cent higher than the established cartel rates.

Direct short-term loans are an important financial instrument in *France*. To a greater extent than elsewhere in Europe commercial banks are inclined to extend short-term credits against promissory notes that are then rediscounted with the central bank. This type of loan can be executed at a low interest rate because of the rediscountability of the borrower's promissory note. To qualify for rediscounting the note must be drawn with a maturity of no longer than ninety days and carry three signatures. Despite the restriction regarding maturity, notes are frequently renewed for up to 270 days and up to eighteen months if covering purchases of equipment with a lien. It is also possible in France to arrange special rediscountable credits when financing purchases in connection with government contracts. France's Caisse Nationale des Marches de l'Etat guarantees working capital credits for companies engaged in government work. To obtain such credits the international concern must apply both to its bank and to the CNME. The company must estimate its monthly payments and deduct from these payments all anticipated receipts from the government. The financing is based on the difference between these two magnitudes. The financing cannot exceed, however, 20 to 25 per cent of the total value of the contract. Usually prefinancing credits are provided on a ninety-day renewal basis for up to one year. When the government is making late payments, the contractor may apply for interim financing until payments are received. The maximum financing available in connection with late payments is 90 per cent of the contract value. The cost of both CNME guarantee plans is the same. In 1968 the cost was 6 per cent, including the commercial bank's commission for discounting.

Undertakings, or deferred tax payment financing, is another special short-term financing technique available in France. Under this arrangement short-term loans in an amount equivalent to the company's taxes or customs duties payable are obtained when a covering bank guarantee is issued in favor of the state authorities. Under such arrangements short-term loans with a maturity of up to 120 days can be obtained covering the full amount of taxes and customs duties payable. This practice, like rediscountable note financing, is uncommon elsewhere in Europe.

Arbi Loans

International Interest Arbitrage Financing (Arbi loans) is available to the international firm that wishes to augment expensive or scarce local short-term financing. Arbi loans involve the use of external sources of short-term capital to obtain local short-term financing. The object is to obtain loans in another country where money is abundant and cheap and to convert these borrowings into the desired local currency. Simultaneously the borrower arranges a forward exchange contract to provide for reconversion of the local currency into the foreign currency of original denomination at the time when the need for additional financing expires. The cost of the Arbi credit consists of the interest on the foreign loan and the charges associated with the forward exchange contract. If the foreign currency is selling at a discount in the forward market, the cost of the forward exchange contract is negative; the firm repurchases the foreign exchange required for repayment of the original loan at a rate below the initial conversion. It is not surprising, therefore, for astute firms to borrow abroad occasionally when funds are required at home at rates in excess of local costs. Conditions in the forward market permit the companies to realize profits on foreign exchange transactions that more than offset the unfavorable interest rate differentials. The commercial banks' role in Arbi loans is multifaceted. The banks act as foreign lenders in some instances; they advise or serve as intermediaries in the trading of foreign exchange. Clearly, effecting these arrangements with dispatch and care requires a considerable degree of expertise and close contact with parties in the international money markets.

Factoring

Factors buy a company's receivables, thus accelerating the conversion of claims against customers into cash. If the factor buys the receivables without recourse, he assumes the risk associated with customer default. Additionally he performs a number of credit investigation and collection functions normally conducted by the company. Consequently factoring is more expensive than most other methods of short-term borrowing. Notwithstanding the higher cost, factoring is frequently attractive to the international concern for whom credit investigation and collection in foreign countries are problematic. Factoring in Europe has grown in importance in recent years. In *England* receivables are acquired both with and without recourse. Typically the cost consists of a 1 to 2 per cent flat turnover commission in addition to a discount equivalent to 1 to 2 per cent in excess of the bank rate applied to the amount of financing made available. In *Switzerland* subsidiaries of commercial banks have become active in the factoring field, and charges are comparable to the fee structure in the U.K. In the other European countries factoring is conducted on a modest scale although there are signs that suggest significant expansion will occur in the near future. International Factors, Ltd., has been formed as a joint venture between the Boston Financial Corporation, an Edge Act subsidiary of the First National Bank of Boston, and two British banks. With numerous influential commercial banks in many countries as affiliates, International Factors is in a position to provide customers with credit checks and factoring privileges on an expeditious and efficient basis. The phenomenal growth of this company portends widespread use of factoring in the future.

MEDIUM-TERM NATIONAL CURRENCY FINANCING

Any of a number of considerations may indicate the desirability of supplementary short-term borrowing with medium- or long-term financing. Seasonal liquidation of receivables or inventory requirements may be impracticable or undesirable. Investment in plant or equipment may suggest longer-term financing if repayment depends on cash flows generated from operations rather than asset liquidation. Outstanding debt obligations may require refunding or stock may need to be repurchased. Commercial banks extend medium-term credits in a number of forms—renewable overdrafts, bridge loans, medium-term loans, and rediscountable medium-term loans.

Renewable Overdrafts

Under the basic overdraft arrangement the borrower agrees to repay the amount overdrawn plus various charges discussed earlier by the end of an agreed upon period, usually one year. Yet based on many commercial banks' practice of extending overdraft privileges from year to year, the renewable overdraft becomes a medium-term financing tool. Renewable overdraft facilities are more widely used in those countries where medium-term lending is relatively underdeveloped or nonexistent.

In the *U.K.* and *Italy* commercial banks regard themselves primarily as working capital lenders although international firms can obtain renewable overdrafts to finance medium-term receivable needs and investment in fixed assets. The interest charges for renewable overdrafts are comparable to the rates for simple overdraft facilities. Although the semi-permanent or renewable overdraft remains common in Britain, a number of banks have begun to extend prearranged medium-term credits. Thus, differences in medium-term lending between British banks and their counterpart on the Continent where banks make direct medium-term loans are disappearing. Commercial banks in Belgium, France, Germany, and Switzerland provide direct-term loan facilities for their customers although in Italy, as in the U.K., renewable overdrafts are common.

Bridge Loans

Bridge loans are renewable short-term loans which can be used as medium-term financing for extended periods. The purpose of the bridge loan is to provide interim financing while the borrowing company is in the process of obtaining medium- or long-term financing, usually from a noncommercial banking institution. Under the basic short-term loan agreement the borrower obtains financing by signing conventional promissory notes that are renewed until the permanent financing substitute has been arranged. When the alternative financial arrangement is completed, the bridge loan is repaid, typically in a lump sum. The interest rates charged on bridge financing are basically those of short-term loans. The rates are subject to revision each time the short-term loan is renewed.

Although commercial banks in *Germany* extend direct medium-term loans as indicated earlier, the banks play a larger role in assisting firms to obtain medium-term credits from other lending institutions. The commercial banks arrange private loan placements and negotiate mortgage loans from insurance companies and savings banks. Bridge financing is usually extended by German commercial banks in these instances, whereas the banks act as agents in identifying substitute sources of financing for borrowing companies. In *Italy* commercial banks do not extend direct medium-term credits although such accommodations are frequently available at lending institutions affiliated with the banks or from public sources. As in Germany, it is common for the Italian banks to handle all the arrangements with the medium-term lending institutions while extending bridge credits until the arrangements are approved. The cost of the bridge financing in Italy is tied to the short-term loan rate but also depends on the kind of collateral pledged. Commercial bank bridge financing is not so well developed in the other European countries as in Germany and Italy.

Medium-Term Loans

In extending medium-term loans (loans maturing in one to seven years) commercial banks pay particular attention to the borrowers' anticipated sources of repayment and, to this end, tend to view critically the cash flow prospects stemming from enterprise operations. Typically the repayment schedule is geared to the estimated operating cash flows of the borrower during the period the loan is to be outstanding. Rates of interest for medium-term loans are usually higher than for short-term loans although, as in the case of short-term financing, the rates are typically linked to the central bank rate. The conditions of the medium-term loan are set forth in a formal agreement between the international concern and the lending bank. Requests for collateral are more prevalent than in short-term lending because of the additional risks involved. Additionally, the lending bank is more likely to impose restrictions and conditions on the operations of the borrower. Real estate or equipment is commonly pledged to secure the medium-term loan. Facilities for direct medium-term lending are available in Belgium, the U.K., Germany, the Netherlands, and Switzerland.

In *Belgium* commercial banks offer medium-term loans for periods of up to ten years although loans for longer than seven years are uncommon. The interest rates on medium-term loans are based on those established by Société Nationale de Crédit à l'Industrie (SNCI), a semipublic institution, in order to qualify for a government subsidy in connection with the interest charges. In granting a medium-term loan, a Belgium commercial bank will normally insist on collateral and may require in addition a guarantee from the parent company. Usually repayment is scheduled for equal monthly, quarterly, or annual installments. The banks are often willing, however, to extend a grace period at the outset. The government subsidy, available under the 1966 incentive program, provides interest rebates for up to five percentage points during five years and in addition may guarantee up to 75 per cent of the recoverable debt. The net effect of the government subsidy is to reduce the effective rate of interest paid by the borrower on loans granted to finance either buildings or equipment. Although the commercial bank charges may be as high as 8 to 9 per cent, the effective cost to the borrower due to the subsidy may be as low as 3 to 4 per cent. Applications for government subsidies are submitted to SNCI by the lending bank together with detailed descriptions of the projects financed.

As suggested earlier, *British* commercial banks have begun to extend medium-term loans to credit-worthy borrowers. The medium-term loans in England are rarely for periods in excess of five years and are repayable according to accepted schedules that in turn are tied to estimated cash flows. The interest rate usually is 1½ per cent above the bank rate, placing borrowing costs late in 1968 in the 9¼ per cent range. Medium-term direct loans are most commonly extended to firms purchasing machinery and equipment manufactured in England.

In *France* commercial banks are willing to extend medium-term credits to established firms purchasing equipment or buildings. Medium-term loans in France are most often made by means of a series of staggered notes that are rediscountable for a portion of or for the entirety of the tenor. Interest rates on medium-term financing are higher than for the rediscountable facilities offered both by commercial banks and Crédit National, a semipublic institution. In late 1968 rates were in the 8 per cent range in contrast to 6¼ to 6½ per cent for rediscountable notes. In *Germany* medium-term loans mature within six months to four years. Direct medium-term loan financing has become more important in recent years although the rates tend to be 1 to 1½ per cent higher than for overdrafts after including commitment fees. Additionally, the German banks serve as investment advisors and underwriters to borrowing clients and, as such, frequently arrange private loan placements and negotiate mortgage loan arrangements with institutional investors.

In *Switzerland* medium-term loans are difficult to obtain. A substantial portion of bank medium-term lending resources are allocated to the construction industry. This phenomenon is attributable largely to tightness in recent years in the mortgage market. When medium-term loans can be obtained, the interest rate is tied to the rediscount rate but is not firm beyond the first year. Loans in excess of SF50,000 maturing in two years or longer are subject to special taxes as are debentures. These taxes include a 1.2 per mill issuance tax levied for each year or fraction thereof up to a maximum of 1.2 per cent for ten years or longer, and a 30 per cent withholding tax on interest paid by the borrower. The first tax element is shared equally by the borrower and the lender.

In *Italy* and the *Netherlands* commercial banks usually do not provide direct medium-term loan financing. Rather, the banks concentrate on the collection of deposits and the extension of traditional short-term credits. Nonetheless, the commercial banks become involved in the medium-term market via the activities of their affiliated medium-term credit banks.

Rediscountable Medium-Term Loans

Commercial banks in *France* extend a sizable amount of medium-term lending on a rediscountable basis. The borrowers' promissory notes are rediscounted with the central bank or a semipublic institution. This type of financing is usually granted with maturities of up to seven years. After the commercial bank has approved an international concern's loan application, the Bank of France and Crédit National, a semipublic institution, consider whether the credit is eligible for rediscounting. Crédit National bases its decision on the credit-worthiness of the applicant, the value of the proposed investment within the framework of the government's economic objectives, and the availability of alternative sources of credit to the borrower. The cost of rediscountable medium-term financing in late 1968 was 6.25 per cent for five years, 6.75 per cent for six years, and 7.25 per cent for seven years including commissions. When requested, grace periods of up to two years are extended. However, the Bank of France must approve the repayment schedule ultimately agreed upon. Other European countries have not developed a comparable medium-term rediscount facility.

Link Financing

Link financing enables international concerns to participate in the international money markets, thereby supplementing local sources of business financing and frequently lowering financial costs. Linked to lenders from another country, an international concern in a tight money country can indirectly tap external sources of credit. The lender who is located in a different country where money is plentiful may be induced to deposit redundant liquid assets with a bank in the borrower's country. The time deposit can be earmarked for a stipulated borrower, e.g., the local subsidiary or affiliate, or channeled through a money broker to any borrower of good credit standing. The original lender deposits the money in a bank abroad and gets a higher interest rate than at home. In addition to the interest rate differential, the lender usually receives a fraction of the broker's premium. This return must be adjusted for the cost of protection against foreign exchange risk to measure the true yield to the lender; the lender typically will hedge his position in the forward exchange market. Normally, however, link financing is arranged only when exchange risk is absent or minimal and, consequently, the cost of cover is relatively low. In some instances a premium and extra profit is obtained by the lender on the forward contract. From the borrower's point of view, interest is paid to the local bank and a fee is paid to the broker. Nonetheless, he is able to supplement otherwise available local financing and frequently at reduced costs when compared with the rates of local nonbank sources. The local commercial bank profits from the interest differential between the local deposit rate and lending rate; and at the same time the broker benefits from the fee charged the borrower. Hence all parties gain from the transaction. In order for the link to work between a low interest rate country and a high interest rate country, the latter country must have a sound currency or, at a minimum, a well-developed forward exchange market so that currency risks can be hedged. Usually link transactions are arranged for periods of one year or less although renewals at maturity are frequently obtained.

LONG-TERM FINANCING

Long-term financing is used primarily in connection with the purchase of fixed assets—i.e., plant and equipment. When a commercial bank evaluates a long-term borrowing request, it attaches less importance to the company's liquidity position than in short-term or intermediate-term lending. Its primary concern is the earnings capability of the company over the time period of the requested loan since repayment normally will depend on successful operations. It analyzes the international concern's long-term market potential, management, technological position, labor conditions, and prospects. Security is usually required. European commercial banks become involved directly, or indirectly through affiliates, in several aspects of long-term financing—long-term lending or debt flotations, equity financing, and intermediary activities such as public and private placement of securities for local companies and international concerns.

Long-Term Debt Financing

In direct long-term lending the obligations to commercial banks take the form of promissory notes usually secured by a pledge of specific assets such as plant, real estate, and equipment. A parent guarantee is usually required of the international concern. Repayment of the loan is customarily accomplished through cash generated from operations, refinancing or a combination of both. Characteristic repayment schedules depend on the agreement between the company and the commercial bank. In most cases regular monthly, quarterly, or annual installments are required although repayment terms are sometimes tied to income or cash flow projections. Although there are exceptions, interest rates on long-term loans tend to be higher than for medium-term financing, and the differential is usually greater than in the United States.

In *Belgium* commercial banks provide long-term loan financing for periods in excess of ten years, although such credits are comparatively rare. Late in 1968 rates were in the 9 per cent range. The banks usually extend this type of loan on a secured basis. The type of collateral depends on the company's credit standing and potential for growth. The main types of collateral are the following: a mortgage, a bank or second company guarantee, or a foreign parent corporation guarantee. Direct long-term lending in *Germany* is usually supplied by the commercial banking system. Long-term credit consists of loans which mature in four years or longer and the interest rate on long-term loans is approximately the same as for medium-term financing. In other European countries including *England, France, Italy,* and the *Netherlands,* commercial banks do not extend direct long-term loans. However, Italian and Dutch commercial banks extend long-term loans through affiliated long-term credit banks. In *Switzerland,* commercial banks extend long-term loans but only in exceptional cases.

Equity Financing

Equity is another form of direct long-term financing that is provided by commercial banks in certain countries. Through equity participation, the commercial bank becomes a partial owner of the enterprise and is entitled to a residual claim against the earnings of the concern. Thus the bank shares in both the risk and profitability of the company being financed.

German commercial banks, the prototype of the universal bank, are allowed to take equity participations in any type of concern. The commercial banks in *Germany* engage in all types of activities normally restricted to investment banks in other countries. Usually there are no restrictions on banks regarding the size of permissible equity participation. The *French* commercial banking system is permitted to take equity participations of up to 20 per cent in commercial and industrial corporations. However, the large commercial banks almost never take equity positions directly, preferring to place their investment capital in affiliated institutions where there are no restrictions on ownership and where administrators have been trained to manage such operations. In other countries, such as *Belgium, England, Italy,* the *Netherlands,* and *Switzerland,* commercial banks do not engage in direct equity financing. However, banks in some of these countries have affiliated institutions, e.g., the investment trusts in the Netherlands, which do take equity participations.

Intermediary Activities

Perhaps more important than direct involvement is the role commercial banks play as intermediaries. They are the principal link between the company or international concern that requires long-term finance and the individuals or institutions supplying this type of financing. The role of the commercial banks in most instances consists of assisting investors in the purchase of securities of the international concern being financed. In this connection they become involved in both public issues and private placements.

Through underwriting arrangements the commercial banks purchase the securities (stocks or bonds) of a company or international concern for resale and, by assuming the underwriting risk, assure the issuing company of a definite amount of long-term financing. Commercial banks usually form syndicates to market the purchased securities, especially when the issues are large. In this way diversification of risk is achieved and, in addition, sale is facilitated. Under the syndicate arrangement several commercial banks act as underwriters, each liable for an agreed upon portion of the issue. The originating commercial bank acts as manager of the syndicate and makes all the arrangements including selection of other commercial banks that are invited to join the syndicate. The cost of marketing securities through public placement depends on several factors such as popularity and standing of the issuing company with the investment public, type of security being offered, and the size of the offering.

Private placement consists of selling whole issues to an individual investor or to a small number of institutional investors such as insurance companies, pension funds, and mutual funds. Commercial banks play the important role of middlemen between the borrowers of funds and the suppliers of funds. In this regard the bank locates appropriate buyers for the securities, carries on negotiations for the seller, and advises both parties regarding terms. The advantages of private placement for the borrower relates to flexibility and speed with which funds can be obtained. Private offerings are flexible in relation to timing, size of borrowing, and covenants. In addition private placement is sometimes less expensive for the international concern than public offering. Underwriting risks are eliminated; marketing activities are limited; and registration and related expenses of public offerings are avoided. The cost of private debt placement consists of interest charges, finders fees to commercial banks which act as agent, legal charges, and revenue stamps. The intermediary activities of European banks both with regard to public issues and private placements are annotated below.

The financing of industrial and commercial concerns through public offerings is not very common in *Belgium*. This is due to the fact that public agencies obtain most of the funds supplied in the capital market. A 20 per cent withholding tax on dividends and interest levied on individual investors also discourages private firms from entering the market. The cost of floating securities through a public offering depends on the financial situation of the company and the volume of financing required. In general the cost of floating issues varies from 7 per cent to 8 per cent of net proceeds for common shares and from 2.7 per cent to 3.5 per cent for bonds. Private placements are relatively unimportant since institutional investors are subject to regulations that restrict their activities in corporate securities.

The capital market in *France* is relatively weak. Savings are lower than in other European countries and institutional investors are required to hold a high percentage of their funds in securities of public agencies. However, the government's Leca commission ruled in 1968 that institutional investors can acquire more corporate securities and reduce their percentage of investments in government bonds. The decision was designed to strengthen the capital market and to allow commercial banks to place bonds on a wholesale basis with large institutional investors instead of on a retail basis with small investors. Commercial banks play an active role in the placement of corporate securities in *Germany.* Corporate securities play a prominent role in the portfolios of large institutional investors such as insurance companies. The commercial banks help with the listing as well as the initial purchase and sale of securities. In addition, they maintain an orderly market by buying or selling shares from inventory, thus dampening price fluctuations in the aftermarket. The fees charged by commercial banks are 2 per cent to 2.5 per cent for underwriting both bonds and shares and 1 per cent for listing the securities on the exchange. For bonds an extra 0.25 per cent charge is levied due to interest payment handling expenses. German commercial banks also play an important role in private placement of unsecured notes with insurance companies, especially when the bond market is weak. A number of large loans (DM30 to 50 million) have been privately placed by a syndicate of banks.

Long-term financing on the *Italian* capital market is difficult. There are several adverse factors such as high issuance costs, a 30 per cent withholding tax on dividends, and restrictions on the volume of funds that insurance companies can invest in corporate securities. The portfolios of insurance companies consist mostly of bonds of public agencies. By law insurance companies can invest only up to 15 per cent of reserves in common shares. Commercial banks underwrite securities either by themselves or by forming consortia with medium-term affiliates such as Mediocredito, Centrobanca, and Efibanes. For a common stock issue, handling costs approximate 2.25 per cent. In the *Netherlands* commercial banks underwrite bonds and stocks that are offered publicly in the capital market. The banks are also active in negotiating private placements with large institutional investors. Insurance companies hold in their portfolio sizable amounts of listed corporate securities. In addition the insurance companies participate in private placements arranged by the commercial banks.

Commercial banks act as *Switzerland's* main underwriters and stockbrokers for public offerings. Additionally they play a leading role in private placements. The most important group of commercial banks, the Big Three formed by the Swiss Bank Corporation, Union Bank of Switzerland, and the Swiss Credit Bank, handle a sizable proportion of all public issues. These banks like to float issues of large, widely held concerns. The underwriting fee charged by commercial banks depends on market conditions, size of offering, and the issuer's standing. It can range from 1.5 per cent to 2.5 per cent for bonds and is usually in the 2.5 per cent range for stocks. The federal stamp duty is 2 per cent for bonds and 1.2 per cent for equity issues. Additional charges include publication, printing, and quotation costs. Although private placement is normally more expensive than public offerings in Switzerland, simplicity and time saving account for the frequent borrower preference of the private placement route.

In *England* the underwriting of public issues is not conducted by commercial banks, but rather by the merchant banks that are members of the Issuing House Association. In addition merchant banks engage in consulting, administration of investment trusts, and merger negotiations. The role of the merchant bank in England is comparable to that of the investment bank in the United States. In contrast to most European countries, the United States and Britain separate commercial banking and investment banking functions.

FOREIGN CURRENCY FINANCING

Eurocurrencies

Eurocurrency is one of the most discussed financial innovations of the last decade. It is the sole truly international money market undisturbed by the rules and restrictions of any national authority. Any convertible currency available for borrowing earns the "Euro" label once it is banked outside its native country.

Eurodollars are dollar deposits borrowed by financial institutions outside the United States. The dollar funds may be used as dollars or converted into other currencies. Eurodollars represent about 80 per cent of Eurocurrency operations, the balance consisting mainly of British pounds (Europounds), Deutsche marks (Euromarks), and, to a lesser extent, other European currencies such as French and Swiss francs (Eurofrancs). The Eurodollar market has grown impressively in recent years. The size of the market in 1964 was $8 billion, and it grew to an estimated $20 billion by 1969.

Perhaps ironically, the Trosbank, the State Bank of the USSR, and other Communist countries' central and official trade banks, were the first to engage in a sizable volume of transactions in Eurodollar deposits. These institutions began to transfer dollar holdings to Europe, fearing the funds might become blocked in the United States. Using their correspondents, in particular the Moscow Narodny Bank of London and the Banque Commerciale pour l'Europe du Nord of Paris, the Communist banks offered dollar funds to European banks on a short-term deposit basis at very attractive rates.

The major attraction for depositing dollars outside the United States has been the normally higher interest rates paid abroad. The United States commercial banking system, subject to the Federal Reserve Board's Regulation Q, is not permitted to pay interest on demand deposits and is restricted with regard to interest payments on time deposits. Large commercial banks operating efficiently in wholesale transactions are able to attract dollar deposits and operate profitably on small spreads in interbank deposits. London, with the expertise of its financial institutions, has emerged as the focal point for Euro operations. The wholesale nature of the Eurodollar market is illustrated by the size of loans extended. A typical loan may amount to $5 million. However, larger loans, sometimes as large as $50 million, have been extended to single borrowers by groups of commercial banks active in this market.

The interest rate charged in the Eurodollar market depends on general supply and demand conditions in the market, the credit standing of the prospective borrowers, and the maturity characteristic of the loans. Prime borrowers are able to take loans at relatively low spreads above the London interbank rate for Eurodollars. For example, the major oil companies can borrow at ½ per cent per annum above the London interbank rate. The spread increases to 1 to 1¼ per cent per annum for medium- and small-sized firms. Recently, a new practice has evolved regarding the rate basis for borrowings. Traditionally, if six-month advances were being negotiated, the rate charged would be the London interbank offering rate for the day of drawdown, plus the appropriate spread. However many large and prime companies objected to this procedure, as not infrequently they were the victims of abnormal upward rate fluctuations due to technical considerations of the London money market rather than real increases in the cost of money. As a result, if the day of drawdown or rollover of a loan fell on a day when purely technical factors increased the cost of Eurodollars, a company might be saddled with an abnormally high rate for six months. Accordingly, some banks now offer their better customers rates based on the average interbank rate over the last five banking days prior to drawdown, or some similar rate averaging method.

The real cost of Eurodollar borrowings is almost always lower than the cost of domestic dollar borrowing, even though the stated rate of interest may be higher. This results from the fact that Eurodollars are loaned out simply for the spread, whereas domestic borrowings usually require compensating balances of anywhere from 10 per cent to 20 per cent on the amount of outstandings. A 20 per cent compensating balance requirement increases the effective cost of domestic borrowing by 25 per cent so that a 6 per cent loan with a 25 per cent compensating balance in reality costs 7½ per cent. A 6 per cent loan with a 10 per cent compensating balance requirement has an effective cost of 6.66 per cent.

Short-Term Eurocurrency Financing

Short-term Eurocurrency financings encompass the major part of the Eurodollar lending business. Since most international borrowers tend to be among a bank's large and well-known clients, the loans are usually made on an unsecured basis and with a minimum of documentation. In order to maintain low costs and efficient operations, care is taken to avoid documents that are subject to local stamp taxes or similar charges. Transactions are usually arranged by telephone and confirmed by an exchange of letters. Short-term Eurocurrency borrowing is generally committed under one of the banking arrangements described below.

Most short-term Eurocurrency financing by international companies is conducted under previously established *lines of credit*. After investigation of a client's credit standing, the commercial bank establishes a maximum loan balance—a Euro line of credit. Advances under a line of credit are usually made against notes with maturities of 90 or 180 days. Lines of credit are reviewed annually on the basis of the borrower's credit standing and overall banking relationship. Under a short-term *revolving credit* arrangement, a commercial bank agrees to provide standing credits with a specified maximum outstanding at any one time. The interest charges are based on prevailing rates at the time borrowing takes place. Firms also borrow Eurocurrencies on an *ad hoc* basis without having previously established lines of credit.

To qualify for a Eurocurrency credit, the international concern must demonstrate credit-worthiness. The lending commercial bank requires assurance of the borrower's ability to generate a sufficient and dependable cash flow in dollars or an easily convertible currency to repay the Eurodollar loan. Frequently the parent company is asked to guarantee the repayment of the Eurodollar loan in the event that the international subsidiary defaults on its commitment. This requirement is especially important when the international concern is operating in countries where there are controls over the repayment of debt in foreign currencies. Short-term Eurocurrency borrowing costs are roughly comparable to national currency interest rates in Europe. However, they have been higher than corresponding borrowing costs in the United States. There is a relationship between United States and international interest rates due to arbitrage. However, in times of crisis this close relationship does not necessarily hold.

Medium-Term Eurocurrency Financing

With the growth in availability of Eurocurrencies, commercial banks have begun to extend medium-term Eurocurrency loans for the financing of medium-term needs. There are two principal forms of medium-term Eurocurrency credits: a *revolving Eurocurrency credit* is a confirmed line of credit beyond one year. It guarantees the borrower of the availability of specified amounts of Eurocurrency for the duration of a period, usually between three to five years. The actual borrowing is typically made against renewable notes with 90- to 180-day maturities. The interest rate is established at every renewal interval in accordance with prevailing market rates. For prime credit names, the credit agreement may specify that the borrowing will be made at the lending bank's best commercial rate or some fraction higher depending on the international borrower's credit standing. In consideration for the commitment to extend medium-term credits, the commercial bank normally charges a fee of about ½ per cent per annum on the unused portion of the commitment. This charge, as well as the interest on the outstanding portion, is usually payable on a quarterly basis. The important advantage of Eurocurrency revolving credits is that the commitments can be terminated at the borrower's request on short notice (thirty days).

Another avenue of medium-term financing open to international concerns consists of Eurocurrency term loans. The Eurodollar term loan is basically a Eurocurrency medium-term credit without the revolving feature and with the addition of an agreed upon amortization schedule. The interest rate charged on this type of loan is usually subject to revision every 180 days. Eurodollar term loans are very flexible since they allow for prepayment of the loan on interest adjustment date. Fixed rate Eurodollar term loans are sometimes extended to international concerns of prime credit standing. The advantage of this type of loan is that the international borrower knows his interest cost in advance. However, the interest rate is usually higher than the existing short-term rate to compensate the commercial bank for the uncertainty associated with future adverse changes in the interest rate. In general Eurodollar term loans are used to finance investment projects with established cash flow schedules. The maturity schedules for these loans vary from three to five years.

Long-Term Eurocurrency Financing

Commercial banks play an important role as intermediaries in long-term Eurocurrency financing. They frequently assume the underwriting function in the flotation of Eurobonds for companies or international concerns seeking additional long-term finance. Eurobonds are Eurocurrency securities that are floated in the international capital market. Eurobond financing is used mainly to facilitate expansion involving fixed asset commitments. Eurobonds have also been floated to assist in the acquisition of companies. One such case involved the takeover of Deutsche Erdoel by Texaco in 1967. The deal was arranged by exchanging $179 million of Eurobonds maturing in twenty years for the stock of the German company. This transaction represented the largest Eurobond issue to date. In 1968, the most active year to date, more than $2 billion of Eurobonds were issued by foreign subsidiaries of United States-based companies. The potential size of the Eurobond market is unknown due to the anonymity of ultimate suppliers. The commercial bank, merchant bank, or investment bank that manages the underwriting forms a syndicate or consortium with other commercial banks and financial institutions. Usually these syndicates are large, even for issues involving small amounts. For a $10 million issue as many as fifty-six institutions in ten countries have participated. The international investors who buy the Eurobonds are predominantly wealthy individuals from Europe, Latin America, Asia, and the Middle East. Eurobonds are designed to provide anonymity for these investors, freedom from currency controls, and exemptions from withholding taxes. Most of the Eurobond issues are denominated in dollars. The German mark and the Swiss franc are next in importance.

Two basic types of Eurocurrency debt have been issued—straight Eurobonds and convertible Eurobonds. Straight Eurobonds have been floated during periods when the market has been characterized by strong investor interest. Maturities for the straight bonds have ranged from five to twenty years. Issuing prices have been adjusted in relation to coupon rates to make issues attractive for investors. In general the interest rates on straight bonds have been 1.5 to 2 per cent above the interest rate on convertible bonds. However, these rates have characteristically been lower than corresponding interest rates for similar instruments in the national capital markets of Europe. Interest rates usually reflect market conditions, borrower standing, and the investor response to the currency of denomination. The underwriter's fee is usually 2.5 per cent of the total nominal amount of the loan. Additional expenses are normally incurred in connection with listing, publicity, printing, and marketing.

Eurobonds convertible into parent stock have become increasingly prevalent, as the market for straight debt has weakened. International investors are inflation conscious and prefer securities that maintain the purchasing power of money. The convertible privilege provides such a hedge. Convertible Eurobonds havs been floated in the international capital market with maturities in the ten to twenty year range. The fee charged by commercial banks in the public offering of convertible Eurobonds has approximated 2.5 per cent. The 2.5 per cent covers a 1.5 per cent selling commission, a .5 per cent underwriting fee, and a .5 per cent management fee. Additional expenses have raised the total cost to 3 per cent of issue value.

OTHER FOREIGN CURRENCY FINANCING

Multicurrency Loan

The multicurrency loan is a special line of credit arrangement under which a commercial bank stands ready to lend up to a specified amount in different currencies, not only Eurodollars, subject to the availability of funds at the time they are actually needed by the international concern. The multicurrency line is arranged with commercial banks that have extensive branch or affiliate networks in different countries. This type of loan is extended to the parent company and its designated subsidiaries, usually in countries with freely convertible currencies. Under this arrangement the bank's headquarters opens a dollar credit line for the parent company, and designated subsidiaries have a qualified right to borrow and repay in local currencies. Thus the commercial bank assumes foreign exchange risks in making a particular currency available, and the multicurrency loan provides a powerful borrowing tool for international financial managers. It is an appropriate borrowing tool for covering the working capital needs of subsidiaries in different countries where the subsidiaries' access to lenders is limited. The parent company is usually required to guarantee the multicurrency credit and the guarantee typically specifies that, in the event of default at maturity, the parent will repay the dollar equivalent of the local currency borrowing at the rate of exchange then prevailing plus interest payable and any other expenses involved.

Medium-Term and Long-Term Credit Banks

In several countries where medium-term and long-term financing is not supplied directly by commercial banks, affiliated institutions have emerged to fulfill borrowers' longer term needs. The leading medium-term bank in *France* is the Societé Financière Européenne. It is sponsored by Banque Nationale de Paris, Bank of America, Algemene Bank Nederland, Kommerzbank A.G., Banco Nazionale del Lavoro and Barclays Bank Ltd. There are no long-term credit banks sponsored by commercial banks in France. Long-term loans, especially for the purchases of equipment, are provided through Crédit National, a semipublic institution. In *Italy* commercial banks have established banks which provide both medium- and long-term financing. Included among the medium- and long-term credit institutions are such banks as Mediobanca, Efibanca, and Interbanca. These institutions extend loans at interest rates of about 7¼ per cent plus a commission of ¼ to ½ per cent per annum. The actual interest rate and the commission rate depend on market conditions, the maturity of the loan, and the credit standing of the international borrower. Funds are made available for plant modernization and expansion. Similarly, in the *Netherlands* medium-term loans are granted by companies affiliated with commercial banks. Usually the rate of interest is not fixed but fluctuates with the central bank rate. Generally a commitment fee and a turnover commission on total debits or credits are charged to the borrower. A long-term credit bank, the Nationale Investeringsbank (National Investment Bank), has been established by commercial banks with government support. Usually medium- and long-term loans are collateralized.

Edge Act Companies

Edge Act companies are affiliates of United States commercial banks, chartered to engage exclusively in foreign operations. Among other activities, Edge Act companies provide financing to international industrial concerns—both loans and equity capital. They provide venture capital to new enterprises as well as capital to assist in expansion, modernization, or reorganization of established concerns. The loans provided range from short to intermediate maturities. These loans frequently contain an extra incentive or sweetener—that is, an agreement allowing common stock participation either through conversion, purchase, or the exercise of options. Thus the Edge Act affiliate is able to participate in the growth and profitability of the international company being financed. The equity sweetener compensates for the risk inherent in the investment situations. The interest rates for loans are dependent on the risks of the venture, money market conditions, the nature of incentives, and the general outlook for the international concern. The equity investments are sometimes sold by the Edge Act company after the situation has matured. This enables the company to invest in new situations that require risk capital. The leading Edge Act subsidiaries of United States banks include Bamerical International Financial Corp., Banker's International Corp., Chase International Investment Corp., Chemical International Finance Corp., Continental International Finance Corp., First National City Overseas Investment Corp., Manufacturers Hanover International Finance Corp., and Morgan Guaranty International Finance Corp.

THE EUROPEAN PATTERN AND FINANCIAL PRACTICES IN THE REST OF THE WORLD

The previous discussion has suggested that financing practices of commercial banks on the Continent are more extensive and variegated than those of British or United States commercial banks. The differences in banking philosophy have historic origins. These differences and their origin help to explain the financial practices that have subsequently evolved in other parts of the world.

In the nineteenth century the emerging British commercial banks were chiefly deposit-taking institutions that granted short-term credits for working capital needs. If capital was required for permanent investment, and if it was not privately available, other intermediary sources were contacted such as issuing houses, underwriters, company promoters, and investment trusts. Commercial banks did not become involved except perhaps as agents. By way of contrast, in continental Europe commercial banks provided comprehensive financing due to the fact that industry and capital markets were in a relatively underdeveloped state. Rapid growth in population and industrial development in Europe increased the demand for capital dramatically. In the absence of specially conceived institutions to satisfy the burgeoning need for risk capital, investors and government called on the commercial banks to assist in financing the expansion. Thus continental banks became active agents in promoting economic development. Banks in some countries became "universal," i.e., active in all facets of financing activity. The best examples of universal banking are the *Swiss* and *German* commercial banks which today may receive deposits, extend loans and credits in all maturities, deal in foreign exchange, underwrite securities offerings, assist in the placement of securities, and invest in the equity instruments of clients. By way of contrast, the British commercial banks, as historically, restrict their activities to the receipt of deposits, and the extension of loans and credits, usually short term. The British commercial banks are standard deposit banks. They are not permitted to engage in capital flotations, in prefinancing of investments or the ownership of stock in nonfinancial businesses. Only recently have British commercial banks begun to provide prefinancing of a medium-term nature. As deposit-seeking institutions, the British banks have developed extensive branching networks.

In *Belgium, France,* and *Italy* commercial banks are basically modified deposit banks. They engage in capital flotations, but do not provide substantial prefinancing, invest in shares, or assume underwriting risks. In the *Netherlands* the commercial banks are a mixture of the deposit and the universal bank styles. Dutch banks engage in capital flotations and assume issue guarantees. In the *United States, Australia,* and *Canada* commercial banks follow the Anglo-Saxon tradition of British banks, acting chiefly as deposit banks. In each of these countries, however, deposit banks have become active in prefinancing, and substantial volumes of credits are of a medium- and long-term nature.

To a considerable extent the basic distinctions between deposit banks and universal banks are beginning to fade. Today deposit banks are attempting through the vehicle of affiliated institutions to become active in numerous fields not directly serviced by them. In *Britain* commercial banks are buying interests in merchant banks that are active in the investment field. In *Italy* and the *Netherlands* commercial banks have established medium- and long-term credit banks. In the *United States* several commercial banks have incorporated Edge Act affiliates that in turn hold equity investments in ventures outside the United States, assist in securities underwritings, and extend long-term loans. Commercial banks are entering fields until now the province of other financial institutions—e.g., leasing, factoring, and installment financing.

Banking Practices in Asia and Africa

In the nineteenth century the colonial powers established banks throughout Asia and Africa and in so doing profoundly influenced lending practices on these continents. The most common short-term borrowing instruments in *Asia* are overdrafts, discounted bills and short-term loans. In *Japan* overdrafts are uncommon because they are ineligible for refinancing at the central bank. Short-term loans and discounting are more common in *Japan*. In *India* overdrafts may be renewed annually without periodic retirements. Short-term loans are not available in *India*, and discounting is less important than overdraft facilities because of higher costs. In the *Philippines* overdrafts are usually renewed although they must be cleared up periodically. Discounted bills and short-term loans are uncommon in the *Philippines*.

The most common medium- and long-term credit instrument in Asian lending is the term loan. Medium-term loans may take the form of renewable short-term loans (e.g., *Japan*) or of straight term loans (e.g., *India*). Long-term loans usually are of a straight renegotiated nature. When commercial banks are unable to provide medium- and long-term loans directly, they may extend such credits through affiliated companies as in the *Philippines*. In Asia commercial banks provide additional specialized financing through affiliated companies such as development corporations. Underwriting facilities are provided directly by commercial banks (e.g., *India*) or through affiliated companies (e.g., *Philippines*). In *Japan* commercial banks do not engage in underwriting.

Commercial banks in *Africa* closely follow the colonial pattern established by the European mother countries. The most common short-term credit instrument is the overdraft. In *South Africa* overdrafts constitute well over 80 per cent of total credit operations. Overdraft charges are computed on daily outstanding debt, and they are usually two points higher than the central bank rate. In *Nigeria* commercial banks extend working capital and inventory loans in addition to basic overdrafts. Short-term facilities in *Egypt* are essentially limited to working capital overdrafts. Medium- and long-term financing are not commonly provided by commercial banks although renewable overdrafts frequently serve as a substitute. Commercial banks extend medium- and long-term credit through affiliated institutions as in South Africa. Most longer term credits, however, are extended by state-owned development corporations (e.g., *Nigeria* and *Egypt*). Underwriting activities and equity participations fall outside the province of commercial banking activity. These are sometimes performed by affiliated companies as in *South Africa*. Sources of equity funds may be found also in state-owned corporations (e.g., *Nigeria* and *Egypt*).

The banking structure in *Latin America* is perhaps best characterized as one of a relatively few with large numbers of branches geographically dispersed throughout the individual countries. The main credit instruments used by the banks in short-term financing are the overdraft, discounted bill, and short-term loan. More specifically, discounted bills are the customary short-term financing device in *Brazil* where overdrafts and straight loans are difficult to obtain. Similarly in *Argentina* overdrafts are rarely used although both discounted bills and short-term loans are common. In *Mexico* overdrafts can only be obtained when a formal agreement has been arranged in advance. The agreement, which is required by law, specifies the repayment terms. Short-term loans and discounted bills are the usual short-term financing devices in Mexico.

Term loans are the most common medium-term financing device in *Latin America.* The principal sources of term loans in *Brazil* and *Argentina* are the state development banks, since commercial banks are reluctant to commit themselves in view of the prospects for substantial erosion of currency purchasing power. Nonetheless, the commercial banks are frequently willing to renew short-term loans that serve as medium-term borrowing substitutes. In *Mexico* commercial banks will extend loans for one to two years that usually can be renewed at rates then prevailing. Latin American commercial banks extend medium- and long-term financing facilities primarily through affiliated companies called financieras. This financing institution complements the activities of commercial banks. The financieras are not closely regulated as are commercial banks and may charge higher rates for term lending. Underwriting activities are usually performed by commercial banks or affiliated institutions such as investment banks in *Brazil* and *Argentina,* and financieras in *Mexico.* Underwriting charges are typically high by United States or European standards. Commercial banks can take equity participations directly in *Mexico* or indirectly through affiliated institutions such as financieras in *Argentina* or investment banks in *Brazil.*

Summary

This chapter has described the lending and investment activities of commercial banks *vis à vis* the international enterprise. For purposes of illustration, characteristic instruments and credit terms from selected European countries have been analyzed. A variety of short-term national currency instruments are used—the overdraft, discounted bills, short-term loans, rediscountable loans, and underwritings—although relative popularity of the instruments varies from country to country. In the medium-term maturities renewable overdrafts, bridge loans, and medium-term loans are employed. Various commercial banks play a diverse role in the long-term market—extending loans directly or through affiliated institutions, acting as agent and consultant in private placements, underwriting as well as selling debentures and common stock, and supplying venture capital with equity participations. In countries that restrict the scope of commercial banking activity, many banks have formed, acquired, or combined with nonbank institutions permitted to engage in a more extensive list of activities. The resourcefulness and imagination of commercial banks in the financing of international enterprise is also evident in the Eurocurrency money and capital markets in which the banks play a leading role. In the Eurocurrency money market commercial banks extend lines of credit, establish standby credits, loan any of a number of Eurocurrencies on an *ad hoc* basis and facilitate Arbi loans and link financing transactions. Additionally, some banks extend multicurrency lines of credit, lend Eurocurrencies medium-term, and assist in the underwriting or private placement of Eurobonds for international clients. Many commercial banks have established affiliates or branches in other countries in order to tap the Eurocurrency market and to better serve international clients. At the same time joint venture alliances have been formed between commercial and investment banks of different countries to mobilize resources and exploit new banking markets. As banks learn from each other and competition intensifies, the distinctions in practices among countries are beginning to fade. Commercial banks are discovering better ways to mobilize and utilize the world's financial resources, and the new insights are of enormous value to the banks' growing list of clients classified as multinational corporations.

BIBLIOGRAPHY

Association of Austrian Banks and Bankers. "Commercial Banks in Relation to Medium and Long Term Credit," 16th International Banking Summer School. (Vienna: Brider Rosenbaum, 1964).

"Banking in Africa," *The Banker's Magazine*, March 1966.

"Banks and Factors: Partners in Finance?" *The Banker*, February 1968.

Benett, R. A. "U.S. Banks' International Branches, Offices and Subsidiaries," *American Banker*, February 29, 1968.

Brown, C. V. *The Nigerian Banking System*. (Evanston, Ill.: Northwestern University Press, 1966).

"Development Banks in Mexico," *Review of the Economic Situation of Mexico*, February 1965.

"Edge Act Firms Multiply," *The Journal of Commerce*, December 11, 1967.

Einzig, P. *The Eurodollar System*. (New York: St. Martin's Press, Inc., 1966).

Eurodollar Financing. (New York: Chase Manhattan Bank, 1968).

"Factoring's Breakthrough Year," *The Banker*, February 1968.

Fehrenbach, T. R. *The Swiss Banks*. (New York: McGraw-Hill Book Co., Inc., 1966).

"Financing Foreign Operations," *Business International*, New York, 1968.

"Five Hundred Largest Banks in the World," *American Banker*, July 31, 1968.

"Foreign Operations of United States Banks," *Bank Stock Quarterly*, December 1967.

"How Business is Financed in Europe," (New York: First National City Bank, 1966).

Institute of Bankers. *Banking Trends in Europe*. 17th International Banking Summer School. (Rochester, England: Staples Printers, Ltd., 1965).

"Investing, Licensing and Trading Conditions Abroad," *Business International,* New York, 1968.

"Japan–A Survey," *The Banker,* May 1968.

Klopstock, F. H. "The International Money Market: Structure, Scope and Instruments," paper presented at a meeting of the American Finance Association, December 28, 1964.

Meyer, L. "The World's First Money Market," *Fortune,* April 1968.

"Money and Banking in Africa," *Africa Report,* May 1966.

Nehrt, C. L. *International Finance for Multinational Business.* (Scranton, Pa.: International Textbook Company, 1967).

Ohka, S. "The Japanese Banking System," *The Canadian Banker,* Autumn 1966.

Olakanpo, O. "Commercial Banking in Nigeria," *The Bankers' Magazine,* January 1965.

Orsingher, R. *Les Banques dans le Monde.* (Paris: Payot, 1964).

Reimann, G., and E. F. Wigglesworth. *The Challenge of International Finance.* (New York: McGraw-Hill Book Co., Inc., 1966).

Richardson, D. "Investment Companies Throughout the Free World," *Financial Analysts Journal,* January-February 1965.

Richebacher, K. "The German Banking System," *Journal of the Institute of Bankers,* December 1964.

"Structure of Banking in South America–A Survey," *The Banker,* September 1967.

Tamagna, F. "The Pattern of Change in Latin American Banking," *Banco Nazionale del Lavoro Quarterly Review,* March 1965.

Venkatzraman, K. *Local Finance in Perspective.* (New York: Taplinger, 1965).

Case 15
MEXICANA DE GAS, S.A.

On November 1, 1968, the manager of a branch of Banco Industrial Mexicano, located in Toluca, Mexico, called on Mexicana de Gas, S.A., a prospective client. In substance the gas company informed the branch manager that its business was to buy gas containers and gas and resell them at a substantial profit. The company bought the containers from a specialized producer and the gas from the government and sold them at retail. It also engaged in the wholesaling of gas installations. Mexicana de Gas, S.A. expressed its desire to work with the branch and requested a line of credit for discounting trade bills accepted by its customers. To justify the line it provided audited financial statements for 1965 and 1966. The company did not typically have large inventories, except for the normal stock of containers and working material for installations. When it obtained a big contract from the government for an installation, it kept bigger inventories. It also maintained a fleet of thirty vehicles in order to supply the gas, containers, and installation materials.

On November 2 the branch requested and received a telephone credit checking from the company's local bank and an agency report. The same day, November 2, the Toluca branch telephoned the head office in Mexico and strongly recommended approval of a 1 million peso line for discounting Mexicana de Gas' trade acceptances with up to eighteen months maturities. The bills, discounted with full recourse to the company, were to be drawn primarily on large and well-known companies (in one instance a government organization like FOVI, a government construction company for cheaper homes) to which the company sold complete gas installations.

On November 9 the head office telephoned the branch requesting clarification about whether Mexicana de Gas, S.A., was a wholesaler or contractor of gas. Questions were also asked regarding the kind of paper to be discounted and the high inventories that had prevailed at certain times in the past. The head office also asked if satisfactory checkings had been received from the company's present bank.

On the same date the branch responded stating that the company was both a contractor and a wholesaler of gas; when it contracted for an installation for building, it usually supplied gas for all the apartments therein. A major portion of the contracting work was done for government sponsored construction firms and a minor portion for private companies and persons such as bakers, tortilla producers, and clubs or organizations with water heating problems. The branch mentioned the fact that gas was also distributed to private homes.

All acceptances were to be discounted only after the branch had been satisfied that the drawees' credit standing was good. The branch also stated that very satisfactory checkings had been received from the company's bank in Toluca.

On November 15 the head office approved the line as requested but emphasized that it was for the discounting of approved trade acceptances only.

On November 16 the head office approval was received by the branch, and on the same day Mexicana de Gas, S.A., sent in trade acceptances drawn on and accepted by five of its customers for a total of 1,205,000 pesos.

On November 20 the 1,205,000 pesos proceeds of the bills discounted were credited to the company's newly opened account and were drawn by check shortly thereafter. Subsequently the branch credited the company's account for 110,000 pesos in bills discounted on December 1, and the funds were withdrawn almost immediately.

On December 19 the branch informed head office by telegram that it was likely that Mexicana de Gas would be forced into bankruptcy by one of its creditors and that the bills discounted were probably drawn on weak drawees. In a letter to the home office dated January 2 the branch indicated that the drawees probably would be unable to pay the bills at maturity if at all.

Case 16
THE TORQUE CORPORATION

The Torque Corporation, headquartered in Kansas City, was a major producer of four-wheel-drive commercial and passenger vehicles. The Company did all of its manufacturing within the United States, but exported its products throughout the world. For many years international sales were made by Torque's traveling representatives. By the mid-1960's, however, franchised dealerships owned and managed by foreign nationals were used in many countries. Torque representatives concentrated on areas without dealers or worked with new dealers who were developing new exclusive territories.

In May 1966 Sr. Jaime Brito, Torque's dealer in Ecuador since 1961, visited Kansas City to discuss methods of expanding sales in that country. Brito was one of Ecuador's leading businessmen, with interests in construction and real estate ventures, bakeries, and a department store. His fortune was considered to be one of the largest in the country, and his wife was related to a prominent government official. The operational responsibilities for Brito's dealership were assumed by his cousin, but Brito followed all of his commercial interests very closely.

Torque sold on ninety-day delivery terms to Brito and most other Latin American dealers. Dealers maintained a limited display inventory and normally ordered vehicles from Kansas City for each local sale. To the Ecuadorian retail customers, terms were ordinarily cash with up to ninety days to pay. Brito went to Kansas City in 1966 determined to gain better credit terms for himself and for his customers. His arguing point was that the extension of credit would immediately open a sizable new Ecuadorian market for Torque.

Torque trucks were priced at the local currency equivalent of $4,000 to $10,000 and its cars at $4,000 to $6,000. A number of industrial buyers was able to purchase new vehicles for cash, but relatively few small businesses or families in Ecuador could afford cash payments of these amounts. (Exhibit 1 provides a brief statistical summary of the Ecuadorian economy.) Hence Brito believed that his sales volume would at least double if he were able to offer his customers one-to-two-year credit terms.

Torque had a financing program for sales in the United States and Canada similar to General Motors Acceptance Corporation. Its sales in Western Europe were often financed by customer loans from local financial institutions. In Latin America Torque had limited its financing to support of dealers, providing them with loans with which to establish sales and maintenance facilities and to purchase vehicles for show and demonstration. The latter included financing for the importation of one to four of the Torque models—the number of show vehicles being dependent on the size of a dealer's market potential. The Company's Latin American credit policy reflected first the absence of local credit institutions and sufficient information about a prospective customer's credit ratings;

and second, Torque management's belief that it did not possess the know-how to establish or to manage captive foreign finance companies, nor did it wish to divert resources to develop them. The company's Latin American expansion had been relatively recent, and in most areas sales had not reached a level which Torque managers considered to be large enough to worry about arranging financing for potential customers who were not able to pay cash.

Torque's worldwide sales volume was about 170,000 vehicles a year. Almost three-quarters was accounted for by the United States and Canadian operations. Of the remaining 45,000 vehicles, about 50 per cent were sold in Europe, 10 per cent in the Far East, and 40 per cent in Latin America. Ecuador's share of the Latin market was about 8 per cent (800 vehicles), which represented $5.2 million in annual sales. Most of the latter sales were made to the larger companies or wealthy Ecuadorians.

Brito believed that many of the smaller local companies wanted to buy Torque trucks and cars if attractive credit terms could be arranged. The problem was that credit sales to Latin Americans were usually impossible because the local financial institutions were not able to provide a sizable volume of this financing. Ecuador had only two financieras, one small development bank, nine locally owned commercial banks, and three that were foreign owned. Credit was generally restricted to short-term loans, with maturities of up to a maximum of one year and at 11-12 per cent rates.

When Brito met with Sam Jeffrey, Torque's South American sales manager, and William Martin, vice-president for international sales, the Ecuadorian immediately asked the others if Torque were planning to change its policy of financing sales in Latin America. Martin reiterated the reasons for the firm's traditional pattern of selling in overseas markets, but he did indicate that new approaches might be taken to expand foreign markets because management resources were increasingly available for developing Latin American and Asian markets. Torque was planning to make market studies of these areas to determine the suitability of its product line and the potential market size. It was very likely, Martin said, that Torque would add dealers in areas where they were not extant and might go into cooperative advertising and promotion with existing dealers.

Brito felt new approaches in financing should also be considered because the German and Japanese vehicle producers were offering attractive credit terms to dealers and their customers, and it appeared likely that Torque's two United States competitors in Ecuador might begin to extend credit in the near future. (Exhibit 2 describes the United States' programs intended to improve the facilities for financing exports to foreign markets.)

Brito also told the American executives that the Ecuadorian government had recently tightened its import regulations so that importers were required to place a deposit with the Central Bank before an import permit could be issued. For imported goods on "List I" (heavy industrial goods necessary for the development of the economy, which included Torque's trucks) a 30 per cent deposit would be required. "List II" goods (consumer goods—including Torque's jeep-type autos) required a 140 per cent deposit. Brito believed that measures designed to discourage nonvital imports would seriously damage the dealer's ability to offer vehicles on credit because so large an amount of funds would be tied up in the predeposits. The new restrictions would serve to reinforce the existing tendency of limiting sales to cash customers. Brito asked if arrangements could be made to help finance the preimport deposits so his working capital could be conserved.

Martin replied that Torque was not in the financing business. He said, however, that he would consider financing dealers on a revolving basis, utilizing the FCIA or Eximbank insurance plan which was available to United States companies (see Exhibit 2). Under these programs American banks finance the export sales by buying the importer's interest-bearing notes from the exporter with the payment guaranteed in part by Eximbank, or insured in full by the Foreign Credit Insurance Association (FCIA). A fee or premium to the guaranteeing entity must be paid by either Torque or by the importer, and in many cases a commitment fee of about ½ per cent per annum must be paid to the bank on any unused portion of the credit extended. In all cases, Torque would be obliged to participate in 10-30 per cent of the credit, although it could sell its participation to the bank on a recourse basis. While this possibility aroused some enthusiasm on the part of Brito, he was essentially disappointed and could not understand why Torque would not become more interested in financing, which would increase sales.

Several days later during lunch with a long-time friend, a New York banker, Brito expressed his discontent with Torque's financial policy. The banker explained that many American firms were reluctant to enter into foreign financing because of their lack of expertise and their fear of lending to customers in areas where it is difficult to obtain credit information. The banker then suggested to Brito that he talk with the bank's international investment subsidiary, which might have an interest in investing funds in an Ecuadorian finance company.

Brito followed the advice and met with officers of DBIC, the bank's Edge Act subsidiary that was permitted under the law to hold equity stocks in foreign corporations (see Exhibit 3). Brito explained his situation and admitted to having an interest in founding an Ecuadorian finance company with the hope that Torque would subscribe to a part of the capital stock. He himself might take a share, and he wondered if the Edge Act subsidiary might be interested in financing and/or investing in such a venture.

The DBIC officers were very interested. They explained that they had investments in finance companies in Venezuela and the Philippines. The one in Caracas operated as a consumer finance company for durable goods, and the Philippines company operated chiefly to finance the sales of American firms to that country. In each case DBIC financed the finance company with a loan that was convertible into options for about one-fifth of the equity capital.

Brito returned to Ecuador to investigate the climate for establishing a finance company. He was again impressed by the fact that the commercial banks' terms were too high to finance his working capital requirements, even the import predeposits; and the local banks were unwilling to lend funds to a finance company that would be competition. In terms of locating finance capital from other sources, Brito learned that under Ecuadorian law, any institution that makes loans to anyone other than its shareholders is considered a bank and thereby subject to federal regulation, reserve requirements, and so on.

He forwarded this information to DBIC, which agreed to consider how financing might be arranged in Ecuador. DBIC split the task into two parts: financing predeposits and financing sales. The Edge Act bankers believed the former problem could be solved if DBIC's parent bank would extend a line of credit to Brito's dealership which would be used to finance the import deposit requirement when vehicles were purchased from Torque. This arrangement would work unless the Ecuadorian government formulated additional legislation that would require predeposits to be financed out of local capital. Such additional legislation was considered unlikely unless Ecuadorian importers were found to be circumventing the predeposit requirement on a large scale.

DBIC believed that the latter problem—financing sales—could be solved by creating a local finance company in which the vehicle dealer would become a shareholder. The local finance company could loan funds to the dealer, who in turn could extend credit to his customers. DBIC also suggested an additional solution for Brito's problem—bringing dealers of other goods into the proposed finance company as shareholders so that a number of Ecuadorian merchants could indirectly offer consumer credit on a regular basis. Under this arrangement the newly created finance company would issue bills of exchange denominated in sucres, selling the bills to wealthy Equadorians. A local dealer who was active in the bills market expressed confidence that a finance company backed by such names as DBIC, Brito, and Torque would be able to issue bills in an amount equal to twice the amount of subscribed equity capital. The bills would mature in 80 to 190 days and could be rolled-over without difficulty under current market conditions. The prevailing effective cost of bills financing was 11 per cent per annum.

Brito received DBIC's comments with interest but some skepticism. For one thing, Ecuadorian law requires a corporation's stock to be fully subscribed at incorporation though only 25 per cent had to be paid in at that time. He was concerned that this requirement might prevent other dealers from participating, for most of them had little free working capital and would probably be reluctant to secure their subscriptions by personal guarantees. Another possible problem was that Torque might not agree to support a company which was also financing other dealers even though the others were not competitors. Brito also knew that as compensation for their support, DBIC would ask for a convertibility feature whereby its loan would be made convertible into a stock option (at par value) for perhaps a 20 per cent share of capital. This would be expensive financing, and other potential shareholders might balk.

Nevertheless Brito believed that there should be some approach which would achieve the kind of financing he desired. In November 1966 in a letter to William Martin at Torque, Brito made the following points:

1. It was bad business for Torque if it failed to take advantage of the market available for credit sales in Ecuador. Sales volume would at least be doubled if moderate financing terms could be offered.
2. If Torque would not change its policy, he hoped to promote a company to finance the installment paper of his dealership and possibly other noncompetitive dealers in Ecuador.
3. Ecuadorian law required full subscription of stock, 25 per cent of which had to be paid in immediately. The finance company could loan only to its shareholders.
4. DBIC's possible role as financier of operations was described.
5. Would Torque be interested in supporting this finance company through equity, loans, or introduction to United States banking institutions?

Martin realized that it was time for Torque to examine its Latin American selling policy and asked Sam Jeffrey to make an extensive report addressing the following points:

1. Should Torque consider direct financing of sales to dealers and/or customers in Latin America (and in Ecuador)?
2. Should Torque consider a captive finance company for Latin American consumer sales?
3. If a captive finance company appeared to be an attractive possibility, should Torque invest in Brito's proposed finance company?
4. From Torque's viewpoint, what are the most desirable characteristics for Brito's proposed company?
   (a) Membership: Brito's dealership alone, or the inclusion of other non-competitive dealers?
   (b) Sources of capital and operating funds: DBIC, Torque, Brito, other private investors, other American exporters, or government agencies?

To assist Jeffrey, Martin asked Torque's treasurer to have his staff prepare a report analyzing Brito's proposed finance company in which the questions above and the following points are considered:

1. What financing is available from Export-Import Bank, AID, the IMF, the World Bank, the International Finance Corporation, the Inter-American Development Bank?
2. What investment guarantees are available from AID?
3. What is the nature of exchange risk in Ecuador and methods by which it could be hedged?

EXHIBIT 1

Selected Data on Ecuador Economy*

The incomplete statistics and the data available on certain recent economic trends lead to the conclusion that Ecuador's economic growth lost some of its impetus in 1965. The growth rate of the gross domestic product, which had climbed to 6.6 per cent in 1964, probably dropped to 5 per cent in 1965, which represents an increase of less than 2 per cent if taken in conjunction with the population growth rate. The weakening of Ecuador's economic growth can be ascribed to the increasing difficulty of placing its principal export commodity on the world market.

The end of 1964 already marked a reduction in the operations of the principal company purchasing Ecuador's bananas, which was reflected in a sharp drop in banana exports. The above trend persisted in 1965 and was aggravated by the dock strike in the United States and by a gradual decline in the actual sales prices. Ecuador is estimated to have sustained a loss of about 20 per cent in the value of its banana exports for the whole year. However, since the exportable volume of production was maintained and even increased slightly in relation in 1964, failure to sell to the usual markets resulted in serious wastage. This has served to accentuate the need to seek new export markets, since the levels of consumption of bananas in North America and Western Europe seem to have reached saturation point. Attention is drawn to the fact that the major distributor of this fruit in the United States has recently been urging people to eat more Central American bananas.

In spite of the reduction of nearly $20 million in the value of banana exports, total foreign exchange receipts remained at virtually the same level as in 1964, i.e., about $150 million. This was due to the increase in the value of coffee and cocoa exports, since the reduction in world prices (slight in the case of coffee but more serious for cocoa) was amply offset by the larger volume of production and exports.

The lack of impetus in external demand for Ecuador's production as a whole was counteracted by the stepping up of domestic investment in industry and the execution of infrastructure works for the expansion of social services. Imports for that purpose increased by over 20 per cent, although this increment seems to be attributable in part to the effects of speculation based on the revision of the import tariff, with the new version going into effect at the end of the year.

The growing deficit on the merchandise account was aggravated by the heavy incidence of net payments under the head of insurance and freight and of remittances abroad in the form of private capital servicing. The result of all this was an unprecedented deficit of nearly $90 million on current account.

In 1964 Ecuador began to apply its overall Economic and Social Development Plan for the ensuing decade, the target being an annual growth of 3.5 per

* From *The Latin American Economy in 1965, Excerpt from ECLA Survey,* United Nations.

cent in the per capita gross product. The strong tendency of its external operations to show a deficit and the technical and organizational difficulties in impeding the increased use of external resources previously envisaged, culminated in 1965 in proposals for a revision of the goals set forth in the Plan. In spite of a sufficient number of investment projects and the growing accumulation of balances available from earlier loans, the above-mentioned factors seem to have impeded the use of external financing in 1965 on any greater scale than in 1964, except in the case of housing construction, for which $5 million were utilized (only 11 per cent of the foreign aid envisaged was made use of in 1964). Disbursements against external loans are estimated at $20 million in 1965, compared with $12 million in 1964.

For the development of the fiscal sector, 1965 showed a larger deficit than 1964. This is attributable to the marked rise in fiscal expenditure and to the fact that the recently implemented tax and customs tariff reforms have not yet yielded sufficient additional resources. The deficit in 1965 is estimated at 1,200 million sucres. In order to cover it, recourse was had to internal loans, and the floating debt was increased.

Table 1

Ecuador: Product, Consumption, Investment and External Sector

	1960	*1963*	*1964*	*1965**	*ANNUAL GROWTH RATES 1960-65*	*1963-64*	*1964-65*
	Millions of 1960 sucres				*Percentages*		
Gross domestic product	14,060	15,421	16,432	17,254	4.2	6.6	5.0
Total investment	2,081	2,256	2,805	2,993	7.5	24.3	6.7
Fixed investment	1,856	1,928	2,285†	2,440	5.6	18.5	6.8
Public	882	704	806		-2.2‡	14.5	
Private	974	1,224	1,479		11.0‡	20.8	
Total consumption	11,925	12,534	13,745	14,750	4.3	9.7	7.3
Public	1,813	2,004	2,202	2,422	6.0	9.9	10.0
Private	10,112	10,530	11,543	12,328	4.0	9.6	6.8
Exports of goods and services	2,530	3,207	3,084	3,214	4.9	-3.8	4.2
Imports of goods and services	2,476	2,576	3,202	3,703	8.4	24.3	15.6

Sources: 1960-64: Central Bank of Ecuador, *Memoria del Gerente General correspondiente al ejercicio de* 1964; exports and imports: ECLA, on the basis of International Monetary Fund, *Balance of Payments Yearbook*; 1965: ECLA, on the basis of piecemeal indicators.

* Provisional figures.

† Estimates.

‡ 1960-64.

The above facts led the Government to establish an agency called the "Economic Front" ("Frente Económico") to revise the Development Plan and limit certain items of public sector expenditure.

Investment in electrification projects and highways has been practically at a standstill since 1963, but the funds invested in education and public health have gradually risen. Housing construction has continued to increase in 1965, but will probably fail to offset the drop in public investment caused by the postponement of several projects. Altogether, total investment went up very little in real terms, and the coefficient with respect to the gross product remained unchanged.

The relatively favorable weather conditions in 1965 permitted an increase in the potato, wheat, barley, maize, and sugar cane crops. The exportable output of coffee and cocoa also increased, although on a smaller scale. The overall per capita index for agricultural production rose by 3 per cent, and that for food items by nearly 7 per cent.

Table 2

Ecuador and Latin America: Estimated Average Annual Growth Rates Compared, 1950-1965

	PER CENT CHANGE IN TOTAL GNP			*PER CENT CHANGE IN GNP/CAPITA*		
Area	*1950-1955*	*1955-1960*	*1960-1965*	*1950-1955*	*1955-1960*	*1960-1965*
Ecuador	5.3	4.6	4.3	2.4	1.4	1.0
18 Latin American Republics	5.1	4.9	4.5	2.3	2.0	1.6

Source: U.S. Agency for International Development.

Table 3

Ecuador and Latin America: Per Capita GNP In Constant 1965 Prices, 1950-1965 (dollar equivalents)

	PERIOD								
Area	*1950*	*1952*	*1954*	*1956*	*1958*	*1960*	*1962*	*1964*	*1965*
Ecuador	177	189	200	197	201	212	212	222	222
18 Latin American Republics (avg.)	292	301	316	328	348	359	370	382	390

Source: U.S. Agency for International Development.
Ecuador Average for 18 Latin American Republics

Table 4

Ecuador and Latin America: Selected Economic Indicators, 1965

	POPULATION			AREA		POWER	TRANSPORT	
	Total (millions)	Rate of growth	Density	Total (1,000 sq. miles)	Agricultural land as per cent of total	KWH per capita	Miles improved roads*	Motor vehicles (1,000's)
Ecuador	5.0	3.0	44	112	12	107	58	36
18 Latin American Republics	12.0	2.9	30	406	24	400	76	283

Source: U.S. Agency for International Development.
* Per 1,000 square miles

Table 5

Ecuador: Selected Economic Indicators, 1960-1965

	PERIOD											
Indicator	1960	1961	1962	1963	1964 I	II	III	IV	1965 I	II	III	IV
Exchange rates												
Official rate	15.15	18.18	18.18	18.18	18.18	18.18	18.18	18.18	18.18	18.18	18.18	18.18
Free rate	17.50	21.70	22.10	18.53	18.71	18.64	18.51	18.52	18.54	18.78	18.73	18.52
Int'l liquidity*	40.80	38.30	43.20	51.60	52.20	49.80	53.20	51.60	41.60	38.00	44.70	46.00
Gold	20.00	19.20	19.10	18.70	18.50	11.20	11.20	11.20	11.20	11.20	11.20	11.20
IMF tranche	3.80					3.00	3.00	3.00	3.00			
Foreign exchange	17.00	19.10	24.20	32.90	37.70	35.60	39.00	37.40	27.40	26.80	33.50	34.80
Cost of living (1958 = 100)	102	106	109	115	117	121	121	120	121	124	125	124
Exports	2,281	2,110	2,701	2,704	612	610	670	680	NA	NA	NA	NA
Bananas	1,447	1,381	1,707	1,547	414	429	330	338				
Coffee	329	243	376	329	43	40	177	130				
Cacao	321	250	283	356	71	91	54	63				
Rice	56	48	11	66	10	8	1					
Imports†	1,520	1,531	1,532	2,029	487	709	687	790				

Source: IMF *International Financial Statistics.*
* In millions of United States dollars
† In millions of sucres.

EXHIBIT 2

Export Insurance Programs

To promote and encourage American exports, two programs available to United States firms offer nonrecourse financing (i.e., the exporting firm can offer credit terms to the importer, and the exporter will not have to assume the credit risk of lending to the importer).

One program is the guarantee plan of the Export-Import Bank that is operated in conjunction with United States commercial banks. The importer pays at least 10 per cent in cash and signs a series of promissory notes promising to pay the remaining amount to the exporter in equal installments at regular intervals. The exporter then sells these notes to a commercial bank for cash, and the bank collects on them. In effect the bank has extended the credit.

It should be noted that the bank purchases only 70 to 90 per cent of the value of each note because the Eximbank requires the exporter to participate up to 10-30 per cent in extending credit. Meanwhile the bank has obtained an agreement that the Eximbank will guarantee payment of the "later installments" (the last half of the installments of a one-year to three-year credit, or all but the first eighteen months of a longer credit). Because a commercial bank can be assured of collecting on these later notes, it is more willing to finance exports.

For the guarantee, a fee must be paid to the Eximbank by either the exporter or importer, depending on the arrangements made. The fee ranges from $.21 to $5.29 per $100 financed, depending on the foreign country, amount of risk, and the length of credit. For exports to Ecuador, the fee would range from $.48 per $100 financed for one year to $2.01 per $100 financed for five years. The exporter would be required to participate in at least 10 per cent of each note.

Banks may purchase the exporter's participation also, but the extra amount will not be guaranteed by the Eximbank, and it must be with recourse to the seller if the importer defaults.

The other program available is through the Foreign Credit Insurance Association. Under this program the exporter himself obtains an FCIA policy insuring payment of an importer's notes. FCIA insurance covers *all* maturities.

The exporter may if he wishes assign his policy to a commercial bank, which will buy the notes. Again the exporter must participate for 10-30 per cent, though the bank may purchase the participation with recourse to the exporter. FCIA insurance costs about 25 per cent more than an Eximbank guarantee.

EXHIBIT 3

Edge Act Corporations

The Edge Act, Section 25A of the Federal Reserve Act, was named after Senator Edge (R., N.J.) who sponsored the legislation in 1919. The law permits United States banks to form subsidiaries that may conduct certain international financial transactions that are prohibited to the parent banks.

Edge Act corporations may invest in foreign equity, grant loans overseas, finance imports and exports, pay and collect obligations, and deal in international securities and in foreign exchange.

Parent banks may invest no more than 20 per cent of their capital and surplus in Edge Act subsidiaries. An Edge Act may lend to or invest in any one firm up to 50 per cent of its capital and surplus unless the Edge Act is engaged in banking. If the Edge Act is in banking (taking any type of deposits), this limit is 10 per cent.

Some Edge Acts do medium-term export financing, but most tend to leave this to their parents and concentrate on investment banking. Their development loans usually have some provision for stock options, a special finance fee, profit-sharing, special bonus shares, or other "sweeteners."

Case 17
NOZZACK CORPORATION

The Nozzack Corporation is a multinational industrial concern in the plastics and synthetic fiber fields. Activities outside the United States are concentrated primarily in Europe and contribute 35 per cent of total company revenues. On April 12, 1967, James Duncan, president and chief executive officer of Nozzack, attended a President's Club luncheon at the Waldorf Gastronomy. During the luncheon some of Mr. Duncan's friends mentioned receiving letters of commendation from President Johnson for aiding the United States balance of payments by raising capital abroad. Nozzack's French affiliate had recently submitted a request for additional funds, and Mr. Duncan wondered as he listened to his friends whether this was the appropriate time for his company to float an offshore issue.

For the most part Nozzack's foreign affiliates had financed their growth through retained earnings and parent equity contributions. Typically, foreign sources of capital had been avoided because of high interest costs except to facilitate the day to day operations of the affiliates. Financing of the French affiliate was in some respects atypical in that rapidly expanding working capital requirements had forced the affiliate to utilize continuously its line of credit at a local French bank. The French affiliate had established a revolving line of credit for the French franc equivalent of $10 million. The French bank reviewed the rate of interest on a quarterly basis and currently charged Nozzack 6 per cent. Although the line was to expire in 1969, the affiliate had the option of negotiating a two-year term loan at that time. In addition to extending credit to the French affiliate, the local bank provided a number of extremely useful ancillary services.

After reviewing the French affiliate's capital expenditure program for 1967 and 1968, Nozzack's treasurer, Leonard Karbern, recognized that the existing financial arrangements were insufficient. The French affiliate proposal to expand its manufacturing facilities and related plant and equipment expenditures, together with working capital requirements, indicated a need for $15 million of external financing. The required $15 million was in addition to the existing $10 million line of credit and anticipated inflows from operations. After the board approved the French affiliate's capital expenditure program, Mr. Karbern contacted domestic commercial bankers in an attempt to obtain funds for the projected plant and equipment requirements. The treasurer was confident that the company's French banking source would accommodate the increased working capital requirement and that adequate leeway existed under the President's Guidelines Program to finance the fixed assets from domestic sources.

At Mr. Duncan's suggestion, however, Mr. Karbern began to explore the possibility of a $15-25 million off-shore bond issue. If the company raised only $15 million, it would be necessary to maintain the existing $10 million revolving credit line, whereas a $25 million issue would enable the affiliate to extinguish the existing line of credit. In April 1967 the rate of interest on Eurodollar bond issues was 6½ per cent, approximately fifty basis points above the 6 per cent rate Nozzack was paying for its existing bank credits in France.

On April 15, 1967, Mr. Karbern arranged an appointment with Sam Rolles of Klein Brothers, Menn, Nozzack's traditional investment bankers in New York. Mr. Rolles was particularly well qualified to advise Mr. Karbern regarding off-shore bond issues for he had arranged several such financings for Klein Brothers on previous occasions. Before meeting with Mr. Rolles, Karbern reviewed a speech on the European capital markets, which appears as Exhibit 1. The meeting with Rolles was informal, for Rolles and Karbern had known each other from business school and had subsequently worked together on Nozzack's domestic issues. The conversation proceeded much in the following manner:

Len: Would it be safe to assume that the growing list of off-shore financings by American companies has been a response to the Guidelines Program and the Interest Equalization Tax?

Sam: Yes. Most American-based companies that have issued bonds in Europe have needed additional funds to finance the expansion of their foreign operations; the Interest Equalization Tax (IET) and the Guidelines Program have effectively precluded reliance on domestic sources of capital.

Len: To what extent is the off-shore financing phenomenon explained by companies trying to emulate others?

Sam: Not appreciably. The issues we have seen during the past two years have been floated by top-rated companies. (See Exhibit 2.) The treasurers of these companies have been concerned primarily with obtaining sufficient capital to keep from stunting the growth of their affiliates overseas. Following the leader hasn't been a big factor. Perhaps a few issues have been based on prestige rather than economic considerations but not the majority.

Len: What can you tell me about foreign dollar bonds?

Sam: Foreign dollar bonds are issues denominated in United States dollars and sold to nonAmericans. They have been by far the most important development in financing foreign operations since the IET closed off New York as the traditional center for international issues. During 1966 foreign dollar bonds accounted for more than 80 per cent of the volume of foreign issues. There have been three types of issues—the fifteen-year guaranteed sinking fund debenture, the five-year guaranteed note, and the guaranteed convertible debenture. During 1965 and early 1966 all of the dollar bond issues were fifteen-year obligations. During 1966 the trend moved toward five-year notes and convertibles as the market for straight debt with long maturities thinned.

Len: I seem to recall that a lawsuit was filed against one of the companies that issued a convertible overseas.

Sam: Yes. Stockholders of Indiana Standard have brought suit, contending that the company paid exorbitant rates overseas. (See Exhibit 3). This is the only case, however, that has been called to our attention.

Len: What will a dollar issue cost in today's market?

Sam: Comparative costs of issuance look something like this for a $25 million issue. (Exhibit 4.) Either the five- or fifteen-year notes could probably be sold at par with a 6 per cent coupon. A convertible would obtain a favorable reception in this market with a 5 per cent coupon; conversion would be permitted at a 15 per cent premium over current market prices of parent company stock.

Len: The convertible would enable local nationals to acquire Nozzack stock. This might help our European affiliates combat hostility to foreign investment. Isn't the intent of the United States government to assure that issues exempt from the interest equalization tax remain in the hands of nonAmericans? How do you make sure that the stock obtained through conversion stays overseas? And if you can't, what is the extent of our liability?

Sam: The underwriters attempt to distribute the bonds in such a fashion that they will remain in European portfolios. Inevitably there will be some leakage but in any event you are not responsible for the ultimate pattern of ownership.

Len: Can an issue be floated abroad without a parent guarantee?

Sam: Unfortunately the parent guarantee is essential to the success of this type of bond issue. There has been only one issue that wasn't guaranteed and about 90 per cent of the buyers were confused on this point. European institutions are quite conscious of corporate names and consequently unwilling to lend solely on the strength of subsidiaries.

You should also consider the possibility of a franc issue in the French capital market since the proceeds are to be used in France. The French have recently instituted exchange reforms in an effort to make it easier for foreign companies to raise money there. (Exhibit 5.) Local issues are usually underwritten by commercial banks that in turn place the bonds in the investment portfolios of their clients. The French market like the Swiss market is limited by government regulation both with respect to the timing and size of issues. Issues must be placed on an official waiting list, and it often takes up to two years to obtain final government authorization. Foreign company issues find themselves in competition with issues of various French government agencies, and the latter are naturally given higher priorities.

Len: Shifting the subject momentarily, I noticed that Wade, Williams, and Washburn (another investment banking firm) ran an ad in *Fortune* last month emphasizing their expertise in off-shore financing. I know that one of your leading people recently left Nozzack and became a partner over there—and has been doing quite a job. What can you offer me that Wade, Williams, Washburn can't?

Sam: (Smiling.) Certainly the newness and complexity of these off-shore issues makes the choice of underwriters more critical than for the typical domestic floatation. Timing, syndication, and control of the selling group is made less certain by the physical and cultural difference between the United States and Europe. Communication and transportation problems are more complex. International political considerations play a greater role in timing and distribution. I feel that we have had a great deal of experience with this type issue, and our excellent overseas connections provide more certainty in control of the underwriting group and distribution of the bonds. Let me ask you a few questions, even though they are rhetorical. Do you want to turn your financing over to someone who doesn't know the subtleties of the market? Do you want to entrust your financing to a banking firm that has only a passing familiarity with your history, corporate scope, and financial structure? Do you want to hinder what has been a good and mutually beneficial relationship with your present bankers? Now, Len, you know that I can only mention these considerations so bluntly because of our long and close friendship. I have the best interests of your company at heart. If I didn't we'd soon be out of business.

Len: Thanks, Sam. I do appreciate this last bit of advice. I have about two weeks in which to make a decision about rolling over our credit line in France. I think I should inquire further into the possibility of a French franc issue with my commercial banking friends in Paris. I'll give you a call toward the end of next week to tell you of our current thinking.

As Leonard Karbern left the offices of Klein Brothers, Menn, the details of the international bond issues were fresh in his mind. There didn't appear to be much difference between a foreign dollar issue and a French franc issue since most of the proceeds would be used in France in either event. Given the recent switch in attitude by the French government on foreign exchange restrictions and his knowledge that recent French franc issues had carries 5½ per cent coupons, the French market seemed attractive. The task remained of identifying and recommending the most appropriate instrument, or combination of instruments, to Mr. Duncan.

EXHIBIT 1

The European Capital Market

Talk by Robert L. Genillard, Partner, White, Weld and Company, Resident in Zürich, at the Midyear Meeting of the American Petroleum Institute San Diego, California, June 2, 1966*

It is not only a privilege to be addressing such a distinguished audience but a pleasure, particularly in view of the fact that the industry which you represent has been one of the great and fascinating adventures of the twentieth century. In recent times of monetary difficulties resourcefulness has, in a much more modest way, also proved rewarding in international finance.

I would like to divide my presentation in three parts: First, a review of recent events and their significance. Secondly, I would like to deal with practical aspects, describing the actual size, scope and workings of the European Capital Market. Finally, I would like to draw some conclusions and invite your questions.

I must start by defining my subject because there is no such thing as a European Capital Market. On the one hand, there is an international one, which is a composite of many factors stretching geographically well beyond Europe. On the other hand, there are the various internal national markets of European countries. The international market operates in international currencies acceptable to foreign investors, principally the dollar. The local markets function in their own local currencies and under the national laws and regulations applying in each country. But the international market operates, to use an expression which *Fortune Magazine* quoted last month, not so much in the air as in the ether. It has no set residence, no real domicile as yet. Since the introduction of the Interest Equalization Tax the center of gravity for international long term issues has tended to shift from America to Europe and this activity has given rise to the term European Capital Market. It is premature, but hopefully, and most importantly against its critics, this international market operating with great freedom may well, if the present evolution can continue, serve as the foundation for a future truly unified and supranational European Capital Market. If this were to happen a considerable contribution to the further economic development of Europe will have been made.

Let's examine the national markets first. I am sure it is obvious to you that in Europe, while aggregate figures of savings and capital floatations are fairly impressive, they represent a total of many separated and isolated markets. According to official figures the combined savings of the European Economic Community Countries, Switzerland and the United Kingdom reached in 1963 $75.7 billion, that is about 70 per cent of the gross formation of capital in the United States. The rate of savings in these countries has been high, namely 22.6 per cent

* Reprinted by permission of White, Weld and Company.

of the gross national product against only 18.1 per cent in the United States. On this base, new issues, public and private, in the various European markets reached in 1963 some $11 billion which is again about two-thirds of the total of new issues in the United States. More recent official figures are not as yet available, but estimates indicate that these ratios have continued to prevail, by and large, on the higher levels of economic activity achieved since 1963. One of the objectives of the treaty of Rome is the liberalization of the flow of capital and while remarkable progress has been achieved in freeing trade, very little headway has been made on connecting capital markets in the common market or in Europe generally. In the absence of a unified European Capital Market the capacity for absorbing foreign issues in each national market depends on foreign exchange controls, different issue and withholding taxes and a variety of other legal and administrative complications. Furthermore, local capital markets are dominated by domestic economic interests and policies.

Until 1963 long-term financing in Europe had to be undertaken primarily at the local level, and those European borrowers, mostly governments or their political subdivisions who had requirements which could not be met by their local markets went to New York, but also to Switzerland and to London for sterling area operations. These were the principal markets where they could with varying degrees of freedom or difficulty float with reasonable frequency loans of sufficient size and on acceptable terms. The freest and biggest market was New York. Yet because of S.E.C. requirements, listing procedures and other administrative complications it was only readily accessible to governmental borrowers primarily. The Swiss market had requirements more easily compatible with the wishes and practices of private borrowers. It accommodated many public and private ones alike but the rhythm, rate and size of issues was strictly controlled and held down to figures manageable for the Swiss economy. Today it remains a highly regulated market where rates are still deliberately kept at a comparatively low level by a policy of carefully spacing issues, so that it is only available for any one borrower, infrequently and for relatively modest amounts. It is however a very well organized market.

Oddly enough, although loans were floated in New York because after the war it was the largest center of excess capital and the freest market, and although rates on foreign issues were materially higher than on domestic issues, foreign bonds were bought in only modest proportions by American investors. While in a few cases, such as for Australian and Japanese issues, something like half or more of the issues went into the hands of American investors, many more issues of other borrowers, mostly European governments, were taken up to a large extent, sometimes over 75 per cent, by foreign investors.

In defining and describing the market for dollar bonds of foreign issuers, it might in fact be worth emphasizing the point that the market for such bonds has been one in which the demand has been largely from nonresidents of the United States, and that, in the case of new issues registered with the S.E.C. and described as having been offered in the New York or U.S. market, the facts have been that, while available for purchase in the U.S., such bonds were largely absorbed by nonresidents of the U.S. The enactment of IET effectively put an end to the ability of U.S. residents to purchase such offerings, thus confining the market for such issues to non-resident purchasers. In other words, the imposition of IET did not require the creation of an entirely new source of demand for so-called foreign dollar bonds--rather, it effectively barred U.S. investors from the market, leaving only the market demand from outside the U.S. which had been the more important all along. This, of course, necessitated the development of new marketing techniques to facilitate the syndication and offering of dollar issues entirely outside the U.S. I exclude from this description Canadian issues as well as those of the World Bank and more recently the Inter American Bank which were sold primarily to U.S. investors and at rates well below those prevailing for other foreign issues.

These peculiar conditions in a climate of constant improvement in international communications and understanding could only have remained unchanged if an increasing amount of these foreign issues had been sold domestically to U.S. investors or if American investment banking firms had gone abroad in substantial number and integrated themselves into foreign local markets, by developing foreign networks of distribution. This latter course is what my firm chose to do several years ago, in the belief that the floating of international issues would sooner or later internationalize itself. This process was greatly accelerated, however, by a historical accident, namely the institution of the IET. It is not my role here to discuss the merits or drawbacks of this tax, and I shall just limit myself to mentioning one of the paradoxes which it created in my particular industry. The IET marked the first major post-war reversal in the process of economic liberalization which created so much prosperity and which the very United States did so much to promote, but it caused Europe to discover that a sizable international market could function there and one in which European bankers could play a role in spite of the severe handicaps under which they have to labor in their domestic markets. Thus one can say that the IET has, paradoxically, greatly accelerated the internationalization of investment banking and thereby helped to broaden the international capital market. In 1962 for instance only some $550 million of international bonds were floated in New York and in Europe. By 1964 this volume had climbed to $980 million and 1965 saw a further rise to $1.2 billion. And while in 1962 the participation of European bankers in the underwriting of international dollar issues was practically non-existent, today they have become active in the field and acquired experience which should serve them in any future European supranational market.

Naturally this evolution is not taking place without growing pains. For many European bankers their entry into this field required their acquainting themselves with a number of syndication techniques new to them but, more importantly, many of them had to feel their way around to attempt to locate ultimate buyers and attempt to cope with aftermarket problems. In fact, there are still many deficiencies left in these areas and the mistakes which have been made and continue to be made have given support to those who favor some form of regulation of the market. But in their analysis of the problems many of the critics have confused the symptoms of the illness with its causes and this is a point to which I shall revert shortly. Some of the real difficulties are structural problems which only time can remedy. For example, there are still no European investment bankers with a network of offices throughout Europe handling local distribution, making an after-market and in general gaining firsthand local expertise. In spite of excellent communications, activity remains regional and bankers must continue to rely on the knowledge of their correspondents in other markets than their own. But this process of local integration which my firm embarked on several years ago, will undoubtedly gain momentum among European investment bankers. Recently several of them have joined us in the all-important field of making secondary markets in Europe, which is highly desirable because there is a very important need to keep broadening the aftermarket in line with the increase in new issues. The future growth of the primary market will depend heavily on it. Another favorable development which can be ascribed to the IET and which should have a lasting effect on the market is the advent of substantial borrowings by private corporations. Prior to the arrival on the scene of U.S. companies as borrowers in the international market governmental borrowers dominated the scene. While it is undeniable that the borrowings of U.S. companies have displaced a number of foreign borrowers, this must be viewed as a temporary phenomenon. The lasting effect will undoubtedly be that major international companies in Europe will in the future find it easier to borrow in the international market. My firm was instrumental in bringing to market in Europe the first straight dollar debt issue by a fully private European company, the first dollar straight debt issue of a Japanese private corporation, the first such issue for a U.S. company, and also the first issue convertible into shares of an American company. We are now working on a similar convertible dollar issue for a major European company, using a Luxembourg vehicle, and this example may well be followed by others before long. It is noteworthy that all of these developments have occurred in the last three years only.

Let us now turn to an examination of the various specific financing possibilities which are available to an international company in Europe. I shall not deal with short-term commercial bank borrowings in domestic markets because this is not my field and I think you will agree that it is a fairly cut and dried subject with regard to availability and costs.

The Eurodollar market is also probably quite familiar to you. It has become a pool of short-term funds of some $10 billion in which rates are not subject to any official controls and the freedom with which it operates makes it structurally comparable to the international bond market. Like the latter it cannot be said to be domiciled in any one jurisdiction. London is the biggest center, but it is only a clearing place for nonresidents lending their balances to London banking firms who relend them to other nonresidents. This market which was viewed with some reservations by monetary authorities at the outset is now well accepted. It is in the process of being further institutionalized by issuance of negotiable certificates of deposit in bearer form by the London Branch of the First National City Bank of New York and in which my firm will make a secondary market. Initially C/D's of up to 120 days are being offered but as the market develops and other banks join in, longer maturities will undoubtedly be sold. This will give banks a more stable base of Eurodollar deposits and therefore permit them to lend them for longer periods. On the other hand, these C/D's will represent the first truly international money market instrument, and thereby undoubtedly broaden the Eurodollar base. Considering that large issues of medium-term notes have recently been floated publicly in the international market, a more complete spectrum of fully negotiable maturities is beginning to emerge from thirty days to twenty years, which is a most constructive development. At this time very sizable amounts of credit are available in Eurodollars generally up to one year, but occasionally longer. A prime international borrower would at the moment pay between 6¼ and 6½ per cent for one-year money. External markets in European currencies have been developing parallel to the Eurodollar one, at rates related to both the Eurodollar ones and those prevailing in the countries of origin of these currencies.

I hope that you will agree that in the limited time available there is no point in discussing the internal capital markets which are open only to resident corporations. I am sure that all the treasurers of your local affiliates and subsidiaries have reported to you pretty thoroughly as to what your local subsidiaries can do in their domestic markets in local currency. Since this category of capital markets which are inoperative for a foreign borrower, whether by recent or long standing policies or merely by physical inadequacy of the market itself, embraces most of Europe at the moment, this leaves us for all practical purposes to examine the German market, the Swiss market, the Dutch market, and the international market.

Germany is experiencing a serious liquidity shortage. Rates have been rising sharply and first class corporate borrowers have had to pay around 8 per cent for long term funds. There are many reasons which account for such a rate. One of them was the imposition of a 25 per cent withholding tax on interest paid by German borrowers to foreign bondholders which resulted in massive liquidation of German bonds by foreigners who had been very large buyers in previous years. The German capital market is the freest of any European one. Germany and Switzerland are the only two countries in Europe which enjoy complete freedom from foreign exchange controls and thus qualify for the definition of full convertibility under Article 4 of the International Monetary Fund.

To overcome the German withholding tax problem German companies have been borrowing through foreign income financing vehicles, principally Luxembourg subsidiaries. However, Germany does not impose any withholding tax or other formalities with regard to interest paid in DM by non-German borrowers. They are also exempted from the German tax on new issues. Rates for AAA internationally-known borrowers on foreign DM loans have been close to those prevailing in the international market in dollars. The volume of such DM issues has been limited, however, and lately some concern has developed among investors about the possibility of Germany having to reverse its 5 per cent revaluation. This worry seems premature but a more fundamental concern has been the somewhat unnatural exercise of issuing a foreign bond denominated in DM at a rate of interest much lower than those prevailing for domestic DM bonds. Therefore such external DM bonds are only of interest to foreigners and if the latter at one time lost their willingness to hold such bonds in DM they would have no one to sell them to as German investors would only be interested in acquiring them at a much lower level, in line with domestic rates. This has already been reflected at times in limited marketability for such issues, although German bankers have made a serious effort to try and improve the aftermarket by supporting some of these issues from time to time. However, taking a longer view, if ever the German level of interest rates came into line with that of the international market, Germany could become one of the most active and attractive markets in which to float international loans denominated in DM.

The Swiss market remains the strongest and cheapest, although it is getting increasingly difficult for international borrowers to raise money therein, as the National Bank has been restricting the number of loans sharply in order to avoid further upward pressure on rates of interest. The Swiss approach in this regard is fairly simple. The country is too small to risk that its currency be used as an international reserve currency like the dollar for international financing operations. The Swiss economy would be swamped by the movement of funds which could develop as a result. Therefore by keeping interest rates on foreign loans low, which in any case ties in with a number of domestic policies, investors are discouraged from buying massive quantities of international securities denominated in Swiss francs. This is achieved by restricting the number and the size of issues, which is easy because the National Bank must authorize them and because all issues are handled by a cartel led by the big three commercial banks which so far has a virtual monopoly on the business. At present the waiting line can make for a delay of over a year in coming to market and the amount of any given issue seldom exceeds the equivalent of $10,000,000. The yield for the investor on AAA issues is around 5 per cent and if all expenses and issue taxes are included the net cost for the borrower is around 5.50 per cent on average life which usually runs around twelve years, with a final maturity normally of about fifteen years. The Netherlands followed in the past policies which in a number of respects were similar to those of Switzerland but it now finds itself in a considerable credit squeeze with the result that the National Bank has virtually closed the capital market to international issues and the situation is expected to last for some time. In any event, internal long term rates have risen above those of the international market.

Let us now turn therefore to the international market. Its real size is difficult to ascertain for reasons I shall explain shortly but I would expect it this year to accommodate some $1.5 billion of floatations. When it comes to describing where it is located and how it functions, matters get complicated. There is little reliable data on who purchases international bonds. The knowledge is empirical and belongs to those who have been placing and trading in such bonds over the years. While institutional interest in such securities has been growing,the larger portion of straight debt issues is still taken up by wealthy individuals around the world whose funds are traditionally administered by banks principally in Switzerland, Belgium, Holland and Great Britain and American firms such as mine. While it is true that a large part of the securities find their way to Swiss banks, the figure often mentioned being more than 50 per cent, the direct role of Swiss banks in distributing and selling such securities to their clients has been diminishing in recent years. The larger depositors of securities in Swiss banks have become increasingly sophisticated and developed their own financial contacts outside of Switzerland, often using Swiss banks only as custodians. Also many international financial organizations outside of Switzerland have taken interests in Swiss banks, set up holding or financial companies there, or made other financial affiliations in Switzerland. As a result an increasing amount of business booked in Switzerland is controlled from outside of the country. These remarks are not meant to minimize the placement role of Swiss banks which remains considerable. In fact they still rank ahead of any other national group of financial institutions in this field. But I did wish to underscore the complexity of determining the origin of purchases in the international market, and also that the process of internationalization to which I have been frequently referring has spared no one, not even the Swiss banking industry, one of the finest, but also one which has guarded sovereignty in its national market most jealously. The wealthy individuals I have mentioned are not only Europeans but also South Americans, Middle and Far Easterners who fear inflation or political risks in their own countries and want a fair return on their money combined with freedom from taxation. One prominent investment banker commented that perhaps the international market should be called instead the "émigré market." And the respected London weekly, *The Economist*, at one time dismissed the whole market as nothing more than a haven for tax dodgers. This misses the market's significance and its promise. In the view of national governments it is no doubt very important that everybody pays his taxes on time, but from the point of view of world economic development this is not the case and if Arabian sheiks are willing to bet on General Electric convertible debentures or the European Investment Bank bonds it would seem part of wisdom to let them. However, there are not only individuals in the picture. As the market has broadened, more institutions have been attracted to it not only with offshore funds which they wish to invest without immediate taxation. Insurance companies, investment trusts, pension funds and the like are increasingly coming into the picture. The convertible securities have contributed importantly in diversifying the sources of funds. Of course with the market stretching from Hong Kong to Zürich via Beirut and Caracas the problem of good distribution is a most delicate one and a number of recent issues have shown how easy it is to misjudge the size of the market and the mood of investors. In giving my estimate of one and a half billion dollars in floatation for 1966 I am assuming that American issues will continue to represent an important part of the total. There is no question that the quality of American borrowers and in some cases their willingness to grant conversion privileges has attracted additional money which would not have flowed into this market otherwise. So far this year $638 million of internationally syndicated issues have been floated. Of this total 40 per cent were for American companies. The currencies in which these issues were denominated broke down as follows: $ 79 per cent, DM 10 per cent, £/DM 3 per cent, Units of Account 8 per cent. Foreign Swiss franc issues are not included because they are not internationally syndicated. The total floated so far in 1966 was Swiss francs 194 million, or $45 million, against $79 million for all of 1965.

This leads me to an important point which is the significance of the currency in which the bonds are stated. The overwhelming preference of investors continues to be for issues denominated in U.S. dollars and which enjoy by far the broadest markets. In 1965 the breakdown of floatations among the various currencies was $ 66 per cent, DM 25 per cent,£/DM 6 per cent, U/A none. The dollar remains the primary international reserve currency of governments as well as private investors and whatever balance of payments problems the U.S. is now experiencing, the confidence of investors in America remains high. For years the best investment opportunities for international investors have been in American securities. However, because the dollar is only the most desirable and convenient vehicle in such loans, where in so many cases the borrower is foreign and the lender is foreign, other formulas have been put forward. The Unit of Account is an attempt to create a composite vehicle of all European currencies in order to create a currency with the widest possible acceptance and insure the holder against devaluation risks. The idea is certainly interesting. No real European supranational market will develop fully until there is a unified European currency. However, the complexity of this formula and the fact that it has not been widely accepted by monetary authorities has not permitted it to emerge as the ideal forerunner of a common European currency. The market for such issues is not at this time of a size that will permit a borrower to tap it on a regular and substantial basis. There were $10 million of issues floated in Units of Account in 1964, none in 1965 and $48.5 million in 1966 so far, which although still comparatively little is an encouraging revival.

Now if we turn to the question of listing of these issues we find ourselves in a fairly theoretical area. Even when the New York market was open to foreign borrowers and all issues floated there were listed on the New York Stock Exchange, a great deal of the trading in such issues was done in the over-the-counter market, especially where the larger part of the issue had been distributed abroad. My firm has specialized in the trading of these securities for over thirty years. It has been our experience before the IET as well as after that 90 per cent or over of all the trading in these securities takes place over-the-counter. Therefore one may ask, why should they be listed at all? Well, because a listing does permit investors to have an official record of prices, but more importantly, because in the case of the major exchanges, listing requirements are a guarantee of proper and continuing disclosure of financial information to investors. Also a listing is frequently required for the security to be eligible as an investment for certain types of institutional investors. Investors have shown a distinct preference for issues which are quoted on leading exchanges, and in the case of issues in dollars, they have preferred a New York listing. However, it must be observed that certain European borrowers, while realizing that they can secure the best terms in an issue stated in dollars, may be unwilling to meet New York listing requirements and on these grounds choose a European listing. However, while a listing is necessary and some listings make more sense than others, let me make clear that no listing will give any guarantee of a good aftermarket for an international issue. The market will remain for a long time primarily an over-the-counter one, simply because investors are in so many different places that resident brokers will never be able to compete with the few specialized trading institutions that are able to cover simultaneously many countries and even different continents.

Next I should comment on the size of individual issues and here we must divide the subject in two parts, straight debt issues and convertibles. A number of investors in the latter do not buy the former. As an illustration, a British investor who buys foreign securities must acquire the necessary currency from another British investor. There is at present a premium of well over 20 per cent on the so-called investment dollar. Yields on sterling bonds are higher than those of international issues of prime borrowers and if you subtract 20 per cent therefrom there cannot be any interest for a British resident to buy an international straight bond. On the other hand, such an investor will buy convertibles because he looks primarily to the value of the conversion feature into equity, matched with a higher current yield and better downside protection than on the shares. Similar considerations apply to a number of other European countries. In addition for those investors for whom the yield on the bonds is not subject to immediate taxation, whereas the divident of the shares in which the bonds are convertible is subject in the case of U.S. stocks to a withholding tax of up to 30 per cent, the gain in yield is sufficient to attract a number of investors who would otherwise not be buyers of fixed income securities. My firm has come to regard any floatation of a straight debt issue in the international bond market as a large one if it exceeds $25 million. Experience over decades has shown, even with the recent growth of the market, that the composition of investors' portfolios, their geographical distribution, the number of investors themselves and the absence of a substantial institutional segment, make it difficult to have a successful floatation in excess of this figure. In fact, in many cases the wiser range is normally between $15 and $25 million. Issues of less than $15 million, beside the higher incidence of fixed costs, pose problems of marketability, but these can be overcome with sinking funds starting early and which can be graduated in order not to alter substantially average life and therefore true costs to the borrower. Such an early sinking fund may be distasteful to many a borrower but it is of considerable importance, particularly if he intends to float several issues in a short interval. Markets in international bonds are still not very broad and many investors are very conscious of the value of the support of a sinking fund in the aftermarket, which is always conspicuous in comparative price performance of different issues. Thanks to such features it has been possible to float publicly issues even as small as $6 million, with a good aftermarket performance. As regards the size of convertible issues it is much more difficult to generalize because the appeal of a convertible is after all as individual a proposition as is the situation of the company in the shares of which the issue is convertible. However, one can say here quite safely that regardless of the attractiveness of the underlying equity and assuming terms of issue which are not over-generous, any issue of over $30 million is over-ambitious at this time.

Since I have the privilege of addressing a highly sophisticated financial audience I am not going to deal with the relative merits of straight debt issues versus convertibles under conventional circumstances. Let us only look therefore at the problem in the international market. Those international investors who buy straight fixed income securities are by and large a conservative and cautious lot. Thus straight debt issues can only be floated in a weak market by the larger and better known companies. A lesser known and smaller company but with a good record of growth for its common stock earnings and a good outlook can, however, float a convertible. A straight debt issue in the international market is often sold as much on the familiarity of investors with the borrower's name as on statistical considerations. Possibilities however for educating buyers on the attractiveness of a conversion option into equity are substantially better. This does not mean that only AAA companies can float straight debt issues but simply that for borrowers of lesser standing timing is more critical. Nevertheless investors have shown such a strong preference for issues of United States companies that in the case of the latter possibilities for floating straight debt issues remain quite broad. At this time for example there would be no difficulty in floating a $20 million issue with a maturity of fifteen years of straight debentures for a middle sized U.S. company with an AA debt rating, with a coupon of 6¼ per cent to yield the investor around 6.30 per cent to maturity. A company rated single A might require a yield around 0.15 per cent higher, while an AAA internationally known company could come out with a 6 per cent coupon to yield 6.20 per cent to maturity. Since I am mentioning specific terms I should refer to those applicable to convertibles but here generalizations are much more difficult because so much depends on the characteristics of the underlying shares. However, assuming an average size company with a reasonable debt to equity ratio and a good but not spectacular growth record and prospects, a yield to the investor of 5 per cent with a conversion premium of between 12 and 18 per cent is at this time an approximate range of terms for an issue of between $20 and $25 million.

Examining further straight debentures versus convertibles, I should mention that for the company which, as a matter of policy, wishes to increase distribution of its shares abroad, the convertible issue has much merit. A straight distribution of shares to foreign investors does not give any guarantee under the balance of payments program of the United States because the buyers can turn around the next day and sell their shares back to American investors. There is no guarantee either as to how well or how poorly this stock is going to be distributed by foreign intermediaries as their proficiency in distributing American shares varies widely. The foreign convertible issue on the other hand cannot be sold back to U.S. investors without payment of the IET. Of course, in the long run such bonds may be converted by foreign investors. As you know, in a U.S. domestic convertible issue conversion does not take place at least until the convertible debentures are selling without conversion premium, which normally only occurs when the underlying shares have risen considerably and often also after substantial increases in dividend have taken place. The same holds true for the foreign convertible but in addition it must be remembered that many investors have a considerable advantage in holding them longer because of the difference in taxation favoring the interest, which is not subject to a withholding tax, while the dividend is.

In fact, the performance of foreign convertibles of American companies in a declining stock market has been much better than in domestic American issues. The high yield of the debentures free of withholding tax has supported their price even though the underlying shares dropped and the conversion premium increased. Many such issues which were offered initially at a conversion premium of say 15 per cent have not gone down very much although the conversion premium has risen to 25 per cent or more. This by the way does not mean that new issues can be floated at a starting conversion of 25 per cent without increasing going coupon rates, but simply that these securities have shown excellent downside resistance. Thus the chances of an early flow back to the U.S. of the underlying shares through conversion are limited and one can assume that if an investor has held his debentures for a number of years, he will have taken during this time a keen interest in the earnings and performance of the company and its shares, so that by the time he is ready to convert he might be a good long term holder of the stock.

For companies which are not prepared to float long term straight debt or convertible issues there remains the possibility of raising medium-term funds, up to around five years at this time, in a public issue in small denominations or privately with larger denominations but then for a somewhat shorter duration and for a smaller total. There is no real international private placement market in Europe for long term debt, such as is known in the United States. Some domestic European markets have institutional private placement markets in local currency, but with few exceptions they are very limited and in general not accessible to foreign companies and in many cases not even to their local subsidiaries in the present climate. In the international market the only private placement possibilities are among the larger investors who operate in the international public bond market. This obviously makes for a restricted audience. Nevertheless at present it is possible to raise amounts of the order of $10 million and in a few cases up to $20 million in a private placement providing the duration does not exceed much more than three years. If raising money for longer periods is desired without going outright to the longest term available in Europe, there is the possibility of floating notes in small denominations and with basically many of the characteristics of the longer term public bond issues. This is a much bigger market and amounts of $20 to $30 million or even more can be raised by first class borrowers without difficulty. The costs of such note issues for five years is at this time very similar, when all expenses are included, to the cost of a three year private placement. At present a prime U.S. corporate borrower could raise either type of money at an effective cost including all expenses of between 6 3/4 per cent and 6 7/8 per cent.

If we now summarize the review of terms, the prime U.S. company wishing to raise money for the medium-term privately or publicly, or long-term publicly, is therefore faced with borrowing costs on average life, including issuing, legal, administrative and other costs, which are not very far apart, except for convertibles. The choice is therefore heavily dependent on your outlook on two related subjects: the U.S. balance of payments and the future evolution of interest rates in Europe.

The latter are likely to remain high as has been the case historically, particularly if European economic development continues at a rapid rate. The need for capital in Europe is phenomenal. As an illustration, my firm is a member of a financing consortium, with six other leading European Investment Banks, called Pipeline Finance. We estimate that in the next five to six years the building of pipelines alone in Europe will require outlays of $6 to $7 billion. If added pressure is placed on European sources of funds by the United States balance of payment situation, rates could well move still higher, although one must assume that sooner or later rates materially in excess of those now prevailing must in the end have a deflationary effect bringing about an automatic correction in the rate structure. In the short and medium run it is difficult however to see rates easing and, while it is not my role here to discuss the United States balance of payments, there seems to be a rather broad consensus at this time that the problem will not be corrected as quickly as had been hoped.

I would like to conclude by saying that the international capital market which has emerged in Europe has been a fine example of the benefits of international collaboration by bankers in a fully competitive climate. While lip service has been paid to the unification of European capital markets, little has been done officially in practice as yet in this direction and the international capital market in Europe is making its own significant private contribution thereto, by knitting together the European investment banking community which until only a few years ago was working in largely isolated compartments. We live in an age where anything not subject to some form of control is almost automatically suspicious. Yet freedom and sharp competition have given rise to ingenious new techniques in the international market in Europe, which permitted raising $1.2 billion in 1965, greatly easing the strain on domestic credit markets. These new techniques and the international teamwork will be of great value to European capital market unification when governments are ready to follow the leadership which the private investment banking community has displayed in this field. As regards the criticism which is heard in some quarters about American companies pre-empting an important part of the international market in Europe, I find it somewhat gratuitous. The United States has contributed in a very important measure to the economic development of Europe in the post-war years. One of the meaningful factors in this connection was heavy direct investment by the United States in Europe financed from U.S. domestic sources and parallel thereto the fact that Europe was able to draw on the United States' market very substantial amounts of short- and medium-term credit and to a lesser but not negligible extent long-term funds at a time when this money was critically needed for development. The current reversal in this process should form part of a normal economic ebb and flow, in a climate of international collaboration and interdependence. Admittedly, it is to be regretted that it should have been the very United States which took the first important post-war restrictive measure on capital movements in the form of the Interest Equalization Tax. However, so long as this is not the beginning of a new philosophy but merely an interim measure, while the fundamental problems are being tackled, then surely the critics are being emotional. In any case, let me assure you, as a European, that private European investors at large, individuals and institutions alike, have given ample proof of their confidence and their liking for American industry and for its role in Europe by investing heavily in the international issues of U.S. companies, and a large segment of the European banking community has done likewise by underwriting them.

EXHIBIT 2

Foreign Debt Offerings Subject to U.S. Interest Equalization Tax Issued by Finance Subsidies of U.S. Parent Companies

	OFFERING									
	Equivalent dollar amount	*Currency*	*Rate*	*Price*	*Yield to maturity*	*Conv. price*	*Conversion premium over market at offering*	*Current market*	*Bid price current yield to maturity*	*Current conversion premium*
Medium Term issues	(000)									
(1) Allis Chalmers International Finance Corp. 6 5/8%, February 1, 1972	$15,000	$	1/25/67	100	6.52%	—	—	102 - 3/8	6.04%	—
(1) Ameribas Holding S.A. 6 5/8%, December 15, 1971	15,000	$	12/15/66	99½	6.64	—	—	103 - ¾	5.78	—
(1) Cabot International Capital Corp. 7%, September 15, 1971	10,000	$	9/13/66	99	7.12	—	—	103 3/8 - 4	6.01	—
(1) Cities Service International Capital Corp. 6 3/8%, June 15, 1971	25,000	$	6/ 1/66	99¾	6.34	—	—	103¼ - 4	5.40	—
(1) Continental Oil International Finance Corp. 6 3/8%, May 1, 1971	20,000	$	4/21/66	99¾	6.34	—	—	101 7/8 - 2 3/8	5.75	—
(1) General Electric Overseas Capital Corp. 6¼%, July 1, 1971	25,000	DM	6/28/66	99 5/8	6.25	—	—	102¼ - 3	5.57	—
(1) Goodyear International Finance Corp. 6¾%, October 1, 1971	20,000	$	9/27/66	99	6.88	—	—	103 3/8 - 4	5.78	—
(1) Hercules International Finance Corp. 6 5/8%, December 1, 1971	25,000	$	11/ 9/66	99½	6.64	—	—	102 3/8 - 3 1/8	5.93	—
(1) Honeywell International Finance Co. S.A. 6 5/8%, November 1, 1971	15,000	$	10/19/66	100	6.52	—	—	103 3/8 - 4	5.67	—
(1) Marathon International Finance Co. 6¼%, February 15, 1972	20,000	$	1/31/67	99¾	6.22	—	—	101¾ - 2½	5.74	—
(1) Sun International Finance Corp. 6 5/8%, January 1, 1972	10,000	$	12/14/66	99½	6.64	—	—	101 7/8 - 2¼	6.06	—
(1) Union Oil International Finance Corp. 6¼%, March 1, 1972	15,000	$	2/16/67	99½	6.28	—	—	101 7/8 - 2 3/8	5.71	—

EXHIBIT 2 (cont.)

	OFFERING									
	Equivalent dollar amount	Currency	Rate	Price	Yield to maturity	Conv. price	Conversion premium over market at offering	Current market	Bid price current yield to maturity	Current conversion premium
Long Term Issues										
Amoco Oil Holdings S.A. 5¾%, October 1, 1985	$25,000	$	9/30/65	99½	5.79%	—	—	97 7/8 - 8½	5.94%	—
Avon Overseas Capital Corp. 6¼%, February 1, 1981	15,000	$	1/27/66	97½	6.51	—	—	100½ - 1¼	6.20	—
Cincinnati International Finance Corp. 6¼%, March 15, 1976	6,000	$	3/22/66	97	6.67	—	—	99 5/8 - 100¼	6.31	—
Cynamid International Development Corp. 5¾%, September 1, 1980	20,000	$	9/10/65	98¼	5.93	—	—	98½ - 9¼	5.91	—
(1) DuPont Europa Holdings, S. A. 6%, November 1, 1980	25,000	DM	11/ 3/65	100	5.91	—	—	100¼ - 1	5.88	—
(1) DuPont Europa Holdings, S. A. 6 3/4%, February 1, 1982	25,000	DM	2/ 8/67	99½	6.72	—	—	103¼ - 4¼	6.30	—
(1) General Motors Overseas Capital Corp. 6¾%, December 1, 1976	31,250	DM	1/ 5/66	99½	6.71	—	—	103¼ - 4¼	6.19	—
W.R. Grace Overseas Development Corp. 5 3/4%, November 15, 1980	20,000	$	11/17/65	97¾	5.98	—	—	97 - ¾	6.08	—
Honeywell International Finance Co. S.A. 6%, February 15, 1981	15,000	$	2/ 2/66	96	6.42	—	—	100¾ - 1½	5.92	—
(1) IBM World Trade Corp. 6%, January 2, 1981	30,000	DM	12/15/65	100	5.91	—	—	101½ - 2¼	5.75	—
International Standard Electric Corp. 6%, March 1, 1986	15,000	$	2/24/66	95	6.45	—	—	100¾ - 1½	5.93	—
Mobil Oil Holdings S.A. 5¾%, June 15, 1980	28,000	£/DM	6/16/65	97	6.06	—	—	92¼ - 3	6.64	—
Philips Petroleum International Investment Co. 6%, January 15, 1981	25,000	$	1/17/66	98	6.21	—	—	100¾ - 1½	5.92	—
Transocean Gulf Oil Co. 5¾%, October 1, 1980	25,000	DM	10/10/65	98½	5.90	—	—	94 - 5	6.43	—
Uniroyal Holdings S.A. 6%, July 31, 1980	14,000	£/DM	7/22/65	97	6.31	—	—	95¼ - 6¼	6.54	—

Convertible Issues											
Bankers International (Luxemburg) S.A. 5%, June 1, 1986	$20,000	$	5/10/66	100	5.00%	60	14.8%	108½	- 9¼	4.34%	10.3%
Bristol-Myers International Finance Co. 4½%, December 31, 1980	15,000	$	12/13/65	100	4.50	57½(3)	18.6	131	- 33	1.92	8.8
Clark Equipment Overseas Finance Corp. 4½%, March 1, 1981	15,000	$	3/ 1/66	100	4.50	39(3)	15.6	93¼	- 4¼	5.19	28.1
John Deere Overseas Capital Corp. 5%, June 15, 1986	20,000	$	6/14/66	100	5.00	75½	9.4	111¼	- 12	4.14	13.9
Federated Department Stores International Co. 4½%, December 15, 1985	20,000	$	12/13/65	100	4.50	82	14.9	98	- 9	4.66	30.7
General Electric Overseas Capital Corp. 4¼%, December 1, 1985	50,000	$	12/ 7/65	100	4.25	131	15.0	92¼	- 3¼	4.89	42.3
W.R. Grace Overseas Development Corp. 5%, April 1, 1986	15,000	$	3/18/66	97½	5.20	65	15.5	104	- 5	4.68	25.8
International Harvester Overseas Capital Corp. 5%, April 1, 1986	15,000	$	3/22/66	100	5.00	55½	11.8	102 5/8	- 3 3/8	4.79	53.9
International Utilities Overseas Capital Corp. 5¼%, June 1, 1986	12,000	$	5/11/66	97½	5.45	32	8.5	99¼	- 100¼	5.31	19.3
(2) ISE Finance Holdings S.A. 4½%, March 1, 1986	15,000	$	2/24/66	100	4.50	82	15.7	115¾	- 16¾	3.37	6.4
Marathon International Finance Co. 4½%, March 1, 1986	25,000	$	2/24/66	100	4.50	63	15.6	113¼	- 14¼	3.54	4.2
Monsanto International Finance Co. 4½%, October 15, 1985	25,000	$	10/20/65	100	4.50	91(3)	13.9	91¾	- 2¾	5.20	84.0
Owens-Illinois Overseas Capital Corp. 5%, January 15, 1977	20,000	$	1/17/66	100	5.00	62¾	8.2	108½	- 9½	3.94	12.5
Pepsi Co. Overseas Corp. 4½%, March 1, 1981	30,000	$	2/16/66	100	4.50	93	14.6	104¾	- 5¾	4.05	14.3
Warner-Lambert International Capital Corp. 4¼%, March 1, 1981	15,000	$	2/23/66	100	4.25	46	17.6	114¼	- 15¼	3.00	5.6

(1) Annual coupon; all other issues have semi-annual coupons. Yields have been adjusted to a semi-annual payment.
(2) Adjusted.

EXHIBIT 3

News Story Published in The Wall Street Journal
February 8, 1966

HOLDERS UNIT SUES TO BAR INDIANA STANDARD BORROWING OVERSEAS AT 'EXCESSIVE' RATES

New York – The Government's voluntary guidelines aimed at encouraging U.S. companies to raise foreign investment capital overseas came under indirect attack from a group holding stock in Standard Oil Co. (Indiana).

The Sylvia Martin Foundation, Inc., a New York institutional investor holding 200 shares of Indiana Standard stock, said it has begun legal proceedings seeking to block Indiana Standard from raising money abroad at "excessive interest rates." Murray S. Bornstein, New York attorney, acting for the foundation, said the suit has been served on American Oil Co., an Indiana Standard subsidiary, one of several defendants in the action.

The case could indicate that a U.S. company planning foreign outlays may face the uncomfortable choice of either violating the Federal Government's directives or risking a suit from its stockholders.

In the action, the foundation describes as "exorbitant" the 5¾% interest rate and initial discount price of 99½% of the principal Indiana Standard received on sale of $25,000,000 of bonds in Europe last fall. The group asserted the money could have been raised in the U.S. for about 4½% interest.

Sale of the bonds last October was "in part in response to President Johnson's voluntary program for improving the U.S. balance-of-payments position," said Richard J. Farrell, vice president and general counsel of Indiana Standard.

"Prudent business judgment dictated this kind of borrowing at this time for business purposes overseas, and we are pleased with the results" Mr. Farrell asserted. "The funds obtained are enabling us to proceed with our planned program overseas which we expect to contribute to future earnings for our stockholders."

Mr. Farrell said that the company has no present plans for selling additional securities abroad. He also confirmed that the suit had been served on the New York office of American Oil.

While Commerce Department officials were clearly interested in the development, they declined any immediate comment on it. The Washington view was that, presumably, the legal challenge won't prove anything but an unwelcome complication in the Administration's intensified efforts to reduce the outflow of dollars into direct foreign investments.

Defendants in the stockholder suit are Indiana Standard, and two wholly owned subsidiaries, American Oil Co., chief domestic operations subsidiary, and Amoco Oil Holdings, S.A., set up in Luxemburg to raise foreign capital; and officers, directors and agents of those companies. The legal action, scheduled to be filed in supreme court for New York county, a state court, on receipt of defendants' reply, will seek to enjoin the defendants from sale of future bond issues abroad, and to account for "losses" on the initial bond sale.

Prior to establishment of the Federal guidelines a year ago, there was almost no borrowing overseas by U.S. companies, a New York investment firm notes. But since the guidelines went into effect a year ago, U.S. companies have borrowed about $100 million abroad, and have announced plans to raise another $100 million, the firm declares.

Last December, President Johnson further stiffened the restraints on private lending and investment abroad in an effort to reduce this year's outflow of U.S. dollars for direct foreign investment to about $2.4 billion from an estimated $3 billion in 1965. This is being done in an effort to reduce the nation's balance-of-payments deficit—the amount by which U.S. receipts of goods and funds from foreigners fall short of the flow of U.S. goods and funds abroad. This deficit totaled about $1.3 billion in 1965.

Oil companies will account for about $2.3 billion of the about $7.3 billion U.S. companies will invest in foreign operations this year, although much of this comes from cash flow of foreign subsidiaries, which doesn't count in the balance of payments. Oil companies also held about one-third of the about $44 billion in direct investments by U.S. companies abroad in 1964, the latest year for which statistics are available.

But borrowing overseas has been undertaken by a wide range of U.S. companies. Among those selling public issues abroad in the last year are American Cyanamid Co., Avon Products, Inc., Bristol-Myers Co., Du Pont Co., Federated Department Stores Co., General Electric Co., W. R. Grace & Co., Gulf Oil Corp., Honeywell, Inc., International Business Machines Co., Monsanto Co., Phillips Petroleum Co., Socony Mobil Oil Co. and U.S. Rubber Co.

EXHIBIT 4

Comparative Costs

Security	*5-year guaranteed note*	*15-year guaranteed sinking fund debenture*	*Convertible bond*
Coupon	6%	6%	5%
Size of issue	$25,000,000	$25,000,000	$25,000,000
Organization expense of financing subsidiary	$ 500	$ 500	$ 500
Issuance expenses:			
Gross underwriting commission	500,000 (2%)	625,000 (2½%)	625,000 (2½%)
SEC registration fee		5,000	5,000
Reimbursement of underwriters' expenses	50,000	50,000	50,000
Legal and accounting expenses	20,000	30,000	45,000
Printing and engraving	20,000	45,000	50,000
Fiscal agent or trustee's fee	6,000	10,000	15,000
	$ 596,000	$ 765,000	$ 790,000
Listing expenses:			
New York Stock Exchange	$	$ 4,000	$ 4,000
Luxembourg Stock Exchange	3,000	3,000	3,000
	3,000	7,000	7,000
Registration under Securities Act of 1934		500	500
Estimated total expenses	$ 599,500	$ 772,500	$ 797,500

EXHIBIT 5

Press Release From
Ambassade de France
Service de Presse et d' Information
972 Fifth Avenue, New York
February 1967

FRENCH EXCHANGE CONTROLS ABOLISHED AS OF JANUARY 31, 1967

Practically all remaining French exchange controls have been abolished by a law dated December 28, 1966, implemented by a decree of January 27, 1967. This law constitutes a landmark since it makes the franc totally convertible after a period of restraints starting in 1939 and extending over 27 years. Freedom of transactions has now become the rule. In particular:

1 - Resident and nonresident firms and individuals may open franc or foreign currency accounts in France or abroad, without restriction or distinction;

2 - All foreign exchange operations are now permitted to resident companies and individuals;

3 - Imports to France no longer require prior domiciliation with banks, and repatriation of foreign currency proceeds are no longer necessary for French exports;

4 - Exportation and importation of money, gold and securities are free.

This policy reflects the belief of the French authorities that the balance-of-payments situation should be managed through fiscal and monetary instruments rather than through restraints on exchange transactions.

The freedom of transfers covers all assets, including gold, and is now similar to the system applied by neighboring countries (Federal Republic of Germany, Belgium, Switzerland).

This liberalization of financial transactions does not detract from existing policies concerning foreign investments and some other forms of capital movements.

a - *Direct investments in France* by nonresidents as well as *direct investments abroad* by French residents still have to be declared to the Finance Ministry. This does not apply to the purchase of less than 20% of the listed stock of a company, or to investments made with the profits of a resident company. No formal authorization is required, but the Minister has two months in which he may request the postponement of the transaction or waive his right to do so.

b - In order to prevent capital inflows from defeating credit policies, *borrowing abroad*, over two million francs ($400,000) for a single borrower, is subject to prior approval of the Ministry of Finance. Foreign lending and borrowing by banks is not subject to any restriction.

c - In view of the capital resources available, *foreign issues* on the French market require approval by the Ministry of Finance under similar conditions as issues by French companies.

The few controls thus maintained are motivated by both balance-of-payments and economic policy considerations.

For compiling balance-of-payments data, banks will have to report exchange transactions, above a certain amount, but only for statistical purposes.

A decree of January 27, 1967 laid down the new rules for patents and licenses transactions.

Sources and Instruments of International Finance: Part II

9

In the previous chapter the diverse activities of commercial banks and affiliated institutions in supplying capital to the international enterprise were discussed. In this chapter attention is focused on governmental and international bodies that also provide financing.

Many governments overtly seek to achieve balanced national economic development. Usually this development is promoted by encouraging specific types of industrial development or by discouraging excessive industrial and manpower agglomeration in certain regions of a country at the expense of economic development in depressed areas. In their desire to promote economic development in backward areas and to stimulate specific types of industrial activity, governments have passed industrial investment legislation that facilitates the financing of new and established enterprises. Although this legislation varies in character from country to country, it usually provides for medium- and long-term financing through government institutions, guarantees for funds supplied by private lenders, subsidies, and fiscal incentives. These activities of national governments are discussed in the first section of the chapter. A second section is concerned with the activities of regional and national development banks. Then private finance company activities are analyzed. Finally the chapter examines the financial assistance programs of the World Bank group.

NATIONAL GOVERNMENT FACILITIES

The financing supplied by local commercial banks is oftentimes supplemented by state-owned or semipublic institutions in the latter's attempt to achieve public policy objectives. While governments extend direct loans for industrial projects, they usually work through specialized institutions such as industrial development banks. The development banks in turn usually extend credits of five to ten years' duration to facilitate the establishment of new industries or the expansion and modernization of existing ones. The government loans may be offered at normal market rates or at reduced rates for projects satisfying the requirements of national policy. In addition, the development banks often are empowered to make equity investments in suitable projects, although they generally avoid accepting a controlling voice in management.

Many governments also provide guarantees for loans or parts of loans extended by third parties to industrial companies for the establishment, expansion, or conversion of industrial activities in depressed areas. Offered to the institutions which finance the industrial activities, the guarantees provide assurances relevant to business risks or regarding the availability of foreign exchange required for servicing credits denominated in external currencies. Guarantees that safeguard remittance privileges may also be supplied to the industrial investor.

Subsidies are another facet of governmental activity designed to encourage the establishment of specific industries or firms in depressed areas. Subsidies may take any number of specific forms:

1. Outright cash grants of government funds to finance part of the cost of land, plant, or equipment
2. Reduced interest rates or rebates of interest paid to third parties
3. Infrastructure investment—e.g., roads, electric power, or other facilities required to support the commercial venture
4. Subsidized training of unskilled workers or rehabilitation of workers with obsolete skills
5. Total or partial reimbursement of costs associated with transferring labor to new establishments in selected areas.

Governments can indirectly supply financing for industrial investment through fiscal measures such as tax exemptions or reductions. Such measures are one of the simplest and most widely used governmental tools to encourage private industrial investment. In effect the tax exemptions or reductions are a gift in the amount of the tax benefits. These awards may apply to otherwise taxable income, dividend remittances, or property assessments. Sometimes countries offer larger exemptions to industries that are considered to be critical *vis à vis* national economic priorities or that use local raw materials. New investments are often eligible for accelerated depreciation or depreciation in excess of original cost. This option is particularly attractive in industrial sectors characterized by rapid technological obsolescence. Additionally, investment tax credits are sometimes offered that permit the recipient firm to offset a certain percentage of total investment cost against taxable income. The net effect is an interest free loan from the government for the period of tax deferral. Having outlined the basic characteristics of national governmental programs, we can now turn to specifics in selected countries.

Belgium

The main government and semipublic institutions that offer medium- and long-term financing in *Belgium* are the Caisse Génerale d'Epargne et de Retraite, the Société Nationale de Crédit à l'Industrie (SNCI), and Société Nationale d'Investissement (SNI). Caisse Génerale d'Epargne et de Retraite is the state savings bank. This public institution may supply both medium- and long-term loans and hold company bonds in its portfolio. Credits usually extend for periods of five to fifteen years, and the interest charges are dictated by the Société Nationale de Crédit à l'Industrie. SNI is occasionally a source of industrial financing. Société Nationale de Crédit à l'Industrie (SNCI) is the most important medium- and long-term financing institution. Medium-term loans are awarded for periods from five to ten years. Long-term loans typically range in maturity from seven to fifteen years although twenty-year maturities are not uncommon. Principal is usually repaid in annual installments, often with a grace period of one or two years. SNCI may finance 100 per cent of the expansion of top priority projects in Belgium. The effective interest rate for these credits late in 1968 was approximately 8 per cent including commissions. The loans are usually secured, the type of collateral depending on the borrower's financial status and growth potential. Société Nationale d'Investissement is a specialized institution that provides equity for enterprises excluded from the capital market. This institution can subscribe to as much as 80 per cent of total venture capital. Its voting power, however, is restricted to 20 per cent of total stock or 40 per cent of the represented shares, whichever is lower. SNI invests in new enterprises or existing ones regardless of whether ownership is in the hands of nationals or foreigners. Additionally SNI is active in underwriting and guarantee programs. Its investments are of a temporary nature, and it offers joint venture partners an opportunity to purchase its stock at cost plus accumulated interest.

Industrial investment legislation provides special financial incentives for industrial enterprises that conform with national economic development objectives. These include firms that build or expand industrial capacity or that establish research and development centers. The incentives are also available to trading organizations that assist industrial enterprises. In addition the government regards the coal-mining section of the country as depressed, and therefore industrial firms that establish facilities in this area are entitled to extra incentives.

Industrial firms are entitled to a state guarantee covering total financing provided by public credit institutions and covering as much as 75 per cent of commercial bank credits that are not secured. The government offers subsidies in the following forms:

1. Firms are entitled to interest subsidies on long-term loans of up to five basic points for a period of five years. In rare cases industrial corporations obtain subsidies for the entire first two years' interest charges. The amount of long-term borrowings eligible for interest subsidies is restricted to 50 per cent of total investment. This allowance is increased to 75 per cent for investments in the coal-mining region.

2. Outright, tax free, cash grants are offered to finance portions of new industrial ventures that rely solely on equity capital. The maximum cash grant obtainable is equivalent to the interest subsidy that could have been received had the required capital been borrowed.

3. Industrial concerns are allowed to lease plants or buy them on an installment plan at attractive rates. The Belgian government also extends to new investors a five-year real estate tax deferral, a waiver of registration taxes on equity capital, and double depreciation for an initial period of three years.

England

The main government institutions in the *U.K.* that provide medium- and long-term financing are the Industrial Reorganization Corporation and the Board of Trade. Industrial Reorganization Corporation (IRC) extends medium- and long-term loans to industry and holds minority equity interests. The loans provided by IRC are for enterprises engaged in projects deemed in the national interest. The Board of Trade is an important supplier of term loans of up to ten years. These loans are also restricted to companies that meet objectives of national policy.

The U.K. provides financial incentives to industrial concerns engaged in "qualifying industrial processes" and to firms that invest in areas with high unemployment such as the "development areas" and northern Ireland. The financial facilities extended to industrial projects that meet national policy objectives are outlined below.

Although the British government does not extend guarantees for term financing to industrial enterprises, firms can borrow directly from the Board of Trade and the Industrial Reorganization Corporation. Industrial enterprises engaged in qualifying industrial processes are entitled to cash grants for the purchase of most fixed assets. The amount of the available grant is 20 per cent of total costs in most geographic regions. It runs as high as 40 per cent in the development areas and up to 45 per cent in northern Ireland. Grants are paid directly by the Board of Trade. They must be deducted from the purchase price of the assets financed in calculating depreciation for tax purposes. The government through the Ministry of Labor provides assistance in transferring labor to new locations and for manpower training. Industrial firms in development areas have the opportunity to rent prebuilt government factories or to have factories constructed especially for them. Rent is subsidized for the first ten years, and the company is entitled to a purchase option at a future date. New investment in machinery that is not eligible for cash grants is entitled to a 30 per cent write-off in the first year. Industrial buildings are entitled to a 15 per cent initial depreciation allowance plus a capital allowance of 4 per cent per year.

France

In France the main government bodies that provide term financing for industrial projects are Crédit National, Regional Development Associations, and Crédit Hôtelier. Crédit National (CN) offers the most important facilities for long-term financing and is the channel for discounting medium-term loans obtained from commercial banks. CN extends loans from eight to twenty years although loans for more than fifteen years are uncommon. Loans from this institution require collateral, usually a mortgage, a bank guarantee or parent guarantee, or listed securities. The maximum credit obtainable from CN is equal to 30 per cent of the borrower's assets and 50 to 60 per cent of the market value of securities deposited as collateral. Interest rates during late 1968 were in the 7 to 8 per cent range. The charge for the unused portion of a loan is about .5 per cent. Regional Development Associations (RDA) are joint stock companies formed under the control and assistance of the federal government. These institutions specialize in the financing of industrial projects in specific geographical areas. They offer long-term loans of up to twelve years duration. Because of their limited resources these institutions provide only complementary financing for industrial investments. Crédit Hôtelier specializes in the financing of hotel construction. Additionally it supplies long-term industrial credits. This organization extends credits of up to 50 to 65 per cent of total capital requirements for industrial projects up to a specified maximum. Long-term loans may be extended for up to twenty years, but rarely mature beyond fifteen years. In late 1968 the interest charges were 7 per cent plus a 1 per cent commission payable when the loan agreement was signed.

The French government under industrial investment legislation extends credit to enterprises that create employment in areas of chronic unemployment or in areas classified as economically underdeveloped. Credit is also extended to firms whose activities assist in the decentralization of industry. Investments in five geographic regions are eligible for the credits as well as for other government incentives. The French government does not have a guarantee program for industrial financing.

Nonetheless, industrial enterprises can borrow directly with Crédit National, Regional Development Associations, and Crédit Hôtelier. They can also obtain loans from the Social and Economic Development Fund managed by Crédit National.

Companies investing in top priority regions, i.e., regions with high unemployment and ailing industries, are entitled to outright cash grants. The grants may run as high as 25 per cent for new investments or resumption of discontinued operations and up to 15 per cent for expansion or partial conversion. In addition companies which cooperate with the government's industrial decentralization policy by setting up headquarters outside the Paris region are entitled to a cash grant from 5 per cent to 15 per cent of total cost. Cash grants in France are not tax deductible. Moreover, financial assistance is available for the training of workers. This assistance includes outlays for course materials and a portion of salaries paid to workers and instructors for a period of up to six months. In addition there is an allowance for the expenses incurred in connection with transferring workers. The fiscal incentives for industrial enterprises established in regions with high unemployment consist of a 25 per cent initial depreciation allowance on buildings and a reduction of the transfer tax on real estate transactions from 16 per cent to 4 per cent. The other regions with lower priorities are eligible only for the reduction in transfer taxes. In addition local authorities may exempt or reduce licensing taxes for a period of up to five years.

Germany

Kreditanstalt für Wiederaufbau (KFW) is Germany's government institution that provides term loans for automation, reconversion, modernization, and new investment. KFW concentrates on the financing of large-scale projects for basic industry, public utilities, and infrastructure. Nonetheless, small industrial projects are also eligible for KFW financing. KFW offers its loan facilities to private firms through the borrower's commercial bank. Loans usually mature in ten to twelve years although longer maturities are obtainable. Interest rates in late 1968 were in the 7 per cent range.

German industrial investment legislation establishes financial incentives for industries that contribute to national economic policy. Special financial incentives are available for industries erected in the East German border region, federal development areas that include low income districts, and federal development sites that consist mainly of small towns. Additional benefits are available for investments in the coal-mining areas in the Ruhr and in West Berlin.

Industrial enterprises with new or expanded facilities in federal development areas are entitled to credit guarantees for financing obtained through commercial banks. These guarantees are offered under the European Recovery Program. In addition the provincial authorities in the Ruhr area offer guarantees for credits extended by commercial banks in connection with the purchase of industrial sites. Cash grants of up to 15 per cent of total investment are awarded industrial firms that establish, expand, or modernize facilities along the East German border and in federal development areas as well as to firms that establish new facilities in the federal development sites. These cash grants are nontaxable. Loans at subsidized rates may be obtained in lieu of cash grants. These subsidized credits are limited to 50 per cent of capital investment and carry a 3.5 per cent interest rate and fifteen year maturity for building and a 4 per cent interest rate and ten year maturity for machinery. These incentives are offered to firms establishing, expanding, or modernizing plant and equipment along the East German border and in federal development areas and for firms setting up new industries in federal development sites.

Credits at subsidized rates, in addition to cash grant received by the industrial firms, are provided for under the European Recovery Program by the Kreditanstalt für Wiederaufbau and are administered through the commercial banking system. The rate of interest is 5 per cent for investments along the East German border, and maturities are limited to twelve years for equipment and twenty years for buildings. A 6 per cent rate is applied to investments in the development areas and sites. The maximum ERP subsidized credit is DM500,000. With reference to investments in the coal-mining sections of the Ruhr region, subsidized credits of up to 30 per cent of total investment are provided by ERP at a 6 per cent interest rate. The maximum financing that can be arranged with public funds is 60 per cent of total investment. In West Berlin ERP credits are available at a 5 per cent interest rate covering up to 30 per cent of the industrial project. The ceiling on financing with public funds is 50 per cent of total investment in this region. The local government of the Ruhr extends subsidized credits for up to DM1 million at a 4 per cent interest rate to industries that employ former coal or steel workers. The Federal Unemployment Insurance Agency extends credits at 4.25 per cent for up to ten to twelve years. Other sources of funds are Marshall Plan and European Coal and Steel Community funds that are available at interest rates in the range of 4.5 to 6.6 per cent for ten to twenty years.

Interest subsidies are another financial incentive available to industrial firms. Companies expanding or converting industrial plant and equipment along the East German border are eligible for either an 8 per cent of total credit interest rebate in the first year or a 3 per cent of total credit interest rebate payable during each of the first three years. Financial assistance in the form of subsidized land or utilities and free construction of roads or rail links is typically provided for by the different local authorities.

Special write-offs of 50 per cent of machinery and 30 per cent of plant in the first three years are awarded to firms that invest along the

East German border. A special write-off of 75 per cent of total plant and equipment is allowed during the first year for firms that invest in West Berlin. Additionally special tax reductions are available to firms in West Berlin. These tax incentives include a 20 per cent reduction in corporation tax, a 30 per cent reduction in income and wage taxes, and a 4.2 per cent reduction in value-added taxes. Investment tax credits are offered to investors in the Ruhr area and in West Berlin. In the Ruhr area, which is the industrial center of Germany, companies that employ displaced coal miners and steelworkers are entitled to a 10 per cent investment tax credit in the first year. More generous tax credit incentives are available in West Berlin. These include a 20 to 25 per cent investment tax credit for investment in machinery and a 30 per cent tax credit for investment in research and development.

Italy

Italy has a well-developed system of government bodies and semipublic institutions that supply medium- and long-term capital to industry. These institutions are either national or regional in scope. The main national institutions are Istituto Mobilaire Italiano, Banca di Credito Finanziario, Ente Finanziario Interbancario, Istituto Ricostruzione Industriale, and Societa Finanziaria Ernesto Breda. The regional bodies include Istituto per lo Sviluppo Economico dell'Italia Meridionale (ISVEIMER), Istituto Regionale per il Finanziamento delle Industrie in Sicilia (IRFIS), Credito Industriale Sardo (CIS), Istituto per lo Sviluppo delle Attivita Produttive (ISAP), Ente Siciliano per la Promozione Industriale (ESPI), and Societa Finanziaria Industriale Rinascita (SFIRS).

Istituto Mobiliare Italiano (IMI) is the single largest medium- and long-term lending institution. This government body supplies approximately one third of Italy's term loans. IMI extends credits for expansion, modernization, and establishment of new industrial enterprises. The lending period is from five to twenty years although most loans fall into the ten- to fifteen-year maturity range. Security is commonly requested and usually includes a first mortgage or other guarantees. Interest rates in late 1968 were in the 6 to 9 per cent range. In addition IMI is empowered to take equity participations.

Banco di Credito Finanziario (Mediobanca) is a governmental institution controlled by the banks of national interest. This institution specializes in medium-term loans for periods usually ranging from one to five years. It also engages actively in the underwriting of bonds in the Italian and European capital markets. Interest rates are similar to those of IMI. Ente Finanziario Interbancario (EFIBANCA) is a semipublic institution controlled by the government that also has Italian and foreign bank participation. EFIBANCA specializes in industrial financing although its volume of operations has been limited to date.

Istituto Ricostruzione Industriale (IRI) is the largest government holding company and is empowered to supply venture capital to industry. This body controls important industrial sectors either through wholly-owned corporations or through joint ventures involving the private sector. In some cases IMI eventually sells its equity participations after the industrial enterprises are operating successfully. This is most likely for investments in depressed areas. Aside from the venture capital supplied, the advantage of having IRI as a venture participant is that the institution's involvement facilitates obtaining orders and contracts from the large number of companies controlled by the IRI group.

Societa Finanziaria Ernesto Breda (SFEB) is also controlled by the government and is another supplier of venture capital to industrial corporations. This public financial institution is usually interested in majority control or 50–50 joint ventures. Nonetheless, SFEB can provide capital through a subsidiary and offer to joint venture partners an option to buy out SFEB participation after the industrial concern is well established. This possibility is usually reserved for industries located in the southern part of Italy.

There are three specialized regional financial institutions established by the Cassa per il Mezzogiorno as the executive instrument for implementing development plans of the Italian state, especially in the southern region of the country. These institutions, ISVEIMER, IRFIS, and CIS, work closely together with the public law institute and local banks. The working capital supplied by these institutions is obtained from the interest on the funds assigned to the Cassa. The funds are distributed to the three specialized bodies on predetermined pro rata bases. ISVEIMER, IRFIS, and CIS also provide medium- and long-term loans to industries located in the southern region, Sicilia, or Sardinia.

Istituto per lo Sviluppo delle Attivita Produttive (ISAP) was created to provide equity capital to industries establishing in the south. ISAP may only acquire minority positions. Industrial projects are evaluated in terms of profit outlook and in terms of potential contribution to the economic development of the region. Ente Siciliano per la Promozione Industriale (ESPI) is another specialized governmental body that supplies equity to industrial enterprises, in this instance, to firms operating in Sicily. This institute may take either majority or minority capital positions. It is empowered to provide up to 100 per cent of equity and, in addition, is allowed to supply term loans to industries in which it participates. ESPI may sell its equity holdings to joint venture partners when the businesses are established. Societa Finanziaria Industriale Rinascita (SFIRS) is another governmental institution founded to provide venture capital to industrial plants in Sardinia. This organization is restricted to minority positions in industrial projects that satisfy the requirements specified by the economic plan.

Industrial investment legislation in Italy provides special financial benefits for industries that promote economic development in depressed areas. The two regions singled out as underdeveloped zones are the southern part of Italy and some depressed or mountainous areas in the central and northern part of the country. Higher priorities are given to industrial projects in the south than elsewhere. The financial incentives take a number of forms. Although the government dos not guarantee loans, firms establishing industrial facilities in depressed areas may borrow directly from the government-controlled institutions, particularly from the Cassa per il Mezzogiorno's regional institutes that provide the special financial facilities for such industrial ventures. Outright cash grants are also made available by the Cassa per il Mezzogiorno to industries that establish or expand operations in southern Italy. The cash grants amount to a 20 per cent of total cost for basic utilities, buildings, and roads, and up to 25 per cent of industrial project cost in connection with commitments to plant and equipment. Local authorities in Sardinia award cash grants of up to 40 per cent of total cost of equipment, 66 per cent of total cost of land and roads, and 66 per cent of the total cost of basic utilities during the first ten years, as well as a 66 per cent rebate on all sea transportation for the first three years. Subsidized credit is offered to firms in the Mezzogiorno area—a 4 per cent interest rate if fixed investment is below L6 billion ($8.6 million) and a 6 per cent rate if the fixed investment exceeds L6 billion. These subsidized credits may cover as much as 70 per cent of total investment in plant and equipment. The maximum maturities for the credits are ten years for expansion and conversion projects and fifteen years for new industrial projects. In addition there are subsidized credits for inventory purposes. Subsidized credit in the central and northern regions is available for small and medium-sized companies that set up new industrial facilities or expand or convert existing facilities. These credits are awarded at a 5 per cent interest rate for up to ten years. The subsidized loans may cover as much as 70 per cent of total industrial projects for up to ten years. Interest subsidies are offered to industries in the regions of Trentino-Alto Adigio and Friuli-Venezia Giulia. This subsidy takes the form of a 3 per cent interest rebate.

If a firm invests in the Mezzogiorno region, it is entitled to tax exemptions and reductions. These incentives include a ten-year exemption of the General Income Tax Category B and the Corporation Tax and a 5 per cent reduction in both the turnover tax on plant and equipment and consumption tax on electricity. Small- and medium-sized firms in the central and northern regions are eligible for a ten-year waiver of direct income taxes.

Netherlands

Nationale Investeringsbank (NI) is the Netherland's principal source of medium- and long-term financing. A government-controlled institution, NI is jointly owned by the government and a group of private banks and institutional investors. Although term loans are extended for up to twenty to twenty-five years' duration, the usual range is five to seven years for medium-term loans and ten to fifteen years for long-term loans. NI will provide up to 75 per cent of term financing requirements for industrial projects. Interest rates are approximately one percentage point in excess of rates quoted in the capital market, although NI imposes no assessment in regard to unused portions of term loans extended. This semipublic institution's terms are generally more flexible than those of commercial banks and affiliated institutions.

Industrial investment legislation in the Netherlands is designed to improve the distribution of industrial employment throughout the country, to develop the economic structure in backward regions, and to reduce the pressures on the Randstand Holland, the industrial center of the western region. Considerable financial assistance is offered to enterprises that establish industrial operations in the backward regions. The backward areas consist of twenty development sections located mainly in the eastern portion of the country. The Dutch government provides additional benefits to firms with operations in the Limburg province where there are displaced coal miners.

The Dutch government extends guarantees to industries establishing operations in the development areas. These guarantees that apply to borrowed principal and interest enable industrial firms to obtain medium- and long-term financing with the National Investeringsbank. For investments that contribute significantly to the national economy, the government guarantees repayment of required financing and assures payment of a minimum dividend to financial institutions making investments. Additionally, the government, which may make an equity investment in the project, agrees to sell its interest at a future date to other participating investors. Outright cash grants for 25 per cent of total investment in plant and equipment are awarded to companies setting up new industrial facilities in depressed regions. The maximum amount obtainable is $3 million except for industrial investments in the Limburg region where there is no such ceiling. Interest subsidies are available to industrial firms which promote economic development when these firms are financed by private third parties. The subsidies provide for interest rebates of up to 3 per cent per annum for a maximum duration of fifteen years. Usually the financing of at least 50 per cent of total investment is eligible for such rebates. Additional financial assistance is provided by local authorities in the custom building of plants for rental or installment purchase and the construction of roads and worker housing. Fiscal incentives in the form of reduced tax rates and special depreciation allowances are awarded on a case by case basis.

The United States

Several United States governmental institutions play a leading role in the financing of international business. The financing facilities are made available because of the desire of the United States government to provide economic assistance to foreign countries while at the same time serving the objectives of national policy. The key institutions include the Agency for International Development, the United States Department of Agriculture, and the Export-Import Bank, all of which attempt to foster this double objective of United States foreign policy.

The *Agency for International Development,* a subdivision of the State Department, was created in 1961 under the provisions of the Foreign Assistance Act to extend technical and economic assistance to the less-developed areas of the world. A precondition for assistance from AID is a sound local policy for self-help measures in order for grants eventually to be converted into loans, repayable in dollars at low interest rates, often with long maturities. The principal programs for implementing AID financing of international enterprises are the Development Loan Program and the Cooley Loan Program. The purpose of the Development Loan Program is to promote the economic development of friendly less-developed areas, emphasizing assistance in long-range plans and programs designed to develop economic resources and increase productive capacities. The loans are long-term with both principal and interest repayable in dollars, requiring only a reasonable prospect of retirement. The direct development loans are made available to international corporations through a two-step technique that permits the host country government to act as the first borrower on a soft-term basis and the international corporation to act as the sub-borrower. Indirect development loans through local development banks have also been extended to international concerns in cooperation with AID. AID supplies dollar loans to the local financial institutions which, in turn, extend loans in local currency to the international concerns. The chief characteristic of these development loans is that they make available longer maturities and lower interest rates than would otherwise be the case. The local governments agree to repay the development loans made through development banks and other financial institutions. The repayment schedule to AID may extend beyond twenty years at 5.5 to 6 per cent rates of interest.

The so-called Cooley Amendment Funds are local currency funds received in payment for export sales of agricultural products sold either under the Mutual Security Act or under the Agricultural Trade Development Assistance Act. AID, in turn, loans these local currency funds to American firms and subsidiaries that are engaged in business development and trade expansion in the host country. These loans are also extended to private firms in the host country whose activities facilitate the expansion of overseas markets for American agricultural products. No loan may be extended under this program to a local firm that exports products in competition with American products in the United States or whose products compete with United States agricultural commodities. Loans of Cooley funds are made at interest rates comparable to those prevailing in purchaser countries and they carry no maintenance-of-value clauses. The maturity dates are generally flexible and depend on the nature of the project. Generally, guarantees are not required, although in some cases a local bank or parent company guarantee is demanded.

In addition to administering the Cooley Amendment funds, AID also operates programs that insure qualifying investors against inconvertibility, expropriation, or confiscation, war, revolution, or insurrection. The general characteristics of these programs have been discussed in chapter 4 and need not be reiterated. It should be noted here, however, that AID announced in July 1968 the availability of insurance against political risk for qualifying investments in private development banks, finance companies, and other intermediate credit institutions. The coverage includes losses due to damage from war, revolution, or insurrection, or losses from expropriation or inconvertibility of local currencies into dollars. For example, a $700,000 investment by a Massachusetts investment company in a Korean intermediate finance corporation has been backed by $2,800,000 worth of AID specific risk guarantees in the first application of the new liberalized rules for political risk insurance. Previously, AID political risk insurance for this type of investment was no different from insurance covering ordinary loan and equity investments for industrial enterprises. This new development finance insurance extends coverage to investments made by the intermediate credit institutions in developing countries as well as to United States investments in the development finance companies themselves. This broadened coverage provides insurance similar to that offered to United States-based financial institutions, and should encourage United States risk capital firms to organize in developing countries. The liberalized contracts have recently been offered to United States branch banks in developing countries and to other leading United States institutions.

Another agency of the United States government that provides financing under its Private Trade Credits Program is the Department of Agriculture. Private trade credits are long-term local currency loans made with funds obtained through the sale of available United States agricultural products. An international concern that seeks local currency financing first sells the available United States agricultural products. Private United States traders make the agricultural commodities available to the firm through a line of credit extended by the United States Commodity Credit Corporation. Upon completion of the sale, the international firm may invest the funds obtained from the sale in projects previously approved by the Department of Commerce's Foreign Agricultural Service (FAS). This program gives priority to projects which create new or expanded markets for United States farm commodities. It discourages projects involving commodities, the sale of which will adversely effect the future trade in the particular commodity between the United States and the foreign country. Private trade credits are extended for up to twenty-year maturities. Interest rates are similar to those which the United States

Treasury pays for comparable maturities. In no case are the rates lower than for AID financing. These long-term loans are particularly attractive in countries where money is tight and interest rates are relatively high. The borrowing concern must, however, guarantee the credit and bear the exchange risk.

The *Export-Import Bank,* whose role is to supplement and encourage rather than compete with private capital, is one of the largest suppliers of investment funds to international concerns. By way of capitalization the bank is authorized to have outstanding at any one time dollar loans, guarantees, and insurance not in excess of $13.5 billion. In addition the bank is authorized to have capital stock of $7 billion and to borrow from the United States Treasury on its own obligations up to $6 billion at any one time.

The purpose of the bank is to aid in financing and to facilitate exports between the United States and foreign countries. Specifically, this entails long-term direct financing to facilitate the purchase of United States manufactured equipment and services used in the implementation of industrial projects in foreign countries, as well as long-term financing to various foreign financial institutions for relending purposes. These foreign institutions, in turn, make loans to companies to facilitate the purchase of United States manufactured goods and services.

In this type of long-term direct financing the bank expects a reasonable equity participation by the borrower—approximately half of the total cost of the project. Such loans mature within five to twenty years and interest rates are approximately 6 per cent per annum.

Recently a few transactions meeting the Eximbank standards and initiated by United States suppliers have been developed and financed by commercial banks that have participated substantially for their own account and have obtained Eximbank's comprehensive guarantees for the remainder. Notable examples of this type of transaction have concerned the sales of jet aircraft and locomotives.

There are other areas in addition to export financing in which Eximbank assistance may be applied. Eximbank is in a position to make emergency foreign trade loans to foreign governments, thereby assuring continuity of trade from the United States when temporary dollar shortages threaten to disrupt it. Also, in certain cases the bank covers political and credit risks involved in the sale abroad by United States firms of technical services, such as architectural services, engineering studies, and reports on economic surveys. Also in this context are guarantees that are made available in connection with United States equipment leased abroad, or equipment on consignment awaiting sale. The agency also provides war risk and expropriation insurance for United States commodities owned by United States citizens and located in friendly foreign countries. This insurance has made possible many shipments of cotton, wheat, barley, and tobacco.

In summary, the bank is a key source of financing abroad when private sources are not available. In making commitments the bank requires confirmation that the capital will be profitably used and reasonable assurance that it will be repaid. The projects must be economically justifiable and must contribute to the economic development of the country while at the same time improving the country's foreign exchange position.

REGIONAL AND NATIONAL DEVELOPMENT FINANCE

National Development Finance Companies

The private development finance institutions, often called development banks, are set up to provide term debt and equity financing in economies where there is a strong private sector to generate the demand for such financing and a distinct gap on the supply side of the capital market. There are three general ways a development bank may fulfill its role:

1. Provide long-term debt and permanent capital
2. Perform an investment banking function through private placements and underwriting such new issues as the incipient capital market can bear
3. Supply management consulting services on a fee basis.

A most significant function of a development bank is to help strengthen the money and capital markets. Providing medium- and long-term financing, this type of bank relieves commercial banks from the task of rolling over short-term money, thus helping to enlarge and strengthen the money and capital markets.

A second major function of private development banks is the promotion of industries essential to the sound economic growth of a given country. The more successful development banks have not only been forceful in tailoring existing proposals into workable form but have also been instrumental in structuring and promoting new enterprises.

A third key function of a private development bank is to provide professional guidance to aspiring entrepreneurs and infant industries. Creative assistance is essential in guiding the formation of new enterprise, providing technical, marketing, and financial know-how. Providing professional assistance helps to safeguard the bank's loans and investment position.

The banks may concentrate on a single economic sector or be multipurpose. In some cases they provide short-term working capital credits, but normally they do not compete with commercial banks, preferring to supplement the short-term loans of these institutions with equity and medium-term capital.

The capital structures of development banks vary from institution to institution, but generally the equity is a mixture of national interest, taking up 51 to 75 per cent, and international interest accounting for the balance. The IFC (International Finance Corporation) generally accounts for 15 per cent of the international participation. As a rule of thumb, the equity/quasi-equity/debt ratio is 1/1.5/3. The quasi-equity is debt secured on a long-term basis, generally over twenty years from institutions such as the World Bank, the International Development Association, AID, and the InterAmerican Development Bank or local government institutions. The medium- to long-term debt is generally secured from government institutions or participating foreign banks or other private investment companies such as ADELA.

In March 1967 the United States Federal Reserve System revised Regulation M which concerns the foreign activities of United States national banks. Under Regulation M United States banks with foreign branch systems are permitted, through their local branches, to invest up to 7 per cent of their total deposits in development banking institutions. Although development banks are intended to be profitable, they have typically been conspicuously unsuccessful in this regard. The incentive for foreign private institutions to participate, however, is not primarily return on investment, but rather the opportunity for good public relations through participation in the development of local economies. Additional incentives include contacts with the business leaders on the Development Bank Board and deposits gained as a result of establishing credit relationships with the institution. Even though profitable operations are not the primary objective, a development bank with good management can show adequate returns on capital if sufficient leverage is attained, tax benefits are received, and dividends are not restricted.

A successful development bank has two primary characteristics. First, it is able to locate capable investment-oriented, administration-minded managements; and, second, it can find a sufficient supply of economically viable projects to allow management to be selective while continuing to generate the volume of projects necessary to utilize available resources. Quasi-equity subscriptions amounting to 100 per cent to 130 per cent of paid-in capital is a key to adequate leverage. This capital is typically provided by the host government or AID in the form of a low or interest-free local currency loan that is subordinated to all other debt and paid-in capital in the case of liquidation. Usually there is a lengthy grace period of fifteen to twenty years. When long-term credit lines from sources such as the World Bank or Kreditanstalt are as high as four times the equity capital base, resources equivalent to twelve and a half times the paid-in capital base can be put to work for the shareholder. A portion of new income is transferred annually to a net worth reserve to assure that the equity base and earning power will be maintained when the quasi-equity is repaid. For proper protection and control it is essential that hard currency liabilities be counterbalanced by hard currency assets, that equity investments not exceed net worth, and that operating expenses be properly controlled.

By way of example, a particularly aggressive development bank is the

Pakistan Industrial Credit and Investment Corporation (PICIC) which was established in 1957 to provide medium- and long-term finance in local and foreign currencies for Pakistan's private enterprises. In 1962 it reported share capital of $6.5 million, 60 per cent of which had been contributed by local Pakistani shareholders and 40 per cent by individual foreign shareholders including a 5 per cent IFC participation. In more than ten years with large-scale support from the World Bank group PICIC has helped to finance more than $378 million of projects. When all projects now approved have been completed, total investments will exceed $672 million.

PICIC's main contributions have been sanctioning of loans and making direct equity investments. It has primarily assisted medium- and large-size firms. Almost 60 per cent of PICIC loans have exceeded $520,000 in size. Medium- and long-term loans have been negotiated at a 6½ per cent rate for local currency loans and 7½ per cent for foreign exchange. It is in connection with industrial concerns' foreign exchange requirements that foreign participation has been most beneficial, providing more than $224.2 million since PICIC's inception.

The industries favored by PICIC include jute mills, which have received close to 23 per cent of total resources, food products with 22 per cent, and cotton and textile with 20 per cent. PICIC has also contributed substantially to the development of other industries such as chemicals, pharmaceuticals, cement, glass, paper products, and inland waterways and shipping.

The most significant characteristic of PICIC's lending activities is that over half of the bank's loans have been made to new enterprises, an essential feature in developing countries. The bank has also proven instrumental in promoting better utilization of by-products of existing industries. For instance, PICIC has encouraged sugar mills to find new uses for molasses produced from sugar cane and other industries to find ways of making hardboard from cotton stalks, particle board from jute stalks, oil from rice bran, and viscose from bamboo.

Besides supplying private capital, PICIC has involved itself in industrial promotion, feasibility studies, and expansion of the local capital markets by underwriting joint stock companies and encouraging the public to become investment conscious. At the same time PICIC has sought to train Pakistanis in the techniques of development banking. PICIC is a good example of what national development banks can contribute to local economies.

Three hundred and forty-eight development finance institutions from sixty-six countries are listed in the 1967 Global Directory of Development Finance Institutions. Eight of these institutions are classified as "regional" as distinct from national. The most obvious distinction between the regional and national development finance institution is implicit in the name. The regional institution can serve as local points for the regional and subregional cooperation that is essential in promoting economic integration. Aspirations of the regional groups are neither national nor global, but rather reflect a regional outlook. Their purpose is to accommodate the financial needs of regional projects that fall outside the scope of local development banks. The regional banks also are interested in extending preferential assistance to the poorer and less-developed nations in their regions that receive less financial help than the relatively more developed areas while, at the same time, promoting regional industrialization through diversification of production.

Although their basic objectives are the same, the various regional institutions differ considerably due to the peculiarities of the specific areas in which they operate. For instance, the European Investment Bank is essentially an instrument for the financial integration of the European Economic Community. Its task is essentially one of promoting and harmonizing common financial, monetary, and fiscal policies of the members, with the desired goal of instituting a joint central bank. The problems and successes experienced by the EIB are distinctly different from those faced by similar institutions in developing countries. For instance, the Inter-American Development Bank, the financial vehicle for the Alliance for Progress, is entrenched in the promotion of Latin economic integration. Organized in 1967, the Asian Development Bank, which is in an embryonic stage, consists of a partnership between the developing and the developed nations of Asia, with strong guidance from and dependence on the United States and Japan. The African Development Bank has faced the most difficult problems and therefore has been the most ineffectual as a regional source of capital. It is basically a consortium of recipient countries each with overwhelming needs of its own. Due to the bank's rigid exclusion of nonregional partners, the African Development Bank is drastically undercapitalized, understaffed, and lacking in adequate financial know-how.

The European Investment Bank (EIB) was founded in 1958 under the terms of the Treaty of Rome, which formed the European Economic Community (EEC). EIB was to become the bank of the Common Market, and its objectives were to assist in reducing differences in economic development among the countries within the community, to provide financing to industrial sectors in difficulty as they adjusted to the economic effects of integration, and to provide financing for projects of interest to two or more national governments.

EIB has become the single most important international supplier of long-term credit to Common Market members and, as such, is a valuable source of supplementary financing. Its services are particularly useful to international firms establishing new industrial facilities or expanding existing facilities in the less-developed areas of the Common Market, Greece, and Turkey. By managing the resources of the European Development Fund, the EIB is also the agent for providing the Common

Market's financial support to associated members in Africa and other territories overseas. This facility could be expanded if closer relations with the African Development Bank were to evolve in the future.

As is true of several other government institutions we have discussed, EIB extends financing for industrial projects only if credit from other sources is unavailable. EIB does not purchase equity in the ventures it finances nor does it assume any management responsibility. Its funds are made available only for specific projects which must first be approved by the government of the country in which the project is to be implemented, even though a government guarantee is not required. The borrower typically receives the required financing from EIB in currencies chosen by the bank, and repayment is to be made in the same currency. Alternatively, the borrower selects the currency of one of the member countries and the bank specifies in which currency repayment is to be made. The interest rate charged by EIB depends upon the type of project being financed and the maturity characteristics of the loan. In late 1968, EIB loans were in the 7 to 7.5 per cent range. Long-term loans usually mature in eight to twelve years with an initial grace period of two to four years. The proportion of financing that EIB is prepared to supply is to some extent dependent on where the industrial project is located. Generally, projects in associated countries and territories obtain larger proportions of financing than those in European member countries. In reality the resources of EIB, whose authorized capital is $1 billion, are too small in relation to the financial institutions of its members for the institution to fulfill its assigned role as the bank of the Common Market. In addition, the financial integration hoped for originally has not materialized.

The Inter-American Development Bank (IDB) is a regional financial institution established by nineteen Latin American nations and the United States in 1960 to promote more effective economic development within the member countries and to assist the countries in achieving better utilization of resources. IDB has three capital categories which its members tap—the Ordinary Capital Resources Fund, the Fund for Special Operations, and the Alliance for Progress' Social Progress Trust Fund for social development projects in Latin America. Special financial facilities are available for projects with high social value, and the financing for such projects is channeled by the Fund for Special Operations through the member governments. IDB extends loans directly to private enterprise through the Ordinary Capital Resources Fund. This fund is earmarked for projects that further Latin America's economic development.

In many respects IDB's lending activities are patterned after those of IBRD, IDA, and IFC. IDB financing is available only when capital is not available from private sources on reasonable terms and is unavailable for more than 50 per cent of total project cost. Projects financed with IDB funds must be approved by the government of the country in which the project is to be located even though government guarantees are not normally required for projects being financed. Preferential treatment is given to projects that further the economic integration of Latin American countries, and financing may be disbursed for procurement anywhere. Loans may be made in local currency to cover local costs and in external currencies to finance imported machinery and equipment. Loan repayment is in the currency borrowed, and hence the borrower is saddled with the exchange risk. Unlike the IFC, the IDB does not make loans for working capital purposes. The basic interest rate on IDB's ordinary capital resources loans is 6.5 per cent per annum on amounts disbursed, and in addition there is a commitment fee of 1 per cent on undisbursed balances. In the case of nonmember currencies, loans may carry service commissions and commitment fees of 1 to 2 per cent. Maturity of IDB loans may range from seven to twenty-five years, but generally the range is from eight to twelve years for industrial projects.

The Asian Development Bank is a regional financial institution dedicated to promote the regional economic cooperation and development of Asia. It was founded by several Asian nations in partnership with the United States, Britain, West Germany, Switzerland, and other European countries. International enterprises may take advantage of a number of financial facilities made available to them by the Asian Bank. Long-term debt financing is provided directly by the Asian Bank without government guarantee. In other instances, the bank lends to Asian national banks which relend to enterprises through their respective development agencies. The bank supplies risk capital in certain instances and assists with public offerings in others. The interest rates for long-term financing charged by the bank are slightly higher than those of the World Bank. The bank occasionally extends loans with over thirty-year maturities and at interest rates below normal levels. The lending criteria used to select industrial projects are similar to those practiced by IFC and IDB, as the standards of the latter institutions were used as models for the Asian Bank.

Even though the bank was solidly backed by the United States-Japanese partnership, which contributed $200 million, the bank's charter is by no means dictated by the two countries. The bank's program and framework have been worked out by purely Asian committees which have occasionally sought the advice of other interested groups such as the IDB, the United Nations, and United States representatives. Organized in 1967, the bank can be expected to commit additional funds initially to projects conceived earlier, such as the Indus River project sponsored by the World Bank. As the bank moves into new projects in this troubled area of the world, tremendous subregional cooperation will be required, bringing to bear all available resources and local institutions.

The African Development Bank was founded under the Treaty of Khartoum as a regional institution whose purpose was to promote economic and social development of African independent states, either individually or jointly. The African Bank is authorized to stimulate the investment of both public and private capital on the African continent. The bank is authorized to make long-term loans to industrial investors and underwrites equity offerings for projects. These activities are directly available or, alternatively, take place indirectly through public and private development agencies. Due to its rigid policy of excluding non-regional participants, the bank suffers from severe capital limitations which in turn restrict its ability to lend and invest in national and multinational projects. In April 1967 the bank announced its first loan of $3 million for the improvement of two trunk roads in Kenya, connecting the existing roads in Uganda and Tanzania.

Although each of the regional institutions is distinctly different, many problems and requirements are common. They are all confronted with the arduous task of establishing themselves as financial institutions capable of tackling the complex duties imposed by member countries while, at the same time, fulfilling their primary objective as suppliers of capital to new and expanding industries. To meet their needs these institutions must rely heavily on external financial institutions, such as the World Bank Group, and acute competition for funds among the banks is likely to develop if a better system of coordination of the regional institutions on a global level is not found.

PRIVATE INVESTMENT COMPANIES

Another important and relatively new source, which has assumed much of the initiative in financing the requirements of developing economies, is the private investment company. Although the main emphasis of private investment companies during the experimental years has been in underdeveloped areas, these companies, depending on their nature, can also operate in developed nations. The best way to illustrate the role of private investment companies is to describe the development and activities of a few prominent firms. The pioneer in this field is the Rockefeller International Basic Economy Corporation (IBEC) which has operated globally since 1947. Adela Investment Company, S.A., is one of the newer creations whose activities are restricted to opportunities in Latin America. The newest company formed on the same principle as Adela is the Private Investment Corporation for Asia (PICA) which began operations in January 1969.

The International Basic Economic Corporation (IBEC) was founded in 1947 by Nelson Rockefeller. Its aim was to upgrade the economies of developing countries by lowering food prices, building sound housing, mobilizing saving, and fostering a better distribution of the profits of economic progress. IBEC, which takes equity positions in sponsored companies, has founded almost 200 separate companies in thirty-three countries. Included are supermarkets, agricultural services, milk processing and distributing companies, mutual funds, middle income housing projects, poultry breeders, and manufacturing concerns.

In the earlier years—1947–55—IBEC concentrated its activities mainly in Venezuela and Brazil. In Venezuela a subsidiary (VBEC) was created to establish four different companies for farming, fishing, wholesaling, and milk production. By way of contrast, IBEC has chosen to assist firms in Brazil that specialize in services to upgrade farm production. IBEC set up five key companies specializing in hybrid seed production, hog production, grain storage, helicopter crop-dusting, and a mechanized agricultural service. IBEC lost money with these first experiments mainly because it spread itself too thin and was unable to identify the appropriate link in the marketing chain. More important than the losses, however, was the experience gained, which has facilitated a major functional expansion into new areas. The IBEC supermarkets started in Brazil were successful and have prompted the establishment of other supermarkets in Puerto Rico, Italy, Peru, and Argentina.

The mutual funds in developing economies have also been successful. The mutual fund experiment began in Brazil with an attempt to channel private savings into promising investment prospects. This idea was duplicated in Colombia, Argentina, and Chile. Experience has suggested that, with government and capital market stability, the funds can perform well despite inflation. With instability and acute inflation, however, the funds are unable to maintain performance. The fund idea has recently been applied in Thailand and Spain.

Housing is another area in which IBEC has been able to develop new concepts and approaches. The first housing experiment was in Puerto Rico in the mid-fifties with the construction of low-cost concrete homes. In ten years IBEC has built over 10,000 homes in Puerto Rico and the same method has been used successfully in Iraq, Iran, Chile, Peru, and Mexico.

These are only a few examples of the areas which IBEC has entered. Through past experience the company has been able to amass expertise in marketing, production procedures, and organization. The company's early losses are largely attributable to ineffectual management and lack of knowledge and information. Nonetheless, successful application of private capital to economic and social growth of developing countries remains heavily dependent on environmental stability and on the financial and political maturity of local governments.

Adela Investment Company, S.A., (The Atlantic Development Group for Latin America) is one of the newest and most exciting adventures of private enterprise applying itself to the capital and professional needs of developing areas of the world. Adela's main purpose is to make long-term investments in Latin American industrial and commercial projects in order to promote structural development in the local economies. Incorporated in 1964, Adela has authorized capital of $50 million, most of which is paid-in. In addition to its own capital, Adela seeks to generate external funds through a multiplying effect. It attempts to obtain at least eight dollars for every one it invests, through joint participations with local and international investors and private and public financing institutions and by virtue of funds raised in various capital markets. Adela's shareholders include more than 160 major industrial companies, banks, and financial institutions. To encourage each shareholder's active interest and involvement, Adela has required each investor to subscribe for at least $100,000, but to assure a wide distribution of share holdings, the maximum participation is limited to $500,000.

Adela prides itself in being an investment company rather than a financing institution that derives its income from interest, dividends, and capital appreciation. Its primary purpose is to provide equity capital. The company also engages in debt financing and underwriting activities alone or in conjunction with others, using its own resources or funds obtained from local or international financing institutions. When Adela provides debt financing, it is usually coupled with an equity participation or at least with equity features such as stock options, conversion rights, or profit incentives.

Because of its objectives, Adela provides more than financial assistance. It also attempts to meet the primary need of management assistance and technical know-how. In 1965 Adela incorporated the Adelatec Technical and Management Service Company as a wholly-owned subsidiary to provide professional services in the field of economic planning, market research, marketing, engineering, manufacturing, finance, and administration. These services are provided for the study and development of internal projects and also are made available to the managements of existing companies to assist with problems of an organizational or technical nature.

Adela's main goals are to identify investment opportunities in Latin America, to develop and make capital investments in private enterprises, and to encourage and support active participation of private capital in the economic growth of Latin America. The firm attempts to mobilize the knowledge, energy, and resources within and outside of Latin America, while using its own resources as seed capital to translate opportunities and feasible projects into profitable enterprises. When investing in new projects or existing companies, Adela, in contrast to IBEC, does not seek financial control or management responsibilities.

Adela's project turnover is generally from five to seven years. Because direct investments do not ordinarily offer sufficient profitability, Adela places its uncommitted capital in short-term Latin American paper (two to three years) or makes its excess capital available for debt financing. Also, within the last year, Adela has gone into underwriting activities. Basically, there are three categories of activity: long-term investment, medium-term lending and financing, and short-term paper transactions and underwriting. Presently, Adela is committed to seventy-five projects in eighteen different Latin American countries for a total of $50MM (60 per cent equity, 40 per cent loan). Adela operates regional offices throughout Latin America whose responsibility is to identify viable investment opportunities.

In summary, Adela has acted as an entrepreneur, and as such has attempted to demonstrate that assisting private enterprises of a developing continent can be both profitable and instrumental in raising the living standards of the population. Adela believes that private enterprise has a responsibility and unique opportunity and can be more effective than government due to its freedom from political considerations. As a private organization, it is able to offer the key elements traditionally associated with highly motivated and forward looking private enterprise.

The Adela philosophy is implemented through careful evaluation of projects, active support of effective management, and continued supervision of projects through their implementation, start-up, and operating stages. Once Adela is satisfied that a project is economically justifiable, commercially viable, and financially attractive, it is not a silent partner, but rather follows closely the development of the enterprise through board representation, periodic progress and financial reports, and frequent inspections by its resident representatives and central staff members.

Adela not only receives proposals submitted to it by third parties but also takes the lead in identifying promising investment opportunities, develops them from inception into bankable propositions, and carries them through to ultimate execution and operation. This work involves prefeasibility surveys, pinpointed feasibility studies, searches for interested partners, and arrangement of appropriate financing with investors and lenders in and outside Latin America. Cases in point are the $90 million Olancho forestry project in Honduras and the $50 million Borregaard rayon pulp project in Brazil. Adela may be the instigator of such projects although it may not make capital investments, rather recovering its costs through fees charged for services provided.

In addition to its investment activities, Adela is engaged in a broad range of functions not directly related to specific projects but equally important insofar as the achievement of its long-range objectives are concerned. These objectives are directed to areas such as economic integration, promotion of legislation, assistance to multinational companies, encouragement of agri-business enterprises and development of local capital markets.

Adela has been a vital, vigorous, and highly regarded financial institution with project commitments of over $40 million in all twenty countries in the hemisphere. Total Adela resources approach $80 million. The success and significance of Adela's achievements have prompted many of its sponsors to apply the same concept elsewhere. As recently as 1967 a new multinational private investment company was formed to carry out the same Adela role in Asia. This new "Asian Adela," called the Private Investment Corporation for Asia, will facilitate capital investments in private enterprises in the less-developed Asian countries. Under the leadership of the Japanese private representatives, and with head offices in Tokyo, this new company will be owned one third by private Japanese businessmen, one third by United States firms, and one third by firms from Europe, Canada, and Australia.

It was scheduled to commence operations January 7, 1969, with authorized capital of $40MM. It will work alongside the newly created Asian Development Bank and other development agencies and banks in the area. Its investment criteria and goals are almost identical to those of Adela in that, by operating on a sound business basis, it will attempt to further economic growth by mobilizing human and financial resources within and outside the Asian area and channeling these resources into productive private enterprises that will prove economically viable and beneficial to overall economic development.

Of course the problems Adela has faced will be even greater for PICA. In Latin America there are nineteen countries, all with the same language, except for Brazil, and comparable cultural heritages. In Asia there are sixteen countries, all with different languages and distinctly different cultures. Moreover, the Latin American population is only one-eighth as large as Asia's, and the Latin economies are relatively more advanced industrially. Except for Japan, Asia is likely to remain, for decades to come, primarily a collection of agri-economies whose main concern is the growing, processing, and marketing of agricultural products.

Be that as it may, PICA members will attempt to pool their resources and talent and show how private capital can create a multiplier effect, generating investments substantially in excess of the limited sums directly employed. Where governments cannot and will not provide the resources needed to upgrade the living standards and development capital markets, PICA will attempt to assume this role and responsibility.

The three aforementioned examples of private investment companies should illustrate what has been done and what can be expected from this sector in the future. The companies have similar motivations. They are attempting to prove that by working with sound business principles the private sector can be extremely effective in meeting the challenges of developing economies.

THE WORLD BANK GROUP

The World Bank is a multilateral governmental institution conceived after the devastation of World War II for the purpose of fostering economic reconstruction. Since the reconstruction of Europe, this institution, together with the other closely related agencies of the UN system, has become the chosen multilateral instrument of governments for providing external capital on a global basis to help finance the development of new and economically impoverished countries of the world.

The World Bank Group is composed of three institutions, the International Bank for Reconstruction and Development (IBRD), the International Finance Corporation (IFC) and the International Development Association (IDA). The latter two organizations were formed later to meet the specific needs of the developing nations. Although IBRD is allowed to set its own interest rates and other terms, its philosophy and methods of operation have been geared to follow sound banking principles rather than to become involved in "soft loans" or hidden grants. This policy of "hard loans" has left unfulfilled many needs in less-developed countries for resources to finance good projects which nonetheless are unable to support loan repayment schedules with conventional terms. Therefore, the other two institutions—IFC and IDA—were established to supply external capital on a soft loan basis.

The members of the World Bank make capital subscriptions according to their economic strength. The Bank funnels its loans through governments, government agencies, and private enterprises of each of the member countries with the objective of assisting these countries with economic growth. The main emphasis of the bank has been to finance large government infrastructure-type projects, with approximately one third of its development loans going to electrical power, one third for transportation improvements (highways, railroads, air, waterways, and pipelines), and one third for agricultural projects, steel production, education, and general development purposes. Total subscriptions of the World Bank are $23 billion, of which over $2.3 billion has been paid-in, partly in gold or dollars and partly in local currency. The rest is subject to call should the need arise. This capital subscription was never intended to finance all of the bank's operations, and the institution has borrowed heavily in the world markets by issuing bonds. Although these bonds for the most part are denominated in dollars, more than half are held outside the United States.

The IBRD provides capital when it is not available through private sources on reasonable terms. If the borrower is not a government, the bank requires the guarantee of the member government concerned. In its lending the bank never assumes the total cost of the project or program, preferring to provide only the foreign exchange costs involved in the purchase of imported goods or services. The bank's loans are amortized over a period of years, determined by the specific type of project. Its terms also allow for a waiting period before repayment of principal commences. The normal interest charge in late 1968 was approximately 6 per cent, with a commitment fee of .375 per cent on any undisbursed portion of the loan. The rates charged bear some relation to fluctuations in current rates in the capital markets. The maturities generally run from eighteen to twenty-five years with a grace period of up to five years.

Traditionally, the bank has refused to lend to state-owned manufacturing and mining industries while at the same time extending many loans for government infrastructure projects and state-owned transportation, communications, and electric power industries. This policy has also been extended to state-owned development banks, even though many of these banks have engaged chiefly in lending to private industry. Due to this policy the bank's activities in Latin America have been relatively limited in relation to need. In June 1968 the World Bank policy was changed to permit loans to industrial projects and development finance institutions that are owned or controlled by governments. This new pronouncement has been viewed as a major step forward which should permit the bank to move more flexibly into Latin America.

The *International Development Association* (IDA), an affiliate of the World Bank, and member of the Group, was established in 1960 to "promote economic development, increase productivity and, thus, raise standards of living in the less-developed areas of the world." As distinguished from the World Bank, its role is to provide financial assistance for projects which require longer periods of amortization and lower interest rates than those offered by the World Bank itself. It lends money to countries that are otherwise unable to borrow and allows repayment in local currencies. All World Bank members are eligible to join IDA and more than ninety-six countries have done so, contributing more than $1.8 billion to its resources. Its funds are entirely separate from the World Bank, and it extends development credits to the less-developed countries on exceptionally favorable terms. The same public and private entities that borrow from the World Bank are also eligible for IDA financing. Presently the agency has extended more than one hundred credits to some thirty countries for a total of approximately $1.6 billion to finance electric power, road construction, harbor dredging, inland port construction, irrigation, drainage, flood protection projects, school construction, small private industries, and water supply improvement.

The IDA is at liberty to charge interest but so far has extended credits for up to fifty years with no interest. Amortization begins after a five-year grace period and 1 per cent of the principal is repayable annually for the next thirty years. There is a .75 per cent annual service charge to cover the agency's administrative costs. IDA assistance may take the form of agency credits combined with World Bank loans or alone. Although IDA has funneled its credits mainly to the less-developed countries, the agency is also capable of providing credits to projects in developed areas of the world.

The *International Finance Corporation* is the third member of the

World Bank Group, established in 1956 to supplement the World Bank's role in development finance through debt or equity participation. It enters projects in association with nationals of the countries in which the projects are located, or with foreign private investors, or a combination of both. In contrast to the World Bank which requires government guarantees, the IFC is not permitted to accept a government guarantee of repayment. This restriction is one of the reasons for IFC's existence. It supplies loans and equity capital directly when funds cannot be obtained from private sources on reasonable terms. By statute the IFC is not allowed to invest its funds in an undertaking which is more than 25 per cent owned or operated by local government.

Structurally the IFC is divided into two main departments that correspond to the two areas of major activity. The first concerns development finance companies, which the IFC is prepared to help establish, expand, or reorganize. It is prepared to assist in setting up companies in geographic areas where there are gaps in the local capital and money markets, and where local support is strong enough for such institutions. The IFC has currently invested in twenty-seven development finance companies in twenty-two countries with a total commitment of approximately $18.6 billion. IFC interest usually consists of 15 per cent to 25 per cent of total equity with preference for 15 per cent. IFC accepts Board Representation only if all other members concur and when IFC feels its contribution might be constructive to operations. As an institution, IFC is less interested in profits in terms of dividends than in well-managed operations which will be successful as a consequence of the medium- and long-term risk capital that is supplied. Working with a relatively small but well-trained staff of experts, IFC carefully scrutinizes each investment proposal and keeps in close touch with ongoing projects.

The second department and area of activity of the IFC is the industrial project section. In this area the IFC provides risk capital to companies that require financing in order to expand, modernize, or diversify existing operations. The corporation also helps to finance the establishment of new ventures. It has invested primarily in manufacturing industries but is prepared to consider projects in numerous other areas such as agriculture, service industries, public utilities, and tourism. IFC funds are available for either foreign exchange or local currency expenditures involving fixed assets or working capital. In many cases IFC collaborates with joint venture participants from either the foreign or local private sectors. The main consideration concerns whether the project is sound and has a high priority in the country concerned.

The interest rates charged by IFC are established on a case-by-case basis. The corporation considers in this regard the risks involved, the amount of IFC's participation, and the industrial project's expected rate of return. In addition IFC charges a commitment fee of 1 per cent per annum on the undisbursed portion of the loan. IFC loans are usually granted for maturities in the range of five to fifteen years. Most IFC's participations to date have been concentrated in the more-developed among the less-developed nations. In addition to loan and equity participations, IFC sometimes enters into standby or underwriting agreements in support of public and private placement of shares. In this context the corporation also helps international corporations to find additional financing from private and governmental sources.

The sister organization of the World Bank, the *International Monetary Fund* (IMF), was formed in the postwar period to promote international monetary cooperation and balanced growth of world trade. Membership in the fund is a prerequisite of World Bank membership. Financial operations of the IMF are in the form of drawing rights and standby credits to member countries. It is a multilateral organization designed to assist member countries during periods of short-term balance-of-payment problems. The fund does not lend to specific projects but because it promotes international economic and exchange stability in its member nations, it contributes invaluably to the quality of international investments.

Even though commercial banks and other private investors cannot directly participate in the IMF credits, many governments drawing from the fund have simultaneously negotiated loans from private sources. In many cases the private lenders recognize the existence of a satisfactory agreement between the borrowing country and the fund as a healthy incentive for investment. Additionally, the IMF is an excellent source of technical assistance on fiscal and credit policy for the less-developed countries.

Summary

This chapter has surveyed the principal sources of medium- and long-term financing available to the international enterprise exclusive of commercial and investment banks. Most national governments have developed financial programs that are intended to stimulate particular types of private investment and industrial activity in specific regions. Directly or indirectly through affiliated institutions, the national governments usually supply medium- and long-term loans to investors with qualifying projects. Many governments accept equity participations that sometimes can be retired at the private investors' option when assistance is no longer required. Additionally, the governments offer a wide variety of fiscal incentives, cash grants, and guarantees for qualifying investments. Similarly, motives relating to economic development have prompted international and regional bodies such as the European Investment Bank, the Inter-American Development Bank, and the Asian Development Bank to supply capital to new and expanding industries.

The role of private venture capital firms, such as IBEC and Adela, has been extremely important in stimulating economic activity in the private sectors of developing economies. Finally, the World Bank Group—IBRD, IFA and IDA—in collaboration with the IMF has both directly and indirectly supplied capital and managerial assistance to private investors whose projects are expected to contribute significantly to the economic development of sponsoring countries.

BIBLIOGRAPHY

Adler, Robert W., and Raymond Frech Mikesell. *Public External Financing of Development Banks in Developing Countries.* (Eugene, Ore.: University of Oregon Books, 1966).

Aids to Business—Overseas Investments. (Washington, D.C.: Agency for International Development, 1964).

"The Asian Bank Gets Down to Work," *International Management,* August 1968, pp. 26–28.

Barzanti, Sergio. *The Underdeveloped Areas within the Common Market* (Princeton, N.J.: Princeton University Press, 1965).

Black, W. "UK Investment Incentives and the 1965 Finance Act: Regional Implications," *Scottish Journal of Political Economy,* February 1967.

Bloch, H. S. "Regional Development Financing," *International Organization,* No. 1, 1968.

Calvo, R. A. "Financial Aspects of Latin American Integration," *Bank of London and South America Review,* June 1968, pp. 312–22.

Common Markets Around the World. (San Francisco: Bank of America, 1965).

Curtis, Michael. *Western European Integration.* (New York: Harper & Row, Publishers, 1965).

Diamond, W. "Development Finance Companies," *Finance and Development,* June 1965, pp. 97–102.

Dominci, G. "Credit Policy for the Development of Southern Italy," *Review of the Economic Conditions in Italy,* November 1964, pp. 438–54.

Farer, T. I. *Financing African Development.* (Cambridge, Mass.: The M.I.T. Press, 1965).

Financing Foreign Operations. (New York: Business International, 1968).

Financing U.S. Exports and Overseas Investment. (Washington, D.C.: Machinery and Allied Products Institute, 1964).

Friedmann, Wolfgang Gaston, *et al., International Financial Aid.* (New York: Columbia University Press, 1966).

Fuchs, H. *Financing Industrial Development in Latin America.* Text of Remarks, 16th World Trade Conference, Louisville, November 11, 1965.

Gordon, David Livingston. "Coordinating Aid to Developing Countries," *Finance and Development,* June 1966, pp. 129–35.

Grenier, David. "The International Finance Corporation," *Westminster Bank Review,* May 1966, pp. 21–31.

Homan, J. L. "The Merger of the European Communities," *Common Market Law Review,* March 1966, pp. 397–419.

International Information Center for Local Credit, *Government Measures for the Promotion of Regional Economic Development.* (The Hague: M. Nijhoff, 1964).

Keith, C. K. *Foreign Tax Policies and Economic Growth.* (New York: Columbia University Press, 1966).

"Latin America and Financial Integration," *Comercio Exterior de Mexico,* October 1965, pp. 3–4.

Lovel, A. H. "How Should Overseas Aid Be Given," *Lloyds Bank Review,* April 1966, pp. 19–32.

Martellaro, Joseph A. *Economic Development in Southern Italy.* (Washington, D.C.: Catholic University Press, 1965).

McDaniels, John F. *International Financing and Investment.* (Dobbs Ferry, N.Y.: Oceana Publications, Inc., 1964).

Mikesell, Raymond Frech. *Public International Lending for Development.* (New York: Random House, Inc., 1966).

Nehrt, Lee Charles. *International Finance for Multinational Business.* Scranton, Pa.: International Textbook Co., 1967).

Patrick, Hugh T. "Financial Development and Economic Growth in Underdeveloped Countries," *Economic Development and Cultural Change,* January 1966, pp. 174–89.

"Regional Organizations and Financial and Technical Cooperation," *Temas del BID,* April 1964.

Reimann, Guenter, and Edwin F. Wigglesworth. *The Challenge of International Finance.* (New York: McGraw-Hill Book Co., 1966).

Robinson, R. *African Development Planning.* (Cambridge, Mass.: Cambridge University Overseas Committee, 1964).

Stoneham, P. E. "The Asian Development Bank," *Australian Quarterly,* March 1967, pp. 77–84.

Weaver, James H. *The International Development Association.* (New York: Frederick A. Praeger, Inc., 1965).

Weil, Gordon Lee. *A Handbook on the European Economic Community.* (New York: Frederick A. Praeger, Inc., 1965).

Case 18
TOWNSEND AND COMPANY

In April 1967 Ian Blackman, a prominent Jamaicar businessman requested financial assistance from Townsend and Company (a computer softwear firm headquartered in London) in acquiring all the stock of the Jamaicar Investment Company (JIC), a Jamaicar holding and management company that owned 99.8 per cent of the common stock of the West Indian Sugar Company (WISC)—the largest sugar mill in Jamaicar. JIC also owned about 75 per cent of another medium-sized sugar mill in Jamaicar and 100 per cent of a small cement plant and jute bag manufacturing plant.

WISC was the key to the deal because its estimated annual after-tax earnings exceeded £292,000 after paying over £150,000 to JIC for management fees.[1] All of the other subsidiaries of JIC were expected to earn about £65,000 and paid no management fees to JIC. JIC and its subsidiaries were then owned by Juan Gonzales (born in Venezuela but now a Jamaicar citizen) and a group of his relatives. Mr. Blackman for many years had been working for the Gonzales family in a number of capacities and in 1967 was president of JIC and all its subsidiary companies. Mr. Blackman was at the same time president of Kingsly Bauxite Company, one of the largest corporations in Jamaicar (total assets £25,000,000). In 1966 Mr. Blackman had successfully negotiated on behalf of the Gonzales family and their associates the purchase of the Kingsly Bauxite Company from Jamaicar Public Utilities.

(Ian Blackman, age 43, was a native of Jamaicar. He was educated at the University of West Indies and was well-known throughout the island for his prowess in the game of cricket as a university student. Since graduation from the University, Ian Blackman had been working for Juan Gonzales and representing him and his many interests throughout the island.)

Mr. Blackman explained to Townsend and Company that the Gonzales family wanted to dispose of JIC because the sugar and related companies owned by JIC had gone deeply in debt during the previous election year to both government and private lending institutions in Jamaicar. He explained that the Gonzales family had been for many years the principal supporters of the Republic Party. The Gonzales family had strongly supported the Republic Party candidate, John Brownley. During the campaign for premier a year ago, the Gonzales family contributed heavily to Brownley's campaign and persistently attacked the opposition candidate, Dudley Stampler, in its newspaper, *The Jamaicar Standard*. In the 1966 elections Brownley lost, and the newly elected premier, Dudley Stampler, announced his intention to reduce the political and economic strength of the sugar bloc that had traditionally supported the Republic candidates and was led by the Gonzales family. During the administration of John Brownley, the loser in the election, businessmen with the proper connection received all types of lucrative favors. So when Dudley Stampler took office the government was in an economic and moral mess. Stampler went to work with vigor, launched an all-out attack on government corruption and drafted plans to get the sluggish Jamaicar economy moving again. Once installed in office Stampler did not wait long to counterattack. He contended that the Gonzales family had received "loans, credits, and accommodations" from the government amounting to £5 million.

Although the JIC companies were not yet in arrears on their debt to government lending institutions, it was feared that their credit lines might be withdrawn. Mr. Blackman explained his plan as follows:

1. He would organize a new company called Trans-Jamaicar Investment Corporation (TJIC). The paid-in capital of TJIC would be nominal (about £6,500) and Mr. Blackman would purchase 55 per cent of TJIC shares. He planned to

[1] Jamaicar is part of the sterling bloc, and the Jamaicar pound equals $2.80.

sell a total of 15 per cent to three prominent Jamaicar businessmen (a bank president, a hotel owner, and a wealthy real estator). Mr. Blackman thought that these minority Jamicar investors would be needed to give the company a financially reputable and politically neutral board of directors. Mr. Blackman offered the remaining 30 per cent to Townsend provided that Townsend lent TJIC £65,000 at 8 per cent interest repayable over five years. He explained that he needed U.K. investors to add further strength to the financial and political independence of the new company that would take over JIC and its subsidiaries.

2. Once TJIC was organized Mr. Blackman planned to buy the JIC companies from the Gonzales group under terms and conditions to which the Gonzales group had already agreed. The total purchase price would be £3.3 million payable as follows: £65,000 on date of sale; £65,000 within thirty days of date of sale; and £3.17 million in equal annual installments over ten years plus interest at 6 per cent on the unpaid balance. However the Gonzales group was indebted to JIC for £2.35 million (resulting from advances to stockholders) that they would repay over ten years with interest at 6 per cent. Thus the net cash payment to the Gonzales group would be only £950,000 plus interest, of which £820,000 would be payable over ten years.

3. TJIC would use the proceeds of the Townsend loan as the source of funds for the £65,000 down payment to the Gonzales group. The additional £65,000 due within thirty days would be advanced to TJIC by WISC. The net annual payments of £82,000 plus interest to the Gonzales group would be generated out of the profits of JIC's management contract with WISC. (JIC incurred only £35,000 of operating expenses while earning over £150,000 of management fees annually.)

No reliable financial statements for the JIC companies were available, and it was virtually impossible to reconstruct the earnings of the JIC companies in recent years. However, an appraisal of the companies' assets had been performed in early 1967 by The British Appraisal Company, and a complete list of the companies liabilities was available. Audited balance sheets were being prepared, but there would be no audited income statements available until after another year of operation. Copies of the audited balance sheets of JIC and WISC as of June 30, 1967, are attached.

In explaining why he believed that WISC could earn almost £300,000 annually after taxes and after paying management fees to JIC, Mr. Blackman drew up the following pro forma income statement:

Export sales to U.S.: 650,000 piculs[2] @ 1.866	£1,213,000	
Domestic sales: 225,000 piculs @ £1.333	300,000	
Molasses sales	40,000	
Total sales		£1,553,000
Cost of sugar sold @ £.75 per picul	667,000	
Gross profit		886,000

[2] A picul equals 139 pounds of raw sugar.

Management fee to JIC (10% sales)	155,000	
Other general and administrative expenses	63,000	
		218,000
Operating profit		668,000
Interest expense		250,000
Net income before taxes		418,000
Provision for taxes (30%)		125,400
Net income after taxes		£292,600

A brief investigation of the sugar industry and of known costs in WISC confirmed Mr. Blackman's estimates of WISC earnings. The Jamaicar sugar industry consisted of twenty six sugar mills with each sugar mill under contract to mill all the sugar cane grown by independent farmers in its geographic district. The mill received 35 per cent of all sugar produced as its compensation for milling the farmers' cane.

There were about 22 million hectares of sugar cane planted in the WISC district in 1967. At the historical average yield of about 115 piculs of raw sugar per hectare of sugar cane, WISC could expect a total district production of about 2.5 million piculs—of which about 875,000 piculs (35 per cent) would be mill share sugar available for sale by WISC. Under the Jamaicar quota system WISC had a permanent United States quota of 560,000 piculs and a domestic quota of 225,000 piculs. The remaining WISC mill share sugar was classified as reserve sugar to be converted to United States or world export sugar or domestic sugar. In recent years, however, all reserve sugar had been sold to United States buyers under deficit quota allocations (representing unfilled quotas of other countries supplying sugar to the United States). If not sold to United States buyers, reserve sugar would have to be sold in the world market.

The assumed price of £1.8 per picul was the equivalent (under current exchange regulations) of $6.50 per cwt. on the New York Sugar Exchange. It was the announced policy of the United States Department of Agriculture to stabilize United States raw sugar prices at about $6.50 per cwt. World sugar prices were about $3.00 per cwt. in 1966. Domestic sugar prices were liable to minor fluctuations but had traditionally been about £.533 per picul below United States export sugar.

Mr. Blackman also explained to Mr. Townsend his plan to refinance the extremely heavy short-term debt of JIC and WISC. He first pointed out that raw sugar is a highly bankable commodity, and he was confident that WISC could continue to roll over about £1.4 million of short-term bank loans and advances on sugar sales. A consortium of United States commercial banks had offered to advance WISC up to 80 per cent of the FOB value of each year's export sugar sales on a revolving basis. These advances would be in the form of promissory notes and would be secured only by a bond guaranteeing shipment to be issued by an insurance company owned by the Gonzales group.

In addition Mr. Blackman indicated that he had obtained a verbal commitment from a leading London bank to lend WISC £2 million repayable in equal amortizations over five years provided that WISC could get Jamaicar banks to guarantee payment by issuing stand-by letters of credit to the London bank. Mr. Blackman said he already had assurances from the presidents of two Jamaicar banks that they were agreeable in principle to participating in the stand-by letter of credit.

Finally Mr. Blackman said that he was offering Townsend & Company an opportunity because of Mr. Townsend's excellent reputation in Jamaicar. Townsend (president and controlling stockholder in Townsend & Company) had been the first foreign aid director in Jamaicar while working for the U.K. Foreign Service in the early 1950's. Mr. Townsend left the government service after his Jamaicar assignment to start Townsend & Company, a computer software company. By 1966 Townsend & Company had expanded into a variety of nonfinancial businesses that it managed in the service and marketing fields. It also held as investments substantial minority interests in four companies—two of which were domiciled in Canada. Net worth was about £1 million, and the company had no long-term debt. £350,000 of the company's £1.2 million of assets consisted of cash and marketable securities. The company had not conducted business in Jamaicar theretofore.

EXHIBIT 1

Marshall, Hartwell and Peet Co.
Certified Public Accountants
490 Kingsly, Jamaicar

The Board of Directors
Jamaicar Investment Co., Inc.
Kingsly, Jamaicar

We have examined the balance sheet of Jamaicar Investment Co., Inc., as at June 30, 1967. Our examination was made in accordance with generally accepted auditing standards and accordingly included such tests of the accounting records and such other auditing procedures as we considered necessary in the circumstances.

We were engaged as the company's auditors in July 1967.

In our opinion the accompanying balance sheet presents fairly the financial position of Jamaicar Investment Co., Inc., at June 30, 1967, in conformity with generally accepted accounting principles.

October 19, 1967

Assets			
Current assets			
Cash on hand and in banks		£ 103,085	
Accounts receivable:			
Trade	36,138		
Others	216,288		
Total	252,426		
Allowance for doubtful accounts	123,541		
Net		128,884	
Loans receivable from West Indian Sugar Co., Inc. (Note 2)		410,000	
Due from shareholders - current (Note 3)		235,000	
Total Current Assets			876,969
Due from Kingsly Cement Co., Inc.			14,360
Investments in shares of stock - At Cost (Note 1)			
West Indian Sugar Co.		640,000	
Mobay Sugar Mills		122,625	
Industrial Co., Inc.		153,400	916,025
Office furniture and equipment - At cost less accumulated depreciation of £5,114			263
Other assets			
Due from shareholders - net of current portion shown above (Note 3)		2,115,000	
Marginal deposits (Note 4)		23,333	
Total Other Assets			2,138,333
Total assets			£3,945,950
Liabilities and Stockholders' Equity			
Current liabilities			
Accrued taxes and expenses		£ 7,109	
Bank overdrafts		6,462	
Dividends payable		2,912	
Accounts payable:			
Trade	£ 7,411		
Others	83,486		
Total		90,897	
Current portion of long-term debt (Note 4)		23,333	
Notes payable to bank (Note 2)		510,000	
Deposits on future sales (Note 5)		276,949	
Total current liabilities			917,662
Long-term debt			
Loan payable to Bank of Nova Scotia — net of current portion shown above (Note 4)			70,000
Due to affiliated companies			
West Indian Sugar Co., Inc.		1,909,677	
Mobay Sugar Mills		877,600	
Industrial Company, Inc.		21,701	
Total due to affiliated companies			2,808,978
Stockholders' equity (Note 1)			
Capital stock— 7 par value a share			
Authorized—133,810 shares			
Issued and outstanding—46,101 shares		322,707	
Deficit (Note 6)		173,395	
Net stockholders' equity			149,310
Total liabilities and stockholders' equity			£3,945,950

Notes to Financial Statements

1. The company became a wholly-owned subsidiary of Trans-Jamaicar Investment Corporation in July, 1967. The company owns 99.8 per cent of the common stock of the West Indian Sugar Company, 75 per cent of the common stock of another medium-sized sugar mill in Jamaicar, and 100 per cent of the common stock of a cement and jute bag manufacturer. The investments in the subsidiaries are recorded at cost in the financial statement which is £900,000 less than the company's equities in the net assets of its three subsidiaries.

2. A short-term bank loan of £510,000 with interest at 6 per cent was secured to provide temporary working capital. Of the total loan, £410,000 was advanced to the company's subsidiary West Indian Sugar Company.

3. Promissory notes receivable from stockholders totaling £2,350,000 at June 30, 1967 are due in ten equal annual installments of £235,000 plus interest at 6 per cent per annum.

4. Promissory notes payable to the Bank of Nova Scotia with interest at 6 per cent annum totaling £93,333 at June 30, 1967 are due in annual installments of £23,333. The company has deposited £23,333 in a segregated account as security for the repayment of the loan.

5. The company negotiates contracts for the sale of all sugar produced by its subsidiary West Indian Sugar Company. At June 30, 1967 total advances of £276,949 had been received from customers on contracts for future delivery.

6. The company's deficit represents dividends paid in excess of accumulated net earnings.

EXHIBIT 2

Marshall, Hartwell and Peet Co.
Certified Public Accountants
490 Kingsly, Jamaicar

The Board of Directors
West Indian Sugar Company, Inc.
Kingsly

We have examined the balance sheet of West Indian Company, Inc. as at June 30, 1967. Our examination was made in accordance with generally accepted auditing standards and accordingly included such tests of the accounting records and such other auditing procedures as we considered necessary in the circumstances.

We were engaged as the company's auditors in July 1967 when all the shares of the parent company of the West Indian Sugar Company, Inc., were purchased by Trans-Jamaicar Investment Corporation. Prior to the purchase, Appraisers (Jamaicar) Inc., an affiliate of the British Appraisal Company, was requested to make an independent appraisal of all property and equipment, except constructions in progress, as of March 31, 1967. In view of the material differences between net book values and current replacement costs less accumulated depreciation, these appraisal figures which were partly used as a basis in arriving at the total consideration paid by Trans-Jamaicar Investment Corporation, have been set up in the balance sheet of the West Indian Sugar Company, Inc.

In our opinion, the accompanying balance sheet presents fairly the financial

condition of the West Indian Sugar Company, Inc., at June 30,1967, in conformity with generally accepted accounting principles, except for the change in the method of valuing property, plant, and equipment.
October 19, 1967

Assets	
Current assets	
Cash on hand and in banks	£ 6,319
Advances and accounts receivable—planters (net of allowance for doubtful accounts of £57,000)	30,990
Accounts receivable—others	8,002
Notes receivable (net of allowance of £5,350)	615
Inventories:	
Molasses—at market	39,308
Materials and supplies—at cost (net of allowance for obsolescence of £6,500)	106,677
Materials and supplies in bonded warehouse and in transit	72,666
Recoverable deposits	534
Prepaid expenses	63,800
Total current assets	£ 328,911
Due from Jamaicar Investment Co., Inc.	1,909,677
Property, plant, and equipment (Notes 1 and 2)	
Land	218,855
Land improvements	6,870
Buildings	475,573
Mill, machinery, and equipment	2,975,209
Rolling stock and transportation equipment	1,656,501
Furniture, fixtures, and office equipment	48,925
Total	5,381,933
Less accumulated depreciation	2,443,470
Net	2,938,463
Constructions in progress	53,149
Total property, plant, and equipment	2,991,613
Sugar quota rights (Note 3)	223,566
Other assets	
Due from officers and employees	10,541
Rights of way—unamortized balance	2,171
Other receivables—(net of allowance for doubtful accounts of £1,350)	618
Investments—at cost	91
Total other assets	13,421
Total assets	£5,467,188

Liabilities and Stockholders' Equity

Current liabilities	
Bank overdraft	£ 43,166
Accrued taxes and expenses	133,449
Accounts payable	129,923
Acceptances payable (net of applicable marginal deposits of £3,950)	54,777
Loans payable	
Banks	1,049,870
Jamaicar Investment Co., Inc.	410,000
Others	938,333
Current portions of long-term debts (Note 2)	
Development Bank of Jamaicar	250,086
Jamaicar National Bank	41,357
International Products Company	7,865
Other current liabilities	10,773
Total current liabilities	3,069,599
Long-term debts (net of current portions shown under current liabilities) (Note 2)	
Development Bank of Jamaicar	608,325
Jamaicar National Bank	140,304
International Products Company	39,326
Total long-term debts	787,955
Reserves	
Off-season costs and expenses (Note 4)	133,333
Retirement gratuity	15,283
Contingencies	34,000
Total reserves	182,616
Stockholders' equity (Note 1)	
Capital stock—no par value	
Authorized, issued, and outstanding—400,000 shares	601,532
Deficit (Note 5)	(250,442)
Surplus arising from revaluation of capital assets (Note 1)	1,075,928
Total stockholders' equity	1,427,018
Total liabilities and stockholders' equity	£5,467,188

	Current portion	*Non-current portion*
Development Bank of Jamaicar—due in quarterly installments of £62,522 plus interest at 6% to November 30, 1970	£250,086	£608,325
Jamaicar National Bank—due in semiannual installments of £20,678 plus interest at 5 3/4% to December 15, 1971	41,357	140,304
International Products Company—due in annual installments of £7,865 plus interest at 6 1/4% to May 1, 1972	7,865	39,326
Total debt	£299,308	£787,955

Notes to Financial Statements

1. The company is a subsidiary of Jamaicar Investment Co., Inc., that owns 99.8 per cent of the company's common stock. An independent appraisal of all of the company's property and equipment, except constructions in progress, was made by Appraisers (Jamaicar) Inc., an affiliate of the British Appraisal Company as of March 31, 1967. In view of the material differences between net book values and current replacement costs less accumulated depreciation, the appraisal figures have been set up in the balance sheet. As a result, property, plant, and equipment was increased by £1,075,928 with an offsetting surplus arising from revaluation of capital assets.

2. Long-term debt, which is secured by substantially all of the company's property, plant, and equipment consists of the following:

3. Costs of securing permanent sugar quota rights under the Jamaicar quota system totaled £223,566. No amortization of the sugar quota rights is recorded.

4. The company provides a reserve during its selling season to cover general and administrative expenses during the off-season period.

5. The company's deficit represents dividends paid in excess of accumulated net earnings.

Import and Export Financing*

10

The exportation of goods and services has historically been the most important form of international commerce. While the volume of foreign direct investment has increased recently at a more rapid rate than have exportations, the latter nevertheless account for far larger inflows of funds to the lending country than do the fruits of direct investment—i.e., dividends, royalties, and fees. The intent of this chapter is to familiarize the reader with the institutional arrangements and credit instruments relevant to import and export financing. The chapter includes a discussion of bank and nonbank sources and forms of financing, short-term and extended-term credit arrangements, and the role of governments in assisting or restricting the types of financing that may be used.

The first section of this chapter describes the functions of banks, other private financing organizations, and government in providing short-term financing. The unique advantages and disadvantages of each financial instrument, as well as some basic methodology, are indicated. The second section of the chapter deals with medium- and long-term refinements of basic instruments. Most important, this section discusses the causes and effects of the blurring of the three distinct categories of

* This chapter was written by Lawrence Broadwell under the direction of the authors.

financing set forth earlier. More often than not, governments, banks, and private nonbank financiers pool their resources to make medium- and long-term credits possible, and this cooperative effort has substantial impact on the provisions of and requirements for financing. A brief, final section places the role of export and import credits in perspective and summarizes some of the considerations a credit applicant must take into account in selecting the proper form of financing.

THE ROLE OF COMMERCIAL BANKS

For the vast majority of importers and exporters, whether they seek outside funds or rely on their own resources to finance transactions across national boundaries, the commercial banking system will supply the services that make financing of any sort possible. For the exporter who is able and willing to extend his own credits, United States banks and to a lesser extent European banks are able to provide *credit information* so that the seller can choose terms suitable to the risk in dealing with each customer. For regular customers most large banks also provide at cost or free of charge, foreign market research, information on exchange rates and tariffs, import and export regulations, licensing procedures, and political and economic conditions.

Banks also put the international businessman in contact with foreign lawyers, distributors, agents, and brokers who are able to provide key services to the trader. Upon the customer's request, a bank will also obtain the names of dependable suppliers of raw materials.

By far the most important contacts of the bank are its correspondents abroad. By writing letters of introduction to these foreign banks, the domestic bank can open many doors for the trader who wishes to explore overseas opportunities for himself. In this regard, two large banks use a *Traveler's Letter of Credit,* which provides a prospective importer assurance of receiving foreign exchange equivalent to the total amount of credit arranged with his local bank. The Traveler's Letter enables him to offer a supplier the nearest thing to cash, and therefore can be used to negotiate price reductions that more than compensate for any interest charges.

An impression of the value of correspondent and branch relationships can be gained by noting the geographical areas covered by some of the larger networks. One American bank, Chase Manhattan, cooperates closely with more than one thousand foreign banks. The largest network is maintained by Barclays DCO of Great Britain, which has more than four thousand branches, most of which are in the Mediterranean area and in nations formerly associated with the British Empire.

In addition to the above services, commercial banks perform several routine operations that are essential to their role as advisers and financiers in international commerce. Foreign exchange trading, collecting foreign bills, discounting and loaning against bills payable abroad, and opening letters of credit constitute the indispensable core of trade financing in most countries. Unlike the provision of information and contacts, these services entail explicit charges, and the banks make a substantial part of their earnings from these operations.

Charges for the various bank instruments used in financing international trade vary sharply from country to country. It should be kept in mind, however, that the importer or exporter probably will pay more than the nominal charge for bank service received, possibly in the form of required deposits of noninterest-bearing compensating balances for lengthy periods. By investing these funds, the banks reap sizable profits; at the same time they retain security for the customer's letters of credit, discounted acceptances, and loans against collections.

Bank services are not without cost to the customer. Good relations with the bank entail considerable indirect charges. Frequently other organizations can provide contacts or information at less cost. The government in the importing or exporting country, for example, is usually most accommodating. Why then do traders usually prefer to deal with banks? Briefly, the following advantages in relying on banks apply. Banks are committed to the customer; their services are generally quicker, more informal, and tailored to the customer's needs. Finally, there is some information a trader does not wish his government to know, especially where exchange controls are applied; bank officers can normally be relied upon to keep such data confidential.

BASIC INSTRUMENTS

Bank Drafts

Through the use of drafts or bills of exchange, an exporter may employ his bank as the collection agent on accounts the exporter himself finances. The bank forwards the exporter's bills to the foreign buyer either directly or through a branch or correspondent and then converts and/or remits proceeds of the collection back to the exporter. In the case of a *sight draft,* which is payable upon presentation to the importer, remission of the face value of the draft is made within one or two weeks. The cost of financing in this case is equal to the total of bank fees, cable and postal charges, and any additional charges imposed by the governments of the importing and exporting nations.

Most often shipping documents and title to the merchandise do not pass to the buyer until payment is made to the collection agent. Most banks will await the arrival of the merchandise before presenting drafts, so the buyer has an opportunity to make certain that the documents are in good order and conform to the sales contract underlying the transaction.

When an exporter draws his draft on the foreign buyer, he will complete a lengthy set of *instructions* to the bank. These instructions cover the tenor or usance of a *time draft*, setting the time or date after initial presentation when payment must be made. Importantly, the instructions prescribe the currency for payment, and thus determine on whom will be placed the burden of insuring against the risk of exchange fluctuation.

The documents certifying title and conditions of shipment are normally entrusted to the collecting bank together with the exporter's draft. Occasionally clean drafts unaccompanied by documents are given to the collector and the remaining forms are sent directly to the buyer. In most cases, however, the exporter will prefer to ship all forms at once and keep the title within the exclusive control of his agent until payment is received or the draft is *accepted*. By accepting the draft the importer exchanges his formal promise to pay the draft at maturity for possession of the goods.

Documentary drafts are clearly preferable if bank financing is sought. Enclosure of documents enables the bank to attest to the correctness of all charges, including insurance and freight costs. In addition, the exporter cannot use his draft as security for a loan unless the bank can hold title over the goods in transit. Possession of the proper documents makes the bank an "innocent" title-holder, immune in most legal disputes between buyer and seller. This immunity can be an important inducement for the bank to provide credit to the exporter.

The possibility of extending credits beyond the period required for shipping merchandise has already been mentioned. Bills of exchange are frequently drawn with tenor of thirty, sixty, and ninety days or more. In such cases delivery is made against acceptance or a formal promise to pay rather than actual payment.

Normally the buyer's acceptance is simply noted on the original draft, which then becomes a negotiable instrument—a "trade acceptance"—and suitable for discounting by the seller with his bank. If a bank adds its acceptance to that of the importer, and if the bank has a strong reputation in international trading circles, the seller will possess what is termed a "prime banker's acceptance." Such an instrument can be discounted at ½ per cent to 1 per cent below the prime rate of interest because a ready market for acceptances exists among large companies with temporary excess cash. The short-term, self-liquidating banker's acceptance offers a secure, convenient, and profitable investment for these cash holdings.

Whenever such an acceptance is sold or discounted, the seller adds his endorsement on the back of the draft. In the event of the importer's unwillingness or inability to pay at maturity, the holder of the acceptance will have *recourse* for the full amount of the draft from the last endorser. Only those who have added a qualified endorsement, stipulating that no recourse against them will be allowed in case of default, are exempted from the obligation. An exporter who chooses to dispose of the acceptance without recourse, however, will have to settle for a lower price.

If the exporter does not wish to hold the draft to maturity, he may negotiate to sell it at a discount in the market described above. In some cases negotiation will consist only of looking up the current rate in the New York Times. In most cases, however, the discount from the amount on the face of the draft will be derived from careful consideration of the time remaining before maturity, the credit standings of the exporter, importer, and all endorsers, whether the endorsements are qualified or recourse is allowed, and the political and economic conditions extant in the importing nation.

The time draft, or as it is more commonly termed the *usance* draft, is particularly useful where a lengthy quarantine of imports is required by the purchaser's government. Unless the buyer can obtain advance payment from another party on resale of the goods while they are still in quarantine, he is likely to request such extended credits as the exporter, in consultation with his bank, is willing to allow. Whether or not the buyer's request is granted depends chiefly on the seller's estimation of his trustworthiness and the probability of exchange blockage or devaluation by his government. If the seller decides to provide credit after delivery, the bank handling collection abroad will release the shipment in accordance with its instructions.

Retaining a measure of control over the goods after their release is often considered necessary. Trust and warehouse receipts can provide a measure of control when the buyer's formal acceptance is deemed to be insufficient security. Warehouse receipts convey title and are negotiable in most instances, whereas with a trust receipt the bank releases the goods in trust to the importer who, in turn, indicates the bank's security interest in the goods.

Under the terms of a sight draft, goods are only released upon payment of the draft. Where a time draft is supplemented by a trust or warehouse receipt, goods are not completely released until the draft is paid. Through the trust receipt the correspondent bank can retain nominal title to the merchandise while allowing the buyer to use and even to resell the goods. In most countries the trust receipt protects against a lien on the assets of an insolvent importer, as long as due notice is given to his creditors and the property is readily identifiable. The latter requirement, however, may render a trust receipt valueless where, for example, a shipment of grain has been mixed into a large bin of identical staples. The trust receipt also fails to protect against the deceit or fraud of a dishonest importer. If, for example, the trustee sells the goods and disappears, in most countries the trustor cannot recover against an innocent buyer.

The warehouse receipt offers a different kind of security. The title is transferred to the importer, but control of the merchandise is placed in the hands of an independent warehouseman. In many countries it is better to keep the goods under lock and key in this manner than to settle for mere title. But both instruments have unique advantages in different countries, and the adaptation of laws to the growing volume of international trade is constantly changing the trader's preference between the two. Widespread adoption of the Uniform Commercial Code in the United States, for example, has significantly limited the effectiveness of the trust receipt, a fact that is yet unrealized by many exporters in this country.

There are three main reasons for using drafts in international trade. First, they provide written evidence of obligations in terse and comprehensible form. Second, drafts enable both parties to the transaction to reduce the costs of financing and to apportion the remaining costs equitably. When an exporter has good relations with his bankers or when he holds an acceptance from a reputable firm or bank, he may choose not to finance the credit himself and seek immediate payment for his draft or acceptance. Third and more important, the drafts are negotiable and unconditional, that is, their authenticity is not subject to disputes which may arise among drawer and drawee concerning the underlying transactions.

A number of methods are open to him. Nonbank sources will be evaluated later in this section. The possibility of selling or discounting acceptances has already been discussed. The exporter may also borrow from the bank using his drafts as collateral. Bank loans against either sight or time drafts can be made on one of four bases: [1]

1. Where the nature of the trade and circumstances of shipment are such as to make the schedule of payment and remittance from abroad extraordinarily precise, the bank may feel confident enough to *discount* a draft at a flat rate. The rate will be computed from the collection fees of the discounting bank and its foreign correspondent, the cost of bill stamps, and the rate of interest for the time the loan is outstanding. Despite the growing precision of international transport schedules, discounting has fallen into disuse.

2. The *liquidation* or cash advance basis contrasts sharply with the discounting procedure. Instead of deducting the charges beforehand, the bank lends an exporter the full amount of his draft on a foreign buyer. As soon as payment is remitted to the lending bank, charges are computed and billed to the borrower.

[1] Morgan Guaranty Trust Company, *Export and Import Procedures,* New York, Morgan Guaranty Trust Company, 1965, p. 26; *see* also William S. Shaterian, *Export-Import Banking: The Documents and Financial Operations of Foreign Trade,* New York, The Ronald Press Co., 1956, pp. 278–281 (discounting), and pp. 283–284 (advances).

3. The exporter may also borrow on a *note* basis, pledging his drafts currently in collection by the bank as collateral. This method is more informal than the others listed here, and the terms and amount of the exporter's borrowing may be altered easily to meet his needs.

4. The *acceptance* basis is used primarily by large-volume traders and frequent customers of the bank. At the same time the exporter draws his drafts on buyers abroad, he draws a time draft on his own bank. The bank accepts his draft and discounts it at the rate for prime banker's acceptances. As is true for other acceptances, the bank may then resell the acceptance and pay the holder from the proceeds of the loan at maturity.

With respect to qualifying for credit in any of the above forms, it should be appreciated that normally advances against collections are not made for amounts of more than 100 per cent of collections in process. Only with the cash advance is there much uncertainty about the total cost of the loan. At the same time, however, the cash advance is attractive because it provides prompt payment, enabling the exporter to obtain his money immediately.

In deciding whether or not to finance the collection of an exporter's draft payable abroad, the bank will consider several factors. Obviously, the good credit standing of both parties to the transaction is a *sine qua non,* as is the borrower's good relations with his bank. Complete insurance coverage is also important. Banks frequently insist on warehouse to warehouse coverage against accidental loss or damage to the merchandise. Policies for political risks may also be required for shipments to areas where conditions are unsettled. The coverage of political risk will be discussed later.

A full set of instructions with the draft and full documentation on the shipment are requirements. If the bank is to accept the goods in transit as collateral, it will insist that control over the goods when they arrive abroad be given to the party in possession of the documents: i.e., the bank's foreign correspondent. The bank might also wish to examine the contract underlying the sale to see whether the merchandise is readily marketable at its destination. The requirement that the goods be readily marketable staples is often restated in interdepartmental memoranda of the larger banks.[2] Generally it is demanded in inverse proportion to the credit-worthiness of the exporter.

The bank will usually be receptive to a loan request that covers only the time period required for shipping and, within a short period after arrival, resale of the goods. Banks dislike "prefinancing" the assembly of exports for a thinly capitalized merchant. They generally abhor any attempt by the exporter to "stretch" the terms offered to the buyer be-

[2] Frank Sauter, *Random Notes on Commercial Credits,* vol. 2, New York, First National City Bank, 1963, p. 16.

yond the period normally required for process and resale. In essence, banks prefer short-term, inherently self-liquidating loans that are readily rediscountable when the lender itself is under pressure.

Although commercial banks can be of great value to both buyer and seller, there are some risks they may not be prepared to take in collecting foreign receivables. Where tremendous amounts of money are involved the risks of dealing in foreign exchange, for example, are likely to be left to the trader. The bank will not automatically protect its customer from the effects of exchange blockage in the importing country nor from losses on exchange rate fluctuation and devaluation. There are, however, several steps importers and exporters can take to protect themselves. First, they can carefully select the currency in which the draft is to be denominated. If dollar reserves in the importing country are running low, for example, an American exporter can make his draft payable in another hard currency that is in plentiful supply there. This may protect at least one of the parties from the effects of a deteriorating exchange rate.

Importers and exporters can also protect against devaluation loss by contracting with their banks to buy or sell forward exchange at a fixed rate. In many nations, however, the exporter's risk of foreign exchange blockage by authorities in the importing country can be very great, and it is difficult to obtain a hedge against this risk. Where local exchange control authorities forbid immediate payment of sight drafts in foreign currency, exporters commonly instruct their banks to accept local currency deposits pending the availability of exchange, with the importer's promise to assume all exchange risks. It is important to remember that even when this promise is kept, the credit must be involuntarily extended over an indefinite period, with the exporter taking all the real risks.

Most other risks arising in the use of drafts on a foreign buyer are caused by a misunderstanding of the bank's role in collections. Banks do not guarantee collection; the exporter retains all commercial risks. The bank is responsible only to make sure that all documents appear to be in order; the unwary importer may still find himself obligated to pay the bank for goods that have been damaged in transit or even mislabeled. The bank is in effect an innocent holder for value and immune to suits arising from the manufacturer's malfeasance.

The exporter may also find that his loan or advance against a draft is abruptly recalled when the importer refuses to take delivery, to accept the draft, or dishonors his previous acceptance. Unless acceptance has been made, the exporter must bring suit on the basis of his contract with the buyer; he cannot sue on the basis of his rejected draft. With a dishonored acceptance, endorsers will be able to recover from the seller where the acceptance has been discounted with recourse. But the exporter will also be able to bring suit against the importer on the basis of the acceptance, which constitutes a clear promise to pay. Nonetheless, the commercial risks are by no means eliminated through the use of drafts and bank facilities. Conceivably, the exporter can wind up not only involuntarily financing the storage of goods abroad, but financing the costs of a lengthy court battle as well.

Letters of Credit

In order to cover both the exchange and commercial risks of foreign trade financing, the exporter may require his customer to open a letter of credit (L/C) at a given bank. Alternatively, the buyer may obtain the letter on his own in order to induce more favorable treatment by the exporter. In brief, a letter of credit is an undertaking given by a bank to a seller to honor the seller's drafts drawn on it if they comply with the restrictions as to terms and amount contained in the L/C and are accompanied by the required documents. The mechanics of a letter of credit transaction are shown in the chart on page 387.

Asking for a letter of credit is somewhat like seeking a loan. Like the bank that loans against drafts for an exporter, the issuing bank may require compensating balances, a measure of control over the goods shipped, and evidence of both parties' credit standing. Where the importer already has a substantial line of credit at the bank, opening the L/C presents no difficulties. The amount that may be drawn under the L/C is simply deducted from the total available on the credit line. While fees on L/C's are low in the United States, they can be very high in Europe and in the less-developed countries, ranging as high as 2 per cent of the maximum amount available under the L/C. Additionally, in many LDC's the importer must deposit a stipulated percentage of the face amount of the loan in a noninterest bearing account. If the importer does not have an established credit line, he must provide additional security to the issuing bank. Bills of lading may be consigned directly to the bank, which will then have unconditional title to the merchandise and control over it until payment is received. Trust receipts may also have to be offered to the bank. Even if the buyer must provide prepayment of part or the full amount of the credit, however, he will still find the L/C valuable.

The L/C gives three primary benefits to the importer. First, where prepayment is necessary, he is much better off depositing the price of the shipment with his bank than with the seller; if the seller is unable or unwilling to make proper shipment, recovery of the deposit from the bank is not difficult. Second, where prepayment is not required, bank financing through the L/C is comparatively inexpensive for the importer. Third, because the credit standing of the bank is substituted for that of the buyer, the importer may be able to bargain for a lower price and better terms; in effect, the buyer removes the commercial risk for the exporter in return for other considerations.

Even greater benefits are conferred on the exporter. He is assured of payment immediately after shipping the merchandise if the L/C calls

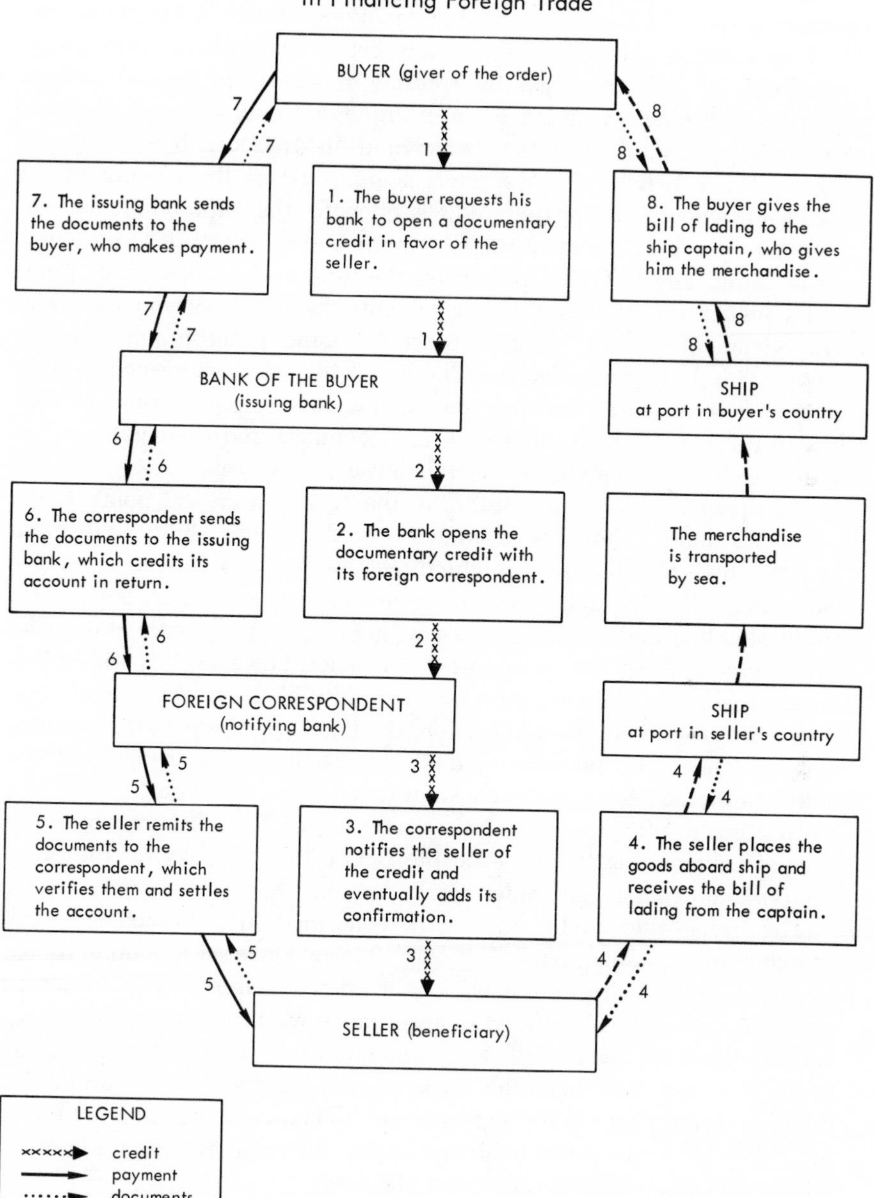
The Traditional Practice in Financing Foreign Trade
BUYER (giver of the order)
1. The buyer requests his bank to open a documentary credit in favor of the seller.
BANK OF THE BUYER (issuing bank)
2. The bank opens the documentary credit with its foreign correspondent.
FOREIGN CORRESPONDENT (notifying bank)
3. The correspondent notifies the seller of the credit and eventually adds its confirmation.
SELLER (beneficiary)
4. The seller places the goods aboard ship and receives the bill of lading from the captain.
SHIP at port in seller's country
The merchandise is transported by sea.
SHIP at port in buyer's country
5. The seller remits the documents to the correspondent, which verifies them and settles the account.
6. The correspondent sends the documents to the issuing bank, which credits its account in return.
7. The issuing bank sends the documents to the buyer, who makes payment.
8. The buyer gives the bill of lading to the ship captain, who gives him the merchandise.
LEGEND
credit
payment
documents
merchandise

for sight drafts. Where the credit calls for time drafts, he receives a banker's acceptance, almost as good as cash, upon presentation of draft and documents. If drafts may be drawn in the currency of his country, and the L/C is issued or "confirmed" by a domestic bank, the seller will encounter none of the exchange risks mentioned in the last section.

The format of the L/C has gradually been standardized, although the possibility of differing legal interpretation persists in several nations. There is a striking resemblance, for example, between a Circular Sterling Credit issued by an Australian bank [3] and an American bank's letter of credit. The beneficiary, or exporter, is informed of the amount of the credit, on whose account the credit is opened (the importer's), and the dates before which shipment must be made and drafts must be presented to the bank. The L/C also prescribes the time of drafts (sight or time) and a precise description of the documents that must accompany drafts. The documents, for the most part, are the same as those normally presented with drafts for collection. The list of the standard terms is a short general description of the shipment; detailed description would be useless to the bank, which deals only in documents and does not conduct a thorough inspection of the merchandise in any case.

The specification of revocability of the L/C is a critical point. If the buyer has doubts about the transaction or the seller's ability and intent to fulfill his obligations, he might direct his bank to issue a *revocable* letter of credit. Through this instrument, the bank attests to the buyer's credit standing and affirms its own willingness to pay drafts authorized by the credit. From the viewpoint of the seller, however, this willingness to pay is sharply circumscribed by the ability of the buyer to withdraw the credit. Indeed, at any point before the bank actually pays the exporter in accordance with this form of L/C, the credit can be revoked *without notice* to the beneficiary. The constant danger that the exporter may take costly steps to place goods in transit only to find himself bereft of assurance of payment makes the revocable L/C extremely risky for the beneficiary. The experienced trader rarely uses it.

The *irrevocable* credit, advised or confirmed by a branch or correspondent of the issuing bank, is the usual form. Once set in motion by the buyer, the machinery of the bank will operate automatically to accept and process documents offered in accordance with the terms of the L/C. Second thoughts, even violent remonstrations by the buyer, are of no avail. The bank will thereafter insist on accepting authorized drafts, for it has its own reputation for dependability to maintain. An unhappy buyer must then recompense his bank or sacrifice his collateral, his trade reputation, and his good relations with the bank.

Notice of the credit in his favor is usually transmitted from the opening bank to the exporter through a branch or correspondent near the beneficiary. This second bank may be asked only to *advise*, or inform, the

[3] Shaterian, *op. cit.*, p. 405.

beneficiary without undertaking responsibility to any party. Alternatively the second bank may be requested to *confirm* the credit, thus adding its own promise to accept or to pay the exporter's draft to that of the first bank.

An advising bank may also negotiate to discount the banker's acceptance held by the exporter after presenting a time draft to the bank designated in the L/C. A confirming bank, on the other hand, is obligated to do so. The exporter sometimes considers this obligation to be very valuable. He therefore may seek to have a L/C confirmed at his own expense at a local bank. In most cases the local bank will consider the proposition virtually riskless and confirm for a nominal fee.

When a letter of credit is denominated in the currency of the exporting country and is confirmed by a local bank that has been designated as the drawee for the exporter's drafts, the exporter is said to have a *straight credit*. In such cases the beneficiary will either receive immediate payment on his sight draft or discount the acceptance of his time draft at leisure with no danger of losses through foreign exchange blockage or fluctuations. When the exporter holds a *negotiation credit*, denominated in foreign currency and designating a foreign bank as drawee, he is free to discount his time drafts at the local bank that offers the best terms. Although recourse to the beneficiary may be demanded by the negotiating bank, its rate will be determined by the bank's evaluation of the issuing bank's guarantee of acceptance.

A third form of L/C is the *circular commercial credit*. Like the other two forms, the circular credit hinges on the irrevocable obligation of a foreign bank; but here the guarantee is not supplemented by the advice or confirmation of a local bank. Drafts are denominated in foreign currency and drawn on a foreign bank generally well known to the beneficiary and local banks. Time drafts may be sold or discounted locally at the discretion of the beneficiary. Circular credits are used extensively by Australian banks.

It is estimated that more than one quarter of the drafts and documents presented to banks under letters of credit contain discrepancies or omissions of some sort. No matter how minor the error, banks will refuse to pay or accept a draft when the requirements of the L/C are not met precisely. If the receiving bank overlooks the mistake and the buyer refuses to *waive* his rights to specific performance, the paying bank will have to exercise its right of recourse; this prospect is unpleasant for both parties.

A good portion of the errors and omissions caught by the bank are quickly corrected by the exporter. In many cases, however, the discrepancy cannot be eliminated, and more formal action is required if the transaction is to be completed. At all times the issuing bank will act according to the instructions of its customer, the importer, regarding discrepancies. If the buyer agrees to waive a requirement, the seller may count himself fortunate; at most, he has had to finance the transaction two or three days longer than anticipated and pay for a few cables.

If the importer refuses to waive, the situation becomes more complex. Unlike less formal methods of consummating a transaction, the preparation of documents under a L/C cannot be adjusted easily to handle last minute contingencies. If an amendment is contemplated, all parties—importer, exporter, issuing bank, and confirming bank—must agree to it. At the very least, settling on amendments takes time and trouble. The trouble is compounded for the seller, however, who is prevented from obtaining payment or financing for his time draft. Occasionally, the importer will need title to the shipment as badly as the exporter needs cash. This fortunate convergence of interests will spur both parties to a quick and amicable settlement. More often the party that is more thinly capitalized comes out on the short end.

In many countries minor mistakes and omissions will be accepted by the bank if the seller places a *guarantee* with it. The exporter promises to hold the bank blameless and make a full refund if the buyer refuses to waive a requirement of the L/C. By giving this guarantee, however, the seller removes the protective umbrella of the L/C. His own credit is placed on the line instead of that of the banks and the buyer.

Variations on Basic Instruments

The Far Eastern Authority to Purchase is a formidable instrument that resembles a letter of credit in form but not in effect. It is intended to enable a trusted agent to gather together goods for shipment, or to secure scarce commodities in an extreme seller's market situation by making, in effect, a down payment in a form which legally binds the seller to supply the goods in the future. Procedurally, drafts are drawn on the buyer, and the bank is simply conveying its willingness to negotiate the exporter's drafts on the buyer. This promise is of little value if the exporter already enjoys a sizable line of credit at a local bank. His bank is more likely to subtract the amount advanced to the exporter from its credit line than it would be if an L/C were involved. The obligations of the buyer and issuing bank are not unconditional as under the L/C, and this fact is reflected in the size of the discount by the exporter's bank. The negotiating bank will insist on the right of recourse to the beneficiary.

Regardless of the use of drafts negotiated under a "Far East Clause," delivery of documents will be made only upon payment. Insistence on the so-called *D/P draft* (documents released against payment), requiring payment before delivery, protects both the exporter and the bank. The Authority to Purchase does not warrant sufficient confidence on the exporter's part to draw a time draft and allow delivery against the buyer's acceptance of the draft; this practice, or the use of a *D/A draft* (documents released against acceptance) requires more security.

The authority to purchase may be deemed attractive when the issuing bank is known to take special care in assessing the applicant's creditworthiness. The Far Eastern bank of issue will also extend important services to the buyer and seller. The bank will clear the shipment through customs, arrange and pay for warehousing the goods until the draft matures. The importer will pay a hefty rate of interest along with the face amount of the draft at maturity; but the exporter can obtain immediate payment without taking responsibility for these services even when the right of recourse is exercised.

Contrastingly, authorities to pay are issued by a foreign bank to allow the exporter rather than the buyer to draw drafts on a local bank. Negotiation is commonly done without recourse, a comparatively rare occurrence under the authority to purchase. Again, however, the obligation of the drawee bank is not unconditional. There is little difference between the authority to pay and the revocable L/C. The buyer may therefore offer an authority to pay when he anticipates a sharp drop in market prices in the near future. If he does not feel constrained by the underlying contract for sale, he will take advantage of the new buyers' market and withdraw his promise.

In the absence of any credit security the exporter will find his chief asset in the authority to pay to be its protection against foreign exchange risks. As with L/C's opened on behalf of importers in soft currency countries, the opening bank will clear the transaction in advance with exchange control administrators. Hence the authority is as effective in this respect as the L/C.

Occasionally a foreign bank designated as payee under a letter of credit will request an authority to pay from the importer's bank. The authority is sought as evidence of the buyer's intent to waive a specific right under the terms of the credit. In effect the payee is asking the buyer: "Will you give me the option to pay the beneficiary of your credit if he fails to meet the following requirement?" The exporter's ability to discount his draft will hinge on the reply.

In the same class as the authorities to purchase and pay are *Standby L/C's.*[4] They usually allow for sight drafts to be drawn at any time during a specific period up to a maximum amount and accompanied only by a simple statement that the beneficiary is owed a certain amount by the opener of the L/C.

In the United States and most other capitalist nations, the basic framework for export-import financing provided by private banks allows for considerable flexibility and imagination. Credits are not classified simply as revocable or irrevocable, confirmed or unconfirmed. They are also listed as export or import credits, assignable or nonassignable credits, and revolving credits, which in turn may be described as cumulative or noncumulative and/or periodic. For present purposes, the distinction between export and import credits is meaningless. The export credit estab-

[4] *Ibid.*, pp. 415–417.

lished for the seller is identical to the import credit established by the buyer.

A L/C may be *assigned,* thus giving a negotiating bank authority to pay all or part of the credit to a third party. This party is designated by the beneficiary of the L/C. The beneficiary of an assignable credit is usually not the manufacturer of the goods shipped. The assignable L/C is frequently used by thinly capitalized middlemen who cannot pay their suppliers in cash. With their own poor financial standing precluding bank loans to pay suppliers, these middlemen seek to transfer credits proffered by their foreign buyers to the suppliers.

Importers and banks are generally wary of such requests. In most countries custom or law has prevented the transfer of credits not expressly made assignable. In no case may a credit be assigned more than once, although different parts of a *divisible* credit may be assigned to different parties. These precautions have been taken to protect the importer. His contract is with the exporter even if the exporter is only a broker or export merchant. The importer may have means to offset malperformance by his beneficiary; if so, he will not relish the thought of losing this influence and having to trace through a maze of transfers to correct an error on his order.

The advantages of an assignable credit to an exporter are as follows: First, despite his poor credit standing and slim capital reserves he can obtain financing for his transaction. Second, he is able to keep his customer and supplier dependent on him by substituting his own invoices for those of the manufacturer; so long as suppliers and customers do not know each other's identity, they are dependent upon the good offices of the exporter.

The *revolving credit* is used to cover a series of transactions over a specified period of time. This credit is valuable where the importer is unwilling to open a single letter of credit to cover each shipment from a frequent supplier over a period of months or years. By establishing a revolving credit the bank sets a limit on the credit available at any one point, but allows the retirement of earlier obligations to replenish the importer's credit line. So long as the importer properly retires acceptances at maturity, the credit is more or less automatically extended.

Revolving credits are either cumulative or noncumulative. If cumulative, the beneficiary can make up in later periods whatever he fails to ship under the credit in the current period. Of course if the credit is noncumulative, the exporter who fails to produce documentary drafts covering an amount equal to the total credit in each period has simply lost a sales opportunity.

The cumulative provision of a revolving credit is intended to limit or increase the total liability of an importer in any one period. A kindred purpose is served by the periodic revolving credit. This form of credit sets the time limits within which partial shipments must be made by the exporter. For example, if the credit is good for a year and covers a total of thirty equal shipments, the periodic credit may stipulate that no more than three shipments may be made in any month. The purpose of such a provision is to restrain the importer's inventory at manageable levels.

As previously indicated, commercial banks usually prefer short-term, self-securing, and self-liquidating loans. Nonetheless, many influential customers are able to use the banks' collection and acceptance facilities for longer-term, essentially unsecured credit extensions. Financing has been extended to cover increasingly longer periods after shipment, by lengthening the maturities of time drafts and acceptances. Other devices are employed to increase the availability of financing prior to shipment.

Under circumstances kindred to those giving rise to the assignable credit, the *Back to Back* credit was developed to finance the acquisition of materials. When the buyer refuses to allow assignment or transfer, the prospective exporter will approach his own bank with his irrevocable L/C and try to open a domestic L/C on behalf of his supplier. The exporter's ability to meet his obligations on the second L/C hinges on the importer's prompt payment or acceptance of drafts drawn under the original L/C. The difference in invoice values between the first and second credits represents the exporter's profit. The cost of this arrangement to the exporter will equal the bank's charge for opening the domestic L/C plus, where applicable, its discount on his acceptance.

If a discrepancy in documents or some unforeseen contingency delays the exporter's proceeds, however, he may be placed in a desperate situation. Typically the chain reaction that follows default anywhere along the line will injure all parties with the possible exception of the original supplier or manufacturer.

The *red clause* represents still another method of financing the procurement of supplies for resale abroad. When inserted into a L/C, this clause authorizes the exporter to make drawings against the total amount available under the L/C. The risk of default by the exporter is borne entirely by the importer, who contracts to repay the unpaid advance and all interest charges accruing thereon. For obvious reasons the red clause is used only when the importer is dealing with his own purchasing agent or someone he can trust completely. The clause may be necessary because the agent is in turn dealing with shoestring operators who need immediate cash payment. The red clause is safer than providing an itinerant agent or broker with cash, and at the same time it enables the agent to take quick action when an opportunity arises.

Production-export credits [5] seem to offer the prospective exporter the soundest and often the cheapest means of financing the early stages of a transaction. The exporter arranges a loan from his bank after receiving notification of the importer's irrevocable L/C in his favor. The exporter must produce a bona fide sales contract, prove that he can meet its requirements, and show that his customer is both legally bound and natu-

[5] Wilbert Ward and Henry Harfield, *Bank Credits and Acceptances,* New York, The Ronald Press Co., 1958, pp. 115–116.

rally inclined to pay in due course. If satisfied with the exporter's assertions, the bank will finance the acquisition of materials, assembly, and shipment by accepting and discounting a draft on itself. The exporter's bank will time its placement so that the acceptance will mature when the transaction is completed. In Germany the procedure differs in that exporters may simply be granted *overdraft* facilities. In many countries, the use of overdrafts is restricted or forbidden by law.

To qualify for either acceptance or overdraft financing of the production period, the exporter must have an exceptionally strong credit position. He might also have to submit to restrictions imposed by the bank. For example, the bank may specify the currency in which drafts are to be denominated; the bank may also take a lien on goods in production.

Financing after shipment, or *refinancing*, is a category that may include all extensions of credit to an importer. In Great Britain,[6] for example, refinancing involves two distinct operations. This bank first accepts the usance draft of a foreign buyer, then pays the seller's sight draft. Discounting the buyer's accepted usance draft provides the funds with which to pay the seller's sight draft.

Refinancing on an acceptance basis is also done by banks in the United States. The effect upon the importer is the same as what would have occurred if he had opened a time credit at the outset. The buyer must, however, pay a second commission for refinancing.

In Germany the financing of imports through the stages of shipping and resale may be performed by the *Lombard loan*.[7] When "Lombarding" a bank may become more than a mere holder of title for value. Goods can be consigned directly to the banks, which releases them to the importer on presentation of a warrant similar to a trust receipt.

The goods or a portion thereof are legally owned by the bank until the importer sells them. Only at the point of sale is the importer's obligation to repay the bank actualized. A specified percentage of the resale price, plus interest on the loan, is then remitted to the bank. If the bank does not wish to hold the loan to maturity, it may rediscount the loan with the *Deutsche Bundesbank*.

The Lombard loan is particularly desirable when the possibility of a drop in the value of an import exists. Loans may cover up to 80 per cent of the invoice value of a shipment. The first 20 per cent of any loss on resale is borne by the importer, but the bank takes the loss on any further decline in value. Lombard loans are therefore very popular in financing bulk importation of perishables. Interest rates are higher than those on acceptance credits, but usually below the rates for other business loans. Kindred participations by private banks have occurred in Great Britain,

[6] For U.S. practices, *see* Sauter, *op. cit.*, vol. I, pp. 76–77; British practices are well explained in H. H. Thackstone, "The Methods of Financing Foreign Trade," in *Banking and Foreign Trade*, Oxford, International Banking Summer School, 1952, pp. 142–143.

[7] Passing reference to the Lombard loan is made in Lee C. Nehrt, *Financing Capital Equipment Exports*, Scranton, Pa., International Textbook Co., 1966, p. 52.

where the plan has also served to limit risk as well as provide financing.

American banks are often legally restrained from creating acceptances that do not arise directly from domestic or international trade. Transactions wholly within the borders of another country are supposedly out of bounds. There are important exceptions to this rule, however, especially in the treatment of consignments. Even after goods are landed and stored on consignment to an agent in France, for example, an American bank may still open a L/C for a French purchaser of the goods.

In such cases drafts on the American bank may be drawn up to six months tenor. Occasionally the differential between interest rates on French loans and discount rates on American acceptances may be so great that the Frenchman will take the full six months available to him. Perhaps also the importer anticipates a sharp alteration in exchange rates that may warrant either immediate payment (or even "leads") or the longest maturities possible ("lags").

Summary of Bank Instruments

The influence of leads and lags on financing provides a suitable introduction to a summary of this section. The speculative participation of importers and exporters on the exchange markets has tremendous impact on the relative popularity of various financial instruments, as well as on the balance of payments among nations. Selection of the proper instrument, offering the proper maturity, might reduce the real cost of an import by one-half the original amount.

In evaluating the various forms of bank and nonbank financing, traders will closely examine each method or instrument in the light of:

1. Anticipated trends in exchange rates
2. Interest rate differentials between countries and between instruments offering the same protection
3. The burden on managerial time involved in the use of each method.

Illustrative of this last consideration, small firms with busy executives may prefer to entrust all export sales to a confirming house or a broker. Even though bank services may seem cheaper, management simply does not have the time to fret over correspondence, documentation, insurance, or negotiation of acceptances. With these factors in mind, we may begin our assessment of nonbank methods of financing international trade.

PRIVATE, NONBANK SOURCES OF SHORT-TERM FINANCING

Export Merchants

One alternative means of financing exports is to work through export merchants or confirming houses. Many exports from the United States before World War I were handled in this manner.[8] Wherever credit in-

[8] Shaterian, *op. cit.*, pp. 3–7.

formation on foreign buyers is inadequate or banks are unable to provide credit facilities, manufacturers may resort to these institutions.

As may be gathered from the previous sections on assignable and back to back credits, transactions between manufacturers and export merchants have only a remote relation to the question of export financing. Such transactions may properly be classified as domestic sales; only a small price adjustment and special packing distinguish the export merchant's order. Export merchant's purchases from domestic suppliers are therefore excluded from further consideration in this study.

Open Account

Sales on open account are perhaps the least complicated of all foreign trade transactions. The buyer simply charges his purchases, and his account is carried on the books of the exporter like any other receivable. The exporter assumes the full burden of risks of foreign exchange blockage and buyer default or insolvency.

Where the importer is allowed to pay in his own currency and payment schedules are erratic, the exporter may not even be able to cover adequately the risk of exchange rate deterioration on the forward market. Collections from foreign customers are sometimes difficult and costly. The absence of a contract on many sales compounds the legal hazards facing the exporter who extends credit on open account. For these reasons, open account terms are extended only to dependable customers in nations that are relatively free of economic and sociopolitical problems.

Cash in Advance

Diametrically opposed to the lax collection methods implied by the extension of credit on open account is the exporter's insistence on advance payment by the buyer. This method, of course, places the full burden of financing on the importer. Foremost among the reasons for demanding full or partial advances [9] is the importer's poor credit standing or reputation for misdealing. At times, however, the exporter's fear of exchange blockage or political upheaval in the importing country may outweigh considerations of individual credit-worthiness. Where the credit standing of the buyer is marginal, the exporter may demand cash in advance if the sale involves goods specially manufactured for the importer that cannot be easily disposed of on the open market. Sometimes the buyer himself will offer cash in advance of shipment; he may wish to get his funds out of the country before exchange restrictions are imposed, or he may be trying to foster good relations with the seller for future negotations. Resistance of both importers and foreign exchange control authorities in the buyer's country has kept the volume of advance payments to a minimum.

[9] John M. Dyer and Frederick C. Dyer, *Export Financing: Modern U.S. Methods*, Coral Gables, Fla., University of Miami Press, 1963, p. 16.

Consignments

Merchandise for export may be consigned to or placed in the hands of the exporter's own agent or subsidiary; an independent broker, agent or import house may also take possession at the direction of the exporter. Consignment to the latter group raises most of the same problems encountered in open account transactions. A recent survey by Morgan Guaranty Trust Company, entitled *Export and Import Procedures,* contains a complete list of precautions to be taken in dealing with both groups.

Factoring

If an American merchant has trouble collecting on open account sales, or if the banks are unwilling to collect notes receivable or loan against them, the exporter may turn to a factor.[10] Factors' rates on domestic accounts are believed to be much higher than those of banks, but not without good cause. Factors are often approached as a last resort by businessmen who need funds badly and/or have little hope of collecting. In some industries, however, factors are frequently used as collection agents and short-term lenders. Where a firm's notes and receivables are discounted with recourse to the borrower, rates are more reasonable.

According to recent reports, factoring has taken a very different course in international trade. Edge Act Corporations' financing against receivables on a with-recourse basis provides competition to factoring houses. Although one authority described "the total financial resources of the Edge Act Corporations as too small for them to become an important source of financing in the future,"[11] the statement seems misleading. It fails to mention the possibility of parent banks' contributions to the capital bases of these corporations. The statement also fails to take into account some of the more recent innovations by commercial banks and factors. A network of firms providing factoring services in several countries has been organized to compete directly with the extensive networks of commercial banks. The network, International Factors Group, claims that its charges are nominal, its resources extensive, and the savings to its clients considerable.

The main advantage in using international factors is their swift and inexpensive credit investigation and collection on foreign receivables. Even if an exporter chooses not to discount his foreign receivables with a factor, he can still utilize the factor's facilities to estimate a prospective account's credit-worthiness. If he discounts his receivables without recourse, many factors will assume all risks—business and political—of nonpayment except where a dispute exists between parties to the transaction. In discounting without recourse, the factor will insist on authorizing all

[10] Nehrt, *op. cit.*, pp. 98–100.
[11] *Ibid.*, p. 100.

credit extensions. If credit is granted by the factoring house, it will pay the exporter immediately and collect a service fee and interest for the agreed length of the credit. A cutoff point is also set, indicating the date beyond which the factor must assume all costs if the buyer remains in default.

By using such a network of international factors, an exporter is able to take the initiative in credit sales and assure that his terms accord with local practice and competitors' offerings. At the same time, the small firm can avoid the costs of a foreign credit and collection section. Where the sale is in a country serviced by a network like the International Factors Group, the exporter can permit payments in local currency, thus offering considerable incentive to buy his product and letting the factor assume the task of currency conversion as well.

THE ROLE OF GOVERNMENT: REGULATION AND SHORT-TERM FINANCING OF INTERNATIONAL TRADE

State Trading

The extent of active participation of governments in short-term financing varies tremendously from country to country. In the Soviet Union and Eastern Europe where almost all trade is financed by state trading and manufacturing organs, the use of private financial institutions has thus far been precluded. Private commercial banking is not allowed in these countries, and individual transactions are made within the framework of intergovernmental trade agreements. Payments for Eastern Bloc transactions have been made in commodities specified in barter agreements and accounted for in "clearing units," which normally have no monetary value outside of the agreement. Clearing units do become important and West European banks may play an important role, however, when a substantial imbalance in trade develops despite the dictates of the agreement.

"Switch trading," or the elimination of these imbalances in barter trade between two or more nations, consists largely of matching up the material needs of traders outside the agreement nations with surpluses within the bloc. It calls for great knowledge and negotiating skill on the part of its practitioners. Only a few banks, most of them in Zurich and Vienna, will take on the obligations of switch trading.[12] Although switch traders are naturally secretive about their deals, and although some switches are complex beyond the layman's comprehension, the underlying principles of switching are simple. For example, in the reconciliation of an imbal-

[12] The following articles on switch trading give a good outline of procedures: "How Switch Trading Works," *The Economist*, January 14, 1967; "East-West Trade Pulls a 'Switch,'" *Business Week*, March 11, 1967.

ance in barter transactions between Brazil and Rumania, both countries, having currencies of little value to prospective trading partners, have attempted to husband their hard currency reserves by circumventing the foreign exchange market. Brazilian coffee and Rumanian machinery are therefore given arbitrary unit prices in "clearing dollars," and it is agreed that $1,000,000 in commodities would be exchanged in the following year.

Within a few months, however, the Rumanians have built up a sizable credit in unneeded coffee. By the end of the year, the Brazilians were clamoring for Rumania to buy $500,000 worth of coffee. To meet its obligations and at the same time to dispose of the unwanted goods, Rumania could enlist the services of a switch trader. A Rumanian official calls one of the Viennese bankers and offers him $500,000 (clearing) in coffee at a discount of 30 to 40 per cent. The trader, having ascertained the actual value of the coffee (in real dollars), calls European businessmen and other contacts who might pick up the credit. Eventually he finds a buyer who is willing to take the coffee and offers 65 per cent in hard currency for the corresponding credit in clearing dollars. The broker makes 2 per cent on the deal by setting his own discount at 37 per cent. Rumania receives 63 per cent of its $500,000 credit in hard currency for the coffee it has earned with its machinery exports. Another European importer takes the coffee and pays $500,000 minus a 35 per cent discount. All parties gain with the possible exception of Brazil, which may shortly find itself undersold in world coffee markets by the unexpected dumping of its own produce.

For the purposes of this study, the importance of both barter and switch trading is slight. Their volume, as closely as it can be measured, is a very small part of international trade. The probability of a private Western manufacturing corporation participating directly in such a deal is small. Switch deals are usually conducted on the level of bankers and brokers, and barter trade seldom appeals to private importers and exporters. When private corporations export directly to a nation in the Communist Bloc, they generally do business on a cash basis or with the aid of the government credit insurance and guaranty programs described below.

Government Credit Insurance and Guaranty Programs

As stated earlier, thorough insurance coverage is of critical importance in arranging for external financing. Without insurance the disposition of goods in transit or in the hands of a foreign buyer is in doubt. Unless the trader can offer a safe form of collateral, he will not obtain advances against collections abroad. In this context it is easy to understand the importance of government credit insurance and guarantees.

Government insurance policies and programs in the more developed countries of Western Europe, North America, and Japan are similar. In most of these countries the government cooperates with private insurance firms to augment the types of coverage and to insure poor risk propositions. The dominant concern of government has been political risk coverage, and the extent of such coverage has mushroomed over the past decade.

In the United States [13] the Export-Import Bank has restricted its repayment guarantees chiefly to medium-term credits, but it offers a preshipment guaranty to cover the production period for American exports as well. This guaranty of loan repayment is made to the exporter's bank, enabling the exporter to obtain advances against his foreign orders. Eximbank also provides political risk insurance for consignments held abroad and in rare cases will itself advance funds to an exporter.

Even more active in the short-term field, however, is the Foreign Credit Insurance Association. FCIA offers two types of short-term coverage in cooperation with the Eximbank: [14] comprehensive risk insurance and political risk insurance. The comprehensive policy covers commercial risks of buyer insolvency and default, as well as everything covered in the political risk policy. The latter policy insures against alteration of foreign government regulations that prevents importation, charges arising from diversion of shipment for political reasons, war and civil disturbance, and all forms of governmental expropriation and destructive interference.

Under these policies, 90–95 per cent of losses are recoverable so long as:

1. Payment for the export was to be made in United States dollars
2. No negligence of the exporter is evident
3. At least half of the value of the shipment is traceable to United States labor and materials
4. The loss is not insurable under another policy
5. Loss is properly reported within eight months
6. No dispute between buyer and seller as to responsibility for loss is left unsettled.

With a special amendment up to 60 per cent of losses due to a buyer's refusal to take delivery may be recoverable. In no case, however, are losses due to exchange rate fluctuation or devaluation insurable.

The average cost of the comprehensive policy is $.50 per $100.00 of invoice value. The exporter may apply for FCIA policies directly or through his own broker; he will receive a rate quotation and notice of the total amount insurable (on a revolving basis) on the basis of the infor-

[13] Morgan Guaranty, *op. cit.*, pp. 55–58; "Selling Abroad with Credit Insurance," an FCIA pamphlet (no facts of publication given); and "Washington Agencies That Help Finance Foreign Trade," 4th ed., New York, Bankers Trust Co., 1964, pp. 5–7. These publications appraise the FCIA and Eximbank programs.

[14] Francis X. Scafuro, "A Review of U.S. Export Insurance," New York, FCIA, undated, unpaginated.

mation on his application form. He may at the same time request coverage of goods shipped on consignment, of sales from consigned stocks abroad (at half the regular premium rate), and of goods in production. If he accepts the FCIA rate and terms, the exporter will make an advance premium deposit; he then remits a monthly premium along with a regular report describing his shipments covered by the policy.

Two principal drawbacks are sometimes attributed to FCIA-Eximbank policies. First, an inordinate length of time is required to process applications, and an applicant may risk losing his customer if he waits for FCIA approval too long. Second, the burden or paperwork on applications, monthly reports, and claims is considerable. At times banks or foreign freight forwarders can relieve this second burden but only for a price.

The FCIA program has been explained because it is fairly typical of the programs offered in major industrial nations. Credit insurance schemes in other countries will be examined later in this chapter. As one can well imagine, once a comprehensive policy is obtained the exporter will have far less difficulty financing his foreign transactions than he would have without insurance or with only a commercial risk policy.

Government Financing for Selected Exports

Since well before the Industrial Revolution governments have for various reasons subsidized or financed the exportation of certain commodities. The reasons for this financing vary widely. Perhaps the industry involved was depressed or was in danger of becoming depressed, e.g., the agricultural sector in the United States. Or perhaps exportation of the commodity made some real or imagined contribution to total welfare and national political power; hence the subsidization of fine linen exports in eighteenth-century France. Most often the reason seems to have been a combination of the above, as was the case of Eximbank loans for arms purchases in the United States.

Whatever the reasons, some methods of government financing are among the most complex encountered in international trade. Indeed, flat rebates and subsidies are being replaced in many places by more subtle forms of aid. The provision of foreign exchange to importers at favorable rates by exchange control authorities and the use of multiple exchange rates to maximize export earnings, for example, go beyond mere government regulation. The meticulousness with which applications for foreign exchange are prepared in countries like Brazil should demonstrate amply that classification of commodities for import or export is often tantamount to financing. If an import falls into the right category, it might cost the buyer half as much as it would bring on a free market.

The penchant for complexity is not confined to exchange control authorities in less-developed countries. Few programs can rival the American method of financing agricultural exports in intricacy. The Department of Agriculture, the Commodity Credit Corporation, the Agency for International Development, Eximbank, and private enterprise all take a hand.

It is not the purpose of this chapter to describe in detail the special financing available in different countries for particular commodities. Suffice it to say that in almost every nation sectors of industry deemed crucial to economic development are good candidates for special, low cost government financing. Often this financing entails considerable burden for the recipient in terms of detailed applications and time-consuming interviews. Nonetheless, the benefits are generally conceded to outweigh any direct or implicit costs.

Both individually and in cooperation with such multilateral institutions as the World Bank and International Development Association, the governments of several industrial nations provide indirect financing for exports through buyer credits and loans to less-developed countries. The United States, which pioneered in the organization of development loan funds, once again provides an exemplary program.[15] In a recent year loans to foreign buyers accounted for nearly one billion dollars in exports, or roughly 4 per cent of American sales abroad. The share of AID financing tied to American exports grew from 50 per cent to 85 per cent between 1960 and 1964.

Most procurement by recipients of AID loans is conducted through the regular L/C channels. Exporters may discover sales opportunities by keeping track of AID purchase authorizations to foreign buyers; these are described in several government publications and press releases. Where the submission of bids is required by the foreign borrower, AID will also finance preliminary studies by American bidders and ensure that all bids are given consideration.

To qualify as a supplier to AID loan recipients, the United States exporter usually must show that 90 per cent of the value of his product is of American origin. AID will normally refuse financing to foreign applicants who wish to buy luxury goods, goods which are specifically denied importation into the United States, or goods which on balance are imported into this country. Payment to United States exporters is made immediately in dollars upon presentation of drafts and documents to the bank issuing or confirming a L/C. The only document not regularly needed in L/C transactions is the AID Supplier's Certificate; the importer will advise his supplier of the specific form of this document required in each case. Exporters must also maintain complete records of their AID-financed sales for examination by government auditors.

In any appraisal of the effect of tied loans and development financing on international commerce, it must be noted that significant departures

15 AID, *Commercial Exports under A.I.D. Programs,* Washington, D.C., Office of Material Resources, 1965.

from the normal rules of *caveat emptor* are usually implied. Occasionally an exporter will be called upon to justify a price quotation with an extensive cost breakdown. For greater assurance of payment an exporter must sacrifice time and money to keep abreast of sales opportunities and to prepare documents. The foreign freight forwarder or combined export manager can be of great help to inexperienced firms. But the burden is still on the exporter.

The loan recipient frequently must bear a kindred burden. It is often alleged that in order to receive a development loan, an importer must first prove that he does not need it. The prospect of opening his books to the agent of a foreign government also may be distasteful to an importer. In return for the loan and the protection he receives, the importer must take pains to justify his choice of suppliers, if indeed he has a choice at all. Despite these drawbacks, financing of this sort is increasingly important and will be discussed further in the following sections on medium- and long-term financing.

MEDIUM- AND LONG-TERM FINANCING

The distinctions between bank, government, and private nonbank financing are less precise in the medium and long ranges. How, for example, would one classify the Export Procurement Corporation of New York, a confirming house (similar in some respects to the export merchandising firms that dominated American trade before World War I) that deals almost exclusively in nonrecourse discounting of FCIA-Eximbank insured notes? EPC has been lumped together with factors and international banks, and it competes directly with both.[16]

In Japan the distinction between public and private financing is even more tenuous. Branches of foreign banks and the so-called city banks, which monopolize foreign trade financing, act as agents for the government Export-Import Bank when dealing with medium- and long-term maturities. The private banks will provide credit only for the uncovered portion of the Japanese Eximbank participations and charge very high rates for this service. All credits are insured with the Ministry of International Trade and Industries (MITI).[17]

A kindred arrangement prevails at this time in West Germany. The Hermes Bank serves as a government agent on questions of medium- and long-term insurance coverage. A consortium of banks called the Ausfuhrkredit-AG or AKA offers varying types of credit to exporters and apportions participations among its members when large credits are requested.

[16] Paul Hirsch, Export Procurement Corporation, interview with the author in New York, August 1, 1967; Nehrt, *op. cit.*, pp. 99–100.

[17] Nehrt, *op. cit.*, p. 25.

Private Financing

A few methods and instruments remain wholly in private hands. One device, the *deferred payment credit,* is used increasingly by American commercial banks to circumvent Federal Reserve provisions forbidding the use of banker's acceptances to extend credit offerings beyond 180 days. An American exporter may, for example, present shipping documents to his bank on the understanding that the bank will accept his 180-day draft at a specified future date. This arrangement has worked to the satisfaction of foreign importers and with the grudging consent of the banks, but exporters are somewhat less satisfied. Exporters are virtually unprotected between the date of shipment and the date of acceptance. Other banks will not discount his draft without collateral, and the accepting bank is under no obligation to discount the draft before the acceptance date. There is also the possibility that a dissatisfied or dishonest importer can delay payment even longer with a court injunction before the bank can accept and discount the draft.[18]

A less complicated method of medium-term bank financing is available for German exporters. For customers of good standing German banks will increase overdraft facilities on the understanding that the purpose of the loan is to extend export credit. As with short-term overdrafts, this form of financing is very expensive. A similar practice is found in the United Kingdom.[19]

Another alternative available to most exporters is to roll over loans using promissory notes of foreign buyers as collateral. By using only short-term loans, exporters are not locked into a single interest rate over a long time period; therefore they may choose between short- and long-term maturities according to their evaluations of interest rate trends. An inevitable risk is incurred in selecting shorter maturities. In the first place, funds might not be available at all. Second, terms and rates may be quite unfavorable at renewal time.

A final method of bank financing, implied above, is the use of medium- and long-term loans. Using his buyer's notes as collateral, the exporter can time his loan payments to run concurrently with the maturities of these notes. Generally long-term loans against foreign promissory notes entail interest rates second only to rates on overdrafts. Banks will also insist on full insurance coverage and/or a guaranty from a reputable bank or government agency in the importer's country.

Private nonbank sources of financing for medium- and long-term credits are rare. Factors are less active in the purchase of medium-term receivables than they are with maturities of less than six months. One study lists only three factoring organizations in New York that as of September 1966 were willing to discount medium-term bills, drafts, and

[18] Sauter, *op. cit.,* pp. 63–75.
[19] Nehrt, *op. cit.,* p. 51.

notes without recourse to the exporter. It is possible for an American exporter to obtain FCIA or Eximbank permission to dispose of the uncovered portion of his credits through these factors. By discounting the insured or guaranteed portion with a commercial bank or factor on a nonrecourse basis, the exporter can realize quick payment and eliminate his credit risk entirely.[20]

Government Participations

The vast majority of medium- and long-term financing methods involve participation by government agencies or international institutions. It is useful in this regard to distinguish between suppliers' and buyers' credits. Suppliers' credits are exporters' borrowings from local credit institutions: e.g., advances against foreign promissory notes and drafts drawn on and accepted by the importer. An excellent description of buyers' credits (also known as financial credits) from a recent United Nations survey on this subject is reprinted below:

> Buyers' credits are granted directly to the foreign buyer by a credit institution or a consortium of credit institutions in the exporting country in order to enable him to purchase capital goods or services from suppliers in that country on a cash basis, the government of the exporting country guaranteeing repayment under the official export credit insurance scheme. Buyers' credits are relatively substantial, generally exceed five years and are granted in connection with large-scale projects.[21]

Another distinction of note is the proper definition of "medium" and "long" terms. No single definition is universally accepted as yet. In the United States, Federal Reserve restrictions on the use of banker's acceptances provide a convenient dividing line between the short and medium ranges at 180 days. For practical purposes, however, some American bankers define short-term financing to include maturities up to one year in length.[22]

The United States, the United Kingdom, and most other capital goods exporting countries use the definition of medium term that includes maturities between six months and five years. The Italian government, however, sets the lower limit at one year. France is unique in placing the lower limit of so-called medium-term financing at two years. The upper limit of five years is widely accepted, except with regard to the sale of jet aircraft, where seven-year loan maturities are considered medium-term.[23]

[20] *Ibid.*, pp. 98–99.

[21] United Nations, *Export Credits and Development Financing*, New York, U.N. Department of Economic and Social Affairs, 1967, pp. xii–xiii.

[22] Statement of W. E. Page, senior vice-president of Morgan Guaranty Trust Co., before the Senate Foreign Relations Committee hearings on *East-West Trade*, Part II, February 24–26, 1965, Washington, D.C., G.P.O., 1965, p. 89.

[23] Nehrt, *op. cit.*, pp. 3–4.

The above definitions and distinctions are important because they affect the availability of credit in general and the selection of financing methods in particular. In the gradual shift from a seller's to a buyer's market in the postwar period,[24] for example, capital goods exporting nations first resisted pressures from their own exporters and from the governments of less-developed nations for a greater volume of credit and longer maturities. As competition between sellers in different nations grew more intense, however, governments began financing, insuring, and guaranteeing longer and longer maturities to promote exportation. As tied development loans were implemented and bilateral and multilateral aid programs gained momentum, buyers' credits began to replace sellers' credits as the dominant form of financing. Government postures on medium- and long-term credits became crucial to both importers and exporters, who sought for different reasons to get more government support for longer maturities. Despite the resistance of credit insurers, as expressed through the Berne Union (Union d'Assureurs des Credits Internationaux), competitive conditions have required the provision of broader insurance coverage to handle a larger volume of medium- and long-term credits.

Indicative of the pressure on governments to provide more competitive export credit insurance is the record of Italy's insurance system. Tracing its history back to enabling legislation in 1912, one finds few changes between the time the government commenced insuring exports in 1927 and the beginning of the postwar buyer's market. More recently, however, changes seem to be unfolding at an increasing rate. In 1953 and 1961, the system was changed considerably, and reorganization was again proposed in 1965. One provision in particular stands out among recent changes in the Italian insurance system. All exporters domiciled in Italy, whether controlled by foreign or domestic interests, can qualify for medium-term insurance on exports. In attracting foreign investment and improving the nation's balance of payments, this provision can be expected to help Italy's economic development considerably. Like the United States, Italy balances public and private efforts in its insurance system. A government agency, the INA, handles political risk coverage, whereas commercial risks fall within the purview of SIAC, a consortium of private companies.

The Japanese scheme for export credit insurance has been even more volatile. The basic insurance law has been amended in two out of every three years since its passage in 1950. Coverage is ostensibly available to foreign firms domiciled in Japan, but stringent entrance requirements for alien investors has sharply limited the use of this clause. More important has been another facet of the insurance system that protects the businessman against his own miscalculation. If a Japanese

[24] For an account of postwar market conditions and their effect on credits, *see* United Nations study, *op. cit.*, pp. xi–xvii; and Claudio Segré, *Medium-Term Export Finance*, Rome, Banca Nazionale Del Lavoro, 1958, pp. 5–16.

exporter overestimates the amount of goods he can sell on consignment abroad, he can recover a portion of the resulting loss through one of the government policies. On the negative side, the government imposes a "whole turnover" requirement on many clients, so that an exporter must insure all credit sales—even those on which he feels the risk is negligible—if he wants to insure one.

The sharpest contrast between the Japanese and American systems lies in their supporting organizations. Unlike the quasipublic, cooperative plan in the United States, the Japanese credit insurance apparatus for medium- and long-term coverage lies wholly within the sphere of government. The Export Credit Insurance Section of the Ministry of International Trade and Industry issues comprehensive, commercial, and political risk policies. The Insurance Section is authorized to make annual drawings from a special account created by law for its use. Parliament also sets the maximum liability for export credits. The maximum liability for general export insurance coverage grew from 110 billion yen to 1.2 trillion yen between 1957 and 1966. Not only is the government relatively liberal in its coverage, but it is also quick and efficient in its operations. The Japanese exporter, unlike his American counterpart, need not lose time in the processing of applications and claims by a number of private and public agencies.

Thus export credit facilities are changing substantially and rapidly in response to pressures of competition. With these changes importers and exporters adjust their preferences among financial instruments accordingly. Until very recently facilities for rediscounting medium-term notes in the United States were comparatively underdeveloped.[25] This inadequacy made commercial banks reluctant to discount these notes, and their reluctance was reflected in high interest rates. Although it is too early to measure the full impact of Eximbank rediscounting, one may reasonably expect that a greater number of exporters will turn from borrowing on domestic assets to discounting their medium-term promissory notes from foreign buyers. Even if their choice boils down to a selection between medium-term borrowing on domestic assets or discounting *with recourse* at roughly the same rate, exporters are likely to choose the latter method. A primary consideration in this choice, of course, is that the exporting firm's contingent liability on the discounted notes need only be mentioned in a footnote on the balance sheet. Direct borrowing, in contrast, adversely affects the firm's debt-equity ratio and might contribute to a rise in the cost of capital for the exporting firm.[26]

Export Financing in the Centrally Planned Economies

As the finale to the discussion of medium- and long-term financing, we may return to the unique methods of financing foreign trade em-

[25] For accounts of Eximbank's recent rediscounting innovations, *see International Commerce,* August 22, 1966, p. 14; and *The New York Times,* January 30, 1967, p. 1.
[26] Segré, *op. cit.,* p. 30.

ployed in the Communist Bloc. For the short term, barter trade was dismissed as anomalous and of little importance to private importers and exporters. This may be an acceptable oversimplification with regard to short-term financing, but it would be a glaring error to apply the same argument to medium- and long-term credit agreements with the Soviet Bloc.

In some ways barter trade is a very suitable means for conducting transactions involving capital goods.[27] A large proportion of Soviet exports to less-developed countries consists of heavy, expensive machinery. Sale of this machinery requires flexible financing arrangements with importers as well as some device to cut through the distortions of multiple exchange rates and inconvertibility. Barter agreements fulfill both requirements with little complication.

Distortions are already so rife in many less-developed countries that any method of financing that circumvents the foreign exchange markets in these countries is bound to be an improvement. Developing nations are relieved of the need to husband foreign exchange reserves in order to service debts. Credit repayments may be arranged in shipments of traditional exports or industrial goods, *including goods produced on the machinery imported.* This last provision may be used to assure the continuing commitment of the exporter to the efficiency of the equipment.

Although these transactions usually involve the exclusive participation of public agencies, some East European states have offered similar terms to private firms.[28] Despite the many *caveats* to be followed in dealing with government trading organizations, barter agreements seem to provide an acceptable framework within which financing can be arranged in certain less-developed countries.

CONCLUSION

The extension of credit on imports and exports is of vast importance to both parties in a transaction. For many importers the ability to continue operations hinges on the lag between payments by their customers and remittances to foreign suppliers. For exporters, willingness and ability to extend credit are crucial determinants of sales volume and the economies of scale enjoyed by the firm. Evidence of this connection has been provided in a recent survey by the United States Treasury Department.[29] This survey noted a very high correlation between the extension of credit and volume of sales; of the 2,869 American exporters surveyed, the 758 firms offering credit to foreign customers accounted for over 75 per cent of all American exports.

[27] U.N. Study, *op. cit.*, pp. 107, 109.

[28] *Ibid.*, p. xiii.

[29] National Foreign Trade Council, Inc., "Survey on Export Financing," Brochure No. 3212, New York, September 23, 1966, p. 2.

Unfortunately several important forms of credit seem to be the exclusive province of heavily capitalized buyers and sellers. Even with capital goods exportation, where one would expect that widespread government support and low cost insurance programs would make financing available to all exporters, smaller firms often are forced to carry foreign accounts on their own or to offer no credit at all. In 1966 Lee C. Nehrt reported that American exporting firms carried an average of one year's foreign receivables on their books. Small firms in this category, however, were forced to carry receivables for an average of 1.3 years, allegedly because external financing was not available.[30] The size of an individual order may also affect the availability of financing. At least for medium-term credits, it is alleged that banks and government agencies do not want to bother with small credits [31] despite their importance to small but efficient manufacturers.

In light of the above factors, we may summarize some of the more important considerations in selecting a method to finance exports and imports. In dealing with outside sources of financing, all costs—direct and implicit—must be weighed carefully: the costs of compensating balances, extra paper work, and outside controls must be quantified as far as possible. The size of the firm and the amount of credit needed to finance the transaction must be taken into account. The probability of loss arising from political and economic changes must be weighed in selecting both the proper form of insurance and the financial instrument. The effects of borrowing *versus* discounting, with or without recourse, must be assessed beforehand; if the firm's debt-equity ratio would be adversely affected by borrowing, management may wish to discount its acceptance or draft, thus forestalling a rise in the cost of capital. Finally, interest rates on available instruments must be compared.

Almost invariably the banker's acceptance will provide the cheapest means of financing for the exporter and qualified importer. To reiterate, the letter of credit also provides significant reduction of commercial risks for both parties. A growing volume of trade, especially among industrialized nations in the Northern Hemisphere, is conducted on open account. Nonetheless, banks still provide the backbone of international trade through networks of foreign branches and correspondents. For these reasons and others mentioned earlier in the study, the letter of credit will be the most popular instrument for financing international transactions for many years to come.

In appraising any method of financing international transactions with medium- or long-term credits, a firm will pay particular attention to the following questions. First, how important is the question of financing to the importer? What is the probability that the transaction will not take place without an extension of credit? This is an important

[30] Nehrt, *op. cit.*, p. 117.
[31] Segré, *op cit.*, pp. 18–19.

consideration for both parties. Especially for capital goods exports, the manufacturer may require extensive prefinancing before he can even consider a sale. Similarly, the importer's need for financing might drive him from a low cost supplier to a seller who offers longer credit terms.

Second, will the cost of borrowing to the importer be more or less than the cost of discounting or borrowing against his note by the exporter? Naturally both parties will want to minimize the cost of outside borrowing, and a mutually beneficial arrangement might be possible. For example, the exporter may help his customer obtain a low cost buyer's credit or development loan from government or international agencies. If such funds are available, both parties will want to consider how much control they wish to sacrifice to reduce borrowing costs. Government participation, for example, often requires a 10 to 20 per cent down payment by the importer; the exporter may also have to hold 10 or 20 per cent of the outstanding liabilities of the importer without insurance or guaranty.

Third, what type of insurance policy is necessary or desirable? Where a whole turnover stipulation in a low cost insurance program requires the applicant to insure all transactions regardless of risk, the exporter must determine whether the saving on a few shipments is worth the extra expense on others. In particular, both parties will want to examine the cost of various types of coverage in relation to the reduction of borrowing costs attributable to holding such coverage. In Italy this analysis is somewhat complicated because government and private insurance institutions do not provide complete, medium-term commercial risk policies for exporters; to be fully covered, therefore, the exporter must ask his customer to obtain a guaranty on his behalf at a local bank.[32]

Finally, both parties will want to examine the expressed and implied costs of each method of financing. The procedure for evaluating medium- and long-term financial instruments is largely the same as the one described at the end of the section on short-term financing. Careful attention to risks and opportunities in the movement of exchange rates is even more essential in the study of longer range financing.

[32] *Nehrt, op. cit.*, pp. 64–65.

BIBLIOGRAPHY

American Bankers' Association, Credit Policy Committee. *A Banker's Guide to Financing Exports.* (New York: American Bankers' Association, 1963).

Bankers Trust Company. *Washington Agencies That Help Finance Foreign Trade,* 4th ed. (New York: Bankers Trust Company, 1964).

Brown, James S. "Eleven Ways of Financing U.S. Agricultural Exports," *Foreign Agriculture,* September 5, 1966.

Dyer, John M., and Frederick C. Dyer. *Export Financing: Modern U.S. Methods.* (Coral Gables, Fla.: University of Miami, 1963).

"East-West Trade Pulls a 'Switch,'" *Business Week,* March 11, 1967.

First National City Bank. "Your New Export Markets Abroad and How to Reach Them." (New York: FNCB, 1964).

International Banking Summer School. *Commercial Banks in Relation to Medium and Long Term Credit.* Dr. H. H. Haschek, admin. ed. (Vienna: Brüder Rosenbaum, 1964).

International Commerce, November 28, 1966, pp. 6–10.

Morgan Guaranty Trust Company, *Export and Import Procedures.* (New York: MGTC, 1968).

National Foreign Trade Convention, Proceedings of the 53rd. (New York: National Foreign Trade Council, 1967).

National Foreign Trade Council, Inc. "Survey on Export Financing," bulletin no. 3212, September 23, 1966.

Nehrt, Lee C. *Financing Capital Equipment Exports: A Comparative Study of Medium-Term Export Financing.* (Scranton, Pa.: International Textbook Co., 1966).

Sauter, Frank. *Random Notes on Commercial Credits.* (New York: First National City Bank, 1960, vol. I, and 1963, vol. II).

Scafuro, Francis X. "A Review of United States Export Credit Insurance." (New York: FCIA and Bank of America [International], undated).

Segré, Claudio. *Medium Term Export Finance: European Problems and Experience.* (Rome: Banca Nazionale Del Lavoro, 1958).

Shaterian, William S. *Export-Import Banking,* 2nd ed. (New York: The Ronald Press Co., 1956).

Thackstone, H. H. "The Methods of Financing Foreign Trade," *Banking and Foreign Trade.* (Oxford: International Banking Summer School, 1952), pp. 125–150.

United Nations, Department of Economic and Social Affairs. *Export Credits and Development Financing.* (New York: United Nations, 1967).

U.S. Congress, *East-West Trade,* Parts I and II. Hearings before the Senate Foreign Relations Committee. 88th Congress, 2nd Session (Part I) and 89th Congress, 1st Session (Part II). (Washington, D.C.: Government Printing Office, 1964, I, and 1965, II).

U.S. Congress, *Government Guarantees of Credit to Communist Countries.* Hearings before the Senate Banking and Currency Committee, 88th Congress, 1st Session. (Washington, D.C.: Government Printing Office, 1963).

U.S. Department of State, Agency for International Development. "Commercial Exports Under A.I.D. Programs." (Washington, D.C.: Department of State, 1965).

Ward, Wilbert, and Henry Harfield. *Bank Credits and Acceptances.* (New York: The Ronald Press Co., 1958).

Winter Bank of Vienna. "How Switch Trading Works," *The Economist,* January 14, 1967.

Managing International Fund Remittances

11

The rapid postwar growth of business assets in foreign countries has accentuated the need for international financial managers to make *worldwide* analyses of fund resources and needs. Of key importance among the new and more complex problems in international finance is deciding what proportion of affiliate earnings should be reinvested and what proportion should be remitted to the parent company? This query becomes increasingly critical to firms which already have a significant volume of overseas earnings, fund flows, and assets. The advent of increasing restrictions on the international flow of capital has added a further complication to this question.

A Review of Companies' Current Approaches to Managing International Fund Flows

By way of introduction let us review how multinational companies approach the task of effectively managing international fund flows. The following insights are based on extensive interviews with international division executives in thirty of the largest multinational manufacturers.[1]

[1] For a more detailed account *see* David B. Zenoff, "Profitable, Fast Growing, But Still the Stepchild," *Columbia Journal of World Business,* July-August 1967, pp. 51–56, and "Remitting Funds from Foreign Affiliates," *Financial Executive,* March 1968, pp. 46–63.

The decision regarding the amount of foreign-generated funds to be remitted to the parent company is made almost invariably by parent management. The highest echelons of management believe that only they are in a position to appraise correctly what patterns of remittances are in the best interest of the worldwide company. To be sure, many companies request advice from foreign affiliates on how much each should send home—and often the affiliates' recommendations are closely followed. Nevertheless most headquarters managers are sufficiently apprehensive about either the risks in the foreign environment or the ability of the local manager to perceive correctly the headquarters' point of view to forego their prerogatives to make the final remittance decisions.

HOW MANAGERS VIEW THE FOREIGN ENVIRONMENT

It is probably not surprising that business managers feel more uncertain about the foreign business environment than they do about the domestic scene. The managers usually attribute their uneasiness to three principal factors:

1. Being in international business adds to the number of economic, political, and business variables that warrant review
2. It is more difficult to obtain and evaluate information about conditions abroad.
3. A personal familiarity—a "businessman's feel"—for the foreign operating climate in which their companies have investments is lacking.

In response to the higher level of riskiness which they perceive in the foreign environment, most managers have developed both a strong aversion to holding corporate-controlled funds overseas and an acute awareness of the extent to which their equity funds abroad are exposed. Equity from the parent company's viewpoint is normally considered to include a subsidiary's net worth and its long- and short-term debt to the parent. Being exposed is construed to be synonymous with vulnerability to partial or total loss in dollar value.

To avoid being overly exposed abroad (irrespective of how an individual company makes this determination) a wide variety of practices are followed. Many firms limit severely the amount of their initial dollar commitment by keeping the capitalization of the subsidiaries small; some subsequently refuse to provide additional company funds other than through reinvestment of local earnings. Many companies press subsidiaries to maximize their use of local debt sources as the primary means of adding to working capital or for capital expansion purposes. *The majority of firms do not permit their foreign subsidiaries to keep locally-generated funds that are in excess of agreed upon working capital requirements.* Other things being equal, this is the most commonly followed dividend decision rule observed in the sample companies.

With this rule of thumb as a starting point the financial managers of most large multinational companies decide on the exact amount of fund remittances after they have evaluated one or more variables within the firm and/or in the business environment.

For many firms there are a number of methods by which funds can be transferred from one country to another. Dividends, royalties, management fees, repayment of intercompany loans, and interest on these loans are the most prevalent. In this regard it is noteworthy that very few make their decisions regarding international fund movements by considering what *mix* of remittance forms would be most suitable to the company's overall interests. Instead the decision regarding dividends is made *independently* of the decision regarding such flows as royalties and fees. The latter have been found to be a function of:

1. The value of the services and benefits provided the foreign subsidiary
2. The amount allowed by foreign taxing authorities as deductible business expenses
3. The total amount of contribution to the overhead of the international division desired from overseas operations (prorated to each subsidiary)
4. The overall corporate tax picture, including the availability of foreign tax credits and the possibilities of remitting funds in the form of dividends.[2]

Dividend decisions are based on the manager's consideration of one or more of the following variables:

The Subsidiary's Fund Requirements

Frequently, the affiliate's fund requirements are one of the most critical considerations. Many companies permit their foreign subsidiaries to retain funds if they are required for short-term working capital purposes or for planned capital expansion within the forthcoming few months. The excess is remitted to the parent.

The Risk of Devaluation

In a large number of firms the possibility of a currency devaluation within six to eight months leads to an evaluation of how various remittance forms—dividends, royalties, management fees—might be utilized to protect the dollar value of the foreign operation. While there is ample evidence of foreign affiliates having accelerated the timing of their remittances or increasing their size, it is noteworthy that many firms

2 These considerations and the entire matter of selecting a mix of remittance forms will be discussed in depth later in this chapter.

normally do *not* direct their subsidiaries to take action of this type. A possible explanation for this approach is provided by the president of the international division of a large capital goods manufacturer:

> Devaluation is virtually impossible to predict . . . in fact, even the economists don't agree; therefore, what can we expect of our own staff?! Over the years, one hears many rumors of devaluation; if every time I heard a rumor I dropped my work and began to worry what to do about it, I wouldn't have the time to perform my regular duties.

The Tax Variable

Another factor that influences the remittance decision of numerous multinational companies is taxation. While no large firm is indifferent to the tax effects of their decisions, not all of them make a serious attempt to minimize the tax liability to the company as a whole.

To illustrate different emphasis among companies regarding tax considerations, it is useful to categorize companies according to their so-called tax objectives:

1. About one-quarter of the firms, the most tax-conscious, make every attempt to minimize the corporation's total tax burden and normally give this consideration higher priority than any others in the dividend decision.

2. For 35 per cent of the companies, taxes assume considerable importance, and the objective of minimizing the corporation's total tax burden is of about equal importance to one or two other factors such as the risk of leaving funds abroad or the subsidiary's requirements for funds.

3. For a little more than one-fifth of the companies, paying taxes to the United States on dividends received from overseas is considered a fact of doing business, and no effort is made to delay or avoid this obligation. Their main interest in taxes is to avoid what are referred to as penalty taxes—those designed to induce or retard income distribution in particular countries. This approach is illustrated by the excerpt from an interview with an executive of one multinational company:

> There are two angles to this tax rate which we should not confuse. One is tax penalties—for paying too high or too low a dividend. That we try to avoid at all costs. But that merely we have to pay a tax on income—and whether we pay it this year or next—they are about the same. This doesn't bother us. There is no substantial loss [in paying U.S. taxes on foreign dividends] unless one considers the loss from the use of the tax money that may have been paid . . . but for a company like ours that has a substantial amount of ready cash, there is no real loss involved. . . . What I referred to earlier [i.e., penalties] was failure to pay a required dividend and incurring a tax that would not otherwise be paid at all, such as Germany. . . . In general, then, we do not compute in detail in advance what the tax situation is when we try to estimate future dividends.

4. A few multinational corporations assign a generally low level of importance to any kind of tax consideration in relation to the foreign dividend decision and rarely base their decisions on analysis of the tax variable. In many such cases this may be because of the relatively minimal amounts involved.

As would be expected, there is a high degree of correlation between the complexity of the analysis that companies put into the tax consideration and their tax consciousness in the dividend decision. Where tax analysis is of importance, the comptroller usually has the responsibility for advising the decision-maker on the tax effects of various payout decisions that are being considered. Depending upon the composition of the overseas operations (i.e., number of affiliates, their location, and their legal forms) and the tax objectives of the firm, the design of the analysis might include the *total* tax burden to the corporation (foreign plus United States taxes minus United States tax credits) that results from different payout possibilities for each of the foreign subsidiaries. And, companies that extend calculations to this level usually go on to compute the optimum foreign dividend—the payout ratio for each of the overseas operations that will minimize the overall corporate tax liability.

The Parent Company's Dividend Policy

Conversations with the financial managers have revealed that for about one-third of the multinational firms, the proportion of parent company earnings that are paid in dividends to the shareholders strongly influence foreign remittance decisions. This guide is utilized by companies in one of two ways. Some firms use the parent payout figure as the payout goal for the overall foreign operations: the same percentage of the total foreign earnings must be remitted to the parent company, even though for any individual subsidiary the amount declared will not necessarily be identical or even close to that target. As a matter of fact, these companies set the overall target and then proceed on the basis: "Where should we get the money?" There is no systematic attempt made to receive a certain percentage of each subsidiary's earnings.

Other companies approach the decision by establishing a payout target for *each* subsidiary identical to the payout ratio of the parent. An attempt is made to adhere to the target rate, although deviations from it are permitted if certain conditions warrant it (e.g., tax effects, devaluation threat). From the available evidence it appears that in the great majority of cases the dividend payouts of overseas subsidiaries are *not* exactly the same as the parent company's. (Of course many countries —India for example—have laws on the percentage of profits that *must* be distributed by subsidiaries.)

Four somewhat related reasons have been suggested for placing so much importance on the parent payout ratio:

1. Cash is required by the parent company to meet its own obligations to stockholders, and the subsidiaries must meet their portion of the obligation by providing their share of the cash.

2. By paying to the parent company the same percentage of its earnings that the latter pays to its owners, the subsidiary is in some intuitive sense demonstrating its value and perhaps worthiness to the ultimate shareholder. This is reflected in the following quotes from discussions at two companies about their dividend policy guidelines: "The parent company gives its shareholders an annual return on their investment; the subsidiaries also have this responsibility." "Every corporation must recognize its obligations to reimburse its shareholders for the use of their investments."

3. For the many companies that have had difficulties in obtaining dividend payments from a portion of their subsidiaries in less-developed countries, the establishment of a *uniform* dividend payout rate throughout the corporate system—justified by the obligation to the stockholders—is hoped to be persuasive enough to gain for these subsidiaries official approval for making the remittance to the parent company. The excerpt below is from an interview with a member of the holding company that manages the international operations of a large multinational corporation:

> International as such is expected to contribute 55 per cent of its earnings to the parent company, and in order to do that it is necessary for us to maintain the policy that the subsidiary companies must also remit 55 per cent of their earnings. The policy also came about on the basis that this could not be criticized in the field. In other words, it would not be unrealistic in the minds of any local government organization to expect at least a 55 per cent distribution of the profits of the local company in that year.

4. In a few companies the, interviewees have indicated that the parent payout ratio provides a *rule of thumb* for foreign dividend remittances; the amount reinvested in the subsidiary seems to them to fulfill the affiliate's requirements while concurrently providing a satisfactory amount of funds to the parent company.

PATTERNS OF DIVIDEND DECISIONS

Looking beyond the question of what the variables are that influence companies' foreign remittance decisions, it is our impression that certain of the variables have greater impact on the decisions of some types of companies than on others. Two broad classes of multinational firms can be distinguished. First are the companies with lengthy experience in business abroad, large numbers of foreign affiliates, a significant portion of total earnings contributed by operations in foreign countries, and the practice of consolidating the results of foreign operations. In the second group are companies with relatively small foreign earnings, few foreign affiliates, and fairly limited experience in international business.

For the first of these groups the foreign dividend decision is observed to be closely tied to a target payout rate—a percentage of the affiliate's earnings after foreign taxes—whereas in the less internationally oriented companies a more thorough job of analysis is normally done, and a combination of the variables described above influence the final decision. Apparently the more international firms are able to rely on past performance as a satisfactory guide to what the current remittances ought to be; furthermore, the large numbers of foreign affiliates probably necessitate utilizing a rule of thumb approach to conserve management time. In contrast, the more analytical behavior of the second group of firms that is less involved and less experienced with foreign business reflects the absence of guidelines and standards tested over the years. And with relatively few foreign subsidiaries, these companies can afford to undertake detailed analyses of the potentially complex remittance decision.

A Recommended Approach to Remittance Practices

An important conclusion which can be drawn from the foregoing summary of corporate practices is that many firms could undoubtedly improve their methods of managing remittances by making a *systematic* appraisal of *all* of the variables relevant to the funds flow decision. It should not come as a surprise to the student of international business that companies follow a *variety* of management approaches and that many of the approaches do not appear to lead to a profit maximizing solution. The field of international financial management is a relatively new one, and many of the prevalent practices reflect this newness. With the rapid growth in direct investment abroad there has not been sufficient time for many companies to study carefully and revise the existing decision-making process.

In attempting to develop a framework for managing transnational remittances attention is focused initially on the questions: "Should funds be remitted by an individual affiliate, and if so, in what amount?" A subsequent stage of analysis is concerned with the *form* which remittance should take. Having decided how much should be transferred, the manager then chooses the method (or methods) of remittance that best serves corporate objectives. The discussion that follows sequentially examines these interrelated facets of the remittance decision process.

SHOULD FUNDS BE REMITTED AND IN WHAT AMOUNTS?

There are two fundamental reasons for transferring funds from a foreign affiliate into the worldwide company capital pool:

1. In order that an affiliate can repay the parent company or one of its sister affiliates for resources that have been made available to it such as components, advice, capital, or finished goods
2. Because the funds can be deployed elsewhere in the company system in a manner that the managers believe is more advantageous to the company as a whole.[3]

There may be an opportunity to earn higher returns in another affiliate or to insure against a loss in the dollar value of funds or inaccessibility of funds if they are continuously held in the country in which they are generated. An elaboration of these fundamental reasons forms the basis for deciding whether or not a foreign affiliate should make a remittance.

An Obligation to Repay the Parent Company or an Affiliate

To earn a return on investment

Why would an affiliate be obliged to repay another subsidiary or the parent company? Perhaps the most obvious answer is that the parent expects to be repaid for funds it has loaned to the affiliate and/or to receive a return on funds that it has invested. The fundamental premise upon which the funds were initially provided was that a satisfactory return would be forthcoming.

To minimize the overall tax liability

As a separate matter the parent company may levy a charge on a foreign affiliate for services rendered. If the services are of an intangible nature—such as payment for a part of the overhead of the international division—the question may arise, of what value can it be to the company as a whole of requiring in effect, "the left hand to pay the right"? The answer may be sought in various areas. From an overall *tax* point of view, the company's best interests may be served as a result of the headquarter's having allocated so-called common costs among the various affiliates that presumably benefit from the services. The parent company as a profit center may calculate that by requiring the foreign firms to make contributions to its overhead expenses, the foreign tax burden is lightened by a greater amount than the parent's tax liability is increased.

[3] Although it is useful to distinguish between these two reasons for purposes of exposition, it is recognized that they are not necessarily mutually exclusive.

To establish a recognizable global practice

As a matter of remittance strategy, the levy of a few thousand dollars for services rendered on each of the affiliates may enable many of them to convince the local host governments that remittances made for this purpose are a necessary and legitimate expense of conducting business. If the local manager in Nigeria, for example, is able to demonstrate to the Nigerian foreign exchange authority or the internal revenue service that the company's Japanese, Thai, and Chilean affiliates must remit to the headquarters a like amount, the Nigerian government may be more willing to permit the local affiliate to make the payment and to deduct it from the local taxable income.

To control foreign operations

Another possible justification for requiring certain types of remittances lies in the realm of retaining control of foreign affiliates. Highest levels of management often complain that the subsidiary staffs are far too engrossed in their own local problems and opportunities to see how the local unit fits into the worldwide pattern of operations designed by the parent company. As a result the international headquarters is constantly searching for effective tools and methods to *remind* the geographically dispersed lower management levels that the capital on which they are operating is that of the parent and that the controlling objectives are those set by the international headquarters. Levying charges for services rendered—even small nuisance charges—can be an effective form of reminder to local managers when they are engaged in the periodic preparation of operating budgets or in the day to day management of the affiliate.

Effective Deployment of Company-Controlled Funds

The second basic approach to answering the question, "Should an affiliate remit funds?" consists of an analysis of how best to deploy funds controlled by the firm among its worldwide operations. Without repeating the arguments of chapters 5 and 6 regarding optimal financial structures and worthwhile investment opportunities, the following section identifies the critical ingredients in the funds deployment-remittance decision. Remittance policy is to a large extent dependent on answers to three questions:

1. *What are the fund requirements of the worldwide enterprise?* For the forthcoming fiscal period what amounts and types of financing will be needed by various affiliates and by the parent company?

2. *What are the fund requirements of the foreign affiliate for which the remittance decision is being made?* What are its needs for both

working capital and capital expansion during the forthcoming fiscal period and thereafter?

3. *What are the possibilities and associated costs of using funds from external sources to fulfill the financial requirements of the parent company and its various affiliates?*

The requirement for worldwide financial planning

When the financial manager looks at the financial plans of individual foreign affiliates, it must be done within the context of a *broad* scope analysis of the corporate system's overall fund position. The manager must decide whether or not the Nigerian affiliate, for example, should proceed with a planned project and finance it in whole or in part with internally generated funds, or if it should remit its capital to the common pool—for use by other affiliates—and either forego the project or alternatively obtain the required capital from local sources. Hence the answer to the Nigerian query must be found *as a part of* the solution to the broader problem of how to provide for the capital requirements of the worldwide enterprise, using the guidelines suggested in chapter 6 as the basis for effective analysis.

Assessing the future accessibility of foreign-held funds

International fund deployment must also be based on the future *accessibility* of company-controlled capital. Countries can be expected to place restrictions on the outward flow of capital when they are experiencing balance-of-payments difficulties; therefore the financial manager must try to forecast whether or not its affiliate in a given foreign country will have any problems in remitting funds in the future,[4] as an important part of deciding if the affiliate's current cash flow should be retained or transferred into the company pool. From the point of view of trying to maximize the utility of company-controlled capital resources, the company as a whole will have suffered in both flexibility and cost if the capital of any of its affiliates is blocked for a period of time and is consequently unavailable for use by another affiliate where it could earn greater returns. The financial manager must therefore analyze the costs and benefits to the company as a whole if a decision is made to remit funds from a foreign subsidiary as a hedge against possible future loss of accessibility to the funds. In these cases the net cost to the company of not remitting is the difference between what the blocked funds will earn and the return which could be earned on these funds if they were employed in another country, or the increased costs of providing alternate financing to an affiliate in another country that otherwise would have used the now inaccessible funds. The net cost of remitting the

[4] *See* chapter 3 for a discussion of techniques of forecasting foreign environmental conditions.

funds is the difference between what they could have earned had they not been transferred and the return that they actually earn elsewhere in the company system.

The risk of loss in dollar value of foreign-held funds

A separate analysis that pertains to the fund deployment-remittance decision is that of the risk of loss in dollar value of funds generated by foreign affiliates. To maximize the value of the parent company equity shares, it is essential that the dollar value of the affiliates' assets be maintained and the dollar value of future earnings be protected. Companies operating in more than one currency are continually incurring the risk of an adverse change in the exchange value of one or more currencies. With respect to the remittance decision the manager must evaluate the likelihood of a depreciation in the exchange rate of a currency of a country in which the company has an affiliate. Chapter 3 provides a guide to making such an evaluation. If there is reason to believe that such a change will occur in the near future, the manager can calculate the benefit that would accrue to the company as a whole of hedging against the loss in dollar value by speeding up the timing of a remittance or by increasing the size of the fund transfer compared to past practice. The benefit of a hedge is based upon the savings in dollar value that occur if exchange rate depreciation actually takes place. If, for example, the equivalent of $100,000 is shifted out of an affiliate as a special measure to guard against depreciation, the savings to the company is $100,000 times the percentage by which the currency value diminishes. But by definition a hedge involves taking a known *cost* to protect against an unknown risk. In this case the cost of the hedge might be the additional expenses to the affiliate of having to borrow local funds in lieu of operating on the $100,000 that was remitted. Or perhaps the affiliate is forced to forego temporarily a project because of the unavailability of funds, and the cost of the hedge is equal to the opportunity cost to the company of the project foregone. The key point in this discussion is that the financial manager should recognize the possibility of loss in dollar value as a part of his decision on remittances and international deployment of funds, and he should, wherever possible, make an analysis of the costs and benefits to the company of alternative courses of action.

Presenting results to the parent company's stockholders

A final consideration in the decision on remittances has to do with companies' practices of consolidating the financial statements of foreign subsidiaries with those of the parent company for public reporting purposes. If the parent company consolidates its financial statements to include all or a large segment of its overseas affiliates, the dividends, fees, and royalty payments actually remitted by the consolidated subsidiaries will *not* have any effect on the reported income of the parent corporation. Hence the management cannot in any sense manage its foreign remittances so as to favorably affect the overall profits reported to the shareholders. On the other hand, to the extent that the parent company's dividend policy is anchored to its present and forecasted earnings [5]—the inclusion of positive foreign earnings in the consolidated statements can be expected to *increase* the amount paid out in the form of dividends, and concomitantly increase the parent's requirements for cash to make the distribution.

When a corporation does not consolidate the results of foreign operations and uses the cost method of reporting, only the remittances of dividends, fees, interest, and royalties from the affiliates abroad are recorded as income in the parent company's profit and loss statement. This reporting practice gives management a certain latitude in deciding to what extent overseas operating results will influence reported corporate earnings. Hence from two points of view—the cash requirements of the parent company and the potential effect on the shareholders' overall best interests—the remittance decision and deployment of funds must account for the consolidation practices of the firm.

IN WHICH FORM(S) SHOULD FUNDS BE REMITTED?

Having considered the variables that influence the decision-maker in his analysis of the questions—"Should an affiliate remit funds, and if it should, in how large an amount?"—attention can now turn to the third fundamental query: "Which form(s) of remittance should be utilized to effect a transfer of funds across national borders?"

In order to provide a useful decision framework for answering this question, the reader must first possess an understanding of the variety of remittance forms that may be selected by a manager in a given situation. The following discussion will commence with a brief review of the remittance methods; subsequently the discussion will focus on the environmental and managerial constraints that serve to restrict the decision-maker's freedom in choosing among the methods of moving funds internationally.

The Variety of Possible Remittance Forms

The available evidence indicates that companies utilize a number of techniques to move funds across national borders from one affiliate to the parent company. A survey of the thirty largest multinational companies has revealed that almost all of them direct their affiliates to remit dividends. Approximately two-thirds of the firms also employ so-called man-

[5] John Lintner, "Distribution of Income of Corporations among Dividends, Retained Earnings and Taxes," *American Economic Review Papers and Proceedings*, May 1956, pp. 97–113.

agement fees. Approximately 40 per cent use royalty payments, and some also utilize export commissions, interest payments, and amortization of credit advanced to the foreign affiliate by the parent company.[6] It should also be appreciated that for many thousands of companies that sell goods and components to their foreign affiliates, an avenue is open to move funds back to the exporting company by virtue of intercompany transfer pricing arrangements.[7]

Table 11–1 summarizes the relative importance of some of the most widely used methods of fund transfers. The data suggest there is an increasing reliance on royalties and fees to supplement dividends and interest payments as remittance methods.

TABLE 11–1

Royalties, Fees, Dividends, and Interest Payments Made by Foreign Affiliates of United States Companies in All Industries, from All Areas, in Total and as a Percentage of Total Remittances, 1957, 1961–1967 (millions of $)

YEAR	TOTAL REMIT-TANCES	INTEREST AND DIVIDENDS	% OF TOTAL REMIT-TANCES	ROYALTIES AND FEES *	% OF TOTAL REMIT-TANCES
1957	$2,950	$2,249	91	$ 241	9
1961	2,715	2,267	83	448	17
1962	3,598	3,050	85	548	15
1963	3,681	3,059	83	622	17
1964	4,426	3,670	83	756	17
1965	4,887	3,963	81	924	19
1966	5,090	4,045	80	1,045	20
1967	5,658	4,518	80	1,140	20

* Note: Royalties and fees include license fees, management fees, service charges, and royalties.
Source: *Survey of Current Business,* various issues.

The dividend as a form of fund transfer

It becomes apparent from reviewing the table that dividend payments have been by far the most important remittance form from foreign subsidiaries. Countries that permit free enterprise within their borders recognize the dividend as a method by which the earnings of a business corporation can be distributed to the shareholders of the firm. Not all countries, however, permit dividends of local corporations to be paid in convertible currencies to the foreign parent companies. Countries char-

[6] See David B. Zenoff, *op. cit.;* and Judd Polk, Irene Meister and L. Veit, *U.S. Production Abroad and the Balance of Payments,* New York, National Industrial Conference Board, 1966, Ch. V.

[7] The data on the volume of intercompany sales is somewhat incomplete. However the reader may wish to consult the *Survey of Current Business,* vol. XLIV, no. 12, 1964, for an indication of the then current volume.

acterized by balance-of-payments problems and relatively small amounts of foreign exchange reserves may be expected to place restrictions on the payment of dividends to foreign companies. The precise types of restrictions vary from country to country, but generally they regulate the size of dividend payments according to either a percentage of the subsidiary's earnings or in absolute dollar amounts.[8]

A dividend must be formally declared by the board of directors of a corporation at one of its meetings, and once declared it may be paid to the shareholders or credited to the account of the owners in lieu of an actual distribution. The latter case frequently occurs when the host government has placed severe restrictions on remittances, and the subsidiary's directors wish to establish the grounds for making future remittances when the restrictions are lifted or modified. In most nations dividends are declared *after* the local corporate income tax has been paid. The decision on earnings distribution is thereby affected by the amount of after-tax earnings possessed by the foreign affiliate. Furthermore, some national taxing authorities also levy a 5 to 15 per cent withholding tax on dividends and other remittances that require foreign exchange. And most countries treat the dividend income received by the parent companies from their foreign affiliates as ordinary income to the parent and thereby taxable at the standard rate for corporate income. These so-called incremental costs to the company associated with transferring funds in the form of dividends must be factored into the decisions regarding the amount and the form by which funds will be moved across national boundaries.

A further complicating factor may arise when the foreign affiliate is jointly owned by the multinational investor and by one or more partners. The principals may have different expectations and objectives *vis à vis* their investment and the percentage of earnings that should be distributed to the shareholders or reinvested in the operation. It is, of course, impossible to generalize about the precise nature of conflicts between partners, but there have been numerous reports that multinational companies characteristically regard their foreign affiliates as long-term investments, whereas local partners have shorter time horizons and wish to begin earlier drawing funds out of the business. The important point to be recognized here is that the decision on dividend remittances must in all probability be tempered by the needs and desires of the other principals in a jointly owned foreign subsidiary.[9]

[8] The most comprehensive source of current information on governmental restrictions of capital movements is the *Annual Report on Exchange Restrictions* published by the International Monetary Fund, Washington, D.C.

[9] For a review of the managerial problems involved in international joint ventures *see* W. G. Friedman and G. Kalmanoff, *Joint International Business Ventures,* New York, Columbia University Press, 1961; *Pros and Cons of Joint Ventures Abroad,* New York, Business International Corporation, 1964.

Royalties and fees as forms of fund remittance

The data in Table 11–1 reflect the importance and increasing use of royalties and fees by United States companies. To a considerable extent these remittance methods reflect arrangements between the parent companies and individual foreign subsidiaries whereby the former makes available patents, trademarks, technical data, know-how, and advice for a consideration.[10] Undoubtedly a large percentage of the total dollar value of royalties and fees in Table 11–1 accounts for the licensing agreements between United States firms and foreign operations in which they own only a *portion* of the equity—often a minority position. (In the case of a jointly owned venture the international investor will, of course, have to obtain permission from its partner to be able to levy charges for any of these contributions.) The agreement insures the United States company of receiving at least some compensation for the resources it has contributed to the foreign subsidiary, perhaps in lieu of a satisfactory amount of dividend payments over which it may have little or no effective control. What is interesting is that a number of companies have also concluded licensing agreements with their *wholly-owned* affiliates abroad. The reasons for undertaking such formal arrangements with a foreign business over which it exercises complete management control will differ from company to company, and it is important that the student of international business recognize what they may be:

1. In order to overcome restrictions that less-developed countries may place on the remittance of earnings by affiliates operating within their borders, some firms will establish a contractual licensing agreement with their subsidiaries as the means of opening up an additional route for international funds flow. Although the existence of a contractual agreement per se will not necessarily persuade the host government to allow the subsidary to remit funds, experience has demonstrated that there is a greater likelihood that restrictions will be modified for what appears to be a legitimate business expense such as a fee for technical information than will be the case for a mere distribution of local earnings.[11] As a

[10] Foreign licensing agreements are discussed in the following sources: L. J. Eckstrom, *Licensing in Domestic and Foreign Operations*, 3rd ed., Essex, Connecticut, Foreign Operations Service, Inc., 1964; Claude McMillan, "The Pros and Cons of Licensing Agreements," *Management Review*, May 1965; C. H. Lee, "How to Reach the Overseas Market by Licensing," *Harvard Business Review*, January-February 1958, pp. 77–81; David Zenoff and James Jepson, "How to Boost Profits from Your Foreign Licensing Agreement," *Business Abroad*, December 1968.

[11] "Where governmental restrictions on the transfer of currency already exist, it has been found that returns on royalties are often looked upon more favorably than the returns of dividends and principal. Not only are royalties smaller in many instances . . . but also there is no possibility that a large sum might be repatriated in a short space of time." Jack Behrman, "Advantages and Disadvantages of Foreign Licensing," *The Patent, Trademark, and Copyright Journal of Research and Education*, March 1958, p. 147.

means of giving the licensing agreement an appearance of a legitimate and necessary business expense for affiliates in countries with exchange restrictions, multinational companies sometimes establish identical agreements with *all* of their subsidiaries abroad, thereby giving individual affiliates some verbal ammunition in negotiating for remittance approval.

2. The existence of a contractual licensing agreement with a wholly-owned foreign subsidary may also have payoffs for the investor in the event of a change in local commercial circumstances. The legal precision that characterizes licensing agreements can be expected to assist the parent company in maintaining its control over the name, patents, trademarks, and techniques that it has made available should there be a change in the ownership of the subsidiary, local infringement of the copyright protection, the establishment of a sublicensing arrangement in a third country, or nationalization of the foreign business assets.

3. From the point of view of minimizing the company's overall tax liabilities, the use of management fees and royalties can in some cases be a better form by which to remit funds than dividend payments. Where this advantage can be gained it is usually the result of the host government's permitting the foreign affiliate to deduct from their taxable income a certain reasonable amount of such remittances as business expenses.

4. The reduction of a subsidiary's taxable income resulting from charges for management services, trademarks, etc., may serve the added function of discouraging additional local competition from entering the same market. In effect the fees may disguise the true earnings potential of the subsidiary.

5. A number of capital exporting countries have recently begun to pressure domestic companies to charge their foreign affiliates for all resources that the parent company makes available. The authorities' interests are in increasing tax revenues and improving their balance of international payments.

6. For internal control purposes companies may find that levying charges on affiliates abroad will help to provide a more clear and meaningful basis on which to evaluate the operations of both the parent company and the individual affiliates (provided that the host country *allows* such charges). The belief is that the allocation of so-called joint expenses is a more reasonable practice than one in which the parent company absorbs them.[12]

Intercompany transfers of goods as a method to justify fund remittances

In addition to dividends, royalties, and fees as methods by which to transfer funds internationally, a considerable amount of funds is moved

[12] Jack L. Goldstucker, "Allocating Costs in International Operations," *Business Horizons*, vol. 8, no. 4, pp. 75–84.

as a result of goods that are sold to a foreign affiliate by the parent company or another of the company's affiliates. Although current data are unavailable, in 1963 United States companies sold approximately $5 billion worth of finished and unfinished goods, components, and supplies to their affiliates in foreign countries,[13] and probably many hundreds of millions of dollars worth in addition were sold by affiliates of the companies to their sister firms in third countries. Intercompany sales are the single most important method of effecting a movement of capital between countries in which companies have operations.

The problems, opportunities, and policy questions involved with the intercompany sale of goods *domestically* are thoroughly discussed—although not thoroughly resolved—topics.[14] Within the strictly domestic business sphere decisions on transfer pricing must be concerned with such matters as the establishment of profit centers within the company, controlling and measuring division performance, motivating division managers, and maximizing overall corporate price competitiveness. In an *internationally* oriented company the same policy questions arise, but the fact that goods will be sold between countries requires the additional consideration of opportunities for *profit placement* and *risk avoidance*. The discussion that follows highlights the specific considerations and problems that must be accounted for by the financial manager in establishing transfer-pricing policy.

From the points of view of maximizing worldwide profits and effecting a satisfactory flow of funds from individual overseas affiliates into the overall company pool of funds, adaptation must be made to five peculiarly international environmental conditions.[15]

1. The rates at which corporate income is taxed differ from one country to another. A company that is engaged in the sale of goods across national boundaries will have certain opportunities to decide in which tax jurisdiction it wishes to take the profits that result from the intercompany sale of goods. If other things are equal, a company's worldwide profitability will be maximized if it ships goods at relatively *low* prices to affiliates located in countries that have relatively low corporate income tax rates.

2. Countries construct different levels of tariffs on goods that are imported into their economies. A company that exports goods from one

[13] Office of Business Economics, *U.S. Business Investments in Foreign Countries: Survey of Current Business,* no. 12, 1964.

[14] *See*, for example, John Dearden, "Decentralization and Intra-Company Pricing," *Harvard Business Review,* vol. 33, 1955, pp. 65–74 and J. Bieman, Jr., "Pricing Intra-Company Transfers," *Accounting Review,* vol. 34, July 1959, pp. 429–432.

[15] The leading study in this area is James S. Shulman, *Transfer Pricing in Multinational Business,* unpublished doctoral dissertation, Harvard Business School, Boston, 1967.

country into another in which it has an affiliate will have its profitability affected by the level of the second country's import duties. Consideration must therefore be given to how an upward or downward adjustment of the price of the internationally traded goods will affect the profit and sales objectives of the firm. Many companies may decide, therefore, to follow the practice of setting a relatively low price on goods exported to countries having high tariff barriers and conversely pricing the goods relatively high when the importing nation has low duties.

3. When a company sells goods to an affiliate that is located in a country that restricts the remittance of funds to foreign parent companies, the company may—within certain limits—bypass the government restrictions by adjusting the price of the goods upward, thereby ensuring a greater outflow of funds from the subsidiary than would otherwise have been possible. Similarly, if the subsidiary is in position to sell goods to another company affiliate or the parent corporation, the seller may attempt to lower artificially the price of the goods, which will in effect place an abnormally large percentage of the profits with the buying affiliate compared to the seller.

It is important at this juncture to note that however wise these transfer-pricing strategies may appear on paper, the ability of the companies to readily bypass the various regulations and restrictions of the interested governments will usually be limited by the countervailing powers of the national authorities. Governments can be expected to try to police these practices and to uncover methods by which enterprises subvert the original intent of the national policies. Nevertheless it is also true that a well-planned policy for worldwide transfer pricing can add significantly to a company's profits and the safety of its funds compared to an *ad hoc* approach to transfer pricing and remittance of funds.

4. Another factor which should temper international pricing strategy is the local borrowing ability of foreign affiliates. Presumably the success that a subsidiary will have in obtaining locally denominated debt funds will be partially affected by its demonstrated earning power and by its financial strength as reflected in a balance sheet. If the decision is made to finance all or part of a particular foreign operation by local borrowing, an ill-conceived transfer-pricing policy of overcharging the affiliate on intercompany sales could damage the subsidiary's credit standing, reduce its reported earnings, and ruin its chances of obtaining the required capital. The important point is that transfer pricing and remittance policies must be designed in conjunction with financing objectives.

5. Problems often arise in deciding on a transfer price when the foreign affiliate to which goods are to be sold is owned *jointly* with one or more other partners. Because the price at which the goods are sold will have a somewhat *different* effect on the profitability of the foreign affiliate

and each of the principals, conflicts frequently have to be resolved in the determination of a fair price. While there are no pat answers to such involved problems, in the long run it is true that companies could eliminate some problems if they would resolve these matters before making decisions to enter into a collaborative business venture.

Repayment of intercompany indebtedness and interest payments as forms of fund remittances

Another widely used method of transferring funds from foreign affiliates to the company pool of funds involves the repayment of a debt owed by the subsidiary to the parent company or a sister affiliate. The use of this particular method of effecting fund transfers is suggested in some cases by tax savings and in others by its effectiveness in bypassing host country restrictions on remittances. Funds received in the form of repayment of principal of an intercompany loan are normally not considered as taxable income of the recipient where the taxing authorities are convinced that an earlier provision of funds to the subsidiary was considered by both to result in indebtedness by the affiliate rather than a forgiveable loan in the event it subsequently is not possible or convenient for the affiliate to make repayment. Some of the host countries that restrict dividend payments have been found to be more lenient with the amortization of a subsidiary's indebtedness. Hence where a loan is outstanding on the books of an affiliate, its partial or total repayment is sometimes an effective rationale for obtaining otherwise unavailable foreign exchange.

A related method to move funds from one affiliate to others is by making interest payments to the lender on the outstanding balance of an intercompany loan. The tax implications of interest payments are different from those of loan amortization. Most host countries will permit a reasonable amount of interest to be deducted from an affiliate's taxable income as a business expense. The remittance itself is then often subject to a 5 to 15 per cent withholding tax levied by the host country, and the funds are considered as ordinary income accruing to the recipient enterprise in the second country. Another value of interest payments in these situations is that they can be used as evidence that the affiliate has a balance of intercompany indebtedness; this could help assure questioning civil servants that particular movements of funds represent amortization of principal and not distribution of income for tax calculation purposes.

Reliance on the international commercial banking networks for assistance in moving funds

The growth of multinational banking as an accompaniment to the emerging internationally oriented manufacturing companies has opened new avenues for moving funds across national borders. While the banks themselves are also limited in their ability to shift funds in and out of countries that have restrictions on such practices, the financial institutions' geographically dispersed networks are sometimes able to arrange for a near equivalent to an actual transfer of funds for a company that requires it. Suppose the ABC company owns subsidiaries in Taiwan and Nigeria. The Chinese operation has been generating a large sum of funds over the past fifteen months, and the parent company decides to shift the affiliate's excess funds to Nigeria where its relatively new operation requires a sizable amount of investment in plant and equipment. The parent's decision to effect such a fund transfer is based on three factors:

1. In both countries there is a threat of currency devaluation.
2. Long-term funds are virtually unavailable in Nigeria.
3. The Taiwan affiliate has no foreseen need for most of its current profits.

Upon applying to the Taiwan government for foreign exchange the ABC affiliate is informed that for the next eight months all remittances by foreign-owned companies will be suspended. What can the company do?

One approach might be to seek an arrangement with the multinational bank with which the company has established relations. The company may find that the bank's branch in Taiwan is in urgent need of deposits to carry on its lending activities in the tight credit environment. Hence the local branch might welcome an opportunity to gain a time deposit as one part of a package designed to meet the manufacturing company's requirements. In return for the deposit in Taiwan the bank might agree to direct its branch in Nigeria to lend the required amount of funds to the company's affiliate in the latter country. The maturity of the loan would be the same as that of the time deposit negotiated in Taiwan. The ABC Company, by availing iself of the worldwide facilities of its bank, will have partially fulfilled its financial objectives. The Nigerian affiliate receives the locally denominated debt funds it requires. From an overall view the company has been relatively successful in protecting its position against devaluation of the countries' exchange rates. If the bank financing had not been arranged, the parent company or one of its foreign affiliates would have been forced to make the funds available to the affiliate in Nigeria, thereby committing foreign exchange in the face of a devaluation; thus ABC would have been vulnerable to dollar losses in both Taiwan and Nigeria. Under the suggested arrangement the locally denominated debt is not vulnerable to devaluation and only the funds banked in Taiwan are exposed.

Hence financial managers can sometimes use the facilities and services of multibranch banks as supplements to or even as substitutes for internal remissions. As illustrated by the formation of the International Commercial Bank, Ltd., described below, several banks have expanded their facilities and have been continuously increasing their services in response to the dynamic growth of direct investment abroad.

> Two U.S. Banks Plan International Unit. . . . Two United States banks disclosed plans yesterday [June 15, 1967] to join three foreign institutions in the formation of an international bank to be based in London and to be called the International Commercial Bank, Ltd. . . . The . . . spokesman said it was expected that the bulk of the clients of the proposed bank would be "multinational corporations" but the new institution would be equipped for all types of banking business. It would specialize in advancing credit for medium and medium long terms. . . . [One of its foreign partners] has 1700 branches in Britain, Ireland, Belgium, France and the Channel Islands. . . . [Another foreign partner] has 470 branches in 250 cities in West Germany as well as offices in eight Latin American, Middle Eastern and African nations.[16]

Other methods of fund remittances

In addition to the forms of remittance already discussed, one additional remittance category warrants brief identification. As companies have grown accustomed to foreign countries that restrict access to their foreign exchange reserves, a variety of rather secretive methods have developed for subverting or bypassing governments' foreign exchange restrictions. Because most of these techniques are illegal in the eyes of the foreign governments, they are obviously not widely advertised by either the companies or the governments, and the authors merely provide an illustrative hypothetical example of what may constitute an approach utilized in some situations.

The Luxury Goods Company and Tractors, Inc. each own manufacturing affiliates in LDC, a Latin American nation with severe restrictions on the use of its foreign exchange reserves. Luxury Goods has excess local currency that it is unable to remit to its parent company or to invest profitably in LDC. On the other hand, Tractors, Inc., a rapidly expanding subsidiary in the same country badly needs working capital funds. Its only sources of added short-term capital are the local financieras, which charge 45 per cent interest per annum. The solution to the problems of both companies may be for them to arrange illicitly for Luxury Goods to give Tractors, Inc., the local currency equivalent of, say, $100,000 in return for a United States bank account transfer of the same amount between the parent companies of these LDC subsidiaries.

The Factors That May Constrain the Manager's Choice of Forms to Effect Fund Transfers across National Borders

Up to this juncture we have reviewed the various methods by which companies may effect a funds transfer between a foreign affiliate that is holding funds and other company affiliates or the parent company. The discussion now focuses on the environmental and internal factors that

[16] *The New York Times,* June 15, 1967, p. 67. *See also* M. Main, "First Real International Bankers," *Fortune,* December 1967.

limit the manager's choice of remittance forms in a given situation as well as the amount of funds that can be remitted. To facilitate the following discussion, the variables that may impede fund transfers will be categorized somewhat artifically into two main groups, "Costs of Moving Funds" and "Restrictions on Fund Movements." The international manager must consider the relevant constraining variables in deciding upon the appropriate remittance amount and mix of remittance forms in each individual case.

Costs of moving funds across national boundaries

Taxation Taxation is a complicated and somewhat difficult consideration since regulations differ among countries and are subject to frequent change. However, tax considerations do lend themselves to systematic analysis and because of their importance should be explicitly analyzed in every remittance decision.

In the broadest sense the goal of management should be to minimize the overall tax liability of the company. In terms of remittance policy this objective implies minimizing the incremental tax cost to the company of moving funds from one tax jurisdiction to another. The critical elements in this task are found in the tax regulations of *both* the host country from which the funds are to be transferred and of the country into which capital is moved. In most cases the host country has two types of taxes that will directly affect remittances: corporate income taxes and withholding taxes levied on dividend, interest, royalty, and fee payments. The corporate income tax is relevant when the choice to be made is between a before-tax remittance such as an interest payment and an after-tax payment like dividends or repayment of principal on intercompany loans.

The key question regarding taxes in the recipient country is: Will there be an additional tax levied by the second tax jurisdiction? Many countries (including the United States) treat dividends, fees, interest payments, and royalties as ordinary income of the parent corporation and therefore taxable at the regular corporate income tax rate. Where the rate is higher than that of the foreign country, there will normally be an incremental tax cost to the movement of the funds. Mention should be made of foreign tax credits that many countries provide for taxes already paid on the same income in other tax jurisdictions. The purpose of this and similar provisions such as tax treaties between countries is to avoid double taxation of the same income. The effectiveness of these exemption devices in minimizing double taxation has been somewhat limited by the differences in the interpretation and definitions used by the various countries in providing foreign tax credits.[17]

[17] For more information on various countries' philosophies and rates of corporate income taxation of foreign-earned income, *see* S. G. Ross and J. H. Guttentag, "United States Taxation of International Transactions," *A Lawyer's Guide to International Business Transactions,* Walter S. Surry and C. Shaw, eds., Philadelphia, American Law Institute and American Bar Association, 1963; Lawrence B. Krause and Kenneth W. Dam, *Federal Tax Treatment of Foreign Income,* Washington, D.C., The Brook-

A simplified illustration of the type of tax analysis that is required in remittance decisions will help to clarify the relevance of the types of taxes discussed above. Assume that a United States multinational company requires approximately $500,000 from abroad to finance a domestic project. After careful preliminary analysis the financial manager concludes that the only sources of available capital are three of the company's foreign affiliates, and moreover that certain factors dictate that only one of the affiliates should be tapped for the funds. The problem is to decide from a tax point of view which affiliate should provide the funds. The German subsidiary with before-tax earnings of $1 million is subject to the local split income tax rate of 15 per cent on distributed corporate income and 51 per cent on all undistributed income and to a 10 per cent withholding tax on dividends. The company's French affiliate also has earned $1 million in the current fiscal period. It is taxed at the normal 50 per cent corporate income tax rate in that country, and its remittances are subject to a 10 per cent withholding tax. The subsidiary in LDC, a less-developed country, has earned a total of $1 million during the past two years without having to pay local taxes because of a tax holiday that the local government provides to new foreign investors. LDC does not have a withholding tax on remittances. The relevant tax consequences of remitting $500,000 from each country are summarized in Table 11–2:

TABLE 11–2

FOREIGN COUNTRY	*DIVIDEND AMOUNT*	*HOST COUNTRY INCOME TAX (If dividend paid)*	*HOST COUNTRY WITH-HOLDING TAX*	*UNITED STATES INCOME TAX **	*TOTAL TAXES IF DIVIDENDS ARE PAID*	*HOST COUNTRY INCOME TAX (If no dividend paid)*
Germany	$556,000	$ 83,400 +226,440 $309,840	$55,600	$134,560	$500,000	$510,000
LDC	500,000			$500,000	500,000	
France	$556,000	$500,000	$55,600		$555,600	$500,000

* Note: Assume for simplification that the United States corporate income tax rate is 50 per cent and that income received from less-developed countries is taxed at the same effective rate as that from the developed countries.

If the German subsidiary is selected as the source of parent company funds, the worldwide tax liability of the company is $1 million. If the LDC affiliate is selected the taxes will total $1.5 million. If the French affiliate is tapped the taxes will be $1,065,600. Hence, under the restric-

ings Institution, 1964; Nathan Gordon, "The Role of Tax Treaties," in *Taxes and International Business*, New York, National Association of Manufacturers, 1964; Confederation of British Industry, *Taxation in Western Europe*, issued yearly.

tive assumptions of this illustration, the best choice for funds is the German subsidiary.

The Cost of Borrowed Funds Another cost that may arise with transferring funds is the interest expense associated with borrowings to finance the subsidiary in lieu of retained earnings. Still another cost which may be attributable to international fund transfers stems from exchange restrictions that are often found in less-developed countries. These restrictions operate to impose a penalty on the use of foreign exchange by requiring the user to pay a premium exchange rate for convertible currencies. In such cases the official par value of the local currency may be LC3:$1, but in order to make a remittance the local affiliate may have to pay four local currency units to obtain one dollar.

Restrictions on fund movements

Host Government Regulations In the category of restrictions that may act to impede the flow of funds across national borders, host government regulations are of primary importance. Some countries limit the size of a subsidiary's dividends by restricting it to a percentage of the affiliate's current earnings or to a percentage of its capitalization. Another form of governmental constraint relates to the government's unwillingness to grant approval for all types and sizes of remittances as tax deductible business expenses. For example, royalty payments in excess of 2 per cent of the affiliate's net sales may not be allowable as expenses in the computation of taxable income. The company may decide to make the remittance anyway but it will forfeit the local tax shield on the excess portion. Similarly, royalty payments and management fees must relate to some prearranged base in order to qualify as tax deductible expenses. Where such rules are in effect the financial manager loses a certain degree of flexibility in the selection among remittance methods for a fund transfer in a given period. The ruling may apply only to what is allowable as a tax deductible expense, or it may provide a ceiling for the payment of certain types of remittances in countries that are rationing their foreign exchange reserves.

Availability of External Sources of Funds A different type of restriction acting upon the remittance decision involves the availability of alternative sources of financing for foreign affiliates. In many of the less-developed countries subsidiaries may be unable—at almost any price—to obtain medium- and long-term financing. Therefore a directive from headquarters for them to remit their current earnings may preclude the subsidiaries from following through on a previously planned expansion program. In some cases funds may be available but be so costly or have so many restrictive covenants that they are unsuitable. In either case the important point is that the ability of a foreign operation to make remittances is based not only on its earnings but also on the availability of outside supplementary sources of capital.

Similarly the size of a subsidiary's remittance may be so large as to raise the cost of borrowed funds or impair its ability to borrow funds locally where funds may otherwise have been available. The affiliate's borrowing capacity may be based on its balance sheet position or relate to its demonstrated earning power. Both of these indicators are affected by the amount and types of remittances that the affiliate is directed to make. Any fund transfer will draw down the cash balances of the enterprise. And any remittance that is in effect an expense of doing business (whether tax deductible or not) reduces reported profits. The point here is *not* that remittances per se are harmful; from the overall company point of view it may be far more important to draw down the affiliate's cash balances than to preserve its borrowing capability. The important point is that the financial manager should tailor the remittance decision to the overall financial plan for the affiliate.

The Partners' Wishes in a Jointly Owned Foreign Venture A jointly owned foreign affiliate may raise serious problems for the multinational investor with regard to remittance planning. The interests of the partners may differ appreciably with respect to the percentage of foreign affiliate earnings that should be reinvested or paid out in dividends and with regard to the amount of outside financing to be used. While there are ways to overcome such problems or to prevent them from ever arising,[18] many companies complain that they must relinquish managerial freedom and flexibility in collaborative ventures.

Implications for the Competitiveness of the Foreign Venture In considering transfer pricing as a strategy by which to control transnational fund movements, one important factor may be the extent to which the pricing arrangements may impede or stimulate the competitive position of the foreign affiliate. If the decision is made to charge an affiliate a high price for the components it buys from the parent company, the implications may be a severe loss in the affiliate's sales volume if it faces a price elastic demand curve, and if the component is an important part of the total value of the final product that the affiliate sells. Transfer pricing has already been discussed as a tool with many possible advantages for the company that sells goods from one affiliate to others in different countries. As such the financial manager must be sensitive to the possible consequences of a particular pricing policy with reference to the multitude of company objectives. In the case of remittance policy a top priority decision to milk an affiliate in advance of an expected exchange devaluation may be suitably achieved through the medium of intercompany sales and appropriate pricing strategy. But if the company also wishes to maintain the affiliate's market position over the long run, then such a transfer pricing approach may not be desirable.

[18] The reader may wish to review the literature on joint ventures, which was cited in footnote 9 of this chapter.

Organizational and Structural Restrictions As a final consideration in this discussion of restrictions on the transfer of funds, one should be cognizant that the type of business, product, marketing methods, legal structure, and function of individual subsidiaries have an important bearing on the type of remittance methods that can be utilized. Obviously where intercompany sales do not exist, the opportunity to use transfer pricing is nil. In some cases, if an affiliate is located in a less-developed country and is owned by a holding company located in a so-called tax haven country, the affiliate may pay dividends to its parent company without subjecting the recipient corporation to any incremental tax. However, if the foreign subsidiary is owned directly by a United States corporation, the dividends are included in the ordinary income of the recipient firm. If it is considered necessary to effect a transfer of funds between a company's subsidiary in Italy and its operations in the Philippines, the manner in which the payment is made depends on such factors as whether or not one affiliate owns the other, sells goods to the other, can provide technical advice to the other, or can obtain governmental permission to make a loan to the other.

A synthesis

The chart on page 438 illustrates the stages through which the remittance discussion has thus far traveled. In stage 1 the manager decides whether or not a given foreign affiliate *should* remit funds—either to the parent company or to another business entity controlled by the firm. Once an affirmative decision has been reached, the task in stage 2 is to decide tentatively on the *amount* to be transferred from the affiliate. This second decision is dependent on such factors as the basic reason for making the remittance, tax rates and regulations, and ability to move funds. In stage 3 the manager considers the *form(s)* in which the remittance can be effected. His analysis considers such factors as the reason for making the fund transfer, the amount of funds to be moved, the remittance forms that are permitted by the respective governments, and the costs and benefits to the company as a whole associated with each of the alternatives.

The relevant variables in a remittance decision are normally too numerous and too interconnected to permit separate consideration of the three basic questions: "Should funds be remitted; how much should be remitted, and in what forms should the remittance be made?" Yet the task of making a final decision can be somewhat simplified throughout the analysis by distinguishing the so-called discretionary aspects of the remittance decision from the elements over which management has no control.

The fundamental reason(s) for making a remittance and a few key environmental characteristics are likely to suggest the remittance amount as well as the form in many instances. If, for example, the parent com-

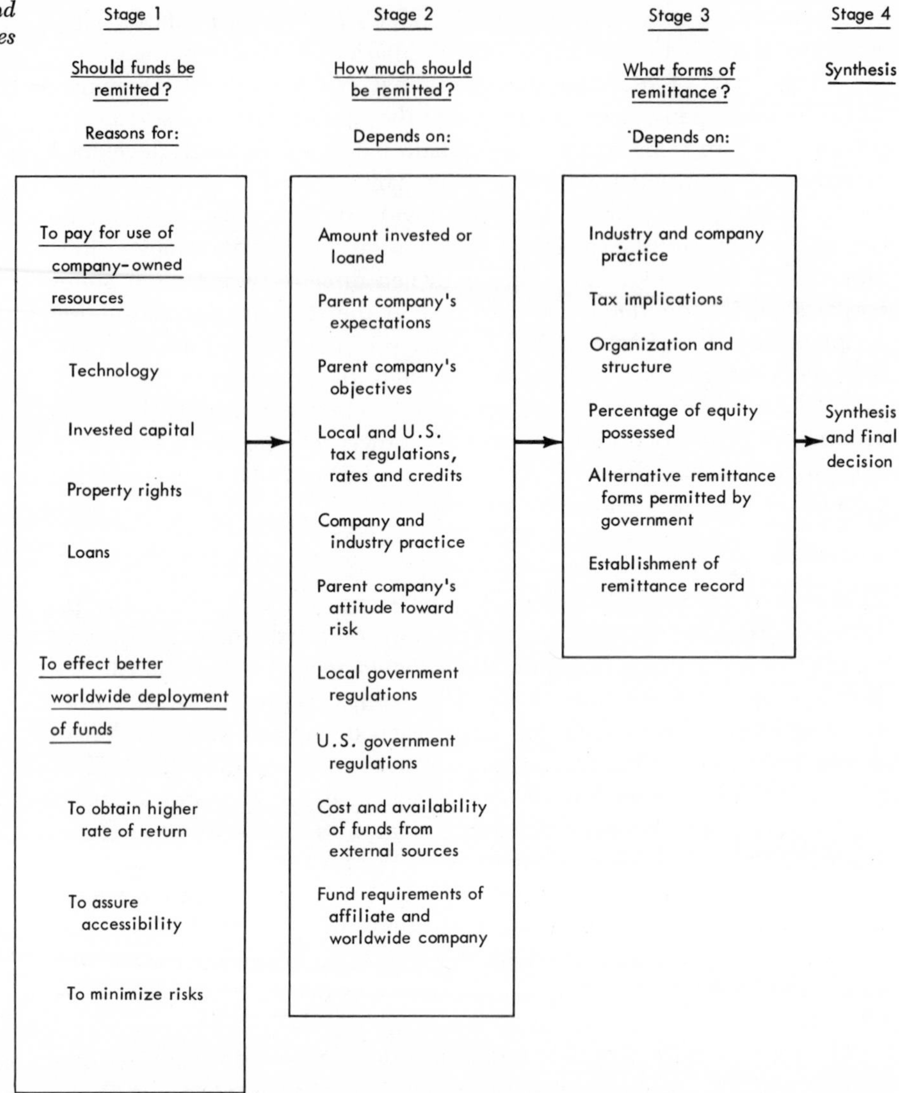

pany charges a flat fee to each foreign affiliate to cover the cost of maintaining a worldwide teletype communication network, the basic reason for the remittance provides the financial manager with both the dollar value of the affiliate's remittance for that purpose and the form (a fee) by which the funds will be transferred. In a similar vein, if a foreign country has imposed controls on the extent to which local companies can utilize the nation's scarce foreign exchange reserves, it is likely that permission to make certain types of remittances such as dividends will be explicitly denied (or limited).

If at the beginning of his analysis the financial manager identifies the variables that limit or preclude discretionary action, he will have been able to arrive readily at a tentative conclusion for a part of the remittance decision, and he will have somewhat simplified his decision task.

In this next broad area of remittance analysis—the area where the financial manager has discretionary authority—it is important at the outset to establish explicitly a system of priorities. The decision maker must identify not only *why* an affiliate should remit funds, but also the relative importance of each of the reasons. Is the firm primarily concerned with avoiding an exchange devaluation, as might have been the case in England in 1967? Or is the main objective to obtain funds from one affiliate so that they can be used more effectively by another? A system of priorities will help to guide the financial manager through each step in his analysis, initially in identifying the relevant environmental and internal variables, and subsequently in weighing the myriad of answers obtained from a cost-benefit analysis.

The key to effective decision making in the remittance area—as is true in all of business management—is *systematic* analysis. The stages of the decision-making progress discussed in this chapter and illustrated on page 438 offer a logical sequence for the manager to follow. As a *minimum* condition the decision process should normally include consideration of all of the variables associated with each of the stages. Where it is possible the relevant factors should be quantified to indicate the costs and benefits to the company as a *whole* associated with a particular course of action. When he has examined all of the alternatives and has calculated their respective merits, the manager should temper these assessments with his own judgmental evaluation of the wisdom of remitting certain amounts in each of the ways being considered. Out of this process of narrowing down the choices the financial executive will eventually be able to select a mix of forms by which to transfer funds and the percentage of the total amount to be remitted using each of the forms. His selection will not guarantee the optimal solution for the firm because of his inability to quantify many of the variables. However, by *explicitly* identifying the relevant variables and by carefully evaluating how they bear on the final decision, the decision-maker can maximize the utility of his own judgment and thereby best fulfill his function to the corporate shareholders.

Summary

The discussion has focused on the opportunities and requirements of a multinational investor to *manage* the international flow of funds between its affiliates and the parent company. Contrary to the practices of many firms that tie foreign remittances to an historically satisfactory percentage of local earnings, the approach recommended in this chapter involves basing the decision upon a complete analysis of the organization's projected sources and uses of funds around the globe, the rationale for transferring funds between affiliates, the costs associated with such movements, and the influence of environmental constraints.

The business manager is counseled to use the following three questions as guidelines to appropriate management of international remittances:

1. Should funds be transferred?
2. How large should the remittance be?
3. Which is the most desirable form for effecting the transaction?

The discipline of answering these questions should insure adequate consideration of the relevant variables.

BIBLIOGRAPHY

Annual Report on Exchange Restrictions. (Washington, D.C.: International Monetary Fund).

Behrman, J. N. "Foreign Licensing, Investment, and U.S. Economic Policy," *The Patent, Trademark and Copyright Journal of Research and Education,* Summer 1960.

Mikesell, Raymond F. *U.S. Private and Government Investment Abroad.* (Eugene: University of Oregon Books, 1962).

Polk, Judd, Irene Meister, and Lawrence Veit. *U.S. Production Abroad and the Balance of Payments.* (New York: National Industrial Conference Board, 1966).

Shulman, James. "When the Price Is Wrong—By Design," *Columbia Journal of World Business,* May-June 1967.

Smith, Dan T. "Financial Variables in International Business," *Harvard Business Review,* January-February 1966.

"Where's the Money? Remitting Profits the Hard Way," *Worldwide P&I Planning,* September-October 1967.

Zenoff, David B. "Remitting Funds from Foreign Affiliates," *Financial Executive,* March 1968.

Case 19
ASSOCIATED FOOD MACHINERY COMPANY (AFMC)

In January 1968 Andrew Fay was hired by the Associated Food Machinery Company to be its new financial vice-president. The company produced and sold a machine part called the *Z*, which was sold to food-processing companies in eight countries. Sales and profits had grown steadily through the 1960's, and were about $28 million and $5 million, respectively, in 1967.

Fay was brought in to manage the company's finances after the former treasurer, John Liebert had retired. Fay was an experienced corporate finance man, and the president's decision to hire him instead of other sales or engineering-oriented executives—as had been the case with Liebert and the present comptroller—was thought by many to be a new approach to boosting the firm's overall performance. In the words of a Wall Street security analyst who had followed AFMC for several years: "The company's president finally woke up to the fact that AFMC has become too big and the opportunities are too great to continue with a basically unimaginative and ill-equipped top management."

In many respects AFMC could be characterized as a "multinational" company. It had subsidiaries in nine foreign countries, its market opportunities were virtually worldwide in scope, and the parent company accounted for only 35 per cent of the total sales and profits – although it was the largest single operating unit. With the exception of the United States operation, none of the other units was completely self-sufficient in the production of the *Z*. Therefore both manufacturing and sales were handled on an integrated worldwide basis. As shown in Exhibit 1, the United States plants produced the three components *A, B,* and *C,* which comprised the *Z,* and they also assembled the *Z*. The parent company exported *A*'s to its Canadian and Mexican affiliates. AFMC Canada manufactured *B*'s and *C*'s, and with the *A*'s imported from the United States, it assembled finished *Z*'s for the local market. Canada also exported all three components to Germany, and *B*'s to the Mexican affiliate. The German subsidiary, the basic unit in Europe, was utilized as a central assembly and distribution point for the continent because of its central geographical location, its duty free entry to other common market countries, and the availability of relatively low cost, skilled laborers. The German affiliate assembled *Z*'s and sold them in the local market as well as to the company's sales subsidiaries in France and England. It was projected that within the next five years sales offices would also be opened in Italy and Belgium.

In Latin America AFMC utilized a Panamanian holding company as the legal parent company for its three affiliates there. Mexico was the key operation, manufacturing *C*'s and utilizing imported *A*'s and *B*'s in its assembly of *Z*'s, which were sold in Mexico and exported to the company's sales affiliates in Brazil and Peru. The Panamanian holding company was founded in the late 1950's when the former treasurer, John Liebert, became intrigued with the possibilities of deferring United States taxation on some of the income earned abroad, via a so-called tax haven holding company. At that time, however, the Latin American operations had been too small to realize any noticeable gains from the Panamanian affiliate, and in 1962 when the United States internal revenue code was revised, Liebert was convinced that the future opportunities for tax deferral were nil. Since then the income of the Latin American affiliates had been funnelled through the Panamanian holding company to AFMC in the United States with virtually no funds withheld in Panama.

Having joined the company at the beginning of calendar year 1968, Fay's first task was to review and reapprove the operating and financial budgets developed by his predecessor. From Fay's reviews and conversations with Liebert prior to the latter's departure, Fay learned that AFMC had relied on a number of rules of thumb for guiding financial practices. One rule was that the company should try to declare 60 per cent of its annual profits after taxes as dividends to its shareholders. Another guide was that the foreign affiliates should remit a like amount to the parent company each year in order to do their share in providing dividends to the company stockholders. The company had not been averse to the use of debt funds, and in fact it had followed a standard practice of requiring foreign affiliates to finance a large portion of their working capital and capital expansion needs through locally denominated borrowings. The prevailing philosophy was that exchange risks should be avoided at all costs, and that, therefore, capital should be borrowed from local sources only. There was no outstanding intercompany debt with the exception of short-term balances; these reflected the sizable volume of interaffiliate trade in components and finished goods. The steadfast rule was that all intercompany accounts must be paid within thirty days. The pricing policy was uniform throughout the firm. Intercompany sales were made at cost plus 15 per cent, and sales to outsiders at cost plus 20 per cent. Cost represented the unit variable cost, in addition to the total overhead of the respective plants, divided by the number of units produced per annum. Exhibit 2 shows the production costs for each component and for the finished product at each manufacturing site; Exhibit 3 depicts the sales volumes and prices of the various components and of the *Z*'s that were sold by each of the AFMC organizations. In 1967 all units were producing at capacity or within 10 per cent of capacity.

A necessary part of the review made by Fay was of the existing scheme of intercompany supply. He was told that it had been designed in 1959 in response to the creation of the EEC and to the then existing tariff rates of each country. Exhibit 4 contains the relevant tariff and transportation rates that existed when Fay assumed his new duties.

The investment required to increase the capacity of an existing AFMC plant or to establish a new one in order to produce any of the components or the *Z*'s is shown in the table below. A company engineer estimated that these figures would apply to any geographical location where AFMC affiliates were extant.

Total U.S. $ Investment Required to Build a Plant

TYPE OF OPERATION	*ANNUAL PRODUCTION CAPACITY (number of units)*					
	10,000	*30,000*	*50,000*	*100,000*	*200,000*	*500,*
Component *A*	$195,000	$ 360,000	$ 470,000	$ 680,000	$1,050,000	$2,100,
Component *B*	220,000	400,000	550,000	800,000	1,400,000	2,900,
Component *C*	230,000	400,000	510,000	800,000	1,400,000	2,900,
Assembly into *Z*'s	90,000	115,000	190,000	260,000	500,000	1,000,
Total investment required to produce *Z*'s	$735,000	$1,275,000	$1,720,000	$2,540,000	$4,350,000	$8,900,

It occurred to Fay that the closely knit international production scheme and the large volume of intercompany sales warranted a close reevaluation of the existing pattern of transfer pricing between affiliates.[1]

For the purely financial area Fay decided that until he was more familiar with the functions of the overseas managers and the nature of the company's operations and problems, he would postpone drawing up a system of reporting and management controls. However, he saw no reason to delay his evaluation of the methods and amounts by which funds were transferred between the affiliates and the United States parent company. His approach to such an evaluation included a brief review of the status and plans of the individual affiliates and of the parent company and a careful inquiry into the bases for the individual units' sales and profitability in the year just ended. The highlights of Fay's review of the affiliates' status and plans are contained in Exhibit 5. Exhibit 6 presents the income tax rates and capital restrictions in each of the countries in which AFMC had operating units.

As Fay:

1. What general factors would you take into consideration in drawing up a plan for moving funds between foreign affiliates and the United States parent company?
2. With the information available to you in January 1968, would you modify the existing company policy of requiring all foreign subsidiaries (except Panama which remitted virtually 100 per cent) to remit 60 per cent of their after-foreign tax income? Why? Of what influence— if any—are United States and foreign income tax rates and regulations?
3. Given the limited amount of information available on marketing conditions how, if at all, could AFMC's pricing policies be altered? What options appear to be open?

[1] In 1967 the company president had commissioned an outside study of the nature of the demand which existed for the product *Z* in each of the countries in which it was then sold. In essence the results showed: (1) The nature of the demand for *Z* was identical in all of the countries. The customers were local or multinational food-processing companies whose production schemes were very similar. There appeared to be virtually no price elasticity of demand for the various *Z*-type products when a producer's price was within plus or minus 4-5 per cent of the average price for it within a given country. A price rise or decrease that was plus or minus 5-10 per cent of the existing average price in a country was expected to lead to a decrease or increase, respectively, of about 18 per cent in the number of units sold by the company having introduced the change. A price change of 10-20 per cent above or below the prevailing average price of *Z*-type products in a country, would produce a 30 per cent decrease or increase, respectively, in the number of units sold.

EXHIBIT 1

AFMC Financial and Production Organization Chart

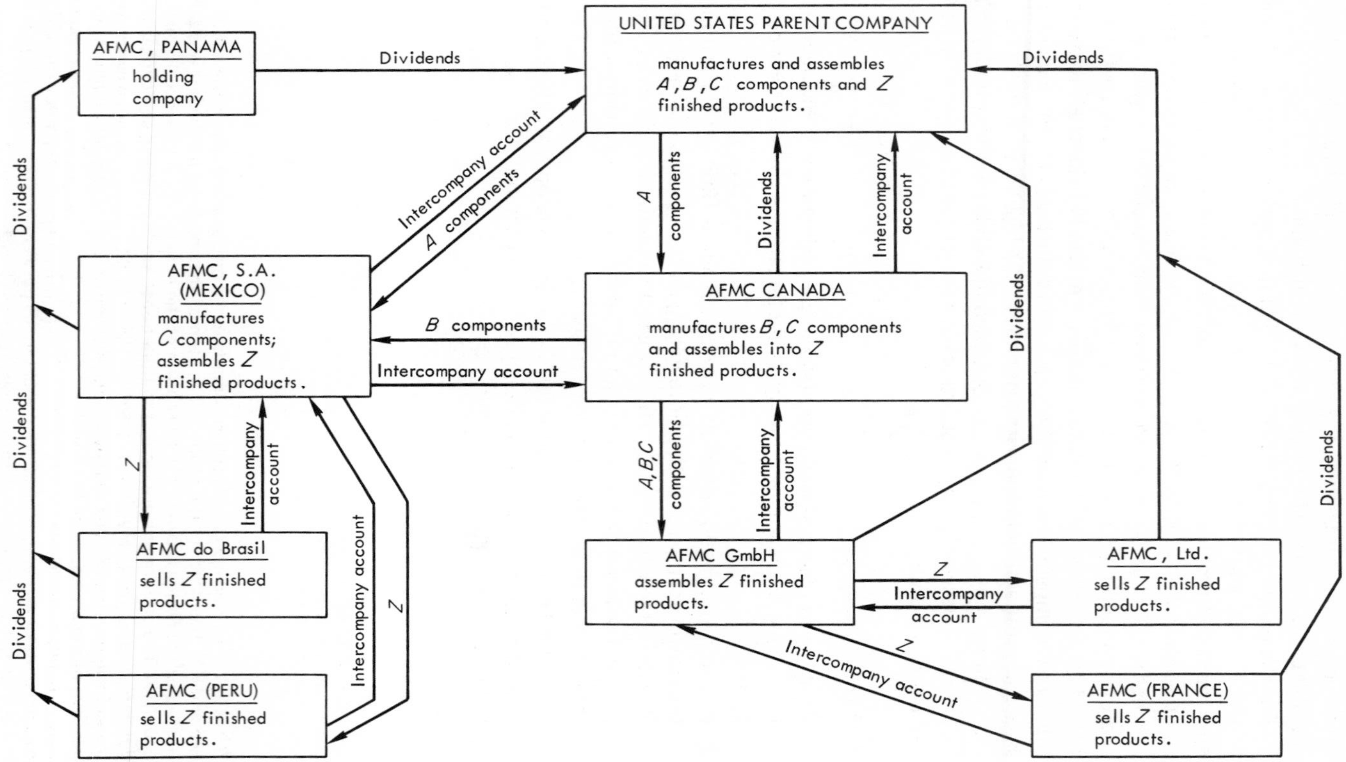

EXHIBIT 2 | AFMC Unit Production Costs for Components And Finished Products at Various Sites

PRODUCT MANUFACTURED	*UNIT COSTS (IN U.S. $) BY LOCATION*		
	Fixed costs	*Variable costs*	*Assembly*
Component *A*	(U.S.) $1	(U.S.) $2	
Component *B*	(U.S.) $1 (Canada) $1.10	(U.S.) $3 (Canada) $3.15	
Component *C*	(U.S.) $1 (Canada) $1.10 (Mexico) $1.20	(U.S.) $1.50 (Canada) $1.60 (Mexico) $1.90	
Z – finished product			(U.S.) $6 (Canada) $5 (Mexico) $2 (Germany) $3

EXHIBIT 3 AFMC Sales Volume, Costs, Prices, and Profits on Component and *Z* Sales by Various Affiliates (1967)*

Unit that sells	*Unit that buys*	*Product and volume*	*Cost in selling country*	*Plus 15% profit*	*Plus transpor-tation*	*Plus duty†*	=	*Landed cost*	*Plus assem-bly*	*Plus local profit†*	=	*Local selling price*
Germany	England	*Z* 100,000	$16.82	$2.52	$.29	$5.80		$25.43		$5.09		$30.52
Canada	Germany	*A B C*	*A* 3.62	.54	.18	.17		13.82	3.00	3.36		20.18
		270,000 of	*B* 4.25	.64	.20	.29						
		each	*C* 2.70	.41	.20	.62						
Germany	France	*Z* 70,000	16.82	2.52	.19			19.53		3.91		23.44
U.S.	Canada	*A* 470,000	3.00	.45	.10	.07		3.62				
U.S.	local mkt.	*Z* 500,000	14.50							3.10		18.60
U.S.	Mexico	*A* 100,000	3.00	.45	.11	.59		4.15				
Canada	Mexico	*B* 100,000	4.25	.64	.16	1.03		6.08				
Mexico	Peru	*Z* 30,000	15.33	2.30	.20	4.41		22.24		4.45		26.69
Mexico	Brazil	*Z* 30,000	15.33	2.30	.30	2.64		20.57		4.11		24.68
Canada	local mkt.	*Z* 100,000	15.57							3.11		18.68
Mexico	local mkt.	*Z* 40,000	15.33							3.07		18.40

* Note: all monetary figures are shown in U.S. dollars.
† Country duties on imports are *ad valorem*, based on the selling price in the country of origin. See Exhibit 4 for relevant tariff rates.
† Local profits are always cost plus 20 per cent.

EXHIBIT 4

Tariff* and Transportation Rates Applicable to AMFC Units (in U.S. $)

COUNTRY FROM WHICH EXPORTED	*TRANSPORTATION RATES PER UNIT*				*COUNTRY INTO WHICH IMPORTED*	*TARIFF RATES PER UNIT*			
	A	*B*	*C*	*Z*		*A*	*B*	*C*	*Z*
U.S.	.10	.10	.10	.30	Canada	2%	4%	9%	25%
U.S.	.11	.10	.10	.31	Mexico	17%	21%	57%	145%
Canada	.18	.20	.20	.58	Germany	4%	6%	20%	45%
Germany	.09	.10	.10	.29	England	8%	10%	7%	30%
Germany	.06	.06	.07	.19	France				
Mexico	.06	.07	.07	.20	Peru	6%	5%	6%	25%
Mexico	.10	.10	.10	.30	Brazil	5%	3%	7%	15%
Canada	.18	.16	.16	.50	Mexico	17%	21%	57%	145%
U.S.	.17	.18	.18	.53	Germany				
U.S.	.18	.19	.19	.56	England				
U.S.	.17	.18	.18	.53	France	12%	16%	7%	35%
U.S.	.21	.22	.21	.64	Brazil	11%	6%	12%	35%
Mexico	.20	.21	.21	.62	England				
Mexico	.20	.20	.20	.60	France-Germany				
					U.S.	7%	8%	8%	25%

* Note: Tariff rates are *ad valorem*, with the rate representing a percentage of the selling price of the unit in the country from which it is exported to the foreign purchaser.

EXHIBIT 5

Excerpts From the Brief Country-by-Country Review by Andrew Fay (all amounts in United States dollars)

1. Canada

Wholly-owned by AFMC. Served the local market with *Z*'s and exported parts to Germany and to Mexico. Imported *A*'s from the U.S. Sales and profits have increased by about 10 per cent a year, and the pattern is expected to continue. Competition is widespread from a number of large and small producers of *Z*-type products, with prices ranging from $18 to $20.50. No reason to worry about inflation or devaluation. In 1968 expected to earn $805,000 before taxes and about $890,000 in 1969. An increase in capacity was scheduled, and fund requirements were $250,000 in 1968 and in 1969. Funds could be borrowed for up to five years at about 7 per cent rate of interest.

2. Germany

Wholly-owned by AFMC. Started primarily as an assembly operation to serve EEC countries, but thus far about one-third of all sales went to the U.K. affiliate. (If U.K. joins the EEC, the steep $5.80 tariff on *Z*'s should be abolished.) Sales increases averaged about 10 per cent a year and are forecasted the same for the near term. Growth should come from France and Germany but not the U.K. Considerable number of competitors within $21.00 to $22.50 price range. No foreseeable balance-of-payments or inflation problems. Expected to earn $765,000 before taxes in 1968 and $825,000 in 1969. $300,000 to be spent this year on increasing capacity and $600,000 in 1969 for same. Six-year, 6½ per cent funds are available locally.

3. England

Wholly-owned. Sales only. Apparently the company has always been afraid to manufacture there because of balance-of-payments crises and the slow growth in the country's economy and industries. Sales have not grown at all in the past four years because (1) our price is high compared to competitors' $27-30 prices, (2) the economy has been generally sluggish, (3) two competitors with local manufacturing affiliates are strong, both in prices and large and effective sales forces. Our ability to hold customers is apparently based on trade relations leverage exerted on a worldwide basis. No inflation problems but continued uncertainty about balance of payments. Pound sterling may have to be devalued again. Profits for both 1968 and 1969 expected to be $510,000. No capital expansion plans. Funds can be borrowed for only one to two years at 9-10 per cent effective cost.

4. France

Jointly owned. Sales only. Newly established in past three years. We went in 50-50 because our partner (French) is an effective industrial goods distributor. He handles marketing, we the supply. Good relations, although with recent rise in sales of *Z* (from 0 to 70,000 units in three years) he wants dividend to be at least 75 per cent of 1968 earnings after French taxes. Many small competitors mostly in $23.50-26 price range. Expect sales to rise to 100,000 units/year in next two years, then level off. No balance-of-payments worries or problems with inflation. 1968 profits expected to be $275,000 and $330,000 in 1969. Planned increases in sales force and sales activities will cost us $300,000 this year and $375,000 next year.

5. Mexico

Wholly-owned. Gradual increase in local market as country becomes more industrialized. Sales and profits should increase by 10 per cent in each of the next few years. Our competition there is one other large producer. Sells his *Z* for $18.75. No balance-of-payments or inflationary worries. Exports *Z*'s to Peru and Brazil. Expect 1968 profits of $260,000 and about $15,000 higher in 1969. No expansion plans.

6. Peru

Wholly-owned sales affiliate. Market small and not much growth expected. Competition supplied by exporters like us. $26.75 price. 15-20 per cent inflation in past few year, expected to continue. Balance of payments somewhat shaky. Might have another devaluation. Expected profits in each of the next two years about $450,000. Local borrowing costs 20-25 per cent for extremely short-term funds and difficult to get.

7. Brazil

Wholly-owned, sales only. Large market potential over next twenty years as country develops. Present growth of profits and sales about 10 per cent a year. Several competitors with same plans as ours for the long run. Their prices $24-26. Expect $410,000 profits in 1968 and $460,000 in 1969. Inflation a bad problem—at least 30 per cent a year. Need additional working capital of $300,000 in 1968 and $350,000 in 1969. Local borrowing, even short term hard to obtain. Pay at least 35 per cent rate of interest. Balance of payments in trouble. Frequent devaluations can be expected.

8. United States

Parent company. Overall growth about 10 per cent per annum. Many competitors. Considerable price competition. $18.50-18.75 range. Board of directors considers 60 per cent dividend payout rate a must. President began program of diversification two years ago to increase sales, profits, and stability. Acquiring smaller companies for cash. Management time spent on international activities and investments was at a cost of $300,000 per year for 1967. Corporate objective: over next ten years become more involved abroad where there appear to be greater opportunities for the *Z*. Expected domestic earnings before taxes to be $1,707,000 in 1968 and $1,860,000 in 1969. $2,500,000 in acquisitions planned for this year and same for next. Long-term funds available in U.S. at about 6½ per cent.

EXHIBIT 6

Corporate Income Tax Rates and Restrictions On Capital Transfers in Countries In Which AFMC Organizations Were Located

Country	*Corporate income tax rate*	*Restrictions*
U.S.	.48 (see note below on foreign tax credits and method for calculating tax on foreign income)	none
Germany	.15 on distributed income, .51 on undistributed income	none
Canada	.50	none
Mexico	.52	none
England	.40	none
France	.50	none
Brazil	.30	No dividends presently possible; remittances permitted only for royalties up to five per cent of sales-- if government considers them to be "legitimate."
Peru	.35	Dividends limited to eight per cent of after local tax income. Royalties up to 2 per cent of sales.
Panama	0	none

Note on United States Taxation of Foreign Income:

1. The United States government recognizes the right of foreign governments to levy a tax on the income earned by United States-owned enterprises located in foreign tax jurisdictions. However, for its own citizens the United

States applies the principle that it can tax income earned in a foreign country. In order to preclude a combined foreign and United States taxation rate on foreign source income that is greater than the normal corporate rate in the United States, the United States government allows a credit against United States income tax liability which is virtually equal to the amount of foreign taxes already paid on the same foreign income.

2. With the exception of undistributed income of so-called foreign base companies, which will be explained below, the United States does not tax income earned abroad by United States-owned companies until the funds are actually remitted to the United States parent company. For income remitted by affiliates located in the economically advanced countries, the amount of United States tax liability is calculated in the following manner: The dividend received from abroad is grossed up to include the foreign income taxes paid by the foreign company—which are attributable to the dividend—and the entire amount of the tax is allowed as a credit against the United States tax liability. Assume, for example, that the United States tax is 50 per cent, the foreign tax 30 per cent, and all of the foreign subsidiary's after-tax profits are remitted; the United States tax would be $20 based on these calculations:

Foreign income	$100
Foreign tax	30
Dividend	70
Gross up	30
Amount included in United States income	100
United States tax	50
Foreign tax credit	30
Residual U.S. tax	$ 20

3. Income received from an affiliate located in a less-developed country is handled slightly differently for purposes of calculating the amount of the United States income tax. The foreign tax credit allowed in the United States is based on the formula: dividend/foreign profits before tax multiplied by the foreign tax. No gross-up is used. In the following example the same assumptions are used as in number 2 above.

Foreign income	$100
Foreign tax	30
Dividend	70
U.S. tax	35
Foreign tax credit (.7 x 30)	21
U.S. tax liability	$ 14

4. In those situations where a United States company has an excess foreign tax credit resulting from an affiliate abroad being subject to a higher tax rate than the parent, the credit can be applied against other foreign income that is subject to a lower local tax or as a foreign tax credit carry-over. The foreign tax credit is available only for foreign income and excess profits taxes and tax-

es in lieu of income taxes. United States firms (as was the case with AFMC) can elect to have the foreign tax credit applied on a *composite* basis whereby foreign taxes paid are lumped and the limitation on its use is based on all foreign source income.

5. The exception to the principle that United States income taxes are levied only upon actual distribution of foreign earnings is "foreign base companies." When they receive income in the forms of dividends, interest, sales commissions from related corporations—as opposed to normal "operating income"—the income is considered to be a part of the taxable earnings of the United States parent company, even if not distributed to the parent. Among the exceptions to the rule of automatic United States taxation of foreign base company income are these: (1) If the foreign tax rate is over 47 per cent, the undistributed income is not currently taxed to the United States shareholder; if the foreign tax rate is less than 47 per cent, a required minimum distribution to the United States will provide an escape from the automatic inclusion of all of the foreign base company income with that of the parent company. The schedule of minimum distributions is as follows:

If effective foreign tax rate is (%):	*The minimum distribution percentage is:*
Under 10	90
10-19	86
20-27	82
28-33	75
34-38	68
39-41	55
42-43	40
44-45	27
46-47	14
47 or over	0

(2) The other method of avoiding the foreign base company provision occurs when the income received by the foreign base company is from a less-developed country and is reinvested in the stock or the debt of one or more other affiliates located in less-developed countries, provided such affiliates are more than 10 per cent owned by the United States parent company.

6. Section 482 of the United States Internal Revenue Code states: "In any case of two or more organizations, trades or businesses, (whether or not organized in the United States, and whether or not affiliated) owned or controlled directly or indirectly by the same interests, the Secretary of the Treasury or his delegate may distribute, apportion, or allocate gross income, deductions, credits or allowances between or among such organizations, trades, or businesses, if he determines that such distribution, apportionment, or allocation is necessary in order to prevent evasion of taxes or clearly to reflect the income of any of such organizations, trades or businesses."

The recent increase in foreign investment activity by United States corporations and the ability of many of these firms to shift income via transfer pricing and allocation of common costs among the various affiliates have resulted in a large backlog of Section 482 cases in the Treasury Department. In order to preclude arbitrary administration of the Section, the Treasury agreed to issue regulations that would provide a sound basis for business planning and policies. Thus far little guidance has been provided other than the widespread knowledge that the chief criterion relied upon by the government for granting approval of existing transfer prices is the extent to which price negotiations among affiliates are conducted at arm's length.

Further information on the United States taxation of foreign income can be found in: "Tax Factors in Foreign Business Operations," Harvard Business School Technical Note 71, 1963; James S. Shulman, "The Tax Environment of Multinational Firms," *The Tax Executive*, April 1967, pp. 173-187; Lawrence B. Krause, *Federal Tax Treatment of Foreign Income*, The Brookings Institution, Washington, D.C., 1964.

Management Control of Foreign Operations

12

Designing a control system for an internationally oriented company—as distinguished from a purely domestic business—and then implementing it is complicated by the so-called international variables encountered when business affairs cross countries' borders and are conducted in many foreign nations. As is true with virtually all of the functions of financial management in a multinational business corporation, the control process must account for the influence of the international variables and must be adaptable to their effects on operations and communications. The following brief description of some variables and their possible implications for the firm is intended to clarify the impact that some of these variables may have on the management control process.

It is generally true for most international companies that foreign affiliates are further removed geographically from central headquarters than are the domestic divisions and affiliates. From an operations viewpoint the greater distance may lead to serious problems and complications in logistics. Larger distances often produce increased transportation costs, longer periods of delivery time, and more frequent delays in intercompany movement of materials and goods. One of the implications of these complicating factors may be the necessity of establishing and maintaining closely controlled and strategically planned global inventory management. From the point of view of establishing a management control system—which will be the life blood of inventory management—an elaborate communication mechanism may be required to transmit data from the affiliates to the central logistics staff for analysis and in turn to send directives to the myriad of individual supply, assembly, transportation, manufacturing, and marketing subsidiaries. Anyone familiar with the operations of an integrated international petroleum company can readily appreciate the logistical complexities and the requirements for timely and complete communication.

The greater distances encountered in international business may also limit the effectiveness of traditional domestic methods of communicating results and directives between affiliates and the headquarters. Distance involves time delays and costs of transmission and may therefore necessitate the establishment of

1. Geographically disbursed intermediate headquarters to facilitate information flow
2. Reporting by affiliates on a more frequent basis in order to keep the headquarters in closer touch with actual operations
3. Different methods of reporting and communication from those used in domestic business to overcome difficulties posed by greater distance.

More personal visits between affiliate managers and headquarters staff may, for example, be necessary. One international executive explained his method of overcoming the distance barrier as follows: "We have instituted what we call our 'hot line telex system'; I have a direct line in my office now. . . . I do not have to go through the corporate telex system to get to the European headquarters and to every one of our major locations in Europe. I can write directly to them and receive a reply within half an hour.

Another distinctive variable in international business is the widespread utilization of *foreign nationals* in the management of foreign affiliates. For evidence of the growing use of local nationals and third country nationals in the managerial and technical positions of foreign affiliates of United States companies, one has only to examine the annual reports of any of the largest 500 firms, starting with those of the late 1950's. Typically the reports will highlight the large number of foreign nationals compared to the number of Americans employed abroad. Despite the sizable number of multilingual Europeans and Latin Americans and the growing number of bilingual American managers, the use of foreigners in management nevertheless causes problems in communication and differences in management practices. The reasons for these difficulties are basically three-fold:

1. Cultural differences are still extant, even though international travel and linguistic ability are closing the "culture gap" [1]

[1] An enlightening discussion of the impact of cultural differences on managerial performance is found in James Lee, "Cultural Analysis in Overseas Operations," *Harvard Business Review*, March-April 1966, pp. 106–114.

2. There are still a large number of foreign and domestic executives who are not able to communicate effectively or at all in other than their native tongue
3. The distance barrier will often magnify the problems caused by the subtleties of communicating across languages even among the more cosmopolitan group of international managers.

What often ensues from these complications are misunderstood directives and reports, loss of confidence among managers of different nationalities and languages, subtle but sometimes important differences among the nationalities in their attitudes toward risk, relationships with governments, delegation of authority, disclosure of information and ideas, acceptance of criticism and authority, openness in discussing business problems, and methods of dealing with lending institutions, suppliers, and various service organizations such as management consultants.

The implications for top level management are *not* that these nationality differences per se are harmful, but that they require adaptation. Management control procedures are useful only if they are comprehensible and acceptable by the people to whom they relate. The existence of language and cultural differences within an organization thus raises the important questions:

1. Should a multinational company institute more or less controls over foreign nationals compared to the practice for nationals of the home country?
2. Should a different set of standards be utilized to assess the performance of foreign nationals?
3. Should a separate system and approach to reporting and communication be implemented for managers of different nationalities?

A third relatively unique variable encountered in international operations pertains to *governmental regulations and restrictions.* Although businesses that are purely domestic in orientation are exposed to a large number of government directives and restraints, the firm whose activities extend abroad can anticipate the requirement of adapting to a larger number and wider variety of restraints. Restrictions on the movement of capital, goods, and personnel across national boundaries are peculiar to the multinational company. Minimum requirements for the amount of local value-added, the costs connected with importing or exporting goods, materials, and services, government limitation on the choice of factors of production utilized in a manufacturing operation, and mandatory collaboration with outsiders in the ownership and/or management of investment properties are among the more prominent types of restrictions encountered in foreign operations.[2] In addition the international

[2] For a more complete account of the type of restrictions encountered by international investors, *see* National Industrial Conference Board, *Obstacles and Incentives to Private Foreign Investment,* New York, 1965.

investor must contend with the many differences that exist between host countries' methods of regulating businesses such as taxation principles and codes, industrial relations practices, controls over pricing, limitations on capital structures, and methods of incorporation.

A system of management controls must therefore

1. Provide the highest echelons of management as well as the affiliate managers with a clear picture of the *impact* of these regulations and constraints on the foreign investment
2. Tailor a set of objectives and standards for individual foreign affiliates that account for the influence of the regulations and thereby provide realistic goals for local managers and a clear basis for evaluating performance.

In actual practice a number of companies still rely for management appraisal purposes on the reports that affiliates have prepared for local tax authorities or for the foreign ministries of finance and industry. One cannot normally expect that the design of such financial statements or the amount and type of information that they convey will be adequate for the needs of higher level executives who wish to obtain a clear picture of a subsidiary's operations and financial well-being. Yet they are often used because they are available or because the firm has not had the inclination or time to design different statements that would be more appropriate for internal control ends.

Another variable encountered in international business is the *risk* to the foreign subsidiary of loss or adversity stemming from currency devaluation, price inflation, or exchange controls in the host country. As discussed earlier in this book the possibility that one or more of these environmental problems may develop will often require the affiliate to plan a series of precautionary tactics designed to protect the value of the organization's assets and its earning power. A control system must be designed to help apprise headquarters and affiliate levels of management of the possibilities of such environmental contingencies, as well as for the financial status and operational position of the local subsidiary, so that decisions may be made on whether or not to take remedial action. The control mechanism must also provide a set of standards with which to motivate and evaluate management performance. They must be based upon the type of environmental dangers that are deemed to be extant and the manner in which the subsidiary is affected by their presence. In addition it is likely that special measures must be taken to acknowledge the effect that inflation and/or exchange devaluation can have upon the local currency value of the affiliate's financial statements.

The international manager can also expect to adapt to differences that exist in the business environment of foreign countries. In the broadest sense a company's control system must conform to three major constraints: the corporation's objectives, the organizational structure, and the environmental characteristics.[3] The organizational structure can exert a constraint if the quality of the company's management group is generally low or lower than desired. If management is of high quality, familiar with the modern tools of analysis, and resourceful in problem solving, a control system can be designed and implemented that can have a wide range of benefits to the company as a whole. If, however, at all levels there is a dearth of top caliber international executives, the attempted use of a sophisticated system of management controls may lead to human problems within the organization and far fewer benefits than if a more simple system were tried. Affiliate management may become demoralized, suspicious, frustrated, and disgruntled by having to adapt to a system not thoroughly understood or appreciated; headquarters staff may be incapable of reaping the full rewards from the structure either because they are unable to work with the data supplied or because the data itself is inaccurate or incompletely provided. An example that can be cited in this context is that of the worldwide Singer Corporation. In the early 1960's a new and relatively sophisticated group of top level executives took charge of the company. In their appraisal of international operations they discovered that the quality of many managers in the field precluded the adoption of complex performance standards and evaluative criteria. The method of control decided upon was a system of *simple* standards and reports that was comprehensible to overseas personnel and provided some degree of control for the parent company—rather than trying to force a complicated system where it could not have succeeded.

The reference earlier to the environmental constraint to which an internationally oriented company's control system must conform was intended to highlight the fact that methods of conducting operations and the institutions that form the business scene differ from country to country. In marketing, for example, the channels of distribution for a given product may differ considerably in the country of the parent company and in a second country;[4] in finance the custom in a foreign nation of extending lengthy periods of credit to customers may necessitate a significant alteration in a company's existing rule of thumb for working-capital management; in paying taxes and reporting to the host governmental authorities, a multinational firm may find that country *X* uses a different fiscal criterion than do the countries of the parent company or other affiliates; in industrial relations, subsidiaries in foreign countries may encounter local regulations that prohibit laying off idle personnel during periods of unused manufacturing or sales capacities.

[3] David F. Hawkins, "Controlling Foreign Operations," *Financial Executive*, February 1965, pp. 25–34.

[4] An interesting account of a few of the problems of marketing in foreign countries is provided by M. Sommers and Jerome Kernan, "Why Products Flourish Here, Fizzle There," *Columbia Journal of World Business*, March-April 1967, pp. 89–97.

These environmental differences may require alteration in the timing of fiscal budget activity and reporting, employment of special standards for inventory management, receivables policy, gross margins, capital structure, and the introduction of a complete set of special measures of control that are intended to facilitate adaptation to such differences.

A final variable that is likely to require special approaches to effecting management control over international operations is the difficulty encountered in forecasting changes in foreign environmental conditions. It is generally more difficult to make projections of the business climate abroad than in the country of the parent company—except where the affiliate is located in the United States. The problem usually results from a relative dearth of data and unfamiliarity with sources of data, the small or virtually nonexistent research staff at the affiliate level, and the absence of a businessman's feel for a foreign country when the analysis is carried out at the headquarters level. The difficulty is often compounded by the possibility of inflation, devaluation, or exchange controls abroad that are unlikely in the country of the parent company and therefore not required in forecasting activity.

The major implications of these added difficulties in making projections are:

1. Special techniques must be used to compile and analyze foreign environmental data
2. More difficulty can be anticipated in formulating precise objectives and operating standards for affiliates abroad
3. The measurement and evaluation of foreign results will be more complicated and will frequently require specially devised and often *ad hoc* approaches.

In summary the existence of these international variables necessitates the development of a control system that incorporates the possible effects of these variables on the respective foreign subsidiaries and that focuses on those areas of management that should and can be controlled by each international executive. Internationally oriented companies are complex and diverse in character, and a system that purports to provide control over their far-flung activities must rely upon a sizable *number* of *different* operating standards and reports. The familiar balance sheet and profit and loss statements that are drawn up for foreign tax authorities or the parent company's stockholders are not likely to be suitable for internal management purposes. Designing a system that accounts for the variables discussed above *and* the differences in mission, maturity, and importance of the respective foreign subsidiaries can be painstakingly slow and exceedingly difficult; high-priced outside consultants may be required to get the task accomplished. However, once the standards have been set and the reporting format, schedule, and directions established, the payoffs for headquarters and affiliate management can be very high when implementation of the system is readily facilitated.

Implied in the foregoing discussion were the components of a system of management control for large, multinational companies:

1. Policies that motivate managers at all echelons to strive for established goals
2. A system that ensures that appropriate executives will receive complete and timely data on activities for which they have accountability
3. A procedure for evaluating the results of operations so that the interested corporate officers will be able to appraise management performance and identify the affiliate's problems and major accomplishments
4. An organization that encourages and facilitates a relatively free flow of ideas and information throughout the worldwide system and which can be used as the basis for developing a meaningful dialogue by managers on all of the critical aspects of the organization's being.[5]

Given the unique capabilities of a global business corporation and the many adaptations that it must make to function effectively under diverse and sometimes threatening environmental conditions, the system of management control that is ultimately designed for such an organization will depend on how the following three questions are answered by key executives:

1. Within the multinational structure where should accountability lie for the key functions of management?

2. What special methods can be used to communicate critical policies and information between headquarters and field operations to ensure compliance with objectives established by the chief corporate officers and the establishment of realistic and appropriate goals?

3. What methodology can be developed for use in evaluating foreign operating results and the financial status of the various subsidiaries?

The remainder of this chapter is devoted to approaches which can be used to answer these queries.

ESTABLISHING MANAGERIAL ACCOUNTABILITY FOR KEY DECISIONS

The great care that must be given to decisions on where to locate accountability in a multinational corporation can be explained in terms of two factors: first, business that encompasses both domestic and foreign

[5] There are many slightly different definitions of what constitutes a system of management control. The one used in the text is a summation of the major writers' descriptions of suitable systems. For an appreciation of the possible definitions, the reader may wish to consult Charles T. Horngren, *Accounting for Management Control: An Introduction,* Englewood Cliffs, N.J., Prentice-Hall, Inc., 1965; David F. Hawkins, *op. cit.*

spheres is typically more complex than that confined to the domestic market only. Hence, the choice of where to place the ultimate accountability for a particular function must be based upon consideration of more variables and alternatives than would normally be the case for a purely domestic operation; second, among management specialists there has been a growing adherence to the concept that *specific* tasks and functions should be identified as the responsibility of *specific* managers—or included in a specific profit center—in order to ensure that proper managerial attention is provided to all of the areas that require it. This implies, among other things, that a scheme of responsibility reporting should be used in which information flows between an activity area and the manager accountable for it and performance is judged on the basis of how well the executive performs in those areas *over which he has control.*

In international financial management the question of where to locate accountability arises repeatedly. Who should conduct the capital budgeting for affiliates abroad? Who should establish basic objectives and operational strategies for the respective subsidiaries? Where should policies be set for working capital management, transfer pricing, protection against losses due to devaluation, exchange controls, and inflation? Who should have the right of approval of banks and accountants abroad? The following excerpts from interviews with treasurers, comptrollers, and financial executives of a number of large multinational companies in which these officers were asked to describe the location of accountablity for working capital management are indicative of the range of possible answers and their rationale.

1. Vice-president of a pharmaceutical company: "We want our affiliates to keep a proper inventory and not run out of stock . . . but also to keep their inventories low. We at headquarters help them develop procedures to ensure the latter. There are rare instances—for example if we see that a country might have to institute import controls—when we either rely on the subsidiary to increase its inventory, or we draw their attention to it by asking 'Don't you want to increase your inventory?' It is up to them, however. Whatever they need we will have to see that they get. . . . Fortunately, most of our subsidiaries make enough money so that except for a new operation, we at headquarters do not have to supply them with funds. We agree on minimum balances after they make up a cash budget for the year. When they have more funds on hand than the budget called for, we take it from them. . . . As for the terms of trade which the affiliates extend, the policy is fixed by headquarters, based on local conditions. If an affiliate wants to change the terms, they have to ask for permission from us. Other than that, it is up to them to see that their accounts are collected. Our auditors notice if there are bad accounts."

2. Treasurer of the international division of a food processor: "At one time in the early days we actually tried to handle trade credit from New York. When we first established ourselves in Canada, Mexico, and Puerto Rico, all credit was controlled by headquarters. It then came to a point where it was just impossible for us to sit here and supervise the extension of credit by a foreign organization. The subsidiary would know the customers much better than we, and the overall volume became too great for us. Actually it interfered with the affiliate's selling operations if everything that they received in orders had to be cleared back here. Hence the first change in policy was to shift responsibility for national sales within a country to the local management. They had direct responsibility for credit as far as their local sales went. Where, however, we were still supplying foreign distributors in sizable amounts, credit was still controlled from New York. . . . As far as dividends from the affiliates: for a new affiliate, the local manager makes the decision as to when he feels he is in a position to commence the payment of a dividend. If, however, he did not make a proposition to commence payouts, and we at headquarters felt they were in a position to do so, we would certainly request a clarification as to why they were not paid. For more mature subs, the company policy is for them to pay out 50 per cent of the prior year's earnings. The parent company pays out that amount to its shareholders, and we must therefore maintain that policy for the subsidiaries."

3. Subsidiary manager of a large, international petroleum company: "We can make decisions, for example, on the working capital requirements of the local marketing subsidiary, when we borrow locally from a bank. The amount we can borrow on our own is usually not material in relation to the affiliate's total financing picture. But the minute we get *outside* of the local situation, then we must come back to the parent company for advice because there are several different mechanisms that can be brought into play: to borrow from one or more United States banks, the parent company may elect to do some shareholder financing, and the intercompany accounts may be a source of funds."

4. Financial manager of an internationally oriented chemical company: "In the question pertaining to the decision-making authority in capital budgeting and foreign financing, an important reason for *our* retaining the final say-so at the headquarters is that most of our foreign managers are not experienced in this type of activity. Most of them are men with an engineering or production or strictly sales background in domestic operations; if we send them overseas, they don't have the right kind of experience and judgment to make financial decisions; and also, we can't afford to hire a high-priced financial man locally (because of the relatively small volume of each foreign subsidiary)—either he is not avail-

able or, as in Venezuela, he would cost more than in New York. So we are limited in the type of people that we find feasible to assign abroad; by default we make the decisions here, and they consider it a very great pleasure that we do so."

5. Vice-president of the international division for Europe and Africa: "The basic credit policies are set by the corporation, but only gradually are they being applied to the overseas operations. First they are applied to export sales because all of the foreign affiliates handle substantial export sales from the parent company. We try to get all of these credit terms on the same basis; we are just now beginning to apply modifications due to marketing differences in certain countries. In Italy, for example, we are up against an entirely different mentality, and we will not be able to just superimpose our rather idealistic ideas of credit collection on the Italians. It is a well-known fact that certain Italian companies are bad payers—usually the biggest firms! They ask for 120 or 180 days and then they never pay—they just take another two months or so. They actually use suppliers' credit to finance their working capital. . . . Even the corporate credit staff sees the light. I sent the corporate credit manager over to Europe last month to try to coordinate this better, and he came back convinced that while it would be good to be able to apply the United States system, it is just not practical in Italy. . . . Hence we are going to end up with a very flexible approach that will give a great deal of liberty to the local manager to try to maximize the amount of business he can do, versus the best collections he can achieve."

These excerpts, which refer to only one area of international financial management, provide an illustration of the approaches taken in today's multinational corporations to assign accountability for certain key decisions. The executives' statements suggest that the matter of deciding on the proper location for accountability is made difficult by a number of somewhat conflicting motivations and objectives. For one thing many officers attempt to avoid suboptimal decision making in their areas of responsibility. They would like to locate accountability at a high enough level in the organization to provide the decision-maker with a clear view of all of the relevant facts, all of the alternative solutions, and sufficient perspective to appreciate which of the alternative courses would appear to best serve company objectives. This philosophy is spelled out somewhat in the following remarks of a subsidiary manager in a large international petroleum company:

> You have to recognize that we have three distinct levels of management. The local affiliate is trying to optimize its profits within the country in which it is operating. The regional headquarters is trying to optimize its profits for the region. And the parent company is trying, of course, to optimize profits for the entire operation, worldwide. So each one is looking at a little different picture, and when it is neces-

> sary to reconcile our differences we bring in the *general* interests and ask what is best for the company as a whole. Because that's what our general objective is. . . . If a particular headquarters decision made in the general interest will not optimize the profits of our subsidiary, it is understood at the regional headquarters and the parent company that it is in the general interest to do so, and the managers such as I are not penalized when our performance is evaluated.

A number of experienced international managers are not swayed by the optimization principle for locating accountability. This group of pragmatists argues that it is never possible for *any* decision maker within the company to *really* know which solution will be the optimal one for the entire company. Furthermore, they state, the *cost* of gathering sufficient information on which to base an optimal decision would frequently outweigh the benefits to be gained from being able to select the best over the second-best answer. For these reasons many corporate officers reject the company-wide optimization concept as being a valid criterion for deciding where to locate accountability.

The widespread problem of finding capable experienced managers can be used as the basis for arguing for or against centralizing the key financial decisions in a multinational corporation. On the one hand it can be questioned whether or not the highest levels of management are *really* capable of making better decisions than the lower echelon subsidiary managers. If it happens that the headquarters staff is without adequate staff or are themselves not particularly skillful analysts of the foreign environment, there is no a priori basis for locating accountability at the headquarters. This sentiment was expressed in slightly different terms by the financial vice-president of a large industrial goods manufacturer:

> The decision-making levels for particular types of matters are identical in the international and domestic divisions. This, I believe, is a mistake. I think that the local managers abroad are *more* than just plant managers or sales managers for a particular country. They are the men who in the eyes of the public and their employees *are* our company. They are executives who run a *complete* operation. I believe we usually have higher caliber men in these positions than we normally have domestically. If we do have that kind of man overseas, we should give him more freedom to make decisions. Most of our foreign managers have well-rounded backgrounds—they have been marketing managers, financial managers, and production managers—while in a domestic division there is usually a much greater degree of functional specialization which, I think, justifies the fact that much of the overall decision making is done by men on a higher level who have the background and experience from two or three special functions.

The dearth of qualified personnel that appears to bother almost all large companies can also be used as justification for arguing in favor of centralizing key decisions. If the organization is forced to ration its top caliber managers, the approach that will make best use of them is to place the best men in the spots where the most important policy questions must be resolved and the most critical decisions made. This is likely to lead to centralization of accountability.

One of the forces that work against centralizing key financial decisions and accountability in a large multinational corporation is complexity and size. When a single firm owns many affiliates in foreign countries, it is constantly confronted by a variety of environmental conditions and uncertainties, as well as by many unique business operations each having its own mission, problem areas, experience in international operations, and requirements for assistance from the parent company. The frequent result is to give a greater degree of operating autonomy to the respective affiliates—or at least to those with experienced managers—because headquarters management is unable to provide systematic and analytically based decisions and managerial attention to so many foreign units.

In a similar vein many large companies have found that their highest level personnel are unable to develop a sufficient feel for the foreign environment, which is often believed to be a requisite for providing appropriate support to the affiliates and for assuming accountability for certain financial functions. The top executives are usually occupied with other pressing matters, are unable to make frequent visits to the many subsidiaries abroad, and find that written reports on foreign activities cannot replace visitations as a means for becoming intimately familiar with local conditions. Therefore accountability is frequently placed close to or at the level of the affiliate where "feel" is best developed. Obviously, the question arises, is "feel" necessary for appropriate decisions and for assuming responsibility for an operation? In those areas in which an impersonal judgment may be perfectly suitable, accountability may be safely placed at a higher level of management.

COMMUNICATING OBJECTIVES AND OPERATING RESULTS WITHIN A MULTINATIONAL ORGANIZATION

In addition to deciding where to place accountability for the financial management of international operations, the designer of a system of management controls must also examine the special approaches that can be utilized to enhance the timeliness and quality of communication between the international headquarters and the respective foreign operations. The basic objective is to ensure that lower levels of management are aware of the higher echelon's policy pronouncements and that the upper echelons are aware of what is happening at the affiliate level. The discussion that follows will not become involved in a nuts-and-bolts appraisal of the special techniques of communication that might be used—or that are being used—but rather will focus on the broad approaches available for fulfilling the communication and control objectives.

The most commonly used control technique among domestic and internationally oriented companies is budgeting. Through a combination of affiliate recommendations and top management guidance, a quantitative plan is made for each fiscal period. This budget, as it is usually called, is used as a standard of performance for the particular affiliate, and barring extraordinary circumstances or revision to the plan, the unit manager is expected to meet and fulfill the budget's provisions.[6] The activity of budgeting is considered by many to be an instructive and useful management tool. It disciplines managers at all levels to review established objectives, operating policies, and environmental conditions and expectations. The budget formulation also necessitates a close and continuing exchange between headquarters and affiliate personnel on all of these matters.

The precise format of a company's budget and its contents will of course vary from one company to the next, and from subsidiary to subsidiary—reflecting differences in corporate reliance on the budget, the affiliates' particular objectives, unique operating environments, and areas over which local managers are given control. As an example of the type and timing of budget and control activity that is carried out in large multinational firms, the following is a summary of how a successfully managed, integrated international petroleum company approaches this function:

> For convenience this system of management can be described in terms of separate, but interrelated planning and appraisal/control systems, each of which is programmed and administered on an annual cycle.
>
> 1. *Annual Planning Cycle*
>
> The annual planning cycle starts in mid-January of each year with presentation to the company of long-range *environmental forecasts* and assessments by the regional and operating organizations. These are coordinated by various staff groups in the headquarters as a basis for development of broad business objectives and result in judgments pointing up emerging trends in the economic, raw materials, and finished goods sectors, as well as in the broad areas of international political relationships, population and social trends, technological developments, etc. An integral part of this overall assessment is an appraisal of the company's own capabilities and limitations.
>
> With the environmental assessments that define the risks, constraints, and opportunities of the various geographical areas, the company establishes broad *corporate and investment objectives* for the

[6] There is a complete literature on the general subject of budgeting techniques and rationale. The uninitiated reader may wish to consult either of these sources for an introduction: Glenn A. Welsch, *Budgeting: Profit Planning and Control,* 2nd ed., Englewood Cliffs, N.J., Prentice-Hall, Inc., 1964, ch. 3; Charles T. Horngren, *op. cit.,* ch. 6.

organization as a whole and for each particular area. In late January the company sends these objectives to the regional and operating organizations for guidance in the development of investment projects for the budget year immediately ahead.

Concurrent with the environmental outlook, the regional and operating organizations also submit to headquarters their *long-range demand and supply forecasts* for the products sold and materials utilized in production. The document essentially looks forward three years.

In mid-March the regional and operating organizations submit to the company their *long-range corporate financial outlooks* which provide statements of their objectives and planning assumptions together with forecast results of significant financial and operating items such as capital expenditures, net earnings, cash flow, and operating levels. This document covers the same forward time period as the long-range demand/supply outlook. In September headquarters reviews initial results of the consolidated, worldwide long-range corporate financial outlook. Completion of this document is timed to provide part of the essential framework for New York headquarters review of the affiliates' capital budgets, which start in October.

For the shorter range planning period, the current year, and two years ahead, the headquarters and its affiliates employ two management tools, the *short-range demand/supply forecast* and the *short-range financial forecast*.

Submitted in mid-June and updated at the beginning of the following January, the *short-range demand/supply forecast* furnishes information concerning individual affiliates' current and future supply/demand outlooks for raw materials and finished products. These data are the basic information used to prepare sales projections, financial forecasts, transportation requirement forecasts, and overall product supply programs to carry out the affiliates' plans for the current period. Worldwide coordination of interaffiliate current period raw material, product, and transportation supply programs takes place in New York at the international headquarters.

The *financial forecast* is submitted by the regional and operating organizations in late September of each year and updated the following April. At the regional and operating organization level, the financial forecast serves as an overall plan of operations as well as a means of controlling performance, profitability, and the coverage of indicated financial needs. At the headquarters level the financial forecast is used in evaluating the financial progress of the affiliates worldwide as well as in formulating actions on financing plans and dividends.

Completing the annual planning cycle is the formulation of investment plans and formal *capital budgets* for the ensuing year. Prepared by each affiliate based on its own corporate objectives and with the long-range guidelines available from headquarters as well as the counsel and advice of regional managements, these capital investment projects and programs are submitted to headquarters on a regional basis in October for assessment of technical soundness, interregional coordination, overall evaluation of rate of return, risk, and projected income production, and for evaluation of responsiveness to overall, long-range corporate business and investment objectives. The headquarters' review of proposed budgets is completed in early December, and the views and comments of the company are made available at that time to the regional and operating organizations prior to adoption by the affiliates of their capital budgets for the ensuing year.

2. *Appraisal and Control Cycle*

A directly related and, in effect, integral part of the planning cycle is the appraisal of progress toward objectives and the control of capital budgets and operating programs.

Appraisal by headquarters of progress toward current operating objectives is achieved through a system of *monthly reports* from the regional and operating organizations on monthly and year-to-date results for *earnings* and *operating volumes* (production and product sales). Semiannually current operating plans and objectives are reappraised through the use of the short-range *financial forecasts* submitted to the company in September and April as described previously.

Control of capital budgets is largely decentralized at the affiliate level. The headquarters, however, has established certain limits beyond which budget overruns and additions require the company's review before commitment.

Final appraisal of actual results is accomplished annually by two separate systems:

First, annual reports are submitted in February to the Company, as follows: (A) *Financial statements* are submitted by each of the regional and operating organizations reporting on the financial results of operations for the calendar year just ended as well as the financial position as of year end. (B) For capital budgets *budget expenditure and commitment statements* from the affiliates report status of spending and appropriations against authorized capital investment programs and projects.

Second, a system or program of annual stewardship reviews is employed by the company to appraise and evaluate both financial and operating results as well as major capital investment programs, as follows: (A) In May and June, managements of the regional and operating organizations present to headquarters management a *financial and operating review.* Comparisons are made of the important financial and operating results for the year just ended with results for the previous year as well as with results predicted for the year just ended when the capital budgets for that year were presented. A comparison is also made of the outlook for the current year in relation to the forecast for the current year made the previous fall in connection with the presentation of the capital budgets. (B) Periodically, under its budget reappraisal, the regional and operating organizations are asked to review with the company the actual expenditures and results achieved for major investment projects and programs in relation to funds proposed and results predicted at the time the original budgets for the investments were adopted.[7]

In addition to budgeting there are other forms of exercising control over foreign operations that rely in essence on effective communication. As implied in the foregoing example, *personal visits* made by members of interested management units to their foreign counterparts, superiors,

[7] The information was generously provided by the assistant comptroller of the international headquarters of a large United States multinational company.

and subordinates form an important part of the control process. The purposes of such visits are essentially three-fold:

1. To provide headquarters staff with a clearer impression of operations and management performance abroad and to permit them to convey their ideas and policies to the subsidiary managers
2. To permit geographically separated and culturally diverse managers who normally communicate with each other in written form to meet personally and to discuss matters of mutual interest
3. To encourage and facilitate a free airing of ideas and problems by affiliate managers in the presence of headquarters personnel and to afford the former with an opportunity to explain their operating results.

To achieve these objectives, it is usual that headquarters line and staff personnel will visit individual affiliates and that the general managers, controllers, and financial managers of the subsidiaries will meet with each other—perhaps at a regional headquarters—and with headquarters staff at the parent company. The frequency and timing of such visits can be expected to depend on such phenomena and factors as:

1. The techniques and requirements of preparing budgets
2. The necessity of explaining sizable investment proposals
3. The need for personal explanations of variances from objectives or previous periods' results
4. The requirement for one or more higher level managers to solve a significant problem in a local affiliate
5. The use of refresher courses or management training programs for subsidiary level managers at the headquarters
6. The quality and experience of affiliate managers
7. The relative importance of an affiliate to the company as a whole
8. The number of foreign affiliates owned by the company and the size of the headquarters staff
9. The value placed by top management on personal meetings and first-hand examinations of foreign conditions.

Experienced international managers usually express a genuine interest and enthusiasm for regularly scheduled personal visits—as opposed to just putting out fires—but most complain that they have been unable to put their ideas to work because of the pressures of having to deal with day to day operating problems at home or special problems abroad.

Somewhat related to the use of personal visits in the manner described, a number of large firms have employed *traveling teams of internal auditors* to keep track of foreign operations, to communicate headquarters' directives and ideas, and to provide assistance to subsidiary managers in dealing with specific problems. Audit teams can be sent out on a regularly scheduled or on an unannounced basis. Companies have found many advantages and several potential liabilities in employing these teams.

On the plus side, internal auditors have been able to facilitate the communications between geographically separated units. By virtue of the auditors' widespread travels and grass roots familiarity with operations in foreign countries, they are often able to suggest methods of problem solving and new procedures that have been tested with other affiliates and found to be useful. In addition some top level international executives believe that the ever-present possibility of having the auditors drop in on a subsidiary helps to keep the affiliate managers on their toes at all times. An instance of the effectiveness of internal audit teams was expressed by the comptroller of a large pharmaceutical company:

> The rest of us who merely visit an affiliate do not spend enough time to really learn the *basic* problems; we may get the big problems and an overall view, and we can be helpful in that regard. But an auditor who spends time in a subsidiary can really get into it and find out what the problems are—problems which the local managers didn't even realize they had. Then, with the fresh approach by the outside auditors, the newly discovered and fundamental problem areas can be dealt with in a more effective manner.

Not all multinational firms use these teams, and many of those that do are not altogether satisfied with the results. The teams are expensive to support. Some have *not* noticeably improved the international communications link. In some instances the problems with auditors appear to be a result of a dearth of well-trained and capable personnel who can effectively perform the role of intermediary for the headquarters and affiliates, accountant, and management consultant. The problem seems to be one of recruitment. Highly qualified management talent is not usually receptive to taking on the life of a traveling auditor—living out of suitcases and being constantly on the go. In other cases the problem with auditors is that the system itself or the personalities of the men performing the function are too much like a spy network. Managers at all levels can grow suspicious of the system, resent the visits and advice, and work to undermine the auditors' work—whether or not deserved. A mixed appraisal of traveling auditors is provided below in an excerpt from a conversation with the international division vice-president of a multinational capital goods manufacturer:

> In addition to using the chain of command approach to fixing responsibility, we have internal audit teams which work for the general audit committee of the board of directors. There is a group of thirty to forty auditors who are ensuring compliance with any company directive; they can go to any of my operations and request to see compliance, and they will write in their audit report that goes through the regular chain of command coming up from the field to the audit committee any of their observations which are listed as deviations. The supervisor will then have to check into deviations and report whether

> they should result in changes or modifications of company standards. If an auditor says he thinks things should be done a certain way and lists a deviation, and another responsible manager or I believe things are being handled correctly, we can reject the auditors' recommendation. The audit teams' schedule is known to me but not to my managers. I tell them, though, because I think the managers can learn a lot from the auditors, and the managers travel so much that I want them to be present when the auditors are—at least for part of the time—because usually relations are very good and the auditors will show their preliminary reports to the managers and very often the manager can tell the auditor that corrections will be made and that a report of deviation need not be filed.
>
> The audit approach can sometimes lead to unpleasantness. We have had auditors who were not very diplomatic and perhaps talked behind the manager's back, and tried to eavesdrop.
>
> I think it depends on the background and professional strengths of the auditor involved. Some men have CIA backgrounds and have a habit of playing CIA and this has been commented on by some of the managers. I even have had some difficulties myself, which can become nasty. . . .
>
> I am actually in favor of an auditing system, and we are now working on a scheme for our *own* (the European division) auditing team in Europe, permanently attached to the European headquarters . . . with language ability. This is the only thing we don't like about using American auditors abroad; they don't have any idea about foreign languages. They look at documents and need a translator with them all the time, and this, of course, ties down the local administrative staff.

Another approach now taken by more than thirty-five large multinational companies to shorten the communications distance between the headquarters and foreign affiliates and to get more effective and close control of overseas operations is the establishment of regional headquarters. In essence, these are high level management units that are given line and staff responsibility for the company's investments in a given geographical area of the world. In part the increasing number of these regional headquarters can be considered as a normal—although not inevitable—evolutionary pattern in companies' attempts to organize better to meet the challenges and responsibilities of foreign operations.[8] Starting first with export offices, the large internationally oriented firm typically developed an international division with sufficient staff to manage the growing number of foreign investments. A few companies have gone even further and have restructured themselves into truly *global* patterns of management and control. But most firms have taken a less dramatic step beyond the international division by establishing regional headquarters that are responsible for coördinating and supervising the geographical area's production, finance, marketing, research, and control.

[8] For a review of the organizational changes and options open to management of large internationally oriented companies, *see* Gilbert H. Clee and Wilbur M. Sachtjen, "Organizing a Worldwide Business," *Harvard Business Review,* November-December 1964, pp. 55–67.

From the point of view of the international financial manager, a regional headquarters can have a number of advantages. It shortens the communications distance and minimizes difficulties in communicating between headquarters and the numerous field units. By substituting its own directives for those of headquarters or by relaying pertinent policy memorandums from the parent company, the regional headquarters have been found to be valuable. Their close geographical proximity to the subsidiaries permits the regional director to develop a close relationship with his affiliate managers and to stay abreast of the important environmental and internal problems and changes in the field. This close contact sometimes permits added flexibility in managing foreign operations and more rapid decision making and analytical support for the affiliates. An additional benefit to the system as a whole is the possibility of reducing the flow of data between the subsidiaries and the parent company if the regional headquarters screens and relays reports and communiques coming from both ends of the network.

If, as can be expected, regional staffs are more familiar with foreign operations than were (or are) higher echelons of management, they will be better able to establish realistic standards for the subsidiaries and to evaluate the results of operations. Presumably this kind of familiarity will allow for tighter control over foreign activities.

At this point in international business, it is not possible to accurately appraise the utility and liabilities of regional headquarters. They have been in existence for too short a period for anyone to make definitive statements about them. Thus far the main complaints have been that they may insulate parent headquarters from what is occurring in the field and that they may lead to too much preoccupation on the part of regional and affiliate executives with the welfare of the *region*, sometimes at the expense of the company as a whole.

APPRAISING FOREIGN RESULTS

The third principal requirement of an effective international control system is to develop suitable methods for appraising the operating results and financial status of foreign affiliates. Both the headquarters management and the affiliate managers will need to evaluate the general health of investments, ascertain the relative security in foreign environments, measure the value of investments to the company as a whole, and identify major problem areas. They will also want to evaluate how well affiliates have succeeded in achieving goals for particular fiscal periods, how effectively the local management has performed, consider whether or not extraordinary or special (protective) measures and policies should be instituted, and what modifications of major objectives and short run tactics are warranted. Appraisals of these questions require an effective reporting system and methodology and suitable standards for correctly evaluating available information.

The task of developing an effective reporting system for foreign affiliates has two critical facets: a decision must be made as to what information should be reported, and to whom, and a format must be designed for designated reports. Regarding the former, no generally applicable recommendation can be made here; the guidelines that should be used in making the decision are based on common sense. For whom is the information prepared? With what problems will the report deal? What information is required to solve particular types of problems? What data can be generated to meet the needs of management? The answers to these queries, together with an analysis of the cost of obtaining data, will form the basis for deciding which information needs to be reported and by whom it should be reviewed.

The task of devising a suitable format for reporting operating results is also devoid of a solution that would be universally applicable. Companies must decide for themselves such matters as in which currency(ies) the foreign data should be reported. In this regard management must evaluate the benefits that accrue from having local currency figures as opposed to dollar-denominated ones (if the parent is a United States company), or both sets. The decision on currency translation becomes somewhat complicated if one or more currency devaluations or revaluations in foreign locales are anticipated. Such changes in currency values require a determination of what rate of exchange to utilize in translating reports for internal use. Is the present rate most appropriate? Or is the expected rate more meaningful? In a similar vein how should the existence of price inflation in a foreign host country affect the format for reporting by exposed company affiliates? Without any modification to the basic data supplied by the subsidiaries, will local and higher levels of management be able to properly evaluate how well the unit has achieved its objectives, and what are its more pressing problems and weaknesses? Questions like these require answers before a reporting format can be devised. The solutions that are ultimately reached will depend in part on the purposes to be served by the issuance of particular reports, as well as the impact that price inflation and currency devaluation may have on the financial condition of foreign subsidiaries. A recommended methodology for handling these problems of translation and modification to affiliates' reports is presented in chapter 13.

The related question is how to establish standards for use in evaluating foreign results. The approach that companies decide upon hinges largely on the methods selected for translating local results and for interpreting them. In establishing standards, two general guidelines have proved useful to a number of firms:

1. The development of pro forma statements for foreign operations is very difficult—because of the added difficulties of forecasting environmental conditions abroad—and therefore a company should not rely too

heavily on *absolute* standards for motivating and evaluating foreign management.

2. The country to country differences in environment—which naturally will have a significant impact on the relative successes and problems of individual affiliates—make it exceedingly difficult to compare the operating results of one affiliate with another. No doubt there are circumstances where such comparisons have their merit. But in general the danger and shortcomings in making comparisons argue for another kind of evaluating procedure, i.e., making comparisons between an affiliate's results and the standards that were established for it.

Summary

The process of controlling foreign operations is complicated by such variables as long distances, cultural differences, local business practices, diverse host country regulations and restrictions of commercial transactions, the risks of currency devaluation and the imposition of exchange controls. An effective control system in a multinational company must incorporate the possible effects of the so-called international variables on the respective foreign affiliates. Additionally, the maintenance of control in an internationally oriented organization requires the establishment of accountability for key management functions at all echelons, methods for communicating information and policies between headquarters and field operations, and a system for evaluating the current financial status and past operating results of frequently dissimilar foreign subsidiaries.

From the discussion in this chapter and from the reader's own knowledge of the processes of management control, it should be recognized that the cornerstone of any management control system is the financial reports that hold managers at each level accountable for actions that they can and should influence. To understand what the options are to management of a multinational corporation, it is necessary first to understand the unique accounting problems that are encountered in international business. These are discussed in the following chapter.

BIBLIOGRAPHY

Butler, Jack, and John Dearden. "Managing a Worldwide Business," *Harvard Business Review,* May-June 1965.

Chandler, A. D. *Strategy and Structure.* (New York: Doubleday-Anchor Books, 1962).

Clee, Gilbert, and Wilbur Sachtjen. "Organizing a Worldwide Business," *Harvard Business Review*, November-December 1964.

Fouraker, L., and J. Stopford. "Organizational Structure and the Multinational Strategy," *Administrative Science Quarterly*, June 1968.

Gaddis, Paul O. "Analyzing Overseas Investments," *Harvard Business Review*, May-June 1966.

Hawkins, David. "Controlling Foreign Operations," *Financial Executive*, February 1965.

Lawrence, P. R., and J. W. Lorsch. *Organization and Environment.* (Boston: Harvard Business School, Division of Research, 1967).

Lovell, E. B. *The Changing Role of the International Executive.* (New York: National Industrial Conference Board, 1966).

Mauriel, J. J. "Overseas Performance Evaluation and Control—Is It Time to Examine Your System?" unpublished paper, June 1968.

Organizing for Worldwide Operations: Structuring and Implementing the Plan. (New York: Business International Corporation, 1965).

Pryor, Millard. "Planning in a Worldwide Business," *Harvard Business Review*, January-February 1965.

Smith, G. A., Jr. *Managing Geographically Decentralized Companies.* (Boston: Harvard Business School, Division of Research, 1958).

Steiner, George A., and Warren M. Cannon. *Multinational Corporate Planning.* (New York: The Macmillan Company, 1966).

Zwick, Jack. "Is Top Management Really on Top?" *Columbia Journal of World Business*, Winter 1966.

Case 20
THE WINSTON COMPANY

The Winston Company, headquartered in New York, is a major producer and distributor of products in both the textile and paper industries. Its facilities include integrated textile mills; pulp and paper mills; plants that produce newsprint, folding cartons, jute bags, and boxes; chemical plants; and finishing plants to serve the textile industry. The scope of activities has changed dramatically since Robert Winston started the company in Manchester, New Hampshire, in 1864. Product diversification and geographic dispersion of manufacturing facilities have occurred more or less continuously. In June 1966, annual sales were $500 million.

The company has established manufacturing facilities in eighteen countries, each of which serves a local national market with Winston products. In some countries several plants have been constructed to produce a wide variety of products. A separate, subsidiary company has been formed in each country, and the local manager is responsible for all facets of operations. Although investment proposals must be approved by headquarters management in New

York, the managing director in each country maintains his own professional staff and arranges most aspects of affiliate financing.[1]

In June 1966 Ronald Knowlton, treasurer of the parent corporation, was reviewing the financing plan of the corporation's Nigerian affiliate, Jazwi Mills, Ltd. (JML). JML is one of Winston's largest affiliates. Its 1965 balance sheet and income statement are shown as Exhibits 2 and 3. JML was formed in 1947 to manufacture textiles. (Nigeria had long been an exporter of cotton and an importer of textiles.) During the late forties and early fifties the company expanded into various aspects of the textile business and in 1961 entered the paper business by constructing a pulp mill. Subsequent expansions have concentrated in the pulp and paper fields and in 1963 when Nigeria made the transition from monarchy to republic, JML offered 40 per cent of its common stock to Nigerian interests.

The Winston Company has traditionally taken the position that affiliates should expand only so fast as local earnings and borrowings permit. As the company president has stated on numerous occasions, "Winston has grown without the aid of a 'big brother'; so should the affiliates." This financial posture, according to the president, has helped to assure that unwarranted expansions do not occur in the autonomously managed subsidiaries. Almost without exception, requests from affiliates for parent financial assistance have been turned down.

As Mr. Knowlton reviewed the JML plan, which appears below, he began to wonder whether the "no parent financing" rule should apply to the Nigerian affiliate. Additionally, he concluded that if the basic rule could be relaxed in this instance, it would be highly desirable to develop a list of general conditions under which the rule might be altered for other Winston subsidiaries in the future.

EXHIBIT 1

Jazwi Mills Limited's Financing Program

June 12, 1966

Dear Mr. Knowlton:

In accordance with its six-year plan, the Government of Nigeria is now issuing licenses to manufacturers to produce textiles, chemicals, and paper products up to the amounts of the target figures established in the Plan. JML's application for its newsprint and paper bag expansion have been submitted

[1] Projects costing less than $50,000 can be approved by the managing director without reference to headquarters.

and discussed with the Nigerian Government. During our visit to Lagos on May 10, 1966, we were told that JML's expansions have been approved and that a license would be issued shortly subject to the Finance Ministry's approval of an acceptable financial program. The purpose of this memorandum is to present the various methods available for financing the new construction and working capital.

The overall construction program as presently envisaged amounts to the following for the years 1966-1969:

Construction Program, 1966–69

	U.S. $ (1,000's)
1966	1,382
1967	3,158
1968	5,012
1969	340
Total	$9,892

It is now estimated that the newsprint and paper bag expansions will be completed by April 1969. They will be the second series of major expansions the Company has undertaken since 1962. The fixed assets of the Company have increased $3,151,000 in the four-year period 1962-1965. The new expansions provide for the Company to increase its fixed assets by $9,893,000 during the 1966-1969 period or an average of about $2,474,000 per year, and in 1963 alone the Company plans to spend approximately $5,013,000.

During the period 1962-1965 the Company was able to finance its expansion in fixed assets and working capital as follows:

Source and Application of Funds, 1962–66

	U.S. $ (1,000's)
Source	
Retained earnings	798
Depreciation	451
Increase in capital stock	555
Loans	1,734
	3,538
Application	
Construction	3,150
Working capital	388
	3,538

It has been thought that the new expansion might be financed entirely by borrowing and retained earnings as explained later in this memorandum, and the following is the estimated source and application of funds for the periods 1966-1968 and 1966-1969:

Source and Application of Funds, 1966–68 and 1966–69

	U.S. $ (1,000's)	
	1966-1968	*1966-1969*
Source of Funds		
Retained earnings	617	(208)
Depreciation and development rebate	1,889	4,696
Loans	7,817	7,517
Total funds received	10,323	12,005
Application of Funds		
Construction	9,553	9,893
Working capital	770	2,112
Total funds applied	10,323	12,005

The present construction estimate includes a newsprint plant at a cost of approximately $1.9 million. If JML should decide to forego or delay the manufacture of newsprint until such time as funds are available, the cash requirements could be reduced accordingly. However, the Nigerian Government is known to have under consideration six proposals from competitive firms that are anxious to enter the newsprint field, and the Government has notified JML management that if they intend to proceed with newsprint production, a formal application should be submitted by July 1, 1966.

The profits of the Company during the 1962-1965 period were as follows:

Profits After Taxes

U.S. $ (1,000's)			
1962	*1963*	*1964*	*1965*
282	260	492	584

During the period 1966-1969 the Company estimates its earnings will be:

Profits After Taxes

U.S. $ (1,000's)			
1966	*1967*	*1968*	*1969*
253	753	693	(458)

The principal reason for the decline in profits in 1966 as compared with 1965 and the apparent loss after taxes in 1969 are the absorption against profits of the development rebate. The development rebate is a special allowance made by the taxation authorities for newly installed equipment to the extent of 20 per cent of the installed value of such equipment. It operates as if the Company were granted depreciation to the extent of 120 per cent on the installed value. 75 per cent of any development rebate must be held in reserve and cannot be used for distribution as dividend for a period of ten years.

Earnings for the period after taxes but before development rebate are estimated to be as follows:

Profits After Taxes

U.S. $ (1,000's)			
1966	*1967*	*1968*	*1969*
934	753	693	1,159

In order to determine the funds required and the scope the finance plan should encompass, the attached estimated Balance Sheet, Cash Flow, and Profit and Loss statements were prepared for the years 1966-1969. (See Exhibits 2, 3, and 4.)

At present the Company has an overdraft with Barclays Bank DCO, debentures with the public, and a product loan from the parent company, all of which amount to $1,848,000. In the event funds are borrowed for the whole of the expansion program, it will be necessary for the Company to borrow an additional $7,818,000, which with present borrowing will total approximately $9,667,000 at the end of 1968.

After discussions with the Minister of Finance in Lagos it appears that JML has three borrowing alternatives available to it at the present time:

1. Three international banks have agreed to lend JML, Ltd., up to $5,350,000 on the following terms:

Draw down:	1967–1968
Pay back:	10 equal semiannual installments commencing June 1971 and finishing in December 1975.
Commitment fee:	1/2 of 1 per cent on the unused balance of the loan. A maximum of 8½ per cent and a minimum of 6½ per cent, 1 per cent over New York prime rate during the construction of facilities; after the construction period the interest rate would be 1½ per cent over the New York prime rate.
Guarantee:	The proposed loan would require (a) a parent guarantee, (b) a guarantee by the Central Bank-sponsored Nigerian Development Finance Corporation (NDFC), (c) an ICA guarantee with respect to convertibility, expropriation, etc.

Funds required to cover pound expenditures would be raised through local borrowing or an application to the Export-Import Bank for Cooley Amendment funds.

2. An application could be made to the Export-Import Bank, Washington, asking for a loan of up to $5,350,000 with draw down during 1967-1968 and pay back in 20 equal semiannual installments commencing in June 1971 and finishing in December 1980. Funds required to cover pound expenditure would be raised through Cooley Amendment funds as described above. If our application is reviewed favorably, it would be necessary to negotiate the terms of interest and commitment fee presently estimated to range from 7-8 per cent interest, ½ of 1 per cent commitment fee, and NDFC guarantee with respect to availability of Nigerian pounds.

3. During our visit on May 5 with the Minister of Finance, we were informed that the Government of Nigeria was in the process of negotiating long-term foreign aid on a scale previously inconceivable. If the Government of Nigeria is successful in its negotiations, it may be in a position to release foreign exchange required for the project, and JML would then require only Nigerian pounds to cover its foreign exchange. These funds might be obtained from the Export-Import Bank under the Cooley Amendment whereby Nigerian pounds would be made available and in which case the Export-Import Bank would in all probability require a guarantee covering availability of Nigerian pounds for repayment.

In the event all of the funds required are borrowed, JML would have two problems resulting from the size of the loans:

1. Security required to cover debentures in the event additional debentures are issued.
2. A guarantee with the NDFC that pounds would be available.

The bank has a policy that it will lend via debentures only if the debentures are secured by a first mortgage, the amount of the debentures to be not more than one-half the value of the assets securing the debentures and the loan to be no longer than seven years. The length of the loan is within the period required in the JML finance program, but as the bank will normally lend only up to 50 per cent of the value of the security, it would be necessary that some relaxation in this bank policy be made by the bank if all of the funds required are to be obtained from borrowings and retained earnings.

For 1968 (as shown in Exhibit 1) the new loans in Nigerian pounds are \$3,383,000 and \$274,000 (overdrafts). Because it is possible to increase the overdraft to \$1 million, JML has the flexibility of reducing the long-term loan in Nigerian pounds at the expense of increasing the overdraft. This would make the JML long-term borrowing 56.2 per cent of the assets, which exceeds the bank's security requirements by 6.2 per cent. Exhibit 4 shows the ratio of fixed assets to loans.

The guarantee fee for availability of Nigerian pounds is estimated to run about 1 per cent and can be arranged with NDFC. However, NDFC has a policy of limiting such guarantees to a seven-year period and also requires that the security margin referred to regarding debentures apply to the guarantee coverage. We have explained to NDFC that our loans would be for a period of nine and one-half years in the case of the commerical banks and fourteen years for the Export-Import Bank as suggested by the Finance Ministry. Discussions were held with the President of the Nigerian Development Finance Corporation regarding the bank's attitude about these two problems and we are confident that these can be worked out satisfactorily.

The extraordinary increase in our debt structure is shown in Exhibit 5 by comparing the outstanding loans of the Company at the end of 1965 with those at the end of 1968, the peak borrowing period. In addition, the capital stock and the shareholders' equity are displayed in Exhibit 5 to highlight the debt/stockholders' equity relationship.

Under Nigeria's Six-Year Plan covering the years 1962 through 1968, planned investment of the paper industry is expected to increase by $25 million as compared to an estimated $10 million total investment up to 1965. When JML's recently completed pulp and paper expansion becomes fully operative this year, the Company will be in a position to establish itself prominently in these new and rapidly growing industries in Nigeria. The rapid growth potential of the paper industry in Nigeria has recently attracted the attention of prominent producers in the United States and Europe who have submitted to the Nigerian Government proposals for establishing plants in Nigeria.

None of the other firms as yet has any significant stake in the Nigerian market. JML, with its well-established administrative, sales, and production facilities, therefore has considerable lead over its competitors at the present time. JML also has the benefit of long-established and excellent relations with senior officials in the Government of Nigeria, particularly those concerned with industrial expansion. However, to maintain its predominant position JML must act quickly to expand its operations in those areas where it wishes to exploit fully opportunities offered by the developing Nigerian market.

In the face of rising competition from United States and European producers who have decided that Nigeria is a place for growth and long-term investment, it seems desirable for JML to reappraise its financial abilities in relation to its proposed undertakings described earlier in this memorandum. To complete the program contemplated, JML will need to borrow additional funds equal to four times its present capital or about twice its shareholders' equity. We believe that the Nigerian Company should continue its policy of financing the major share of its growth by borrowing and retained earnings, but the extremely large ratio of debt to capital stock and shareholders' equity is getting out of line when compared to other Nigerian companies of comparable size. This is particularly true when the debt is incurred to provide manufacturing facilities that will not produce operating income for a period of two to three years beyond the dates the funds are borrowed.

On the basis of projections made it is our opinion that JML should expand its capital base over its existing level in Nigerian pounds by 2,800,000 (U.S. $1 million). By the investment in capital stock of this amount, the Company would be able to lower the amount of its secured borrowing requirements enough so that the Company's fixed assets in relation to secured debt would be below the limits set by NDFC. This action would assure the guarantee of the availability of Nigerian pounds by NDFC if the Company borrows from Export-Import Bank or commercial banks and would provide the security required if debentures were sold to provide local funds.

The increase in capital stock of 358,000 pounds (U.S. $1 million) would increase the shareholders' equity by 1968 to approximately $5,729,000, and the secured loan ratio to shareholders' equity would be 1.2. This new issue of capital stock would require an investment by the parent company of $600,000 and Nigerian shareholders of 143,000 pounds (U.S. $400,000). If approved this investment should be made during the last half of 1967 or early 1968 depending upon the rate of construction expenditures.

Since its independence the Nigerian economy has moved to a new plateau of industrial growth from which it is expected to develop at an accelerated rate. In spite of this rapid growth the Government has maintained its stability and appears to be dealing successfully with major social and economic problems with which it has been and continues to be faced. Repatriation of profits is permitted freely and all obligations and agreements entered into by the Nigerian Government over the years have been honored.

JML has also developed rapidly in the last few years and has reached a new level from which it expects to achieve an increasingly greater growth rate. In fact JML's profits during the last five years had an overall average annual growth rate of 16 per cent. This record is indicative of the type of operation that JML has enjoyed and will be capable of maintaining.

It is our intention to present an application for a loan of the United States dollars and Nigerian pounds to the Export-Import Bank as soon as possible, and it would facilitate the presentation if a decision could be made about the parent equity commitment as soon as possible. Detailed calculations have not been completed for all phases of the expansion at this time, but we believe it advisable to have an agreement in principle that at least $1 million of the funds should be raised by an issue of capital stock.

Very truly yours,
Richard Merschell
Manager, JML

The Winston Company
Jazwi Mills Limited
Estimated Comparative Balance Sheets
1965-1969 ($1,000's)

	(actual) *1965*	*1966*	*1967*	*1968*	*1969*
Assets					
Cash	142	544	950	708	1,158
Accounts receivable – trade	743	850	945	958	1,248
Inventories	1,778	1,976	2,078	2,126	2,590
Total current assets	2,663	3,370	3,973	3,792	4,996
Fixed assets	4,196	5,578	8,737	13,754	14,087
Investments	21	21	21	21	21
Goodwill	208	208	208	208	208
Total assets	7,088	9,178	12,939	17,771	19,315
Liabilities, Capital Stock, and Surplus					
Accounts payable – trade	471	553	710	720	878
Accrued liabilities:					
Income taxes	225	106	323	296	
Other liabilities	107	166	166	166	
Dividend payable	204	173	183	183	183
Total current liabilities	1,007	998	1,382	1,365	1,227
New Loans:					
In pounds		150	850	3.393	3,322
In U.S. dollars		163	2,320	4,543	4,587
NDFC – overdraft	278	815	732	274	172
Debentures – bank and public	347	694	608	520	434
Barclay's bank loan	394	305	209	116	22
Parent loan	827	827	827	827	827
Reserve for development rebate	100	781	781	781	2,397
Reserve for depreciation	803	1,209	1,608	2,012	3,202
Surplus and surplus reserve	1,387	1,291	1,678	2,000	1,179
Capital stock	1,944	1,944	1,944	1,944	1,944
Total liabilities, capital stock, and surplus	$7,088	$9,177	$12,939	$17,765	$19,313

EXHIBIT 3

The Winston Company
Jazwi Mills Limited
Estimated Comparative Income Statements
1965-1969 ($1,000's)

	(actual) *1965*	*1966*	*1967*	*1968*	*1969*
Net sales	4,870	6,077	7,881	7,990	10,401
Cost of net sales	2,982	3,694	5,068	5,148	6,268
Gross margin	1,888	2,383	2,813	2,842	4,133
S.A.D. expense	677	784	819	863	1,060
Operating income	1,211	1,599	1,994	1,979	3,073
Less: other charges	2	(55)	(28)	(206)	72
interest on loan	40	109	252	521	651
Income before depreciation and tax	1,169	1,545	1,770	1,664	2,350
Development rebate	17	680			1,616
Depreciation	144	406	398	404	1,190
Income before income tax	1,008	459	1,372	1,260	(456)
Income tax	426	204	617	566	
Income after income tax	582	255	755	694	(456)

EXHIBIT 4

The Winston Company
Jazwi Mills Limited
Estimated Statements Of Cash Flow
1966-1969 ($1,000's)

	1966	*1967*	*1968*	*1969*
Cash beginning of year	142	544	950	708
Add:				
Income before depreciation and tax	1,544	1,769	1,663	2,348
Proceeds new financing:				
New Loans: Nigerian pounds	150	700	2,533	112
U.S. dollars	163	2,156	2,223	44
NDFC – overdraft	537			
Debentures – bank	347			
Total additions	2,741	4,625	6,419	2,504
Deduct:				
Income tax payments	323	401	593	296
Dividends paid	379	357	366	366
Construction	1,382	3,158	5,012	340
Repayment of:				
New loans, pounds				174
U.S. dollars				
NDFC – overdraft		83	458	101
Debentures – bank		86	86	87
Barclay's bank loan	91	93	93	93
All Other – net	163	40	51	595
Total deductions	2,338	4,218	6,659	2,052
Change in cash during year	403	407	(240)	452
Cash – end of year	545	951	710	1,160

EXHIBIT 5

The Winston Company
Jazwi Mills Limited
Ratio of Fixed Assets And Shareholders Funds to Borrowings ($1,000's)

	December 1968	*Assume stock issue*	*After stock i* *December 1*
Gross fixed assets	13,749	1,000,000	13,749
Borrowings to be secured			
New loans: pounds	3,383	(335)	3,048
U.S. dollars	4,543	(665)	3,878
Present debentures	521		521
Total to here	8,447	(1,000)	7,447
Less: additional overdraft available	726		726
Total loans to be secured	7,721	(1,000)	6,721
Borrowings as a % of fixed assets	56.2		50.1
Per cent in excess allowable by bank	6.2		0.1
Capital stock	1,944	1,000	2,944
Surplus and reserves (incl. development rebate)	2,785		2,785
Total shareholders' equity	4,729	1,000	5,729
Secured loans	7,721		6,721
Ratio of secured loans to	1.6		1.2
shareholders' equity	4.0		2.3

EXHIBIT 6

The Winston Company
Jazwi Mills Limited
Comparative Capital Structures ($1,000's)

	1965	*1968*	*Differe*
Bank overdraft	278	273	(5
Debenture–NDFC		173	17
Debenture–public	347	347	
Hanover bank loan	394	116	(278
Parent product loan	827	827	
New Borrowings			
In Nigerian pounds		3,383	3,38
In dollars		4,543	4,54
Total	1,846	9,662	7,81
Capital stock	1,944	1,944	
Debt ratio to capital	.95	4.97	
Shareholders' equity (Incl. capital stock)	3,432	4,729	
Debt ratio to shareholders' equity	.54	2.04	

Managerial Accounting for Operations Abroad*

13

Meaningful financial reports are the cornerstone of effective management. Intelligible financial data are especially important in international business where operations are usually supervised from a distance. Regrettably the data supplied headquarters management are frequently unsuitable for evaluative purposes. Statements prepared in accordance with generally accepted accounting principles do not adequately communicate the effect of inflation on operations. The procedures used to translate business results from one currency to another oftentimes obscure the real business environment and currency effects normally conveyed in financial statements. Additionally, the characteristic format of income statements does not readily facilitate evaluation of performance in terms of designated authority. This chapter examines the characteristic deficiencies of generally accepted accounting principles in the international field and prescribes certain techniques for adjusting financial data in order that headquarters management can better appraise performance and motivate local personnel.

THE EFFECT OF INFLATION ON THE FINANCIAL STATEMENTS

The postwar period has been characterized by inflation ranging from 3 to 5 per cent per annum in most industrialized countries to 25 to 60 per

* The section of this chapter dealing with inflation draws upon unpublished materials contained in a First National City Bank memorandum prepared by D. A. Austin, assistant manager, Overseas Division, First National City Bank, New York, N.Y.

cent in several South American and southeast Asian countries. Past and present deterioration in the value of monetary units complicates the process of measuring financial performance. For example, the conventional matching of expenses and revenues to compute profits is susceptible to misinterpretation if various elements in the income statement reflect different monetary values. Where expense elements are stated in the monetary units of earlier periods, it is entirely possible that a company may be losing ground in real economic terms despite substantial reported profits. Likewise it is hazardous to compare sales or expense figures of a company for a period of years unless the figures are adjusted to reflect the intervening changes in price levels. Other complications in financial statements can also be traced to inflationary forces. The major problems can best be examined in the context of an illustration that is presented below:

Example: The Reliable Affiliate

The hypothetical Reliable affiliate anticipates revenues and expenses in the forthcoming year to be as follows, provided that there is no inflation:

	LOCAL CURRENCY
Sales	400
Cost of goods sold (includes 10,000 of depreciation)	250
Labor	120
Profit	30

The beginning and ending hypothetical balance sheets in local currency units are as follows, again presuming that there will be no inflation. The current exchange rate is two local currency units to one United States dollar.

	BEGINNING	*ENDING*
Cash	0	40
Receivables	100	100
Inventory	60	60
Total: current assets	160	200
Net plant and equipment	90	80
Total assets	250	280
Payables	30	30
Bank loan	40	40
Net worth	180	210
Total liabilities and net worth	250	280

These balance sheets reflect the following additional assumptions:

1. Receivables remain unchanged at three months sales
2. Inventory remains unchanged at three months purchases
3. Payables remain unchanged at one and half months purchases

4. A United States dollar loan of $20,000 is payable at the end of the year, the amount including principal and interest
5. Volume of sales in physical units is unchanged.

It is clear that if Reliable's projections materialize, the affiliate will generate sufficient cash by the end of the year to repay the bank loan on schedule provided that there is no inflation. The net cash inflows (equal to profits plus depreciation) are forty of local currency, which is adequate to repay the twenty-dollar bank loan at the two-to-one exchange rate.

However, let us now relax our original no inflation assumption and presume that on the first day of each of the last three-quarters of the year the costs of goods sold and labor increase by 10 per cent. These increases are simultaneously matched by 10 per cent increases in selling prices. Moreover, the prices of fixed assets appreciate 10 per cent. The price index during the year is as follows:

	1st QUARTER	*2nd QUARTER*	*3rd QUARTER*	*4th QUARTER*
Price index	100	110	121	133

Let us further assume that these price changes have no effect whatever on the pattern of business operations. The physical volume of sales, purchases, and inventory remains the same. Receivables remain at three months sales and payables at three months purchases.

According to conventional accounting principles, the Reliable affiliate would not adjust its accounts to reflect this inflation on any regular basis, although in some countries periodic adjustments are permitted under local reporting statutes. Assuming no adjustment, let us trace the inflation through the local currency accounts to see how the company's financial position is influenced. The quarterly income statements will now be as follows:

	1st QUARTER		*2nd QUARTER*		*3rd QUARTER*		*4th QUARTER*		*TOTAL*
Sales		100.0		110.0		121.0		133.0	464.0
Beginning inventory	60.0		60.0		66.0		73.0		—
Purchases	+60.0		+66.0		+73.0		+80.0		279.0
Closing inventory	−60.0		−60.0		−73.0		−80.0		
Cost of goods sold *		60.0		60.0		66.0		73.0	259.0
Labor cost		30.0		33.0		36.0		40.0	139.0
Depreciation		2.5		2.5		2.5		2.5	10.0
Profit †		7.5		14.5		16.5		17.5	56.0

* We assume that the company uses the FIFO rule for costing its inventory.
† For the sake of simplicity it is assumed that the company is not subject to taxes.

The beginning and quarterly balance sheets will now appear as follows:

	BEGINNING	END OF 1st QUARTER	END OF 2nd QUARTER	END OF 3rd QUARTER	END OF 4th QUARTER
Cash	0	10	14	19	23
Receivables	100	100	110	121	133
Inventory	60	60	66	73	80
Total current assets	160	170	190	213	236
Plant and equipment	90	87.5	85	82.5	80
Total assets	250	257.5	275	295.5	316
Payables	30	30	33	37	40
Bank loan	40	40	40	40	40
Net worth	180	187.5	202	218.5	236
Total liabilities and net worth	250	257.5	275	295.5	316

Assuming that the exchange rate remains constant and no dividends are remitted, Reliable's net worth increases by LC56, as the comparative balance sheets indicate. The profits realized during the four quarters account for this increase in net worth. Although unit sales are identical to the company's original forecast, reported profits of LC56 exceed the original profit estimate of LC30 due to the inflation.

Yet has the affiliate really exceeded expectations? Although price increases have kept up with rising costs, one aspect of the financial statements leaves room for doubt. Notwithstanding its inflationary pricing policy, Reliable is unable to generate sufficient cash to repay its dollar loan; the year-end balance sheet indicates a cash balance of only LC23 in contrast to the balance of LC40 shown in the original projected balance sheet.

What has happened is that a substantial part of increased local currency profits has been reinvested in inventories and receivables due to the increases in costs and sales prices per unit. The following cash flow statement pinpoints this effect:

SOURCES		USES	
Inflow from operations	66	Increase in Receivables	33
Increase in payables	10	Increase in Inventories	20
	76	Increase in Cash	23
			76

Yet this explanation of increased investment in receivables and inventory is erroneous in an important respect. The purchasing power of the current assets has declined although the financial statements are insensitive to this phenomenon. In point of fact the company has not increased its investments in receivables and inventories in real terms. Although the local currency value of these accounts has risen, the investment in receivables and inventories has not increased if valued in terms of constant purchasing power. (Accounts receivable of LC133 ÷ by 1.33 = LC100, or the beginning receivables balance; and inventory of LC80 ÷ by 1.33 is equal to the beginning inventory balance of LC60.)

In effect Reliable's increased profits are largely attributable to the fact that revenues are expressed in higher monetary units than the cost of goods sold units, reflecting the time lag between purchases and sales.[1] Especially significant is the fact that it has been necessary for Reliable to reinvest a substantial portion of its profits in receivables and inventories merely to sustain the business–i.e., to preserve its investment in working capital.

Another source of distortion in Reliable's financial statements is attributable to depreciable fixed assets. The problem caused by depreciation is that the annual charge is derived from the cost of the fixed assets that may have been purchased many years before the year in which the depreciation charge is made. Consequently the monetary units in which revenues are expressed represent different real values from the monetary units in which the depreciation charge is expressed, and therefore the units are not comparable.

To illustrate, assume that the Reliable Company purchased all its fixed assets at the beginning of the prior year for LC100, which included the cost of installation. It was anticipated that the assets would have a ten-year economic life and that there would be no salvage value. Using the straight-line method, the company charges LC10 to depreciation each year or LC2.5 each quarter. Let us further assume that the cost of fixed assets has increased in line with the general price level and that it would now cost LC133 to replace Reliable's fixed assets. Under these circumstances the annual depreciation charge based on historic costs understates the real current cost of fixed asset use.

By adjusting all the local currency accounts, it is possible to appraise the Reliable Company's operating performance in real terms.

First net income is recomputed using the ending price level index (1.33 to 1). In these terms quarterly operating results are identical and thus appear as follows:

Price Level Adjusted Income Statement

	QUARTERLY	*ANNUAL*
Sales	133.3	533.3
Cost of goods sold	(80)	320.0
Labor	(40)	150.0
Depreciation (2.5% of 133)	(3.3)	13.3
Net income	10.0	40.0

However, the LC40 of price level adjusted profit overstates the company's operating achievement by virtue of the loss in purchasing power

[1] This tendency is accentuated by the company's FIFO costing procedure; however, the problem persists regardless of the cost flow rule which the company selects.

sustained on net monetary assets.[2] To the extent that cash balances, receivables, and perhaps inventories are held in inflationary environments, a loss in purchasing power is incurred. On the other hand, the loss sustained on these assets is partially offset by a gain on monetary liabilities.

Reliable's loss on net monetary assets can be calculated as follows:

Net monetary assets (beginning) †	93.0
Add: sales	533.3 *
	626.3
Deduct: purchases of merchandise	(320.0) *
labor	(160.0) *
	(480.0)
Indicated net monetary assets (ending) ‡	146.3
Actual net monetary assets (ending) §	116
Loss in purchasing power (146.3–116)	30.3

* From price level adjusted income statement (page 489).
† Beginning balances (see page 486) adjusted at 1.33 to 1

add:	cash	0
	receivables	133
deduct:	payables	(40)
		93

‡ What net monetary assets would have been had there been no loss in purchasing power.
§ Ending balances (see page 488).

Reliable's operations can now be placed in perspective with the aid of the following price-adjusted, comparative balance sheets:

Price Level Adjusted Balance Sheets *

	BEGINNING	ENDING
Cash		23.0
Receivables	133.0	133.0
Inventory	80.0	80.0
Total current assets	213.0	236.0
Plant and equipment	133.0	133.0
less accumulated depreciation	(13.3)	(26.6)
Net plant and equipment	119.7	106.4
Total assets	LC 332.7	LC 342.4
Current payables	40.0	40.0
Bank loan	53.2	53.2
Net worth:		
Beginning balance		239.5
+ Net income		40.0
− Loss on monetary items		(30.3)
Ending balance	239.5	249.2
Total liabilities and net worth	LC 332.7	LC 342.4

* In terms of monetary units at end of period.

[2] Net monetary assets are defined here as cash and receivables less liabilities denominated in the local currency.

The beginning assets, liabilities, and equity accounts are restated in terms of the monetary unit at the end of the period to obtain comparability. (Note that the loan denominated in dollars is valued in terms of its ending local currency equivalent; had the loan been denominated in units of local currency, this step would have been unnecessary.) Similarly the accumulated depreciation account is revised to reflect 10 per cent utilization of ending fixed asset costs (133).

Since the company has not repaid its loan or declared dividends during the year, it is possible to isolate the factors contributing to the growth in net worth by comparing the beginning and ending balance sheets. With the exception of cash, plant and equipment, and net worth, the balance sheets are identical, and therefore the company's improved position can be explained by analyzing these three accounts.

Originally the company expected the plant and equipment account to decline by LC10 due to the 10 per cent annual depreciation charge. In point of fact, net fixed assets declined LC13.3 on a price-adjusted basis, reflecting the increased cost of fixed asset utilization occasioned by rising replacement costs.

Since the receivables and payables balances did not change, the LC23 of accumulated cash reflects the extent to which cash receipts exceeded cash charges during the year.

To calculate real profits it is necessary to subtract the LC30.3 loss on monetary items (calculated on page 490) from the LC40 of price-adjusted net income (calculated on page 489). The remaining figure of LC9.7 indicates the value of Reliable's accomplishments in real terms. In other words, Reliable earned LC9.7 after providing for the maintenance of asset purchasing power.[3]

The reader might naturally raise the question as to whether price-adjusted profits could not be more easily derived by merely using the price index to deflate quarterly profits. For example, Reliable's quarterly profits might be deflated by 10 per cent, indicating profits of LC49.40 for the year. Several problems are inherent in this method and account for the substantially different profit conclusion. The approach ignores the erosion of purchasing power of monetary assets. Additionally it is insensitive to the rising replacement cost of fixed assets as well as holding gains derived from locally denominated debt.

[3] The simplified illustration for the Reliable Company has assumed that prices and costs move in unison. In point of fact it should be remembered that inflation is unlikely to affect prices and costs equally. Consumer goods, industrial goods, raw materials, various imports, various exports, land, buildings, and other broad categories of goods typically experience dissimilar degrees of price increase even under free market conditions. Government controls and subsidies are likely to accentuate these differences, and consequently the degree of distortion in the profit and loss figure computed using conventional accounting procedures is likely to be greater (or less) than the Reliable illustration suggests.

THE POSITION OF PROFESSIONAL ACCOUNTING BODIES

The problems caused by inflation have been widely recognized within the accounting profession. Accounting organizations in many countries have organized study groups to reexamine generally accepted accounting principles with reference to the question of inflation. The resulting studies have tended to focus on the propriety and implications of adhering to the historic cost principle during periods of changing price levels.

By and large the study groups have suggested that accounting procedure be altered to recognize the changing value of the monetary unit. Although the recommendations have differed in detail, the studies clearly reflect a consensus that any of a number of alternatives would be preferable to ignoring the price level problem entirely.

Although in some instances the professional organizations have unofficially approved the researchers' conclusions, accounting groups with few exceptions have not so far adopted the recommendations of their study groups.[4] In the absence of a clear lead from the accounting profession, management has been left with a choice between retaining the historical cost principle or adopting some method that is not generally accepted for tax or reporting purposes. Concerned with the deficiencies of conventional accounting procedures in periods of inflation, several companies have adopted alternative methods in order to obtain more accurate data for internal decision making and to present more useful information to outside interest groups. The numerous procedures that are used fall into four main categories:

1. Some companies such as U.S. Steel set up special capital reserve accounts for the segregation of reported profits equivalent to the depreciation understatement. Although reported profits remain the same, this procedure communicates the necessity of retaining a portion of the inflated profits to maintain assets in real terms. Other companies segregate a larger portion of profits to reflect other inflationary effects as well.

2. Some European-based companies calculate the amount of depreciation deficiency and charge this amount directly against profits so that reported profits are partially price-adjusted. This type of adjustment may be limited to depreciation or also encompass inflation's impact on other cost and revenue accounts.

[4] A few exceptions are worth noting. The Argentine and French governments have passed laws permitting companies to compute depreciation for tax purposes according to asset revaluations based on government price level coefficients. Although Scotland has not passed asset revaluation laws for tax purposes, the Institute of Chartered Accountants in Scotland has held that a departure from historic costs does not necessarily require a qualification of the auditor's report.

3. A few companies such as Indiana Telephone present both price-adjusted accounts and conventional accounts in their reported statements. In these instances the adjustments are normally complete, although different methods and presentation formats are used.

4. A few companies use price-adjusted accounts for both managerial and reporting purposes and provide conventional accounts only when regulatory authorities request them.[5] The best known of these companies is the Dutch firm, N.V. Philips Gloeilampenfabrieken, which accounts for its worldwide activities on this basis.

Companies within these four groups follow different procedures in making and reporting the price adjustments. Some companies, for example, apply a general price level index to ascertain the amount of adjustment required, whereas others use different indices to reflect relative price movements for various asset categories. Some South American countries publish official sets of coefficients each year that are used as a basis for asset revaluation.

Yet we would mislead the reader were we to suggest that price-adjusted statements regardless of type are commonly used. Such methods are still very exceptional, and there seems to be no trend toward extensive use of price-adjusted financial data despite powerful arguments in its favor.

The advocates of price-adjusted accounts support their position with the following arguments:

1. Real profits and losses can only be determined by matching revenues and expenses expressed in identical monetary units
2. Marginal decisions regarding wage negotiations, pricing policies, and dividends are improved if they are based on realistic profit figures
3. Price-adjusted accounts facilitate proper emphasis on the maintenance of asset purchasing power.

Those who oppose price-adjusted accounts argue that:

1. Adjusted accounts are not generally accepted by the accounting profession or by regulatory and tax authorities
2. Historic costs are the only objective and thoroughly comprehensible standard
3. There is not a generally accepted method of making the necessary price level adjustment.

Adoption of price level adjusted accounting methods is likely to be slow. Yet inflation is almost certain to continue in most countries, whether

[5] Tax authorities in most countries base their assessments on unadjusted figures and regulatory authorities such as the SEC—who have refused to accept inflation-adjusted accounts.

it be 2 to 4 per cent per annum or the 20 to 30 per cent variety. Company management should be cognizant of the distortions that arise when conventional accounts based upon historical cost principles are used in inflationary conditions and revise their assessments of operating progress and financial condition accordingly.

The problems and the extent to which analysts of financial statements should be on their guard are neatly summarized in the auditor's report of the Indiana Telephone Corporation (ITC). ITC shows conventional accounts under Column A and inflation-adjusted accounts under Column B. Part of the auditor's opinion reads:

> In our opinion, the accompanying financial statements shown under Column A present fairly the financial position of the company . . . and the results of its operations for the year then ended, in conformity with generally-accepted accounting methods supplied on a basis consistent with that of the preceding year. In our opinion, however, the accompanying financial statements shown under Column B more fairly present the financial position of the company and its results of operations since recognition has been given to variations in the purchasing power of the dollar.

TRANSLATION AND MANAGERIAL ACCOUNTING

For a variety of reasons it is frequently desirable to express the results of foreign operations in a single currency. Headquarters management, principal banks of account, tax officials, regulatory authorities, and shareholders desire a single frame of reference for all company operations regardless of geographic origin. By translating the financial accounts of various affiliates from local currencies into the currency of the parent, one can better measure the relative contributions and commitments of various geographic areas. Moreover, translation enables companies to incorporate the effects of current (or proposed) cross currency transactions such as imports, exports, and dividend remittances into the financial statements.

Three alternative translation procedures have been proposed and are used in preparing statements that reflect both parent and affiliate operations. The first and most commonly used procedure is to translate current assets and liabilities of foreign affiliates at the current rate of exchange and all other assets and liabilities at the historical rates of exchange—that is, the rates prevailing when the assets were acquired and liabilities incurred. Revenue and expense elements in the income statement are translated at the average exchange rate applicable to each month of operation (or alternatively, using a weighted average exchange rate for the entire period) with an adjustment to record depreciation expense at the exchange rate prevailing when the respective fixed assets were acquired. Realized gains or losses on foreign exchange are charged against or credited to operations. Unrealized losses are also charged against current operations but "unrealized gains should preferably be carried to a suspense account, except to the extent that they offset prior provisions for unrealized losses, in which case they may be credited to the account previously charged." [6] Under this method the net current assets are deemed to be exposed to the risk of devaluation, regardless of their form, while devaluation does not affect fixed assets and long-term liabilities. Cash, receivables, and inventory are treated equally under devaluation and short-term liabilities offset devaluation losses by reducing net current assets. On the other hand long-term liabilities are not regarded as offsets to devaluation losses except to the extent that these liabilities mature within the current period. This method is described in detail in chapter 12 of Accounting Research Bulletin number 43 of the American Institute of Certified Public Accountants and is regarded as the generally accepted translation procedure in the United States and in many other countries.

An alternative method recommends that a distinction be made between accounts which are of a financial nature and those that are physical in nature.[7] It is suggested that all financial assets and liabilities be translated at the current exchange rate whereas physical assets, including inventory, land, plant and equipment, be translated at historic rates. In contrast to the generally accepted current method, this financial method presumes that holdings of inventory do not involve a loss from devaluation, since hopefully inventories will appreciate in local currency to approximately the same extent that the foreign exchange value of the currency depreciates. Additionally, locally denominated debts are regarded as offsets to potential foreign exchange loss regardless of the maturity of the debt.

Still another translation method has been advocated by the Accounting Principles Board, a group of professional accountants and scholars charged by the AICPA to issue its own pronouncements on accounting principles. In its opinion number 6, the Accounting Principles Board takes exception to the general rule that long-term receivables and long-term liabilities must be translated at historic exchange rates and allows the translation of these items at current exchange rates. This opinion permits an alternative translation procedure, although it does not revoke the traditional method of translating foreign currencies. Thus the Accounting Principles Board in its recommendation adopts one element of the Hep-

[6] AICPA, Accounting Research and Terminology Bulletins, final edition, New York, 1961, p. 113.

[7] See Samuel R. Hepworth, Research Report, no. 36, National Association of Accountants.

worth thesis—namely, that both current and noncurrent locally denominated liabilities be translated at the current rate—without accepting other elements of this proposal.

IMPLICATIONS OF THE TRANSLATION METHODS

Certain differing implications of the three translation methods as guides to policy are obvious. Under the current method there is no inherent advantage in holding inventory in preference to cash or receivables, nor in financing by local borrowing unless the resulting liabilities are short term. By way of contrast the method advocated by the Accounting Principles Board makes no distinction between short-term and long-term debt. Regardless of maturity locally denominated liabilities provide a hedge against current assets that, regardless of form, are deemed to be exposed to the risk of devaluation. Hence management can ignore the maturity characteristics of local debt in attempting to avoid foreign exchange losses. The third method advocated by Hepworth insists that foreign exchange exposure is related to the composition of current assets and that management in attempting to minimize foreign exchange losses should divert its commitments from financial assets—cash, receivables, and marketable securities—to physical assets that will appreciate in value in terms of local currency.

To better understand what traditional translation procedures accomplish, let us recast the original data for the Reliable affiliate in accordance with these procedures. Recall our original assumption that the cost of goods, labor costs, fixed asset prices, and selling prices increase 10 per cent on the first day of each of the last three quarters of the year. Let us now also assume that on the same days the local currency is devalued 10 per cent against the dollar.[8] The price indices and the exchange rates during the year are as follows:

	1st QUARTER	*2nd QUARTER*	*3rd QUARTER*	*4th QUARTER*
Price indices	100	110	121	133
Exchange rate to $1	2.00	2.20	2.42	2.66

Assets and liabilities (not adjusted for price level changes) are translated to United States dollars at the current exchange rates except that fixed assets and dollar loans are translated at the rates prevailing when they were acquired or incurred.

[8] In our earlier discussion of the Reliable affiliate, we assumed that exchange rates remained constant and analyzed the affiliate solely in terms of the local currency.

Beginning and fourth quarter balance sheets appear as follows:

	BEGINNING IN LC	*TRANSLATION RATE*	*BEGINNING IN $*	*4th QUARTER IN LC*	*TRANSLATION RATE*	*4th QUARTER IN $*
Cash		2:1		23	2.66:1	8.64
Receivables	100	2:1	50	133	2.66:1	50.00
Inventory	60	2:1	30	80	2.66:1	30.00
Total: current assets	160		80	236		88.64
Plant and equipment	90	2:1	45	80	2.00:1	40.00
Total assets	250		125	316		128.64
Payables	30	2:1	15	40	2.66:1	15.00
Bank loan	40	2:1	20	40	2.00:1	20.00
Net worth	180		90	236		93.64
Total liabilities and net worth	250		125	316		128.64

Each of the translation methods is wedded to the traditional accounting premise of holding constant the historic costs of fixed assets. Fixed assets are valued at historic costs following the logic which is well developed in the accounting literature.[9] In effect, the translation methods presume that the local prices of fixed assets will increase as the exchange rate deteriorates, and consequently that inflation-devaluation will have no net effect on the value of fixed assets.[10] Using traditional translation procedures Reliable's plant and equipment at the end of the fourth quarter are valued at eighty units of local currency (LC90–10 of depreciation). Assuming that the exchange rate was 2:1 when the plant and equipment were originally acquired, these assets are translated into $40 using the historic rate.

Recall that the plant and equipment account was revalued at 106.40 units of local currency when the account was price level adjusted (see page 490). If the price-adjusted plant and equipment figure of LC106.40 is translated at the current exchange rate of 2.66:1, plant and equipment is valued at $40, or precisely the value ascertained using conventional translation procedures that disregard changes in local prices and apply historic exchange rates to historic book values. Thus the rise in prices of plant and equipment during inflationary conditions is assumed to be matched by depreciation of the local currency that reflects the domestic inflation. For this reason it is asserted that fixed assets serve both as an inflation and devaluation hedge.

[9] See for example, Staff of the Accounting Research Division, "Reporting the Financial Effect of Price Level Changes," AICPA Accounting Research Study, no. 6, New York, American Institute of Certified Public Accountants, 1963.

[10] The financial method extends this line of reasoning to all physical assets thus including inventories as well.

Let us now turn to the translated profit and loss statement. The revenue and expense items are translated at the applicable quarterly rates of exchange, except that depreciation is calculated at the rate prevailing when plant and equipment were acquired (at the 2:1 rate). Working with the local currency quarterly income statements that appear on page 487 one can readily verify that translated profits are $15 for the year or $3.75 per quarter; the sales and costs figures with the exception of depreciation are translated at the applicable quarterly rates, whereas a $1.25 depreciation charge is made for each quarter using the 2:1 historic rate.

The net worth reconciliation now appears as follows:

Beginning net worth	$90.00	(from translated balance sheets)
Profit	$15.00	(from translated income statements)
Ending net worth	$93.64	(from translated balance sheet)
Unrealized foreign exchange loss	($11.36)	(derived figure)

The translated accounts indicate dollar net improvement of $3.64 for the four quarters comprised of $15 in profits and ($11.36) of unrealized foreign exchange losses. These conclusions are identical to the price-adjusted results that appear on pages 489 and 490. (LC40 of profit less LC30.3 of losses on net monetary assets translated at the ending rate of 2.66:1 equals $3.64.) The identity is attributable to our assumption that internal price levels and exchange rates move together equally and simultaneously.

Unfortunately empirical evidence tends to invalidate the assumption upon which the accuracy of the conventional procedures depend—namely, that inflation and devaluation move together simultaneously. If this assumption is correct there should have been, for example, a steady devaluation of European currencies against the dollar during the last twenty years since inflation in Europe has generally been higher than in the United States. Not only has the anticipated devaluation not occurred, but the Deutsch mark and the Gilder have been revalued upwards in relation to the dollar. Nor is the assumption any more accurate in the case of countries that have experienced much higher rates of inflation than has Europe. Brazil is a case in point. During the recent past the cruzeiro has remained at 2,200 to the dollar during a twelve-month period when internal prices have risen more than 40 per cent per annum.

This is not to deny, of course, that there is a relationship between currency depreciation and domestic inflation. Over a long period it would be difficult to imagine circumstances in which the dollar-cruzeiro exchange rate could remain stable while inflation continued at 40 per cent per annum. Yet for a substantial period of time the economic forces that affect the rate of exchange—e.g., the external payments position of a country—can operate independently of the forces that determine the rate of domestic inflation. In some instances the forces may even operate in different directions. Even if the direction of change is the same, however, it is rarely appropriate to assume that precise correlations between inflation and devaluation exist, which is the basic premise of the translation procedures.

To the extent that the prices of fixed assets do not move with the depreciation of the currency, the presumed inflation-devaluation offset will be incomplete or more than adequate. If the increase in local prices of fixed assets exceeds the devaluation, the conventional translation procedures will understate the actual value of these assets. Conversely, if currency depreciation exceeds the rise in local prices, the translation method will result in balance sheet overstatement relative to actual local values. Hence financial statements of affiliates abroad that are translated in conformity with generally accepted methods are subject to distortion to the extent that local inflation is not matched by depreciation of the local currency.

Ignoring price level changes and translating in accordance with generally accepted procedures has several other serious shortcomings. A fluctuating foreign exchange rate may produce inventory translations that distort operating results between accounting periods. For example, assume that the Reliable affiliate's parent ships inventory to the affiliate during the third quarter when the exchange rate is 2.42:1 and that the inventory remains unsold as of the fourth quarter balance sheet date at which time the exchange rate has deteriorated to 2.66:1. The inventory has a United States dollar cost of 20 and consequently the Reliable affiliate records the receipt of imports by charging purchases (inventory) with LC48.4 ($20 × LC2.42) and posting an appropriate current United States dollar liability. Let us further assume that the Reliable affiliate has a normal markup of 50 per cent above cost and therefore expects to sell the imported inventory for 72.6 of local currency.

Using the traditional translation methods the LC48.4 of inventories are translated at the current rate at the end of the fourth quarter into approximately $18.20 (LC48.40 divided by 2.66). Therefore a foreign exchange loss of $1.80 is recorded in the accounts, and the annual profit figure is lowered by the same amount.

If we presume that the inventory in question is sold for 72.6 of local currency during the first quarter of the subsequent year as originally intended and that the applicable rate of exchange during this first quarter is 2.66:1, the sale is translated into roughly $27.29. This means that the gross margin on the sale will be reported as $9.09 during the subsequent year ($27.29 minus $18.20) although it should be reported as $7.29 ($27.29 minus $20), which is the real difference between cost and selling price in dollars. Thus the translation procedure has resulted in an understatement of the first year's profits and an overstatement of profits in the subsequent year. In point of fact there has been no foreign exchange loss during the first year since the decline in the foreign exchange rate from 2.42 to 2.66 simply has reduced the originally anticipated gross profit margin to $7.29 ($27.29 minus $20). The foreign exchange loss reported during the first year is also misleading by virtue of the likelihood that Reliable's imported inventory will appreciate in terms of local prices and that the affiliates may very well be able to sell the inventory for more than 72.60 units of local currency as originally planned. To the extent that Reliable is able to increase its selling prices, the foreign exchange loss reported by the company is misleading.

The differences between the financial statements prepared according to conventional translation methods and price-adjusted statements are naturally greater if one drops the assumption that price levels and currency depreciation are fully offsetting. Yet even if there were no differences between the conclusions conveyed by conventional and price-adjusted statements, the financial statements prepared using traditional translation methods are of limited usefulness to management. The meaning of the foreign exchange loss (or gain) element deduced from the comparative net worth accounts provides little insight if calculated without adjustments to reflect changes in internal price levels. Indeed, the foreign exchange gains or losses on local currency long-term debts are susceptible to misleading reporting if traditional translation methods are followed. Decisions regarding tax policy and the selection of appropriate financing instruments are not logically served by the conventional ground rules. Routine international business decisions such as pricing under conditions of changing local price levels and foreign exchange rates, capital expenditure policies, and determination of the appropriate foreign exchange exposure are difficult to make using financial data translated by the traditional methods.

THE RECOMMENDED APPROACH

Because of the distortion and limited insights inherent in traditional translation methods, a translation procedure known as the net assets method is advocated. Under this method all items except the net worth account and external debt are translated at the current rate of exchange. Used in conjunction with price level adjustments this method applies the current rate of exchange to all account items. The combination of price level adjustment and translation at current rates makes it possible to distinguish four significant figures—operating results in the local currency, the effects of inflation, the effects of devaluation, and the combined net effect of operations, inflation, and currency depreciation. Unlike the methods described earlier, the net assets method when used in conjunction with price-level adjustments recognizes the probability of disparate movements in domestic prices and foreign exchange rates.

To demonstrate the insights conveyed by this approach, let us again return to the Reliable illustration. As previously, let us assume that the

Reliable affiliate's costs and prices rise simultaneously at a 10 per cent rate at the beginning of the second, third and fourth quarters. Therefore, the local currency balance sheet and income statement appear precisely as before (see pages 488 and 487). If we assume that plant and equipment actually have a current net replacement cost of approximately LC106.40 at year end, the price-adjusted balance sheet is as shown on page 490. By comparing the beginning and price-adjusted fourth quarter balance sheets, the reader can assess both the ordinary operating results in terms of local currency and the effects of inflation on these results. Working with the price-adjusted accounts, it is possible to assess Reliable's performance after providing for the maintenance of affiliate assets.

In many instances it is unnecessary for headquarters to carry analysis of Reliable's results further. Local currency figures are sufficient for most managerial purposes. If devaluation has occurred, however, management may wish to distinguish the effect of currency depreciation on the affiliate's operations. This subsequent stage of analysis is accomplished by translating the price-adjusted balance sheet figures at the ending rate of exchange. Let us examine the financial statement implications of the "net assets" method under three different ending exchange rate assumptions: no devaluation, devaluation from 2:1 to 2.66:1, and devaluation from 2:1 to 3:1. Our analysis assumes that when devaluation occurs, it does so before the fourth quarter balance sheet data. The translated balance sheets appear as shown on page 502.

Comparison of the beginning and ending net worth figures translated into dollars reveals the extent to which the alternative exchange rates have affected the Reliable affiliate. Earlier (page 491) our price-adjusted calculations indicated LC9.7 of net income after adjustments for losses on monetary items; the equivalent dollar profit under the assumption that price increases are exactly matched by exchange rate deterioration (2.66:1) is \$3.64. Thus, if the rate of exchange deteriorates to 2.66:1, the company experiences no further loss or gain on translation since price level increases precisely offset exchange rate depreciation. Net worth increases in an amount equivalent to price level adjusted profits (\$3.64).

On the other hand, if the exchange rate remains at 2:1, the Reliable Company's position is relatively better at year end in two respects. First, adjusted profits are \$4.85 instead of \$3.64 since the company experiences a smaller loss on monetary items. Second, the firm experiences an exchange gain of \$36.35 due to the purchasing power erosion of locally denominated liabilities.

Yet if the exchange rate deteriorates to 3 to 1, the company's position at year end is substantially worse. Net profits are only \$3.23 by virtue of significant losses on monetary items. Also, an exchange loss of \$12.43 is incurred. Because price increases have not kept pace with exchange rate deterioration the company is \$12.43 worse off than if net worth had been converted into dollars prior to the inflation-exchange rate spiral.

Ending Balance Sheets Based on Various Exchange Rate Assumptions

	IN LOCAL CURRENCY *	*IN $'s 2:1* †	*IN $'s 2.66:1* †	*IN $'s 3:1* †
Cash	23.0	11.50	8.64	7.67
Receivables	133.0	66.50	50.00	44.33
Inventory	80.0	40.00	30.00	26.67
Total current assets	236.0	118.00	88.64	78.67
Net plant and equipment	106.4	53.20	40.00	35.47
Total assets	LC342.4	$171.20	$128.64	$114.14
Current payables	40.0	20.00	15.00	13.34
Bank loans (in $'s)	53.2	20.00	20.00	20.00
Net worth:				
Beginning balance	239.5	90.00 ‡	90.00 ‡	90.00 ‡
and net income	40.0	20.00	15.00	13.33
gain on monetary items	(30.3)	(15.15)	(11.36)	(10.10)
gain on exchange	—	36.35 §	0 §	(12.43) §
Ending balance	249.2	81.20	43.64	30.80
Total liabilities and net worth	LC342.4	$171.20	$128.64	$114.14

* Price-level adjusted (see page 490).

† Alternative $/LC exchange rates assumed for comparison.

‡ The dollar equivalent of net worth at the beginning of the period is calculated by applying the beginning exchange rate LC2:$1 to the beginning LC balance of 180 (see page 488).

§ The foreign exchange gain (or loss) is a derived or "plug" figure. It can be verified by subtracting the dollar value of beginning net worth and external debt from the dollar equivalent of these items translated at ending rates:

Dollar value of beginning net worth and dollar loan (page 486)

	LOCAL CURRENCY	*TRANSLATED AT BEGINNING RATE*
Loan	LC 40	$ 20
Net worth	180	90
Total	LC220	$110

Dollar equivalent at end of period with various assumed rates

Price-adjusted opening balances (see page 490)

	LOCAL CURRENCY
Loan	LC 53.2
Net worth	239.5
Total	LC292.7

Translation of 292.7 into dollars at various ending rates

LC2: $1	=	$146.35
LC2.66: $1	=	$110.00
LC3: $1	=	$ 97.57

Exchange gain (or loss):

	ENDING VALUE		*BEGINNING VALUE*		*GAIN (OR LOSS)*
LC2: $1	$146.35	—	$110.00	=	$ 36.35
LC2.66: $1	$110.00	—	$110.00	=	0
LC3: $1	$ 97.57	—	$110.00	=	$(12.43)

CONCLUSION

It is apparent from the previous discussion that substantial information is required to cast financial data in the prescribed format. Predictions of the degree of inflation and likely devaluation (if any) are required before pro forma balance sheets and income statements can be prepared. These predictions provide the basis for detailed line-by-line analysis of all account items. To illustrate the type of analysis required, we list some questions that should be raised when considering the profit and loss statement:

1. When are the various cost components expected to increase in price and by how much?
2. Is the labor cost subject to expected government action; is there a contract in force?
3. Are raw materials costs expected to rise? If so, when and by how much?
4. Are raw materials imported and therefore subject to foreign exchange and tariff uncertainties?
5. Is there a stockpile of inventory that will mitigate the effect of higher material costs, and what will be the effect on the profit statement?
6. What adjustments in the depreciation charge need to be made, if any, to allow for rising replacement costs? What other inflation adjustments, if any, are planned?
7. What is the effect of inflation on borrowings? Are there premiums payable on local currency debt, and is the loss in local currency on foreign currency debt taken into account?
8. What are the likely tax consequences of any inflation adjustments that may be made?
9. Above all, given steadily increasing costs, can the affiliate raise its prices without difficulty? Will competitive conditions allow it? Is there competition from imports that may prevent the desired price increase? Will the government limit price increases? Is the demand for the product inelastic so that price increases can be made without causing a reduction in unit demand?
10. When will devaluation occur and to what extent?

Detailed analysis along these lines must be undertaken to insure that projections in local currency are as realistic as possible. Transactions moving through the exchange market must be translated into the local currency using the expected, applicable rates of exchange. This facet of the analysis explicitly identifies the increased local currency outlays associated with importing, remitting dividends, and servicing international debt.

In countries where inflation and devaluation are important enough to pose the types of problems discussed above, financial statements are subject to considerable distortion. Both deteriorating internal prices and devaluations are symptoms of economic problems and the existence of these problems makes the predictions on which pro forma financial statements depend very difficult. For example, it is less easy to predict corporate tax rates in inflationary economies than is the case in the United States where changes will tend to be small and infrequent. Or again, a new political regime determined to slow the inflationary spiral may take a variety of unpredictable steps such as price controls that may seriously affect an affiliate's profits and cash inflows. Notwithstanding the difficulties inherent in projecting financial statements under these circumstances, analysts must deal with the problems to the best of their ability. Indeed, forecasting is more important in these environments than in stable situations since it is of the utmost importance that management identify problem areas and adopt corrective management measures wherever practicable in order to deal effectively with the volatile environment conditions.

RESPONSIBILITY ACCOUNTING IN INTERNATIONAL OPERATIONS

The success (or failure) of an overseas affiliate is usually attributable to several parties either directly or indirectly concerned with its operations. Typically the local manager plays an active role in obtaining or producing products for sale in the local market. He may also be responsible for exports and for maintaining the value of affiliate assets.

At the same time, aspects of affiliate operations can sometimes be traced to local government mandates or the efforts of local partners. Such factors as tax concessions, liberal depreciation allowances, and favorable exchange rates for imported machinery and materials often are attributable to the efforts of outsiders.

Still other aspects of affiliate performance are the result of policy decisions and actions taken by headquarters personnel. Frequently headquarters supplies technical and managerial assistance to an affiliate with or without the consent of local management! Headquarters may assist in the establishment of transfer prices among various affiliates and make product loans or advances to facilitate affiliate expansion. The resulting fees, interest charges, cost-price relationships and allocation of headquarters overhead influence the affiliate's reported profitability. Additionally the affiliate's financial structure and related costs may, on the one hand, be attributable to local management decisions, or, alternatively, be a function of headquarters policy.

In order to motivate properly and appraise performance of local managers, it is necessary to unravel the various factors contributing to affiliate performance and to isolate the elements subject to local authority. In this fashion it is possible to devise performance measures that are suitable for the appraisal of local managers. Appropriate appraisal measures can be devised by modifying the traditional profit and loss statements, substituting functional captions for the traditional revenue and expense elements. One possible format is outlined below:

Revenues (in local currency units)
  Revenues as they appear in traditional profit and loss statement plus (or minus) adjustments to eliminate unrealistic transfer-pricing effects.

Expenses (in local currency units)
  Cost of goods sold (as it appears in traditional profit and loss statement except that extra costs due to local government policies or local partners are excluded)
  plus: depreciation, adjusted to reflect current cost of fixed asset replacement
  plus: cost savings attributable to local factors (e.g., special concessions)
  minus: extra costs attributable to local factors
  plus: general and administrative expenses (as it appears in traditional statement except that headquarters charges are eliminated)
  plus: headquarters G & A charges
  plus: selling expenses

Operating profits before interest and taxes (in local currency units)
  less: local interest expense
  less: interest expense on external debt

Operating profits before taxes (in local currency units)
  less: local taxes
  less: actual (or imputed) taxes in country of parent

Operating profits after taxes (in local currency units)
  less: inflationary loss (or gain)
    loss due to erosion of purchasing of monetary assets
    gain due to holdings of nonmonetary assets
    gain due to locally denominated liabilities
  less: devaluation loss (or gain)
    [realized (or unrealized) on translation into parent currency]

Frequently transfer prices are established among affiliates to minimize unfavorable tax consequences. Any such transfer prices are adjusted to reflect the true contribution of the affiliate in question. The operating expenses are separated into elements attributable to local management, outside parties, and headquarters. Depending upon whether headquarters management desires to hold the local affiliate accountable for either headquarters charges or the activity of other outside parties, these cost elements are either included or excluded from the operating profit performance measure. Next local taxes are included and, again depending upon management philosophy, a charge is made against affiliate management in recognition of realized or deferred United States tax liabilities.

Thus far the income statement has been reconstructed using local currency data and ignoring the effects on operations of changes in the internal price level. It is now desirable to isolate the effects of inflation on operations, using price-adjusted figures as advocated earlier. There are four separate aspects of the inflationary adjustment:

1. The loss due to erosion of purchasing power of monetary assets—i.e., cash, receivables, LC marketable securities, and perhaps inventories [11]
2. The gain due to appreciation in local currency of nonmonetary assets
3. The incremental depreciation charge to reflect the rising cost of fixed asset replacement
4. The gain arising from monetary liabilities denominated in local currency.

The reason for distinguishing between the elements of inflationary loss (or gain) is that aspects of the total loss (or gain) may fall outside the scope of local management purview. It is desirable to identify and hold local managers accountable for the steps that they can take to minimize inflation's eroding effects.

Frequently affiliate financial policy is dictated by headquarters management, and local managers have little influence with regard to the added costs or benefits derived from certain financing plans during inflationary conditions. Similarly the composition of affiliate assets is often determined by the inherent characteristics of the business or by headquarters management, and consequently the local manager has only limited authority to cope with inflationary pressures. The performance measures used to appraise local management should recognize the extent to which local managers have freedom of action.

In most companies local personnel have some discretionary authority with reference to cost-price relationships and therefore can take steps to minimize the adverse effects of inflation even though the degree of asset exposure to inflationary pressures and related financing plans may be outside their control. Some companies permit their local managers to discontinue or curtail selling efforts whenever the latter believe that the added

[11] To the extent that inventories rise in selling price in local currency, an inflationary loss is avoided.

costs of carrying receivables in inflationary conditions outweigh the benefits of added sales. In many firms local managers have some control over asset composition, and the extent to which this authority is exercised properly can be appraised in the context of nonoperating, holding gains (or losses) attributable to the erosion of asset purchasing power during inflationary conditions. Still other firms delegate total authority to local managers in determining asset composition, financial arrangements, and sales policy under inflationary conditions. Consequently, aspects of the total inflationary loss (or gain) can be charged to local management only after the local manager's authority to deal with inflationary pressures has been carefully analyzed.

Similarly the nature of finance charges levied against local management should logically depend upon the authority vested in local management to make financial decisions. If, for example, headquarters selects the financial instruments and related currencies of denomination for affiliates, headquarters personnel should be held accountable for specific financing costs. Premiums paid to borrow in local currencies and gains arising from local borrowing during periods of inflation should be reflected in headquarters performance measures. If headquarters personnel specify the amount of affiliate debt and choose between borrowing sources—i.e., local or international—then headquarters rather than the local affiliate is the logical party to be held accountable for the true cost of financing incurred by the affiliate. Effective financing costs are a function of both nominal rates and price level changes. Hence both nominal financial charges and indirect gains (or losses) attributable to specific financial instruments should be eliminated from the local affiliate performance measure.

At the same time profits of local affiliates should be sufficient to cover financing costs even though actual financial expenses depend on headquarters decisions. In order to reflect this expectation an imputed finance charge should be substituted for the actual financial expenses incurred by the affiliate. This imputed charge might reflect the average cost of capital for the corporation at large.

Under other circumstances financing problems may be left for the respective local affiliates to resolve. In these instances the affiliates should be held accountable for actual financing costs. Charged with the authority for selecting optimal financial plans, the local affiliates can be expected to minimize effective financial costs that in turn depend on nominal rates of interest, inflationary pressures, and, in the case of externally denominated debt, on the rates of exchange that are applied when international debt is serviced. The information conveyed under three captions—interest expenses, gain due to locally denominated liabilities, and devaluation loss—provide a basis for evaluating local management's financing achievements.

Summary

Financial statements prepared in accordance with generally accepted accounting principles do not convey sufficient information for meaningful appraisal of foreign operations. This chapter has dealt with some of the major deficiences characteristic of the conventional accounting statements. Specifically, distortions caused by inflationary conditions have been noted and procedures involving price level adjustment have been advocated to compensate for the distortions. Additionally the problems inherent in conventional translation procedures have been discussed and an alternative net asset procedure has been suggested that, in conjunction with price adjustments, is intended to remedy the characteristic deficiencies of traditional translation techniques. Finally the chapter has suggested the need for a revised profit and loss format to be used in appraising affiliate performance and has outlined the specifications of such a format.

In focusing on managerial accounting issues, this chapter has ignored several important international accounting questions. For example, the chapter has not dealt with the reporting question regarding whether parent and affiliate financial statements should be consolidated. Likewise the important related question regarding when affiliate profits should be reflected in the parent profit measure has been disregarded. These and other international accounting questions are resolved by management in collaboration with auditors, legal advisors, tax officials, and regulatory authorities. Our concern has been deliberately restricted to managerial accounting questions relating to the compilation of data that will enable headquarters management to improve their appraisals of performance and to establish appropriate incentives for local personnel. In conclusion it should be emphasized that the prescribed adjustment to conventional financial statements requires outlays of managerial time and money. Although the authors are of the opinion that the costs are not likely to be prohibitive in view of the valuable insights obtained, it is important to recognize that the modifications are warranted only if anticipated benefits outweigh related costs.

BIBLIOGRAPHY

American Institute of Certified Public Accountants. *Professional Accounting in 25 Countries*, New York, 1964.

Anderson, David S. "Communications Problems of Financial Reporting," *Journal of Accountancy*, April 1963.

Barnes, William S. "Guides to International Operations," *Harvard Business Review*, November-December 1965.

Binger, Martin O. "Translation of Financial Statements Expressed in Foreign Currencies," *Arthur Young Journal*, January 1964.

Bomeli, Edwin C. "Management Reviews by Scandinavian Accountants," *Journal of Accountancy*, July 1964.

Bourn, A. M. "Economics and Accountancy," *Accountancy*, March 1966.

Business International. *Accounting Practices in Fluctuating Currency Countries*, Business International Management Monograph, no. 4, New York, 1963.

Donner, Frederic G. "The World-Wide Corporation in a Modern Economy," *Canadian Chartered Accountant*, January 1963.

"The Economic Approach to Accounting," *Journal of Accountancy*, March 1963.

Elliot, E. Witlard. "The Lower of Cost or Market Test for Foreign Inventories," *NAA Bulletin*, February 1965, sec. 1, pp. 12–17.

Forsstrom, Borje. "Finnish Accountancy and Increasing International Capital Movements," unpublished technical paper, Session B, *VIII International Congress of Accountants*, New York, 1962.

Fredrikson, Eric Bruce. "Reporting International Operations," unpublished Ph.D. dissertation, Columbia University, 1963.

Furlong, William L. "Minimizing Foreign Exchange Losses," *Accounting Review*, April 1966.

Gillespie, Gwain H. "Foreign Accounting Problems," *Quarterly* (New York: Touche, Ross, Bailey & Smart), June 1964.

Hepworth, Samuel R. *Reporting Foreign Operations*, Michigan Business Studies, vol. XII, no. 5 (Ann Arbor: University of Michigan, 1956).

International Finance Corporation. *Accounting and Financial Reporting*, pamphlet, 1964; *Illustrative Form of Audit Report*, pamphlet, 1965.

Johansson, Sven-Erik. "An Appraisal of the Swedish System of Investment Reserves," *International Journal of Accounting*, Fall 1965.

Kafer, Karl. "European National Uniform Charts of Accounts," *International Journal of Accounting*, Fall 1965.

Kircher, Donald P. "Now the Transnational Enterprise," *Harvard Business Review*, March-April 1964.

Kleerekoper, I. "Some Aspects of Accounting and Auditing in the Netherlands," *Accountants' Magazine*, October 1959; November 1959.

Kocan, Peter. "Geographical Distribution of Earnings and Assets," *Journal of Accountancy*, June 1963.

Kraayenhof, Jacob. "International Challenges for Accounting," *Journal of Accountancy*, January 1960.

Leagyel, S. J. "Standardized Accountancy Considered Internationally," *Accounting Research*, July 1949.

MacNeill, James H. "Accounting for Inflation Abroad," *Journal of Accountancy*, August 1961.

May, George O. *Financial Accounting*. (New York: The Macmillan Company, 1956).

Mueller, Gerhard G. *Accounting Practices in Sweden*. (Seattle: College of Business Administration, University of Washington, 1962).

Mueller, Gerhard G. "Accounting Problems of International Corporations," *Canadian Chartered Accountant,* April 1965.

———. *International Accounting.* (New York: The Macmillan Company, 1967).

———. "Valuing Inventories at Other than Historical Costs—Some International Differences," *Journal of Accounting Research,* Autumn 1964.

"Multinational Companies: How U.S. Business Goes Worldwide," Special Report, *Business Week,* April 20, 1963.

National Association of Accountants. *Accounting Problems in Foreign Operations,* NAA Research Report, no. 36, New York, 1960.

Oppenheimer, H. H. "Reporting Undistributable Foreign Borrowings," *New York Certified Public Accountant,* February 1962.

Shilinglaw, Gordon. "International Comparability of Accountants," *Accountancy,* February 1966.

Solomons, David. "Economic and Accounting Concepts of Cost and Value," Morton Backer, ed., *Modern Accounting Theory.* (Englewood Cliffs, N.J.: Prentice-Hall, Inc., 1966), pp. 117–140.

"Unilever-World Trader in a Shrinking World," *Forbes,* November 1, 1962.

Van Vlerken, J. H. M. "Financial Reporting in Holland," *Canadian Chartered Accountant,* November 1965.

Watt, George C. "Management Accounting Problems in Foreign Operations." *Proceedings, 1960, Institute on Private Investments Abroad.* (New York: Matthew Bender & Co.).

———. "Unrealized Foreign Exchange Gains Arising from Funds Borrowed in Local Currency," *NAA Bulletin,* February 1965, sec. 1, pp. 3–11.

Wells, Michael T. "Devaluation and Inflation and Their Effect on Foreign Operations," *Accountancy,* August 1965.

Wilkinson, Theodore L. "Can Accounting Be an International Language?" *Price Waterhouse Review,* Summer 1963.

Yu, S. C. "Microaccounting and Macroaccounting," *Accounting Review,* January 1966.

Case 21
STABILITY, INC.

Stability, Inc. was founded in the mythical republic of Bellerivia on January 1, 1964. On December 31, 1967, its condensed balance sheet was shown in Exhibit 1. All figures are stated in Bellerivian doubloons, a decimal currency represented by the $ symbol.

Stability, Inc. does only a wholesale business, with no manufacturing operations. All wages and salaries are charged to expense as earned. Inventory is valued on the first-in, first-out (FIFO) basis.

Prices were stable during the first four years of the company's life. The general price index on December 31, 1967, was 100 – the same as it had been on January 1, 1964. Early in 1968, however, the government of Bellerivia launched large-scale rearmament and social welfare programs. These activities were financed mainly by government borrowing from the Bellerivian central bank, which was allowed to treat the government's promissory notes as part of its required legal reserves. Taking prices at January 1, 1964, as 100, the general price index changed as follows during the year:

Date	*General price index*
January 1, 1968	100
First quarter average	110
Second quarter average	130
June 30, 1968	140
Third quarter average	150
Fourth quarter average	170
December 31	180
1968 average	140

The company's trial balance, on an original cost basis, was as follows on December 31, 1968:

	Debits	*Credits*
	(in thousands of doubloons)	
Cash	190	
Accounts and notes receivable	1,400	
Inventories	4,250	
Plant and equipment	2,210	
Accumulated depreciation		521
Accounts and notes payable		1,550
Capital stock		2,000
Retained earnings, Dec. 31, 1967		2,700
Sales		15,400
Cost of goods sold expense	12,250	
Salaries and other current expenses	1,750	
Depreciation expense	121	
Totals	22,171	22,171

Purchases during 1968 were as follows:

Quarter	*Historical cost (thousands of doubloons)*
1st	2,750
2nd	3,250
3rd	3,750
4th	4,250
Total	14,000

Under the first-in, first-out inventory method, the goods in the December 31, 1968, inventory were those purchased at various times during the final quarter of 1968. The ending inventory represented the same physical quantity as the January 1, 1968, figure. During the year, purchases and sales of physical units of goods were the same in each quarter.

The major part of the plant and equipment, costing $2,000,000 was acquired on January 1, 1964, when the business was founded. Depreciation had been recorded on this part of the asset account at the rate of 5 per cent a year. On June 30, 1968, additional equipment costing $210,000 was acquired. It was expected to have a useful life of 5 years, but depreciation was recorded for only a half year in 1968.

At a meeting early in 1969 the board of directors was considering the question of how large a cash dividend to pay.

Questions

1. Prepare a balance sheet, an income statement, a source and application of funds statement, and a cash receipts and disbursements statement for 1968 on the basis of historical cost.
2. Prepare the same statements for 1968 on a price-level adjustment basis.
3. Compute the gain or loss from holding monetary assets in 1968.
4. Compute the gain or loss from holding inventories and fixed assets during 1968. What is the meaning of your answer?
5. How do the procedures used for adjusting account balances for general price-level changes resemble the procedures for translating the accounts of a foreign business subdivision into the domestic currency? In what major ways do the two types of procedures differ?
6. What policy should Stability, Inc. follow if it wishes to minimize the gain or loss on monetary accounts?
7. How can the management of Stability, Inc. use the adjusted financial information? What are its shortcomings?

EXHIBIT 1

Stability, Inc.
Condensed Balance Sheet
December 31, 1967
(in thousands of doubloons)

Assets		
Current assets		
Cash	$ 400	
Accounts and notes receivable	1,500	
Inventories	2,500	
Total current assets		$4,400
Fixed assets:		
Plant and equipment (cost)	2,000	
Deduct accumulated depreciation	400	
Total fixed assets		1,600
Total assets		$6,000
Liabilities		
Current liabilities		
Accounts and notes payable	$1,300	
Total liabilities		$1,300
Stockholders' Equity		
Capital stock	2,000	
Retained earnings	2,700	
Total stockholders' equity		4,700
Total equities		$6,000

Case 22
INDUSTRIAS BRASILERIA ELECTROMETALÚRGICA, S.A.

Historical

Established in the mid 1950's, Ind. Brasileria Electrometalúrgica, S.A., is a major Brazilian manufacturing company of electric implements. Purchases by its related company, Metales, Inc., have accounted for 60 per cent of its total production. Historically, the Company has relied on imports for its materials, but a new national hardware company presently under construction will supply its future material needs.

Because of rampant inflation over the past several years, historical values of sales and earnings have very little meaning when evaluating the trend of IBESA's past performance. In the past, sales in physical volume have been fairly stable—about 10.6 thousand tons except in 1965 when sales fell almost 30 per cent. However, sales in cruzeiros have increased substantially from Cr1,001 million in 1962 to Cr4,812 million in 1965 reflecting higher sales prices.

It is clear from the "Historical Operating-Nonoperating Cash Flow Statement" (Exhibit 1) and the "Historical Comparative Statement of Financial Condition" (Exhibit 2) for 1963-1967 that IBESA has been able to pass on successfully any inflationary cost increases almost immediately to its consumers because of its monopoly position. This is reflected in the fact that its margins have remained stable and that the Company has been able to generate sufficient cruzeiros internally and, with interim short-term debt financing, to fully repay its long-term debt of U.S. $1.7 million from Exim Bank and to meet other nonoperating needs.

The interim statement of September 30, 1966, shows IBESA in good shape financially with a current ratio of 2.92 accompanied by a very high cash balance and no long-term debt. The steady improvement in IBESA's working capital position is seen from 1962-1966 in the current ratio strengthening from 1.21 to 2.92. At September 30, 1966, IBESA has a debt to equity ratio of .25 on a net worth of Cr5,796 million (U.S. $2,602 thousands).

Expansion

The Company has proposed plant expansion that will double its existing capacity and will exceed the demand from its traditional hardware market. The expansion, which has been engineered by an American Company, is the smallest addition that will provide desired efficiency. An engineering firm predicts that the highly automated new unit will result in a doubling of production with only a 25 per cent increase in the existing operating staff. The long-run strategy of IBESA is to maintain a supply of electric implements to hardware consumers to meet the normal growth in the market of 10 per cent annually. The excess production mentioned above will be sold to small Brazilian consumers until the growth of traditional wholesale markets absorbs the increased production. The traditional market is protected by a 15 per cent duty that is considered adequate to eliminate imports.

The total cost for construction and equipment is forecast at U.S. $4 million consisting of U.S. $800,000 for imported machinery and U.S. $3.1 million for construction and locally manufactured equipment. The Company's projections of Operating and Nonoperating Cash flow for 1966 to 1972 are shown in Exhibit 3. Basically, the Company's projections show that sales will almost double in 1968 to U.S. $6 million immediately following plant completion in 1967 and with the same favorable rate of growth projected for net income of U.S. $1 million in 1968. Thereafter, sales are projected at a steady growth of 9 per cent annually and net profits at 19 per cent of sales. No inflationary effects are incorporated in the projections.

Banco De Labora De Curitiba Analysis

After a thorough study of the proposal prepared by the Company, the projections have been revised. The most significant revision as shown in the bank projections of Operating Nonoperating Cash Flow Statements (Exhibit 4) and the Comparative Statements of Financial Condition (Exhibit 5) is a one-year delay in construction and the resulting provision for an additional 20 per cent escalation for the construction and local equipment cost. Additionally the equity injection, sales increases, and capital expenditures have been deferred by one year. Further, the working capital needs and sales increases have been adjusted on a more conservative basis in line with the Company's historical experience.

The construction will be undertaken over two years in 1967-1968, and the financing is planned to be supplied from the following sources:

Means of financing	*Equivalent U.S. % in thousands*	*%*
Bank debt	2,278	57
Internal generation	1,260	32
New equity issue	450	11
Total project cost	3,988	100

Of the total bank debt, 37 per cent or U.S. $838 thousand will be supplied by Exim Bank, and the balance will be in cruzeiro loans from Brazilian national agencies guaranteed by commercial banks.

As reflected in the Bank projections (Exhibits 4 and 5) a cash shortage occurs during 1968. To cover this shortage the Bank has included in its projections an additional U.S. $1 million loan in 1968 to provide liquidity during the construction period. This prospective loan involves a total commitment of four years with repayment in 1970 (U.S. $400 thousand) and in 1971 (U.S. $600 thousand).

Taking all of the Bank revisions into account, Exhibit 4 shows the Company with a cash generation available to meet nonoperating needs of U.S. $480 thousand in 1966, U.S. $344 thousand in 1967, U.S. $802 thousand in 1968, U.S. $1,160 thousand in 1969, U.S. $1,200 thousand in 1970, and U.S. $1,506 thousand in 1971. Although negative changes in cash of U.S. $240 thousand occur in the first year of construction (1967) and of U.S. $324 thousand in 1970 due to heavy debt repayment and dividends, there is no serious deterioration in IBESA's operating cash position. Nevertheless the coverage during the payout period (1969-1971) is fairly thin, although some leeway may be afforded in the magnitude of dividend payments.

The effects of potential inflation are ignored in the analysis since over the duration of the loan the Company can be expected to increase its selling prices (as in the past) not only to offset higher costs due to inflation, but also to preserve a constant profit margin (i.e., the Company's profits are to be expected to be maintained in real terms). Furthermore the analysis assumes that the rate of depreciation of the Company's local currency earnings are presumed to be sufficient to buy the same amount of dollars, notwithstanding the deterioration of the exchange rate. On the basis of these assumptions, the ability of the Company to repay its dollar debt can be judged by constructing projections in dollars, and the problems of inflation and currency depreciation can then be ignored because they will offset each other.

Questions

1. Does the historical summary of income statements (Exhibit 1) represent a reasonable measurement of past performance? How could it be improved?
2. Do the Bank projections (Exhibit 4 and 5) seem reasonable and complete? Would you amend the method of projection, assuming that estimates of future physical production are substantially accurate?
3. What additional information, if any, is required before making a decision on a $1 million term loan to provide liquidity during the Company's expansion program?

EXHIBIT 1

CIA Brasileria Electrometalúrgica
Historical Operating–Nonoperating Cash Flow Statement
(amounts in 1,000's of U.S. $)

	For the year			
	1963	*1964*	*1965*	*1966*
Net sales	1,703	366	4,464	4,812
Cost of goods sold	956	240	2,644	2,904
Selling, general, admin., exp.	134	23	306	244
Deprec. and other noncash charges	165	27	990	530
Other income	10	1	24	54
Other expenses				
Income taxes	154	39	446	320
Net income	284	38	54	868
Depreciation	165	27	424	530
Other noncash charges				
Funds flow	449	65	478	1,398
Less: operating cash needs				
inc/(Dec.) required cash				
inc/(Dec.) receivables	140	(13)	652	266
inc/(Dec.) inventory	64	(30)	942	356
inc/(Dec.) prepaid expenses	5	(4)	20	(5)
Total	209	(47)	1,614	617
Plus: operating cash sources				
inc/(Dec.) accounts payable	(34)	(10)	186	(120)
inc/(Dec.) accruals taxes	186	40	340	236
inc/(Dec.) customer advances	(184)			
Total	(32)	30	526	116
Cash flow	208	142	(610)	897
Sale of equity				
inc. long-term debt		184		
inc. short-term debt		94	266	
Sale of marketable sec.				
Compulsory loans				
Total	208	278	(344)	897
Capital expenditures	36	3	4	86
Dividends		12	102	
Reduction long-term debt			88	326
Reduction short-term debt				76
Inv. and adv. subs. and affiliates	60	(38)	110	226
Total	96	(23)	304	714
Net increase (decrease) in cash and marketable securities	112	301	(48)	183

EXHIBIT 2 **CIA Brasileria Electrometalúrgica**
Comparative Statements of Financial Conditions

Description	*12/31/62*	*12/31/63*	*12/29/64*	*2/28/65*	*2/28/66*	*9/30/66*
Current assets	643	825	**957**	2,410	3,479	4,239
Current liabilities	527	476	599	1,391	1,432	1,454
Working capital	116	349	358	1,019	2,047	2,785
Long-term debt	274	224	409	3,325		
Tangible net worth	536	1,023	1,067	3,379	4,424	5,797
Net sales	1,011	1,717	366	4,465	4,812	3,967
Net profit	125	314	19	645	867	620
Assets						
Cash	169	143	315	159	583	1,633
Marketable securities						
Receivables	265	405	393	1,045	1,311	1,252
Inventory	195	260	231	1,173	1,528	1,307
Prepaid expenses	11	17	13	33	28	27
Total current assets	640	825	952	2,410	3,450	4,219
Net fixed assets	583	733	989	2,533	2,135	2,577
Inv. and adv. subs. and affiliates						
Compulsory loans	107	167	129	239	465	657
Intangibles						
Total assets	1,330	1,725	2,070	5,182	6,050	7,453
Liabilities						
Notes payable banks	362	134	227	494	418	182
Accounts payable	165	131	121	307	187	278
Taxes payable		149	181	459	442	532
Accruals		24	30	66	267	281
Current long-term debt		38	39	65	117	180
Total current liab.	527	476	598	1,391	1,431	1,453
Total long-term debt	267	226	405	431	195	204
Total sub. long-term debt						
Total long-term liab. and rvs.						
Preferred stock						
Common stock	400	700	700	2,466	2,466	3,233
Capital surplus	10	25	44	481	979	996
Earned surplus	126	298	323	433	979	1,567
Exchange loss						
Total liabilities and net worth	1,330	1,725	2,070	5,182	6,050	7,453

EXHIBIT 3 CIA Brasileria Electrometalúrgica
Operating–Nonoperating Cash Flow–IBESA Predictions
(amounts in 1,000's of U.S. $)

	For the year					
	1966	*1967*	*1968*	*1969*	*1970*	*1971*
Net sales	3,771	3,771	6,135	6,681	7,078	7,571
Cost of goods sold						
Selling, general, admin., exp.						
Deprec. and other noncash charges			NA			
Other income						
Other expenses						
Income taxes						
Net income	561	424	1,107	1,308	1,385	1,521
Depreciation	177	127	533	533	533	536
Other noncash charges						
Funds flow	738	551	1,640	1,841	1,918	2,057
Less: operating cash needs						
inc/(Dec.) required cash						
inc/(Dec.) receivables	234	(220)	720	125	105	125
inc/(Dec.) inventory	(64)	(23)	17	17	20	19
inc/(Dec.) prepaid expenses						
Total	170	(243)	737	142	125	144
Plus: operating cash sources						
inc/(Dec.) accounts payable	(5)	95	51	25	33	43
inc/(Dec.) accruals taxes	76	(86)	159	252	87	51
inc/(Dec.) customer advances						
Total	71	9	210	277	120	94
Cash flow	639	803	1,113	1,976	1,913	2,007
Sale of equity	270	200				
inc. long-term debt	939	396				
inc. short-term debt	219	178				
Sale of marketable sec.						
Compulsory loans	73					
Total	2,140	1,477				
Capital expenditures	1,706	2,283		72		30
Dividends			400	533	667	667
Reduction long-term debt	174		502	202	105	105
Reduction short-term debt			100	300	100	
Inv. and adv. subs. and affiliates						
Total	1,880	2,283	1,002	1,107	872	802
Net increase (decrease) in cash and marketable securities	260	(806)	111	869	1,041	1,235

EXHIBIT 4 **CIA Brasileria Electrometalúrgica**
Operating–Nonoperating Cash Flow Statement–Bank Projections
(amounts in 1,000's of U.S. $)

	For the year					
	1966	*1967*	*1968*	*1969*	*1970*	*1971*
Net sales	3,067	3,771	3,771	4,900	6,400	6,820
Cost of goods sold						
Selling, general, admin., exp.						
Deprec. and other noncash charges						
Other income						
Other expenses						
Income taxes						
Net income	460	570	570	900	1,200	1,350
Depreciation	175	125	125	525	530	530
Other noncash charges						
Funds flow	635	695	695	1,425	1,730	1,880
Less: operating cash needs						
inc/(Dec.) required cash						
inc/(Dec.) receivables	141	169		167	360	280
inc/(Dec.) inventory	129	155		250	330	260
inc/(Dec.) prepaid expenses						
Total	270	324		517	690	540
Plus: operating cash sources						
inc/(Dec.) accounts payable	50	60		96	128	100
inc/(Dec.) accruals taxes				165	75	50
inc/(Dec.) customer advances	65	(85)	110			
Total	115	(25)	110	261	203	150
Cash flow	480	346	805	1,169	1,243	1,490
Sale of equity		270	180			
inc. long-term debt		1,145	1,780			
inc. short-term debt						
Sale of marketable sec.						
Compulsory loans						
Total		1,415	1,960			
Capital expenditures	20	1,575	2,640		70	
Dividends					500	650
Reduction long-term debt	175			700	900	800
Reduction short-term debt						
Inv. and adv. subs. and affiliates						
Total	195	1,575	2,640	700	1,470	1,450
Net increase (decrease) in cash and marketable securities	295	160	125	469	(227)	40

EXHIBIT 5

CIA Brasileria Electrometalúrgica
Curitiba, Brazil
Comparative Statement of Financial Conditions—Bank Projections

Description	*12/31/66*	*12/31/67*	*12/31/68*	*12/31/69*	*12/31/70*	*12/31/71*
Current assets	2,015	2,099	2,197	3,159	3,524	4,075
Current liabilities	699	927	1,476	1,947	2,056	1,506
Working capital	1,316	1,172	721	1,212	1,468	2,569
Long-term debt		891	2,230	1,329	525	420
Tangible net worth	3,044	3,811	4,628	4,975	6,135	6,828
Net sales	3,067	3,771	3,771	4,900	6,400	7,571
Net profit	460	567	567	887	1,153	1,360
Assets						
Cash	693	453	551	995	670	685
Marketable securities						
Receivables	664	833	833	1,103	1,463	1,743
Inventory	658	813	813	1,061	1,391	1,647
Prepaid expenses						
Total current assets	2,015	2,099	2,197	3,159	3,524	4,075
Net fixed assets	1,543	3,395	5,912	5,387	4,926	4,394
Inv. and adv. subs. and affiliates						
Compulsory loans	185	205	225	245	265	285
Intangibles						
Total assets	3,743	5,699	8,334	8,791	8,715	8,754
Liabilities						
Notes payable banks						
Accounts payable	292	352	352	447	576	675
Taxes payable	407	321	431	599	675	726
Accruals						
Current long-term debt		254	693	901	805	105
Total current liab.	699	927	1,476	1,947	2,056	1,506
Total long-term debt		891	2,230	1,329	524	210
Total sub. long-term dent						
Total long-term liab. and rvs.						
Preferred stock						
Common stock	2,816	3,087	3,267	3,267	3,267	3,267
Capital surplus						
Earned surplus	2,291	2,857	3,424	4,311	4,931	5,624
Exchange loss	(2,063)	(2,063)	(2,063)	(2,063)	(2,063)	(2,063)
Total liabilities and net worth	3,743	5,699	8,334	8,791	8,715	8,544
Lease rentals						
Contingent liab.						
Gross fixed assets	3,157	5,137	7,780	7,780	7,852	
Deprec. allowance	1,614	1,741	1,867	2,393	2,925	

EXHIBIT 6

Price-Level Index and Cruzeiro/Dollar Exchange Rate (1962 – 1966)

Year	*Cost of living index (1963 = 100)*	*Exchange rate (cruzeiro – dollar)*
1962	58	475
1963	100	620
1964	187	1,850
1965	302	2,220
1966	443	2,220

Case 23
IBM

IBM is the largest single factor in the business machines industry, and in the past two decades it has put together a classic record of growth. Recently two trends have affected the financial results reported to stockholders. The first was a gradual increase in computers sold, a development forced on the company under the terms of a consent decree. The second was a dramatic growth in international operations.

Consent Decree–1956:

In 1952 the United States Department of Justice filed an antitrust complaint against IBM charging monopolistic practice in the punch card and card tabulating industry. The claim that the company controlled 90 per cent of the card industry was denied by IBM management, and they announced their intention to fight the suit. However, in 1956 the company, while making no admissions of any violations, consented to the entry of a judgment settling all issues raised by the antitrust suit. Under the provisions of this Consent Decree, IBM agreed to divest itself of that part of its tabulating card manufacturing capacity in excess of 50 per cent of the total national capacity. IBM was also required to change its previous policy of only leasing equipment, to a policy giving customers the option to lease under contracts terminative after one year or to buy the equipment at a reasonable price.

One of the results of these provisions was to increase the ratio of sales revenue to rental revenues. This increase has been moderate, however, because most customers prefer to lease expensive data processing equipment so they can change to newer models as they are developed. Further, there are often tax advantages to leasing. The breakdown of sales versus service and rentals (as presented in the 1965 Prospectus for the Employees Stock Purchase Plan and including the consolidated foreign subsidiaries) is as follows:

	(in millions)				
	1960	1961	1962	1963	1964
Gross income from sales	$ 523	$ 714	$ 830	$ 797	$ 928
Gross income from services	1,294	1,488	1,761	2,065	2,311
and rentals	$1,817	$2,202	$2,591	$2,862	$3,239
Cost of sales	$ 332	$ 436	$ 449	$ 379	$ 381
Cost of service and rentals	468	538	649	747	843
	$1,800	$ 974	$1,108	$1,126	$1,224

IBM World Trade Corporation:

A recent magazine article asked the question, "who grows faster than IBM?" It suggested the answer—the IBM World Trade Corporation, a wholly-owned subsidiary that operates directly or through foreign subsidiaries in countries outside of the United States. IBM World Trade's growth under Arthur K. Watson has given a tremendous boost to the earnings of the parent corporation.

In the years prior to 1961 IBM carried IBM World Trade on the balance sheet at cost and included in its earnings only the cash dividends received from IBM World Trade Corporation. As of January 1, 1961, IBM began to include in its earnings the net earnings of IBM World Trade, which represented the cash dividends, royalties and income received by it in the United States less expenses and foreign and United States income taxes. The undistributed earnings of IBM World Trade's subsidiaries continued to be excluded. At this time IBM World Trade stopped paying cash dividends to IBM; instead these funds were reinvested to aid in financing continued worldwide growth. In 1964 IBM changed to a worldwide consolidation basis, providing for deferred taxes on undistributed foreign earnings. (See Exhibits.)

A comparative summary of the results of the operations of the IBM World Trade Corporation and its foreign subsidiaries is as follows:

	(in millions)				
	1960	1961	1962	1963	1964
Gross income from sales, service, and rentals in foreign countries	$372	$498	$653	$788	$933
Net earnings for year:	$ 49	64	87	105	124
Portion of above net earnings included in IBM net earnings (earnings of IBM World Trade excluding subsidiaries)	$ 12	19	25	32	Consolidated

SRA Acquisition:

In 1964 IBM acquired all the capital stock of Science Research Associates in exchange for 128,841 shares of stock. This combination was treated as a pooling of interests.

Prior Year Restatement:

When IBM went to a worldwide consolidation and included Science Research Associates, it restated prior years earnings to make them comparable. Net income figures were as follows:

	(in millions)	
	As restated on new basis	*As reported*
1963	$364	$290
1962	305	241
1961	254	207
1960	205	168

EXHIBIT 1

Consolidated IBM Statements of Income and Retained Earnings
For the Year Ended December 31 (As Reported)
(in millions)

	1960	*1961*	*1962*	*1963*	*1964 worldwide consolidation*
Gross Income from sales, service, and rentals	$1,436	$1,692	$1,925	$2,059	$3,239
Cost of sales, service and rentals, operating expenses, and development and engineering expense, exclusive of depreciation and amortization	(889)	(1,040)	(1,185)	(1,232)	(1,880)
Depreciation of rental machines, depreciation and amortization of plant and equipment	(218)	(249)	(278)	(283)	(475)
Interest on long-term indebtness	(15)	(15)	(15)	(15)	(23)
Amortization of goodwill					(3)
	$ 314	$ 388	$ 447	$ 529	$ 858
Other income	18	16	19	23	39
	$ 332	$ 404	$ 466	$ 552	$ 897
Dividends received from IBM World Trade Corp.	12				
Net earnings of IBM World Trade Corp.		19	25	33	
Interest Received from IBM World Trade Corp.	2	3	3	4	
Net earnings before income taxes	$ 346	$ 426	$ 494	$ 589	$ 897
Provision for U.S. Federal income taxes (and foreign income taxes in 1964), estimated	178	219	253	299	466
Net earnings for the year	$ 168	$ 207	$ 241	$ 290	$ 431
Retained earnings, January 1	209	322	507	665	1,185
Undistributed net earnings of IBM World Trade Corp. Jan. 1, 1961		41			
	$ 377	$ 570	$ 748	$ 955	$1,616
Cash Dividend	55	63	83	118	166
Retained earnings, December 31	$ 322	$ 507	$ 665	$ 837	$1,450

EXHIBIT 2

Consolidated IBM Balance Sheets
At December 31 (As Reported)
(in millions)

Assets	*1960*	*1961*	*(in millions)* *1962*	*1963*	*1964* *worldwide consolidation*
Cash	$ 57	$ 75	$ 98	$ 86	$ 127
Marketable securities, principally U.S. Treasury, at lower of cost or market	263	248	366	625	725
Notes and accounts receivable —less reserve	144	183	222	329	546
Accounts receivable and unreimbursed expense on military products contracts	76	70	59	39	
Inventories-at lower of average cost or market	32	37	44	47	118
Prepaid insurance, taxes, etc.	5	15	6	8	22
Total current assets	$ 577	$ 628	$ 795	$1,134	$1,538
Investments in and advances to IBM World Trade Corp.	82	179	203	241	
U.S. Treasury securities maturing in 1965-valued at cost plus accrued discount	23	23	24	24	
Other investments	2	1	1	1	10
Factories, buildings, other property-cost					
Land	24	25	30	32	43
Buildings	203	221	246	274	388
Less: reserve for depreciation	(72)	(85)	(96)	(107)	(135)
Factory and office equipment, rental machines and parts	1,566	1,749	1,856	1,946	3,284
Less: reserve for depreciation	(869)	(973)	(1,075)	(1,172)	(1,833)
Patents and goodwill	1	1	1	1	14
	$1,535	$1,769	$1,985	$2,374	$3,309

EXHIBIT 2 (cont.)

Assets	1960	1961	(in millions) 1962	1963	1964 worldwide consolidation
Liabilities and Capital					
U.S. Federal income taxes (and foreign income taxes in 1964) -estimated	$ 109	$ 132	$ 154	$ 185	$ 331
Less: U.S. Treasury securities	(89)	(111)	(128)		
	$ 20	$ 21	$ 26	$ 185	$ 331
Accounts payable and accruals	118	137	153	172	286
Loans payable					21
Total current liabilities	$ 138	$ 158	$ 179	$ 357	$ 638
Deferred income taxes					28
Reserves for employees' indemnities and retirement plans					19
Long-term indebtedness	425	425	425	425	370
Capital stock-par value $5.00 per share	650	679	716	754	804
Retained earnings	322	507	665	838	1,450
	$1,535	$1,769	$1,985	$2,374	$3,309

Note: Foreign assets and liabilities have been converted to U.S. dollars at year-end exchange rates, except the factories, office buildings, rental machines and parts, other property, and long-term indebtedness which have been converted at approximate rates prevailing when acquired or incurred. Income and expense items have been converted at average rates of exchange prevailing during the year, except depreciation and amortization which have been calculated at the approximate rates prevailing when the properties were acquired.

Conclusions

14

The purpose of this book has been to provide a description of existing corporate practices within the realm of international financial management and to develop a decision-making framework for the financial manager of a firm whose resources are worldwide. The emphasis throughout has been placed on the environmental forces that distinguish international transactions from purely domestic business. The discussion has focused on methods for adapting business planning and practice to the international business environment. The concluding chapter extends the analysis into the future. With a five to ten year look into what the future may hold for the internationally oriented company, the discussion concentrates on the possible implications for international business and international financial management. The purpose is to provide a framework for assessing the possible future directions and trends of where the multinational corporation will be in the 1970's and what special adaptations will be required.

INTERNATIONAL TRADE

There are a number of reasons to believe that the volume of international trade will continue to expand during the forthcoming five to ten years and that thousands of companies will be able to increase the amount of goods and services that they are able to sell to foreigners. As the world's population increases, the advantages of trade among nations and national specialization in production of goods and services are increasingly appreciated and promoted by governments. Legislative and transportation barriers to the international flow of goods are being gradually lowered through international negotiation and technological improvements, and new and improved approaches to financing international transactions are being developed. One may assume that at least a 5 per cent increase in world trade will be evidenced annually.

For internationally involved companies the expectation is that not only the volume but the patterns of international trade will provide new commercial opportunities and requirements for adaptation. In part the new patterns of trade are likely to result from a lowering of the present barriers to the exchange of goods with the eastern bloc countries. It is now generally recognized by businessmen and government policymakers that a vastly increased volume of East-West trade is commercially desirable. The task at hand therefore involves finding the means to permit interested parties to engage in such trade. While the barriers are formidable,[1] none appear to be insuperable provided that public opinion and national economic policy on both sides are strongly in favor of moving ahead in this area. Should national policies continue to be directed towards the opening of commercial channels between the East and West, the main problems for the 1970's will include improving the East's ability to sell its output in western markets and providing the means by which the East can finance its imports from the West. Obviously these problems are interrelated, since both refer to the limited stock of reserve assets owned by the East and to their presently inadequate ability to borrow the means of payments or to earn them.

A variety of evidence lends support to the expectation that a significantly larger volume of East-West trade will occur in the 1970's. The medium-term financing that has recently been arranged by the European Economic Community to facilitate exports to the East[2] and the possibility of significantly increasing the supply of medium-term credits through government and private financial institutions, *if* the United States and eastern bloc governments formally signify their intent to open trade channels, provide reason for optimism. The growing public support for engaging in commercial intercourse with the East and

[1] For a review of the post-World War II trends and issues in East-West trade relations, *see* Mose L. Harvey, *East-West Trade and U.S. Policy*, National Association of Manufacturers, New York, 1966; Jack Behrman, "A Reappraisal of US-USSR Trade Policy," *Harvard Business Review*, July-August 1964; A. Nove, "Something There Is That Doesn't Love a Trade Wall,' *Columbia Journal of World Business*, Winter 1966; Marshall I. Holdman, "Businessmen Appraise East-West Trade," *Harvard Business Review*, January-February 1966.

[2] "East-West Trade," *World Business*, The Chase Manhattan Bank, N.A., January 1968.

the limited but growing record of commercially viable and successful deals between firms of the West and state trading institutions in the East also point to an expanding volume of such transactions.

The prospect of trade with the East poses new challenges for the international financial manager. He may be expected to arrange medium- and long-term export financing through new and untried sources; to enter into switch-trading as the means of putting together an exchange of goods,[3] to negotiate with state trading institutions, and to facilitate transactions between the company's Western European affiliates and the East rather than directly between the parent company and Eastern nations. Involvement with the East is also likely to encourage several companies to enter so-called coproduction agreements where the western partner in an East-West collaboration provides the technical, organizational, managerial, and a part of the financial resources required to produce western-style goods with eastern labor, materials, supervision, and in factories located in Eastern Europe or the Soviet Union.[4] Because the Western partner is expected to assume most of the responsibilities for marketing the output of these factories in international markets, the Western financial manager will presumably be required to arrange for export financing and the bulk of the financing required by the operation; he will also encounter unique problems in connection with managing the firm's assets and arranging to remit funds from state-controlled countries.

Another phenomenon of international trade that is likely to introduce somewhat new opportunities and problems for the multinational firm is the growing number and increased size of regional trading groups. Since the establishment of the EEC in the late 1950's, there has generally been an increasing appreciation and enthusiasm for the potential gains from countries forming free trade areas, customs unions, and common markets. To date, three major trading groups have evolved in addition to the European Common Market: EFTA, LAFTA, and the CACM, and there have been several ill-fated attempts by less-developed nations to achieve some degree of economic integration. Although the technical, political, and administrative difficulties associated with the establishment of regional groups are formidable, the prospects of increased market size, more attractive investment opportunities, a wider range of goods and services for local consumers, less reliance on the outside world for desired goods, and greater opportunities for specialized production have induced the formation of numerous study groups to examine whether or not various other nations (be they industrialized or

[3] For a discussion of "switch-trading" *see* Charles H. Baudoin, "The Use of Switch Financing to Facilitate East-West Trade and Investment," *American Review of East-West Trade*, June 1968.

[4] The "coproduction" scheme and its future possibilities are discussed in Emile Benoit, "Business Partnerships With Communist Enterprises?" *Worldwide P and I Planning*, November-December, 1967.

less-developed) should seek entry into some type of bloc and how such a group would best be managed.

Establishing a viable association of this type is a lengthy process as is the maturation of existing groups. One cannot expect the 1970's to bring a doubling or tripling in the number of successful common markets or trade associations. However, owing to the attractions that such unions have, it is probable that during the next five to ten years a few new unions will evolve, the formation of others will be planned, and the existing ones will grow in size and perhaps change in form or with regard to the rules by which they operate.

For the internationally committed firm, the trend toward regional integration may lead to changing opportunities and warrant new or modified approaches to marketing, production, and financial management. The increased trade and specialization that integration provides will normally intensify the competitiveness of the individual firm, create more pressure for product adaptation, increase the requirements for local service facilities, and erect more formidable barriers to the goods of outside exporters. The economic unions, in opening larger markets, afford the firm the possibility of enlarging sales, introducing wider product lines, and using more sophisticated product styles. For the financial manager these trends are likely to necessitate additional export financing, operating with different profit margins, changed working capital requirements, and longer extensions of credit. Additionally, the manager must plan for increased direct investment abroad, larger funds flow associated with export activity, establishing relations with new financial institutions, and modifying business practices in accord with the new restrictions and opportunities stemming from the development of common commercial regulations.

INTERNATIONAL INVESTMENT

In addition to the anticipated opportunities for trade expansion, one might expect continued growth in opportunities for overseas investment in plant, equipment, research, and service facilities in foreign countries. Foreign markets will grow as per capita incomes rise and as population expands. In many cases, as has been true in recent years, exporting will cease to be the most effective method of reaching these markets. An increasing number of companies will in the future be manned by those who are imbued with the desire to see their firms take on an international image. Hence the coming years should bring a continuation of the post World War II growth of business assets in foreign markets. The question that arises in this context is *where* will this expansion take place?

In attempting to answer this question, it is tempting to rely on the historical pattern wherein a large percentage of the export and foreign direct investment activity has been in foreign countries whose market characteristics were the most similar to those of the capital- or product-exporting economy. While the rationale for such behavior is likely to be as valid in the future as it has been in recent years, one might hypothesize that changing environmental circumstances will nevertheless bring about some modifications in the investment pattern of the 1970's.

A number of internationally oriented companies have recently begun to discover that their existing manufacturing facilities in Europe and Canada are adequate to meet projected production and marketing volume in the early 1970's. Competition in these markets has intensified in recent years with the influx of foreign capital and the growth of local firms. Profit margins and the rate of return on foreign investments have declined from former periods. It is believed that future profitability will come largely through the introduction of new products rather than the increased sales of existing ones. Therefore, for a significant number of firms no new sizable investments in Europe or Canada, aside from periodic retooling, will be warranted.

The bulk of the flow of funds to Europe and Canada in the 1970's may therefore reflect investments by companies that heretofore have not invested abroad on a sizable basis or those old-timers that have important new products to introduce to foreign markets. There may also be more numerous small and medium-sized supply and service firms that will follow their large domestic clients abroad to avoid losing their business in both markets. Coupled with these trends, it is also possible that more investor attention will be focused on manufacturing opportunities in the developing economies. Large numbers of LDC's are beginning to take on market characteristics similar to those of Canada and Europe in the 1950's when the postwar United States foreign investment activity began. With a growing middle class, enlarging urban centers, developing channels of distribution and other required marketing institutions, many LDC's are increasingly likely to receive larger inflows of direct investment. The inducements to foreign investors in countries such as Brazil, Australia, the Philippines, Mexico, Greece, Israel, Ireland, Spain, Portugal, India, Pakistan, and Turkey also include: increasing exposure to the goods and services produced and demanded in the economically more advanced countries, slowly growing per capita incomes of the lower classes, greater evidence of political stability, and overall a more favorable investment climate.

As the new investments are made, the trend may be toward less foreign ownership and control of foreign affiliates. Multinational investors will not be happy about giving up control over their foreign affiliates, but they are likely to adjust in a positive manner to the changing terms that will make foreign investment acceptable to the recipient countries.

Similarly, a continuation of government controls over the form and volume of foreign direct investment in capital exporting countries may force multinational investors to settle for partial ownership of new affiliates as the only manner of continuing foreign expansion under capital export constraints. For these reasons a proliferation of joint ventures and distribution of ownership through the sale of common stock to local investors can be expected during the next five to ten years,[5] as well as an increasing amount of foreign licensing, turnkey operations, and management contract activity. Additionally an increasing number of multinational investors will list their equity shares on foreign stock exchanges. The move will be one of several ways investors can cater to foreigners' demands for more voice in the management of companies that have invested in their economies and more opportunity to share in the profits of such ventures. Foreign listing of parent company shares will also be expected to enhance the firm's general reputation among local consumers and make it better known to the foreign financial communities.

Paralleling the anticipated volume and the patterns of growth in foreign direct investment will be the expansion of service organizations on a global scale. Management consultants, commercial banks, investment banks, advertising agencies, and accounting firms will increasingly commit themselves to foreign clients, including the overseas affiliates of their domestic clients.[6] For the international executive the continuing expansion of service agencies should result in a broader range of services of the type now available to the parent company, greater availability of data on foreign environmental conditions, and better quality advice on how to solve the problems faced by the international company.

For the international financial manager in particular, the services of these outside consultants and specialists will be welcomed inputs. They will assist in the analysis of the foreign business climate, design of capital structures for foreign affiliates, identification of attractive sources of funds around the world, management of affiliates' current assets, and control over widely disbursed company resources. Of special relevance to the financial manager is the commitment of the banking community to their multinational clients. As these national and international institutions expand in size and geographical coverage, the corporate investor may expect numerous aids. The banks will be able to provide more extensive services such as receivables collection, preparation of payrolls, and counsel on foreign acquisitions. The bank's

[5] A discussion of management contracts and turnkeys can be found in Peter P. Gabriel, *The International Transfer of Corporate Skills: Management Contracts in Less Developed Countries,* Harvard Business School Division of Research, Boston, 1967.

[6] This trend is discussed in Marvin Bower, "Personal Service Firms Venture Abroad," *Columbia Journal of World Business,* March-April 1968.

foreign affiliates will be able to provide larger sums to meet their local clients' growing financial requirements. A wider range of investment instruments for the corporations' temporarily idle foreign funds will be offered. Through their global size and worldwide management, the banks will be increasingly able to match clients' requirements for simultaneously placing and obtaining funds for geographically separated foreign affiliates. In this regard it should be anticipated that an increasing number of multinational investors will decide to acquire their *own* foreign banking institutions and finance companies.[7] The overall objective will be better financial management with such specific advantages as reduction in intracompany float, greater flexibility in investing idle cash balances, enlarged local financing capability, and financial service for the company's clients.

Although banks, management consultants, and public accountants will in the future be better able to provide timely and more complete data on the foreign environment, the corporate financial manager cannot assume that his task of forecasting environmental changes will be eased. Rather, the improved accessibility to data should assist him in making more accurate and perhaps more rapid environmental projections. So, too, the international manager can expect that the requirement for staying alert to the possibilities of foreign expropriation, devaluation, exchange controls, or inflation will not diminish in the 1970's. The basic economic and political forces that undergird government decisions to take foreign-owned assets or change the par value of their currencies are just as likely to be extant in the forthcoming five to ten years. Although the international payments system will be gradually modified in form and capacity to meet the growing needs of international commerce, the uneven distribution of international liquidity among one hundred-plus nations, the unpredictability and instability of flows which affect countries' current and capital accounts, and the high level of foreign debt service obligations are likely to continue to cause governments to take a variety of steps—among them exchange controls and exchange rate devaluation—to alleviate pressures and solve severe problems.

Similarly the risk of creeping expropriation or outright seizure of private property remains a distinct threat in many countries. In industrial nations experiments with socialism and fears about foreign domination of local industry can prompt restrictive state actions. In the less-developed nations nationalism, political instability, immaturity, unpleasant histories of colonial exploitation, emergent commercial self-reliance in certain industries, and inappropriate activities by foreign investors are apt to result in some form of expropriatory action. In addition, the threat of involvement in military conflict, which in turn necessitates government

[7] A brief discussion of such an arrangement is found in "Dow Chemical Banks on a Global Formula," *Business Week*, April 2, 1966, pp. 84–94.

control of the private sector, remains a distinct possibility for many countries.

NEW APPROACHES TO MANAGEMENT

With the passage of time the rigors of managing a worldwide enterprise and the experiences gained in doing so are likely to produce a number of new characteristics of management in multinational companies. During the 1970's the upper echelons of management of many internationally oriented firms will be filled from a growing list of executives whose careers have included assignments with both the parent company and the overseas affiliates. These managers may speak two or more languages and may have been exposed to international management training in graduate schools or management institutes. As corporations' policies are increasingly influenced by these executives, the following kinds of subtle changes in the tenor of company behavior might emerge:

1. A more mature appreciation of the possibilities and risks in expanding foreign operations
2. A keener awareness of the possible business implications of environmental changes abroad
3. A greater likelihood that the corporation and its activities will be viewed in terms of a global operation, as compared to a domestic company with sizable foreign investments
4. Greater awareness of the requirements for exerting management control over overseas affiliates, with an understanding of the limitations of conventional approaches as well as the difficulties of developing a specially suited system for the foreign operations
5. More accurate assessment of the advantages and difficulties to be encountered in employing increasing numbers of foreign nationals in the highest management positions in local and third country affiliates and in the parent company
6. Better perspective regarding the requirements and liabilities inherent in developing good relations with the host government where the the company has investments
7. A better assessment of the caliber of management that is needed at the affiliate level, of the advantages and weaknesses associated with various degrees of centralized decision and policy-making in large, international organizations, and of the costs and benefits associated with foreign inspection visits by headquarters personnel.

The emergence of the internationalist group of managers should result in greater analytical capabilities and more sophistication in management than formerly. The executives' experience in managing foreign operations, analyzing foreign environmental conditions, and assessing the outcomes of various decisions that have been made are expected to produce improvements in executive performance. The increased quality and quantity of outside advice rendered by banks, consultants, and the academic community combined with a broadened appreciation of the possibilities of developing and using a comprehensive analytical approach to international decision making lend support to such expectations about the quality of management.

The possibility of employing foreign nationals in the management of the parent company was mentioned earlier. During the 1970's an increasing number of largely international firms will have begun to employ foreign nationals. Managers will grow in wisdom and experience with foreign operations. Many headquarters executives will have had close personal relationships and encounters with important foreign nationals who have been employed in responsible overseas positions; hence operations can become increasingly global—as opposed to English, French, or American—with regard to policy and philosophic orientation. Furthermore, sensitive executives will recognize the need to promote foreigners from the affiliate to the headquarters levels of management or else risk losing them to other firms. Concurrently the growing number of foreign nationals who are being trained in the finest schools of business and management institutes in Europe, United States, and Canada will provide the multinational companies with additional evidence of the foreigners' professional competence and potential. This phenomenon will reduce the gap between the perceptions of business, methods of management, and ability to communicate that characterize managers of various countries.

Tangentially the rush in the middle and late 1960's by American companies to employ foreign nationals almost exclusively in the technological and managerial positions of their foreign subsidiaries—except for, perhaps, one or two top positions in each affiliate—may result in a relative *dearth* of United States internationalists in the 1970's. If a large company that, for example, employs 30,000 persons in the United States and 15,000 abroad used only about 100 Americans in the middle and upper echelons of foreign affiliate management during the 1960's, then the organization will have only the 100 from whom to select in filling the hundreds or even thousands of parent company management posts with internationally oriented personnel. The remaining positions will go either to foreign nationals, United States nationals with the traditional domestic outlook and training, or United States nationals who have had only one or two brief overseas assignments.

Given these changes in the characteristics of management and the projected environmental changes and trends described earlier, the methods used to manage multinational corporations in the 1970's can also be expected to develop new features. Perhaps the most noteworthy will be the shift by a large number of companies from multinational in name to multinational in philosophy. The late 1960's found a few European and United States companies reporting this change, but by far the great majority of firms with international commitments were of the type where domestic operations were of greater importance in terms of sales and profitability and therefore received more managerial attention and a disproportionate share of corporate resources. Clearly these firms were at about the halfway point in the organizational evolutionary process. Companies often entered the international field relatively unnoticed with small export operations and an unimportant export department. At some point in these firms' development they may become truly global operations—where the country of the parent company provides an important but not overwhelming share of the company's earnings and receives only a commensurate share of the firm's financial resources and management attention.

It is likely that many companies that earned one-quarter to one-third of their total consolidated profits abroad during the 1960's and that continued to invest large sums abroad throughout the decade will find that by the early 1970's the overall size of their foreign operations and the complexity of managing them will require the adoption of a truly multinational organizational structure and management approach. These evolvements will likely be speeded by a number of factors. The influence of the continued government restrictions over international transactions, the complexities involved in operating within these constraints, and the close control of foreign affiliates that is required to insure their compliance with host or lending country policies should be important. The rapid improvements in data processing and the increased utilization of E.D.P. are likely to mean that

1. Headquarters management will have *more rapid access* to information about foreign affiliates' current performance
2. Executives will have *more data* with which to evaluate international operations
3. Increased use of operations research techniques will be made for managing affiliates' cash balances, accounts receivable, and credit policies, and the international flow of corporate funds
4. In general, foreign operations will be *managed* by the headquarters on a *current* basis.

This will be in contrast to the 1960's, where companies were one to two months behind in obtaining and analyzing affiliates' profit-and-loss statements and balance sheets and were forced to rely heavily on rushed visits by headquarters' executives to put out the fires in subsidiaries as well as on somewhat inflexible budgeting procedures as the sole guides for future fiscal performance.

A global approach to management may first be reflected in a redesign of the entire organization so that functional responsibilities, where appropriate, are more centralized on a regional or worldwide basis. The marketing manager will be responsible for *all* of the firm's activities (or for those in his region of the world). The financial manager will control *all* of the financial function, and so forth. Staffed with men whose careers have included domestic and foreign assignments, policies and operating decisions will be made on the basis of the company as a whole, rather than the domestic division being one unique entity and the international division another.

More accurate planning and logistical coordination should occur. Worldwide or regional materials supply, manufacturing, assembly, and sales will be more centrally managed. Capital budgeting and funds flow management will increasingly become a centralized process where the concept of a company-wide pool of funds will be used by many firms as a policy guideline. More attempts will be made to design policies and make decisions in the best interests of the worldwide enterprise. No longer will that Thai affiliate be simply allocated a lump sum of investment capital each fiscal period or a percentage of its previous year's earnings and directed to proceed with its request for a plant addition. The decision on that Thai plant will be a part of an *overall* review of the company's investment opportunities in Thailand, England, the United States, etc., and the funds available to the entire organization, funds that may have been generated by the Japanese affiliate or the French subsidiary or borrowed in Canada.

Commensurate with the growth of foreign investment and the concept of global management will be growth in managerial resources available at both the headquarters and affiliate levels. In the 1950's and 1960's most companies' foreign involvements were too small to permit employment of large staffs and high caliber executives at various points in the international divisions. The requirements and scale of worldwide operations in the 1970's should elevate the management of international transactions to a first-class status. This trend should, of course, also reflect the growing number of suitably trained businessmen who are able to perform the dual roles of internationalist and functional specialist.

It should be recognized that the corporate adaptations to international business as well as those of the individual manager are a part of an *unending* response to changing opportunities and changing environmental conditions. The organizational structure, analytical techniques, and decision-making framework employed at a given point in time by a multinational company can be expected to change, as do circumstances and corporate objectives. In this book the authors have endeavored to assist in the development of international financial managers by offering a concept of corporate financial management suited to the needs of the multinational corporation as it moves into the third decade of the era of international business.

Index

A

D

F

G

H

I

J

K

L

M

N

S

T

U

V

W

Z